ENDORSEMENTS

Bill Hull, Talbot Seminary graduate, and Founder and President of "Choose the Life Ministries." He is one of America's premier authors on "discipleship," with some nineteen books in print, including his popular trilogy, *Jesus Christ Disciple Maker*, *The Disciple Making Pastor*, and *The Disciple Making Church*. Bill pastored in the Evangelical Free Church of America for 20 years, and spent eight years as the U. S. Director for the Evangelical Free Church of America. He currently writes, teaches, and serves as adjunct professor at several leading evangelical seminaries.

> It is rare and unique for someone to provide such a treasure trove of great writing; I am so glad Don Ekstrand has done it. He has taken years to pour through his mind and soul some of the Church's greatest truths. I am sure it has done more for Don than anyone else, but it is a spiritual feast for all that read it. I recall Eugene Peterson lamenting after attending a contemporary church leadership conference—"All the God had been sucked out of him." Peterson went home and read Karl Barth for several days and it refreshed his soul. I think Don's work can do the same for us when so much of our spiritual diet is fast food-read, and be nourished.

Ronald Youngblood, Professor Emeritus of Old Testament and Hebrew, Bethel Seminary San Diego. Dr. Youngblood has been an author, editor and pastor-teacher for more than fifty years. He was one of the translators of the New International Version (NIV), the executive editor of the New International reader's Version (NIrV), and the recipient of a

"Gold Medallion Book Award" by the Evangelical Christian Publishers Association.

> *"Soul Transformation" is a highly commendable painstaking work by my longtime friend, Don Ekstrand, one of God's choice servants. In it he chronicles the encouraging periods of faith and light and joy in the Lord, as well as those discouraging periods of doubt and darkness and despair. His story is the experience of every Christian who truly wants to know and obey our Lord. Scripturally based and experientially validated, Ekstrand's latest book is a must read for every believer.*

Darryl DelHousaye, President of Phoenix Seminary, and Pastor Emeritus of Scottsdale Bible Church in Scottsdale, Arizona, where he pastored for some 25 years. Darryl is the author of several books and maintains a rigorous preaching and teaching schedule.

> *I recommend "Soul Transformation" to any fellow believer who has a deep desire to become a growing disciple of Jesus Christ. Maturity comes with an understanding of the Scriptures and Don Ekstrand has served us well by taking us on a liberating journey of biblical discipleship. Your faith will be greatly encouraged through this enlightening work—be prepared to grow!*

Sam Talbert, Talbot Seminary & Dallas Seminary graduate, retired pastor of 36 years. Sam now serves as a missionary and teacher with Walk Thru the Bible, Unveiling Glory Ministries, Perspectives on World Missions, E3 Partners Mission Organization, and Global Media Outreach

> *When Don invited me to write a paragraph for his book, "Soul Transformation," I figured it to be a simple, straight forward task. I planned to lay it out and examine it by cruising the perimeter making observations, much like a spectator observing a football game from the sidelines. I wasn't at it more than a few minutes before I realized that standing on the side lines was simply not a possibility. I found myself in the middle of the offensive line in a major spiritual battle. As I looked into the eyes of the enemy across the line, his eyes were full of*

anger and his muscles were bulging, and I could see that I was going to get my spiritual butt kicked on every play. I knew I needed help! What Don has done for us in this book is not only lay out a training regimen that insures spiritual victory, but he give us an understanding of those spiritual dynamics whereby we are able to put the adversary of our soul on his back side. Through this incredible read, you will learn to be an overcomer yourself, and an encouragement to all those around you, thus causing the gospel to move forward.

Scott Wilson, Western Seminary graduate, and the Pastor of Calvary Church in Foristell, Missouri. Scott has been faithfully serving in the local church for some 30 years, and together with his wife Shari are the proud parents of six children who love Jesus.

The writer of Hebrews compares the life of faith to a "race." Every Christ follower has a unique race to run that is set before him and marked out by God. The race each has to run is an extremely challenging one; it is filled with steep uphill climbs, difficult and exhausting terrain, and long stretches that seem to have no end in sight. Our goal is to run it well with endurance, and Jesus' goal through it all is to perfect us and transform our lives into His image. Learning from the life experiences of some of the greatest saints in the history of the church, "Soul Transformation" describes how we partner with God to run this race. Only you can run the race God has for you. The key is to keep your eyes on Jesus, the author and perfecter of faith. This book by Ekstrand will be a treasurehouse of encouragement to you through all the ups and downs of life.

Steve Barduson, Dallas Seminary graduate, founder and president of Barduson Architects in Phoenix, and former pastor at a new contemporary church-plant in Arizona. Today, Steve is one of America's leading architects specializing in houses of worship—his functional designs facilitate worship and community in significant new ways. Steve serves at a church he designed from the ground up, "Mountain Park Community

Church," and together with his wife "Maggie" and their five children reside in Phoenix.

> *Having known Don for some 30 years, I can say that this book and its intense topic is also a product of a man of God who has grappled with its content with a fervent zeal, second only to his love for his Savior. He lives these words, believes these words, and loves those in his flock. This significant work on Sanctification is a new generation's "A Long Obedience in the Same Direction" and "Knowing God."*

Kent Marshall, Talbot Seminary graduate, and Director of the dynamic campus ministry "International Students Inc." (ISI) at Texas A&M University. Kent and his wife Judy have been serving the international student community now for more than 35 years.

> *As my best friend in seminary, Don Ekstrand began his spiritual encouragement in my life nearly forty years ago, and it continues on in a powerful way with his latest book, "Soul Transformation." Your faith and your life will be significantly enriched as you identify with the spiritual realities presented in this book. Your heart will be fed, and your soul will be transformed as you ponder these incredible truths.*

Scott Brown, Asbury Seminary graduate, and Lead Pastor of New Valley Presbyterian Church in Phoenix, Arizona.

> *In "Soul Transformation," Don provides a feast for hungry and thirsty souls by summarizing some of the best writings of current and classic authors on the subject of sanctification by grace, and the reality that genuine liberation and sanctification comes through living in light of our justification. I cannot encourage you too much to read this book again and again!*

Jeff Meyer, Phoenix Seminary graduate, Senior Pastor of Arizona Community Church, Tempe, Arizona.

> *"Soul Transformation" provides a valuable resource for every Christian who truly desires to grow and mature through the toughest challenges*

of life. Reading and considering the timeless insights and wisdom of those who have traveled the road of faith long before we have, and have experienced those painful spiritual realities that are common to the most committed believers, Ekstrand's book provides us with a very clear picture of what that journey is truly all about.

David Brewer, Jerusalem University and Biblical Theological Seminary graduate. David has been an adjunct professor of OT Hebrew and NT Greek at several Christian colleges, universities and seminaries for more than 20 years, and has been on staff with *Life in Messiah International* for the past 22 years.

Don was my college pastor in the early 1980s. I regularly thank the Lord for the impact his excellent Bible teaching had on me spiritually during those highly formative years. To this day, Don has continued to impact my life through his masterful work, "Soul Transformation." You will find this book a tremendously liberating study on God's transforming work of grace in your life.

SOUL TRANSFORMATION

The Sanctification Experience of the Believer

Donald W. Ekstrand

Copyright © 2012 by Donald W. Ekstrand

Soul Transformation: The Sanctification Experience of the Believer
by Donald W. Ekstrand

Dr. Donald W. Ekstrand
3116 S. Mill Ave., #417
Tempe, AZ 85282

Printed in the United States of America

ISBN: 9781624194429

Library of Congress Cataloging-in-Publication Data
Ekstrand, Donald W.
Soul Transformation: The Sanctification Experience of the Believer
Includes bibliographical references and glossary
Library of Congress catalogue number—this number is pending
1. The Transformed Soul. 2. The Sanctification Experience. I. Title

All rights reserved solely by the author. The author guarantees all contents are original and do not infringe upon the legal rights of any other person or work. No part of this publication may be reproduced, stored in a retrieval system, or transmitted in any other form or by means—electronic, mechanical, photocopy, recording, or any other—without prior written permission from the copyright holder. The only exception is brief quotations in printed reviews. The views expressed in this book are not necessarily those of the publisher.

Unless otherwise indicated, Scripture references are the author's own paraphrased translation.

For more information about the author and this book, visit his website:
http://www.TheTransformedLife.com
http://www.TheSanctificationExperience.com
http://www.IntroToChristianity.com

To contact the author personally, you can email him at:
SoulTransformation@yahoo.com

www.xulonpress.com

Be sure to read the author's first book, *Christianity: The Pursuit of Divine Truth*

THIS BOOK IS DEDICATED TO . . .

The love of my life and my very best friend . . .

Barbara

My two beautiful daughters and adorable twin granddaughters . . .

Kelly & Michelle and Brooke & Makenzie

Those strategic "voices of faith" God has used in my life down through the years . . .

Warren Thompson *Guy Davidson*
Jim Rosscup *Dan Baumann*
Ron Youngblood *Sam Talbert*
Frank Anderson *Janet Anderson*
Scott Wilson *Steve Barduson*
Paul Metcalf *David Walls*
Kent Marshall *Ken Koch*

QUOTES FROM SOME OF MY FAVORITE AUTHORS

On sin—*As long as you see your sins as a detriment with regard to your acceptance before God, you will negate the work of the cross in your life.*
—Martyn Lloyd-Jones

On loving God—*If we do not love God enough to be contented, our natural desires will bring us into revolt against God . . . if we are not content and grateful, we are not loving God as we should; rather we are desiring other things . . . a quiet disposition and a thankful heart at any given moment is the real test of the extent to which we love God at that moment.*
—Francis Schaeffer

On being bruised—*The condition of those with whom God deals are "bruised reeds," not "big trees." As believers we need bruising so that we may know ourselves to be "reeds," not "oaks."*
—Richard Sibbes

On suffering—*The only thing that has taught me anything is suffering; not success, not happiness, not anything like that . . . the joy of coming in contact with what life really signifies is suffering and affliction.*
—Malcolm Muggeridge

On affliction—*I bear willing witness that I owe more to the fire, and the hammer, and the file, than to anything else in my Lord's workshop. I sometimes question whether I have ever learned anything except through the rod. When my schoolroom is darkened, I see most.*
—Charles Spurgeon

TABLE OF CONTENTS

INTRODUCTION — xviii
This explains the purpose of the book—very enlightening.

1. **SPIRITUAL DEPRESSION** by Martyn Lloyd-Jones — 1
   Lloyd-Jones was former pastor of Westminster Chapel in London; he died in 1981. He was known as the "greatest Bible expositor in the English-speaking world in the twentieth century."

2. **A SCANDALOUS FREEDOM** by Steve Brown — 31
   Brown is a very popular Professor at Reformed Theological Seminary in Orlando. He is one of the most transparent theologians in America! He tells it like it is!

3. **HOLINESS** by John Charles Ryle — 55
   Ryle wrote this book to counter some fashionable but dangerous teachings about sanctification in the 1800s—he was a great student of the Puritans.

4. **THE BRUISED REED** by Richard Sibbes — 75
   This is one of the most comforting books I have ever read as a believer. The "Heavenly Doctor Sibbes" brings the reader right into the presence of God.

5. **FELLOWSHIP WITH GOD** by Martyn Lloyd-Jones — 89
   This subject desperately needs a "clear voice," and that is precisely what Lloyd-Jones gives us—no more wallowing in uncertainty! A must read!

6. **GLORIOUS FREEDOM** by Richard Sibbes — 113
   Sibbes was one of the most influential figures of the Puritan movement in the 1600s. His writings spoke to the heart; he was Charles Spurgeon's favorite author.

7. LET NOT YOUR HEART BE TROUBLED   129
   by Martyn Lloyd-Jones
   Lloyd-Jones was the pastor at Westminster Chapel in London for thirty years. His books have brought profound spiritual encouragement to millions worldwide.

8. SOUL-DEPTHS AND SOUL-HEIGHTS by Octavius Winslow   139
   Winslow spoke at the opening of "Spurgeon's Tabernacle" in London in 1861. He was a brilliant scholar with a great heart and love for people—that is rare!

9. THE SOUL'S CONFLICT by Richard Sibbes   153
   Sibbes was known as "The Heavenly Doctor Sibbes" because of his loving heart. His books speak directly to the believer's soul—very powerful teaching.

10. THE DISCIPLINE OF GRACE by Jerry Bridges   181
    Bridges has been on staff with "The Navigators Collegiate Ministry" since 1955. He's a disciplined student of the Word, and one of my favorite seminary professors.

11. HOLINESS BY GRACE by Bryan Chapell   195
    Chapell is president of Covenant Theological Seminary and nationwide lecturer; he is a favorite writer of J. I. Packer, Steve Brown, and Jerry Bridges.

12. ENJOYING THE PRESENCE OF GOD by Martyn Lloyd-Jones   207
    Dr. Martyn Lloyd-Jones is one of the "best Christian authors" of the 20th century. His books challenge, inspire, and motivate believers in their "walk with God."

13. ALL THINGS FOR GOOD by Thomas Watson   223
    Watson was one of the Church's great leaders of the Puritan era in England. His writings have encouraged believers around the world for more than 300 years.

14. WHEN YOUR WORLD FALLS APART by David Jeremiah   241
    Jeremiah has a national daily Christian radio program called "Turning Point." His near death experience has given him a wonderful heart from which to teach.

15. SHATTERED DREAMS by Larry Crabb   275
    This well-known psychologist and Bible teacher is founder of "New Way Ministries." Through brokenness God has used Crabb to share the significance of "suffering."

16. **TRUE FACED** by Bill Thrall, Bruce McNicol, and John Lynch — 305
These three gentlemen are co-leaders of the organization "Leadership Catalyst." Their teaching on the issues of "pleasing God" vs. "trusting God" is profound.

17. **THE NEW NATURE** by Renald Showers — 329
Showers serves on the faculty of several Bible Colleges and is a renowned writer. He clearly articulates what the Bible teaches about the subject of sanctification.

18. **WALKING BY THE SPIRIT** by Donald Ekstrand — 357
The ministry of the Holy Spirit is another area in which the Christian community is suffering terribly from a lack of good teaching—why the confusion? Study this!

19. **TRUE SPIRITUALITY** by Francis Schaeffer — 383
Schaeffer was America's pre-eminent Christian philosopher in the twentieth-century. He founded the international ministry called "L'Abri Fellowship" in the Swiss Alps.

20. **SLAVE** by John MacArthur — 423
MacArthur is president of "The Master's College and Seminary" in California. His books and radio ministry have impacted millions of lives all around the world.

21. **CHRISTLIKE** by Bill Hull — 439
Hull is one of America's foremost authors on the subject of Christian discipleship. He was the U.S. director for the Evangelical Free Church of America, and founder of "Choose the Life Ministries."

22. **SIN & MAN'S ETERNAL PURPOSE** by Donald Ekstrand — 465
Temptation and Sin are monumental issues in every believer's life; yet, here again, we find a dearth of good teaching on these subjects in our churches. This is a tremendously enlightening and liberating study!

EPILOGUE — 491

BIBLIOGRAPHY — 497

GLOSSARY — 501

INTRODUCTION
(The Purpose of the Book)

Years ago I had the privilege of attending one of "Francis Schaeffer's" national conferences on the integrity of the Christian faith—it was a memorable time for me as a young seminary student. Dr. Schaeffer was an "icon" to many of us in those days. A few years later I was honored to serve as a regional director for him at one of his conferences. Much of what Schaeffer taught made an impact on my life—up until that time I had never heard anyone give such a profound philosophical defense of the Christian faith. Those were exciting days for a young man just getting started in ministry. Like Schaeffer, I prayed and thought through what the Scriptures taught, and reviewed my own reasons for being a Christian—I learned afresh that there were totally sufficient reasons to know that the infinite-personal God does exist and that Christianity is indeed true. Upon graduating from seminary I entered a lifetime of Christian service and ministry.

The first twenty years of ministry for me were in one of the so-called "mega-churches" of America, and everything seemed to go just as I had imagined. It was a thrilling, successful time of ministry. I loved ministering to college-age young people, and was privileged to see some fifty-five of them enter into fulltime Christian service. And then I began to experience some of the *"difficulties of ministry"* I had seen so many of my contemporaries go through. It seemed like the next fifteen years were "full of problems"—parishioner issues, staffing issues, board issues, pastors falling into sin, pastors on ego trips, and finally outright betrayal by a friend. I had never experienced anything like that . . . naturally, I prayed about it all, but things only continued to spiral downward. I remember confiding in a friend of mine I had grown close to over the years—he had experienced many of the same issues. I recall saying something like this to him: "If I had experienced these things *early on* in ministry, I can't imagine I would have stayed in it." Obviously, God knew how weak and feeble I was, so He spared me a lot of angst in those early years, but now He was about to take me to another level in my Christian walk. At this stage of my growth, I felt like I had come to the point where I was at least doing "fairly well" spiritually—though the horse I was riding on wasn't exactly "pure white," it was at least "light beige" in color . . . or so I thought.

Suffice it to say, "troubles" continued to mount, and the more I prayed the worse things seemed to get. You've probably heard the old expression: "Cheer up, things could be worse!" Sure enough, I cheered up, and things did get worse! Like everyone else, I began to question . . . everything. "God, what in the world is going on in my life? I thought I was on Your side. What did I do?" Many of you have probably asked the same kinds of questions—especially, those of you who have traveled this road for any significant period of time. It is inevitable for those of us who take this path in life—but I didn't realize that then. Somehow I thought by "doing the right things," essentially life and ministry would be an enjoyable, positive experience. In spite of all the testimonies to the contrary, I must have felt that those were not the "rule," but the "exceptions"—and as we all know, we are not the exceptions. Well, as my world grew "darker," so did my soul—I had never experienced a *"season of darkness"* in my soul before. Oh, there were challenging moments from time to time, but nothing at all like I was now going through . . . this was a monumental challenge for me. Though I would cry out to God . . . nothing would happen. Why was God being so "cruel" to me? I remember thinking, "If I treated people I love the way God treats me, they'd dump me in a minute!" How can a loving God treat me so "lousy"? The more water that went under the bridge, the worse things seemed to get . . . and finally, God had me right where He wanted me—sitting on the bench, so-to-speak, "all by my lonesome." Don't get me wrong—my wife was there with me, but the *"spiritually dark times"* we go through in life, we essentially go through "alone;" these are "one on one times" with just ourselves and God. Only God accompanies us during the spiritually dark parts of the journey.

Alas, I came face to face with something Scripture calls "the flesh" . . . couldn't believe it was as corrupt and rotten as it was. The truth of the matter is, there isn't "one ounce of good" in it. None. I remember thinking, "How in the world did I ever get this sinful?" I thought I rode a white horse! I guess I had always wanted to think that there was "some measure of good" in me. Not so. Nada. The challenge before me was that of discovering who this "old man" really was down deep . . . and what God had to say about all this. So I began to study—hour after hour, day after day, month after month—regarding this issue of the *"believer's soul."* I reviewed all my seminary notes—all five years of it— and not much seemed to stand out as to what I was now experiencing. I strongly identified with what Francis Schaeffer said: "I saw that the problem was with all the teaching I had received after I came to Christ, I received *'very little'* about what the Bible says regarding the meaning of the finished work of Christ for our present lives." Wow—that's exactly what I felt. For some reason, I had never gotten a good grasp of the old *"sin disposition"* that was in me, that inhabited a dark room in my soul. Admittedly, it was something that always bothered me, and frightened me to a degree, but I was largely ignorant of exactly how it operated in my life . . . so, like most believers, I tried to "lock the cellar door on it" and as much as was humanly possible keep it bound and tied up. Little did I know, you can't lock the door on the flesh. So here I was, just God and me, and the next thing I knew He was escorting me down into that "dark cellar" to examine what was there. He used some of the writings of the "great pillars of the faith" to reveal to me things I had never learned—things dealt with in pulpits all over America in a "very shallow manner." Why the shallowness, I thought—those men are no different than you and me. For the most part, we are all products of the same institutional (seminary) teaching and training. However, for some reason the "spiritual struggles and seasons of darkness" we go through as believers received very little attention in the seminary classroom—probably because most of the professors either hadn't yet experienced it in its fullness, or hadn't yet taken the time to study the issue and find answers to the hidden questions of the heart. That may not be a fair assessment, but I'm pretty sure there is a little truth to it. At any rate, gradually the "Son" began to shine in my life again, and the "song" in my heart returned (Ps 40:1–3). I describe how this happened a little later on in this *Introduction*.

Many Christians question whether or not it is possible for the soul of genuine believers to be overwhelmed with fear, despair and darkness. The testimony of Scripture suggests that it is. Many of the great saints of the Bible experienced extremely difficult times . . . times of confusion . . . times of doubt . . . times of spiritual darkness . . . times when they felt desperate . . . times of personal pain and despair . . . and times when they experienced no comfort or consolation from God at all. Some believers would have us think the entire Christian experience should be nothing but a positive, encouraging, victorious one—but the teachings of Scripture don't support that view. In spite of his incredible triumph over the prophets of Baal, **Elijah** fell into deep despair (1 Kg 19:4). **David,** a man after God's own heart, experienced significant suffering (some the result of his own sin) and frequently endured great despair (Ps 6:1–7; 10:1; 13:1–2; 22:1–2; 32:3–5; 38:1–22; 42:5, 6, 9, 11; 43:2, 5; 44:24; 69: 1–3; 142:1–7; 143:6–7; also read Ps. 88). **Jeremiah** time and again cried out to God in pain and despair; he didn't understand his suffering; his messages were a failure; worst of all, God Himself seemed distant and uncaring to him; his enemies were both inside and outside himself. Jeremiah never doubted that God was real, but at times he seemed to doubt God's sovereignty, and felt He was being unfair—he actually wished he had never been born; this happened more than once (Jer 11:18–23; 12:1–6; 15:10–21; 17:9–18; 18:18–23; 20:7–18).

Spiritual depression, despair and darkness are such pervasive maladies in believers' lives, they are often referred to by Christian psychologists as *"spiritual common colds."* The process of my own spiritual formation and sanctification has been characterized by periods of joyful victory and frustrating defeat. **C. S. Lewis,** in his book *A Grief Observed,* concluded that the spiritual darkness he experienced in the death of his wife "Joy" was a sort of divine shock treatment. He writes: "Nothing less will shake a man, or at any rate a man like me, out of his merely verbal thinking. . . . He has to be knocked silly before he comes to his senses. Only torture will bring out the truth. Only under torture does he discover it himself." Likening his former faith to a house of cards, Lewis concludes, "the sooner it was knocked down the better; and only suffering could do it" (Lewis, *Grief Observed*). Lewis experienced both the emotional and the intellectual pain of absence—not just the absence of his wife, but the immense absence of God. What disturbed him most was not the thought that God does not exist, but thought that He does exist, and that He may inflict pain from motives that we don't perceive as positive or even ethical. A vivid cinematic example occurs in Robert Duvall's movie *"The Apostle,"* when evangelist Sonny Dewey, who has had his own share of darkness, paces up and down in his room, abusing God in a loud voice, "I love you, Lord, but I'm mad at You!" Lewis ultimately decided that the pain he experienced had a redemptive sanctifying purpose in his life. The truth of the matter is, *God does to us whatever needs doing, even though it is often painful.* Our incomplete, prejudiced, and generally inadequate ideas of God must be shattered in order for us to have any hope of contact with the real God. If our ideas of God are inaccurate, they are like building a house with cards—God will knock the building flat. And He will knock it down as often as proves necessary. This is the supreme end toward which a "dark night of the soul" pushes us.

Many Christian psychologists use the book of Job to illustrate what depressive symptoms look like in real life—*Job* experienced extreme sadness (3:20; 6:2-3), desire for death (3:21; 7:15-16), sleep disturbance (7:4), pessimism about life (14:1), helplessness (3:26), viewing life as worthless (9:21), physical signs of distress (16:8; 17:7), loss of appetite (6:6–7), hopelessness or despair (6:11; 7:7; 17:1, 15), weakness of body and resolve (6:12–13), anger (7:17–19), loss of self-esteem (9:21), fear of suffering (9:28; 10:19; 17:6), bitterness (10:1), sense of rejection (19:13–20). Throughout each of these passages Job reached a point of despair that can technically be described as being severely clinically depressed because of the seriousness of his symptoms and the length of their duration. The believer becomes victorious in the process of sanctification and overcomes his *"dark night of the soul"* little by little as he sees Satan's lies for what they are, and replaces them with the truths of Christ. Darkness in the soul essentially is an absence or deficiency of light; and for most Christians it is a vast interior landscape of loneliness and abandonment. Even in the midst of our loved ones and friends we persist in feeling desperately alone. Many authors conclude that it is this pervasive sense of abandonment and loneliness in the midst of a crowd that is the essence of the dark night of the soul. In short, spiritual darkness is the medium through which we learn about our own suffering, and in doing so, we pursue the essence and purpose of our unique presence here in this life.

Doubt often comes when we let our circumstances control us—when great difficulties come we begin to doubt God's love and lose confidence in His sovereignty, and that ultimately weakens our character. The reality is this: *"negative circumstances initially have a negative impact upon us spiritually;"* that is, when we first encounter trials, discouragement is our first response. We see this time and again in the lives of saints throughout Scripture. Our immediate response is almost always negative because our default mode is the *flesh*—that is our first responder—it is only after we prayerfully reflect upon the difficulties of life in the light of Scripture, that we come to the point where we accept them for what they are and discover their redemptive value. Scripture is replete with examples of godly men stumbling in their faith when confronted with trials, and then getting back on their feet after imploring God's help. After **Peter** confidently proclaimed his faithfulness to Jesus, he denied Him with curses and wept bitterly (Mt 26:33–35; Mk 14:66–72). **Paul** "despaired even of life" (2 Cor 1:8), and agonized over his helplessness when struggling against the "flesh" (Rom 7:18–24). To a man, the ***disciples'*** hopes were dashed when Jesus was crucified (Lk 24:13–35); like everyone else, they thought that Jesus was going to free Israel from Roman rule. Their *"misunderstanding"* only served to feed their despair, just as our misunderstandings feed our despair. The disciples did not understand to whom they were truly in bondage, nor did they understand the true purpose of God's plan of salvation. Though God accomplished great things through all of these individuals, as persons of faith there were times that they all experienced their worlds spinning out of control. Christians down through the ages have interpreted trials and tribulations as being signs of *God's disfavor*—the reality is, they are actually signs of *God's transforming presence!* The foregoing biblical examples of the great people of faith illustrate for us that experiences of stress and despair can be times of greatest spiritual growth.

The poet and hymn writer William Cowper, who penned the famous hymn *"There is a Fountain,"* illustrates how dramatically God's grace can interact with our despair in another hymn he wrote called *"The Way."* Cowper was given to long periods of depression. On one occasion, he convinced himself that he had committed the unpardonable sin . . . he left his home on a foggy London night and walked toward the Thames River, determined to commit suicide by drowning. As he walked, the fog grew thicker and he lost his way . . . after several hours of blind wandering, he found himself back at his own doorstep. Astonished at God's intervention, he wrote a poem that later became this beloved hymn—

> *God moves in a mysterious way His wonders to perform;*
> *He plants His footsteps in the sea, and rides upon the storm.*
> *Judge not the Lord by feeble sense, but trust Him for His grace;*
> *Behind a frowning providence He hides a smiling face.*
> *Blind unbelief is sure to err and scan His work in vain;*
> *God is His own Interpreter, and He will make it plain.*

Job's story provides a framework for understanding this seemingly precarious, conflicted, hostile world in which we live. God allowed Satan to *test* Job (Job 1)—so also, this accuser of the brethren *tests our* *faith*. Every believer has a personal enemy, Satan, who consciously seeks to make him or her feel their faith is empty (1 Pet 5:8–9; Eph 6:10–12). But just as God set limits to what Satan could do to Job (Job 1:12), He also sets limits to what Satan can do to us (1 Cor 10:13; Lk 22:31–32). Suffering is the hardest and most complicated issue that believers have to face; the suffering Job was subjected to was so intense, it is hard for us to even imagine the depth of his pain . . . and the extremity of Christ's suffering is without parallel; His suffering was so severe that the Incarnate One Himself cried out to His Father in great agony, *"My God, My God, why have you left Me alone?"* How awful to feel that God is no longer near you, and not know why He has left you alone—this is the worst of all life's experiences. From the time of Adam and Eve, man has tried to escape suffering in every form. Suffering is a part of the human experience. Every adult either already has or will face grief and despair at a *significant level,* be it during the course of life or at the end of life—plans fail, loved ones die, and hopes are crushed. Because people often feel they don't deserve the suffering they are going through, it generally ushers in a bewildering despair—incidentally, when believers view suffering strictly as a repercussion for sin, they completely miss the primary purpose of suffering in their lives. Scripture teaches that believers suffer, not because they are being *punished* for some wrong, but because this is the instrument by which God *transforms* them into the image of His Son. Suffering is a vital component in God's plan of salvation (Acts 14:22; Rom 5:3–5; 8:17, 36; 2 Cor 1:5, 7; 4:8–9; Gal 6:17; Phil 1:29; 3:10; Col 1:24; 1 Th 3:3; 2 Tim 1:8; 2:3, 10, 12; Heb 12:5–11; Jam 1:2–4; 1 Pet 4:1, 12–13, 17–19; 2:21; 5:10; Rev 1:9). Remember, as believers we are to "die to self"—since when is death a pleasant experience?

Do we all experience the same degree of "suffering"? No, of course not—some will be martyred for their faith (since the first century some 43,000,000 Christians have died simply because they believed in Christ) . . . in all likelihood, the vast majority of us will not suffer martyrdom, but each of us will experience a significant degree of suffering in some way—be it through a debilitating illness or physical infirmity . . . a family or relational problem . . . divorce, betrayal, malicious slander or rejection . . . loneliness, unemployment or financial loss . . . being the victim of some crime or catastrophic loss . . . a mental or psychological disorder . . . or a time of reckoning on our deathbed—each of these experiences can produce a tremendous amount of pain and despair in a person's soul. Some of life's events are a great mystery to us . . . things happen in life that are way beyond our understanding . . . we do not know everything. There is coming a day, however, when we will fully understand that *everything* we went through in this life was a part of God's great and perfect plan for us (Rom 8:28), and that God used satanically induced despair to strengthen and refine us in our love for Him and for one another. The sufferings of this life not only make our temperament more like the person of Christ, but they also serve to detach us from the things of this world.

It is not at all uncommon for believers to buy into the idea that following Christ should bring a pleasant, trouble-free life—this is a very common misconception. We are often inclined to choose a holy life for what we get out of it—our own *personal happiness* is of tremendous importance to us. It is natural for us to think that a holy life should bring with it a substantial degree of personal happiness, security, success, health and wealth. According to Scripture, however, those are the wrong reasons for choosing to live a holy life. Though there are times when these things may be ours in abundance, that will not always be the case. Therefore, we have to be extremely careful not to link *circumstances* with a holy life. This can have disastrous consequences, because one day our lives will lack some or many of these qualities, and then we will doubt God's goodness. Job made this mistake, and just like you and me, it led him to question God's goodness (Job 29-31). We must always remember that trials and problems and tribulations have a *transforming purpose* in God's economy. Therefore, we must live a holy life for only one reason—"it is God's will for us"—as such, our prayer in all things must be, "Thy will be done, Lord, not mine."

Misunderstandings can gnaw at our souls as we seek for solutions to impossible situations. The prospect of future suffering and sorrow can paralyze our souls and place us in a state of near despair. It has been rightfully said that the greatest suffering in the soul is the kind when we thirst for God and find ourselves deprived of the awareness of His presence—there is no greater pain than when God seems distant and far away. We see this internal suffering in the lives of Peter and Paul as doubts assailed them—at times they were weary and Paul speaks of his anguish and weariness of soul as a sting of the flesh. *Internal suffering* can be more purifying than any other form of pain because we are forced to cope with it. We can distract ourselves and forget about a sprained ankle or a broken arm, but when depression, discouragement, dryness, weariness, sadness, worry and fear assail us, they hound us wherever we go. Mother Angelica in her book *"Healing Power of Suffering,"* says the "key" to experiencing God's healing is understanding *why* God permits suffering in the soul. She says interior trials sanctify us slowly, and carry within them the power to change us for the better—it is in the soul, in our personality and temperament, that change must occur if we are to reflect the image of Jesus. We can have cancer and be completely healed, but never change . . . we can experience victory over some difficult situation, but never change . . . but when our pain is inside our soul, and we cooperate with God's grace in using it, then it has the power to change us . . . and it is in our souls that God does His most magnificent work. Angelica goes on to say that . . .

- *Mental anguish* makes us depend upon His wisdom.
- *Doubts* increase our faith when we act according to our beliefs rather than our reason.
- *Fear* makes us trust God's providence and hope in His goodness.
- *Anxiety* leads us to distrust ourselves and release our problems to an all-loving God.
- *Worry* makes us realize our helplessness and instills a desire in us to fully depend upon God.
- *Discouragement* over our imperfections makes us strive for holiness with greater determination.
- *Uncertainty* as to our future makes us look forward to the Kingdom of Heaven.

- *Dryness* makes us patient as we seek to love God for Himself.
- *Disappointments* detach us from temporal things and serve to make us focus on eternal things.

My own personal mistake was grounded in the "experiences" I had as a young believer. Over the years, God had blessed me in a number of ways—there were few negatives and a lot of positives—and these tangible expressions of His love for me had influenced my *practical theology* to a degree; though my *biblical theology* had remained true to the text, I obviously had wandered in the practical outworking of that theology. Clearly I understood that *suffering* was a part of the equation, but deep down I also knew (or wanted to know) that *blessing* was also a part of the equation—I have placed these two terms in juxtaposition to each other to simply make a contrasting point, though ultimately these two concepts are not mutually exclusive; suffering is actually an incredible blessing, because it is used by God to transform us into the image of His Son. Continuing to develop my previous point—apparently, the spiritual experiences I had gone through in life, had caused me to gradually drift toward a more *"mechanical faith;"* that is, "if you do this, such and such happens"—essentially, it is the idea that if you do "right" God blesses, and if you do "wrong" God judges—thus my faith in practice became somewhat "mechanical." By the way, there are plenty of passages in Scripture that support this kind of thinking—throughout the Old Testament narrative God blessed obedience and judged disobedience (Ex 23:22–27; Lev 26:3–13; Deut 28:1–14; 28:15–68; Is 48:17–19; Ps 1:1, 4; 33:12; 84:12; 112:1–2; 119:1–2), and then there is that well-known New Testament dictum, *"we reap what we sow"* (2 Cor 9:6; Gal 6:7; Matt 25:14–29—also cross reference the proverbial wisdom of Scripture: Prov 11:14, 25–31; 12:24–25; 13:4, 11; 14:23; 15:1, 22; 21:5, 13, 23; 22:6, 8; 28:13, 27; 29:13; Job 4:8; Hos 8:7; 10:12–13). Though these teachings are indeed true, we must be careful that we don't misapply or misinterpret these truths, or insist on "reaping" soon after we have sown—you don't harvest a field of wheat the day after you sow the seed. In the spiritual realm, the rewards surely follow faithful sowing "in due season" (Gal 6:9)—we must also be mindful of the fact that some of our reaping will not occur until the life hereafter (Heb 10:36; 11:10, 13, 16, 39; Rev 21:10ff).

The principle of "sowing and reaping" is a fundamental truth about the universe—it is not a theory . . . it is an unalterable law. In the final analysis, nobody outwits it, and nobody escapes it. There are no exceptions. The principle of sowing and reaping is so entrenched in societal thought that it has actually become a popular axiom—frequently, you will hear people say: "You reap what you sow . . . what goes around comes around . . . garbage in, garbage out." It is a straight "cause and effect" principle. But when we insist on applying this truth only to the temporal realm we run into problems, because things don't *always* work that way—the problem most people have is that they don't include the eternal dimension in their thinking. By the way, when we maintain that positive conditions are a sign of *God's favor*, and negative conditions are a sign of *God's disfavor*, the reality of life itself will eventually teach us that this is not always the case. Down through the ages believers have struggled with the idea that wicked men often prosper (Ps 73), and that righteous men often suffer (Job; Jn 9). Nevertheless, most Christians generally come to the same conclusion that the adherents of every other religion come to—that *blessings* are a sign of God's favor, and that *trials* are a sign of His disfavor, and that "God" or the "Supreme Reality" (or whatever name you choose to give Him), ultimately determines what we reap. Every religion in the world operates under just such an economy—God is favorably disposed toward those who do good, and unfavorably disposed toward those who do bad (Jam 4:6). Hinduism and Buddhism refer to this principle as *"karma;"* which, essentially, is the belief that in every action there is a consequence. The Hindus go so far as to apply this to every action, word, and thought—all of these are accounted for in the next life (reincarnation). Why is it that *all religions* embrace the "law of sowing and reaping"? Because God has placed His moral laws, the certainty of a future judgment, and eternity in the hearts of *all men*—as such, all religions have the same moral foundation, a system of rewards and punishment, and some kind of afterlife.

A natural outgrowth of this principle, is that we are all predisposed to thinking that God operates much like we operate—when someone treats us good, we return the favor . . . when someone treats us bad, we take offense to it. People like people who treat them good, and don't like people who treat them bad. Thus it is natural for human beings to assume that God operates in a similar fashion. The "law of sowing and reaping" supports this kind of thinking—even the most casual observer would conclude that this is a fairly good description of the way things *generally* go in this world—that the world essentially operates under the old maxim "what goes around comes around" in life. Hence, the vast majority of people live their lives with the understanding that *"what they do"* significantly influences *"what they experience"* in life. Because they want their lives to be as comfortable and trouble-free as possible, they do what is necessary to insure the best possible outcome (at least to a modest degree); obviously the more disciplined the individual is, the more effort he puts forth to make sure that this indeed is the case—this is the reason we eat healthy food, get ample sleep, exercise properly, go to the doctor for an annual check-up, purchase insurance, study for exams, change the oil in our cars, lock the door when we leave home, turn off the lights in the day-time to lower your electric bill, respect others and treat them nice, answer phone messages from friends, and take steps to prevent any other problem we think might happen. Principally, people do things to insure that they will reap positive benefits . . . they don't purposefully do things that will ultimately bring pain and discomfort into their lives; i.e., they don't intentionally plant "weeds" in their garden. Furthermore, the religious person applies the principle of sowing and reaping to every facet of life, and actually seeks God's help to do those things that will bring the "greatest good and blessing" into his life.

Let me apply this popular theological view to my own "financial stewardship." Though some in the charismatic community teach a *prosperity doctrine*—a kind of selfish stewardship where you give that you might receive—that was not at all the direction I was leaning . . . but the way God had *blessed* me suggested that He was taking care of my financial needs; so I began to naturally assume that God was blessing me financially because I was being faithful to Him with what He had given to me (Mt 6:33; Lk 6:38). This is a very popular teaching here in the western world. The danger with this kind of thinking is that it creeps into every other area of life, and God becomes a kind of *"celestial vending* *machine"*—you do *this* and this happens . . . and you do *that* and that happens . . . if you have devotions in the morning, God blesses (peace, joy, and prosperity!) . . . if you don't have devotions, God doesn't bless (woe is me! trials and problems!). I remember a time as a young man in ministry when I went to the airport to pick up a missionary friend who was arriving back in the states from Africa—because no one else on our church's staff volunteered to pick him up, I said I would. So here I was . . . the good guy! riding a white horse! doing the right thing! even though I also had a tight schedule! Well . . . as I was traveling down the freeway on my way to the airport, a large truck in front of me kicked up a good sized pebble that cracked my windshield. The thought came into my mind, "Lord, why did you let that happen? I chose to do the right thing, and this is what I get for it?" Obviously, God didn't audibly respond back to me, but He left this frustrating little issue on my plate for me to stew over for a good awhile—"Why would God have let that happen?" I wondered. "Was there a reason for it?" As you can see, that little incident got me to thinking about "spiritual cause and effect" issues—"connecting the spiritual dots" if you will.

The past ten years became the "crucible" for me. God was now elevating my game to a new level. No longer would He let me be content with a practical theology that really didn't mesh with *reality*. He was now going to "force my hand," as it were, to deal with issues as they really were. Keep in mind, up until this point, God had predominantly operated in my life in a *"revelatory manner"*—that is, He would clearly reveal His will and direction to me as the need arose. If I was to make a "change in ministry," He would make it very clear exactly what I was to do—I refer to this mode of operation as being *"revelatory;"* His answers didn't require supra-high levels of spiritual discernment. I recall as a young man making my first "ministry decision"—this was my prayer: "Lord, I'm not one of Your brighter students; I want to do Your will, but I'm a novice at this sort of thing, so You need to make it very clear to me exactly what it is You want me to do." Guess what? God was very clear as to what He wanted me to do! Well, for years God *clearly revealed* His will to me when I would ask Him. Then the Lord brought into my life a set of circumstances that really challenged the *practical outworking* of my faith. In the past ten years, I have been betrayed by a friend, and subjected to persecution in the marketplace for my faith (it cost me a teaching position in one of the local secular colleges—in that particular situation, however, it was clear that Satan played a role in that). The betrayal issue was a more difficult issue for me—I spent a couple of months on my knees coming to terms with what had happened, and processing the need to not only forgive my friend, but to also ask God to bless him (I was strongly convicted on that point); though he had clearly made a mistake, he was still a brother of mine. God was gracious, and I came through those two episodes rejoicing in His goodness. And then came, what I like to call, *"the time of my testing."* In short, after a lifetime of reasonably *faithful stewardship* (my wife and I tithed faithfully and sacrificially, and lived a more frugal lifestyle than the norm), my wife and I pretty much *lost everything we owned*—we had a couple of clients walk on debts owed to us in the amount of about $150,000 . . . we lost $51,500 through a $230 million ponzi scheme that a number of our friends had also become involved in . . . we lost our home to foreclosure . . . we lost both of our businesses, in which we had invested our life's savings . . . we lost our 401k . . . we lost all three of our automobiles . . . and we incurred an outstanding debt of some $284,000 (I remember that number well!). Ultimately, we sold most of our possessions and settled the entire debt at about 25 cents on the dollar (we chose not to file bankruptcy). The two years it took to settle everything seemed like a lifetime. By the way, we didn't get an "easy way out" of this mess . . . we actually got a "very long difficult way out," including a court battle (which was not nearly as joyful as one might think, given the fact that we won it).

All the while, we were on our knees . . . daily and often . . . yet God never seemed to show up. The process only seemed to get worse and the way out more exasperating. At this point, I began to reflect on all I had learned over the years, and why everything now had gone south. It was actually too much to really get angry about—anger seems like an appropriate response for smaller problems . . . not for bigger problems. Bigger problems take all of the wind out of your sail . . . they knock the props out from under you . . . they take your breath away . . . they suck the life out of you . . . they leave you despairing and bewildered . . . they make you question everything . . . there is simply no energy left to be angry. What else can a Christian do but importune the throne of God? If you're a realist, there really isn't anything else a believer can do. What can you do? Run from God? Insist that the world become what you want it to be? Obviously, those choices are not reasonable; read the book of Jonah. At any rate, God had me right where He wanted me—on the bench. Without going into more details, I began seeking "God's new direction for my life"—my mantra was, *"God, Anything! Anywhere!"*—which essentially meant, "Lord, just get me out of this mess! I will do anything and go anywhere!" I was hanging on to the *hope* that God was going to deliver me, just like He did Job, and restore my little fortune! Sounds good, right? No such luck! God was silent . . . not a peep . . . not a whisper . . . not even a still quiet voice . . . nothing . . . just absolute silence! I remember thinking, "What in the world am I going to do? Obviously, I can't just sit and do nothing!" By the way, I couldn't find a job of any kind no matter how much I tried. And there in the midst of this *dark winter* in my soul, God was at work . . .

It was time to get into the Word and rethink everything I had learned as a believer. Wow . . . this was going to be a journey. I started all the way back at square one. Being unemployed gave me the opportunity to study the Word *fulltime*. God had never been silent and unresponsive to my cries before—but He was now—obviously He had a *purpose* in all this. This was my season of *spiritual darkness*—little did I know, countless others had traversed this wilderness road before me. Throughout this *spiritual winter* experience, I knew God was there, even though He was silent; but His silence was exasperating and frustrating to me—I so much wanted to see the evidence of His love again. I felt the need to start over and reconstruct my faith from the ground up . . . concluding that I must have erred somewhere along the way in my thinking. Initially, I compiled about nine hundred pages of single-spaced notes . . . I studied the Word along with several commentaries and books of theology . . . and slowly the foundation of my faith was reaffirmed and substantiated . . .

but God was still not going to release me from this journey of discovery. He would now have me plunge into the major issues of what I like to call *"soul transformation,"* and the believer's experience regarding his journey of holiness and sanctification. This incredibly enlightening chapter of my life took me back to the writings of the puritans, and many of the great aging saints of the last two hundred years. These men were refreshingly transparent, open and honest, which was tremendously meaningful to me. They delved into those *sticky spiritual issues* that have troubled the human soul since the fall of man. What a liberating feast God had prepared for me.

This book that is now in your hands is a product of that search. It doesn't necessarily include the years of preliminary research that I did through various commentaries and books of theology—at least not directly—but it does include the reviews and summaries of some of the most significant books and studies on the subject that I was able to assemble the past couple of years. The process I use when reading a book is this—if I find the book an encouragement to my heart, I go through it a second time critically, underlining and high-lighting and making marginal notes. The third time through the book, I identify the major teachings of the book. After that, I then do a "summary" of the book—*that is the end product that this particular book contains.* These "notes," if you will, represent those issues that were particularly meaningful to me when I studied them; such notes become sources of encouragement to me later on—they're like a spiritual diary for me—and every time I re-read one of the summaries, my soul is nourished; that's how significant these subject matters are for me personally. I have read this series of summaries at least a dozen times from cover to cover—not only because I ended up printing it, but also because of the need to "remember" and "reflect upon" what I had learned. From my perspective, the information this book contains is *critical* to the believer's well-being . . . so critical, that I can't imagine not reading these summaries many more times throughout the years God still has planned for me. After forwarding several of these "summaries" to friends of mine, and getting positive feedback from them, I felt the need to put a number of them into a single book.

So, rather than having others read twenty-two of the most select books on *"Soul Transformation,"* they can read the "meatiest portions" of those studies in a single volume.

The style of writing that I use when doing summaries is a kind of "devotional style"—as such, the material is meant to be read in a reflective meditative manner. It should also be noted, on occasion I took the liberty to expand and clarify some of the issues the various authors taught; you will find these supplemental studies offset with a "border" around them—my intention was always to complement their material, not to argue against it or develop some totally unrelated topic. In addition, I made the "lead statements" in every paragraph **bold**, to assist the reader . . . and then <u>underlined</u>, *italicized*, and **emboldened** words and phrases to help communicate and highlight the major concepts that are presented. Hopefully, you will find these writing features helpful as well. Another element I included is a <u>*Glossary of Terms*</u> at the end of the book; a study of these terms will prove most helpful to those not familiar with them. Furthermore, for those interested in identifying the location from where I got the material, I placed within each study the *"page numbers"* of the author's book where he discusses the matters presented—for instance, if you go to "page three" of the first summary, you'll notice (9–35) at the end of the first paragraph—that means all of the material "preceding" those numbers was taken from *pages 9–35* of Martyn Lloyd-Jones' book, *"Spiritual Depression."* The material which follows that to the end of the first paragraph on "page four" was taken from *pages 36–63* of his book, and so on. Should you decide to reference the material, you can do so by reading those particular pages.

The "topics" I have covered in this book all relate to the ongoing transformation, liberation, and sanctification of the believer's soul. The various issues presented not only include the positive experiences the believer goes through on his spiritual journey, but the negative experiences he goes through as well—these experiences range from joyful to painful, gratifying to frustrating, encouraging to debilitating. There is also a presentation in this book of the unilateral work God does in the believer's heart (irrespective of the believer's input), and the work He does in the believer's life as a result of the believer's faithful cooperation. By discussing such topics, it is only logical that the targeted audience to whom this book was written is "believers." The believer should know that without a firm understanding of the issues presented in this book, he is simply left to struggle without answers, and combat the enemy of his soul with insufficient weaponry; hence, the expressed purpose for my writing this book. My heart bleeds for those Christians who "wander aimlessly" in their Christian life—in a sense, they are like sheep without a shepherd; they are ignorant of many of the *sobering spiritual realities of life,* as well as all God has really done for them as one of His children, all He is continuing to do for them, and all He is going to do for them in the future. My frustration with "western (American) Christianity" is that it is *overly simplistic;* it teaches only one side of grace; it lacks a cohesive theology of holiness; it lacks a theology of adversity and suffering; and it offers no teaching at all on the critical issues of "darkness in the soul" and "seasons of darkness"—consequently, it leaves the struggling believer bewildered, frustrated and oftentimes guilt-ridden. Furthermore, its teachings on faith, struggling with the flesh, and walking in the Spirit are *very shallow* at best.

My heart not only grieves for parishioners, but also for "pastors." Our seminaries, for the most part, have done a reasonably good job of teaching us about the fundamentals of the faith, and have given us a good overview and introduction to numerous biblically related subject matters—studies in theology, original language studies (Hebrew and Greek), hermeneutics (science of literary interpretation), church history, missions and evangelism, discipleship, philosophy and ethics, Christian education, pastoral care ministry, spiritual leadership, biblical counseling, and various courses on books of the Bible. Being as nearly "every discipline" needs at least one course, and some two, three or four courses, that limits the amount of time one can give to some of the more critical issues like *soul transformation.* Therefore, from my perspective, our seminaries have not dealt sufficiently with the matters presented in this book—spiritual formation, spiritual development, and the nuances of spiritual growth—they simply do a piecemeal study on the "spiritual disciplines" that are needed in the believer's life. Let me give a word of exhortation to pastors at this point: I would like you to read through this entire book before you start preaching on the material that is in it. One thing is certain, you will find a significant amount of material in this book to preach on. If you will read through the entire book first, you will gain a better perspective on the subject matter as it is presented, and enhance your ability to communicate it with greater clarity. Obviously, none of us as pastors come to this subject with an "empty cupboard"—we have all agonized over these issues for years . . . Lord willing, this book will shine a light on these issues in a new and refreshing way for you. My heart's position is that you preach *"Soul Transformation"* issues at least once a month. It has been well said, "If you speak to discouragement, you will never lack for an audience." You and I both know that the Christian community in America is "hurting terribly;" they are desperately crying out for answers that bring peace to their souls. They are tired of spiritual pretense and inadequate answers, so be transparent in your preaching, and expound upon those issues that deal with *"pain in the soul."*

It should also be noted, this book does not contain a number of "extreme positions" that only a radical few endorse, or that are suspiciously questioned by conservative theologians. The teachings in this book reflect those of some of the most respected Christian writers since the reformation. They have long been recognized by many in the Christian world as being "pillars of the faith." They include ***seventeenth thru nineteenth century writers***—Jonathan Edwards, John Owen, Thomas Watson, George Whitefield, Charles Spurgeon, John Newton, John Bunyan, Alexander Maclaren, Dwight L. Moody . . . ***twentieth century writers***—Oswald Chambers, G. Campbell Morgan, A. W. Tozer, Henry A. Ironside, Donald G. Barnhouse, Martyn Lloyd-Jones, C. S. Lewis, John R. W. Stott, Warren Wiersbe, Francis Schaeffer, James Montgomery Boice . . . and ***contemporary writers***—James I. Packer, Ravi Zacharias, R. C. Sproul, Charles Ryrie, Alastair Begg, Eugene Peterson, John MacArthur, David Jeremiah and Charles Stanley. Furthermore, those ***Christian colleges and seminaries*** in America that favorably align themselves with these teachings are—Moody Bible Institute, Wheaton College, Dallas Theological Seminary, Trinity Evangelical Divinity School, Reformed Theological Seminary, Gordon-Conwell Theological Seminary, Talbot Graduate School of Theology, Western Seminary, Southwestern Seminary, Denver Seminary, Phoenix Seminary, Westminster Theological Seminary, and Calvin Theological Seminary, just to name a few. I listed the names of individuals and institutions above to give those who are less theologically discerning "confidence" in the credibility of the various positions that are presented in this book.

As the author of this book, perhaps a brief introduction is appropriate. I was born in Calgary, Canada in 1943; my parents and grandparents grew up on farms in Scandinavia and Canada, and we immigrated to the states in 1948. The evangelical community in those days was highly conservative and legalistic—*"certain behaviors"* were the distinguishing characteristics of spirituality. If you struggled with "sin," you were viewed as near apostate—as such, Christians lived their lives putting on a "good front." It was an interesting era—western society in those days exhibited a lot of admirable qualities, and people basically kept their problems "in house." So there was a degree of moral discipline back then that no longer exists in today's society. Hypocritical? Perhaps. In part. Nevertheless, back in the 50s people essentially subscribed to a Judeo-Christian ethic—they were outwardly polite, respectful, moral and kind. It was an age of *conformity*. Once the mid-60s arrived, however, *nonconformity* fast became the mood of the day (Judges 21:25), and every diabolical behavior imaginable exploded onto the scene—profanity, drugs, sex, questioning authority, and being unashamedly transparent—obviously, these behaviors affected the Christian community as well, both for good and for bad. For the most part, the vast majority of clergy back then were still "old school," because this new *independent spirit* came upon us so quickly. As such, the people in the pew learned to live compromising lives, and before long this transparent spirit of nonconformity also crept into the church; and therein lay the challenge of the day. It was precisely during this time in our culture that I recommitted of my life to Christ—what followed were some forty years of ministry, both in the pastorate and the college classroom. Though believers, in large part, still try to *"smile"* their way through life (as in the past), the spiritual battles within are becoming more and more evident even on their faces—society itself is becoming increasingly debased, degenerate, and corrupt. The hearts of believers across the broad spectrum of Christendom are *"crying out for answers"* to the real problems of the soul—superficiality no longer cuts it when you are genuinely hurting. Fortunately, it is in just such an environment that God's Spirit is best able to do His quickening work in the soul.

I have borne my soul in this book for your benefit, and have been as transparent as I can be with my thoughts and convictions. My prayer is that God will use the teachings of some of the greatest Christians writers in the history of the Church to further *"fan the flame"* in your heart for true spirituality. God willing, that indeed will be the case. Stoke the flame within, my friend.

In the good yoke,
Dr. D. W. Ekstrand

CHAPTER 1

A summary of the book...

"SPIRITUAL DEPRESSION"
by Martyn Lloyd-Jones (1899–1981)

The psalmist David writes, "Why are you cast down, O my soul" (Ps 42:5)—David was sad, troubled, perplexed, disquieted, unhappy and spiritually depressed—a very common condition; obviously he felt overwhelmed within himself. David was an *introvert*—many of the greatest saints are introverts; the *extrovert* is generally a more superficial person. In the natural realm there is the type of person who is always analyzing himself, analyzing everything he does. The danger for such people is to become "morbid." The great Henry Martyn was this type of man—he was a highly introspective introvert who suffered from an obvious tendency to morbidity. Introspective individuals seem to be highly centered on themselves. When believers become depressed it is because their focus is upon themselves—"they forget about God"—hence the psalmist says to himself, "Hope thou in God!" (Ps 42:5)

Notice the psalmist addresses himself—"he talks to himself," and herein he discovers the cure. The main problem in the whole matter of "spiritual depression" in a sense is this—we allow our "self" to talk to us instead of *"talking to ourself."* Most unhappiness in life is due to the fact that we "listen to ourselves" instead of "talking to ourselves." David, in effect, says, "Self, listen for a moment to what I have to say—why are you so cast down?" The main art in the matter of spiritual living is to know how to handle yourself, question yourself, and preach to yourself—you must remind yourself who God is, and what God has done, and what God has promised to do—this is the essence of the treatment in a nutshell. We must understand that this *"self"* of ours (this *other man* within us) has got to be handled; do not listen to him! turn on him! speak to him! remind him of what you know! So rather than listening to him and allowing him to drag you down and depress you—*you must take control!*

Deliverance from spiritual depression begins with an understanding of "justification"—not sanctification, as one might suspect. "This is life eternal, to know Thee, the only true God, and Jesus Christ, whom Thou has sent" (Jn 17:3). As a believer, are you truly enjoying God? Is He the center of your life? He is meant to be. If He is not, you are living in sin—that is the essence of sin. Remember the "good news"—God made *Christ* to be the propitiation for our sins—that is, God made Christ responsible for our sins; they were all placed upon Him and God dealt with them and punished them in His Son. So Christ is our salvation—we accept Him as our Deliverer and Savior by faith. God then imputes Christ's righteousness to us. ***Here is the great exchange: He takes our wickedness and gives us His righteousness!*** To get rid of "spiritual depression" you must say farewell to your past! No matter how dark the stains may be, they have all been blotted out! It is finished! Never look back on your sins again! They will only "depress" you! ***If you focus on your sinfulness, you will only conclude that "you are not good enough!"*** And whether you believe it or not, *nobody* is good enough—that is not the issue. The issue is not our goodness; the issue is God's goodness.

It is only when we truly trust Christ that true happiness and joy are possible for us. Deliverance is not found in making resolutions to live a better life; it is not found by studying, fasting, grieving or praying. Salvation is simply a matter of faith in Christ. You must repeatedly tell yourself, "I rest my faith on Christ alone, who died for my transgressions to atone." Remember, a man is justified (made righteous) by "faith"—not by the "deeds" of the Law—your works and behavior have nothing to do with your being saved. Furthermore, since we are "eternally saved by faith," our salvation is not maintained by "good works." *As long as you see your "sins" as a detriment with regard to your acceptance before God, you will negate the work of the cross in your life,* because you will live as though "your sins" really have not been fully dealt with. This is a *"critical issue"* for many Christians—they have been "set free" from the prison of sin . . . their prison cell has been unlocked . . . yet they continue to live in it! Jesus is the Savior of *sinners,* among whom, writes Paul, "I am foremost of all!" (1 Tim 1:15). (9–35)

It is sad and tragic that so many Christians are frustrated and miserable—The Protestant Reformation brought peace and happiness because the central doctrine of "justification by faith" was rediscovered. One of the most remarkable miracles our Lord performed was the healing of a "blind man" (Mk 8:22–26). When Jesus spat upon His eyes, He asked the blind man what he saw—he said he saw "trees walking." Though one can say that the man was *no longer blind*, yet he obviously did not see perfectly—that description is precisely where most Christians find themselves; they are disquieted and unhappy because of this lack of clarity regarding the doctrine of "justification by faith." They simply see men as "trees walking"—there is confusion in what they see; they don't understand certain basic truths. What they do is mix-in their own ideas with spiritual truth, and stop studying the Bible and praying.

What is the cure? In the illustration above, what saved the "blind man" was his *absolute honesty*—he fully submitted himself to Christ, and did not object to further treatment. Conversely, our response must be similar: "I want the truth whatever it costs me." The blind man listened to Jesus and his sight was *fully restored*—"he saw every man clearly." If you are unhappy about yourself—go to Christ, go to His Word, wait upon Him, plead with Him, hold on to Him, and ask Him in the words of the hymn—

> *Holy Spirit, Truth Divine, Dawn upon this soul of mine;*
> *Word of God, and inward Light, Wake my spirit, clear my sight.*

Spiritual depression or unhappiness in the Christian life is very often due to our failure to realize the greatness of the *gospel*. Some think that it is merely a message of "forgiveness;" others conceive of it as only "moral" in nature. The truth of the matter is, the gospel is a "whole view of life"—it is not partial or piecemeal—consequently the "whole man" must be involved in it—the *mind*, the *heart* and the *will*. There is a danger in having a purely "intellectual" experience, just as there is a danger in having a purely "emotional" experience—many Christians are content to simply live on their "feelings" (their head isn't engaged at all). By the way, we must put things in the right order—mind, heart, and will. "Truth" must be first—once we know the truth, it will move the heart, and once the heart is engaged, your greatest desire will be to live it. The *heart* is always to be influenced through the *understanding*, which in turn will work upon the *will*. (36–63)

Paul wrote to Timothy, "Keep the faith and a good conscience; some have suffered shipwreck with regard to their faith" (1 Tim 1:19). That lack of balance is one of the great causes not only of unhappiness, but of failure and of stumbling in the Christian life. Many suffer shipwreck because their soul is troubled, but every Christian will experience a *"troubled soul"*—the Christian life is a "fight of faith," a "test of faith," and the devil will do all he can to rob us of our joy and make our lives miserable. Where believers go astray is that they tend to focus on their *performance* (they are preoccupied with themselves), rather than on their *relationship to God* (justification). When we come back to the gospel of grace, it is all a matter of belief or unbelief—the problem is *unbelief*; the solution is *belief*. If you find yourself dwelling on your "sin," you have not fully resolved in your heart the work of Christ on the cross—*"the blood of Jesus Christ keeps on cleansing us from all sin"* (1 Jn 1:7—present tense!). That is what happens when you become a believer—believe it! We must be very clear about "justification"—not only do we experience the "forgiveness of our sins," but we have also been "declared righteous" by God Himself. Ultimately it all comes down to this—*the real cause of "troubled souls" is the failure to realize that we are "one with Christ"—"united with Christ."* We died with Christ . . . we have been buried with Christ . . . we have been raised with Christ . . . and we are now seated in heavenly places in Christ! (Rom 6:3–11; Eph 2:6). Paul says we are to "reckon these things as being so" (Rom 6:11). If you are looking at your past and your sins and you are depressed, it means that you are *listening to the devil*. Rejoice in the grace and mercy of God that has blotted out your sins and made you His child. Stop looking at yourself and begin to enjoy *Him!* By God's grace you are what you are—it is all *"grace!"* Become absorbed in the "grace and love of God" and you will forget all about yourself—it will deliver you from self-interest, self-concern, and from depression (which is the result of focusing on self). (64–105)

The number one subject that brings people to counsel with their pastor is the "problem of feelings;" which is really natural, because we all desire to be *"happy."* Nobody wants to be miserable. Our feelings, and emotions, and sensibilities obviously are of vital importance to us—we have been made in such a way that they play a dominant part in our make-up. Probably the biggest problem for people worldwide, is their inability to handle their *"feelings and emotions."* Timothy was a naturally nervous person who was given to *depression*—both things are often found in the same person. We all have certain problems in the Christian life—every man has his own burden to carry—those who are more naturally given to introspection are more often given to depression. The danger comes in submitting to our *"feelings"* and allowing them to govern and control our lives. Obviously, if you are guilty of sin, you are going to "feel miserable"—"the way of the transgressor is hard" (Prv 13:15). If you break God's laws and violate His rules you will not be happy.

There is only one recourse: "Go to God at once, and bare your soul"—acknowledge your sin and believe that because you have done so, He really does forgive you. Avoid the common mistake of concentrating too much on your *feelings*—this is an extremely common error frequently made by Christians; they are too preoccupied with their "feelings"—the dynamic of the flesh is "feeling," and the dynamic of the Spirit is "faith"—we are called to "believe God's Word" even when our feelings send us another message! You have to speak the Word of God to yourself—"Why are you cast down my soul? Hope in God . . . believe what He has said . . . trust Him" (Ps 42). Scripture says, "Blessed are they who hunger and thirst after righteousness"—not after happiness! *Seek for happiness and you will never find it; seek righteousness and you will discover you are happy!* Do you want to experience true happiness? There is only one thing to do—*seek Christ*. He is our joy and our happiness. Seek Him, seek His face, and all other things shall be added unto you (Mt 6:33). (107–118)

There is no part of the Christian life that is without its "dangers"—Not only do we have to contend with "our enemy Satan," but we also have to contend with "our old nature." The parable of the *Kingdom of Heaven* in Matthew 20:1–16 is about a landowner who "hires laborers" to work in his vineyard at all hours of the day, including the "eleventh hour"—and each of them was paid the same wage. Those who worked "several hours" thought they should receive more than those who only worked one hour. The landowner responded, "Did I not pay you what you agreed to? Is it not lawful for Me to do what I will with my own money? Is your eye full of evil because I am good? So the last shall be first, and the first last." The principle of this parable is this—the Christian life is *all of grace* from the beginning to the end. Jesus is the landowner in this parable—and what we see here is that *it is never too late to be saved!* The question is this: Why did those who worked longer hours *"feel cheated"*?

1. Their *"attitude"* towards themselves and their work was wrong—They had "happily agreed" to accept what Jesus paid them; thus something is wrong with their "attitude." These men were clearly conscious of everything *they* did—they had their eyes on *"themselves."*

2. They were *"assessing"* their work—They were keeping an account of others also, and keeping a careful record of all they did and how long they had been working. The Lord is concerned with that kind of attitude—it is fatal in the Kingdom of God. He detected it in Peter's statement: "We have left all and followed Thee, what do we get?" That kind of attitude is entirely antithetical to the realm of the Spirit and of the Kingdom. This parable exposes men for who they really are—they are men with a *"very selfish spirit."* There was not

the slightest bit of "rejoicing over how gracious the Lord was with others." They had completely forgotten the *"principle of grace"*—they felt they were entitled to more than the others; as such, they were clearly "upset!"

3. <u>They began to *"murmur"*</u>—Their happiness and joy were completely gone, and they "murmured" because they felt they were not being treated fairly; they actually felt they were being dealt with harshly. What a tragic thing it is that Christians should be *murmuring* when they should be *rejoicing* in Christ. That is not all—their murmuring led to "having contempt for others" and "being jealous of others." It is the same principle of the "elder brother" in the parable of the Prodigal Son. The attitude of the laborers was *"selfish and self-centered."*

4. <u>They had a feeling in their heart that the landowner was *"unjust"*</u>—The Christian is often tempted by the devil to feel that God is *not being fair*. What a miserable thing "self" is. The devil comes to us and we listen, and we begin to doubt whether God is just and righteous in His dealings with us. *"Self"* needs to be exposed for what it is—it is the greatest enemy of the soul, and it leads to misery and unhappiness! Many of us in reading these "charges" against the laborers are still siding with them in their response! Our *flesh* still is not convinced they were wrong! We are still prone to question God's method of operation, and whether or not He is really being fair! That is the essence of the flesh!

What is the cure for this problem? It is to understand the controlling principle of the Kingdom of God—the principle is that in the Kingdom of God everything is essentially different from everything in every other kingdom. Jesus says in effect, the Kingdom of God is *not like* that which you have always known; it is something completely new and different. The first thing you have to realize is that "if any man be in Christ he is a new creature, old things are passed away, and all things become new" (2 Cor 5:17). The entire realm in which we now live is different. It has nothing to do with the principle of the old life. All of our thinking as Christians has to be different. We must stop bringing all of our *"old* *ideas"* to the table. There is nothing so "wrong" as the spirit which argues that "because I do this, I have a right to expect something in return." God is not a celestial vending machine. There is nothing you can do to manipulate Him. No matter what you do, be it praying or anything else, you must never argue that because you have "done" something, you are "entitled" to get something. Never! We must get rid of the *bargaining spirit* that says, "if I do *this* then *that* will happen." Such thinking makes faith mechanical. Remember, even our "rewards" are of grace! God doesn't need to give them to us! In short, to think in terms of "bargains" and to "murmur" at unacceptable results, implies a distrust of God—watch your spirit lest you harbor the thought that God is not dealing with you justly or fairly. This is an extremely common problem.

Do not keep a record or an account of your work! Give up being a bookkeeper. In the Christian life we must desire nothing but *"His glory!"* nothing but to *"believe Him!"* nothing but to *"please Him!"* Leave the bookkeeping to Him and to His grace. Let Him keep the accounts. The truth is, there is nothing so gracious as God's method of accountancy. Be prepared for surprises in this Kingdom. The truth is, you never know what is going to happen! The last shall be "first"—think about that! What a complete reversal of our materialistic outlook—everything in God's kingdom is upside down! When Jesus separates the "sheep" from the "goats" on judgment day (Mt 25:31–40), He will say to us His sheep, "To the extent that you served one of the least of these brothers of Mine, you served Me—come inherit the Kingdom prepared for you!" We will be totally surprised by many of our acts of kindness and service. This life is all of grace! "By the grace of God we are what we are!" The secret of a happy Christian life is not only to realize that it is all of grace, but to "rejoice in that fact!" (120–132)

Jesus asked His disciples, "Where is your faith?" The whole issue here is the problem and question of the nature of faith. Many believers are often troubled because they have never clearly understood the nature of faith. Remember all believers have been given the "gift of faith," that enables us to believe on the Lord Jesus Christ for salvation, but that does not mean that they fully understand the nature of faith. Though faith is given as a "gift," from there on we have to do certain things about it—there is a vital difference between the *gift of faith* and the *walk of faith* or the life of faith. God starts us off in this Christian life and then we have to walk in it—*"we walk by faith, not by sight"* (2 Cor 5:7). When Jesus rebuked the disciples during the storm that raged on the sea of Galilee (Mk 4:35–41), He did not rebuke them because of their alarm or their terror, but for their *"lack of faith."* Jesus marveled at their "unbelief." The disciples had done everything they could in the storm, but it did not seem to be of any avail. Here is a critical point: *Jesus rebuked them for being in that state of agitation and terror while He was with them in the boat!* A Christian should never, like the worldly person, be depressed, agitated, alarmed, frantic, not knowing what to do. Paul said, "I have learned to be content in whatever circumstances I am in" (Phil 4:11). That is what the Christian is meant to be like. The Christian is never meant to be carried away by his feelings and "lack self-control"—whatever his circumstances. That is why the disciples were so alarmed, agitated, miserable and unhappy.

The disciples' condition also implied a "lack of trust and confidence in God"—Jesus said in effect: "Do you feel like this in spite of the fact that I am with you? Do you not trust Me?" Remember the words of the disciples: "Teacher, do You not care that we are perishing?" (Mk 4:38). Such a response shows a lack of faith in Christ's concern and care for us—as such, we become agitated and disturbed. It is the same response as the unbeliever. The issue is this: We must never allow ourselves to be agitated and disturbed whatever the circumstances, because to do so implies a "lack of faith and confidence in Christ"—at this point we simply do not believe God. One might call this kind of situation *"the trial of faith."* Take the eleventh chapter of Hebrews—every one of those men was "tried." They had been given the gift of faith and great promises, and then their faith was tried. Peter says the same thing: "Though you are distressed by various trials, the reason for the trials is that the *proof of your faith*, being more precious than gold which is perishable, though it be tested with fire (tried), might be found to result in praise and glory and honor at the revelation of Jesus Christ" (1 Pet 1:6–7). That is the theme of all Scripture.

Storms and trials are a vital part of life for the believer—they are allowed by God for a reason . . . our faith is being *tried—proven—tested—purified.* James says, "Consider it all joy when you encounter various trials" (Jam 1:2). Paul writes, "Unto you it has been granted for Christ's sake, not only to believe in Him, but also to suffer for His sake" (Phil 1:29). Jesus said, "In this world you will have tribulation; but take courage, I have overcome the world" (Jn 16:33). Likewise Paul also says, "Through many tribulations we must enter the kingdom of God" (Acts 14:22). When everything seems to be against us; when the Lord Himself appears to be utterly unconcerned; when we are fearful and desperate; when we may even be in danger of our lives—that is where the real trial of faith comes in. In just such circumstances, follow the words of the Christian poet—

> *When all things seem against us*
> *To drive us to despair,*
> *We know one gate is open*
> *One ear will hear our prayer.*

What is the nature of "your faith"? Observe our Lord's response when dealing with His disciples in the midst of the storm—He knows perfectly well that *"they have faith."* The question He asks them is this: "You have faith—but where is it at the moment?" That gives us the "key" to understanding the nature of faith. First, faith is not merely a matter of *"feeling"*—it can't be, because our feelings change from one minute to the next; as such, our faith would be there one minute, and gone the next. Faith involves the *"mind,"* the understanding—it is a "response to truth" (truth implies intelligibilia). Faith is not something that acts automatically or magically. Faith has to be exercised. Faith does not come into operation by itself, you have to put it into operation.

So, how does one put faith into operation? The first thing you must do when you find yourself in a difficult position is to *refuse to allow yourself to be controlled by the situation*—that was the disciples problem; they allowed the situation to control them. Faith is a refusal to panic. That is the very nature of faith—it is a refusal to panic, come what may. Faith has been described thus: ***"Faith is perpetual unbelief kept quiet"***—faith does not allow unbelief to surface. Genuine faith does not entertain the temptation—it immediately rejects the temptation—by considering temptation, you allow it to *"take root"* in your heart. Believers do not have the capacity to fully consider temptation and then turn away from it, because it *"engages the flesh!"* Satan isn't stupid! He knows if you will just "listen" to him and consider what he has to say—he's got you!!! Faith immediately responds to difficult situations with these words: "I am not going to entertain these thoughts! And I am not going to be controlled by these circumstances!" Right out of the shoot, you take charge of yourself! and pull yourself up! and control yourself! You do not let your thoughts wander into Satan's territory! You assert yourself! *Now* is the time to control your thinking! You need to remind yourself *immediately* of what you believe and what you know! That is faith—it holds on to truth, and reasons from what it knows to be fact. That is the way faith reasons. The foundation stone of faith is *Truth—God's Word—Scripture*. Faith reasons, "All right, I see the waves and the billows . . . BUT (and then you remind yourself of ultimate reality—"truth") God is God, and He is in charge. To reiterate, the most important step you can take when faced with a difficult situation, is to *"immediately reject the temptation and refuse to consider it,"* and then *"affirm what you know to be the truth,"* including the acknowledgment of your own weakness. Faith agrees with everything God says about reality—and that includes the need for you to be utterly dependent upon Him. Here is an example of what to say—

> *God, all things seem to be against me to "drive me to despair." I don't understand what is happening, but this I know—I know that You loved me so much that You sent Your only begotten Son into this world for me. You did that for me while I was an enemy, a sinful rebellious alien. I know that Jesus loves me and gave Himself for me. I know that at the cost of His life's blood I have salvation and that I am now Your child and an heir to everlasting life, joy and peace. I know that.*

Faith argues like that—it amounts to "logically thinking through what we know to be true." Faith reminds itself of what the Scripture calls "the exceeding great and precious promises." Faith says, "I cannot believe that

God who has brought me so far is going to let me down at this point. It is impossible, because it would be inconsistent with His character. So faith, having refused to be controlled by circumstances, reminds itself of what it believes and what it knows to be true. Jesus in effect said to His disciples, "Where is your faith? You have it! Why don't you apply it?" ***Bring all you know to be true of your relationship to God to bear upon it***—then you will know full well that He will never allow anything to happen that is ultimately going to be harmful to you. Remember the words of Paul: "God causes all things to work together for *good* to those who love God." Not a hair of your head shall be harmed. He loves you with an everlasting love. You may not have a full understanding of your predicament, but this you know for certain—*"God is not unconcerned."* God permits everything that happens to you because it is ultimately for your good. That is the way faith works—but you have to exercise it. You refuse to be moved. You stand firm in your faith. "This is the victory that overcomes the world—*our faith!"* (1 Jn 5:4).

By the way, God honors the "smallest degree of faith." The disciples, even though they were in a "state of panic," still had a sufficient amount of faith to make them do the right thing in the end—*they went to Jesus!* They still had some kind of feeling that He could do something about it, and so they woke Him and said, "Master, are You not going to do something about this?" That is very poor faith you may say, very weak faith indeed—but it is faith, thank God! Scripture says, *"even faith like a grain of mustard seed"* is valuable because it takes us to Christ! When you finally come to Him in your despair, He may rebuke you for not reasoning things out (which is mature faith), and ask you why you did not apply your faith, and question why you have behaved as if you were not a Christian at all? And then you hear Him say, "I would have been so pleased if I could have watched you stand firm in the midst of the hurricane or storm—why didn't you?" He will let us know that He is disappointed in us and will rebuke us; BUT, praise to Him, *He will still receive us!* He does not drive us away! He did not drive His disciples away—He received them—and He will receive you and me as well! And incredible as it may seem, He will not only receive us, but He will bless us and give us His peace! How can it be that our God is so gracious and kind and forgiving? Jesus rebuked the wind and the sea, and it became absolutely calm—think of it—He produced the condition they were so anxious to enjoy . . . in spite of their lack of faith!!! Such is the gracious Lord that you and I believe in and follow—that He is truly "gracious" in His dealings with us is really "too wonderful" for words. Though we stumble hourly, and stumble terribly, still He never rejects us or gives up on us, and He forever remains faithful to us—even when we are faithless! Why? Because we are His children—and He cannot deny Himself! (2 Tim 2:13). (135–147)

Matthew 14 describes Peter's experience of "walking on the water" (Mt 14:22–33). Like the previous story of the disciples in a storm tossed sea, this incident also concentrates on the nature and the character of faith. Here again we see Jesus commanding and controlling the elements. Peter bids Jesus to have him come to him on the water—He starts off so well, so full of faith . . . then He gets into trouble and ends up being a miserable failure, crying out in desperation. How quickly it all happened. We are told in this story *when Peter "looked at the wind and the waves" he became afraid and began to sink*. The circumstances began to occupy his attention . . . the conditions hadn't changed . . . the wind and the waves were there before he started to walk on the water . . . so there was no new factor . . . yet Peter got into trouble and became frightened and desperate. Why? The answer is that the trouble was entirely "in Peter." Our Lord gives us a precise diagnosis—it was *"little faith!"*

Peter's great characteristic was his energy and his capacity for quick decision, and his active personality. He was enthusiastic and impulsive, and that was the thing that was constantly getting him into trouble. The trouble with this kind of person is that he tends to act without thinking—*his faith was not based upon sufficient thought*. The difficulty with him was that he did not think things all the way through, he did not work them out right. In the Gospels, he was always the first man to volunteer—he was always first in everything, and that was his trouble. The apostle Paul had to rebuke Peter over the fact that he did not work out the question of justification by faith only, as he should have done. He had no excuse, because he was the first man to admit the Gentiles into the Christian Church—you remember the Cornelius incident (Acts 10). It was a tremendous thing for a Jew to bring a Gentile into the Church. What was the matter with Peter? He accepted a position without working out all its implications—this is a very common cause of spiritual depression.

Conversely, when Peter looked at the waves "he began to doubt"— Peter led himself into doubting by "focusing on those things that are in juxtaposition to faith"—he focused on the waves—and that temptation gave birth to sin, and he sank. We will always be *tempted* to let "problems" overwhelm us—and when they do, they cause us not to trust. By the way, doubts are *not* incompatible with faith. Some people seem to think that once you become a Christian you will never doubt—that is not so; Peter still had faith even though he doubted—Jesus said to him, "O ye of little faith." We are all tempted to "doubt"—*doubting is a sign of "weak faith,"* and all of us from time to time *"struggle with faith."* That is the *great fight* for the believer (1 Tim 6:12); and make no mistake about it, it is a fight! The key is not to let doubts "master and control us"—when they do, that is a spiritual warning sign that we need to *"grow more in our faith;"* obviously, we want to be a people of "great faith," not "weak faith." Great faith is a knowledge of the Lord Jesus Christ and His power, and a steady trust and confidence in Him—faith begins and ends with a knowledge of the Lord—not a feeling, or an act of the will. Christianity is Christ, and Christian faith means believing certain things about Him and knowing Him. It is precisely here where many Christians are troubled—their "lack of faith" (weak faith) is the root cause of their unhappiness.

So, the great antidote to spiritual depression is the "knowledge of Christ," and a knowledge of Christian doctrine—and you get that in His Word. You must take the time to learn it! The tragedy of the hour is that people are far too dependent for their happiness upon *"meetings and fellowship,"* and that is why so many Christians are depressed and miserable. Their knowledge of the "truth" is defective. Jesus said, *"knowing the truth will set you free"* (Jn 8:32). It is the truth that frees—the truth about Him, His Person, and His work.

Great faith "persists in looking at Christ—the Author and Perfecter of our faith" (Heb 12:2). Faith says, "What God has begun to do He can continue to do." The beginning of the work was a miracle; so if He can initiate a miraculous work when we were at enmity with Him, He has the ability to keep it going—"Be confident of this very thing, that He who began a good work in you will perfect it until the day of Jesus Christ" (Phil 1:6). *Remember this, you will "never doubt" if you look at Christ and are clear about Him*—without Him we are utterly hopeless. It doesn't matter how long you have been a Christian, you are "dependent" upon Him for every step—*"without Him you can do nothing"* (Jn 15:5). We can only conquer our doubts by looking steadily at Him, and not looking at our doubts. Remember, *"we walk by faith"* (2 Cor 5:7)—and that means living with our eyes on Christ, because we need Him all the time. That is the Lord's method—He does not give us enough "manna" for a *month;* we need a fresh supply *every day,* so start your day with Him and keep in touch with Him throughout the day. That was Peter's fatal error—he looked away from Him. Remember, you are walking on *turbulent waves* and the only way to keep walking is to keep looking at Him—by the way, He will never let you sink! "Now to Him who is able to keep you from falling, and to make you stand in the presence of His glory blameless with great joy" (Jude 1:24). (148–160)

"You have not received a spirit of slavery leading to fear again" (Rom 8:15)—That is one of the most significant statements found in all of Scripture. Why did Paul ever make that statement? He was anxious to save these Roman Christians from a *spirit of discouragement.* A spirit of bondage, a spirit of defeat, is always threatening us in the Christian life. The problem is "dealing with sin"—there is sin within and without, and a host of potential failures in the Christian life—a failure to realize certain truths; a failure to realize what is possible for us as Christians; a failure to understand doctrine; and a failure to persist with the application of faith—*FAITH MUST BE APPROPRIATED! Paul's fear is that they might have a "slave-like attitude" toward the Christian life—a "higher law" if you will—where the believer thinks of the Christian life as a "great task" which they have to take up and to which now they are to apply themselves.* In other words, holiness becomes a *"great task"* to them, and they begin to plan and organize their lives and take up certain "disciplines" in order to enable them to carry it out. This attitude is seen in a classic manner in Roman Catholicism and her teaching—in the whole idea of *"monasticism"*—where the cultivation of holiness and the spiritual life becomes a *full-time occupation* that you must devote yourself exclusively to, and have your rules, to enable you to live it. According to Paul—that is nothing but a *"spirit of bondage"* that ultimately brings with it a *"wrong fear of God"*—a fear that hath torment; it regards God as a taskmaster; as someone who is constantly watching them to discover their faults; a stern Lawgiver who metes out punishment accordingly. So the fear is also a "fear" at not fulfilling the task that they have been given. That is why they thought the spiritual life could only be lived if one segregated himself from the world—hence, they have *"no joy"* because the gigantic nature of the task is something that fills them with a spirit of fear; furthermore, they actually fear themselves and have a fear of failure. It is a "no win" proposition all the way around; a miserable existence. They say something like this—"I have come into this Christian life, but the question is, *"Can I live it?"*

Paul says, "You need not live in a spirit of bondage." Why not? Because the *Holy Spirit* is in you and He will empower you and strengthen you. "God is at work in you both to will and to do of His good pleasure" (Phil 2:13). *We must look to Him and rely upon Him—as we believe and wrestle, He enables and empowers us . . . He transforms our outlook . . . and we lose the spirit of bondage.* Because God cares for us, our desire should not be to *keep the law,* but to *believe the Father.* There is nothing that promotes holiness as the realization that we are "heirs of God and joint-heirs with Christ," that our destiny is certain and secure, that nothing in all creation can prevent it. Realizing that, we purify ourselves even as He is pure, and we conclude that there is no time to waste (1 Jn 3:1–3). Do not worry about what you feel; the truth about you is glorious. Believe in the salvation of the Lord and prevail. (163–189)

"Do not grow weary in well-doing, for in due time you shall reap" (Gal 6:9)—The ills of the spiritual life are always the same, they never vary though their particular guise may differ, and the cause of it all is the "devil." After years of following Christ, and the thrill of new discovery suddenly seems to have gone, many believers are often beset with trials and difficulties . . . and *weariness* sets in. At this stage of development in the Christian life the believer says to himself, "Well whatever happens I'm going on; I'm not giving in; I will not lose heart"—so they go on, but they go on in a hopeless, dragging condition. Resigning oneself to such a fate is the greatest danger of all—one of the great temptations of the devil is to get God's people to *"lose hope."* Many Christians at this point just move forward in a formal spirit and as a matter of duty—wearily trudging along. Actually, if we regard the Christian life as merely a wearisome task or a duty to be performed, and we have to goad ourselves to get through it, somewhere along the way we got off the "narrow road" and got onto the "broad road." ***Go back to the beginning of your life and retrace your steps to the gate through which you passed***. Look at the world in its evil state, and look to the hell to which it was leading you, and then look forward and realize that you are sent into the midst of the most glorious campaign a man could ever enter, and that you are on the noblest road that the world has ever known. Read the "last chapter" of this book!

When the world becomes too much for us, we are immersed too much in our problems—look ahead to the eternal glories gleaming in the distance. "Set your affections on things above and not on the things of earth" (Col 3:2). "Be steadfast, immovable, always abounding in the work of the Lord, knowing your labor is not in vain in the Lord" (1 Cor 15:58). *Go on with your work whatever your feelings; God will give the increase; He will send the rain of His gracious mercies as we need it; there will be an abundant harvest—look forward to it—you will reap!* (Gal 6:9). Remember Jesus—"who for joy set before Him, He endured the cross, despising the shame" (Heb 12:2)—that is how He did it. The absolute glorious certainty of the future moved Him to endure the cross. Remind yourself of your blessed Master . . . look to Him and ask Him to forgive you for ever having allowed yourself to become weary . . . and you will find that you are again thrilled with the privilege and joy of it all, and you will hate yourself for having grumbled and complained, and you will go forward still more gloriously until eventually you hear Him say, "Well done, good and faithful servant; enter into the joy of the Lord. Come, you blessed of My Father, inherit the kingdom prepared for you from the foundation of the world!" (Mt 25:34). (191–202)

Peter wrote his second epistle to encourage people who were discouraged, to the point they began to *"doubt their faith;"* they were barren and unfruitful, and had "forgotten that they had been purged from their old sins" (2 Pet 1:9). These are Christians Peter is writing to, but they are downcast, unhappy, and shaken by doubts. Their faith did not fill them with joy and certainty, and they were not growing in the knowledge of the Lord (2 Pet 3:18). Why are they this way? The ultimate case is a *"lack of discipline;"* and that stems from having a *"wrong view of faith."* Peter exhorts them to "apply all diligence in adding to their faith" (2 Pet 1:5). They seemed to have had a kind of *"magical view of faith"*—the idea that as long as they had faith all would go well, and that their will would automatically work in their lives. Peter tells them that faith needs to be supplemented by virtue, knowledge, temperance, patience, godliness, brotherly kindness, and charity. They had one formula only—as long as they *"look to the Lord"* there is nothing else to do. They felt that any attempt to do anything else is dropping back to the *"salvation by works"* position. This is a very common error even in the church today. But Peter says, *"You must supplement your faith!"* Growing in faith does not happen automatically! Fight the fight of faith! (1 Tim 6:12; 2 Tim 4:7).

Most Christians live their lives seriously "lacking in discipline." The most difficult thing in life is to "order your life" and "manage your life"—if we don't we will cave to the danger of *"drifting."* Obviously, there are a myriad of things that can distract us—newspaper, television, meetings, work, chores, hobbies, internet, sports, etc. The fact is everyone of us is *"fighting for his life"*—fighting to possess and master and live his own life. **We all have the time—the whole secret of success in this respect is to *"take that time and insist that it is given to this matter of the soul,"* instead of to these other things!** Peter says, "apply all diligence," "make every effort," "be zealous to do these things." If you read the lives of the "greatest saints," the number one characteristic in their lives was *"discipline and order."* Hebrews says, *"God is a rewarder of them that diligently seek Him"* (Heb 11:6). We must be diligent and zealous in our seeking. Those who have never experienced a *"warm heart"* have never really sought it. And those who have experienced it believed in the culture and discipline of the spiritual life. If you are an unhappy and depressed Christian it is more than likely that it is all due to a "lack of discipline." You must "insist" upon the disciplines of *Scripture, Prayer, Study, Worship,* and *Meditation.* Furthermore, we must then be diligent to **supplement our faith with—**

1. *"virtue"*—its meaning here is moral energy, power and vigor

2. *"knowledge"*—this means a kind of insight, understanding and enlightenment of the truth

3. *"temperance"*—this means "self-control" over every aspect of your life

4. *"patience"*—patient endurance to keep on through every discouragement

5. *"godliness"*—which means paying careful attention to our relationship with God

6. *"brotherly kindness"*—our relationship to our fellow Christians

7. *"charity"*—love toward those who are outside the faith (202–216)

Peter wrote his first epistle to address the matter of "spiritual depression"—the *"heaviness"* they felt because of the manifold temptations they were experiencing simply robbed them of their joy. They had a superficial view of Christianity—they thought they should be *"happy all* *day long,"* and not have to go through *"fiery trials."* Obviously, they were totally disillusioned. The truth is, there are a series of *PARADOXES* that the apostle Paul uses to describe himself—"we are *afflicted* in every way, but not crushed; we are *perplexed*, but not despairing; we are *persecuted*, but not forsaken; we are *struck down*, but not destroyed" (2 Cor 4:8–9). Grief and suffering are things to which the Christian is subject; he is not immune to such things. The saints of God are subject to human frailties, grief, sorrow, feeling lonely, failure, and being disappointed. The glory of the Christian life is that we can rise above these things even though we feel them. It is not an absence of feeling—according to Scripture, ***it is a law that the more we resemble Christ in our life and living, the more likely we are to have met troubles in this world***. The godliest saints in history all were subjected to rigorous trials—start with all twelve of Jesus' disciples and the apostle Paul; they were all martyred with the exception of John. And throughout the "Church age" we have a seemingly endless list of saints to whom we could point.

The manifold trials to which we are subjected, writes Peter, are "good for us," because they are part of our discipline in this life and in this world—*God has appointed it so*—in order that He might bring us to perfection (spiritual maturity). Sometimes these things happen to us to *chasten us;* other times it is to *prepare us* for something (like Joseph and David). Notice the words Peter uses—*"if need be"* (1 Pet 1:6)—if a particular thing we are being subjected to proves needful, God will do whatever is necessary. God puts us through times of testing in order that the things which do not belong to the essence of faith may fall off. Furthermore, God develops the *"trust element"* in our faith by trying us. God so deals with us in this life as to bring us to trust Him in the dark when we can see no light at all. Trials happen to us in order that the genuineness of our faith may be revealed (1 Pet 1:6–7); and that is the most important thing. It should be noted that God does not keep us permanently under trial—He knows the right amount that is needed, and when we have responded, He will withdraw it. *It is only for a season.* By the way, the greater and the more genuine our faith, the greater our glory will be.

THE ESSENCE OF FAITH

The idea of faith is concerned with the establishment of "some particular reality" as indeed being trustworthy. The Hebrew word for faith in the Old Testament, *he'emin,* is built upon the word *'aman,* which means to be true, reliable, faithful. The New Testament term for faith, *pisteuo,* further develops the Old Testament concept and denotes the various aspects of the religious relationship into which the gospel calls people—that of trust in God through Christ. The most common characteristic of *pisteuo* conveys a movement of trust going out to, and laying hold of, the object of its confidence. The nature of faith according to the New Testament, rises out of testimony, authenticated by God (Jn 10:25, 37, 38; Acts 2:22; 2 Cor 12:12; Heb 2:4)—therefore faith rests upon the acceptance of that testimony, and lives accordingly. Faith and life are intimately connected in the New Testament. The three major tenets of biblical faith are as follows (Elwell, pp. 431–432):

1. <u>Faith in God involves right belief about God</u>—Throughout the Bible *trust in God* is made to rest on the belief of what He has revealed to humanity concerning His character and purposes. The frequency with which the NT Epistles depict faith as knowing, believing, and obeying "the truth" (2 Th 2:13; Titus 1:1; 1 Pet 1:22) show that their authors regarded *orthodoxy* (right belief) as faith's fundamental ingredient (Gal 1:8–9). Faith and the word *"belief"* are often treated synonymously, which has led to Christians being called *"believers."*

2. <u>Faith rests on Divine testimony</u>—Beliefs are convictions held on the grounds of divine testimony. Whether a particular belief should be treated as a known certainty or a doubtful opinion depends upon the worthiness of the testimony on which that belief is based. The Bible views faith's convictions as certainties and equates them with knowledge (1 Jn 3:2; 5:18–20), not because they spring from supposedly self-authenticating mystical experience, but because they rest on the testimony of a God who "does not lie" (Titus 1:2), and is therefore utterly trustworthy. To *receive* His testimony is to certify that God is true (Jn 3:33), and to *reject* it is to make God a liar (1 Jn 5:10). The Christian faith rests upon the recognition of apostolic and biblical testimony as God's own testimony to His Son.

(continued)

3. <u>Faith is a supernatural Divine gift</u>—Sin and Satan have so blinded fallen human beings (Eph 4:18; 2 Cor 4:4) that they cannot discern the divine testimony of God's Word . . . nor comprehend the realities of which it speaks (Jn 3:3; 1 Cor 2:14) . . . nor arrive at self-renouncing trust in Christ (Jn 6:44, 65) except through the enlightenment of the Holy Spirit (2 Cor 4:6). Only the recipients of this divine teaching, drawing, and anointing place their faith in Christ and abide in Him (Jn 6:44–45; 1 Jn 2: 20, 27). As such, God is the author of all saving faith (Eph 2:8; Phil 1:29).

The author of Hebrews writes, "Faith is the assurance of things hoped for, the conviction of things not seen" (Heb 11:1). This passage describes the true nature of faith, and provides us with the only definition of it attempted in all of Scripture. In short, faith makes things hoped for as real as if we already had them, and it provides unshakable evidence that the unseen, spiritual blessings of Christianity are indeed certain and true. So faith is confidence in the trustworthiness of God, and the conviction that what He says is true and that what He promises will come to pass. Faith has the revelation from God as its foundation—it is not a leap in the dark.

Faith *seems* to involve some kind of "venture" in the minds of most people, even though talk of a "leap of faith" is wholly inaccurate. It is widely held by many that faith goes beyond what is ordinarily reasonable, in the sense that it involves accepting what cannot be established as true through the normal exercise of our naturally endowed human cognitive faculties. The nineteenth century metaphysician "Immanuel Kant" put it this way in his work, *Critique of Pure Reason*—"I have found it necessary to deny knowledge in order to make room for faith." But other theistic philosophers have clearly shown that "<u>faith is not at all contrary to reason</u>." The truth is, faith without reason has no biblical foundation; to deny one is to deny the other. Obviously, one should only trust with good reason, and good reason to trust requires sufficient evidence of the trustee's trustworthiness; thus <u>reasonable trust has its venturesomeness diminished</u>. Reasonable faith arguably needs to conform to *evidentialism*—the requirement generally thought essential to rationality—to hold propositions to be justifiably and evidentially true. So faith and reason are clearly interrelated. If faith consists in beliefs that have the status of knowledge, then faith cannot fail to be rational, and the evidential requirement of reasonable faith is satisfied. In the following paragraphs we will briefly examine the description and definition of faith as it is presented in Hebrews 11:1—

Faith is the assurance of things hoped for—The word "assurance"—*hupostasis*—commonly appears in ancient papyrus business documents, conveying the idea that a covenant is an "exchange of assurances" which guarantees the future transfer of possessions described in the contract. In view of this, James Moulton and George Milligan suggest the following rendering: "Faith is the *title deed* of things hoped for" (Moulton, p. 660). *Hupostasis* is frequently rendered "confidence, substance, reality, or nature" in Scripture (2 Cor 9:4; 2 Cor 11:17; Heb 1:3; 3:14)—to get a fuller understanding of this word, substitute each of these words for "assurance" in the corresponding passage. The word *hupostasis* literally means, "that which is placed under"—thus it refers to the "ground, basis, foundation, or support;" so "reality, substance, existence" are in juxtaposition to that which is unreal, imaginary, deceptive. One could say that *faith imparts reality in the mind* of those things that are not seen, and enables us to feel and act as if they really exist *(Barnes' Notes)*.

Faith works like this in every sphere—Believing that there is a place called "London," leads us to act as if this were so, even though we may never have been there; the belief that we will "earn money" by doing some particular work, leads us to act as if it were so; the belief that we will "inherit something genuinely promised to us by our parents," leads us to act as if it were so. Faith gives the *force of reality* to what is believed. The Christian hopes to one day be perfectly free from sin, be admitted to heaven, and enjoy everlasting happiness—under the influence of faith the believer allows these things to control his mind as if they are certain future realities. God's Word is the principal ground and foundation of hope, and faith is a confident persuasion, expectation, and assurance of those things. In the Greek translation of the Old Testament, the *Septuagint,* this word is translated "foothold" in Psalm 69:2. David here cries out, "I have sunk in deep mire, and there is no foothold"—essentially he is saying there is no ground or foundation under his feet; as such, he feels as though he is about to perish. Faith gives us *substantial footing*—it provides us with a sure foundation upon which to stand. The first century Jewish philosopher, Judaeus Philo, said, "The only infallible and certain good thing is *that faith* which is faith towards God—it is the solace of life, the fullness of good hopes" *(Gill's Exposition)*.

Faith is the conviction of things not seen—The word "conviction"—*elengchos*—occurs in the New Testament only here and in 2 Timothy 3:16, where it is rendered "reproof." It means proof, evidence, or

(continued)

proof which convinces another of error or guilt. The idea behind this word is that the _evidence produces conviction in the mind_ with regard to that which is true. When a man is arraigned in a court of law and evidence is furnished as to his guilt, the idea of *"convincing argument"* enters the case—Barnes suggests this is the meaning of *elengchos* here *(Barnes' Notes)*. Faith in the divine declarations of Scripture provides a _convincing argument to the mind_ of those things that are not seen. But is this a good argument? The infidel naturally says "no." However, when a man who has never been to "London" believes that there is such a place, his belief in the numerous testimonies respecting it which he has heard and read is to his mind a _"good and rational proof"_ of its existence, and he would act on that belief without hesitation. In like manner, the Christian believes what God says—though he has never seen heaven and has never seen his Redeemer, he has evidence which is satisfactory to his mind that his Redeemer and heaven are undeniable realities. Those declarations are to his mind more convincing proof and conclusive evidence than all the reasonings and declarations of the infidel to the contrary *(Barnes' Notes)*. Thus faith is the firm assent of the soul to every part of the divine revelation that it is true.

The "convincing proof" that the declarations of Scripture are indeed true, is ultimately accomplished in the believer's mind and heart by the "Holy Spirit"—He is the Trinity's agent of transmission and communication, and the divine author of faith and Scripture (2 Tim 3:16; Jn 5:37–47; 14:26; 15:26; 16:13; Acts 16:14; Rom 15:4; Heb 12:2 ; 2 Pet 1:20-21; 1 Jn 2:27); without His agency, we would neither come to understand nor respond in to Him in faith. Every word that proceeds out of the mouth of God is revealed, inspired, and authoritative (Mt 4:4). Paul says, "The natural man cannot know or understand the things of the Spirit of God because such things are spiritually appraised" (1 Cor 2:14)—*Spiritual* is in opposition to *Natural* in this verse. The psalmist understood the need for God's illumination of His Word: "Open my eyes, that I may behold wonderful things from Thy Law" (Ps 119:18). Though God gives His children the grace to understand His Word, it is incumbent upon the believer to "accept, believe, trust, and act upon it"—such is our part in the matter of "faith" (Prv 3:5; Heb 1:17; 1 Jn 5:4).

God uses a "variety of methods" in the sanctifying process—"This is the will of God, your sanctification" (1 Th 4:3), "that we should be holy and blameless" (Eph 1:4). God's great concern for us primarily is not our happiness but *"our holiness."* Like foolish children, we often misunderstand God's dealings with us and feel He is being *"unkind to us"*—that, of course, leads to depression and it is all due to our failure to realize God's glorious purposes with respect to us. Scripture tells us that God sometimes promotes sanctification by *"chastening us"*—"whom the Lord loves He chastens" (Heb 12:6). God has His ways of producing holiness in us. Another way God transforms us is through the instruction of *"His Word"* (Jn 17:17; 2 Tim 2:15; 1 Pet 2:2). Paul was given a *"thorn in the flesh"* to keep him spiritually right and to keep him from exalting himself; and through it all Paul learned that "when he was weak, then he was strong spiritually" (2 Cor 12:10); as a result, he then learned to rejoice in infirmity rather than in health in order that God's glory might be promoted. Incidentally, the word *chastise* means "to train"—we tend to confuse it with the word punishment; not so, instead it includes correction, instruction, and rebuke; the essential object of chastisement is to train and develop the child so as to produce maturity.

How does God chastise His children? Most often thru *"circumstances;"* in particular God often uses *financial loss—illness—persecution*. Again, God chastens us that we become partakers of His holiness. There are certain faults in all of us that need to be corrected—spiritual pride; self-dependence; self-confidence; worldly values; fleshly lusts; lack of humility; arrogance; need of patience. The psalmist said, "It is good for me that I was afflicted" (Ps 119:71). We all have to be humbled in order to arrive at humility—and *"failure"* is one of the most effective ways to accomplish this. Think of it this way—it is very difficult to be humble if you are always successful, so God chastens us with failure at times in order to humble us. (218–245)

There are a number of "wrong ways" of reacting to trials, troubles, and chastisement—We can despise them . . . become hardened by them . . . resent them . . . become bitter . . . feel hopeless . . . become angry . . . despair . . . give up . . . grumble and complain . . . or faint under the pressure—"Oh, that I had wings like a dove for then I would fly away and be at rest!" (Ps 55:6). Scripture says, *"Pull yourself together and stop* *behaving as a child"*—stop fainting; stop whimpering; stop crying; stop sulking. "You say you are men, but you continue to act like a child!" Listen to what the Word of God has to say—follow the logic of it; bring intelligence to the Scriptures. The great argument of Scripture is that it is "God" who is doing this, and God is doing it to you because you are His child, and He is doing it for your good; but it only does good when you *"submit to the process"* (Heb 12:4–11; Ps 119:75).

What is the process? The psalmist tells us that God is going to do these things to us by putting us into a *"gymnasium."* That is the original meaning of the word translated *"trained"* (Heb 12:11). It is a wonderful picture. We are told that the very root of this word gymnasium is a word which signifies *"being stripped naked"*—so the picture we have here is of ourselves being taken into a gymnasium and there we are told to strip down, that we may go through the exercises unhindered by our clothing. "Lay aside every encumbrance and sin that so easily entangles you, and run with endurance the race that is set before you" (Heb 12:1). The instructor takes his student and puts him through his exercises in order that he might become a fine specimen of manhood. *When you are naked, all of your flaws and infirmities are exposed,* and the instructor can prescribe the exercises that are needed to correct them.

Listen to the Instructor (Christ), and go through the exercises and training that He has prescribed for you—if you do so, it will "yield the peaceful fruit of righteousness." (Heb 12:11). Submit to the examination of God's Word (Heb 4:12), and when you have been trained you will say as the psalmist said, "It was good for me that I was afflicted—before I was afflicted I went astray; but now I keep Thy Word" (Ps 119:67, 71). Follow after holiness with all your might! pursue it! hunt for it! and you will find it! It should be tremendously comforting to know that you are in God's hands, that He loves you, and that *He is determined to produce holiness in you* and bring you to heaven without spot or blemish (Eph 1:4; 5:27; 1 Th 5:24). Should you not listen to God's Word, He will deal with you in another way (Ps 32:8–9; 138:8). One way or another, *God is going to bring you to heaven a "fit specimen."* Take the training, do the exercises, hurry to the gymnasium, and do what He tells you—practice it all whatever the cost, however great the pain, and enter into the joy of the Lord. (247–259)

"Be anxious for nothing . . . pour out your heart to God . . . and His peace will flood your soul" (Phil 4:6-7). This is one of the most comforting statements in all of Scripture. Therefore, "rejoice in the Lord always!" Paul has shown us how "desiring our own way" produces an unquiet spirit and robs us of our joy. We are to be "anxious for nothing"—*anxiety is all due to the activity of the heart and mind;* this is a profound piece of psychology. What Paul is saying here is this: "we can control many things in our lives and outside our lives, but we cannot control our hearts and minds." *The condition of anxiety, says Paul, "is something which is in a sense outside our control; it happens apart from you and in spite of you."* The heart is the central part of our personality, and the seat of our emotions. A prolific cause of anxiety is the *imagination,* and sometimes it simply runs rampant. We are the victims of our thoughts, and oftentimes they are outside our control and master us. The apostle tells us that this is something which at all costs we must avoid. In the state of anxiety we spend the whole of our time reasoning and arguing and chasing imaginations—and in that state we are useless, and we lose the joy of the Lord.

Psychology says, "Stop worrying and pull yourself together"—that's repression. If you happen to be a strong-willed person you can hold these things from the conscious mind with the result that they then go on working in the subconscious mind. That condition, however, is worse than anxiety itself. What then does the apostle say? "Let your requests be made known to God"—that is the answer! First you *"pray"*—that is the essence of worship and adoration. Then you bring your *"supplications"* to the Lord—the particular things that are troubling you. And you do so with *"thanksgiving"*—we must have positive reasons for thanking God. We thank God for our salvation . . . that He cares about us . . . that He is present in our trouble . . . for all of His provisions . . . that He is at work in us for "good" . . . that He is able to do more than we could ever ask or think . . . that He is faithful to His Word—"we shall be kept whether something happens or it doesn't happen." Remember the glory of the gospel is that God is first and foremost concerned about *"us"*—not about our *"circumstances."*

We tend to be "tyrannized by circumstances" because we depend upon them, and we would like them to be governed and controlled, but that is not the position of Scripture. God promises to "give us His peace, which passes all understanding; and His peace will guard our hearts and minds in Christ Jesus"—so He promises to give us peace in our hearts in spite of the circumstances. Prayer does not mean we are going to "feel better," or that our circumstances are going to be "changed." Furthermore, *prayer* itself is not the vehicle that "does the work"—*God* is the one who gives us His peace. (261–272)

One of the high-water marks of the Christian experience is "learning to be content in all situations." The real meaning of the word translated *"content"* is this—"I have learned in whatever circumstance I am in to be self-sufficient, independent of circumstances and conditions." Paul tells us how he learned to be independent of "the thorn in the flesh," self-sufficient in spite of it. He told Timothy: "Godliness with contentment is great gain" (1 Tim 6:6). *The first thing you have to learn is to be independent of circumstances and conditions—we are not to be mastered or controlled by circumstances.* If you can improve your circumstances rightly, by all means do so . . . but if you cannot, do not be mastered by it; do not let it get you down; do not let it control you; do not let it determine your misery or your joy. We must not depend on our circumstances to make us happy. Paul says, "My life is not controlled and determined by what is happening to me; I am in a state in which I rise above them." One of the greatest tasks in life is to discover how to suffer all things without feeling a sense of grudge or bitterness of spirit . . . to discover how not to be worried or anxious. Paul had experienced every kind of trial and tribulation and yet he was unaffected by them—thus in effect he said, "My life and happiness and joy are not determined or controlled by what happens to me."

Professor Whitehead defined religion thus: "Religion is what a man does with his own solitude." You and I, in the final analysis, are what we are when we are alone. Paul had a love for God that rendered him independent of all that was happening to him—whatever was happening to him, he was content. How did the apostle reach this condition? "I have come to learn [by sheer experience]." Paul learned the important lesson, *"My grace is sufficient for you"* (2 Cor 12:10)—experience is a great teacher; it teaches all of us. Paul had come to learn this great truth by working out a ***great argument***—

- Conditions are always *changing,* therefore I must not be dependent upon them.
- What matters supremely is *my soul* and my relationship with God.
- God is concerned about *me,* and nothing happens to me apart for His approving it.
- God's will and God's ways are a great mystery, and whatever He permits is *for my good*.
- Every situation in life is the unfolding of some manifestation of *God's love* and goodness.
- I must regard circumstances and conditions as a part of God's work of *perfecting my soul*.
- Whatever my conditions may be at the present moment, they are only *temporary*.

Our job is to look for the particular manifestation of God's goodness and kindness in life, and be prepared for surprises and blessings, because "His ways are not our ways" (Is 55:8–9). Paul had learned to find his pleasure and his satisfaction in Christ—his intimacy with Christ grew so deep that he had become independent of everything else. Let this become our first ambition.

The apostle Paul writes, "I can do all things through Christ who strengthens me" (Phil 4:13). A better translation would be—*"I am strong for all things in the One who constantly infuses strength into me."* What Paul is really saying is not so much that he can do certain things himself, but that he is enabled to do certain things by the One who infuses His strength to him. Christ is all-sufficient for every circumstance. The essence of the Christian life is that it is a mighty power that enters into us; it is a life, if you like, that is pulsating in us. It is an activity, and an activity on the part of God. "He who began a good work in you, will perform it until the day of Jesus Christ" (Phil 1:6). God is working out His will in your life—that is what Christians really are (Phil 2:12–13). The Christian life is "God's activity," not merely our activity. ***The life of God in the souls of men—that is who Christians are.*** To be a Christian is to be so vitally related to Christ that His life and power are working in us—that is what it means to be "in Christ." "Christ in you the hope of glory" (Col 1:27). Reflect again upon Paul's words, "I can do all things through Christ who strengthens me" (Phil 4:13). Note "I can" and "through Christ"—both play an integral role in the sanctifying process. *"I live, yet not I, but Christ lives in me"* (Gal 2:20). The Christian life is not a life that I live by my own power—neither is it a life in which Christ does everything—***"both of us"*** have responsibilities. That is the incredible romance of the Christian life. "I am able to accomplish God's purposes because He constantly infuses me with His strength" (Phil 4:13). As my friend Dr. Steve Brown (author of the next chapter) would say, "You think about that." (275–300)

CHAPTER 2

A summary of the book . . .

"A SCANDALOUS FREEDOM"
by Steve Brown

Martin Luther said, "We must preach the good news to each other lest we become discouraged." Jesus said we would know the truth and would be free indeed. As believers we oftentimes find a disconnect between what is supposed to be true and what really is. Much of the *"freedom"* Christians proclaim has the feel of a stuffed dog—it looks nice, but it has become only a semblance of the real thing. When Jesus used the word *"free,"* he employed a term that means *"liberation from bondage."* If Jesus said we're free, we ought to accept His declaration at face value and run with it—but we don't. We continue in our bondage by obeying rules, doing religious things, and being nice—as such, we have sold our heritage of freedom for a mess of pottage.

This might come as a surprise to you—if freedom doesn't include the "freedom not to obey," then it isn't real freedom. The Bible is quite radical—Paul writes, "Where the Spirit of the Lord is, there is freedom" (2 Cor 3:17). Paul said, "You were called to freedom, but do not use your freedom as an opportunity for self-indulgence" (Gal 5:13). He did not want them to use their freedom to sin, but they could—why? Because they were *FREE!* Sometimes we destroy freedom by saying, "We must be careful with this freedom thing—people will take advantage of it." But that is not freedom—that is a new kind of bondage.

The truth is, what repeatedly kills our witness is "pretense," not freedom. It would be so refreshing to say to our unbelieving friends, "I really mess up sometimes, but let me tell you something really good: "God is still quite fond of me! Wouldn't it be great if you belonged to a God like that?" If we were really honest, the world would beat a path to our door. I strongly stand on what the Bible says about freedom—let me give you a radical statement: *"You are really and truly and completely free!"* There is no if, and, or but—you are *FREE!* You can obey or disobey . . . you can run from Christ or you can run to Christ . . . you can be faithful or unfaithful . . . you can cry, cuss, spit, laugh, sing, and dance. You are really *FREE!*

Legend has it Abraham Lincoln went to a slave market and bought a young gal being auctioned off—as he walked off with his "property," he turned to the woman and said, *"You are free."* The woman didn't understand what being free really meant, so she questioned Lincoln. In the end, she asked him if she could do whatever she wanted to do . . . and go wherever she wanted to go? Lincoln responded, "Yes, it means you are really free and can go wherever you want to go." The woman then responded with tears in her eyes, *"Then I think I will go with you."* That is what God has done for us. That is what the Christian faith is all about—*we've been bought with a price by a new Master—and He has set us "FREE!"* Really *FREE!*

Being free means "God will love me no matter what—His love and grace are without condition!" But that does not mean that God is *"pleased"* with behaviors that are contrary to His will—God is only pleased when we trust Him and live by faith (Heb 11:6). God's *fondness* for us is dependent on His love and the cross of Christ—not on my earning it. It is critically important that the believer understand that if you are not faithful, God will not withdraw His blessing from you nor turn His back on you (2 Tim 2:13). God will love you and bless you without condition, without reservation, and without equivocation. You are indeed *FREE!*

If you feel no attraction to a God who loves you without condition, there is something wrong with you. We respond with love to those who love us—if someone likes us, we generally like them back. On the other hand, if someone is always judging, dishonoring, and criticizing us, we want to get as far away from them as we can. *There is something extremely attractive about love.* Not only do we feel attracted to someone who loves us, we find ourselves wanting to please them. Paul says, don't you know that "God's kindness is meant to lead you to repentance?" (Rom 2:4). The truth of the matter is this—*the more we experience God's love and grace, the more we want to please Him.*

Satan obviously doesn't want you to believe that you are really "free!" And those he most often uses to steal your freedom are *"other believers."* Many Christians will require things of you that God doesn't require—they will tell you that God is angry when He isn't, and will try and make you feel ashamed and guilty when you shouldn't feel ashamed and guilty. When the new Christian tries to get out from under the burden of rules, regulations, and righteousness, many churches try to shame them into continuing! *This kind of behavior made Jesus angry.* He said of them, "They tie up heavy burdens and lay them on people's shoulders, but they themselves are not willing to bear them; Woe to you, scribes and Pharisees! *You are hypocrites!*" (Mt 23:4, 15). Says Brown: "I believe we show our depravity less by the bad stuff we do than by our reversion to Pharisaism. It is not our sin that is so bad (Jesus fixed that on the cross), but our stiffness—there is something about religion that can make you cold, critical, and mean. It is a tendency we have to fight all the time."

Freedom threatens "religious people"—it makes it more difficult for them to maintain control. Jesus was not big into *"control."* He said, "Whoever would be great among you must be your servant; even the Son of Man did not come to be served but to *serve* (Mt 20:26–28). Sometimes we think the only thing that will make a Christian "go" is a bit of fear and guilt. Jesus wasn't into the *"authority model"* so much either—He said, "The rulers of the Gentiles lord it over people and exercise authority over them—it shall not be so among you" (Mt 20:25–26). Brown writes,

"Freedom scares religious folks to death because a lot of ego goes into being right and righteous—something in us causes us to feel good when we condemn others"—it's our fleshy nature! The problem with most of us Christians is that we are into *"performance" and "perfectionism"*—we like being able to *"measure up"* and feel good about ourselves. In some perverted way we actually think better of ourselves when we see other people fail and stumble—how sick is that!?—yet the reality is, another person's behavior has nothing to do with how good or bad we are . . . most often it merely brings out the evil in our own hearts. Thus, the Christian life is not about feeling good about *"ourselves"* (pride)—it is about feeling good about *"Jesus!"* (1–24)

If there is no God, there is no value, and we live in a meaningless universe. If there is a God, He is in charge—if there isn't, then you are. What you believe or don't believe about God has profound implications for your freedom. *What you believe about God's nature will largely determine how you live.* Many of us don't live free because we don't believe in a God who loves us enough to give us the gift of freedom. Many believe God is against freedom, opposed to laughter, and easily angered, so we create gods who rob us of our freedom and joy, such as—

1. The magical Santa Claus God—These individuals bring their own agenda to God, expecting him to bless and honor it, and then feel devastated when He refuses to play their little game. What they fail to realize and accept is the fact that *"God is sovereign"*—we don't get a vote—we are asked to accept "His will" in life. The God of the Bible isn't one who *"blesses our agenda,"* and promises to make us healthy, wealthy, and wise—if that is your God you have a serious problem. Millions of Christians live with discouragement, bitterness, and anger simply because they worship a god who doesn't exist. As such there is a large gap for many Christians between what they *"expect"* from their Christian faith, and what they actually *"experience."* They have grown up expecting to see "dramatic evidence" of God working in their lives—if they don't see it, they feel disappointed, betrayed and often guilty. If God exists only to bless our dreams, hopes, and desires, we will either turn away from Him or create a new god.

2. <u>The child-abuser God</u>—When our dreams shatter, we tend to create a child-abuser god. This god makes everything you enjoy sinful, and takes great delight in messing up your life—all for your own good, of course. This god gives failure to those who dare to step out of line. If you believe in such an *ogre god,* you will live in perpetual fear of offending him; if you worship a God who is out to get you, you will never be free—you won't laugh, sing and dance, and you won't cuss or spit! Desire so often proves fruitless, so it seems utterly absurd to continue to hunger or yearn for anything any longer. To hope is to become vulnerable to *"more pain."* These Christians talk more about God's requirements than His grace. If God is really a monster, then when bad stuff happens to me, I will become more bound, enslaved, and angry. If, however, I understand that God is my Father, that He loves me without reservation, and that He knows exactly what He is doing, I will learn how to live in freedom. I might get angry at first, but in the end, I will run to Him and eventually will be able to accept His way in my life, and do so with joy and freedom.

3. <u>The absent God</u>—When you try and fail to worship a god who can't be pleased, then you often create a god who has gone away on vacation—this is the god of *"deism,"* quite popular in the 18th century. *Since God has left the building, he might as well not exist.* The problem with the uninvolved, uncaring, unfeeling god is that he tends to make one uninvolved, uncaring, and unfeeling. This most miserable of all theological views robs one of passion—at least those who believe in the *"Santa Claus God"* can laugh and sing . . . and at least the *"child-abuser God"* solicits some kind of action . . . but, sadly, believers in the *"deist idol"* do nothing.

If the bad stuff in life comes from (or is allowed by) a "monster god," I will continue to seethe with anger. But if bad stuff comes from a *"loving, sovereign God,"* at some point I will rejoice and be free—*but don't expect freedom to come without a struggle.* Until a Christian struggles with the issue of freedom, he or she will remain frightened, obsessive and bound. One has to struggle. Unless you are living a Christian life of denial, you know that many pieces of evidence suggest that the God who is, does not always look as benevolent and as kind as we would like. Most Christians blandly accept the clichés of the faith without dealing with the complexities—*"Jesus loves me, this I know, for the Bible tells me so"* is fine until the doctor tells you that you have cancer, that your business has gone down in flames, that your child has died, or that your spouse has left you for someone better looking and more understanding.

The mind believes only what it has "learned"—the heart believes what it has "experienced." Most of the ideas we have about God arise from a *visceral* rather than a *cerebral* source. If our experience has primarily been a painful one, we will believe in an abusive God who has inflicted that pain. Most of us draw our idea of God from the "experiences" (good or bad) of our lives. Biblical Christians should find out about God from *"Jesus"*—if something we think about God violates what we know of Jesus, what He taught, and how He acted, then that thought *"lies."* In short, *if you want to know what God is really like—look at Jesus.* By looking at Jesus, we discover two crucial facts about God that significantly impact our views of freedom and grace: *He is KIND* and *He is GOD.* If God is the vindictive, angry, abusive deity that many tell us He is, then we have a serious problem—we will live in constant fear, and with very good reason (Heb 10:31). Conversely, a *"user-friendly god"* is not God—that kind of god exists only in our imagination. He certainly is not the God of the Bible.

Many Christians frequently create and worship a benevolent "grandfather god" out of their own desire, because he is a far safer, far less terrifying god. But the God of the Bible is both a *"kind and stern God"* (Rom 11:22). Jesus talked about a *"narrow way"* that leads to life, and a broad and easy way that leads to destruction. And He taught clearly about God's judgment, hell, and the wrath of God. That, dear friend, is not a safe God. At the same time, Jesus showed an incredible *understanding of human weakness and sin.* He said, "Come to me, all who are weary and heavy-laden, and I will give you rest; I am gentle and lowly in heart" (Mt 11:28–30). So is God confused? No! Only by understanding both the rule and the kindness of God do we find great personal balance and freedom. Notice the "bridge" between wrath and love—"For God so loved the world that He *gave* His only Son, that whoever believes in Him should not *perish* but have eternal life" (Jn 3:16). So what does this mean? If you are a Christian, it means that God will never be angry with you again, because He imputed Christ's righteousness to you! How can God be angry at perfection? *"There is no condemnation to those in Christ"* (Rom 8:1). God is both scary *(holy!)* and compassionate *(loving!)*. Now, if you really believed that God was good, and that He was in charge of this mess, and that He never grew angry with you—how would you act? Therefore, if the Son sets you free, you are free indeed! (Jn 8:36). (26–48)

Are you getting much better than you were? With all of the teaching you have received about being obedient, holy and sanctified, is it working in your life? If you are honest, you will probably admit that *"you are not getting much better."* Bryan Chapell in his book *"Holiness by Grace"* tells about the 17th century pastor Walter Marshall who said many in his congregation were *"killing themselves in their efforts to be godly."* The issue of "getting better" is not the point—our "relationship with God" is the point. When we are obsessed with being better instead of being consumed with God's love and grace, we become prideful if we can pull it off and self-centered if we can't. ***The greatest cause for our "not getting better" is our obsession with not getting better***—there is a better way of getting better than *"trying harder!"* Sanctification becomes a reality in those believers who don't obsess over their own sanctification. Holiness hardly ever becomes a reality until we *"care more about Jesus than about holiness"* (performance). Writes Steve Brown—

> *I'm about as good as I'm going to get, and I'm tired of trying. There is hardly anything that will beat you down and rob you of your freedom more than "your efforts" to get better. Writes C. S. Lewis about people trying to live by the law—Either we give up trying to be good, or else we become very unhappy . . . the more you obey your conscience, the more your conscience will demand of you. And your natural self, which is being starved and hampered and worried at every turn, will get angrier.*

Paul addressed the problem of "antinomianism" (living with "no law") when he wrote: "What shall we say then? Are we to continue in sin that grace may abound? No!" While *perfectionism* (living by the law) considerably inhibits our freedom, so does *antinomianism*. The issue we have to resolve is this—we aren't going to get much better; that is, we aren't going to get much better by our own *"self-powered efforts."* When you give up on trying to *"make yourself better,"* you will begin to identify with Paul's problem—"he wanted to do good, but when he tried, he ended up doing the very thing he didn't want to do" (Rom 7:15ff). ***Our focus must be on "grace," because we so desperately need it!*** By the way, *"trying to be perfect"* is a good thing, because if we never exasperate ourselves by trying, we would never know that *"we can't be perfect!"* Here's another good that comes from all this—the fact that you *want* to be better, is a sign that you belong to Christ.

The "desire for perfection" indicates the presence of something in us that gives us that desire. That something is the *"Holy Spirit"*—He is the one who brings us to the point of *"giving up"* on what we simply cannot do. Unfortunately, the desire to be better can become a *"monster"* that robs us of our freedom—the downside of desiring to be better is *"perfectionism"* (i.e., performance). When Paul honestly admitted his inability to do the good he wanted to do, he faced up to his own *helplessness and hopelessness*.

Do you remember "Sisyphus" of Greek mythology? He revealed Zeus's rape of Aegina to her father, and as his punishment, Zeus doomed him for all of eternity to roll a huge stone up a hill, only to have it roll down again each time he tried. *Perfectionist, thy name is Sisyphus!* Don't you wish you could just leave the stupid stone at the bottom of the hill and walk away? Are you tired to trying and trying and trying and trying . . . yet never getting much better? You'll find great relief and freedom in *"giving up!"* By the way, you greatly diminish your freedom when you *"pretend"* to others that you are accomplishing perfection. It is called *"hypocrisy,"* and it is quite injurious to your freedom.

The only people who "get better" are people who know that, if they never get better, God will love them anyway! The corollary to that principle is this: God will not only love you if you don't get better, He will teach you that "getting better is not the issue"—*"His love is the issue!"* *Martin Luther* wrote a letter to his friend "George Spalatin," a Christian brother who worked with him in the Reformation. Spalatin was suffering terribly from enormous guilt about some bad advice he had given to someone—he was devastated and depressed. Luther wrote to him:

> *My faithful request and admonition is that you join our company and associate with us, who are real, great, and hardboiled sinners . . . Christ must be a Savior and Redeemer from real, great, grievous and damnable transgressions . . . yea, from the very greatest and most shocking sins.*

How often have we, like Luther's friend, spent hours "grieving over our lack of perfection"? Our freedom has been taken away because we thought we couldn't be free unless we were perfect! Guilt has only one purpose—to drive us to the throne of grace, where we allow God, if He deems to do so, to change us and make us better. When we allow guilt to do anything other than that, we become perfectionists—miserable, guilt ridden, afraid, and lonely. There is really something quite *"neurotic"* about Christians who spend most of their time *"trying desperately to please God"* who is already very pleased! They don't have any freedom! Writes Steve Brown: "When I stopped working so hard at being better and turned to Jesus, that's when, almost without noticing it, I started getting just a little bit better. So I have decided to get as close as I can to Jesus, who will always love me even if I don't get any better!"

The closer we get to God, the more we see the truth about ourselves and how very far off the destination really is. The truth of the matter is this: "We are better because we are closer to Him; but the closer we get to Him, the less we *feel* like we are getting better"—it may sound crazy, but it is true. Rather than *obsessing about our goodness* God asks us to *hang out with Him* (walk with Him) and see where He leads us—He promises He will never leave us or forsake us. So we can quit worrying about getting behind in our holiness and sanctification. The more we worry about that, the worse we are going to get, but the more we abide with Him, the better we will get—even if we don't know it! Paul tells us, "what God begins, He brings to completion!" (Phil 1:6). That means God's beginning in our lives is the absolute promise that He will continue working to completion. We just have to trust and believe that *"God's Spirit"* is busy at work in us making us like His Son (Phil 2:13). (50–73)

The institution of "religion" can be a very hard taskmaster—it can demand your soul by putting you in a prison of guilt and shame. Religion can make people mean, angry, critical, judgmental, frustrated, miserable and neurotic. Worst of all, religion can keep people from God—it becomes a *"substitute"* for a relationship with God; thus it will kill your freedom. Jesus reserved His harshest criticism for the religious folks who "tie up heavy burdens and lay them on people's shoulders" (Mt 23:4). Jesus said, *"The Spirit of the Lord has sent Me to proclaim liberty to the captives!"* (Lk 4:18). The good news of the gospel is that it offers people freedom, healing, meaning, immortality, and forgiveness—the gospel is not a *"misery pill!"*

The good news is that Christ "frees us" from the need to obnoxiously focus on our goodness, our commitment, and our correctness. Religion has made us obsessively obnoxious! The truth is, the only ones who will ever *"get any better"* are those who know God won't be angry with them if they don't get better! Someone has described the church in America as a nice man standing in front of nice people, telling them that God calls them to be *"nicer"*—which is mere *"moralism!"* By the way, Buddhism is probably better at producing moralists than Christianity. When we become moralists, we miss the good news that *"our righteousness" isn't the point*—that is nothing more than performance-based religion! In other words, we buy into the view that religion's sole purpose is to *"make people good."* Many will argue, "I know atheists who are really nice people, and Christians who are hypocrites"—if the essence of the Christian faith is *"morality,"* then they have a point.

Remember, Paul told us that Abraham was given "imputed righteousness!" **—so were we!** Jesus took care of sin on the cross, and that means all of our sins are forgiven—past, present, and future! Conversely, He has given us *"His righteousness!"* People call it *"cheap grace!"*—listen, if it wasn't cheap, you and I couldn't afford it! If it cost us one thing—commitment, obedience, etc.—it would still be in the store on the shelf. It is a *"gift"* that makes us righteous—and it didn't come cheap—it was purchased with the *"blood of Christ!"*

One of the greatest sins Christians commit is "constantly focusing on their sin." When Martin Luther told his friend Melanchthon, "Why don't you just go out and sin so you will have something to repent of," he was encouraging his friend to *"stop focusing on himself!"* Our sin is not the issue! Fixating on flying purple elephants (which is akin to fixating on the law) won't help! But focusing on the God of grace and love most certainly will! One of the problems of cultural Christianity is that we focus on *"fixing people"* (focusing on their sinfulness); no wonder pagans don't want to be around us! Jesus said to His disciples, "Unless your righteousness exceeds that of the scribes and Pharisees, you will never enter the kingdom of heaven" (Mt 5:20)—the Pharisees were the most obedient religious folks in Jewish culture, and were theologically correct in almost everything they believed and taught—yet that *"wasn't good enough!"* The issue is this—it is not *"our righteousness"* that is the issue, it is *"God's righteousness!"* Now go out and dance, and do it with gusto and with freedom! (74–92)

Religious professionals have to wear a number of "masks" to keep their jobs. The masks we wear bind us to a role that kills the very freedom Christ died to give us. Sadly, most of us view ourselves from the perspective held by others—this constitutes our *"self image"*—as such, we deal with life based on this *"faulty self-image."* If we don't know our true selves, we will live in a prison of *"false expectations,"* that means we will try to live up to *"others' expectations"* instead of living out who we really are. Jesus is not into good or bad self-images—*He's into reality!* The only valuable self-image is the one that reflects the reality of who we truly are; anything other than that, good or bad, is a lie—and we eventually will have to face the truth. Because *"grace runs downhill,"* it is very important that you not stake out your territory at the top of the hill. If you come to the place where you think you are wonderful and good and spiritual, when you really aren't, your *"wake-up day"* is coming!

A common mask for many of us former legalists is the "mask of guilt." Whenever we wear that mask, we are horribly bound, and our prison bars make us miserable and depressed. The masks we wear—be them masks of unreality, superiority, or inferiority—take away our freedom. Start by trying to deal with the *"truth"* of who you are. As Paul wrote, "For by the grace given to me, I say to everyone not to think of himself more highly than he ought to think; rather be sober in your thinking" (Rom 12:3). Many of us don't feel that good about ourselves. The prayer God almost always answers is this: "Lord, show me Yourself"—He'll show you how much you are *"loved!"* After that, and only after that, does God show you the stuff you need to know about who you really are. You can handle any truth when you know *"you are really loved and valued!"*

A true self-image includes some "positive and negative" aspects. It is extremely important that you get your self-image from Jesus—He will never lie to you, and He will always love you. Don't ask your enemy to tell you the truth about yourself; instead go to Jesus, He loves you and will tell you the *absolute truth* . . . and He will always temper that truth with His kindness and His grace. Once you know *"God's unconditional love"* and the *"truth about yourself"*—you will rest easy, and you will be free! You may think *if people really knew you*, they wouldn't want to be around you, therefore you should just keep on pretending. But *"that's a lie"* from the pit of hell!

When the requirements for acceptance in any particular group, require us to act in certain ways, we tend to fake it. Allow me to let you in on a secret—*"Nobody fits the mold!"* When we give the impression that we have it altogether, and live 100 miles from any known sin . . . when we seem to be anything other than what we are—*sinners saved by grace*—we do a great disservice to one another, and we become bound to the masks instead of freedom in Christ! Here are the facts—*You need me and I need you! If we aren't honest with each other, those needs will go unmet!* Christ can give you the freedom to *"stop pretending"* to be who you are not! Of course, superficial Christians will probably reject you . . . and religious leaders in control will probably kick you out of their groups . . . but if that should happen, *"Rejoice and Celebrate!"* You have now determined who is and who is not playing games with your mind and your heart. You will discover that it took a lot of *"emotional gasoline"* to keep that mask on—and now you don't have to do that anymore! It is also important that you understand that *"none of our biblical heroes"* were exempt from the necessity of the cross! They were *"all sinners"* just like you and me! If you read the Bible carefully, you will discover that they frequently revealed their sinfulness when they wrote.

The Church should be a place "you can say anything" and know you won't get kicked out . . . where we can confess our sins knowing others will help us . . . where we can disagree and still be friends. *It ought to be the one place in the world where we don't have to wear masks.* By the way, if we took our masks off, the world would flock to our doors! Because *"genuine freedom"* is an attractive commodity! You can't be *"free"* and wear a mask in the presence of unbelievers . . . and our witness is incredibly important! God does not call us to witness about *"our goodness"*—we are called to witness about the *"freedom and joy"* we have found in Christ! Listen, if people think they have to *"be good"* to come to Christ, they will run in the opposite direction! *If we take our masks off, we will attract people to Christ! Wearing masks simply chases them away!* Even though you're afraid to—take off your mask! and "enjoy the freedom God died to give you!" (94–116)

Augustine said: "Do you wish to be GREAT? Then begin by BEING!" Steve Brown writes, "I have spent most of my life trying to find people to put on a *pedestal*—and God has spent most of my life *destroying the pedestals* and reminding me that nobody belongs on one except Him!" Anytime we make another human being more than *"a sinner desperately in need of God's grace,"* God takes great delight in showing us the truth about our heroes. It is very dangerous to worship at any altar other than God's! Some of the biographies of famous Christians should never have been written, because they don't tell the *bad* as well as the *good*—as such, they don't inspire excellence, because they are a *"lie"* and will only make you feel guilty. The truth is, God uses sinful, flawed human beings, because those are the only kinds of human beings He has available to use. One of the wonderful characteristics about the Bible is that God was very careful to allow us to see the *greatness* and the *smallness* of biblical characters. Throughout Scripture, we encounter heroes of the faith with *major flaws . . . serious sin . . . and embarrassing failures*—Adam and Eve, Noah, Abraham, Jacob, Moses, David, Solomon, Rahab, Paul, Peter, etc. The Bible tells the story of "flawed" human beings, and it also tells the story of how God used those flawed human beings in exceptional ways. As Paul said, "We have this treasure in *jars of clay* to show that the surpassing power belongs to God—not us!" (2 Cor 4:7–10). *There are no super-Christians!*

When we deify others, we do a great disservice to them; we rob them of their humanness, forcing them to remain on the very pedestal that will eventually destroy them. When we deify leaders, we force them to live a lie, a lie that will make them both defensive and shallow. The late *Jack Miller,* founder of *World Harvest Mission,* often said that "only the *repentant* have anything to teach God's people." In fact, writes Steve Brown, *"the most genuinely repentant person in a congregation should probably be its pastor!"* When leaders become puffed up with their own importance, their lack of freedom and their loneliness is as much our fault as it is theirs. When Christian leaders act as if they have a hotline to God, don't listen to them—by affirming that kind of nonsense, you allow the leader to stay in a prison where it becomes impossible for him to truly be free. When leadership lacks humility and grace, it can lead to the pride that goes before a fall. Says Brown: *"The only qualification for joining the 'Christian Club' is to be unqualified."*

Charles and Janet Morris in the book *"Jesus in the Midst of Success,"* describe a number of successful Christians who have learned to live by a radically different definition of success. One leader they describe is **Doug Cobb,** founder of the Cobb Report and the president of a venture capital company. They write:

Unfortunately, when "luck" seems to be smiling on us, unseen spiritual dangers often lurk beneath the surface. Cobb, a Christian, says the reason for that is no mystery: **"Success blinds you to your true spiritual condition; people think you're wonderful."** *Even as a believer it's easy to drift into a self-confident independence. It becomes a habit to be always the benefactor, never the supplicant. As one pastor says, tongue in cheek, "It's hard not to feel superior when you really are superior."*

Wise leaders lead, but they don't take themselves so seriously that they consider their decisions the moral equivalent of "God's decisions." Christian apologist, **G.K. Chesterton**, was a great man, but His greatness lay in his humility. "What's wrong with the world?" he once asked. "What's wrong with the world is ME! God has ordained only one Messiah! You're not it! I'm not either!" (118–140)

Steve Brown makes "three startling statements" that will help free you from the power you have given to others. They are as follows:

1. <u>You don't have to pretend to be good, because we all know you're not</u>. When we confess to one another that we aren't good people, the necessity of my demonizing you—because I need to feel good about myself—is no longer a necessity. The apostle Paul said, "Christ Jesus came into the world to save sinners, of whom I am the foremost" (1 Tim 1:15). Paul insisted that no Christian could speak as an *"outsider"* of the human race. Speak the truth ("you're a sinner!") and be free! You won't have to wear a silly mask anymore! What if we really felt that *being human* was ok? What if we no longer had to pretend that we are good? When you don't have an agenda but Jesus, you will be convinced that—

   - We are a lot worse than we think we are, and God's grace is a lot bigger than we think it is.
   - We are really messed up folks whom a sovereign God has decided to love unconditionally.

- Grace always runs downhill.
- Power really is made perfect in weakness.

2. <u>Christians don't have to be right</u>. A big disagreement arose in the church at Rome about eating food offered to idols. Paul advised thus: *"Each one should be fully convinced in his own mind"* (Rom 14:4–5). Don't demonize those who disagree with you—you will end up encasing yourself in concrete and call it freedom. It is hard for those of us who are right to tolerate those who aren't. Only people who get it wrong sometimes, and know they get it wrong, find it easy to be tolerant. God says, *"My thoughts are not your thoughts, neither are My ways your ways"* (Is 55:8–9). If God says that, then it stands to reason that a fairly good chance exists that anybody who thinks he has it all right—in fact is wrong.

3. <u>We don't have to fight a battle already won</u>. Jesus "disarmed the rulers and authorities—and triumphed over them" (Col 2:15). And said, *"Take heart, I have overcome the world"* (Jn 16:33). Christ is the victor. The battle is already over! God won! There is no contest! We don't have to fix anything. God doesn't need our help. He did just fine before we came along, and will do fine long after we are gone. The great thing about being a Christian is that you can forgive, love, and encourage them all, and let God sort it all out. There is a lot of ego involved in being good, and being right. When religion becomes leverage, it ceases to be the religion of Jesus. The gospel of grace takes away the leverage. If God loves me, you can't manipulate me by threatening to take away your love.

All of us are pretty much alike—we're all sinful, afraid, lonely, regretful, sometimes doubting, wrong, angry, loving, hateful, selfish, kind, wounded, very human. Nobody can speak as an *"outsider"* of the human race—we are all sinners—we all have the same problems! (142–190)

Scott Peck tells us that the tendency to avoid problems and emotional suffering is "the primary basis of all human mental illness." Conversely, *Larry Crabb* says, "we all have a place of pain . . . and we try to go anyplace but there; furthermore, in order to get to a place of wholeness, we have to keep on probing and probing at the pain until it gets so bad only God can fix it." The idea that we as Christians can *"avoid pain"* is completely unbiblical. What does the Bible teach? Let's start with Adam and Eve: when they sinned they were "cursed," and what happened to them affected all of us—men must *"work hard"* to eat . . . women must *"painfully"* bear children . . . and all creation is subjected to *"futility."* Jesus said, "In the world you will have *tribulation*" (Jn 16:33). **Jeremiah** felt so down he wanted to give up. **Paul** felt so depressed he despaired of life itself. **Peter** feared others and their opinion of him. And what can we say about **Job's** experience with pain, loss, and rejection? The Spanish contemplative of the 16th century, **Saint Teresa of Avila**, prayed the way many of us may have prayed, "Lord, you would have more friends if you treated the ones you had a little better." In spite of the fact that *"pain and suffering"* are a part of our calling, most of us still try to avoid it any way we can. Most of us live our lives trying to make them as pleasant as possible. You think about that.

We should be aware of what happens when we try to "avoid pain"— We fail to discover the depths of God's faithfulness, and the joy that transcends our circumstances. There is a direct correlation between your willingness to face the darkness of your own pain and your ability to live freely and fully. The freest people in the world are Christians who know that the world is not a nice place—they know about the Fall, about pain, and about sin. And in knowing they find a wonderful freedom. He says to himself, "I'm called to be here and to even suffer sometimes, but I'll face the reality and dance anyway!" Psalm 23—"Even though I walk through the valley of the shadow of death, Thou art with me." If you play games with evil and death, you will never experience the *"sufficiency of Christ,"* and you'll miss out on large chunks of *"grace"* that could have been yours.

Paul was given a "thorn in the flesh"—Most believe it was some kind of physical malady, but whatever it was, *Paul pleaded with God to remove it*—"Lord, this thing is destroying me! I can't stand this thing! Please remove this from me! Lord, if you heal me, I'll give you all the credit!" Here is God's reply: *"My grace is sufficient for you, My power is made perfect in weakness."* In other words, "Paul, if you didn't have the *wound*, you wouldn't have the *power*." One of the most profound realities in life is this: *"What we go through is what makes us successful or great."* The difference between an unbeliever and a Christian when they lose a business, face death, or suffer the pain of loss is *"the way they handle it."* The world can see the difference Christ makes. So when you experience pain—don't run! embrace it! It has shown up so that you will find God! Sometimes that's the only place you can find Him! Remember, nothing in this life is arbitrary—everything happens for a reason—either it drives us to God, or drives us away from God.

I've heard it said over and over again, that "Jesus is all you need;" that's true, but you won't know it is true until Jesus is all you have. *Every broken road leads to God*—so, if you refuse to walk on the broken roads, you'll never get to Him. If you run from pain, you will never know God's wonderful sufficiency and grace. In the middle of a tragedy, God will show up! And you will discover an exhilarating freedom and joy you've never known. When you lose everything, Jesus invites you to laugh and dance and sing in His presence, knowing that *nothing can separate you from Him and His love*. That is the "freedom" Jesus wants us to experience! He sets us free from the bondage of misery! So when pain comes—and it will!—run to it! and you will find you have run into the arms of Jesus! Buck up, face it, embrace it, and know that you and Jesus can deal with it! Then you will laugh and dance in the freedom and the reality of God's sufficiency, and the awesome power that God reveals in your weakness. (142–216)

"I am a failure," wrote a counselee of Steve Brown, "and it has been good for me to be a failure—I have learned so much from my mistakes, and God has allowed me to see Him in a far different and more profound way than I did before. I praise God that He is in charge of every circumstance." Steve Brown said: "I affirmed her belief in God's sovereignty." My friend **Fred Smith** has said the difference between Christians and pagans when both fail is that *pagans blame luck* and

Christians blame God—unfortunately, there is some truth to that. But let me tell you about some other truth—*many Christians live in a prison of failure*, thinking they cannot gain their freedom from that prison. And most of them think they don't deserve freedom. They have lived in the abnormality of a *dark prison* for so long they won't look up at the open door God has given them—an open door into the *light of freedom*.

Steve Brown tells his Seminary students, "If you don't deal with your 'guilt,' you will end up having a ministry of condemnation." He reminds them of what Paul wrote: "There is now no condemnation for those who are in Christ Jesus" (Rom 8:1). I fear too often the church has become an organization of *"guilty people"* with a *"guilty preacher"* telling them they should *"feel guiltier!"* I'm really surprised that any of us ever accomplish anything of note in the name of Christ!

Most Christians never accomplish what God wants them to accomplish because they don't think they *"deserve"* God's good purpose for their lives. Christians often see themselves as bound and helpless sinners, deserving of any punishment an angry God might choose to dish out. A part of that, of course, is true—*we don't deserve anything commendable!* We haven't earned anything good, but that isn't the whole truth! Consider the faulty reasoning that enslaves us—

> *Major premise:* Christians are undeserving sinners.
> *Minor premise:* I'm an undeserving sinner.
> *Conclusion:* I deserve nothing but failure.

While there is "some truth" to such logic, it is only "a small part of the story!" Quite frankly, despite your sin, your unworthiness, and your rebellion—you're going to turn out fine. Our problem is that we have misunderstood the *"gospel"*—we are enormously valuable to God; so valuable that He bought us at the highest price imaginable—the blood of His own Son! And He did that to *"set us free"* from sin and death! We need to know who we are and feel comfortable with that. Our problem is we give the *"law"* a condemning power God never intended—***First*** of all, the law of God is simply a *schematic* for the way the world works; the law of God is the best way to live; and to the degree that you follow it, you will be happy. **Second,** the law of God is a *safeguard*—when you walk in a minefield, you might want to know the location of the mines. The positive side of the law brings happiness; the negative side provides protection. **Third,** the law of God is a *sampler*—it is no secret the laws of Western Civilization are based on the revealed laws of God in the Bible. Those laws point to a just, compassionate, benevolent society, and to the extent that a society does a reasonably proficient job of living by them, that society will echo the way things get done in heaven. When Jesus said we should pray thus: "Thy will be done on earth as it is in heaven," He meant we ought to pray for the "laws of heaven" to be lived out on earth. By the way, things would be a whole lot better if that were to happen.

The "law" was our guardian until Christ came, in order that we might be justified by faith (Gal 3:24). Do you know what the law did for you? In the struggle to keep it, you realized you were in trouble—serious trouble. So the law is the *"tutor"* that brought you to Christ—through the pain of self-revelation, exposed by the law, we came to the throne of grace. The law is not only the *"tutor"* that brings us to Him, it is also the *"glue"* that keeps us there. Paul said that when he wanted to do good things, he couldn't; and when he didn't want to do bad things, he couldn't help it. Paul called it an ongoing problem in his life. He cries out to God, *"Wretched man that I am! Who will deliver me from this body of death?"* And then the wonderful answer, *"Thanks be to God through Jesus Christ our Lord!"* (Rom 7:24). At some point we come to the end of ourselves, and that actually happens quite often—our sin and failure cause us time and again to run to Jesus. We cry out with Paul, "Lord, I'm in trouble! Can You help me?" And Jesus says, "Yes, I can help." The wonderful truth is, *He accepts us no matter how dirty we are!* I can't tell you the number of times I have crept into the throne room of God thinking, *"He's going to really get me this time!"* The Lord responds, *"Come My child. I was wondering when you would come. I was waiting."* And then we discover that *"God's not angry with us!"* How can this be? What an incredible God!

Our relationship with God is not a matter of "reward," but "love." Fortunately for us, God doesn't base our relationship with Him on *"our merit"*—if He did, who among us could stand? The fact that God bases His relationship with us on *"love"* means we can enjoy staggering freedom in His presence. We are *"free"* to be who we are! We don't have to *"perform"* to be accepted! There isn't anything we could do to cause God to "love us less" or "love us more"—nothing! The revelation of your sin—as painful as that is—is a gift from God. God's *"grace"* is the point! It is foolish to think we can present a *"suitable offering of service"* unto the Lord—we simply don't have the wherewithal to do that. Sometimes God gives us the *"gift of obedience,"* and sometimes He doesn't—when God doesn't, He gives us love and forgiveness. When He does give us the gift of obedience, God also gives us an acute awareness that it wasn't us—*it was Him*. Most importantly, God gives us Himself—freely, joyously, and without reservation.

You may be wondering why I left out the guilt, the condemnation, and the promises to get better and better in every way, every day—*I left them out because they aren't in the Bible!* We're all drawn to that stuff, but it simply isn't there. Something about *"religion"* will make you into an insecure, self-doubting, failure-producing worm—it happens with the misuse of the law. You can define yourself by your inevitable failure to live up to the standards of the law, or you can define yourself in terms of God's love, acceptance, and the great value He has put on you. Learn to deal with guilt properly and biblically, because it serves no purpose. Let's review the faulty reasoning concepts we stated on the last page, and correct them—

> <u>Major premise</u>: *Christians are undeserving sinners, and I'm an undeserving sinner.*
> <u>Minor premise</u>: *God's grace is bigger than my sin, and His love is bigger than my failure.*
> <u>Conclusion</u>: *Therefore, I gratefully accept any blessing He deems proper for me.*

If you are not careful, an improper use of the law will confirm your inferiority. When that happens, Satan will rejoice, and you will become as useless as you have come to think you are. Without knowing that God gave us the law as a *"gift,"* then the freedom and success God desires for us will go wanting. The reason for **Tiger Woods** golf success can in large part be attributed to what his father told him: "If you stay *angry with yourself* over a bad shot, you won't be able to prepare for the next one. That's the key—play every shot with the same frame of mind and let go of what happened before." That really is the key to life—*one must live life in the present*. It is our heritage of freedom. The past is the past, forgiven and redeemed; the future is ours, a gift our Father will give us. *God has put us in the present as a place to struggle, succeed or fail, risk, and make a difference.* You are free—really free! You are free because you are forgiven and loved. God is for you and controls all the circumstances of your life! So get moving! (218–238)

It is for "freedom" that Christ has set us free; therefore, stand firm and do not submit again to a yoke of slavery (Gal 5:1). Something about freedom gets lost when you start *"obeying certain rules"* in order to attain it. Says Brown: "I've been walking with Jesus for a long time, and no doubt I've done it wrong a number of times; *but there is something to be said for listening to someone who struggles mightily with being free."* I've gone down several paths that I would like to spare you. Peter said, "Live as people who are free, not using your freedom as a cover-up for evil" (1 Pet 2:16). Paul essentially said the same thing: "You were called to freedom; do not use your freedom as an opportunity for the flesh" (Gal 5:13). Paul said, "All things are lawful for me, but not all things are helpful" (1 Cor 6:12). In other words, you are really free—but don't be stupid about it; don't get bound by your use of freedom.

Says Brown: "If I've tried to do anything in this book, it has been to get you away from obsessing over your sin." The rules are so hard, and there are so many of them. If you get obsessive over rules and laws, you will end up breaking them all. The fact is, one major reason Christians don't obey is they obsess over their obedience. Here's the key: ***Stop making "your goodness" the issue!*** This isn't about you and me; it's about Jesus! When you obsess over anything but "Him"—including being free—you can lose it. *Jesus is freedom, and to the degree you stay focused on Him, you will find yourself free!*

"God has not given us a spirit of fear" (2 Tim 1:7). "God delivers us from our fears" (Ps 34:4). "We don't need to be afraid because God is our strength and our song" (Is 12:2). "The more we are loved, the less we fear; there is no fear in love" (1 Jn 4:18). *Most of us feel afraid*—we feel that we will blow it really bad, so bad we can't be fixed. We fear losing control and doing something stupid. We fear what others think. The truth is—almost anything you do with God that comes from fear is probably wrong. When you live with fear you will miss the joy of laughing and dancing and God's presence.

The Bible says a lot about how "our past" can affect our present and our future. Peter says: "You are a chosen race, a people for God's own possession, that you may proclaim the excellencies of Him who called you out of darkness into His marvelous light . . . you have received mercy" (1 Pet 2:9–10). In other words, *your past is your past.* The past can take away your freedom. God highly values us and has adopted us into His family—that is our reality, and that is how God wants us to define ourselves. For *"freedom"* Christ has set us free! (Gal 5:1). Really free people will make themselves *"servants to others"* that they might win them to Christ (1 Cor 9:19). Free people remain free to give up their freedom. *Martin Luther,* in his book, *The Freedom of a Christian,* said, "To make the way smoother for the unlearned (for only them do I serve), I shall set down the following two propositions concerning the freedom and the bondage of the spirit—A Christian is a perfectly free lord of all, subject to none; and a Christian is a perfectly dutiful servant of all, subject to all" (Lull, p. 586). Regarding our being servants to others—a free mind serves one's neighbor willingly, not because he feels obligated to do so; he serves out of love, because he is *"free to love!"* (240–250)

CHAPTER 3

A summary of the book...
"HOLINESS"
by J. C. Ryle (1816–1900)

Bishop J. C. Ryle's *"Holiness"* is one of the finest theological works ever written. Ryle wrote *"Holiness"* in 1877 to answer some fashionable and dangerous teachings about sanctification, the Christian's struggle with sin, and the so-called deeper life. By the second half of the nineteenth century several varieties of perfectionist and second-blessing doctrines had been gradually gaining grass-root popularity in evangelical circles around the world—*John Wesley* taught "complete sanctification;" **Charles Finney** taught "perfectionism;" *Robert Pearsall Smith* taught "perfectionism;" and **Hannah Whitall Smith** taught a toned-down "Wesleyan perfectionism combined with Quaker quietism;" the believer's only duty is to trust God and rest in the Lord; the key words were *surrender*, *yield*, *trust*, and *rest*. Smith's deeper-life teaching emphatically denied that sanctification entails any kind of *struggle*—victory was characterized as life on a "higher spiritual plane" where temptation would cease to trouble the consecrated person. But Scripture never speaks in such terms—we are commanded to "flee" and "resist" (1 Cor 6:18; 10:14; 1 Tim 6:11; 2 Tim 2:22; Jam 4:7). The same year Mrs. Smith's book was published, the **"Keswick Convention"** was founded in England to promote a similar view of holiness. Again, these are *"totally passive"* approaches to sanctification which essentially promise an easy, instant pathway to victory over all known sin. The movement can be summed in the slogan, *"Let go and let God."* Sadly, the errors of this movement are still causing much confusion today in evangelical circles. (7–14)

J. C. Ryle was born into privilege (his father inherited a fortune); he attended Oxford University. John Charles Ryle's hopes for a career in public service were shattered when his family lost their fortune "overnight." He was ordained as a minister in the "Church of England" in 1841 at the age of 25—he became a prolific writer of tracts that were wildly popular.

He who wishes to attain right views about "Christian holiness," says Ryle, must begin with the subject of SIN. Wrong views about holiness are almost always traceable to wrong views about *"human corruption."* Sin is the fault and corruption of the nature of man; as such, man is inclined to evil . . . every human being inherits a heart and nature inclined to evil. Jeremiah writes, "The heart is deceitful above all things, and desperately wicked" (17:9). A "sin" consists in doing, saying, thinking, imagining anything that is not in perfect conformity with the mind and law of God. Says John, "Sin is the transgression of the law" (1 Jn 3:4)—the slightest outward or inward departure from absolute mathematical parallelism with God's revealed will and character constitutes a sin. A man may break God's law in heart and thought, when there is no overt and visible act of wickedness. Even a poet of our own has truly said, *"A man may smile and still be a villain."* Furthermore, there are sins of omission and sins of commission . . . and things we ought to do, and things we ought not to do. The understanding, the affections, the reasoning powers, and the will are all more or less infected. So deeply planted are the roots of human corruption, that even after we are born again, these roots remain alive in the bottom of our hearts, and we never get rid of them until we exit our bodies into eternity.

Sin in the believer's heart no longer has "dominion" over him, because the *"principle of grace"* now rules in him; therefore sin is checked, controlled and crucified. One of the problems men have is that they regard sin as "less sinful and dangerous" than it is in the sight of God—they make

Holiness   57

excuses for it, minimize its guilt, and question its awfulness. Where is the mighty harm? Sin comes to us like Judas with a kiss—the "forbidden fruit" seemed good and desirable to Eve, yet it cast her out of Eden. David's walking idly on his palace roof seemed harmless enough, yet it ended in adultery and murder. Sin rarely seems sin in the beginning. How true it is that the "holiest saint" is in himself a miserable sinner to the last moment of his existence. **Richard Hooker**, a 16th century English theologian who strongly influenced the development of the Church of England, says, "Search all the generations of men since the fall of our father Adam, find one man that hath done one action which hath passed from him pure, without any stain or blemish at all—*the best things we do all have something within them that needs to be pardoned*." For my part, I am persuaded the more light we have, the more we see our own sinfulness, and the more we are clothed in humility. Let us not be ashamed to confess plainly our *state of imperfection*—it is simply admitting reality. (15–44)

The subject of "sanctification" is of outmost importance to our souls. Sanctification is that inward spiritual work that God works in the soul of man by the *Holy Spirit*. The instrument by which the Spirit effects this work is generally the *Word of God*, though He sometimes uses afflictions and providential visitations (1 Pet 3:1). Scripture, Prayer, Meditation, Sermons, Public Worship, and the Lord's Table are the appointed channels through which the Holy Spirit conveys fresh supplies of grace to the soul, and strengthens the work that He has begun in the inward man—furthermore, there are "no spiritual gains without pains." *Our God is a God who works by "means."* A true Christian is one who has not only peace of conscience, but war within—thus believers must not feel they are *not sanctified* because they experience great inward struggle. Such freedom we shall have in heaven, but not here in this world. The heart of the best Christian, even at his best, is a field occupied by two rival camps, and the *"company of two armies"* (Song of Sol 6:13; Gal 5:17).

The holiest actions of the holiest saint who ever lived are all more or less full of "defects and imperfections." To suppose that such actions can stand the severity of God's judgment, atone for sin, and merit heaven, is simply absurd. "By the deeds of the law shall no flesh be justified" (Rom 3:20–28). For all this, however, the Bible distinctly teaches that the holy actions of a sanctified man, although imperfect, are pleasing in the sight of God—"with such sacrifices God is well pleased" (Heb 13:16). Just as a parent is pleased with the efforts of his little child to please him, though it be only by picking a daisy or walking across a room, so is our Father in heaven pleased with the *less than perfect performances* of His believing children—He looks at the motive, principle, and intention of their actions, and not merely at their quantity and quality. (45–57)

Thousands of Christians have buried themselves in some wilderness "monastery" under the vain idea that by doing so they would escape sin and become eminently holy. *They forgot that wherever they went, they carried the "root of evil" with them in their own heart.* True holiness does not make a Christian evade difficulties, but face and overcome them. Christ would have His people show that His grace is not a mere greenhouse plant, which can only thrive under some kind of shelter, but a strong, hardy thing, which can flourish in any relational climate. It is doing our duty in that state to which God has called us—like salt in the midst of corruption, and light in the midst of darkness—which is a primary element in sanctification. Jesus Himself prayed: "I pray not that Thou shouldst take them out of the world, but that Thou shouldst keep them from the evil one" (Jn 17:15).

"Passive graces" are no doubt harder to attain than active ones; conversely, they are precisely the graces that have the "greatest influence on the world." It is nonsense to pretend to possess sanctification unless we follow after meekness, gentleness, longsuffering, and forgiveness. People who are habitually giving way to critical tempers in daily life are constantly sharp with their tongues, disagreeable to all around them, spiteful, vindictive, revengeful, malicious people—all such know little about sanctification. Genuine sanctification is a thing that can be seen—in a word it is *"godly character."*

A comparison of Justification and Sanctification—Whereas Justification is the *work of Christ* only; in Sanctification the *work of believers* is of vast importance—God bids us to fight, and watch, and pray, and work, and strive, and take pains, and labor . . . as believers obey Christ, the Holy Spirit effectuates a change in the inner man; hence it is a *"cooperative effort"* (Phil 2:12–13). Whereas Justification is a finished and complete work, *sanctification is an imperfect and incomplete work* (comparatively), and will never be perfected until we reach heaven. Whereas Justification admits to no growth, sanctification is eminently a progressive work and admits to *continual growth*. Whereas Justification gives us our title to heaven, sanctification defines our position in heaven (cross reference the parable of the "talents"—if we are "faithful" with what God has given to us, we will receive "multiplied responsibilities" in heaven).

The "great testing question" is this: What are our tastes, and choices, and likings, and inclinations? It matters little what we wish, and what we hope, and what we desire to be before we die. Don't just hope for a better tomorrow—Where are you now? What are you doing? Are you sanctified or not? If not, the fault is all your own. Believers who seem at a standstill in their Christian walk, are generally neglecting close communion with Jesus (a lack of cultivating *"intimacy"* with Him).

For another thing, let us not expect too much from our own hearts here on earth—At our best we shall find in ourselves daily cause for humiliation, and discover that we are needy debtors to mercy and grace every hour. The more light we have the more we shall see our own imperfections. Sinners we were when we began, sinners we shall find ourselves as we go on—renewed, pardoned, justified—yet sinners to the very last. Our absolute perfection is yet to come, and the expectation of it is one reason why we should long for heaven. *Though holiness is perfected in heaven, the beginning of it is confined to this world*. While some are satisfied with a miserably low degree of sanctification, and others are content with a mere round of churchgoing, let us follow after eminent holiness—this is the only way to be genuinely joyful in your faith. As a general rule, in the long run of life, it will be found true that *"sanctified people"* are the happiest people on the face of the earth—they get through life most comfortably, and they have solid comforts that the world can neither give nor take away. "Great peace have they that love Thy law;" conversely, "There is no peace for the wicked" (Prv 3:17; Ps 119:165; Is 48:22; Mt 11:30). (58–79)

True practical holiness—Holiness is the habit of *"being of one mind with God"* . . . the habit of agreeing with God's judgment, hating what He hates, loving what He loves, and measuring everything by the standard of His Word. He who most entirely agrees with God, he is the most holy man. A holy man will endeavor to shun every known sin and keep every known commandment. He will have a decided bent of mind toward God, and a hearty desire to do His will. He will feel what Paul felt when he said, "I delight in the law of God in the inner man" (Rom 7:22). A holy man will strive to be like Jesus Christ; he will labor to have the mind of Christ and be "conformed to His image" (Rom 8:29). *A holy man will bear much, forebear much, and overlook much.* A holy man will labor to mortify the desires of his body, to crucify his flesh with its affections and lusts, to curb his passions, to restrain his carnal inclinations. A holy man will endeavor to observe the golden rule, and be full of affection toward his brethren. A holy man will be merciful and compassionate and benevolent toward those around him. A holy man will follow after purity of heart, and seek to avoid all things that might draw him into uncleanness of spirit. A holy man will desire, in lowliness of mind, to esteem all others better than himself; he will see more evil in his own heart than in any other in the world. He will have the same attitude as Paul, *"I am chief of sinners."* Holy ***John Bradford***, that faithful martyr of Christ, would sometimes finish his letters with these words, "A most miserable sinner, John Bradford." A holy man will "do everything heartily as unto the Lord" (1 Cor 10:31); holy persons will aim at doing everything well. A holy man will follow after spiritual mindedness; he will endeavor to set his affections entirely on things above, and to hold things on earth with a very loose hand. To commune with God in prayer, in His Word, and in the assembly of His people, these things will be the holy man's greatest enjoyments. He will enter into something of David's feeling—*"My soul follows hard after Thee; Thou art my portion"* (Ps 63:8; 119:57). (79–86)

Holiness does not eliminate the presence of "indwelling sin"—No, far from it. It is the greatest misery of a holy man that he carries about with him a "body of death," that often when he would do good, "evil is present with him" (Rom 7:21). But it is the excellence of a holy man that he is not at peace with indwelling sin. He hates it; mourns over it; and longs to be free from it. *Sanctification is always a "progressive work," and at its best is an "imperfect work."* The gold will never be without some *"dross"*—the light will never shine without some *"clouds,"* until we reach heaven. The holiest men have many a blemish and defect; their life is a continual warfare with sin, and sometime you will see them not overcoming. The flesh is ever lusting against the Spirit, and the Spirit against the flesh (Gal 5:17; Jam 3:2). But still, in all this, the heart's desire is to press toward it; it is what they strive and labor to be, not what they are. A man may be truly holy, and yet be drawn aside by many an infirmity. Gold is not the less gold because it is mingled with alloy. Writes **John Owen**, *"I do not understand how a man can be a true believer unto whom sin is not the greatest burden, sorrow, and trouble."* Such are the leading characteristics of practical holiness. (87–89)

Scripture commands us to "be holy, even as God is holy" (Mt 5:48), and "This is the will of God, your sanctification" (1 Th 4:3). Paul writes, "Christ died for all, that they who live should no longer live for themselves, but for Him" (2 Cor 5:15). "He gave Himself for us, that He might redeem us from all sin, and purify unto Him a peculiar people, zealous for good works" (Titus 2:14). "We are created in Christ Jesus for good works" (Eph 2:10). "We are predestined to be conformed to the image of God's Son" (Rom 8:29). Jesus said, "If you love Me, keep My commandments" (Jn 14:15). Our lives are a *"silent sermon"* which all can read (2 Cor 3:2)—holy living carries a weight and influence with it that nothing else can give. The day of judgment will prove that many besides husbands have been won "without a word," but by a *"holy life"* (1 Pet 3:1). Therefore, for the sake of others, if for no other reason, let us strive to be holy.

It is so with religion as it is with other things, "there are no gains without pains." That which costs nothing is worth nothing. If we say with Paul, "O wretched man that I am," let us also say with him, "I press toward the mark" (Rom 7:24; Phil 3:14). "Let us cleanse ourselves from all sin, and perfect holiness in the fear of God" (2 Cor 7:1). "I live, yet not I, but Christ lives in me; and the life I now live, I live by faith in the Son of God" (Gal 2:20). "I can do all things through Christ who infuses me with His strength" (Phil 4:13). "Apart from Me you can do nothing—therefore, abide in Me that you bear much fruit" (Jn 15:4–5). (90–108)

"Fight the good fight of faith" (1 Tim 6:12). *"Spiritual warfare"* is the consummate battle that all of us as believers must wage for "our soul." It has its hand-to-hand conflicts and its wounds . . . it has its watchings and fatigues . . . it has it sieges and assaults . . . it has its victories and its defeats . . . and above all it has its consequences. The Christian man is a *"man of war"*—if we would be holy we must fight (Eph 6:10ff; 1 Tim 6:12; 2 Tim 4:7). The true Christian is called to be a *"soldier"*—he is not meant to live a life of religious ease, indolence, and comfort. With a corrupt heart, a busy devil, and an ensnaring world we must *"fight!"*

1. He must fight *"the flesh"*—Even after conversion he carries within him a *"nature prone to evil,"* and a heart weak and unstable as water. That heart will never be free from imperfection in this world, and it is a miserable delusion to expect it to be. To keep that heart from going astray, the Lord Jesus bids us *"watch and pray."* The spirit may be ready, but the flesh is weak (Mt 26:41). There is need of a daily struggle and a daily wrestling in prayer (Rom 8:36; 1 Cor 15:31).

2. He must fight *"the world"*—The "subtle" influence of that mighty enemy must be daily resisted. The love of the world's good things, and to do as others in the world do—all these are spiritual foes. "Friendship with the world is enmity with God"—"The world is crucified to me, and I unto the world." "Whosoever is born of God overcomes the world." "Be not conformed to this world" (Jam 4:4; 1 Jn 2:15; Gal 6:14; 1 Jn 5:4; Rom 12:2).

3. He must fight *"the devil"*—That old enemy of mankind strives to compass one great end—the ruin of man's soul. Never slumbering

and never sleeping, he is "like a roaring lion seeking whom he may devour." "Satan has desired to have you and sift you as wheat." This mighty adversary must be daily resisted. "The strong man armed will never be kept out of our hearts without a daily battle" (Job 1:7; 1 Pet 5:8; Jn 8:44; Lk 22:31; Mt 17:21; Eph 6:11).

Christian warfare is no light matter—"Fight the good fight of faith." "Endure hardship as a good soldier of Jesus Christ." "Put on the whole armor of God, that you may be able to stand against the schemes of the devil." "We wrestle not against flesh and blood, but against principalities and the rulers of darkness." Jesus said, "I came not to bring peace, but a sword." (1 Tim 6:12; 2 Tim 2:3; Eph 6:11-13; Lk 13:24; Jn 6:27; Mt 10:34; Lk 22:36; 1 Cor 16:13; 1 Tim 1:18-19). True Christianity is a struggle, a fight, a warfare. *Where there is grace there will be conflict—there is no holiness without warfare.* Furthermore, we must fight till we die. We may only have comfort in our souls provided we are engaged in the "inward fight and conflict"—it is the inevitable companion of genuine Christian holiness. Do we find in our heart of hearts a spiritual struggle? Do we feel anything of the flesh lusting against the Spirit, and the Spirit against the flesh? Are we conscious of two principles within us, contending for the mastery? Do we feel anything of war in our inward man? Well, let us thank God for it! It is a good sign! It is evidence of the great work of sanctification! The child of God has two great marks he should be known for—his *"inward warfare"* and his *"inward peace."*

True Christianity is a "fight of faith"—Christian warfare is not waged with carnal weapons, but with spiritual ones. *Faith is the hinge on which victory turns; success depends entirely on believing.* The Christian *is* what he is, *does* what he does, *thinks* as he thinks, *acts* as he acts, *hopes* as he hopes, and *behaves* as he behaves, for one simple reason—he *believes* the propositions revealed in the Word. "He that comes to God must believe that He is, and that He is a rewarded of those who diligently seek Him" (Heb 11:6). *Faith is the very backbone of spiritual existence.* There is no such thing as right living without faith and believing. Faith admits of degrees—all men do not believe alike—according to the degree of his faith, the Christian wins victories or loses battles. He who has the most faith will always be the happiest and most comfortable soldier. Nothing makes the anxieties of warfare sit so lightly on a man as the "assurance of Christ's love" and continual protection. The indwelling confidence that Christ is on his side and success is sure. It is the "shield of faith" that quenches all the fiery darts of the wicked one. The more faith, the more victory . . . the more faith, the more inward peace. (Eph 6:16; 2 Tim 1:12; 2 Cor 4:16–18; Gal 2:20; 6:14; Phil 4:11, 13). (109–136)

Which of you, when building a house, doesn't first "count the cost"? (Lk 14:28). Conversely, what does it cost to be a true Christian? Though nearly every Christian desires for more holiness and a higher degree of spiritual life, yet nothing is more common than seeing believers *"fall away"* after a period of time. Little by little their zeal melts away, and their love becomes cold—why? They had never counted the cost. When they find, after a time, that there is a cross to be carried, that our hearts are deceitful, and that there is a busy devil always near us, they cool down in disgust—why? Because they had really never considered *"what it cost"* to be a really consistent believer and a holy Christian. First consider what our salvation cost—it was nothing less than the death of Jesus Christ— we were *"bought with a price"*—the blood of Jesus (1 Cor 6:20; 1 Tim 2:6). What does it cost the believer to be a real Christian? According to the Bible, there are enemies to overcome, battles to be fought, sacrifices to be made, an Egypt (a past love or passion) to be forsaken, a wilderness to be passed thru, a cross to be carried, and a race to be run. *Conversion is NOT putting a man in an armchair and taking him comfortably to heaven*—it is the beginning of a *mighty conflict,* in which it *"costs much"* to win the victory. Consider the following—

1. <u>It will cost him his "self-righteousness."</u> He must cast away all pride and high thoughts of his own goodness—because he has *none!* (Is 64:6; Rom 3:10)—he must be content to go to heaven as a poor sinner saved *"only by grace,"* and owing all to the merit and righteousness of Christ. He must be willing to give up all trust in his own morality, respectability, praying, Bible knowledge, church going, and trust in nothing but Christ.

2. It will cost him his "sins." He must be willing to give up every habit and practice that is wrong in God's sight. He must set his face against it, quarrel with it, break off from it, fight with it, crucify it. He must count all sins as deadly enemies, and hate every false way; all sins must be thoroughly renounced. They may struggle hard with him every day, and sometimes almost get mastery over him, but he must never give way to them. He must keep up a *perpetual war* with his sins until he dies. To part with sin is as hard as cutting off a right hand, or plucking out a right eye—but it must be done. He and sin must *quarrel and battle,* if he and God are to be friends.

3. It will cost him his "love of ease." He must take pains and trouble to watch and stand on guard regarding his behavior every hour; he must be careful over his time, his tongue, his temper, his thoughts, his motives, and his conduct. There is nothing we naturally dislike so much as "trouble" about our religion. We hate trouble . . . but the soul can have *"no gains without pains."*

4. It will cost him the "favor of the world." He must be content to be thought ill of by man if he pleases God. He must count it no strange thing to be mocked, ridiculed, persecuted, and even hated, to be thought by many a fool and a fanatic. Remember, the servant is not greater than his Master (Jn 15:20). We naturally dislike unjust dealing and false charges. The cup that our Master drank must be drunk by His disciples as well. When a ship is in danger of sinking, the crew thinks nothing of casting overboard precious cargo—surely a Christian should be willing to give up *"anything"* that stands between him and heaven. When you feel like your ship is in danger of sinking, you will feel faint of heart and sorely tempted to give up in despair, I bid you, "Persevere and press on!" *A religion that cost nothing . . . is worth nothing!* (137–161)

"Grow in the grace and knowledge of our Lord and Savior Jesus Christ" (2 Pet 3:18). Growth in grace is an essential part of true holiness—it is intimately and inseparably connected with the whole question of sanctification, spiritual health, and spiritual happiness. Growing in grace means a believer's sense of sin becomes deeper, his faith stronger, his hope brighter, his love greater, and his spiritual-mindedness more dominant (2 Th 1:3; 1 Th 3:12; 4:1, 10; Col 1:10; 2 Cor 10:15; Eph 4:15; Phil 1:9; 1 Pet 2:2). He feels more of the power of godliness in his own heart, and he manifests more of it in his life. There are several "marks" by which growth in grace may be known—

1. Increased humility—The man whose soul is growing feels his own sinfulness and unworthiness more every year. He is ready to say with Job, "I am vile;" and with David, "I am a worm;" and with Isaiah, "I am a man of unclean lips;" with Peter, "I am a sinful man, O Lord;" and with Paul, "I am less than the least of all saints—I am chief of sinners" (Job 40:4; Gen 18:27; 32:10; Ps 22:6; Is 6:5; Lk 5:8; Phil 3:12; 1 Cor 15:9; Eph 3:8; 1 Tim 1:15). The nearer he draws to God, and the more he sees of God's holiness and perfection, the more thoroughly is he sensible of his own countless imperfections. The riper he is for glory, the more he sees of the shortcomings and infirmities of his own heart—by the way, they are "many!"

2. Increased faith and love toward Christ—The man whose soul is growing finds more in Christ to rest upon, and rejoices more that he has such a Savior. As he grows in grace, he discovers a suitableness in Christ to the wants of his soul.

3. Increased holiness of life and conversation—The man whose soul is growing gets more dominion over sin, the world, and the devil every year. He becomes more careful about his temper, his words, and his actions. He strives more to be conformed to the image of Christ in all things. He forgets about the things that are behind and reaches forth unto those things that are before, making "Higher! Upward! Forward! Onward!" his continual motto (Phil 3:13). He thirsts and longs to have a will more entirely in unison with God's will.

4. Increased spirituality of taste and mind—The man whose soul is growing takes more interest in spiritual things; the things he loves best are spiritual things; and the ways and recreations of the world

have a continually decreasing place in his heart. Spiritual companions, spiritual occupations, spiritual conversation, appear of ever-increasing value to him.

5. <u>Increase of charity</u>—The man whose soul is growing is more full of love every year—especially his love for the brethren, a growing disposition to do kindnesses, to be generous, sympathizing, tender-hearted, and considerate. A growing soul will try to put the best construction on other people's conduct.

6. <u>Increased zeal and diligence in trying to do good to souls</u>—The man who is growing will take greater interest in the salvation of sinners, mission work at home and abroad, efforts to increase religious light and diminish religious darkness, and he will not become "weary in well-doing." He will just go on working, whatever the results may be—giving, praying, preaching, teaching, speaking, visiting. (163–175)

Growing in grace reflects "greater intimacy" with Christ—It is possible to have *"union"* with Christ, yet have very little *"communion"* with Him. Those who are growing in grace and getting closer to Christ, are laying hold on Him with confidence, as a loving, personal Friend. No man will ever grow in grace who does not know something experientially of the joyful habit of "communion"—we must have personal intimacy with Christ. Many who are growing in grace are unaware of it—like Moses, when he came down from the mountain—their faces shine, yet they are not aware of it (Ex 34:29). Also, if we know anything of growth in grace, and desire to know more, let us not be surprised if we have to go through much trial and affliction in this world. I firmly believe it is the experience of nearly all the most eminent saints. Like their blessed Master, they have been "men of sorrows, acquainted with grief" and *"perfected through sufferings"* (Is 53:3; Heb 2:10). Every branch in Me that bears fruit, my Father *prunes* it that it may bring forth more fruit" (Jn 15:2)—afterwards it "yields the peaceful fruit of righteousness" (Heb 12:11). When *days of darkness* come upon us, let us not count it a strange thing; rather, let us remember that lessons are learned on such days that would never have been learned in sunshine. All circumstances are *"sent* *to us in love"*—we are in God's best school; affliction and trials are both used by God to correct, train and instruct; ultimately, this is all meant to make us grow. (176–190)

He who would be conformed to "Christ's image" must be constantly "studying Christ Himself"—just as sheep must be intimately acquainted with the *Shepherd,* so the sinner must be intimately acquainted with the *Savior.* Let's look at the story of Jesus crossing Galilee in a boat with His disciples—a storm arises, the disciples are frightened, and Jesus is asleep—"Master! Wake up! Care not that we are about to perish?" He arises and rebukes the wind and the waves, and at once there is calm. Notice the following:

1. <u>Being followers of Christ doesn't exempt us from troubles</u>—perhaps the disciples supposed He would always grant them smooth journeys. No. We are all subject to vexations and disappointments. How would the great work of sanctification go on in a man if he had no trial? Trial is often the only fire that will burn away the dross that clings to our hearts. Make up your mind to meet your share of crosses and sorrows—rest assured, they will pay a visitation to you—leave to the Lord Jesus the process He chooses, and be assured that He never makes any mistakes.

2. <u>Jesus Christ is truly and really Man</u>—Though He was equal to the Father, the eternal God, He was also "fully man." He was made like unto us in all things—sin only excepted. He was often hungry and thirsty, faint and weary, sorrowing and hurting. Jesus is perfect Man no less than perfect God. He is not only a powerful Savior, but a sympathizing Savior. *Never forget, your soul's business is in the hand of a High Priest who can be touched with the feeling of your infirmities.* He knows well that world in which you are struggling. Furthermore, He knows well the scheming, cunning enemy (Satan) with which we have to deal. He is no stranger to our sensations. Are you *poor and needy*—so was Jesus . . . are you *alone in the world*—so was Jesus . . . are you *misunderstood and slandered*—so was Jesus . . . are you *tempted*

by Satan—so was Jesus . . . do you ever *feel great agony and conflict of mind*—so did Jesus—"My God! Why hast Thou forsaken Me?"

3. <u>There is much weakness and infirmity even in true Christians</u>—When the disciples were in a state of panic on the storm-tossed sea, they said to Jesus, "Master, carest Thou not that we perish?" Three things characterized their response: 1) There was *impatience*; 2) There was *unbelief*; 3) There was *distrust*. They had witnessed repeated examples of His love and kindness toward them, but all was forgotten in the present danger—fear is often unable to reason from past experience. Most believers get along very well so long as they have *"no trials"*—and they fancy they are trusting Him entirely. But when a trial suddenly assails them, their faith abandons them! The plain truth is that there is no absolute perfection among true Christians so long as they are still in the body. *The best and brightest of God's saints is still compassed aplenty with infirmity.* There is not a just man on earth who comes close to not sinning. Furthermore, no one knows the length and breadth of his own infirmities until he has been *"tempted."* Learn to abate something of the flattering estimate you may have of yourself—you do not know yourself thoroughly—"Let him who thinks he stands, take heed lest he fall" (1 Pet 5:5; Prv 28:14; 1 Cor 10:12). Though as Christians we have true faith and grace, in spite of all the devil's whispers to the contrary, we may also be frequently riddled with doubts and fears. Cross reference the lives of Peter, James, John, Abraham, David. There is quartz mixed in with many a lump of gold; there are *flaws* in the finest of diamonds; yet they do not prevent their being rated at a priceless value. Let us be more quick to see *grace* and more slow to see *imperfection*.

4. <u>Let us learn the "power" of the Lord Jesus Christ</u>—The waves were encompassing the ship, and Jesus simply said to the sea, "Peace, be still." He calmed the sea with a *"word!"* This same Christ has power over all flesh and all creation—let the believer remember as he journeys thru the wilderness of life that his Mediator, Advocate, Physician, Shepherd, Redeemer, is the Lord of lords and King of

kings—that with Him nothing is impossible (Rev 17:14; Phil 4:13). All things were made by Him . . . by Him all things consist . . . He is sovereign over everything . . . "though the earth should melt, and the mountains should fall into the sea, God is in the midst of her, and will not be moved—therefore, be still and know that I am God" (Ps 46). Are you crushed by your circumstances? Perplexed by your seeming unbelief? There is comfort in Christ—He can speak peace to wounded hearts as easily as calm troubled seas.

5. <u>Let us learn how tenderly and patiently and kindly Jesus deals with weak believers</u>—We see this truth in Jesus' words to His disciples, "Why are you so fearful? How is it that you have no faith?" Even after the resurrection, you see the same unbelief and hardness of heart, though they saw their Lord with their own eyes! Even then some doubted! So weak were they in faith . . . so slow of heart were they to "believe all that the prophets had spoken" (Lk 24:25). Yet, what do we see in our Lord's behavior towards His disciples? *You see nothing but unchanging pity, compassion, kindness, gentleness, patience, long-suffering, and love.* He does not chastise them for their stupidity! reject them for their unbelief! or dismiss them for their cowardice! No! He leads them step by step . . . He restores them . . . He sojourns with them . . . He blesses them! and says, "I am with you always, even to the end of the world!" (Mt 28:20). *Let all the world know that Jesus Christ is full of pity and tender mercy. He will not break the bruised reed, nor quench the smoldering wick.* He cares for the sheep of His flock; He cares for the sick and the feeble; He cares for the weakest as well as the strongest. Christ's pledge to them was this: "I will never leave you nor forsake you" (Heb 13:5). Let the world know that the Lord Jesus will not cast away His believing people because of shortcomings and infirmities. The mother does not forsake her infant because it is weak, feeble, and ignorant—right? *Know this, it is "God's glory" to pass over the faults of His people, to heal their backslidings, and to pardon their many faults.* If you stumble, He will raise you up . . . if you err, He will gently bring you back . . . if you faint, He will revive you. Become better acquainted with Jesus; learn to

know Him better, that you may become more happy and more holy. He will be the happiest and the holiest who says, "To me to live is Christ" (Phil 1:21). (191–223)

"Do you love Christ?"—The true Christian is one whose religion is in *"his heart and life"*—he feels his sinfulness and guilt, and repents. He puts off the old man with his corrupt and carnal habits, and puts on the new man. He lives a holy life, fighting habitually against the world, the flesh and the devil. Besides all this, there is one thing in a true Christian that is eminently peculiar to him—"He loves Christ." He not only knows and trusts and obeys Christ, *He loves Him*. If a man does not love Christ, he is not a believer. Jesus said to the Jewish leaders, "If God were your Father, you would love Me" (Jn 8:42). When Jesus rose from the dead he asked Peter this question, *"Simon, son of Jonas, do you love Me?"* He desired to call forth from him a "new confession of faith" before publicly restoring to him his commission to feed the Church. He might have said, "Do you believe in Me?" or "Are you converted?" or "Will you obey Me?" He uses none of those expressions. He simply said, *"Do you love Me?"*—that is the essence upon which a man's Christianity hinges. A true Christian loves Christ for all *"He has done"* for him—He went to the cross for him . . . He redeemed him . . . He called him . . . He has forgiven him . . . He has freed him . . . He has given him light—the true Christian also loves Christ for all that *"He is still doing."* He is daily washing away his many shortcomings . . . He is daily supplying all the needs of his soul . . . He is daily leading him by His Spirit . . . He is daily raising him up when he stumbles . . . He is daily protecting him against his many enemies . . . and He is preparing an eternal home for him in heaven. Where there is justifying faith in Christ, there will always be heart-love for Christ. *If a man has no love for Christ, he has no faith in Christ.* Love for Christ will be the distinguishing mark of all saved souls in heaven. The peculiar marks by which love for Christ makes itself known are these—

1. <u>If we love a person, we like to "think about Him"</u>—Christ comes up in the mind of the believer many times a day (Eph 3:17). Affection is the real secret to faithful religion—the worldly man can't think about Christ much, because he has no affection for Him. The believer

thinks about Christ every day, for the simple reason, that he loves Him.

2. <u>If we love a person, we like to "hear about Him"</u>—We find pleasure in listening to those who speak of Him. The true Christian likes to hear something about his Master (the One he loves).

3. <u>If we love a person, we like to "read about Him"</u>—What intense pleasure a letter from an absent husband gives to a wife; whereas others would see little worth in the letter. Those who "love" the writer read it over and over again. The true Christian delights to read the Scriptures, because they testify of Him whom his soul loves.

4. <u>If we love a person, we like to "please Him"</u>—We are glad to consult His tastes and opinions, to act upon His advice. The true Christian studies to please Him, by being holy both in body and spirit . . . and in thoughts, and words and actions.

5. <u>If we love a person, we like "His friends"</u>—We are favorably inclined to them, even before we know them. When we meet them we do not feel that we are altogether strangers. True Christians regard Christ's friends as members of His family.

6. <u>If we love a person, we are "jealous about His name and honor"</u>—We do not like to hear Him spoken against without speaking up for Him and defending Him. We regard the person who treats Him ill with almost as much disfavor as if he had ill-treated us.

7. <u>If we love a person, we like to "talk to Him"</u>—We tell Him all our thoughts, and pour out all our heart to Him. We find it easy to talk to a much-loved friend. He tells Him everything—his wants, and desires, his feelings and his fears. He asks counsel of Him in difficulty; He asks comfort of Him in trouble. He cannot help but converse with his Savior continually—because He loves Him.

8. <u>If we love a person, we like to "always be with Him"</u>—When we really love someone, we long to be always in their company. The

true Christian longs to have done with sinning and repenting and believing, and to begin that endless life when he shall see Him as He is, and sin no more.

So, do you "love Christ"?—The essence of Christianity is knowing, trusting, and loving Christ who died for us. The Bible plainly teaches us that there can be no true religion without some feeling towards Christ. If you love Christ in deed and truth, rejoice in the thought that you have good evidence about the state of your soul. *Love for Christ, I tell you this day, is an evidence of grace.* Though you are sometimes perplexed with doubts and fears; though you find it hard to say whether your faith is real; though your eyes are often so dimmed with tears that you cannot clearly see your calling, where there is true love, there is faith and grace! (225–246)

"Christ is all"—these three words are the essence and substance of Christianity. If our hearts can fully identify with these three words, it is well with our souls. Christ is the mainspring both of doctrinal and practical Christianity. He who follows after holiness, will make no progress unless he gives to Christ His rightful place. "In the beginning Christ was with God—and in fact was Himself God" (Jn 1:1; Phil 2:6). True Christians were "chosen in Christ" before the foundation of the world (1 Pet 1:20; Eph 1:4); Christ had "glory with the Father before the world began" (Jn 17:5; Prv 8:23). Scripture says that "all things were made by Christ" (Jn 1:3), that "heaven and earth are the works of His hands" (Heb 1:10). There came a day when the world seemed sunk and buried in ignorance of God and sin, and "Christ left the glory of heaven and came down into the world to provide salvation for us—He died for our sins to reconcile us to God, and today is interceding for us at the right hand of the Father. There will come a time when all sin shall be expunged from existence, and there will be a new heaven and a new earth, and we shall reign with Him in righteousness forever. Christ is the beginning and end . . . He is the Alpha and the Omega . . . He is everything . . . so how can we but give Christ all the glory that is due His Name? For Christ indeed is "all!"

Christ is all with regard to our Justification . . . He is all with regard to our Sanctification . . . He is all with regard to our comfort at the present time . . . He is all with regard to our future Glorification . . . and He is all with regard to Heaven—the *"praise"* of the Lord Jesus will be the eternal song of all the inhabitants of heaven. They will shout with a resounding voice, "Worthy is the Lamb that was slain! Blessing, and honor, and glory, and power, be to Him who sits on the throne, and to the Lamb forever and ever!" (Rev 5:12–13). And the *"service"* of the Lord Jesus will be one eternal occupation of all the inhabitants of heaven. We shall "serve Him day and night in His temple" (Rev 7:13). The *"presence"* of Christ Himself shall be one everlasting enjoyment of the inhabitants of heaven. We shall "see His face" and hear His voice and speak with Him as friend with friend (Rev 22:4). His presence will fully satisfy all our wants (Ps 17:15).

Therefore, Christ ought to be all in the "visible Church"—Splendid buildings are nothing in the sight of God if the Lord Himself is not honored, magnified, and exalted. The Church is but a dead carcass if Christ is not "all." *Christ ought to be "all" in our Ministry*—the great work of the Church is to lift up Christ. We are only useful so long as we exalt the great object of our faith—but useful no further. *We are to be "His ambassadors" to a rebellious world.* The Spirit will never honor that ministry who does not testify of Christ—for He is that *"bread"* that feeds the hungry man . . . He is the *"lifeboat"* that saves the shipwrecked soul . . . He is the *"medicine"* that cures the sin-sick soul. Since Christ is the object of our faith, keep your mind dwelling on Him. He that would prove a skillful archer must not look at the arrow, but at the mark. Christ loves His people to lean on Him . . . rest in Him . . . call on Him . . . and abide in Him. In so doing we shall prove that we fully realize that *"Christ is all!"* (247–276)

CHAPTER 4

A summary of the book . . .
"THE BRUISED REED"
by Richard Sibbes (1577–1635)

There is no better introduction to the Puritans than the writings of "Richard Sibbes"—Of him Spurgeon said, "Sibbes never wastes the student's time; he scatters pearls and diamonds with both hands." Richard Sibbes was born in Suffolk, England, in 1577 . . . attended St. John's College at Cambridge, granted a Doctorate in Divinity in 1627, and thereafter was frequently referred to as *"the heavenly Doctor Sibbes"* on account of both the matter and the manner of his preaching. Of him Izaak Walton later wrote, "Of this blest man, let this just praise be given: *heaven was in him, before he was in heaven.*" For his boldness, Sibbes was forced into exile in Holland or New England in 1632. His book,*"The Bruised Reed,"* has been remarkably fruitful as a source of spiritual help and comfort to millions of believers down through the years.

Isaiah 42:3—"A bruised reed He shall not break, and a smoking flax He shall not quench." The condition of those with whom God deals are *"bruised reeds"*—not *"big trees."* The Church is compared to *"weak things;"* to a dove amongst the fowls; to a sheep amongst the beasts; to a woman (the weaker vessel). The bruised reed is a man that for the most part is in some misery; he is brought to see "sin" as the cause of it; thus, he is sensible to sin, *seeing no help in himself.* Affliction in the life of the believer has a healing and purging power. As believers we need bruising so that reeds may know themselves to be *reeds*, and not *oaks* . . . and by reason of the remainder of pride in our nature, to let us see that we live by mercy. **Peter** was bruised when he wept bitterly (Mt 26:75)—"though all forsake Thee, I will not" (Mt 26:33). **David** was bruised until he fully confessed (Ps 32:3–5); **Hezekiah** complained that God had "broken his bones" (Is 38:13); **Paul** needed the messenger of Satan to buffet him lest he should be lifted up above measure (2 Cor 12:7). Hence, we learn that we must not pass too harsh judgment upon ourselves or others when God exercises us with bruising upon bruising. There must be a conformity to Christ, who *"was bruised for us"* (Is 53:5). God is doing a wonderful work of grace in *"broken-hearted Christians."*

Christ will not break the bruised reed, nor quench the smoking flax; but will cherish those with whom He so deals. Physicians, though they put their patients to much pain, will not destroy them; a mother who has a sick and self-willed child will not cast him away. Shall we think there is more mercy in ourselves than in God, who plants the affection of mercy in us? The ministry of Jesus is to *"bind up the broken-hearted"* (Is 61:1). Oh how His heart yearned when He saw His people "as sheep without a shepherd"? (Mt 9:36). He shed tears for those who shed His blood! And now He makes intercession in heaven for *"weak Christians."* He has a heart of mercy and compassion. Shall our sins discourage us, when He appears before God's throne only for sinners? Never fear to go to God—"rejoice in the Lord always!" (Phil 4:4). *Satan sets upon us when we are weakest* . . . Christ most mercifully inclines to the weakest. Likewise, He puts an instinct into the weakest things to rely upon something stronger than themselves for support. *The bruised are brought to see their sin, which bruises most of all . . . and he that is bruised will be content with nothing but mercy from Him who has bruised him.* When God humbles us, we should know that all His dealings with us are for the purpose of turning us back to Him. We must lay siege to the hardness of our own hearts, and cry out for mercy. We should desire that God bring a clear and strong light into all the corners of our souls. By the way, *there is more mercy in Christ than sin in us.*

The Lord knows our frame, and is mindful that we are nothing but "dust" (Ps 103:14); that our strength is not the strength of steel. None are fitter for comfort than those that think themselves *furthest off.* A holy despair in ourselves is the ground of true hope. In God the fatherless find mercy (Hos 14:3). The God who dwells in the highest heavens dwells likewise in the *"lowest souls"* (Is 57:15). Christ's sheep are *"weak sheep."* His tenderest care is over the weakest. The lambs He carries in His bosom (Is 40:11). He said to Peter, "Feed my lambs" (Jn 21:15). Christ was most familiar and open to *"troubled souls."* How careful He was that Peter and the rest of the apostles should not be too much dejected after His resurrection. "Go your way, tell His disciples and Peter" (Mk 16:7). Christ knew that the guilt of their unkindness in abandoning Him had dejected their spirits. How gently did He endure the unbelief of Thomas and stooped so far unto his weakness, as to suffer him to thrust his hand into His side. (1–15)

Christ will not quench the "smoking flax," but will blow it up till it flames. In smoking flax (smoldering wick) there is but a weak little light—and that is mixed with smoke. Faith may be as a *"grain of mustard seed"* (Mt 17:20). Things of greatest perfection are longest in coming to their growth; it comes to perfection little by little. We see in nature that a mighty oak rises from a small little acorn. In the small seeds of plants lie hidden both bulk and branches, bud and fruit. *Christ values us by what we shall be . . . what we are elected unto . . . and what He will make us.* Nothing in the world is of so good use as the least grain of grace—the grace is not only little, but it is mingled with corruption; therefore a Christian is said to be *"smoking flax."* So we see that grace does not do away with corruption all at once, but some is left for believers to fight with. "O wretched man that I am!" said Paul, with a sense of his corruption. In the seven churches of Revelation (Rev 2–3), are called the "seven golden candlesticks" for their light; yet most of them had much smoke with their light. The reason for this mixture is that we carry about us a double principle—grace and nature. When the people of God look upon the remaining corruption within them, they frequently think they have no grace at all. (16–19)

Christ will not quench the "smoking flax"—this spark is from heaven, kindled by His own Spirit. We see how Christ bore with Thomas in his doubting (Jn 20:27); and how He did not quench the smothered light in Peter, when he denied Him with cursing (Lk 22:61). Conversely, we see how Christ cherished the "seven churches" of Revelation, and cherished anything that was good in them. Because the disciples slept due to infirmity, Christ frames a comfortable excuse for them—*"The spirit indeed is willing, but the flesh is weak"* (Mt 26:41). How He bore with the many imperfections of His poor disciples. He uses moderation, tenderness and care, "lest the spirit should fail before Him, and the souls which He hath made" (Is 57:16). The principle is even applied to the stronger believer— "We that are strong ought to bear the infirmities of the weak" (Rom 15:1).

Many are "lost" in this world for want of encouragement. How careful was our Savior of little children, that they might not be offended. Christ plants in young beginners a love which we call their "first love" (Rev 2:4)—He does not expose them to *"crosses"* before they have gathered strength; as we bring on young plants and fence them from the weather until they be rooted. *The best men are "severe" with themselves, but "tender" with others.* Christ refuses none for *weakness,* that none should be discouraged; conversely, He accepts none for *greatness,* that they should be lifted up. Hypocrites need stronger conviction than gross sinners, because their will is bad; as such, their conversion is usually violent—the wounds of secure sinners will not be healed with sweet words. I speak with "mildness" toward those who are weak and sensible to it; these we must bring on gently, and drive softly, as Jacob did his cattle (Gen 33:14), according to their pace. *Weak Christians are like fragile glassware*—it is easily damaged with least violent usage—but if gently handled will continue a long time. We are to respond gently when confronting weaker vessels (1 Pet 3:7), by which we shall both preserve them and likewise make them useful to the church and ourselves. (20–25)

The ambassadors of so gentle a Savior should not be overbearing, setting up themselves in the hearts of people where Christ alone should sit. Too much respect to man was one of the inlets of popery. Christ chose those to preach mercy who had felt most mercy—like Peter and Paul—that they might be examples of what they taught. *Paul became all things to all men* (1 Cor 9:22), stooping unto them for their good. Shall we not come down from our high conceits to do any poor soul good? Shall man be proud after God has been humble? *The brains of men are most often hotter than their hearts.* It is more suitable to the spirit of Christ to incline to the milder part, and not to kill a fly on the forehead with a mallet. The power that is given to the church is given for edification, not destruction. There are many broken spirits who need soft and comforting words. The prophet is told, *"Comfort ye My people"* (Is 40:1). The Holy Spirit is content to dwell in smoky, offensive souls; Oh, that that Spirit would breathe into our spirits the same merciful disposition. The church of Christ is a *common hospital*, wherein all are in some measure sick of some spiritual disease or other, so all have occasion to exercise the spirit of wisdom and meekness. (26–34)

The marks of a "Smoking Flax"—Those that are given to quarrelling with themselves are prone to feed on that disease which troubles them; they delight to look on the dark side of the cloud only. We must not judge ourselves always according to *"present feeling,"* for in temptations we shall see nothing but smoke of distrustful thoughts. Life in winter is hidden in the *"root."* We must look to grace in the spark as well as in the flame—a *"few grapes"* will show that the plant is a vine, and not a thorn. *It is one thing to be deficient in grace, and another thing to lack grace altogether.* What is the gospel but Christ's obedience being esteemed ours, and our sins being laid upon Him—we are brought to heaven under the covenant of grace by way of love and mercy. Under the covenant of grace *"sincerity"* is perfection. A troubled soul is like troubled water; it is full of objections against itself, yet for the most part we may discern some *"smothered sparks"* of the hidden life. There is no mere darkness in the state of grace. Reflect with me for a moment on the presence of heavenly fire—

1. <u>If there be any *holy fire* in us, it is kindled from heaven by the Father of lights</u>. In every converted man, God puts a light into the eye of his soul in proportion to the light of truths revealed to him.

2. The least divine light has _heat_ with it in some measure. Light in the understanding produces the heat of love in the affections. Weak light produces weak inclinations; strong light, strong inclinations. In the godly, gracious men have a spiritual palate as well as a spiritual eye—grace alters the spiritual taste.

3. Where this _heavenly light_ is kindled, it directs in the right way. We must walk by His light, not the blaze of our own fire. God must light our candle (Ps 18:28) or else we will abide in darkness. A little holy light will enable us to keep Christ's Word, and not betray Him.

4. Where this _fire_ is, it will sever things of diverse natures, and show a difference between such things as gold and dross. It will sever between flesh and spirit, and show that this is of nature, and this of grace. _All is not ill in a bad action, nor is all good in a good action._ There is gold in ore, which God and His Spirit in us can distinguish.

5. So far as a man is spiritual, so far is _light_ delightful to him. He truly hates ill and loves good. If he goes against the light discovered, he will soon be reclaimed, because light has a friendly presence within him; as such, he is soon open to counsel.

6. Fire, where it is present, is in some degree _active_. The least measure of grace "works"—it springs from the Spirit of God. Even in sins, when there seems nothing active but corruption, there is a contrary principle, which breaks the force of sin, so that it is not boundlessly sinful.

7. Fire makes metals _pliable_ and _malleable_. Grace makes the heart pliable and ready to receive all good impressions.

8. Fire, as much as it can, sets everything on _fire_. Grace labors to produce a gracious impression in others, and make as many good as it can.

9. Sparks by nature fly _upwards_. Where the aim and bent of the soul is towards God, there is grace. The least measure of it is seen in holy desires, springing from faith and love.

10. <u>Fire, if it has any matter to feed on, enlarges itself and mounts *higher and higher,*</u> and the higher it rises, the purer is the flame. So where true grace is, it grows in measure and purity. A smoking flax will grow into a flame. *As fire gives more light, it gives less smoke.* God will never take His hand from His work, until He has taken away sin from our natures. The same Spirit that purified His holy human nature cleanses us by degrees—He labors to further His end of abolishing sin out of our natures. (35–44)

Much comfort may be brought to the souls of the "weakest" if they will meditate on the following: Sibbes here strives to help the weakened soul overcome those "ordinary objections" and "secret thoughts" that have lodged in their inner man to keep them low. Here are temptations which hinder comfort—

1. <u>Some think they have no faith at all because they have "no full assurance"</u>—It is important to remember that even the fairest fire will have *"some smoke;"* the best actions will smell of smoke; and all of our actions will savor something of the old man.

2. <u>In weakness of body some think "grace dies," because their performances are feeble</u>, their spirits are weakened. They do not consider that God regards the *hidden sighs* of those that lack abilities to express them outwardly. He that pronounces those blessed that consider the poor will have a merciful consideration of such himself.

3. <u>Some are haunted with vile and "unworthy thoughts" of God</u>, of Christ, of the Word, which disquiet and molest their peace. Shall every sin and blasphemy of man be forgiven, and not these blasphemous thoughts, which have the devil for their father? Christ Himself was molested in this way, but Satan had nothing of his own in Christ—Satan's temptations of Christ were only suggestions on Satan's part. To apprehend ill suggested by another is not ill. Christ yielded Himself to be tempted, that He might both pity us in our conflicts, and train us up to manage our spiritual weapons as He did. *When Satan comes to us, however, he finds something of his own in us;*

there is the same enmity in our nature to God, in some degree, that is in Satan himself. By the way, these thoughts, if the soul dwell on them, leave a more heavy guilt upon the soul, hinder our communion with God, interrupt our peace, and put a contrary relish into the soul, disposing it to greater sins. All scandalous actions are only thoughts initially—thoughts are seeds of actions. *Ill thoughts arise from our sin natures.* Some are tempted to think "no one has such a loathsome nature as I have." This springs from *"ignorance"* of the spreading of original sin, for what can come from an unclean thing but that which is unclean? Remember Paul's cry, *"Wretched man that I am! Who shall deliver me from the body of this death?"* (Rom 7:24). Nothing more abases the spirits of holy men than these unclean issues of spirit that are most contrary to God; they produce in us the necessity of daily purging and pardoning grace. Our chief comfort is that our blessed Savior will command Satan to be gone from us, and bring all the thoughts of the inner man into subjection to Himself.

4. Some think, when they become more troubled with the "smoke of corruption" than they were before, that they are *worse* than they were. *The more sin is seen, the more it is hated.* Dust particles are in a room before the sun shines, but they only visually appear when a beam of light enters. Furthermore, none are so aware of corruption as those whose souls are most alive. Let such know that if the smoke be once offensive to them, it is a sign that there is light. *A little fire is fire, though it smokes.* Let us not be cruel to ourselves when Christ is thus gracious. (45–52)

Suffering brings "discouragements," because of our impatience. "Alas!" we lament, "I shall never get through this trial." But if God brings us into the trial He will be with us in the trial, and at length bring us out, more refined. We shall lose nothing but *dross* (Zech 13:9). "You have heard of the "patience of Job"? (Jam 5:11). Yes, but we have also heard of his impatience. *If we hate our corruptions and strive against them, they shall not be counted ours*—"It is no longer I that do it," says Paul, "but sin that dwells in me" (Rom 7:17). We shall be esteemed by God to be what we love and desire and labor to be. Discouragements do not come from God *(the Encourager);* therefore they must come from ourselves and from Satan, who labors to fasten on us a loathing of duty. (53–57)

Weaknesses do not "break covenant" with God, anymore than they break covenant between a husband and wife. Weaknesses do not debar us from mercy; rather they incline God to us the more (Ps 78:39). Christ betroths her to Him "in mercy" (Hos 2:19). *If Christ should not be merciful to our weaknesses, He should not have a people to serve Him.* Let us not give way to despairing thoughts; we have a merciful Savior. Weaknesses are to be reckoned either imperfections cleaving to our best actions, or actions proceeding from immaturity in Christ. We feel our infirmity and grieve for it . . . and in our striving and labor to reform we make incremental progress against our corruption. Our weaknesses, although they are a matter of humiliation, are the object of our daily mortification.

God's children never sin with "full will," because there is a contrary law in their minds by which the dominion of sin is broken, and which always has some secret working against the law of sin. Nevertheless there may be *"so much will"* in a sinful action as may destroy our comfort to a remarkable degree afterwards and keep us long on the rack of a disquieted conscience. To the extent that we give way to *our will* in sinning, to that extent we set ourselves at a distance from comfort. Sin against conscience spoils our joy and weakens our strength; therefore *willful breaches* in sanctification will much hinder the sense of our justification. (58–60)

When we are troubled in "conscience" for our sins, Satan's manner is then to present Christ to the afflicted soul as a most *"severe judge"* armed with justice against us. Let us present Him to our souls as holding out a *"scepter of mercy"* and spreading His arms to receive us. Though we are weak, we are His . . . though we are deformed, yet we carry His image upon us. Christ sees His own nature in us. Who neglects his own members because they are sick or weak? Let us therefore abhor all suspicious thoughts as the product of that "damned spirit," whose daily work is to create division between us and the Son by breeding "false opinions" in us of Christ. It was Satan's craft from the beginning to discredit God with man, by calling God's love into question. Yet for all this, many of us still feel *"God's just displeasure."* Satan not only slanders Christ to us, but he also slanders us to ourselves. Cast yourself into the arms of Christ that you might find Him merciful; He will not put us off when we earnestly seek His hand. He goes before us by kindling holy desires in us—when the prodigal set himself to return to his father, his father did not wait for him, but met him in the way. When He prepares the heart to seek, He causes His ear to hear (Ps 10:17). He cannot find in His heart to hide Himself long from us. *We can never be in such a condition that there will be just cause of "utter despair"—therefore let us do as the mariners do, cast anchor in the dark.* Christ knows how to pity us in the case. *God sees fit that we should taste of that cup of which His Son drank so deep, that we might feel a little what sin is, and what His Son's love was.* Our comfort is that Christ drank the dregs of the cup for us, that our spirits may not utterly fail under that little taste of His displeasure which we may feel. He became a curse and man of sorrows *"for us."* The lower Christ comes down to us, the higher let us lift Him up in our hearts. (61–66)

We are made partakers of the "divine nature;" as such, we are easily induced and led by Christ's Spirit to spiritual duties. Christ's government in His children is a wise and well-ordered government of grace. Christ subdues the heart by His Spirit to obedience . . . He set up His throne in the heart and alters its direction, so making His subjects good. Other princes can make good laws, but they cannot write them in their people's hearts (Jer 31:33). This is Christ's prerogative—*He infuses into His subjects His own Spirit.* The knowledge which we have of Him from Himself is a transforming knowledge (2 Cor 3:18). The same Spirit who enlightens the mind inspires gracious inclinations into the will and affections, and infuses strength into the whole man. Without Christ's Spirit the soul is in a state of utter confusion, but when Christ enters the human heart He establishes a government all His own. (82–90)

When a Christian is "conquered" by some sins, he gets victory over others more dangerous, such as spiritual pride and security. Christ's work in the hearts of His children often goes backward so that it may go forward better. As seed rots in the ground in the winter time, after it comes up better; and *the harder the winter the more flourishing the spring*, so we learn to stand by falls, and get strength by discovering our weaknesses. Let us assure ourselves that God's grace, even in this imperfect state, is stronger than man's free will in the state of original perfection. *Consciousness of our infirmities drives us out of ourselves to Him in whom our strength lies.* Many waters cannot quench a spark from heaven—no affliction without or corruption within can quench it. In the morning, we often see clouds gather about the sun as if they would hide it, but the sun overcomes them *little by little*, till it comes to its full strength. Every one that is "born of God" overcomes the world" (1 Jn 5:4). (91–100)

We must know that, though Christ has undertaken this victory, yet He accomplishes it by training us up to "fight His battles." He overcomes in us by making us wise unto salvation (2 Tim 3:15); and in the measure that we believe Christ will conquer, in that measure we will endeavor by His grace that we may conquer, for faith is an obedient and a wise grace. When we find our souls *declining*, it is best to raise them up by some awakening meditations of the presence of God . . . of the infinite love of God in Christ . . . of the excellency of a Christian's calling . . . of the short and uncertain time of this life . . . and of how little good all those things that steal away our hearts will do us in the long run. The more we make way for such considerations to sink into our hearts, the more we shall *rise* nearer to that state of soul which we shall enjoy in heaven. When we grow careless of keeping our souls, then God recovers our taste of good things again by *"sharp crosses"*—the taste of good things is much easier kept than recovered (cf. the recoveries of David, Solomon, Samson). Of all persons, a man guided by Christ is the best; a man guided merely by will and affection is worst. The happiness of *"weaker things"* stands in being ruled by stronger. It is best for a *"blind man"* to be guided by him that has sight; it is best for *"sheep"* to be guided by man; and it is best for *"man"* to be guided by Christ. *Grace, as the seed in the parable, grows, we know not how;* yet at length, when God sees fittest, we shall see that all our endeavors have not been in vain. *The tree falls upon the last stroke, yet all the strokes help the work forward.* (101–108)

Christ conquers and achieves His own ends, but He does so to some extent "invisibly." His enemies in us and outside us seem to prevail, but He will ultimately bring forth victory in full view of everyone. In that day He will declare to all the world what He is, and then there shall be no glory but that of Christ and His spouse. Truth shall no longer be called heresy . . . wickedness shall no longer go masked and disguised . . . goodness shall appear in its true luster . . . and those that are as "smoking flax" now shall then shine as the noonday sun (Mt 13:43). *As Christ shall not quench the "least spark" kindled by Himself, so will He damp the "fairest blaze"* of goodly appearances which are not from above; those that have been ruled by their own deceitful hearts and a spirit of error shall be brought forth to disgrace. "Woe unto them that call evil good, and good evil" (Is 5:20). *We often fail in "lesser conflicts" and stand firm in "greater ones," because in the lesser we rest more in ourselves; in the greater we fly to the rock of our salvation* (Ps 61:2). Hence also it is that we are stronger after defeats, because hidden corruption, undiscerned before, is now discovered—hence we are brought to make use of pardoning mercy. (109–117)

There can be no victory where there is "no combat"—prevailing will not be without fighting. Where God's government is in truth, it will be opposed. Nothing is so opposed as Christ and His government are—both within us and outside us. Though corruption does not prevail so far as to make void the powerful work of grace, yet there is not only a possibility of opposing, but a proneness to oppose. *It takes much trouble to bring Christ into the heart—there is an army of lusts in mutiny against Him.* The utmost strength of most men's endeavors and abilities is directed to keeping Christ from ruling in the soul—the flesh still labors to maintain its own government. *Can we be so naive as to think that corruption and Satan will yield possession quietly?* When Christ was born in Bethlehem, there was trouble . . . so when Christ is born in any man, the soul will fight against it. Wherever Christ comes He brings division. *Once Christ sets up His government in the soul, He maintains His own government in* *us and sets in motion a battle plan against our corruptions.* Christ will not leave us till He has made us like Himself, and presented us blameless before His Father (Phil 1:6; 1 Th 5:24; Jude 24). No creature can hinder the course of the sun, nor stop the influence of heaven, much less hinder the prevailing power of divine truth, until Christ has brought all under one head, and then He will present all to His Father. What a comfort this is in our conflicts with our unruly hearts, that it shall not always be thus! Let us strive a little while, and we shall be happy forever. (118–128)

CHAPTER 5

A summary of the book...

"FELLOWSHIP WITH GOD"
by Martyn Lloyd-Jones (1899–1981)

We know that *WE ARE OF GOD*, and the whole world lieth with the wicked one (1 Jn 5:19). The theme of John's epistle is the *position* of the Christian, and *his duty* with respect to life in this world. In a "crisis situation" the Scriptures first tell us to *"think/understand"* the incredibly important truth, that as believers we are *"of God."* By the way, unless we accept this definition of a Christian, this epistle has nothing to say to us. Prayer is sometimes an excuse for *not thinking;* an excuse for avoiding a problem or a situation—as such, we often pray that God would "deliver us from our problems." The Bible is not concerned simply with *"making life easier"*—it is concerned with *"having courage to face the world as it is"*—it is a book of "realism"—in it we see the world as it is, at its worst. If the world is "depressing to you," it is because you either do not know or accept the teaching of the Bible. As Christians, we know that we are *OF GOD,* and we are told there are certain things that are always true about the world. Christians are not people who are in a state of uncertainty—scripture tells us who we are, where we are, and what we have—we are not men and women hovering in the dark. *Christians must be absolutely sure of these things!* So, we start with the truth which we believe by faith—there are certain things you and I must *"know"*—mature

Christians don't "doubt" these things; they know exactly where they are and how they stand. These are absolutes. (9–15)

Since we are of God, *WE ARE PARTAKERS OF THE DIVINE NATURE* (2 Pet 1:4); we have been born from above, we have been born of the Spirit, we are a new creation. Those are the basic postulates the New Testament teaches regarding the *"position of the believer"*—as such, there is no consolation for us in difficult times if we do not start from that basis. We know that we are of God—children of God, related to God in that intimate sense, receivers of His very life. Paul says, "I know whom I have believed" (2 Tim 1:12); "I am in Christ" (2 Cor 5:17); "Christ lives in me" (Gal 2:20). The Apostle John starts on this assumption—that *"we know Him."* Are we fully aware of the "new man" within us? One that is entirely different from the "old man" that we were by nature before we knew Christ? Are we aware that there is something about us which we can only explain in terms of God? Can we say in true humility with the apostle Paul, "By the grace of God I am what I am" (1 Cor 15:10). Christians are those who have been called out of and delivered from this present evil world—we have been transferred from the kingdom of darkness (Satan) into the kingdom of light (Christ). Thus we are able to say, "I am aware that this life in Christ is both beyond me and within me, and I can only ascribe it to the grace of God in Jesus Christ."

Writes Lloyd-Jones: "Though I am amazed and astounded when I consider all the sins I have committed, and all my unworthiness—*in spite of it all, I know that I am of God!* God has had mercy upon me and has worked in me the miracle of the rebirth. Another thing I know is that the whole world lies in the power of the evil one; the whole world lies under the dominion and grip of Satan." It is utterly ridiculous to think that the world can be *"Christianized"*—because it is in the power of Satan, and it always will be. Any positive characteristics are merely superficial. The world will always be the world; it will never get intrinsically better; its final outlook will be judgment and destruction. Christians start with that view of the world; therefore they should not be surprised at the state of the world. As such, they should not be made *unhappy* by what they see. So, should we as Christians seek to *"reform the world"*?

No! that is not possible! Do we turn our backs upon it and withdraw from it? No! God does not say that either. Scripture tells us to maintain our Christian position—*be salt and light* (season the world with the love of Christ, and let His truth reign in our lives), restrain evil as much as we can, and pray that His will be done. Though we are in the world that lies in the power of the evil one, yet we may live in the world with inner joy and peace, and live the victorious Christian life—being more than conquerors. (16–19)

As Christians, we live in an extremely evil world that is highly opposed to God; because the world is opposed to God, it will be doing everything it can to drag us down. Thus, we live in a place in which we have to *"fight for our souls!"* That is the reality! From the beginning until today, the Church has gone in two extreme directions—there have been the *"social reformers"* (an impossibility) and the *"monastics"* (they believed in totally isolating themselves from the world—this position is far more common than many believers realize; many Christians "withdraw" from the world, and keep their light under a bushel). The New Testament avoids both of these errors. Christianity is not about "improving the world," nor is it about "renunciating the world"—instead, *it is about living in a world that is in juxtaposition to who we are*—it is of the "evil one," we are "of God." Yet, we can be "more than conquerors!" John says, "These things we write to you, that your joy may be full!" (1 Jn 1:4; Jn 15:11). Christian people in this world are meant to be "full of joy"—not misery. As Christians, we have no right to be in a state of melancholy or unhappiness because the world is as it is. Christians understand that the world is an "evil place" . . . that they have <u>not</u> been given a mandate to *"change the world"* . . . nor are they to simply make the best of a bad situation—that would not be compatible with the New Testament concept of joy. Because we cannot improve the world, we are prone to want to try and isolate ourselves from the world—there are many kinds of monasticism in the spiritual world. (21–27)

How can we be "joyful" in this world? What does Scripture mean by being *"joyful"*? Well, there are three elements of joy—First, joy is a state of *complete satisfaction;* obviously, there is no joy unless we are satisfied.

Second, joy is a *spirit of exultation;* there is a difference between happiness and joy—happiness fully depends upon what "happens" (both terms come from the same root word *"hap"*) in a person's life; joy has a deep heartfelt genuine gratitude element in it. Third, in joy there is always a *feeling of power and strength.* Someone who is truly joyful, in a sense, is afraid of nothing. When you are truly joyful, you are lifted up above yourself, and ready to meet every enemy. "The joy of the Lord is your strength." So, joy is something very deep and profound, something that affects the whole and entire personality. Furthermore, there is only one thing that can give true joy, and that is a *contemplation of the Lord Jesus Christ*—He satisfies the mind, the emotions, and our every desire. So joy is the response and the reaction of the soul to a knowledge of the Lord Jesus Christ. John writes to us that "our joy might be made full, filled to the brim." The joy of the Lord is not dependent upon circumstances, like happiness. Joy is a deep, profound quality that enables us to stay standing whatever may be happening to us. (28–30)

In order for the Christian to have "fullness of joy," he must have *conscious fellowship with God;* that is, he must be abiding in Christ (and that is not a "passive" abiding). There are certain things that hinder the experience of fellowship, that militate against it, and rob us of it—First, there is *unconfessed sin;* it must be confessed; sin will always rob us of a conscious fellowship with God. If we fall into sin (that is, we cease to actively trust—Rom 14:23), we begin to doubt and to wonder, and the devil takes advantage and encourages us in this. Second, there is *lack of love for the brethren;* one cannot love God and disregard fellow believers. Third, there is *love of the world;* a desire for its pleasures (you cannot mix light and darkness). Fourth, there is *wrong understanding about the person of Christ*—false notions concerning Christ result in having a lack of assurance with regard to salvation. It is imperative that believers are "absolutely certain" about the person and work of Christ—that is why Scripture is so emphatic on these subjects. There can be no true joy of salvation while there is a vagueness or uncertainty or a lack of assurance. Though "assurance" is not essential for salvation, it is essential to the *joy of salvation.* If a believer is certain about these things he will *KNOW* that he is a child of God, that he has "eternal life" (1 Jn 1:2; 2:25; 5:13), and that he has "fellowship with God" (1 Jn 1:3-7)—that is, a *conscious* possession of the life of God within us. Again, the hindrances to "knowing these things" are listed above. If you truly desire to know this "joy," you cannot take short cuts in the spiritual life. There is only one way and that is to confront these great and glorious truths, to believe them and to joyfully accept them. There are certain absolutes—the Incarnation, the Atonement, Regeneration, Sanctification, the Doctrine of Sin and of the Devil, and the Doctrine of the Second Coming. As we believe and practice these things, we will experience *"His joy;"* being lazy and careless with the teaching of Scripture results in *"no joy!"* (31–41)

One of the essentials of "true joy" is conscious fellowship with God—sharing in the life of God. This is one of the most *misunderstood* and *misinterpreted* concepts in Scripture—and it should not be! The Devil simply does not want God's people to get a handle on this subject. "Fellowship with God" is probably the most glorious and wonderful truth in all of Scripture. Life outside God is not life, it is merely existence—there is a radical difference between the two. Apart from God we are spiritually dead (Eph 2:1). Those who have become conscious of the fact that they are *"sharing the life of God,"* know what it is to rejoice and know what it is to be emancipated from certain besetting sins which hitherto always got them down—these are the believers who *"overcome the world."* John wants all believers to share this same joy and participate in this same experience. Regardless of individuality or temperament, every believer can know this same experience. Fellowship with God is the result of something that is based upon the belief of an *objective truth*—note carefully: this is <u>not</u> a primarily *subjective experience*. (55–65)

Mature Christians know there is a "radical evil" in life as a result of sin and the Fall; as such, they do not get excited about the various false hopes, and waste their time analyzing political theories. It was the initial act of rebellion that led to all other troubles—that is the story of the Bible. *Men and women were really meant to live in "joyful communion with God,"* but when sin made its entrance on the human stage, that changed everything—now, outside of obedience to God's law, man only experiences turmoil, unhappiness and wretchedness. This is the state of the world apart from God—it is in rebellion against God and therefore produces its own miseries. Because men and women are in a wrong relationship to God, they can never change their condition. As **Augustine** put it—*"Thou hast made us for Thyself, and our souls are restless until they find their rest in Thee."* It is because of sin that we live in a world like we do today. Is there any hope for us? Yes! (66–69)

Is there any hope for the WORLD? According to the Bible the situation will continue as it is. Therefore, what right do we have to expect *"Christian behavior"* from a world that does not believe in Christ? Why would the world embrace Christian principles? It is rank heresy to recommend Christian behavior to people who are not Christian. They are not capable of it! In a world that lies under the power of the evil one you can expect nothing but evil and wars. By the way, if the Holy Spirit stopped "restraining evil" in the world to some degree, things would be vastly worse than they are today (2 Th 2:7). Whether or not the presence of evil and wars is depressing, the business of wise men and women is to face those facts. Before people can live the Christian life they must be made a new creation. The Church's responsibility in the world is to address *"individuals"* one by one, and tell them "the story about the world they are living in." The supreme need of the world, and of every person, is that they *KNOW GOD* (Jn 17:3; 1:10; Phil 3:10; Jer 9:23)—knowing God restores the fellowship man had with God in the Garden of Eden. Because God has dealt with the barrier of sin that separated us from Him, by dying on the Cross for our sins, the *CROSS* becomes the central tenet of the Christian faith. We cannot be reconciled to God without the Cross. The justice and righteousness of God demands that sin be punished; so Christ became the propitiation for our sins (1 Jn 2:2). God laid on Christ the iniquity of us all (Is 53:6). You may not fully understand it (no one fully can), but it is the essence of the message of Scripture—God has done this astounding thing. He has punished our sins "in Christ"—thereby, removing the obstacle. As such, our thoughts of God are entirely changed—we now see that God is a *God of love*. (69–74)

Peter says, "believers have become partakers of the divine nature" (2 Pet 1:4). We have become "children of God" (Jn 1:12). He has made us "new creations" (2 Cor 5:17). He has given us "eternal life" (Jn 3:16). The Christian life is a lot more than just experiencing "forgiveness"—it also means He takes up "residence" in us in the person of the Holy Spirit (Gal 2:20). And He restores the *"fellowship"* we had with God before the Fall. The *summum bonum* of the Christian life—the ultimate goal of all Christian experience—is *fellowship with God*; i.e., communion with God Himself (1 Jn 1:3). Christ did not come to simply save us from hell and to forgive us of our sins, but to have *"fellowship"* with Himself and with the Father.

What is "fellowship with God"? To be in a state of fellowship means that *"we share in things;"* we are "partakers" or "partners," if you like—that idea is intrinsic to the Greek word *koinonia*. Therefore, the Christian is one who has become a "sharer in the life of God." As mentioned above, Christians are "partakers of the divine nature" (2 Pet 1:4). The whole doctrine of regeneration and rebirth—being born again, born from above, born of the Spirit—carry exactly the same idea. Christians are not merely people who are a little bit better than they once were; rather, they are men and women who have received the *divine life!* Theologians aren't sure exactly what it means to *"possess the divine essence,"* other than to say that *in some amazing and astounding manner we know that we are partakers of the divine nature, that the being of God has somehow entered into us. Divinity lives in us!* As Paul says, "I live; yet not I, but Christ lives in me" (Gal 2:20). Though we do not fully understand exactly how this is possible, the Bible clearly teaches that Christ indwells us by the Holy Spirit—so, we are *"sharers in the life of God."* Somehow we are in God and God is in us—it is a great mystical union, expressed in the term *koinonia*. As partakers of God, we are partners with Him, sharers in His interests and in His great purposes. That means we have become interested in partnering with God in His great plan of salvation . . . which would imply that true Christians are deeply interested in God's enterprise in this world—we see the evil forces in this world as being enemies of God, and we are concerned to bring the purposes of God to pass. We meditate, we pray, we do everything that we are capable of doing in furthering the kingdom of light. All of this means that we have come to *know God*—we no longer see Him as a stranger or supreme energy far off in the distant universe. God is now a reality, we know Him intimately, and address Him as *"Father."*

Those who are in "communion with God" know that He is there; they realize His presence; it is an essential part of this whole position of fellowship . . . and this leads to *"confidence"* in speaking to Him. Communion means "realizing the presence of God in your life." God speaks in His own way to our soul; He gives us consolation . . . He creates within us holy desires and longings . . . He reveals His will to us . . . He leads us . . . He opens doors and shuts them . . . and sometimes puts up barriers and obstacles. Hence, as you go forward in this journey called life, you can be completely confident that *God is there*—that is having fellowship with God, knowing that He is there in these various ways, and is superintending the course of our lives, and giving us wisdom and understanding. Furthermore, He supplies us with strength according to our need and according to our situation (Phil 4:13, 19). (75–86)

Having "fellowship with God" is the only way to live a godly life in a world that is opposed to God. Genuine fellowship with God always starts with the *Scriptures*—understanding them. This evangelical doctrine tells us <u>not</u> to look into ourselves (like a mystic), but to look into the Word of God. It tells us that God can only be known in His own way—through the Scriptures themselves—thru objective revelation. In contradistinction to this approach, many during the Puritan period began to put a new emphasis upon the *Holy Spirit*—they put *feelings* before *understanding*, and is referred to as *"Quakerism"* or *"Mysticism."* There were "two approaches"—one was called *"quietism;"* focus on abandoning yourself to God, and God will speak to you. The other approach was to indulge in *"introspection;"* examine yourself and meditate. The evangelical way of experiencing fellowship with God is to go straight to the *"Word"*—know its truth, believe it, accept it, pray on this basis, and exert your whole being in an effort to live and practice it. ***Mysticism*** is an attempt at taking a "short cut" to the great experiences—the way of the ***Scriptures*** is the other way. Jesus said, "Blessed are those who hunger and thirst after *righteousness*, for they shall be filled [with the fullness of

God]" (Mt 5:6). Notice it does not say "blessed are those who hunger and thirst after spiritual experiences or happiness." So rather than focusing on *spiritual euphoria*, start by building the foundation; then you can erect the walls—everything must happen in God's way and in God's time. Start with "Christ's work *for* you" [at the Cross] before you focus on "Christ's work *in* you."

Reasons why the Christian's "communion with God" is so frequently interrupted. The focus of the believer must be on *God*—not *yourself* (your performance)—if your focus is on yourself and your performance, you will inevitably become overwhelmed with troubles. We must always start with GOD—"God is light and in Him is no darkness at all" (1 Jn 1:4). Lloyd-Jones put it this way: *"Half of our troubles arise in the Christian life because we do not start with God.* Most believers *assume* they have a right understanding of God, so they start with *themselves*—yet the Bible constantly reminds us that we must start with God. If we start with *man/ self,* we will ultimately go wrong in our thinking about truth, because we will demand that everything accommodate itself to man. Thus, we must be careful not to start with ourselves. Incidentally, it is very difficult not to start with ourselves, because our whole approach to the gospel and to Christianity naturally tends to be from that *"self-centered"* selfish standpoint—

We argue like this: Here I am in this world with its troubles and I am ill at ease. I am looking for something I don't have. I am aware of my needs and desires. I am aware of a lack of happiness. The tendency for most of us is to approach the whole subject of God and Christian truth in terms of *"my desires and my demands."* What has God to say to me and to give to me? Is there something in this that is going to ease my problems and help me in this dark and difficult world? That is the *"initial fallacy"*—it is almost blasphemy—*we need to "forget about ourselves and contemplate God."* It is important to note that the great characteristic of the cults and of every religion that is not genuinely Christian, is that they tend to approach man in terms of *"his need"*—and seem to give man the thing *"he wants."*

The Christian faith starts with *"GOD"*—The individual is silenced. He is put into the background. Man is not first and foremost. GOD is first—it all starts with Him—"In the beginning GOD;" he is at the center of all things, not man. The very term "theology" should remind us of that—it refers to knowledge of God, not man ("anthropology"). So this is of *supreme importance* to us as we come to consider the whole question of fellowship with God, walking with God, and enjoying the life of God. Once again let me remind you: *Most of our troubles are due to our self-centeredness and concern for* ***ourselves.*** The way to be delivered from "self-centeredness" is to stand in the presence of God and focus on Him. The vital question is this: What is the truth concerning God? (87–98)

To believe in God we must accept the revelation concerning Him (which is the essence of faith), and that revelation is only found in the Bible. Furthermore, there are only two ultimate positions on the ***Bible***—we either regard the Bible as *authoritative,* or else we think it is the *philosophy of humans.* Reason can take us to a certain point, but it will never bring us to a true knowledge of God—it is here that we are left to rely on revelation. Ultimately, we cannot know God apart from the revelation that He has been pleased to give us of Himself. The apostle John starts with the *"holiness of God"*—"God is light, and in Him is no darkness at all" (1 Jn 1:5). Unless we start with the holiness of God, our whole conception of the love of God is going to be false. Many believers have had the sentimental notion of God as a God of love, always smiling upon us, and then when wars and calamities and troubles come, they are baffled and end up turning their backs on religion. The problem was they did not start where the Scriptures start, with the holiness of God. God is utterly and totally holy, righteous and just—"holiness, without which no man shall see the Lord" (Heb 12:14). The statement *"God is light"* means God is absolute holiness and purity. He is of such pure countenance that He cannot behold and look upon iniquity (Hab 1:13); it is the holiness of God that demands the cross, so without starting with holiness there is no meaning in the cross.

Thus, it should not surprise us why so many modern theologians *DISCOUNT THE CROSS*. It is because they have started with the *love* *of God,* rather than *His holiness.* The most "emphatic" statement in the entire Bible is the fact that *God is holy*—"Holy, holy, holy, is the LORD of hosts" (Is 6:3; Rev 4:8). By repeating the word "holy" three times, that makes this statement the most emphatic one in all of Scripture regarding the person and character of God. Therefore, above everything we know about God, first and foremost is the fact that He is *"HOLY!"* With God, love and forgiveness are not mushy things or things that are easily overlooked or compromised—God can only forgive sin as He has dealt with it upon the cross; remember, God is "holy." Starting with the holiness of God ultimately saves us from the terrible danger of also "blaming God" and "criticizing God" in times of trouble. When we misunderstand God, we question, "Why does God do this? Did I deserve this?" When I start with the holiness of God I will never speak like that, because I know at once that whatever may be happening to me is not the result of anything unworthy in God—"God is light, and in Him is no darkness at all"—He is absolutely holy. So whatever may be happening to me is not the result of imperfections in God. *God's "holiness" demands absolute moral perfection in all things*—all moral law and perfection have their eternal and unchangeable basis in God's very nature. The darkness of sin is an eternal violation of God's moral law; as such, it *must* be expunged and expiated—hence, the eternal condemnation of it at the cross. "But God, being rich in mercy, because of *His great love* with which He loved us, [even in our desperately sinful condition], made us alive together with Christ by grace . . . according to the kind intention of His will" (Eph 2:4–8; 1:3–7). So, the *"love of God"* led Him to justly execute His own Son [in our stead] to satisfy *"His holy justice"*—He bore our sin and gave us His righteousness (2 Cor 5:21; Rom 3:24; 1 Pet 2:24). As the hymn writer Charles Wesley said, *"Amazing love! How can it be that Thou, my God, shouldst die for me!?"*

Last, there is only one way to true and lasting joy, and that is to start with the "holiness of God." If I start there, I shall be delivered from every false peace, from every false joy. I shall be humbled to the dust, and see my true unworthiness, and that I deserve nothing at the hands of God. We can do nothing better, every time we go on our knees to pray, than to repeat John's words—*"God is light and in Him is no darkness at all."* And when we feel like rushing into our own desires and complaints, just to pause and approach Him with reverence and godly fear, "for our God is a consuming fire." (98–110)

Fellowship is a position in which two individuals are "walking together along a road"—it's a journey, a companionship. Gen 5:22 says, "Enoch walked with God"—that means he had fellowship with God. Christians walk with God as they journey through this world. There are "two parties" involved here—God and the believer (not a perfect believer—an *"imperfect believer"*—a believer who "sins"). It is as true to say that man is sinful as it is to say that God is light (absolutely sinless, perfect in holiness). The doctrine of sin has never been popular even though it is an integral part of Scripture. Many Christians think sin is actually an *"old-fashioned doctrine"* in which their fathers delighted; as such they think the doctrine of sin has simply made the whole of life *"miserable."* This has caused many to conclude that things are not quite as bad as the Bible and the theologians of the past have made it out to be—"so long as we do our best, and look to God occasionally for a little help, everything will turn out alright." "We must not take these things too seriously; to be a Christian is to be as decent as we can be, and to do good as God assists and helps us." This, in general, is the *"modern attitude"* regarding the doctrine of sin.

The apostle John teaches "three common errors" with regard to the whole question of *SIN*—

1. **If we say that we have "fellowship with God"(1:6)**—As members of the body of Christ, the claim we are making to the world, says John, is that *"we have fellowship with God."* That statement does not mean that we are trying to be decent and moral—it simply means we do have fellowship with God—that is, we share something in common; irrespective of our stumbling and making mistakes. However, *"if we walk in darkness,"* obviously we lie, because we do not have fellowship with God—"walking in darkness" means "we habitually walk or live in the realm or kingdom of sin." The Bible tells us there are two

kingdoms in this world—the *kingdom of God* (light/righteousness) and the *kingdom of Satan* (darkness/sin); these are the *two realms* in which men live, and all believers have been transferred into God's kingdom of light (Col 1:13; Jn 3:3; 18:36; Rom 14:17; 2 Cor 6:14; Eph 5:8; 1 Pet 2:9; 1 Jn 1:7; 2:9–10; Rev 1:6). The Bible goes on to tell us there is a "mighty contention" between these two powers or realms, fighting for supremacy over human beings in this life and world; there is a great clash taking place between the forces of God and the forces of Satan (Eph 6:12). All of us are born into this world under the domination of the *"kingdom of darkness;"* therefore, by nature, we tend to live and think accordingly (sinful self is on the throne). Scripture tells us that *"men love darkness rather than light"* (Jn 3:19). The kingdom of darkness represents everything that is "opposed to God," opposed to His holiness, opposed to His desires for this world, opposed to His desires for humanity.

"WALKING IN DARKNESS"

"Walking in darkness" means that you live in such a way that you rarely have any thought about God at all; He is not the dominating factor in your decision-making; His wisdom and principles are not the controlling principles of your life—that which controls your life are *"self-concerns."* Should the unbeliever think about God, he would think of Him as some benign fatherly person who, generally, is ready to smile upon him in spite of his failures, and who is ready to grant him entry into heaven at the end, because he is a reasonably good person. Obviously, such people are *not in fellowship with God.* Someone whose whole outlook on life is governed by "darkness and worldliness," cannot be walking along the same road with God who is "light." Scripture says it is simply not possible.

---

2. **If we say that "we have no sin," the truth is not in us (1:8)**—This second failure is not realizing that our "very natures" are sinful. The reference here is not to "acts of sin", but to the *"sin nature"* that produces the acts of sin—our sin natures are a continuous source of influence within us. It is essential that one not interpret this verse

as speaking of "individual acts of sin," but rather of a "sinful nature" (or sinful disposition). Apparently, people in the early Church were being swayed by the heresy of **Gnosticism**—they were being taught that Christians were *"delivered from their sinful nature"* and "given a new nature;" therefore, because we have received this new nature, there is no longer any sin in us; as such, if we do something that is wrong, it is not "we" who have sinned—the sin is merely in the "physical body." Hence the heresy of *"antinomianism"* (no law)—as long as you claim you know God in Christ, it is immaterial what you do, because you do not sin, it is simply the flesh or body that sins. That is the view John is countering here. For someone to say that "he does not have a sinful nature" is nothing but self-deception. The fact is, the *"presence of evil"* (a sinful nature) dwells within everyone of us (Rom 7:18); that is, there is something in our essential being that has twisted and perverted everything—it is called our *"sin nature"* or *"sin disposition."* That is why we have sinful thoughts and sinful desires. *Not only do we do wrong as Christians, but our very nature is sinful.* The human heart is "desperately wicked," writes Jeremiah (Jer 17:9), and those who look at themselves and face themselves honestly, know that this is the simple truth about human nature—that at the center of our being we are evil and sinful. To not admit that is simply self-deceit, and evidence that the truth is not in us—because truth in us is like a great flashlight flashing upon the depths of our being . . . all the evil spots and darkness are evident to us.

"WALKING IN THE LIGHT"

The apostle John says, "If we *walk in the light* we have fellowship one with another, and the blood of Jesus Christ His Son cleanses us from all sin" (1 Jn 1:7). Fellowship is never *mechanical;* it is always *organic.* First we must consider what we must do with regard to fellowship, and then we must consider what God does in maintaining the reality of fellowship. Because John uses *"word pictures"* to teach certain ideas (like "light" and "life"), the danger is to misinterpret the pictures, as if John is teaching

> some form of perfectionism. So, what is it that we have to do? First, we must *"walk in the light"* as He is in the light—though the tendency is to interpret this as saying we must be "absolutely perfect" as God Himself is perfect; that is neither possible, nor is it what this passage is teaching. The "key" to understanding this concept is found in the previous verse, where it says, if we *"walk in darkness"* we lie and do not the truth—in that verse we saw that "walking in darkness" meant living in the realm of darkness; being controlled by the ideas of the world and of sin; belonging to the kingdom of darkness and Satan. In other words, the people who "walk in darkness" are not those who constantly commit overtly sinful acts—they might actually be highly respectable and very moral—but they are walking in darkness because they are outside the light of the gospel of Christ. So it is a *"realm"* to which people belong that John is referring to. Therefore when we come to this verse about "walking in the light," we need to interpret it as the antithesis of "walking in darkness." Thus, it does not mean that I claim absolute perfection . . . rather it means that I now claim to belong to a *"different realm"*—to the kingdom of light and to the kingdom of God. I am in it; I belong to it; I walk in the realm of light. As Paul said, "I have been transferred from the kingdom of darkness to the kingdom of God's dear Son" (Col 1:13). So John is saying that every *believer* of necessity is one who is *walking in the light,* and every *unbeliever* is *walking in darkness.* All Christians, however feeble, unworthy and faltering, are people who are—*walking in the light.* As such, all Christians desire to know God better . . . want to please God . . . and are concerned about being holy. The bottom line?—if someone is not "walking in the light," he simply is not a believer.

3. **If we say that "we have not sinned," we make God a liar (1:10)**—If we do not realize that we are sinners and need the forgiveness of God, we are making God out to be a liar. Scripture teaches that "no one is righteous, not one" (Rom 3:10); that "all have sinned and come short of the glory of God" (Rom 3:23); and that "Jesus came to seek and to save that which was lost" (Lk 19:10), to provide pardon and forgiveness of sin by the shedding of His own blood on the cross. If I say I have not sinned, I am also proving that His word is not in

me (because the word of God and His Spirit convicts us of such). To summarize this: *Not to be right about sin means we are still walking in darkness*—we are either lying or deceiving ourselves. If we are in that position, obviously we are not in fellowship with God, because it is an utter contradiction of everything that God is; hence, we are not Christians. One of the most comforting passages in all Scripture for us as believers is this—*all true believers "walk and live in the realm of light"*—not in the "realm of darkness." That does not mean we are "perfect" or "don't sin"—*it simply means that God is an integral part of our lives;* in short, both by God's choice and by our choice, we are now in **partnership** with each other! Thus the "essential difference" between believers and unbelievers is that our **"essence"** is not the same—even though in many respects our behaviors might be quite similar, we no longer share the same essence. (111–121)

When we have "fellowship with God," we walk in the light, and confess and acknowledge our sins. Therefore, it goes without saying, if we are walking with God and having fellowship with Him, it follows of necessity that we shall be more conscious than ever of our sinfulness and our unworthiness—and that is the great problem always with regard to this whole matter of fellowship with God. *When we are in fellowship with God believers sometimes feel hopeless, because they are so conscious of their sin and of the holiness of God, that they conclude, "Fellowship with God is a sheer and utter impossibility!"* Remember, it is the character of light to reveal and expose the hidden things of darkness, and this is supremely true when we walk with God. When we walk with God and when His Word dwells in us, of necessity we are *"convicted of sin"*—everything that is sinful in us is brought to the surface. God's presence within us "convicts of sin." Remember Isaiah's response to the work of God in His heart? *"Woe is me! I am a man of unclean lips!"* (Is 6:5). Likewise, Peter said, "Depart from me, for I am a sinful man, O Lord" (Lk 5:8). That is what happens when we are truly in the presence of God. (135–136)

So the question arises, "What can we do?" We are trying to walk in the light . . . we are doing our utmost . . . we are confessing our sins . . . but that in and of itself *seems* to break the fellowship and make it impossible, because our conscience condemns us and we feel we cannot dwell in such a glorious light! In order to answer that question, we must return to what John writes (1 Jn 1:7, 9)—we now need to emphasize the *"Godward side"* or the Godward aspect. There are two main principles here: first, God has provided to meet our need; and second, we should have assurance in view of God's provision—*"God is faithful and just to forgive us our sins and to cleanse us from all unrighteousness."*

Justification represents "our standing" in the presence of God. Justification states that God regards us as *"righteous"* (just as if we had never sinned)—all because of what Christ has done for us. What God does for us in **Justification** is "remove the guilt of our sins altogether and remove the sins." **Sanctification,** on the other hand, is that condition in which the *"sin principle"* (sinful nature) is being dealt with. Remember, **Justification** does not deal with the "sin principle" which is within us—it deals with the "sins" that we have committed. After our sins have been forgiven, the "sin principle" remains in us. **Sanctification** is the "process" whereby the very principle and the activity of sin within us, is being removed from us—this ongoing process continues throughout the believers life on earth. Furthermore, *God assures us that this work will ultimately be fully completed when Christ returns!* (Phil 1:6). So the difference between Justification and Sanctification is the difference between dealing with the sins that we have committed and their effect upon us, and dealing with the principle of sin (our sinful nature) that still resides within us. (137–138)

Which of these two issues is the apostle John dealing with? Lloyd-Jones says, "Many people are literally on the verge of a breakdown because of confusion on this point, and they begin to feel they are not Christians at all. Verse 7 does not mean that the blood of the Lord Jesus is cleansing the "sin principle" out of us; that it is sanctifying us; and that we are being literally purged from sin as a power until we shall be absolutely free from it. The *"blood of Jesus"* in Scripture always refers to His death on the cross—nothing more—our Lord's death is that which purchased our pardon . . . reconciled us to God . . . atoned for our sins . . . accomplished our justification . . . and removed the guilt of our sin. Whereas sanctification and the lifelong process of our slowly being changed and transformed into the image of Christ, is the work of the indwelling presence of the *Holy Spirit* within us. (139–141)

The Apostle John is interested in both our "fellowship with God" and our "walk with God"—He is not interested in our *"sinful natures"* as such, but in the guilt of sin and the tarnishing effects which sin produces and which interrupts the experience of fellowship. *What he is anxious to show us is that though we are guilty of sins . . . and though we fall into sin . . . we can still have fellowship with God.* It should be noted that the Bible does not teach us anywhere that fellowship with God is made "impossible" because sin still remains in us; if that were true no man who has ever lived would ever have enjoyed fellowship with God. Here is what John is saying—though the *"sin principle"* remains in us, and we still sin, we can still have fellowship with God. But what about the polluting and tarnishing effects of sin? you ask. Ah, says John, "the blood of Jesus Christ cleanses the very guilt and pollution and tarnishing effect of sin, and therefore you will continue to have *fellowship with God*. Committing an act of sin does not change that! Here is where sanctification comes in—the believer's effort to *walk in the light* is part of the sanctification process (becoming more holy); as is the recognition of and confession of sins. The question before us, however, is the issue of seeing ourselves as sinful and then *feeling* as though we do not have fellowship with God. Thus, we think we are unworthy of this fellowship, so what can we do about it?

The Christian, by definition, is always "walking/living in the light" even though he falls into sin. By falling into sin you do *not* return to "walking or living in darkness;" therefore, if you fall into sin you are still in the kingdom of God—it is the shed blood of Christ that still delivers you from the guilt of your sins in the kingdom of God. We might easily apply this principle to our "earthly parents"—when we disobey them, does that nullify "the relationship we have in common with them? Are we not still their children? Do they not still love us? Well, if our earthly

THE BELIEVER'S "FELLOWSHIP" WITH GOD

For years I struggled with the doctrine of the believer's *"fellowship with God,"* and why there was so much misunderstanding in ecclesiastical circles regarding this issue. My question was this: Is every believer in "fellowship with God" or not? And just what is "fellowship with God" really about? Why all the confusion on such a significant issue? Let me state the case clearly—every child of God (every believer) has entered into *"fellowship with God"* as a result of the work of Christ on the cross. No child of God is <u>not</u> in fellowship with God. The NT word translated *"fellowship"* is the Greek word *koinonia*—this term is frequently translated companionship, fellowship, partnership, sharing, and communion. So *koinonia* describes a situation where two or more persons enter into a "partnership" in which they share things in common. Note the strong similarities among the various words that are translations of *koinonia;* in particular, note the "sharing in common" aspect. *Every believer is in "partnership with God," and every believer has become a partaker of the divine nature* (2 Pet 1:4)—regardless of the depth of their spirituality, this relationship is eternally established (Phil 1:6); but that does not mean every believer *"enjoys"* the fellowship/partnership/communion they have with God. Here is the crux of the matter: the less the believer trusts God, and more the believer sins, the *"less joy"* he will experience in his Christian life. Nevertheless, regardless of the *spiritual joy* he experiences, he is still in *partnership* and *fellowship* with God.

Here are some other considerations regarding the believer's "fellowship with God"—all Christians have fellowship with the Father, the Son, the Holy Spirit, and with one another (1 Jn 1:3; 2 Cor 13:14; Phil 2:1; 1 Jn 1:3, 7); as believers we are brothers and sisters! Christ prayed that as His children we would experience the oneness we have (Jn 17:21). Every believer has become a partner with God for righteousness in this sinful fallen world (Mt 6:33). God by His grace called us into "fellowship with His Son" (1 Cor 1:9). As Christians we must "walk in the light" to <u>enjoy</u> His fellowship (1 Jn 1:3, 6). Fellowship with God is essential to fruitfulness (Jn 15:4). It is natural that Christians desire to enter into the fellowship of the Lord's suffering (Phil 3:10). Ultimately, our eternal fellowship with God will be fully realized in heaven's glory (Rev 21:1–4).

parents continue to love us when we wander off, how much more will our heavenly Father? (Is 49:15; Mt 7:11; Rom 8:32–39). *So, when you sin—confess it and move on! and stop fixating on it!* Acknowledge it before God, and in His infinite mercy He will apply the blood of Christ to it; furthermore, He is faithful and just to forgive you your sins—affirm that fact as indeed being the case! That is faith! It is the blood of Christ that cleanses us from the guilt of sin. We are called to *"walk in the light"*—be the children of light that Jesus died to make us—and to *"confess our sins,"* and as we do, so He will bring to bear upon our confessed sin the provision He made on Calvary. As such, we are delivered from that guilt and pollution and from that tarnishing effect of sin, and by faith we can *consciously rejoice in the fact that we have fellowship with God.* At this point the devil comes and says to you, "You're no Christian! You can't walk with Him! Look at all your sin and your guilt!" And he makes you feel like a deplorable, hopeless wreck. But here is the glorious answer to that, and this is our assurance: *"the blood of Jesus cleanses us—it goes on doing so—and will continue to do so—from all sin!"* That is why it is called "Amazing Grace!" It is truly is amazing! Almost impossible to believe!

David was conscious of the pollution in his soul and his need of cleansing in Psalm 51—"Who can take from me the pollution and tarnishing effect of my sin?" We need something that can cleanse us and give us assurance—the blood of Jesus Christ cleanses us! You can trust that! Peter reminds us that we were redeemed by the "precious blood of Christ" (1 Pet 1:18–19). This is our comfort and consolation: "He is faithful and just to forgive us our sins, and cleanse us from all unrighteousness" (1 Jn 1:9). Our comfort and assurance is the very character of God Himself—He has "promised" that if we confess our sins He will forgive us freely (because of the cross). Therefore, have no doubts, says John—rely upon the faithfulness of God to His own word. Furthermore, John adds, *God is "just" in doing so!* The "cross of Christ" is the propitiation for our sins; God is both "just and justifier" (Rom 3:25ff). So, when you are aware of your sinfulness, look to the blood of Christ and see the justice of God. There is power in the blood! You are forgiven! To not believe that is to not believe God! Affirm that reality! And enjoy His fellowship! (141–145)

The "blood of Christ" cleanses us from all sin! That is the gospel of Christ! Remind yourself of that fact! Without Christ and the cross there is no good news—no hope! There is only one way of fellowship and

THE BELIEVER'S "RELATIONSHIP" WITH GOD

Let me use the metaphor of a *"baseball team"* to illustrate your relationship with God. Being a Christian in a way is like "being a member of God's ball club"—He drafted you on to His team, and from day one He has been committed to making you a great ballplayer, even though at this point you hardly know anything about how to even play the game; the reality is, you have never even played the game! So God didn't draft you because you were some great proven commodity! Like many young people you don't adapt easy to the game or to His training techniques; as a matter of fact, sometimes you don't even like the game, so you feel like quitting and just giving up. Sooner or later you find out that that is not an option either—even when you go AWOL (absent without leave), He comes after you and finds you and takes you back to the ballpark! You see, God drafted you on to His team and now that you are on His team, that is never going to change. You are on His ball club forever! Another amazing thing about being on God's team, is that He really likes you—as crazy as that sounds, He really does! How is that possible? Regardless of how lousy a player you are, He keeps working with you and does everything He can to make you a great ballplayer—He encourages you, instructs you, disciplines you, rewards you, pats you on the back, shows you the ropes, spends time with you, is patient with you, and never loses His cool with you, no matter how "lousy a job you do," or how much "grief" you cause Him. He just keeps on loving you and working with you. Why does He invest so much in you? It doesn't make sense. Many years later you find yourself in a "big game," and He looks over and says to you, "You're pinch-hitting!" You can't believe what you're hearing! How can it be? . . . your knees are shaking . . . your mind is racing . . . and you just know you're going to "lose the game" for the team. Then you hear the Coach saying to you, "Don't worry about all that stuff . . . just go up there and give it your best; you'll do fine." Sure 'nuff, you go up to the plate, and in spite of all your inadequacies and frailties, you get a hit, and you drive in the winning run! You're dumbfounded and grinning from ear to ear! "How in the world did that ever happen?" you wonder. Why would Coach have ever put me in the game? How did He know I'd come through with the winning hit? Read through the following scripture passages with this metaphor in mind—Ps 138:8; Phil 1:6; Rom 8:28–31; Lk 15:4–7; 1 Th 5:24; Heb 12:4–11. By the way, don't get so uptight! Relax and enjoy playing the game! You are on His team!

communion with God, and that is through the cross of Christ! There is "one mediator between God and men, the man Christ Jesus" (1 Tim 2:5). Be perfectly clear about Him! The "blood of Christ" is the gospel! Satan was defeated at the "Cross!" And that is where he focuses his efforts: *"remove the cross and you lose the power!"—that is his modus operandi!* Don't be enticed by the devil to see the "cross" as an elementary principle that really isn't that big a deal—that you need to press on to "deeper matters." *The CROSS is the essence of Christianity!* Remember, it is the "blood of Christ" that <u>keeps on cleansing us</u> from all sin! It is His blood that purchased our pardon and forgiveness and reconciles us to God. It is His blood shed on the cross that sets us free from sin and death. "Love, so amazing, so divine!" (147–156)

Once again, fellowship describes a situation where two or more persons enter into a "partnership" where they share things in common. John tells us that "God is light"—in Him there is no darkness at all (1 Jn 1:5). He is absolutely holy. Because God is light, those who desire fellowship with Him must also be pure. Therefore, in order for a person to be in "fellowship with God," he cannot "habitually walk in darkness" (1:6); those who habitually *(present tense verb)* **walk in darkness** have never been saved. On the other hand, those who habitually *(present tense verb)* **walk in the light** are saved, and as a result, have fellowship with God (1:7). So, John tells us here that a man is either in the *light* or in *darkness*—if he is in the *light*, he is a member of God's family; if he is in *darkness*, he doesn't have anything in common with God, because there is no darkness in God at all. To claim fellowship or partnership with God, yet live a life that is in juxtaposition to the truth is a complete contradiction—John calls that a lie (1 Jn 1:6). Those who *walk in the light* (i.e., those who live in such a way that they are enlightened by the truth of who God is) have *fellowship* with one another (this may refer to fellowship with God rather than other believers), and the blood of Jesus Christ **continually cleanses them** *(present tense verb)* from all sin. *(Did you catch that?)*

Only the blood of Christ can cleanse us from all sin, and make it possible for *"imperfect believers"* to have fellowship with a holy God. Be very clear about this! Every believer lives in the realm of light and has continual fellowship with God; but *enjoying* that fellowship requires *"walking intimately with Christ."* Regrettably, many churches teach the idea that believers can actually be "in and out of fellowship with God," depending upon their walk—when they sin, they are said to be *"out of fellowship,"* and when they are walking in faith, they are said to be *"in fellowship."* Though this erroneous view of fellowship is commonly held by many Christians, that is not at all what Scripture teaches. When believers sin, they do not *"enjoy their fellowship"* with Christ, but that does not mean it has been dismantled in some way, or uprooted as a reality in their lives—should believers sin, and that they do often, they continue to be recipients of the life of Christ and have an *"intimate common bond with Him"* (sin does not alter that in any way!) . . . but their enjoyment of that intimate bond is clearly affected; in short, the "partnership" continues, but the joy of that partnership is eclipsed. This is a very critical principle for the believer to understand.

Let's return again to what the apostle John says concerning the believer's "fellowship" with God. To be in genuine fellowship with God (i.e., being a believer) requires that we acknowledge the truth about ourselves. For instance, to deny that we have a *"sinful nature"* means we are simply deceiving ourselves, and the truth is not in us (1 Jn 1:8). Notice that John makes a distinction between *"sin"* (1:8) and *"sins"* (1:9)—*sin* refers to our corrupt, evil nature; *sins* refers to the evil acts we have done. Conversion does not mean the eradication of the *sin nature;* rather, it means the implanting of the *new divine nature,* with power (Holy Spirit) to live victoriously over indwelling sin (sin nature).

In order for us to walk day by day in "joyful communion with God" and other believers, obviously, we cannot be living a life of sin. Hence, we must *"confess our sins"* (i.e, "agree with God about our sins" or, literally, "say the same thing about our sins" that God says about them). The bible teaches that the one who "covers his sins will not prosper; but the one who confesses and forsakes them will have mercy" (Prv 28:13; Mt 6:12). When we agree with God about our sins, we can claim the promise that God will forgive us our sins (He is faithful and just to do so), and also cleanse us from all unrighteousness (1:9). The forgiveness John speaks about here is *parental*—not *judicial*. **Judicial *forgiveness*** means forgiveness from the penalty of sin (death); the sinner is exonerated when he believes on the Lord Jesus Christ—this forgiveness is called *judicial* because it is granted by God as our Judge; so all the sins a believer has or ever will commit are judicially forgiven. Regarding the sins believers commit *after* conversion—(the "price" of those sins has already been paid for at the cross and has been judicially dealt with)—those sins, however, require ***parental forgiveness,*** and that is obtained when we confess our sins (1 Jn 1:9; Mt 6:12). Parental forgiveness restores the believer's *joyful communion and fellowship* with God; remember, the *"joy of fellowship"* is not possible when there is unconfessed sin in the heart.

Finally, writes John, if we deny that we have committed "acts of sin," we are actually calling God a "liar" (1 Jn 1:10). Why is that? God says we all sin and stumble in many ways—which should be pretty obvious to everyone (Rom 7:14–24; Jam 3:2). Denying that we commit sinful acts, indicates that God's Word is not in us; as such, His Word does not effect a change in those individual's lives (1 Pet 1:23; 2:2; Rom 12:2; Col 3:16). So John teaches us here in his First Epistle that fellowship with God is the result of being in a right relationship with Him (i.e., living in the light/being a believer). Therefore, fellowship with God does not require sinless living (which is not possible); rather, it means that as God's children we *strive in a Godward direction* ("walk in the light"), and when we stumble and sin, we acknowledge our sins before Him, and confess and forsake them—and this we do because of the indwelling presence of the Holy Spirit in our lives (Ps 32:3–5; Jn 16:8). If these things are not being done in a person's life, then God's Spirit is obviously not present in that person's life; hence, they are simply not a Christian. By the way, Christians cannot live their lives in complete delusion and separation from God, because the work the Holy Spirit in their hearts simply would not permit such a wayward attitude of indifference (Ps 32:3–5; Ps 51:2–3, 12, 17; Heb 12:4–11).

CHAPTER 6

A summary of the book . . .
"GLORIOUS FREEDOM"
by Richard Sibbes (1577–1635)

The first edition of this work, entitled *"The Excellency of the Gospel above the Law,"* was first published in 1639, four years after Richard Sibbes died. Sibbes examines the fullness of the gospel, and its effect upon those who behold it (by the Holy Spirit). The vitality of the *"new covenant"* brings about spiritual liberty *and* a spiritual likeness to Christ. "Where the Spirit of the Lord is, there is liberty . . . we are changed into the same image from glory to glory, by the Holy Spirit" (2 Cor 3:17–18); i.e., the ministry of the gospel changes the believer from one degree of glory (or grace) to another. We are predestined to be *"conformed to the image of Christ"* (Rom 8:29)—it is the Holy Spirit who does the work in us. Everything in us is flesh by nature—whatever is spiritual and divine comes from the Holy Spirit. The soul without the Spirit is spiritual darkness and spiritual chaos.

Scripture teaches where the Spirit of Christ is, there is "liberty"—we are in *"bondage"* before we have the Spirit. Every man is a *"slave"* until he becomes a believer—it is the sin disposition of man's nature without grace. As ***Augustine*** said in his book *"The City of God"*—"The unbeliever is a slave though he rule"—he has as many lords as he has lusts. Christ frees us by His Holy Spirit, working such graces in us as to make us see the loathsomeness of that bondage. The Holy Spirit works to soften the heart and make it malleable.

Unless the Spirit of God witnessed to my spirit that I am reconciled to God in Christ, and that Christ's righteousness is mine, I could never have been persuaded of it. For the soul thinks, God is holiness itself, and I am a mass of sin—what reason have I to think that God would be favorably disposed to such a wretch as me? God was pleased to make me His child through the cross of His Son, and the Spirit assures my conscience. *Unless the Spirit tells me that the cross of Christ satisfied the Father, I should never believe it*—"to those who are perishing, the gospel is foolishness, but to those of us who are being saved it is the power of God unto salvation" (1 Cor 1:18).

To whom God gives forgiveness, He gives His Spirit to sanctify. The same Spirit that assures me of my pardon for sin, sanctifies my nature and breaks the ruling power of sin in me. Before then the whole life is nothing but continual sinning and offending God—but now there is a gracious liberty of disposition. Because there are remainders of bondage within the believer, due to the double principle of nature and grace, there will be a conflict in every holy duty. The believer is to resist; there is still liberty to "do good." In a wicked man there is nothing but flesh, as such, there is no resistance. We must understand the nature of this *"spiritual liberty"* in sanctification. It is not a liberty freeing us altogether from conflict and deadness; it is not a liberty freeing us from combat; rather, it is a liberty that enables us to fight the battles of the Lord against our own corruption.

Christians must not be discouraged with the stubbornness and unwillingness of the "flesh" to do good duties. If we have a *"principle in us"* to fight against our corruptions, and to get good duties out of ourselves in spite of them, it is an argument for a *"new nature."* God will perfect His own beginnings and subdue the flesh more and more by the power of His Spirit. "Oh," said Jesus, *"The spirit is willing, but the flesh is weak"* (Mt 26:41). Indeed, there is a double hindrance in God's people when they are about holy duties. Christ made an excuse for His disciples—it was not so much corruption [though that was an ingredient] as it was nature itself. Christ saw a great deal of "gold" in the ore, so we see how He excused them. Therefore when we are dull, let us strive—Christ is ready to make excuse for us, if our hearts are right. While we live here there is "sin" in us, but it does not reign; when man has the Spirit of Christ in him, the Holy Spirit maintains a perpetual combat and conflict against the principle of sin within us. God could subdue sin all at once if He saw fit to; but He chooses to humble us while we live here and exercise us with *"spiritual conflicts."* (vii-39)

A part of God's plan in bringing us to heaven, is that each of us experiences "combat within;" God enables us by the Holy Spirit to fight His battles against the flesh. How does this work? "The law of the Spirit of life [i.e., the commanding power of the Spirit of Christ] which commands as a law in the hearts of God's people, sets us free from [the commanding power of] the law of sin and death" (Rom 8:2). The dominion and tyranny of sin is broken by the Spirit of Christ—we are set at a "gracious liberty." In some respects sin does not have complete dominion over us because of grace, as the apostle says. By the Spirit of Christ we are made kings to rule over our own lusts to some degree—we are not kings to be freed altogether from them, but kings to strive against them; we have the liberty to *fight,* and in fighting to ultimately *overcome;* this is *sanctification.* When the Israelites had a promise that God would give their enemies into their hands, the meaning was not that He would do this without their fighting a blow—they would have to fight, but in fighting they would overcome. In like manner, this liberty of sanctification is not a liberty that ends combat with our corruptions, but a *"gracious liberty"* to keep them under control, till by subduing them little by little, we have a perfect victory. Paul says we are called to complete the sufferings of Christ (Phil 3:10; Col 1:24). What greater encouragement can a man have to fight against his enemy, then to know "victory is certain" before he fights?

So, the Spirit brings us out of that cursed kingdom of Satan and sin, and brings liberty into the soul. The Spirit not only frees us *"from* *sin,*" it frees us from the fear of damnation and the terrors of an evil conscience (1 Pet 1:2). Conversely, the Spirit frees us to *"do good,"* and to make the Word of God our counselor—what was a "severe schoolmaster" when we were not saved, is now in the believer a *"wise tutor"* to guide and counsel us. In a sense, the Law actually scared us to Christ. Note the contrast—where the Spirit of God is, there is "liberty of will" in the inward man; where the Spirit of God is not, there is no liberty, "no free will." Whereas we were *"free to do evil"* as unbelievers, we are now *"free to do good"* as believers—we have the ability and the strength to do what is good. The Spirit of God puts a *"new life"* into the soul of a person—it takes away the "stony heart" and replaces it with a "heart of flesh" (Ezek 11:19).

Though God's Spirit works upon the will, it does so by "enlightening the understanding," so that a man does what he does being fully advised by *"reason."* The creature that is without reason is always confined to one manner of working, because it lacks understanding to work in any other way. Unregenerate man cannot *"discern"* that which is spiritual, because he does not have the Holy Spirit in him (1 Cor 2:14). Birds make their nests and bees make their hives always the same way; they have no choice because of their narrow abilities.

Why do we pray "Thy will be done"? (Mt 6:10). Or "take me out of my own will more and more, and conform my will to Thine in all things." The more we *"align our will with God's will,"* the more liberty we have in serving God. Men are mistaken to think the greatest liberty is to have power to do good or evil—such power is the imperfection of the creature—man "fell" because he was free to choose either good or evil—and he chose evil. The soul under the supervision of the *"new nature,"* is "free not to sin" and "free to do good." The understanding is so enlightened, and the will so confirmed and strengthened, that the soul is not constrained by temptation—the essence of which is *"glorious liberty."* Grace is the beginning of glory—it frees the soul from terror and subjection to sin; therefore, the life of glory is begun in grace by the Holy Spirit. (39–51)

The more we know the "gospel," the more we have of the "Spirit" . . . and the more Spirit we have, the more *"liberty"* we enjoy—as such, we should prize the "charter" of our spiritual liberty, *God's Word*. What a blessed condition it is to have this "spiritual liberty"—for if a man has the Spirit of God to set him at liberty, he has the Spirit of God to free him from temptation . . . or if temptation catches hold of him so that he sins, he has the Spirit of God to fly to, to confess his sins and lay hold on the blood of Christ, and experience the pardoning of sin. A child does not need "other motives" to please his father other than the knowledge that he is the child of a *"loving father"*—it is natural. There is a "new nature" in those who have the Spirit of God to stir them up to duty. When a man is in temptation from within or without, he can go boldly to God and pour out his soul to God freely as to a father—this comes from the Spirit of liberty, whereby he is able to cry out to God, *"Abba, Father."* When a "broken soul" goes to God in Christ with boldness (Heb 4:16), this opening of the soul to God is a sign of liberty, the liberty of a child to his father.

The moment a man is "in Christ" and has Christ's Spirit, he has *"another law"* in his soul to rule him contrary to that which was there before—prior to that he was ruled by the *"law of his lusts."* But now that he is in Christ he has a new Master and a new law, which rules him according to the *"government of the Spirit."* "The law of the Spirit of life in Christ has set him free from the law of sin and death" (Rom 8:2). When we find any corruption stirring in our soul, we should go to the Lord in the words of ***Augustine*** and say: "Lord, free me from my necessities; I am not able to serve Thee as I should or would like to; I am enslaved to sin, but I want to do better. I cannot do as well as I want to; Lord, free me from my necessities." Let us complain of our corruption to God—

> *I cannot by my own strength set myself at liberty from this corruption. Lord, give me Thy Spirit to do it. Set me more and more at liberty from my former bondage and from this wickedness that has enslaved me. Lord, Thy office is to "destroy the works of the devil"* (1 Jn 3:8).

It is the office of the Holy Spirit to "free us"—Let this be a comfort to all poor struggling and striving Christians who are not yet set at perfect liberty from their lusts and corruptions. It is the office of the Spirit of Christ as the king of the Church, by His Spirit, to purge the Church perfectly, to make it a glorious spouse—and at last, He will fulfill His own office, and then we shall be freed from all oppositions without, and from all conflict and corruption within. It is called "the liberty of the sons of God" (Rom 8:21). (52–67)

As the sun rises by degrees till it comes to shine in glory, so it was with the "Sun of righteousness." He revealed Himself in the Church little by little—the latter times now are more glorious than the former. Conversely, the apostle Paul compares the administration of the *"covenant of grace"* under the gospel with that of the *"covenant of law"*—by comparison, he shows the administration under the gospel to be more excellent. *"We now behold with open face"* (2 Cor 3:18)—that is, with freedom and boldness, which was not true in the time of the law. They were "afraid" to look upon Moses when he came down from the mount, because his countenance was so majestic and terrifying. But "we all with open face" freely, boldly, and joyfully look upon the glory of God in the gospel. The light of the *gospel* is attracting and comforting; whereas the light of the *law* was frightening and terrifying. We are changed from "glory to glory" (2 Cor 3:18)—the *law* did not have the power to convert, or change people into its own likeness. But now the *gospel,* which is the ministry of the Spirit, has the power to transform and change people into the likeness of Christ—it is a gradual change, not all at once, but from glory to glory, from one degree of *grace* to another; grace is here called *glory*. We are changed from the heart, inwardly and thoroughly, and the cause of it all is "the Spirit of the Lord." The happiness of man consists in communion with God and conformity to Him.

When the time of temptation and conflict with conscience comes . . . and the hour of death . . . Satan will focus completely upon our *"sin,"* especially in the time of despair. Therefore we must be as cunning and focus upon the grace and glorious mercy of Christ. What a comfort this is to sinful man, that in casting himself upon Christ and upon God's mercy in Christ, he yields glory to God. The last end of man is the glory of God—*He made us for His glory*—we hinder God's glory if we do not believe His mercy in Christ to us; therefore, let us yield to Him the glory of His mercy, and let us think that when we do sin we cannot glorify Him more than to have recourse to His mercy. When Satan tempts us to *"run from God"* and discourages us, keep this in mind—**God has set Himself to be *"glorious in mercy"* above all other attributes!** God will account Himself "honored" if we have recourse to Him; let this thought be as a "city of refuge" to you. *"Where sin abounds, grace much more abounds!"* (Rom 5:20). Never let Satan discourage you from going to Christ! "Oh!" you say, "but I have offended Him often and grievously!" What does Scripture say? "My thoughts are not as your thoughts . . . as high as the heavens are above the earth" (Is 55:8–9). With men, offences often cause permanent alienation, but with God this is not so! As often as we go to God for mercy and spread our sins before Him with broken and humble hearts, we will be pardoned! ***It is "God's glorious mercy" that satisfies a distressed conscience.*** If you find your conscience wounded with sin, do not hold back from God any longer—He has glorious mercy for you! We are never in the condition in which we ought to be, unless "grace is glory to us"—and grace is glory to the sinner when he says in his heart, *"Oh, that I might have a drop of mercy!"* It pleases God to condescend and stoop to us poor sinners, to reveal His glory—the glory of His mercy. Jesus said, "Let all who thirst, come to Me and be satisfied" (Jn 7:37). (69–91)

How shall we make the eye of our souls fit to behold the "glory of God"? We must fix our *meditation* upon the glory of God and the excellency of Christ. We must labor to have both the inward and outward hindrances removed. We must labor that the soul be cleansed from all carnal and base passions and desires—only a spiritual soul can ever behold spiritual things. *As the soul must be fixed upon these meditations, so the Spirit of God must sanctify and purge the soul.* The best place to behold Christ is in His Word, with a spirit of faith. Christ tells us to ask pardon for our trespasses *"every day"* (Mt 6:12). Daily, therefore, reflect upon the "everlasting mercy and goodness" of God—though sin produces grief and shame in us, God's glorious mercy recovers and strengthens our faith again; and God's children, after breaches, emerge stronger than they ever were before. Therefore go boldly to the Father, with love and reverence and "with open face," crying, *"Abba, Father"* (Rom 8:15). Never forget this privilege! (92–100)

We are changed into the image of Christ from "glory to glory" until the soul is filled "with all the fullness of God" (2 Cor 3:18; Eph 3:19). God's mercy in Christ is a powerful object that influences and transforms the soul—the state of man after this change is a *"glorious condition."* First, we are in a state contrary to grace and to God—we are dead in our sin (Eph 2:1); the corrupt nature of man cannot enter into heaven (1 Cor 15:50). We must be "born again"—the whole frame and bent of the soul must be new; we must have new judgments, new desires, new affections. There is no Christian that does not desire the grace of sanctification to change him—every believer looks upon his corruption and sin as the vilest thing in the world—remember, you have been "born again!" God has "written His law in your heart!" (Jer 31:33).

The change is especially in "the will"—grace works upon the will most of all. For the bent and desires of the will carry the whole man with it. All grace first comes in through the understanding being enlightened, and then it goes into the *"will"*—thus the grace of the gospel is not mere persuasion and entreaty, but a powerful work of the Spirit entering into the soul and *"changing it,"* and altering the inclination of the will heavenward; whereas corruption of nature turns the soul toward earthly things. Grace alters everything—"old things are passed away . . . all things become new" (2 Cor 5:17). The pattern to which we are changed is *"the image of Christ"*—He is the pattern of all our sanctification. God's children sometimes deface that image by sin—but as a coin that is somewhat defaced, yet still retains the old stamp and is acknowledged as a good coin, so a Christian in the worst condition, still bears the stamp—when once we are God's coin, we never become reprobate silver. Grace is firmly set in our nature in Christ—it is so certain, all the devils of hell cannot obliterate it. Remember, we are predestined to be *"conformed to Christ"* (Rom 8:29; Phil 1:6); He is making us a "glorious spouse" (Eph 5:25–27). Every man by nature carries the image of the devil on him; but Christ came to "destroy the works of the devil," to erase his image and set His own stamp and image upon the soul. Unless Christ changes us into His image, He would not achieve the end for which He came (Rom 8:29–30; Phil 1:6).

Since God's goal is to transform us into the "image of Christ," let us *labor* every day more and more to study Christ, so that by beholding Him we may be transformed into His likeness—*"the sight of Christ is a transforming sight!"* Notice how sweet Jesus was to sinners when they repented; how ready He was to forgive and pardon. Cross reference the woman of Samaria (Jn 4:6–26) . . . the apostle Peter; Jesus never scolded him for his apostasy, or upbraided him for it; He never even so much as "reminded him of it!" He only looked upon him and said, "Do you love Me?" (Jn 21:15)—*He would not "quench the smoldering wick, or break the bruised reed"* (Mt 12:20); that is how gentle and sweet our Savior is. Jesus was sweet to those who were good in the least degree, where there was only a hint of goodness. Jesus was always patient when wronged; even toward those who despised Him! He even shed tears for those who shed His blood (Mt 23:37)—"Father, forgive them, they know not what they do" (Lk 23:34). The Father's response regarding His Son: "This is My Son, in whom I am well pleased" (Mt 3:17).

Christ is alive in the world in no other way than in the hearts of Christians, who have received His grace and who carry the picture and resemblance (image) of Christ in them. The more we grow in love for one another, the more we conform to the original pattern that is Christ. Said the apostle Paul, "I have been crucified with Christ, it is no longer I who lives, but Christ lives in me" (Gal 2:20). The more I know and meditate on this principle, the more I am transformed into the likeness of Christ's death and resurrection. When the soul considers that it is one with Christ, it has the same disposition that Christ has. When I consider how Christ died to purge sin in me, can I, being one with Him, have any attitude other than He had upon the cross? *As He died for sin,* *so I die to sin.* These and similar thoughts are stirred up in a Christian, which Paul aims at in Romans 6 and other passages.

That we may be changed into the "likeness of Christ," let us fix our meditations on Him, and we shall find a change, though we do not know how it happens. As those who are in the sun working or playing, find themselves warmed, so let us set ourselves about *holy meditations,* and we shall find a secret imperceptible change—our souls will be altered, though we do not know how. *There is a virtue that goes with "holy meditation," a changing, transforming virtue.* Can we think of His humility and not be humble? Shall we be fierce when our Savior was meek? Can a proud heart apprehend a meek Savior? No. The heart is suited to the thing apprehended.

To be changed into the "image of Christ," let us look to what "remains" of our own corruptions. Look to our *worldly-mindedness,* to our passions, to our rebellions, to our darkness, and to our deadness of spirit . . . and then go to Christ. I am earthly-minded; He is heavenly . . . I am full of rebellions and lusts; all is at peace in Him. Therefore, I need Thy *heavenly-mindedness,* Thy meekness, Thy spiritual strength. I am weak and dark and dead—shine on me; Thou hast fullness for me. Christ, in love, became a man—He took upon Himself our nature, our base condition (Phil 2:8); He transfigured Himself to our lowliness—shall we not labor to be transformed to be like Him? *Shall He be conformed to us, and we not be conformed to Him?* If Christ gave Himself for us, shall we not give ourselves to Christ? We have the Spirit of Christ in our hearts by the merit of Christ, that we might be transformed into His likeness. Christ died for us, that we might live to Him! Beholding the glory of God in the gospel is a powerful beholding—says He, *"we are changed, by beholding, to the image of Christ."* Shall not the glorious sight of God's mercy and love in Christ work a change in our soul? The *"eye of faith"* apprehending God's love and mercy in Christ, has a power to change—that is the transforming powerful nature of the gospel. Nothing can "change us" but the gospel—"even the lion shall one day lie down with the lamb" (Is 11:6).

Iron is dull and heavy; yet when hot it is bright and pliable. In the same way our dead, dull, inflexible and unyielding souls become malleable and flexible by the love of Christ shining upon them. His love transforms and kindles them. This is how the glory of God's love in Christ transforms us—*the discovery of the abundant mercy in God towards us kindles love to Him, and that love works likeness.* Where there is "dependence upon Christ" there is a desire to like Him. When we see Christ as our husband, that breeds in us the affections of a spouse. No one sees the mercy of God in Christ by the "eye of faith" without being changed.

We are changed "from glory to glory"—by glory here is meant "grace." When we are persuaded of it by the Spirit, who works grace in us, grace is followed by peace, joy, comfort, and many such things which the Scripture counts "glory." *We grow "from glory to glory"*—from one degree of grace to another. Grace is victorious and conquering, prevailing over the corruptions that prevail over ordinary men. It makes a Christian glorious when he brings every thought and affection, and every corruption within him, to the subjection of the Spirit of glory. All the power in the world cannot interrupt God's gracious progress. What is begun in grace will end in glory. Where the foundation is laid, God will be sure to put up the roof. He never repents of His beginnings (Phil 1:6). Solomon said that *the righteous is "like the sun that grows brighter and brighter till it comes to its full strength"* (Prv 4:18). The state of the wicked is completely contrary—it is in a constant state of decline—the sun goes down and down to twilight, and then to darkness, and then to utter darkness; they decline from the darkness of misery, to the eternal, black, dismal darkness of hell. The state of the godly is always in a growing state; it is a hopeful condition; it grows from one state of glory to another. We say of fire, the more it flames, the less it smokes. (101–145)

There is no stopping or standstill in religion—there must of necessity be a desire to grow better and better; glory will grow to even more glory; grace will never cease till it ends in the fullness of glory in heaven—where we are "fully glorified!" The Christian is in a state of perpetual growth; he will ultimately come to full maturity. *In those who are young* there is a great deal of the old nature joined with a little grace. *But in more mature Christians*, the knowledge they have is more pure and more settled, and their love and affection is more refined. There is less "self-love," and the zeal they have is joined with more heavenly discretion; there is less "wild fire" with it. So *grace grows* in purity and perfection, though it is not altogether pure; something savoring of the worst principle in nature will stick to our best performances. Because we always carry flesh with us in this life, every behavior will savor of corruption; yet this is less so in a grown Christian than it is in an immature Christian. We must labor that more grace may appear; and the more glorious we are, the more we will resemble Christ (His image). Conversely, the more we grow in grace, the more we shall prevail with God in prayer. It is a glorious thing when we resist strong temptations—grace is glorious when a Christian holds his own in the worst of times.

The sun is said to be "in glory" when it is high in the sky; there are many clouds in the morning, but when the sun is at its height at noonday, it scatters them all. So a Christian is in his glory when he can scatter doubts, fears and terrors that trouble weak beginning Christians. When we are troubled with various issues, we should labor to be delivered from them, so that grace may be glorious. Grace continues and increases—as the stream with which it is fed is an ever-living spring, so is grace—*where Christ has opened a spring in the heart, He will feed that grace perpetually*. Let no one in whom grace has begun be discouraged—God will continue the work of grace He has begun in you (Phil 1:6). Until grace has grown it is little distinguished from other things; just as there is little difference between weeds and herbs before they have grown. Grace is little at first, as a grain of mustard seed (Mt 13:31). Remember, Jerusalem wasn't built in a day either. Some Christians of a weaker sort want to be in Canaan just as soon as they are out of Egypt! As soon as they have grace in them they want to advance immediately—but that is not how spiritual maturity develops—believers must be content to be led from one state of glory to another, from one degree of grace to another. *Progress is gradual in the new creature*. We don't immediately arrive in Canaan—God leads us through the wilderness, and through temptations and crosses, before we enter into heaven.

Let those who are growing in their faith not be discouraged with their "little beginnings"—It is God's way in this world to bring His children along *"little by little,"* through many stations. As they were led in the wilderness from place to place, so God brings His children by many places to heaven. It is one part of a Christian's meekness to be subject to God's wisdom in this respect, and not to complain that they are not as perfect as they would like to be or as they shall be. Let us labor to be meek and say, *"Lord, since Thou hast ordained that I shall grow from glory to glory, from one degree of grace to another, let me have grace to magnify Thy mercy that Thou hast given me any goodness at all, rather than to complain that I don't have more."*

Let us not be discouraged with seeming "interruptions" in our spiritual growth. God sometimes works by *contraries*—He makes men grow by their decreasing, and to stand by their falls. Sometimes when God will have a man grow He will *allow him to fall*, that by "his fall" he may grow in a deeper hatred of sin and in jealousy over his own heart, and in a nearer watchfulness over his own ways; that he may grow more in love with God for pardoning him, and stronger in his resolution; and that he may grow more in humility. No one grows so much as those who have their growth stopped for a time. *Little interruptions are like "sicknesses"—it draws out the toxins that hinder growth.* It is also important to remember that God looks on Christians not as they are in *"their imperfections,"* but as they shall be when they come to the *"perfect stature of Christ."* Therefore, let us comfort ourselves in our imperfections—at this point we are lame Mephibosheths; a king's son who was lame (2 Sam 4:4; 9:1–13)—*we are spiritually lame and defective, though we are a king's son.* What a comfort is this in our imperfections, that as every day we live in this world cuts off a day of our life, so every day we live brings us nearer to heaven. Is this not a sweet comfort? Comfort yourself with these things.

Because some cannot see themselves as growing, they think they are "not growing" at all. That is only ignorance; we see that the sun moves, though we do not see it moving; we know things grow, though we do not see them growing. So, if we do not perceive our growth from grace to grace, it does not mean we are not growing. God sees that we need to grow in the *"root,"* so He abases us with some infirmity—just as a glorious spring comes after a hard winter, so after a setback, grace breaks out more gloriously. The best man living does not know himself till he comes to temptation and reveals himself to himself. Temptation uncovers corruption and makes it known, and then stirs up hatred for it. It is profitable for God's children to fall sometimes; otherwise they would never be as good as they are. When they see they are foul, they go to wash—this is a mystery; God has it this way for good ends.

The chief thing in conversion is "the desire," the turning of the stream of "the will"—So when some Christians find their "will" and their "desire" good, yet they continue to "fall short" of their purposes, they naturally conclude, "Surely I have no good in me, because I do not have what I want to have"—as if they should have heaven on earth. *It is God's mercy that He would work "the least degree" of grace in such rebellious hearts as we all have; that He would work "any goodness" or change at all in us. It is God's way to bring His children to glory* **"little by little,"** *so that Christians may depend upon one another, the weaker on the stronger, so that they may be compassionate and tender toward one another.* Therefore let no one be discouraged, especially considering that God, whom we desire to please, values us by the "little good" we have, and esteems us by that condition of perfection He ultimately will bring about in us. Let us be of good comfort in any measure of grace whatsoever—it is "good sickness" if it increases patience and humility; it is a "good loss" if it makes us grow less worldly-minded and more humble. (146–171)

Paul spoke to Lydia—but the "Holy Spirit" opened her heart (Acts 16:14). Only the Holy Spirit has the key to unlock and open men's hearts. We speak to the outward man, but unless the inward man is unlocked and opened by the Spirit of God, it is to no purpose. All change, all comfort, all peace is from the Spirit of Christ. The Holy Spirit never stops changing us until we are carried again to Christ—we are prepared, changed and sanctified by the Holy Spirit; *He conveys grace to us "from glory to glory" by degrees.* We have no goodness within us (in and of ourselves), no more than there is moisture in a stone or a rock; therefore, we must acknowledge that in and of ourselves (as Jesus says) "we can do nothing!" (Jn 15:5; Phil 2:13). We must look to God for His Holy Spirit to enlighten and sanctify us, and not despair. It was folly for Peter to presume of his own strength that "though everyone else might forsake Christ, yet he would not" (Mk 14:29–31). God left him to himself, and you see how he fell—so it is with us. We listen and do good works, but the activity and power and strength to make them *"efficacious"* must come from the Spirit of God.

Where the Spirit is—it changes us. The Holy Spirit not only illumines and enlightens, but sanctifies and changes. Wherein He dwells He sanctifies the house and makes it a temple. *Where the Spirit is, it will work.* If the condition is not altered from bad to good, and from good to better, you can pretty much assume the Spirit is not there. *There will always be some discernible operation of the Spirit of God*—as such, we grow from grace to grace, from knowledge to knowledge, from faith to faith, till we come to that measure of perfection that God has appointed for each of us who are in Christ. The Spirit stirs us up to grow from one degree of grace to another—to this end the Holy Spirit dwells in us and guides us (Rom 8:26). He is our tutor, our counselor, our instructor, and our guide. Therefore, let us labor to know the mercies of God in Christ, and be transformed and molded more into His likeness every day. (172–187)

CHAPTER 7

A summary of the book ...

"LET NOT YOUR HEART BE TROUBLED"
by Martyn Lloyd-Jones (1899–1981)

Martyn Lloyd-Jones preached these sermons in 1951 at "Westminster Chapel" in London—These were difficult times for Britain ... WWII was not long over ... people were still anxious and fearful. These sermons were intended to comfort, strengthen and build-up Christians in their faith. Jesus said, "Let not your heart be troubled; you believe in God, believe also in Me" (Jn 14:1)—the disciples became troubled when they heard Jesus would be leaving them; they had never met anybody like Him before, and now He would be going away—they were filled with alarm and concern, and their hearts were deeply troubled.

The greatest need of men and women in this world, is the need for a "quiet heart"—peace of mind, peace of heart, tranquility. We are all restless and disturbed ... there is unhappiness in us, and it is produced by many different issues—illness, accident, disappointment, financial loss, business trouble, illness of a child or loved one, death of someone close to us, war, political chaos economic collapse, etc. Just when we think everything is going well, something suddenly happens, and our whole world begins to shake and crumble. The supreme problem is that of trying to face these things and to achieve a *"quiet heart"*—that is the purpose for the gospel. Some say people should just *"refuse to think"* about their problems, in hopes that they will somehow just go away—"if you're foolish enough to think in this world, then it is not surprising that you are unhappy." Others say be like the animals and *"go back to nature"* and all will be well. Others believe in *"escapism"*—we should fill up our lives with as much as we can—entertainments, etc. Others espouse the philosophy of *"optimism"*—things will eventually evolve into a better life; though there are temporary setbacks, ultimately, things will get better (many try this approach). Then there are those who embrace a philosophy of *"fatalism"*—what will be will be; all the thinking and worrying isn't going to affect it in the least; the trouble with people is that they persist in thinking. Next is the *"psychological method"*—it attempts a kind of positive thinking approach to problem solving—peace of mind is the objective, not necessarily a change in circumstances; we just need to think of beautiful and pleasant thoughts. Then there is the attitude of *"stoicism"*—they say the one thing we must watch is our "feelings;" our trouble is that we all tend to be controlled by our feelings; therefore, we must become scientific, be objective, and control our emotions. Yet another is *"mysticism"*—this is espoused by the cults and religions like Christian Science, Buddhism and Hinduism—they advocate going into the heart of the universe, losing themselves in the spirit that is at the back of everything. In the final analysis, all of the foregoing attempts to deal with painful reality are *"pessimistic and hopeless"*—the actual truth about them is that they are so afraid of life that they dare not think about it; and that is the most profound pessimism I know. So all these views, at best, are devised just to help the individual get through—they simply help us postpone our problems; they do not resolve them; and none of these approaches give us real joy or satisfaction. The greatest criticism is that they all leave the problem up to the individual. (7–22)

Only the gospel can meet and satisfy our deepest need—Read the stories of the apostles, the martyrs and the first confessors. It worked for them, and it continues to work today. What seems to be so entirely different about the gospel, is that it always faces facts, it is always realistic, it never conceals anything. Other teachings and philosophies try to hide the worst from us. The gospel commends itself to me because of its *"truth."* It says, "in the world we shall have tribulation . . . there will be wars and rumors of wars" (Jn 16:33; Mt 24:6). My problem is not my physical flesh, it's in my spirit. I want an explanation of why it is in the position that it is. There has been one in this world who said to us, "Let not your heart be troubled . . . believe in Me," which means, "Come to Me, tell Me your troubles, tell Me all about your difficulty about God, the difficulty of prayer, the difficulty about your weak will and failure." Whatever it is that makes you restless—go to God about it. He is the one who loves you so much, He went to the cross for you. Said Jesus, *"Come unto Me and I will give you rest"* (Mt 11:28). Believe in the Son of God, who has removed every barrier between you and God and who can give you rest and peace here and now. (23–27)

Believe in God—that is the first thing we must do when we are really in a difficult situation. The trouble with us is that we always tend to aim at the *"problem"* directly, and we always look for some immediate consolation and resolution. Illustration: when a man becomes "ill" he generally is not interested in his *"disease"* as such; what he is really interested in is the *"suffering"* that he has to endure because of the illness, which is perfectly natural. *A man who sins suffers remorse; he has agony of mind, and the one thing he wants is to get rid of the agony.* But what he really needs is much more than immediate comfort. Anything that merely gives us RELIEF from the "unpleasant symptoms" of our disease or from our agony of mind is not enough—what we should always be interested in, in every realm, is HEALTH.

It is at this point that we come across the great differentiating characteristic of the Bible—All other methods are simply concerned with giving us *"immediate relief"* from pain; they are all drugs in some shape or form; they just have one interest—to relieve us. Many people come to God in that way, expecting to have some "temporary relief of pain;" something that can make them *"happy."* But the Bible teaches us that happiness and joy and peace and the absence of pain and trouble are always *"by-products"*—the result of something else. Notice what Jesus did "not" say: "Blessed are they who hunger and thirst after *happiness!*" NO! He said, "Blessed are they who hunger and thirst after *righteousness*, for they shall be filled." (Mt 5:6). In other words, if you make happiness your one aim and object in life, it is certain you will never find it; but if you make righteousness as your main aim, Jesus says, you will be filled with happiness! It will follow. (29–32)

We must always begin with "Believing in God." But what does that really mean? To have a troubled heart means that you are *"not believing in God aright."* There is something wrong in your belief. The questions to ask are these: "Is your heart at rest as you look at yourself and contemplate the state of the world?" "Is there peace in your soul as you look to the future?" When we read Hebrews 11 and take a walk through that gallery of heroes of the faith, we see men and women who lived in this world exactly as we do. Yet, they triumphed. They had a joy, a peace and a happiness that all the things they had to endure could not disturb. Why were they able to do this? What was their secret? Hebrews gives us the key—"He that cometh to God must *believe* that He is, and that He is a rewarder of them that diligently seek Him" (Heb 11:6). First, we must *"BELIEVE IN THE EXISTENCE OF GOD."* People who do not "believe in God" try to produce a kind of peace by not thinking at all. Obviously, that is not the solution. Refusing to think just evades the problem. And a "quiet heart" is unattainable. "There is no peace, says God, to the wicked" (Is 57:21)—the *wicked* are "those who do not truly believe in God."

God controls everything—He is the only Sovereign. Nothing happens apart from Him. We must believe that He is able to do everything, that nothing is too hard for Him. Abraham believed that God was able to raise Isaac up from the dead, if need be (Heb 11:19). Mary believed "nothing was impossible for God." Obviously our hearts cannot be quiet until our minds are satisfied—so the Bible answers our minds by telling us things about God to satisfy us intellectually. You might be experiencing a "peace" right now as you read these biblical truths—even though your heart was troubled a few moments ago—God is instructing your heart with the "truth" and is ushering in His peace. God created this world, and at the fall of man sin entered into the human family, and that is the origin and explanation and source of all our ills and troubles. Ultimately, that is a critical part of our belief in God. Scripture goes on to tell us that God is still in His world; He has not turned His back upon it; He is not allowing it to sin itself into utter hopelessness. He tells us that if we *"live His way of life"* we will be blessed; if we don't, we will be cursed (Deut 11:27–29). God loves humanity so much, He entered into our sinful world in the person of Jesus Christ to reconcile sinful man to Himself. This meant he went to the cross to die for our sins, and pay the penalty for our sin. He was buried, and rose again on the third day, and now sits at the right hand of God the Father ever making intercession for us. By placing our "faith" in His atoning work on the cross, we experience His forgiveness, become His children, and receive eternal life. *God in His sovereignty continues to direct and superintend the course of events throughout the universe . . . He allows even cataclysmic things to happen, yet nothing is outside His control.* In the fullness of time God will draw the curtain on human history. He will allow things to go on until a certain fixed point, but a day is coming when He will bring it all to a close. There will be an end of time . . . He will judge the whole world and all its people . . . then He will destroy all evil . . . and then He will make "a new heaven and a new earth" wherein dwelleth righteousness" (2 Pet 3:13). God will have fulfilled His old promise of restoring order out of chaos, giving universal blessing to those who belong to Him. The vital question for each of us is this: Do we believe that? This is part of what it means to "believe in God." To believe in God means that we must believe implicitly in the *"promises of God"*—believing God means obeying God. (32–40)

If you really "believe in God," anything that may happen to you, ultimately, will drive you nearer to God, and anything that drives you nearer to Him is a *"good thing"* for you. When something goes *"wrong"* it drives us to our knees—"It is good for me that I have been afflicted," said the psalmist; "before I was afflicted I went astray" (Ps 119:67, 71).

God sometimes has to chasten us in order to draw us a little nearer to Himself. Whatever happens to you, whatever may be your experience, He has promised "He will never leave or forsake you" (Heb 13:5). Thus, "believing God" means we are ready to commit ourselves and our affairs into His almighty, loving arms. The men and women of Hebrews chapter eleven risked everything upon that belief. Moses forsook the courts of Egypt and all his privileged position. Why? He believed God and had implicit faith and trust in Him. To believe God means an utter, implicit confidence in what He has said about Himself, and in what He has said about what He will do. It means casting yourself entirely upon that promise (Prv 3:5–6). "Let not your heart be troubled" in effect is this: "You find it hard and difficult to believe in Me? Believe in Me. Trust Me." (41–43)

The great need and the quest of all mankind is for a "quiet heart"—"peace." Many people camouflage their troubled souls by appearing to be supremely happy and carefree. How is "true peace" obtained? The biblical method is that we turn our focus from our *"troubles"* and start with *"God."* "Let not your heart be troubled"—Why? *"Believe in God."* Our problem is we are too immersed in the world; too preoccupied with it. What the Bible does for us is drag our attention away from the immediate scene to God—this is not *escapism*. This is radically different from the numerous psychotherapeutic methods that focus on psychoanalyzing your past (sometimes for years!); the Bible simply recognizes that man's fundamental need is *GOD*. When you have got a problem, you take it to the *"Author of problem solving"—GOD*. Jesus is absolutely essential for obtaining a quiet heart—if He has "resurrection power," He has enough power to quiet the little storm in your life. Furthermore, He has placed "His Spirit" in you to do the work—He has been placed in you to comfort you, to help you, and instruct you; so, going elsewhere for help is senseless; it's like using a "bandaid" for heart surgery. It should also be encouraging for us to go to God for help, because He abounds in lovingkindness, and is mindful of our weaknesses and our frailties— "God gives us grace to help in time of need" (Heb 4:16). Jesus said, "He that comes to Me I will in no wise cast out" (Jn 6:37). "Believe in God, believe also in Me." (45–59)

When you encounter troubles in life, you must learn to take your eyes off the problem and turn to God. The problem with us is that with our limited perspective, we let our problems and life overwhelm us—we need to step back from our *"piecemeal view of life"* and see the bigger picture; having a *"whole view of life"* is critically important. Start with Paul's argument in Romans 8:32—"He that spared not His own Son, how shall He not with Him also freely give us all things?" Do not rush at your problem—step back and get God's perspective. Just as in science you go from the *"known"* to the *"unknown,"* in life you start further back with *"certain postulates."* Scripture gives us three main propositions for dealing with life's problems:

1. <u>Life in this world can only be viewed truly in the light of</u> ***"the next world"***—"Let not your heart be troubled . . . in My Father's house are many mansions." Once more, this is a question of *"perspective."* Here we are in this difficult, troubled world of ours, wondering what is going to happen—stop and look at the bigger picture! Life in this world is temporary and transitory. Life is nothing but a great journey; we are simply *"sojourners"* in this life, pilgrims and strangers, travelers (Heb 13:14). Furthermore, life is also full of uncertainty, accidents, trials and tribulations—life is a kind of existence in which you never know what is going to happen next. No security can be obtained (nor is it promised) in this life—therefore, *to live for this life only, and to rely upon it or anything in it, is to deliberately court disappointment;* that is why the twentieth century was such an unhappy one. "Here we have no continuing city" (Heb 13:14). The Bible tells us "why" this is the case—it is all because of *"sin"*—sin makes us try to be independent of God; we think we can get along without Him. It is as if we are saying, "if only we could abolish death (and science is trying hard to do so), then we could make a perfect world!" (63–69)

2. <u>The most important thing for us to concentrate on is</u> ***"the life of the soul"***—We live in a world that is passing away, but we don't know when it will end. The Bible tells us there is something in us that is bigger than life in this world—it is imperishable—and it is called

"the soul." The soul is what matters—not the external life, but the *"inner life."* Jesus said, "Fear not them which kill the body, but are not able to kill the soul" (Mt 10:28). Therefore, concentrate on the life of the soul. Remember the story of the rich, young ruler—God said to Him, "Thou fool, this night *thy soul* shall be required of thee" (Lk 12:19–20). It is the soul that matters.

3. <u>The main function and purpose of life in this world is to prepare us for **"the next life"**</u>—That does not mean that we turn our back on this world, or that we despise life here, or that you resign yourself to life in a monastery—no, we are to live life to the maximum, but never forgetting that the main object of life in this world is to prepare us for "the next life." That is the whole philosophy of the Bible. We are "looking for a city whose builder and maker is God"—we are "strangers and pilgrims in this life" (Heb 11:10, 13). Look at how our Lord lived His life—"Who for the joy set before Him endured the cross" (Heb 12:2). His focus was upon eternity. The same can be said for the Apostle Paul—"For me to live is Christ" (Phil 1:21). Jesus said, "I will come again and receive you to Myself, that where I am, you may be also." "Believe in Me." *"Your soul" is the one thing that matters—that is the secret of a quiet heart.* Jesus said, "What will it profit a man if he gains the whole world, and loses his own soul?" (Mt 16:26). Jesus has gone to prepare a place for you, so be certain of your eternal inheritance (Jn 14:2). Remember Paul's words, "Nothing can separate you from the love of God that is found in Christ Jesus" (Rom 8:38–39). (69–75)

A day is coming when we will "leave this world" and everything else behind, so it is only my soul, my eternal destiny, my relationship to God that matters. The gospel is not about reforming people or making this world a better place, it is about giving people a "new birth," a new life, a new beginning. The effect of the gospel is to enable us to see the nature of life in this world, and to bring us to see that what really matters for us is our soul. There is a kingdom of darkness and a kingdom of light, and these two kingdoms are here together in this world—ultimately these two kingdoms will meet, and then there will be an end (at the Second Coming). Everything that is evil and belongs to Satan and his kingdom will be destroyed, and God will make a "new heaven and a new earth, wherein dwelleth righteousness" (2 Pet 3:13).

If you want rest and peace and a quiet heart in the midst of the darkness, confusion and uncertainty of this world, you will not find it by trusting in ideas on the reformation of this world, for all these things are being falsified before your eyes—you will only find peace in the assurance that "nothing" will ever separate you from the love of God or His presence in your life. The Christian message is not about international relations or world peace—it is about *"knowing God and enjoying Him for all eternity!"* Again, this does not mean that we are indifferent to the world—as Christians we should be concerned about the world—but rather than fixing our attention upon the world and this life, we need to focus on knowing Christ and those things that are eternal (Col 3:1–4). The Lord Jesus said, *"Believe in Me;"* that is, "believe in what I am going to do; take the right view of life as a pilgrimage to eternity; believe that I am coming back to receive you to Myself; believe this, and whatever may happen, know that your eternity is safe!" And till He returns, "continue to carry out the work He has called us to do." (77–135)

When "Hudson Taylor" died, they found in his Bible a piece of paper he used as a kind of bookmark. As he read his Bible, he moved this piece of paper every day. On it was written this prayer—

> *Lord Jesus make Thyself to me,*
> *A living bright reality,*
> *More present to faith's vision keen*
> *Than any outward object seen;*
> *More near, more intimately nigh*
> *Than e'en the sweetest earthly tie.*

CHAPTER 8

A summary of the book . . .

"SOUL-DEPTHS AND SOUL-HEIGHTS"
by Octavius Winslow (1808–1878)

Octavius Winslow spoke at the opening of Spurgeon's Tabernacle in 1861—This study of his on PSALM 130 opens with the *"depths,"* and closes with the *"heights"*—it reflects the depths and heights of every believer's history. Psalm 130 is perhaps the best known of all the Penitential Psalms. It contains the ardent prayer of a man who is distressed by a sense of God's anger against sin—by an earnest, penitent turning to God, he longs for the forgiveness of his iniquities. The Christian life is tortuous and chequered in its course—today it is a depth; tomorrow a height. This experience is common to all saints. Sink as the gracious soul may, it ever finds the Rock of Ages beneath, upon which faith firmly and securely stands. Whatever be the depressions of the believer, it is important to keep in mind his real standing before God—there is not an angel in heaven so dear to God as the accepted believer in Christ (remember, He "died" for the believer!), though earth is still his abode, and a body of sin his dwelling.

A practical lesson grows out of this truth—know "your standing" in the sight of God. The measure of our assured interest in Christ, will be the measure of our faith in Christ—this is the true definition of "assurance" (Heb 11:1). Assurance comes from *truly believing* that Christ is your Savior; conversely, the *object* of our salvation is not our faith, but CHRIST. Faith is but the instrument by which we receive Christ as a sinner. The eye of faith, looking unto Jesus, gradually becomes stronger. All the sinner's merit and worthiness, is centered in Christ—God's "unspeakable gift" of grace will awaken in the soul the assured and grateful acknowledgment, "He loved ME and gave Himself for ME!" How can it be!? Octavius Winslow enumerates some of the *"soul-depths"* into which many of God's people are frequently plunged, in which grace sustains, and out of which love delivers them—

1. <u>Existence and power of "indwelling sin"</u>—While the Holy Spirit renews the soul, He never entirely uproots and slays the principle and root of sin in the regenerate; the root, or principle of original sin remains deeply and firmly embedded in the soil of the soul, springing up and yielding its baneful fruit, demanding incessant mortification, and will remain so until death sets the spirit free. The old inhabitant still resides in the new creature, inflicting upon the soul many a deep and grievous wounds. It is the existence of this fact that constitutes a source of so much soul-distress to the regenerate. When the Holy Spirit inserts the plough more deeply into the corrupt soil of the heart, revealing the hidden, deep-seated evil, the believer cries from out of the depths of his corruption, *"O wretched man that I am! Who will set me free from the body of this death?"* (Rom 7:24). "O Lord, out of the depths of my deep corruption I cry unto You!" (Ps 130:1). "My soul is plunged into great and sore troubles by reason of indwelling sin—pride, self-righteousness, carnality, covetousness, worldliness—working powerfully and deceitfully in my heart, and bringing my soul into great depths of sorrow." *When we first found the Savior, we imagined that the warfare had at last ceased,* that the victory was won, and that, henceforth, our Christian course would be a continuous triumph over every foe, our path to heaven smooth and cloudless. Our real growth in grace is the measure of our growing acquaintance with ourselves. A deeper knowledge of our sinfulness,

and a more intimate acquaintance with the subterfuges of our own heart, has changed our song of triumph into a wail of despair . . . and our cry of agony ascends to God. Don't be surprised at this *"strange thing"* that has happened to you—such *"depths"* have all saints; all are brought into the region of their own heart, where their holiest lessons are learned. Therefore, let not the conflict of indwelling sin plunge you into despair; rather accept it as an unmistakable evidence of your possession of the divine nature, who's existence has revealed the antagonism of the latent evil of your heart.

2. <u>The outbreaks of "indwelling sin"</u>—Were there no indwelling *root* of sin, there would be no outgrowing *fruit* of sin. But where is the true believer who has fully uprooted the indwelling principle of evil? He does not exist. Listen to the language of David: "Wash me thoroughly from my iniquity, and cleanse me from my sin. For I acknowledge my transgressions and my sin is ever before me" (Ps 51:2–3). Listen to Job: "I abhor myself, and repent in dust and ashes" (Job 42:6). Listen to Peter: "Depart from me; for I am a sinful man, O Lord." Listen to Paul: "Sinners, of whom I am chief." Peter went out and wept bitterly—his penitence is a type of all true penitents. Sooner or later God's Spirit calls the wanderer to his feet with the confession and prayer: "O Lord, pardon my iniquity; for it is great. Heal me, O Lord, and I shall be healed." Every heart that knows its own plague will cry just such a confession.

3. <u>Mental darkness and despondency</u>—There are also "depths" of mental darkness and despondency into which gracious souls fall. While the reality of their conversion is undoubted by all but themselves, they seem to have settled down into a spiritual state of despondency and despair in which all evidence is ignored, all comfort refused, and all hope extinguished. Religious delusion is the great characteristic of souls in a melancholy state of *"morbid religiousness"*—in a number of cases the cause is purely physical; an unhealthy condition of any one vital organ may so powerfully act upon the mind and the soul, that it shades the brightest hopes and prospects. Depressed child

of God, be of good cheer—the Lord loves you even in the darkest seasons of life . . . He "died" for you when you were at enmity with Him (Rom 5:8) . . . He knows your frame, and remembers that you are but dust. Your present mental cloud-veil cannot extinguish the heavenly light within you, touch your spiritual life, or separate you from His love. With tenderness and gentleness Jesus deals with the *"sick one whom He loves"*—though you be on the very verge of despair and self-destruction, Jesus is there patiently forbearing and abounding in sympathy and lovingkindness. (vii-11)

The Holy Spirit works "in the soul" the work that Christ did "for the soul"—It was always God's purpose, by the exercise of His grace, to accomplish our entire salvation in Christ; while giving us the responsibility to *"diligently make our calling and election sure;"* thus we are to "work out our salvation with fear and trembling" (Phil 2:12), encouraged by the assurance that "God is also at work in us, to will and to do of His good pleasure" (Phil 2:13). Therefore, to look *"within ourselves"* for spiritual light, joy and hope, is ludicrous—it is to *"Christ"* we are to look; the Author and Perfecter of our faith (Heb 12:2). He is our Redeemer. So we are to turn away from ourselves to Jesus. Jesus said, "Look unto Me, all the earth, and be saved; for I am God, and there is none else . . . I am the door . . . I am the bread of life." Behold the Lamb . . . contemplate His Person . . . study His work . . . feast upon His Word . . . let Him be all in all to your soul.

In many cases "spiritual despondency" may be traced to the idea, incessantly haunting the mind, of having committed the "unpardonable sin." This fear is completely groundless. Holy fear and trembling which the apprehension creates, is of itself a sufficient contradiction of such a thing. Besides, the "unpardonable sin" was that of ascribing to the agency of Satan the divine power by which He wrought His wonderful miracles—note the context. *There are "depths" in Satan's temptations of various degrees; some deeper and darker than others.* Some of the Lord's people are tempted to doubt, and almost deny the work of grace in their soul. Some are tempted to limit the power and willingness of Christ to save them; others are tempted to deny the truth of God's Word, the veracity of His character, and a future life beyond the grave. These temptations are "common to man" (1 Cor 10:13). The Lord will not leave you to perish in these wiles, but will raise you above the depths.

Deep and billowy and dark are often the waters through which the saints wade to glory. The Lord "tries the righteous," and He tries them to make them yet more righteous. For *David* it was in the cave of Adullam . . . for *Daniel* it was in the lion's den . . . for *Joseph* it was in a pit . . . for *Paul* it was in the jail at Philippi . . . for *John* it was in exile on the island of Patmos—it was in these difficult settings where these men were brought into the richest teaching, and the most blessed experiences of their lives. Shall we plead exemption from these depths of trial and sorrow? Remember the words of our Lord, "Those whom I love I rebuke and chasten" (Heb 12:6). The loss that threatens your resources . . . the bereavement that breaks your heart . . . the trial that saddens your spirit . . . the temptation that assails your faith is the "*furnace of affliction*" to prove you. The Lord said, "When you pass through the waters, I will be with thee." Welcome the sanctified discipline of trial and sorrow that *proves* your conversion real. Lord, if your furnace thus refines, and your knife thus prunes—render your gold more pure, and your branch more fruitful.

Remember, just as there are "depths," so there are "deliverances;" and in God's own time those deliverances will come. "Cast now away therefore your confidence, which has great recompense of reward." Did the Lord ever leave His Son to flounder and sink and perish in His depths? Never! *He invariably sends help from above,* takes them in His arms, and gently draws them out of their "many waters," just as He lifted up *Joseph* from the pit, and *Daniel* from the lion's den, and *Jeremiah* from the dungeon. Cheer up then, you sinking, desponding one! Behold the "rainbow" in the clouds—the symbol and pledge of God's covenant faithfulness to make good on His promises, and deliver you out of all your trouble. Let me add a comment regarding Winslow at this point—admittedly his work can be a difficult read at times, so carefully and prayerfully work your way through his material, re-reading sections if necessary.

> *Out of the depths I cry,*
> *Oppressed with grief and sin;*
> *O gracious Lord, draw nigh,*
> *Complete Thy work within.*
> *O listen to Thy suppliant's voice,*
> *And let my broken bones rejoice.* (11–20)

Seasons of soul-depths are ever seasons of "heart-prayer" in the Christian's experience. At no point does the *"divine life"* of the believer so strongly vindicate its nature as then. This was the case here in Psalm 130—*"Out of the depths have I cried unto Thee, O Lord."* Communion with God is the outbreathing of the quickened soul, and no condition can stifle it. Its potency is learned to a great extent when faith is tried, the heart is overwhelmed, and the soul is plunged into the depths. The arrow of prayer springs from the bow of faith, and winged by the power of the Spirit—as such, it overcomes every obstacle. The intensity of prayer raises with the agony of one's spirit; it gathers strength with the anguish of the soul—read Jonah. There is no *"depth"* so profound, no darkness so dense, no need so pressing, no perplexity so great, but from it you may cry unto the Lord, and He will incline His ear. Cries out of depths of soul-distress have a peculiar eloquence and an irresistible success with God. *"My soul hangeth upon God"* (Ps 63:9).

"My soul hangeth upon God" (Ps 63:9)—Let's look for a moment at the *"object"* upon which the believing, sinking soul hangs—it is upon "deity." Some are hanging upon self . . . some upon wealth . . . some upon intellectual powers . . . some upon bodily strength . . . some upon their own self-righteousness. But the believing soul, though a desponding and sinking soul, hangs upon God. "Whom have I in heaven but Thee? There is none upon earth that I desire beside Thee." This is the *"support"* of every gracious soul. Sin-burdened soul, sinking into depths of guilt and despair, come, hang in faith upon this divine, this most sure nail. "When I cannot think of Jesus," said a sick one, "Jesus is thinking of me." The tried and desponding soul can never sink below the everlasting arms of God. God is frequently inclined to permit His children to descend into great "depths" of spiritual and mental conflict, and even temporal need, that He might display His love and power in stooping to their necessity. "I was brought low, and He helped me." No difficulty is too great or too severe to take to Jesus—our strong refuge is *"prayer;"* remember, God's mercy in Christ Jesus is infinite. Sunk though you are in sin and guilt, you have not sunk below the depths of God's love and grace. The prodigal had wandered far from his father, yet, when he came to himself he exclaimed, "I will arise and go to my father"—your heavenly Father waits to enfold you to His loving and forgiving heart! (21–27)

> *Depth of mercy! can there be*
> *Mercy still reserved for me?*
> *Can my God His wrath forbear*
> *Me, the chief of sinners, spare?*
> *I have long withstood His grace,*
> *Long provoked Him to His face;*
> *Would not hearken to His calls,*
> *Grieved Him by a thousand falls.*
> *If I rightly read Thy heart,*
> *If Thou all compassion art,*
> *Now Thine ear in mercy bow,*
> *Pardon and accept me now.*

Prayer is not only necessary when in the "depths," but also to be preserved from them. "Watch and pray" is our Lord's twofold injunction, given amid the most difficult circumstance of His life. We are to pray lest our feet slide and we lose our steadfastness in the faith . . . or else we fall into the depths of Satan, the seductions of the flesh, and the allurements of the world; and plunge into depths of doubt, darkness, and despondency. A true child of God, though he may sadly backslide, and be sorely chastened, cannot finally perish. "I waited patiently for the LORD; and He inclined His ear to me and heard my cry. He brought me up out of a horrible pit, out of the miry clay, and set my feet upon a rock, and established my goings. And He has put a new song in mouth." (27–31)

"If Thou, Lord, shouldest mark iniquities, O Lord, who can stand?" (Ps 130:2)—Some of the most glorious unfoldings of God's character and of Christ's beauty, of divine truth and lessons of the Christian life, are found in those *"soul-depths."* Right and deep views of sin lie at the root of correct and high views of God; and low thoughts of God inevitably engender low perceptions of sin. The Puritan **John Owen** forcibly puts the matter thus: *"The generality of men make light work of sin; and in nothing does it more appear what thoughts they have of God. He that has light thoughts of sin had never great thoughts of God. As men's conceptions are of God, so will they be of sin, which is an opposition to Him. This is the frame of most men; they know little of God; God is not reverenced; sin is but a trifle . . . he who knows not sin's deceit and sinfulness, knows nothing of forgiveness."* It was God's wrath against "sin" that moved Him to crucify His Son! So, in the cross of Christ we see the enormity of man's sin and the greatness of God's love. Hence, you now have nothing to do with your sins—past, present and future—but to "mortify the root and combat vigorously their ascendancy." (31–37)

The believer has need to learn what true and deep "contrition for sin" is—that learning will bring him into a very close knowledge of himself. By the way, the deepest humiliation, the most broken and contrite spirit is not often found in the "high places" where the soul is privileged to walk; it is predominantly found in "low places"—in the deep valleys—where we learn the force of David's prayer: "O Lord, pardon my iniquity, for it is great;" and of Job's acknowledgement: "I abhor myself, and repent in dust and ashes." What depth of meaning then does the psalmist's prayer contain—"If Thou, Lord, should mark iniquities—the depravity of my nature, the sinfulness of my heart, my thoughts and imaginations, my words and actions, my covetousness, worldliness, and carnality—O Lord, how could I stand?" (Ps 130). We must "cultivate" a holy contrition for sin—godly sorrow and holy contrition will preserve your heart pure and tender. Let not one evening pass over your head without examining how your spiritual account stands. "How have I offended Thee, O God? How have I neglected to perform my duties? How have I injured someone with my words? How have I reflected upon that which is most evil?" Let us lament over our transgressions from our inmost souls, and labor to make up tomorrow what we may have lost today. The effect of this holy scrutiny will be humble contrition; though it be a bitter experience, it will yield a sweet fruit. *"Blessed are those who weep and mourn their willful wanderings and spiritual lapses."*

A humble acknowledgment of sin is a consequence of contrition for sin—"I acknowledged my sin to Thee, and my iniquity I did not hide; I said, I will confess my transgressions to the Lord" (Ps 32:5). Why is it that so many of God's saints travel all their days with their heads bowed low? Why do so few attain to the high standard of an "assured interest" in Christ? Why do so many walk in the spirit of legal bondage, know little of their pardon and acceptance? May it not, to a great degree, be traced to their lax habit of "confession of sin to God"? It is because they go day by day, and week by week, bearing the burden of conscious sin and uncleansed guilt. Oh, the great secret of a pure, holy, and happy walk is in living close by God's confessional. This was David's testimony: "When I kept silent about my sin, my body wasted away through my groanings all day long. For day and night Thy hand was heavy upon me; my vitality was drained away as with the fever-heat of summer. I acknowledged my sin to Thee, and my iniquity I did not hide. I said, I will confess my transgressions to the Lord; and Thou didst forgive the guilt of my sin" (Ps 32: 3–5). The gospel reveals Christ as the *"Great Sin-Bearer"* of the sinner—we must see Him "wounded for our transgressions, and bruised for our iniquities," and made a "sin-offering for us"—"He made Him who knew no sin to be sin for us, that we might be made the righteousness of God in Him" (2 Cor 5:21). Let faith rest upon divine word—"Jesus is my Substitute . . . Jesus stood in my place . . . Jesus bore my sins . . . Jesus suffered all and paid my entire debt . . . *herein I rest.*" "There is therefore now no condemnation to those who are in Christ Jesus" (Rom 8:1). (38–46)

"What God is like Thee, that pardons iniquity? There is forgiveness with Thee"—the divine pardon of sin is God's most gracious act. God satisfies the matter of justice Himself, and bears the entire cost of the plan—a cost which the infinite resources of Deity alone could meet. "For as by one man's disobedience many were made sinners, so by the obedience of one shall many be made righteous." And now the chief of sinners may approach boldly the throne of grace and obtain mercy, because of the merits of Christ. "God so loved the world, that He gave His only begotten Son"—how vast the cost! How immeasurable the sacrifice! It cost God the surrender of His own dear Son, sent into the world poor, despised, insulted, and subjected to indescribable tortures of the cross—*"Who is a God like Thee?"* It cost Him the sacrifice of Himself—His last drop of blood; His last breath of life—to purchase for us divine forgiveness. Oh, the redeeming, dying love of Christ, which passes knowledge! *"How can it be that Thou my God shouldst die for me?"* (47–51)

The "moral reformation of our criminals" has long been a perplexing problem, baffling the most astute philosopher and the most benevolent philanthropist—the plan is still an experiment, and in the vast majority of cases when the hardened criminal is pardoned, he relapses more deeply into crime. So pardon has, in the vast majority of cases, not only failed to weaken the force of his depravity, but has proved a stimulus to a bolder conception and a more awful commission of crime. Let us turn to the "divine forgiveness of the sinner"—never has God regretted the extension of His forgiveness to the vilest sinner, because *the grace of pardon conquers him!* The softening, melting, sanctifying influence of the cross has dissolved the congestive power of sin (so to speak) in the heart, which now beats more freely and throbs more intensely with life and love to God, to Christ and holiness. The grace of pardon not only has cancelled the guilt, but it has conquered the power of sin; it has slain the tyrant. "Though your sins be as scarlet, they shall be as white as snow" (Is 1:18). "Who is a God like unto Thee, that pardons iniquity, transgression, and sin?" God's forgiveness of sin furnishes the believer with the most persuasive motive to live a pure, a holy, and a godly life.

The hardest work of man is to "forgive and forget" a wrong done to him—Jesus said, "Who can have tasted the sweetness of God's forgiving love, the 'ten thousand talents' all forgiven, and then go his way and refuse to forgive the 'one hundred pence' owed to him?" Jesus also said, "If your enemy is hungry, feed him . . . if he is thirsty, give him drink."

If one claims to be a disciple of the loving, forgiving Savior, we have a right to enquire, *"Where is your badge?"*—if the response be, "What badge?" we simply reply in the words of the Lord Himself: "By this shall all men know that you are my disciples, if you have love one for another" (Jn 13:34). Let us cease to cherish in our hearts an unforgiving, uncharitable, unforgetful spirit. "Father, forgive us our trespasses as we forgive them that trespass against us" (Mt 6:12). (52–63)

> *Forgive and forget—it is better*
> *To fling every feeling aside,*
> *Than to allow the deep cankering fetter*
> *Of revenge in thy breast to abide.*
> *For the step through life's path shall be lighter,*
> *When the load from the bosom is cast;*
> *And the sky that's above thee be brighter,*
> *When the cloud of displeasure is past.*
> *Though thy spirit swell high with emotion*
> *To give back an injustice again,*
> *Let it sink in oblivion's ocean;*
> *For remembrance increases the pain.*
> *And why should we linger in sorrow,*
> *When its shadow is passing away,*
> *Or seek to encounter tomorrow*
> *the blast that o'erswept us today?*

Sin is a powerful tyrant—Long after its overthrow it still exists in the regenerate a dethroned despot; its sting extracted and its venom destroyed, but still retaining sufficient power to wound and distress the soul. Despoiled of its empire, like the Canaanites of old, it is yet domiciled in the land, making perpetual invasions and assaults on the camp of Israel; demanding on their part sleepless vigilance and perpetual conflict. Thus, the work of sin-mortification and world-crucifixion must go on, that, by a gradual process of defeat, the Canaanites, like the ones of old, are driven out *"little by little,"* until the last enemy is destroyed. It is a blessed height of the soul when the believer can look down upon his old sins and habits, lying mortally wounded at his feet, dying daily to their power and reign. There is no real happiness this side of heaven apart from *"personal holiness."* My soul! let your one and supreme aim be, a loftier standard of personal holiness and unreserved consecration to God. Lord, what is lacking in my grace supply . . . what is weak in my faith, strengthen . . . what is low in my Christian life, raise . . . what is languid and ready to die, quicken and revive, that I may stand complete in all the will of God.

Sin will remain in the regenerate to the last of life, but a "full redemption" awaits him—The moment the Christian is released from the body, he is in a state of perfect holiness as it regards the *soul;* but the full redemption of the *body* is yet to come. "We ourselves groan within ourselves, waiting for the redemption of our body" (Rom 8:23). The time is coming when we shall no longer be chained to a corrupt body, a living corpse, tainted with sin, assailed by disease, suffering, and death. A glorious resurrection awaits us. It will be a "spiritual body" (yet material), a body free from the infirmities of the flesh, and the indwelling presence of sin. (116–121)

The true element of the gospel is "holy joy"—"Behold, I bring you good tidings of *great joy* . . . a Savior has been born!" Think of it—we are SAVED!!! When the soul is "born again," it emerges from its lower life, and ascends into a new divine heavenly life—a life from God and for God; a life in Christ, by Christ, and with Christ. Therefore writes Paul, "For me to live is Christ!" (Phil 1:21). "Old things have passed away; all things become new" (2 Cor 5:17). Who can describe the sacredness and preciousness of this walk? God is love, and to enjoy and dwell in God's love, is to walk upon the highest place on earth, and in closest proximity to heaven. How elevating is this walk! It lifts us above the dark clouds of trial and sorrow that floats beneath, into a high and luminous atmosphere of God's love. Be not satisfied with walking in low shaded places, but climb in faith these high places. **Prayer** *raises the believer into the highest and holiest atmosphere.* Well rewarded is he for his holy toil, who has climbed these sacred stairs, laden with sin, weary with care, pressed with neediness, crushed with sorrow. Ascend, then, this sacred mount . . . walk with God upon these high places . . . cheered and strengthened by Jesus' words: "Whatever you ask the Father in My name, He will give it to you . . . *and your joy will be made full!"*

Remember, whom the Lord loves "He chastens" (Heb 12:6)—It is impossible to interpret the dark and mysterious dispensations of God's providence accurately except in the light of His love. The believer has never known how deeply God loves him until God has afflicted him. It is thus that sanctified sorrows yield to the believer the richest fruit. Wounded in heart, weary in spirit, and weakened in trial, he walks upon his high places of difficulty and danger warily, humbly, and prayerfully. As an old divine remarks: *"The physician attacks the disease, not the patient; his object is to cure the one he causes to suffer."* It is thus that God, whose mercy is infinite, chastises us only to bring us into the way of salvation or to confirm our course in it. Therefore, since you do not become angry with your physician when he sets your broken bones, don't murmur against the Lord, who wounds only for your good. Thus, ascend from the depths of darkness and doubt, of coldness and unbelief, and walk in the *"high places"* of filial fellowship with God. (122–134)

CHAPTER 9

A summary of the book...

"THE SOUL'S CONFLICT"
by Richard Sibbes (1577–1635)

Satan labors to unsettle and disquiet God's children—since he cannot hinder their estate, he will *"trouble their peace."* Of all Christians, Satan is the most successful against "discontented" people; he hammers all his dark plots in their brains. When Joshua was downcast at Israel's turning their backs before their enemies, God reproved him saying, *"Get up, Joshua, why is your face to the ground?"* (Josh 7:10). Once we are "in Christ," we should settle the question of who we are in Him—yet a guilty conscience will be full of objections, and God will not speak peace unto it until it be *humbled*. God will let his best children know what it is to be too bold with sin, as we see in *David and Peter—they felt no peace till they had renewed their repentance*. One of the main things that hinders Christians from "rejoicing" is not being diligent of making their *"calling sure."* We are not to hearken to our own fears and doubts, or to the suggestions of the enemy—but to the Word, and our own consciences enlightened by the Spirit. It is of paramount importance that Christians study to corroborate who they are in Christ. *When the waters of sanctification are troubled and muddy, let us run to the witness of the cross*—it is there where you can untie the knots that keep you from experiencing the mercy of God. Since Sibbes' books are a somewhat difficult archaic read and require careful thought, ponder his writings in a slow, attentive, reflective manner.

A "growing" Christian is always a comfortable Christian—Growing Christians go on to add grace to grace, and the oil of grace brings forth the oil of gladness. Some degree of comfort follows every good action—as heat issues forth from fire. When Christians forget what a *gracious and merciful covenant* they live under, their comfort is hindered.

The psalms, as it were, are the anatomy of a holy man—In the psalms holy men speak to God and their own hearts. In Psalm 42 we have the passionate words of a man with a broken and troubled spirit—"Why are you cast down, O my soul?" David was a banished man because of Saul's persecution. His soul was nearly overwhelmed, yet he recovers himself a little to look up to God for comfort and peace. All of the greatest saints agree that we must pass through *"many afflictions"* before we enter heaven (Acts 14:22); yet according to the diversity of issues and circumstances, there is a different cup measured to every one of us. **Spurgeon** wrote, *"Never was a poor creature distressed as I am."* Regardless of your stature within Christendom, all of us are made of flesh and blood, subject to the same passions, made of the same mould, and subject to the same impressions from without as other men. By reason of the advancement of the most godly in holiness, and their new disposition, they are more sensible in a peculiar manner to those troubles that touch upon their blessed condition of being "in Christ."

God Himself sometimes "withdraws" the beams of His countenance from His children, whereupon the soul even of the strongest Christian is *disquieted;* and God Himself seems to be an enemy to them; perhaps his conscience tells him that God hath a just quarrel against him. There were some ingredients of this divine temptation (as is sometimes called) in David, when God appeared to him as an enemy. Even the Son of God Himself complained in all His torments—"My God, my God, why hast Thou forsaken Me?" (Mt 27:46).

If we look down to the "inferior cause," the soul is often cast down by "Satan"—Being a cursed spirit, he is full of disquiet, carrying hell about in himself, whereupon all that he labors for is to cast down and disquiet others. By his envy and subtlety we were driven out of Paradise in the beginning; and now he envies us the "paradise of a good conscience." When Satan sees a man strongly and comfortably walking with God, he cannot endure that a creature of lower rank than himself should enjoy such happiness. "Mine enemies reproach me," wrote David—there is nothing the nature of man is more impatient of than of the reproaches of a malicious heart and a slandering tongue. *The goal of the devil is to shake the godly man's faith and confidence in God; just as Satan labored to place a divide between Christ and His Father*—"If Thou art the Son of God, command that these stones be turned into bread" (Mt 2:4). By the way, God is nearest to His children when He seems farthest off—God is with them and in them. How was David affected by the reproachful words? Their words were like *"swords"* that pierced him deeply (Ps 42:10). The policy of "popish tyrants" was to keep the people in darkness and keep them *"fearful,"* that they might better rule them for their own ends.

Many Christians think they have "no grace" when they don't feel any—Our *"feelings"* are not fit to judge our state. How many imagine their "failings" to be *"fallings,"* and their "fallings" to be "falling away," and every sin against conscience to be the sin against the Holy Spirit. *Satan enlarges the fancy, to think things bigger than they really are*—Satan also tries to get Christians to see "great sins" as little, and "little sins" as none. Some also think they have *"no grace"* because they have not grown much as a Christian—as such, they focus more on "what they don't have" than "what they do have." Men may be rich, though they are not millionaires or emperors.

If we "neglect" to grow in holiness, the soul will never be soundly quiet, because it will be prone to question the truth of justification; and it is as proper for sin to raise doubts and fears in the conscience, as for rotten flesh and wood to breed worms. *Sin causes storms within and* *without*, and where there is not a pure conscience, there is not a pacified conscience. A conscience guilty of many neglects and of allowing itself to sin, God will suffer us to have *"painful wounds"* that we might experience the preciousness of His balm.

When men rely on outward things for their comfort, their spirit will be "unsettled and disquiet." We are not to build our comfort upon things that have no firm foundation. It is the good desire of the wise man to desire that God remove from us vanity and lies (Prv 30), because such things promise a contentment they cannot yield. *The "heart" becomes the nature of the thing it relies on;* therefore, it is no wonder that worldly men are often downcast and disquieted (Ps 39). The *"cause"* of our disquiet is chiefly from ourselves, though Satan will have had a hand in it—we insist on having *"our will,"* or we will be disappointed in God. Thus, in all our troubles we should first look at *"our own hearts,"* and stop the storm there. It was not the "troubled condition" that so disquieted David's soul, but David yielded to the discouragements of the flesh—which is like "the troubled sea that casts up mire and dirt" (Is 57:20). Satan's sin cast him out of Heaven, and by his temptations "man" was cast out of Paradise—ever since he has labored to cast us deeper into *sin and despair;* if God in His mercy does not stop Satan's malice, he would cast us as low as himself, *even to hell itself.*

When believers are discouraged, they are like an "instrument out of tune," like a body out of joint. Additionally, *"discouragement"* (Satan is its author; as the Holy Spirit is of "encouragement") is a great wrong to God as well, and it makes us conceive *"dark thoughts"* about Him, as if He were an enemy; what an injury it is to so gracious a Father. Discouragement also makes a man forgetful of all former blessings, and stops the influence of God's grace in his life. Men never experience true comfort until they give themselves up to God and His will for their lives. As we yield to discouragement, we lose the joy of life and happiness God wants us to experience. One way to raise a dejected soul, is to hold a *"court of reason"* in the heart, wherein the conscience has an office. It is a *great mercy of God* that we judge matters ourselves, and prevent public disgrace; if this not be done, the matter will be dealt with in God's higher court—the long and short of it is this: *if we judge ourselves, God will not judge us.* (1–44)

Sin is a work of darkness—it shuns not only the light of grace, but the light of reason. Satan could not deceive us, unless we are *"willingly deceived."* Willful sinners are blind, because they put out the light of reason; as such, they are deservedly termed *"fools."* Martin Luther used to say, "Men are born with a 'pope' in their belly; they are loath to give an account, although it be to themselves; thus their wills are a kingdom unto themselves." Of all the troubles, the trouble of a *"proud heart"* is the greatest. A *"godly man"* when forced to be alone can talk with his God and himself—one reason is that his heart is a treasury and storehouse of divine truths; conversely, the *"ungodly man"* differs—he cannot endure solitariness because his heart is empty. We should set ourselves to care most for that which God cares for—*our soul*—and never yield our soul to the ways of darkness. A Christian is not subdued until his spirit be subdued; thus Job prevailed over Satan and all his troubles at length. The soul is that which Satan and his minions have the most spite for. Satan works upon our affections and our affections work upon our *"will"*—we can "thank ourselves" for willingly yielding to our own passions.

A godly man "complains to God," but not of God, rather he "complains of himself"—A *"carnal"* man is ready to justify himself and complain of God; he complains of the grievance that lies upon him, but never regards what is amiss within himself. As in all discouragements, a godly man has the most trouble with "his own heart." (45–99)

Sometimes God allows "corruption" to break out in His children, that they may know themselves better, whereupon grace stirs up in the soul a fresh hatred and revenge against it . . . and lets us see the need for not only having our sins pardoned, but also having our sinful natures purged and cleansed. We should labor that the truth of God may be grafted into our hearts, that there may be a sweet agreement between the soul and all things that are spiritual—that we may be changed into His likeness. Nothing in heaven or earth will work out corruption and change our hearts, but the Spirit of Christ clothing divine truths. When corruption rises, pray it down by claiming the promise of the new covenant, that God would circumcise and cleanse your heart. Herein consists of the believer's comfort:

1. <u>Our nature is perfect *"in Christ."*</u>

2. <u>Christ hath satisfied *"divine justice"* for both the sins we commit and our sin nature.</u>

3. <u>Christ will never stop *"working in us"* until we are perfect in purity and holiness.</u>

4. <u>The Spirit of Christ and truth will eventually dry up the spring of our *"corrupt nature."*</u>

Christians must remember when they are much annoyed with their corruptions, that it is not their particular case alone, but the condition of all God's people, lest they be discouraged. When the Christian looks within he is apt to think, *"no man's nature is so vile as mine"*—be careful, Satan often abuses this thinking toward discouragement and desperation. Many think that corruption is greatest when they feel it most; the truth is, the less we see it and lament it, the greater its presence—the more sight, the more hatred . . . *the more hatred of sin, the more love of grace.* Upon every discovery and conflict, corruption loses some ground, and grace gains upon it.

Among all the faculties of the soul that creates the most disquiet in us, is our "imagination"—Our imaginations become the seat of vanity within us, and the greatest vexation to us, because it apprehends a greater happiness in outward good things than there is. Experience shows us that there is not that "good" in those things which we imagine to be, but contrarily, we find much "evil" in them which we never expected; hereupon the soul cannot but be troubled. *The life of many men is almost nothing but a "fancy" that takes up most of their time—how to please their own imagination.* From hence spring *"ambition,"* and the vein of being great in the world; hence comes an unmeasurable desire of abounding in those things which the world esteems highly. There is in us naturally a competition and desire to be equal or above others, and esteemed among men; wherein being crossed or humiliated is the greatest misery that can befall us.

A corrupt desire of "being great" in the opinion of others, creeps into our religion if we live in those places wherein it brings credit or gain—men will sacrifice their very lives for vain glory; it is an evidence that man lives more to opinion and reputation of others, than to conscience. It mars all in religion when we go about heavenly things with earthly affections, and seek not Christ but the world. The reason why imagination works so upon the soul, is because it stirs up the affections answerable to the good in which it apprehends. Things work upon the soul in this order:

1. <u>Some object is presented.</u>

2. <u>It is apprehended by the imagination as good and pleasing, or evil and hurtful.</u>

3. <u>If it is good, the desire is carried to it with delight; if evil it is rejected with distaste.</u>

4. <u>If it is good, the affections stir up the whole man toward what he imagines.</u>

Jacob was as much troubled with the "imagination" of his son's death, as if he had been dead—imagination, though it be an empty thing, yet it hath real effects. *Superstitious* persons are as much troubled for neglecting any voluntary service of man's invention, as if they had offended against the direct commandment of God; thus superstition breeds false fears, and false fears brings true vexation; it transforms God to an idol, imagining Him to be pleased with whatsoever pleases ourselves—our Lord said, "In vain they worship Me" (Mt 15:9). God blasted all devised types of service saying, "Who required these things of you?" (Is 1:12). We should not bring God down to our own imaginations, but raise our imaginations up to God. The way to *cure* this malady in us is this:

1. Labor to bring the imaginations of our souls into the *"obedience of God's truth"*—because the imagination ungoverned is a wild thing (2 Cor 10:5); it injures the work of God in us, and produces an unquiet and unsettled soul. Many good men are in a long dream of misery; therefore it is necessary that God by His Word and Spirit should erect a government in our hearts to captivate this unordered faculty.

2. Present *"real things"* to the soul, the true riches—whatever is in the world are but shadows of things in comparison of those "true realities" which religion afford; and why should we vex ourselves about a vain shadow? (Ps 39:6). When we trust in nothing, we become as nothing.

3. Give your mind *"true objects"* to work upon—consider the greatness and goodness of Almighty God, and His love to us in Christ; consider the joy of heaven and the torments of hell; consider the Day of Judgment; consider the vanity of all earthly things; and consider the uncertainty of our lives. By meditating on these things, the soul will be prepared to have a right understanding of things. A careful reflection of the *"truth"* sets the compass in our soul pointing due north.

4. The well-ordering of this unruly faculty demands our *"nature be changed"*—as men are, so they imagine, as the treasure of the heart is (Mt 7:35); an evil heart cannot think well. When the "law of God" is written in our hearts by the Holy Spirit, the soul is then inclined and made pliable to every good thought—when the heart is once taught of God to love, we love God not only with our hearts but with our mind as well (Mt 22:37); that is, both with our understanding and imagination. Therefore, our chief care should be, that our hearts may be circumcised and purified so, as they may be filled with the love of God.

5. Even when we have been given a new disposition, yet there is still some *"sickness of fancy"* remaining in the best of us, whereby we work trouble to ourselves, and therefore it is necessary we should labor

to restrain and limit our fancy. Idleness is the hour of temptation, wherein Satan joins with our imagination, and sets it about his own work; our imagination needs the bridle of reason. "Whatsoever things are true, honest, just, lovely, of good report—think on these things" (Phil 4:8).

6. Even the wisest and holiest of men, like David and Solomon, *"suffered their souls"* to be led by their fancies, and their hearts to run after their eyes—they betrayed and robbed themselves of much grace and comfort. Therefore Solomon cries out with grief and shame, "Vanity of vanities" (Ecc 1:2). *Fancy will take fire before we be aware.* Little things are seeds of great matters. It would much avail for the well-ordering of our thoughts, to set our souls in order every morning with some gracious meditations. It is a thing to be lamented that a Christian born for heaven, should be taken up with *trifles*, and fill both his head and his heart with vanity and nothing, as all earthly things will one day prove to be.

7. Satan oftentimes by a *"spirit of illusion"* makes worldly things appear bigger to us, and spiritual things less than they are—as a result, our affections are misled. God will not only call us to account of how we lived, but how we believed, disputed, and reasoned. Our care therefore should be to build our profession upon sound grounds, that the gates of hell cannot prevail against. Many men are so vain that they delight in being flattered, so that their imaginations are pleased. It is just with God that those who take liberty in their thoughts should be given up to their own imaginations, to delight in them, and so reap the fruit of their own ways. *God will even allow the best of His people, when they take liberty with their imagination, to become vexed and entangled with their own hearts.* The greatest and hardest work of a Christian is the well-ordering of his heart and mind. There is no law to bind the inner man but the "law of the Spirit of grace." (100–124)

Men whose "wills" are stronger than their "wits," are wedded to their own ways; as such, they are more pleased to hear that which complies with their inclinations, than a harsh truth which crosses them. God fills such men with their own ways—they flatter themselves and are robbed of the "true judgment" of themselves.

What if neither the word of a friend or the rebuke of our own heart will "quiet our soul"—is there any other remedy? Yes, look up to God. The child of God hath something in him above a man; he hath the *Spirit of God* to guide his spirit. God commanded David to "trust" in Him (Ps 42), and at the same time infused strength into his soul to think of God's command and trust in God's power—David's spirit was moved as it was moved by God's Spirit, which inwardly spoke to him to speak to himself. God's children have a principle of life in them from the Spirit of God, by which they command themselves. Our spirits are the Spirit's agents; the Holy Spirit is a divine agent maintaining His right in us. As God hath made man a free agent, so He guides him, and preserves that free manner of working which is agreeable to man's nature. The Spirit of God opens our understandings to see that it is best to trust in God. David was willing to trust in God, but God wrought that will in him; He first makes our will good, and then works by it. Jesus said, "Without Me you can do nothing" (Jn 15:5). Good desires and actions all come from God.

A Christian, when he is beaten out of all other comforts, still has "God" to run to—The wicked beaten out of earthly comforts, is like a ship tossed in the sea without an anchor. The Christian can wrestle and strive with God, and plead with God by His own arguments. Furthermore, there is a sanctified use of all troubles to God's children—first they drive them out of themselves, and then drive them nearer to God. *A man in the state of grace finds every condition draws him nearer to God.* The Holy Spirit stirs up the *"grace of faith"* to its proper function. When the soul sees itself out of order, then it enjoins this duty of trusting in God. The soul that hath had a saving work upon it, will be always impatient until it recovers its former sweetness in God—*after God's Spirit hath once touched the soul, it will never be quiet until it stands pointed God-ward.* "God will keep him in perfect peace whose mind is stayed on Thee" (Is 26:3). Though the soul be overcome by passion for a time, yet if grace hath once truly seasoned it, it will work itself into freedom again—it is proper for the *sea* to rage and cast up dirt; likewise, when dust gets into the *eye*, it will not become quiet again until the dust be wrought out again. (124–143)

The "unwise man" hopes most for the things of this life—he being most deceived who hopes most. In religion, it is far otherwise—here hope is the main supporting grace of the soul, springing from *"faith in the promises of God."* Trust in God is a remedy against all distempers. *"God alone"* is the only fit foundation for the soul to build upon, for the firmer the foundation, the stronger will the building be; conversely, the higher the tree rises, the deeper the root spreads itself below. So it is with *"faith"*—if the foundation is not firm, the soul cannot build itself strongly upon it.

The most casual and disordered things are subject to "divine providence." The most horrible sin the sun ever beheld—the crucifixion of the Lord of life—was guided by a hand of providence to the *"greatest good."* Although man hath a freedom in working, yet even these are guided by an over-ruling power (Prv 21:1). We must know that God's manner of guiding things is without prejudice—He guides them according to the instincts He hath put into them. God is not only the *"cause"* of things and actions, but also the cause of the *cessation* of them—He is the "cause" of why things are not, and why things are. Nothing is so high that it is above His providence; nothing is so bad that God cannot draw good out of it; and nothing is so wisely plotted that God cannot disappoint it. It cannot but bring strong security to the soul, to know that in the intercourse of all events, both good and bad, God hath such a disposing hand. Whatever befalls us serves His eternal purpose. *All sufferings, blessings, ordinances, graces and gifts are ruled by God.* (144–151)

It is important for believers to know that they are "under a providence" that is above their own. Flesh and blood is prone to expostulate with God, and question His dealings, as we see in Gideon, Asaph, Habakkuk, and others—"If the Lord be with us, why then is all this befallen us?" After some struggling between the flesh and the spirit, the conclusion will be, yet however matters go, "God is God to Israel" (Ps 73:1). God's ways often seem to us full of contradictions, because His course is to bring things to pass by *"contrary means."* "God doth all things according to the counsel of His own will." His will is a wise will, and a sovereign will. The only way to truly have *"our will"* is bring it to God's will—we must align our will with God's will; and that we do through prayer. If we could delight in Him, we should have our heart's desire (Ps 37:4). Thus, David yields up himself to God: "Here I am, let the Lord deal with me as seems good unto Him" (2 Sam 15:26). "Not my will, but Thy will be done." "The will of the Lord be done" (Acts 21:14). *Out of our inferior reasons we may desire that God remove the cup;* but when we look to the supreme reason of reasons, the will of God, here we must stoop and kiss the rod, and humble ourselves under His mighty hand.

He that endures anything will endure it quietly, when he knows it is the "will of God," and considers that whatever befalls him comes from *"His good pleasure."* Those that have not inured themselves to the yoke of obedience, will never endure the yoke of suffering—they fume and rage as a wild boar in a net. *The man who establishes his soul on Christ will bear his afflictions; whereas the other rageth as a fool.* Nothing should displease us that pleases God; neither should anything be pleasing to us that displeases Him. We find by experience that when "our wills" are subject to "God's will," that we delight to do what God would have us do, and to be what God would have us be, that then sweet peace presently riseth to the soul (Ps 37).

When we can say, "Lord, if Thou wilt have me poor and disgraced, I am content to be so; if Thou wilt have me serve Thee in this condition I am in, I will gladly do so. *It is enough to me that Thou wouldst have it so. I desire to yield readily, humbly, and cheerfully, to Thy disposing providence."* The wicked say that calamities rule over men, but Christians have a spirit overruling all calamities. God's kingdom comes where His will is being done. None feel the sweet experience of God's providence more than those who are most resolute in their obedience.

We must not consult with flesh, for "self-love" will deprave all our actions, by setting before us corrupt ends. It considers not what is best, but what is advantageous. Where the aims are good, there God delights to reveal His good pleasure. In what measure any lust is favored, in that measure the soul is darkened. Even wise Solomon, whilst he gave way to his lust, had like to have lost his wisdom. *Nature of itself is wild and untamed, and impatient of the "yoke"*—but as beasts that cannot endure the yoke at first . . . after they are inured awhile unto it, they bear it willingly, and carry their work more easily by it; so the *"yoke of obedience"* makes the life regular and quiet. The more *"passion,"* the less discretion; because passion hinders the sight of what is to be done. It clouds the soul, and puts it on to action without advisement. *Where passions are subdued, and the soul purged and cleared, there is nothing to hinder the impression of God's Spirit; the soul is fitted as a clean glass to receive light from above.* Because it is not in man to "know his own ways," we should look unto Christ, the great Counselor of His Church, for counsel and direction . . . suggesting, "this is the way, walk in it." We owe God this respect, to depend upon Him for direction in the particular passages of our lives, in regard that He is our sovereign, and His will is the rule, and we are to be accountable to Him as our Judge. Only God can see through all our circumstances. After prayer and trust follows the "peace of God" (Phil 4:6–7), and a heart void of division. (151–159)

To know the will of God towards us, and our duty towards Him, we must first have a knowledge of the *"promises of God."* We should not call God's love into question—He not only gives us His promise, but hath entered into covenant with us through the blood of Christ; therefore, there should be no place left for doubting. Why should it not satisfy our souls to look upon promises in the word of God? All our misery is either in having a *"false foundation,"* or else *"reckless building"* upon a true foundation; therefore having so strong a ground as God's nature, His providence, His promises, to build upon, the only way for establishing our souls is *"by trust"*—relying firmly on Him. No man can know truth without the Spirit revealing it to the soul—furthermore, supernatural truths must have a supernatural power to apprehend them (1 Cor 2:14). The Spirit of God must likewise subdue the rebellion and malice of our will, so that it may be suitable to divine things; there will follow not only peace in the soul, but joy and delight surpasssing any contentment the world offers. We should labor for a *"single heart"* to trust in God only, to rely upon Christ only, and to make the Scriptures our rule only—either we trust God alone, or not at all.

It is the "office of faith" to quiet our souls in all the necessities of this life; we have continual use of *trust* while we are here. God trains us up this way, by exercising our trust in lesser matters, to fit us for greater. It pleases God to keep us in a state of *"continual dependence"* upon Him . . . who gives us the grace and spirit of faith needed to sustain our souls. Christians should labor their hearts to trust in God, even when no light of comfort appears either from within or without—when the darkness of the night is thickest, then the morning begins to dawn. *In a hopeless estate a Christian will see some "door of hope" opened*, first, because God shows Himself nearest to us, when we stand most in need of Him—He knows our souls best, and our souls know Him best in *"adversity"* (Ps 31:7) . . . second, because our prayers then are *"strong cries"* fervent and frequent—God is sure to hear us at such a time, which pleases Him well, as delighting to hear the voice of His beloved. To encourage us in difficult times, and to help us trust God more, we should often call to mind the *"former experiences"* of God's goodness. God is so good to His children even in this world, that He trains them up by daily renewed experiences of His fatherly care. *The heart is never drawn to some sinful vanity, or frightening trouble, till faith first loseth the sight and estimation of divine things.*

That "faith" may take the better place in the soul and the soul in God, the heart must continually be taught what little worth everything else is—reputation, riches, and pleasures, etc. Our heart being weaned from these things may open itself to God, and embrace things of a higher nature; otherwise baser things will be nearer the soul than faith. The main scope of God's dealing with His children in any danger or affliction, is to *"embitter all other things but Himself"* unto them. God is very jealous of our trust; therefore it behooves us to take notice, not only of the deceitfulness of things, but of the deceitfulness of our hearts in the use of them. Our nature is still apt to think there is some *"secret good"* in the forbidden fruit.

It is not a simple matter to bring God and the soul together "in faith"—God is not only the object, but the *"working cause"* of our trust; for such is our proneness to live by sense and natural reason. Because *"guilt"* still remains upon our souls for our rebellion and unkindness towards God, it makes us afraid to entertain serious thoughts of Him. *"Lord, increase our faith; help us against our unbelieving hearts."* By *"prayer and holy thoughts"* stirred up in us, we shall feel divine strength infused and conveyed into our souls to trust. The decay of a plant, though it appears first in the withering leaves and twigs, yet it arises chiefly from a *decay in the root*—therefore the better part of wisdom is to look to the feeding of the root. We shall find that the *main breaches* of our lives arise either from false principles or doubts, or mindlessness of those that are true—all sin is a turning of the soul from God to some other seeming good; but this proceeds from a former turning of the soul from God by *"distrust."* As *faith* is the first return of the soul to God, so the first degree of departing from God is by *infidelity*.

We are prone to conceive that to "trust in God" is an easy matter, therefore it is needful that we should have a right understanding of this trust, what it is, and how it may be discerned. True trust is willing to be tried and searched, and can say to God as David, "Now, Lord, for what do I wait? My hope is in Thee" (Ps 39:7); and as it is willing to come to trial, so it is able to endure trial, and to hold out in opposition, as appears in David. *A child that believes his father will make him heir, doubts not that he will provide him food and nourishment, and give him breeding suitable to his future condition;* it is a vain pretence to believe that God will give us heaven, and yet leave us to fend for ourselves on the way. Where trust is rightly planted, it gives boldness to the soul in going to God, for it is grounded upon the discovery of *God's love* first. The greatest honor we can do unto God, is to close our eyes to all inferior things here below, and look upon *"His all-sufficiency."* God seldom makes any promises to His children, but that He exercises their trust in *"waiting long"* before that which is promised is realized—as David waited long for a kingdom, and the world for Christ's coming. (160–185)

When God seems "contrary" to our spirits, where shall we find relief? Everything in a sense is "spiritual"—God, our soul, terrors, the devil, and that which the soul fears for the time being is also spiritual; and not only spiritual, but eternal, unless it pleases God at length to break out of the thick cloud, wherewith He covers Himself, and shine upon the soul, as in His own time He will. *When a man sees no comfort from above*, and sees nothing but evidences of God's displeasure; clouds without, and clouds within, nothing but clouds in his condition; *here he hath need of faith to break through it all*. Upon this, the distressed soul is in danger to be set upon a temptation, called the *temptation of blasphemy*, that is, to entertain bitter thoughts against God, and especially against the grace and goodness of God. To this degree of blasphemy God's children never fully fall, yet they may feel the venom of corruption stirring in their hearts, against God and His ways, and this adds greatly to the depth of their affliction. The way out of this predicament is to *"call home the soul, and charge it to trust in God,"* even though He shows Himself an enemy—He doth but put on a mask with a purpose to reveal Himself the more graciously afterward; His manner is to work by *"contraries."* In this condition God lets in *a few beams of light*, whereby the soul casts a longing look upon God, even when He seems to forsake it. There is nothing more comfortable in this condition, than to *fly to Him*.

Sin may be somewhat "sweet" in the committing . . . but it is "bitter" in the reckoning. When Adam had once offended God, *Paradise itself was not Paradise to him;* the presence of God, which was most comfortable before, was now his greatest terror. Sin makes us afraid of that which should be our greatest comfort—the guilty soul becomes embittered, and interprets all that befalls as the messengers of an *"angry God,"* sent in displeasure to take revenge upon it (Ps 38). Writes Sibbes, "There is not the stoutest man breathing, but if God sets his conscience against him, it will pull him down, and lay him flat, and fill him with inward terrors."

Conceive of "God's mercy" as no ordinary mercy—the greater our sins are, the greater the glory of His powerful pardoning mercy, and His powerful grace in healing will appear. God delights to show His greatness in the greatest things—*"God delighteth in mercy"* (Mic 7:18); it pleases Him. David after his heinous sins, cries not for mercy, but for *abundance of mercy,* "according to the multitude of Thy mercies do away with my offences" (Ps 51:1). Though we fall by distrust, we recover by trust. *If we could sin more than He could pardon, then we might have some reason to despair.* God is infinite in lovingkindness and mercy.

Nothing keeps the soul more down than "sins of long continuance"—because corruption of nature hath gotten such strength in them, *men think it impossible to recover themselves;* they think by necessity they must be *damned;* they see themselves so *hardened,* that they cannot repent; they would give the whole world to have their spirits at freedom from this *bondage and fear.* To keep them from utter sinking, let them consider the *"unlimited mercy of God"*—invincible mercy can never be conquered. We must never think the *"door of hope"* is shut against us; there is nothing more injurious to Christ—in whom a breast of mercy for *"humbled sinners"* is always available. Indeed "where sin abounds, grace does much more abound!" (Rom 5:20). Those that have enjoyed long the sweet of sin, may expect the bitterest sorrow and repentance for sin; yet never give place to *thoughts of despair.* We must go to God, with whom all things are possible, to put forth His almighty power, not only in pardoning, but in subduing our iniquities. He that can make a "camel go through the eye of a needle," can make a high conceited man lowly, and a rich man humble. Therefore never question His power, much less His willingness. He entreats us to *"come unto Him."* If Christ will have us pardon our brother *"seventy-seven times,"* can we think that He will enjoin us more, than He will be ready to do Himself.

Where the "work of grace" is begun, sin loses strength by "every new fall;" for hence issues deeper humility, stronger hatred, fresh indignation against ourselves; more experience of the deceitfulness of our hearts; renewed resolutions until sin be brought under. Nothing will make us more ashamed to sin, than thoughts of so free and large a mercy. It will grieve an ingenuous spirit to offend so good a God. This is our comfort—that the *"plea of mercy"* from a broken spirit to a gracious Father, will ever hold good. When we are at the lowest in this world, yet there are these three grounds of comfort still remaining—

1. That we are not yet in the place of the damned, whose estate is unalterable.

2. That while we live there is time and space for recovering of ourselves.

3. That there is grace offered, if we will not shut our hearts against it.

Is it "too late" for you? Has your hour passed? By nature of the very questions, *"your fear"* shows you want to experience His forgiveness and mercy; that in itself is proof that your time of mercy is not yet out; so rather than betraying yourself to your greatest enemy, like the *"Prodigal,"* run to the Father and experience His embrace. God is more willing to entertain us, than we are to cast ourselves upon Him. (185–196)

It is one of Satan's schemes to keep us in a "barren condition," by having us think we have not *"sorrowed sufficiently"* in proportion to our offenses—that we should labor that our sorrow might in some measure answer to the heinousness of our sins. The truth is, we could not grieve sufficiently to satisfy God for our sins—the *"suffering for sin"* was done by His Son on the cross; as such, God delights not in *"sorrow,"* but in making us vessels of *"mercy."* By the way, sensibleness of the *"want of feeling"* shows some degree of the life of grace.

Another thing that disquiets and casts down the soul, is that "inward conflict" between grace and corruption. It is the trouble of troubles to have *"two inhabitants"* so near in one soul, and these two *strive against one another* (Gal 5:17)—the one carrying us upward, higher and higher, till we come to God; the other pulling us lower and lower, further from Him. This cannot but breed a great disquiet, when a Christian does the things he does not want to do, and is hindered from doing that which he wants to do, or is troubled in the performance of it—"O wretched man that I am!" cries Paul (Rom 7:18-24). All is *"stained"* that comes from us, and it is one main end of God's leaving us in this *"conflicting condition."*

Christ will help us in this "fight" until He has made us "like Himself." "Oh," say some, "I find such *"strong inclinations to sin"* in me, and such weakness to resist temptation, that I fear I shall but shame the cause; I shall one day perish by the hand of Satan, strengthening my corruption." Why are you so troubled? *"Trust in God! Be strong in the Lord! The battle is His! The victory ours!"* Charge the soul to make use of the promises, and *rely upon God* for perfecting the good work that He hath begun in thee. *Corruptions are strong, but stronger is He that is "in us," than that corruption that is in us.* When we are weak in our own sense, then we are strong in Him (2 Cor 12:7)—The Lord perfecteth strength in our weakness! Our corruptions are God's enemies as well as ours, and therefore in trusting them to Him, and fighting against them, we may be sure He will take our part against them. God gave the Israelites' enemies into their hands—but, they had to *"fight it out!"* Why wouldn't one fight when he is sure of help and victory? (196–207)

Whatsoever comfort we have in friends, health, or other blessings—it is all conveyed by God, who still remains, though these be taken from us. As for those miseries which our weak nature is subject to, they are also all under Christ; they come and go at His command; they are His messengers, sent for our *good,* and called back again when they have done what they came for. Therefore look not so much upon them as to Him for strength and comfort. Trust Him then with health, wealth, good name, all that Thou hast. It is not in man to take away that from us which God will give us, and keep for us.

God is never nearer than when trouble is nearest; there is not so much as a shadow of change in Him or His love. If God takes us from business by sickness, then we have a time of serving God by patiently submitting to His will. If He means to use our service any further, He will restore our health and strength to do that work He sets us about. In the mean time, the time of sickness is a time of purging from that defilement we gathered in our health, till we come purer out. *Blessed is that sickness that proves the health of the soul.* We are best, for the most part, when we are weakest. Learn from the apostle Paul: He who raises our dead bodies out of the grave, can *raise our diseased bodies* out of the bed of sickness, if He hath a pleasure to serve Himself by us.

In all kinds of troubles, it is not the "ingredients" that God puts into the cup so much that afflicts us, as it is the ingredients of our *"distempered passions"* mingled with them. The sting and core of them all is sin. Labor to keep out *"sin,"* and then let come what will come—we should not be cast down about outward troubles, but about sin. *Outward troubles* drive us nearer to God, but *"sin"* defileth the soul, and drives it further from God. Whatsoever our outward condition be, if our hearts do not condemn us, we may have boldness with God. In any trouble, our care should not be to avoid the trouble, but the sinful miscarriage in and about the trouble. It is a heavy condition to be under the *burden of trouble,* and under the *burden of a guilty conscience,* both at once. (207–213)

Christianity is a matter rather of "grace"—not a matter of "gifts not received." Moses did not have good speaking abilities (Ex 6:12; 7:1–2); nevertheless, he was chosen over Aaron (who spoke well), to speak for God. It is a business more of the *"heart"* than of the tongue. Most of our disquietness in our calling is that we trouble ourselves about God's work. Trust God and be doing, and leave the rest up to Him. *All our sufficiency for every calling is from God.* The only way to quiet the soul is to lay a charge upon it to trust God—unquietness and impatience are symptoms and discoveries of an unbelieving heart.

Those who truly trust in God, labor to back their faith with "sound arguments"—Faith is an understanding grace; it know whom it trusts, and for what, and upon what grounds it trusts. *He believes best, that knows best why he should believe.* God having made man an "understanding creature," guides him by a way suitable to such a condition. Godly men have reasons for their trust; those reasons are divine and spiritual like faith is. *A heavenly soul is never satisfied, until it be as near to God as* *is attainable*. And the nearer a creature comes to God, the more it is emptied of itself, and all self-aims. Our happiness is more in Him, than in ourselves. We seek ourselves most when we deny ourselves most. And the more we labor to advance God, the more we advance our own condition in Him. (213–223)

When we are at our "worst," we still have cause to praise God; when we are at our lowest, yet it is a mercy that we are not consumed; we are never so ill, but it might be worse with us. "Yet will I praise Thee" (Ps 42). "The Lord afflicted me, but He hath not delivered me to death" (Ps 18:18). *In the worst times there is a presence of God with His children*— God limits what the wicked can do to us (Ps 125:3) . . . God is always present and mixing in some comfort . . . God supports the soul with inward strength so that it will not utterly fail . . . he may be cast out of his happy condition, but never out of God's favor . . . no matter how bad things are now, God will deal graciously with us hereafter. "Is any afflicted, let him pray," said James (5:13). "In the day of evil call upon Me," saith the Lord. *Our lives are nothing but a web of interminglings of crosses and blessings*, standings and failings, combat and victory, wants and favors—therefore there should be a perpetual intercourse of *praying and praising* in our hearts.

It is the nature of faith to "antedate blessings," because we have them in the promise. The very hopes of future good, made David praise God for the present. "Faith is the evidence of things not seen—of things hoped for" (Heb 11:1). Therefore, a true believing soul cannot but be a praising soul; hence, we should be praising God as if we already possess that which has been promised. "No good thing will He withhold from those who walk uprightly" (Ps 84:11). Abraham was an old man before he enjoyed his son of promise; Joseph stayed a long time in Egypt before he was exalted. *God defers*, but His deferring is no empty space, wherein no good is done—while the seed lay hidden in the earth, time is not lost, for winter fits for spring, yet the harder the winter, the more hopeful the spring—winter being only a "preparing time." Cheer up thyself, when the morning is darkest, then comes day. A saint of God continues still waiting, though all things seem contrary to what he expects. What can encourage us more to wait than this, that the good we wait for is greater than we are able to conceive! yea, greater than what we desire or even hope for!

Though "praise" be God's due and our duty, yet it is not so easy a matter to praise God—Music is sweet, but the setting of the strings in tune is unpleasing; our souls will not be long in tune, and it is harsh to us to go about setting them in order. *"Praising"* sets all the parts and graces of the soul to work—it especially requires self-denial, from a conscience of our own wants, weaknesses, and unworthiness; it requires a giving up of ourselves and all we have to God. Those who *know* God aright, will honor Him by *trusting* Him, and those who trust Him will honor Him by *praying*; and those who honor Him by praying will honor Him by *praising*—when we return praises to Him, He returns new favors to us. When we neglect the praising of God, we lose the comfort of God's love—it is a spiritual judgment to lose sight of God's favors. The greatest danger of all is being *"ungrateful"* and *"unthankful."*

Blessing will procure blessing—The soul hath never such freedom from sin, as when it is in a thankful frame; for thankfulness issues from a heart truly humbled and emptied of itself, truly loving and rejoicing in God—*"unthankfulness"* to His goodness, melts a godly heart most of all. Though it be our duty to be good stewards of all God has entrusted to us, *"thankfulness"* adds a luster and a grace otherwise not present. It was a good speech of him that said—"If God had made me a nightingale, I would have sung as a nightingale, but God hath made me a man, therefore I will sing forth the praises of God, which is the work of a saint only."

Little favors come from no small love; the godly are more thankful for the least favors, than worldly men for the greatest ones. Our time here on earth is short, therefore let us study real praises—God's blessings are in *"deed,"* therefore let us bless in *"deed"* also (1 Jn 3:18). Thanks in words is good, but in deeds is better; leaves are good, but fruit is better; and of fruit, that which costs us most. Our whole life should speak nothing but thankfulness; every condition and place we are in should be a witness of our thankfulness; this will make the times and places we live in the better for us. When we are monuments of God's mercy, it is fitting that we should be patterns of His praises; we should think *"life"* is given to us to do something better than mere living—our life is not the end of itself, but the praise of the Giver!

It is God's will that we should "call upon Him when we are in trouble," and it is His promise that He will deliver. When trouble stirs up *prayer*... God's answer to them will stir up *praise*. A thankful disposition is a special help in an afflicted condition. If God expects praise from us, surely He will put us into a condition of praise. God's children, wherein their wills are conformable to God's will, are sure to have their requests fulfilled. When God by grace enlarges the will, He intends to give the deed. When *our wills* carry us to that which *God wills* above all, we may well expect He will satisfy our desires. The living God is a living fountain never drawn dry. If there be no end of our praises, there shall be no end of His goodness. By this means (praise) we are sure never to be very miserable.

Praise is a just and due tribute for all "God's blessings"—It is a debt always owing; upon the due discharge of this debt, the soul will find much peace. This duty is a work of the *heart*—"let all that is within me bless His Holy Name" (Ps 103:1). Consider how miserable life would be without all of God's favors, even without His *"common favors"*—our life would be "dark" without these. Furthermore, in all favors think not of them so much, but of God's mercy and lovingkindness in bestowing them. What would we be if God had not been good to us? How many blessings hath God bestowed upon us, that we never even prayed for? and yet we are not ready to praise Him? This shows too much "self-love." *Who are we that God should single us out for the glory of His rich mercy?* These things well pondered should set the greater price upon God's blessings. As God hath thoughts of love to us, so should our thoughts be of *praises to Him*, and of *doing good in our places to others* for His sake. Think on this: Is there any way I may honor God by relieving, comforting, or counseling someone? "I will do good to them, that they together with me, may praise God" (Ps 118; 2 Cor 1:3–4). (223–241)

We need reason upon reason to steel and strengthen the soul against the onset of "contrary reasons." Because our lives are subjected to many miseries, in soul, body, and estate, so God hath many salvations; if we have a thousand troubles, He hath a thousand ways to help. He saves our souls from sin, our bodies from danger, and our estates from trouble—*our sins only slow the current of His mercy.* "All His ways are mercy and peace to a repentant soul that casts itself upon Him." The *"devil"* in trouble presents God to us as a revenging destroyer—the skill of *"faith"* is to present Him as our Savior clothed with salvation. *He that brought us into trouble can easily make a way out of it when He pleaseth.* We must trust in Him, as David doth, and conceive of Him as salvation—He is our deliverer. If we would lift up our hearts and hands to God, He would lift up our countenance. Salvation is God's work of mercy; humbling and casting down is His strange work, whereby He comes to His work of mercy.

God bids us to "draw near to Him, and He will draw near to us"—When we *draw near to Him,* He will delight to show Himself favorable unto us. While we *strive against an unbelieving heart,* He will come in and help us, so fresh light can come in. If any thing help us, it must be God; and if ever He help us, it must be by casting ourselves upon Him—for then He will reach out Himself unto us in the promise of mercy to pardon our sin, and in the promise of grace to sanctify our natures. So we should thus reason—if we sit still under the load of our sin, we shall die; if we put ourselves into the hands of Christ, we shall live. *God delights to show Himself gracious to those that strive to be well persuaded of Him,* concerning His readiness to show mercy to all that look to Him in Christ. God will never shut His bosom against those that fly to Him in humble obedience. We can never conceive of God too graciously. (242–257)

We prove that God is ours to our souls, when we take Him at His offer (that is faith), when we bring nothing but a *sense of our own emptiness* to Him, and an *understanding of His faithfulness* and ability to do us good. The voice of the faithful soul: "I am my beloved's and my beloved is mine." God will be to us whatsoever we make Him by our faith to be. God is our God when we plant all our happiness in Him, when the desires of our souls are towards Him, and we place all our contentment in Him. *We make God our God when we set up a throne for Him in our hearts, where self-love before had sat on the throne;* when the heart is so unloosed from the world, that it is ready to part with anything for God's sake, giving Him the supremacy in our hearts, making Him our trust, our love, our joy, our delight, our fear, our all. When we cleave to Him above all, depending upon Him as our chief good, He brings contentment to the soul.

When we resign ourselves to "His gracious government," to do and suffer what He will, we will offer ourselves and all our spiritual services as sacrifices to Him. When the soul without hypocrisy can say, *"My God,"* we shall be ambitious of doing that which may be well-pleasing to Him. When we know we are a peculiar people, we cannot but be zealous for good works. *The Spirit of God reveals the "divine interests" to those that are His . . . He knows their souls and feeds them with His hidden manna . . . He sanctifies them to keep them from being led away by the error of the wicked.* Religion is nothing else but a "binding of the soul close to God." (257–263)

If I am in a "perplexed condition," His wisdom is mine; if in *great danger,* His power is mine . . . if I lie sighing under the *burden of sin,* His grace is mine . . . if in *any need,* His all-sufficiency is mine. Says Paul, "My God shall supply all your needs!" (Phil 4:19). What is religion but a *"spiritual bond,"* whereby the soul is tied to God as its own. What a wonderful comfort it is to know that God gave Himself up to be *"ours."* When riches and friends and life itself cease to be ours, yet God never loses interest in us, nor we in Him. When we leave this world, and are no longer seen here, yet we have a dwelling place *"forever with God."* God is ours from everlasting in election, to everlasting in glory. David himself said, "Though his flesh see corruption, yet he will be alive in his God still." A godly man has one grand policy to secure him in all dangers, and that is to *"run to His God"*—his tower of offense and defense. God never fails those that *"fly to Him."* His mercy and truth never fails. Oh consider, if we had all and had not God—we have nothing! If we had all the comforts our hearts can desire, yet if God withdrew Himself, what remains but a curse of emptiness! What makes heaven but the *presence* of God? And what makes hell but the *absence* of God? *Let God be in any condition, yet it is comfortable*—by the way, usually we find more of God in trouble, than when we are out of trouble; the comforts of religion never come till all other comforts fail.

It is our chief wisdom to "know God;" our holiness to "love God;" our happiness to "enjoy God." "Our strength may fail, and our heart may fail, but God is our portion forever" (Ps 73:26). Everything teaches us that our happiness is not in anything but God—our search sends us to God! If God be ours, He goes with us forever—when earth no longer holds us, heaven shall. O then let us labor for a larger faith—if we had a thousand times more faith, we would have a thousand times more increase of God's blessings. *God's people are like Israel at the Red Sea, environed with dangers on all sides—what course have we then to take but only to look up and wait for the salvation of our God?* If God is our God, will He suffer anything to befall us for our hurt? Will He lay more upon us than He gives us strength to bear? Will He suffer any wind to blow upon us but for our good? Will a friend suffer his friend to be injured? No. As Scripture says, "He hath bottles for our tears, and our sighs are not hid from Him." Thus, let us prize the favor of so good a God, who though He dwells on high yet regards things so low. A Christian undergoes more troubles and suffering (especially with his own heart) than others do, but what are these compared to his gains? What returns so rich, as trading with God?

Paul said, "I know whom I have trusted, I have tried Him, and He never yet failed me." Every new experience is a new knowledge of God. When God shows Himself as *"contrary to us,"* remembering an act of God's former goodness will enable us to lay claim unto Him. God's concealing of Himself is but a wise discipline for a time. *It is the nature of true faith, to search and pry into every corner, until it discovers afresh the presence of God.* If God should take advantage of our waywardness, what would become of us? The fact is, God is ever ready to respond with mercy—He delights in being merciful. When God appears as a *"stranger"* to us, we need to follow after Him with faith and prayer; He withdraws Himself, that thou shouldst be the more earnest in seeking after Him. *God speaks the sweetest comfort to the heart in the wilderness.* God is the center and resting place of the soul—said David, "He who dwells in the secret place of the most High, shall lodge under the shadow of the Almighty. I will say of the Lord, He is my refuge and my fortress; my God, in whom I trust." (Ps 91:1–2). "My strength and my heart faileth, but God is the strength of my heart, and my portion forever" (Ps 73:26). (263–295)

CHAPTER 10

A summary of the book . . .

"THE DISCIPLINE OF GRACE"

by Jerry Bridges

The pursuit of holiness must be motivated by an ever-increasing understanding of "God's grace;" or its pursuit will become oppressive and joyless. According to Jerry Bridges, two of the great theological giants on this subject are the Puritan theologian *"John Owen,"* and the 19th century Scottish theologian *"George Smeaton."* It has often been said that in the pursuit of holiness we need to "preach the gospel to ourselves every day." We try to *change ourselves* into robust Christlike specimens, but spiritual transformation is primarily the work of the *"Holy Spirit"*— He is the Master Sculptor. The Holy Spirit's work in transforming us is called "sanctification." The pursuit of holiness sounds like "legalism;" however, grace and the personal discipline required to pursue it are not opposed to one another. Because we find it difficult to believe that God would bless us and use us in the midst of a "bad spiritual day," deep down we somehow believe God's blessing on our lives is conditioned upon our *"spiritual performance."* So, when we have had a *bad day*, there is virtually no doubt in our minds that we have *"forfeited God's favor"* for some period of time, at least until the next day. Such thinking reveals that, although we are saved by grace, we earn or forfeit God's blessings in our daily lives by our performance. The truth of the matter is, there is never a day when we can stand before God on our own two feet of performance—not an hour! Even the best works of believers are shot through with sin. It's been said that every time the great 19th century preacher **"Charles Spurgeon"** stepped into the pulpit, he did so with the silent prayer, "God be merciful to me a sinner" (Lk 18:13). Here is an important spiritual principle that sums up these thoughts:

> *Your worst days are never so bad that you are beyond the* **reach** *of God's grace . . . and your best days are never so good that you are beyond the* **need** *of God's grace.*

We are not only SAVED by grace—we also must LIVE by grace—Only a continuous reminder of the "gospel of God's grace through Christ" will keep us from falling into the "good-day/bad-day" kind of thinking. We must *"consciously"* reflect upon the gospel of God's grace to us *every day*, or we will start focusing on "our performance" or start "feeling guilty." When we focus on *"our performance,"* we move away from grace . . . and then we try to relate to God directly on the basis of "our performance." Conversely, it is only the blood of Jesus that will cleanse us from a "guilty conscience." When we apply the gospel to our hearts every day, it frees us to be brutally honest with ourselves and with God—we can call sin exactly what it is, regardless of how ugly or shameful it may be, because we know that Jesus bore that sin in His body on the cross. Some fear this emphasis on the gospel might simply "harden them in their abuse of God's grace"—the truth of the matter is, the last thing those who struggle with sin and failure need, is to have more guilt laid upon them. It is tremendously *liberating* to know that our sins are forgiven, no matter how much we stumble and fall, that God still does not count our sins against us (Rom 4:8). That's the incredible *"good news"* of the gospel.

Preaching the gospel to ourselves EVERY DAY addresses both the "self-righteous Pharisee" and the "guilt-laden sinner" that dwells in our hearts. We must come to terms with the fact that *God's grace is greater* *than all our sins*. Repentance is one of the Christian's highest privileges—a repentant Christian focuses on God's mercy and God's grace, not on his behavior. When we fail—and fail we will!—the Spirit of God will work on us and bring us to the foot of the cross where Jesus carried our failures. By the way, we fail when we shift our attention away from grace and mercy. (7–27)

In the parable of the Pharisee and the Tax Collector (Lk 18:11–12), the Pharisee was self-righteous, and the Tax Collector was painfully aware of his sinfulness—he cried out, "God be merciful to me the sinner." Christians tend toward one of two opposite attitudes—either they have a *relentless sense of guilt*, and frequently dwell on their besetting sins . . . or they have a *degree of self-righteous satisfaction* with their Christian life. Jesus told this parable to those who were confident of their own righteousness. It is interesting to note that Jesus said the Tax Collector went home "justified"—the same Greek word used for "righteous." The two most dominant "character traits" for believers in the New Testament are *love* (the primary Christian character trait) and *humility* (there are nearly 40 references to humility in the NT); after love and humility, there are at least 25 other Christian virtues mentioned. Believers should simultaneously view themselves as *"saints and sinners"*—what we are "in Christ" is saints; what we are "in ourselves" is sinners. Therefore, while we should always rejoice in the righteousness we have in Christ, we should never cease to feel deeply for our own sinfulness and subsequent unworthiness. (29–43)

At salvation, the righteousness of Jesus Christ is imputed or credited to us forever—We are declared righteous solely on the meritorious work of Christ on the cross. Our standing in Christ's righteousness is never affected to any degree by a good-day or a bad-day performance. Unless we learn to *"live by faith in the reality of Christ's righteousness,"* our *perception* of our standing before God will vary depending on our good or bad performance. Faith in Christ and a reliance on ourselves, even to the smallest degree, are mutually exclusive. Because we have a tendency to vacillate in our faith due to our frequent failures and sins, we feel like we are under condemnation . . . that God is not for us, but is actually against us . . . and we think He is the one who is bringing charges against us—so crafty is the work of Satan in our minds and hearts! Remember, Satan is the "accuser of the brethren!" (Rev 12:10; Rom 8:33). Scripture says, "there is *no condemnation* to those who are in Christ Jesus" (Rom 8:1). Therefore, at such times we must *"preach the gospel"* to ourselves; that is, we must *"affirm"* what God has declared to be true about our justification (righteousness) in Christ. Scripture also tells us that "God is for us!" (Rm 8:31). So when our conscience tries to defeat us with guilt, we must bring the verdict of our conscience into line with the verdict of Heaven—by faith we must remind ourselves that our guilt has been borne by Christ.

The death of Christ secured for us not only "freedom from the penalty of sin," but also deliverance from the "dominion of sin" in our lives. Romans 6:1–14 is the primary passage in Scripture that deals with "freedom from the dominion of sin"—verse 2 says, *"we died to sin"*—the aorist tense indicates this is a completed action that occurred in the past (at the cross)—the fact is every believer has died to sin; we cannot die any more to sin than we already have, and our awareness of this fact does not make it any more true or not true. When we died to sin, we died to a status wherein we were under bondage to the tyrannical reign of sin. The following question, however, naturally arises: "If we died to sin's dominion, why do we still struggle with sins in our daily lives?" All **unbelievers** live in the dominion or *realm of sin*—they live under its reign—they have not died to sin; as such "they are alive to sin," and everything they do is in accord with the "sinful constitution that rules in their soul"—the individual himself rules his own life, and he would never think of submitting to the lordship of Christ. To understand the unbeliever's diabolical position, look at Paul's definition of sin (Rom 14:23—unbelief). All **believers,** on the other hand, are "new creations"— they have God's Law (a holy constitution) written upon their hearts, and are indwelled by the Holy Spirit; they are alive to God, and live in the *realm of grace* by the power of the Holy Spirit. (45–91)

Scripture says we are in the process of "being transformed" into the image of Christ (2 Cor 3:18)—The Greek term translated "transformed" is actually the word *"metamorphosis"*—it is the same word that describes the transformation of a caterpillar into a butterfly; this is the word Paul uses to describe the *"spiritual transformation"* that takes place in the life of a Christian. The term that is used by theologians to describe the process of transformation is *"sanctification."* Sanctification is the work of the Holy Spirit in us whereby our inner being is *"progressively changed"*—freeing us more and more from sinful traits and developing within us over time the virtues of *Christlike character*. Though sanctification is the work of the Holy Spirit, it does involve our whole-hearted response in *"obedience"* and the regular use of the *"spiritual disciplines"* that are instruments of sanctification. The work of sanctification is a *"cooperative"* work—God directs and we cooperate by following His lead—though the principal work of sanctification is accomplished by the Holy Spirit (as it is in justification), we also play a critical part in it (Phil 2:12–13; 1 Cor 3:6). Believers are called to trust and obey God—faith and obedience are two sides of the same coin.

Sanctification actually begins at "conversion"—at the *"new birth"* the principle of *"spiritual life"* is planted within us. This work was prophesied by Jeremiah and Ezekiel, where God said, "I will write My laws on your hearts" *and* "I will give you a *new heart* . . . I will put My Spirit in you to make you walk in My ways" (Jer 31:33; Ezek 36:26–27). Paul describes regeneration this way: "If anyone is in Christ, he is a *new creation;* old things have passed away, and all things become new" (2 Cor 5:17). He also writes: "He saved us by the washing of regeneration and the renewing by the Holy Spirit" (Titus 3:5). Note the radical change that is explicitly described in each of these passages. God puts His law in our minds and write it on our hearts—that is, He gives us a *"new disposition;"* so instead of being hostile to God's law, the believer now actually delights in it. Jesus said being "born again" means to be *"born of the Spirit"* (Jn 3:6, 8)—therefore the act of regeneration (new birth) is solely the work of the Holy Spirit; it is entirely a work of grace. Regeneration, then, is the beginning of *"sanctification"*—the process whereby we are being transformed into the likeness of Christ (2 Cor 3:18).

Sanctification is a "life-long process" whereby we are changed "from glory to glory" (2 Cor 3:18); that is, as the Spirit of God works in us, we progress from one stage of glory (or grace) to the next. A part of the process includes an *"inner conflict"* between our "sin nature" (called "the flesh") and the "Holy Spirit." Paul says, "The flesh sets its desire against the Spirit, and the Sprit against the flesh; these are in opposition to one another, so that you may not do the things that you please" (Gal 5:17). Paul elaborated on this struggle in greater detail in Romans 7:14–25, where he said such things as, "I know that nothing good lives in me, that is, in my sinful nature; for I have the desire to do what is good, but I am simply not able to do it" (Rom 7:18).

The presence of sin in the believer involves "conflict" in his heart and life. It is absolutely futile to argue that this conflict is *abnormal*—because *sin* is still resident in every believer along with the presence of the Holy Spirit; as such, there is a *"warring tension"* in the heart of every believer. There must be a constant and increasing appreciation in the mind of the believer, that though *sin* is obviously still resident in him, *it is not his master*. As one theologian put it—

> *It is one thing for sin to live in us;*
> *it is quite another for us to live in sin.*

Sin is like a *defeated army* that, instead of surrendering and laying down its arms, it fades into the countryside, from which it continues to wage a *guerrilla war* of harassment and sabotage against the prevailing government forces. Sin as a "reigning power" in our life has been defeated—but it refuses to surrender! If we are going to *"pursue holiness"* we must accept the fact that there will be continual tension within us between *our desires* and *our performance*. As British theologian *J. I. Packer* so often says, "Our reach will always exceed our grasp."

To reiterate, it is the "Holy Spirit" who transforms us into Christ's likeness—The verb *"being transformed"* (2 Cor 3:18) in Greek is *passive*, meaning that the action is being done *"to"* us—not *"by"* us. This does not mean we are without responsibility—as believers we are called to "cooperate with Him" and "do what He asks us to do;" but in the final analysis the Holy Spirit is the one who works deep within our character to change us (numerous passages teach this—1 Th 2:13; 5:23-24; Phil 1:6; Heb 13:21; 1 Pet 1:2). The principle is clearly taught by Paul when he says, "I planted, Apollos watered, but God was causing the growth" (1 Cor 3:6). As believers, we have the "responsibility to obey God," but our obeying is not the *"direct cause"* of the outcome—God is the one who effectuates the outcome. We may plant seeds in the ground and water, but we do not *"cause"* the growth—that is the work of God. When we are "obedient" to God, He honors His Word by making it fruitful and efficacious—as such, He is the *"Great Mover"* behind our action—He is the *"Effectuator!"* With that understanding, we must be mindful of *"our responsibility"* in the sanctifying process—God gives us instructions to follow—when we follow (obey), He blesses; when we don't follow, He does not bless. Conversely, when we don't follow His instructions, He has ways to get us to do so. When King David refused to "deal with his sin," God applied "sufficient pressure" to him to get Him to obey (Ps 32:3-5 and Heb 12:5-7). God told David, "Don't be like the horse or the mule who has no understanding, whose trappings include a bit and bridle to hold him in check" (Ps 32:9). The message is pretty clear: God will put a bit in your mouth and a bridle on you—"if He has to"—to get you to obey Him. Remember the words of the psalmist: "Know that the LORD Himself is God; it is He who has made us, and not we ourselves; we are His people and the sheep of His pasture" (Ps 100:3). God's goal is to make us *like His Son* . . . and that *He will do,* one way or the other (Rom 8:29; Phil 1:6; 2:13; Heb 13:21)—be it with our faithful cooperation, resulting in much joy and peace . . . or our being stubborn and less cooperative, resulting in little joy and more scourging (Heb 12:5-11; 1 Cor 3:1-15). The choice is ours: either we can choose to be cooperative, or we can choose to be less cooperative. (93-109)

The greatest commandment in the Bible is to "love God with our entire being"—We are to love Him with all our heart, soul, mind and strength (Mt 22:37; Deut 6:5). "If you love Me," Jesus said, "you will keep My commandments" (Jn 14:15; 1 Jn 5:3). The equating of *obedience to God* with *love to God* is a prominent feature of the book of Deuteronomy as well (Deut 10:12–13; 11:13; 11:22; 19:9; 30:6,8; 30:19–20). The fact is, our love to God will always manifest itself in obedience to Him. The writer of Hebrews says, "Without faith (believing God) it is impossible to *please God"* (Heb 11:6). How can one say he loves God, yet refuses to obey Him or believe Him? Remember, "not believing" someone is akin to calling that person "a liar"—obviously that is not going to *please* someone. Imagine your spouse or your best friend truthfully telling you something, and then you respond with, "I don't believe you"—would you actually expect them to be *pleased* with you? Then how then can you expect God to be pleased with you when you refuse to believe Him, or obey Him, and call Him a liar? Inherent in the concept of "faith" is *action*—not mere *mental ascent* (Jam 1:22; 2:14, 19, 20)—so, if we really love God, then our desire is to *please* Him by believing Him and obeying Him. Essentially, love is a *"motive;"* without love our obedience would be "self-serving." Negatively, I may fear God will *punish me* if I do not obey; hence I choose to obey . . . and positively, I desire that God *bless me*—thus I choose to obey. Conversely, there are other lesser motives like pride, or consequences, or self-esteem . . . but "love" is the supreme motive.

The key to obeying God is "developing our love for God"—Scripture teaches, "We love God because He first loved us" (1 Jn 4:19); thus, our love to God can only be a response to His love for us. If we do not believe God loves us, we will not love Him—no human being genuinely loves someone who does not love them; only God can love like that. Therefore, to love God, we must believe that He is *for us*, not *against us* (Rom 8:31), and herein is the "hick-up" for most believers—*they are not absolutely certain that God "loves" them;* they have a difficult time persuading themselves that God really does love them—why is this the case? *Because they know they do not deserve His love.* A *"tender conscience"* is a great advantage in the pursuit of holiness, because it is so *sensitive to sin;* but this same tender conscience can load us down with a tremendous *burden of guilt* and a sense of condemnation—therefore it is difficult to believe that God really loves us; because we know we are unlovely. James Fraser on this subject said, "Human nature is so formed, that it cannot love any object that is adverse and terrible to it"—that means, we cannot love God if we think we are under His judgment and condemnation. ***The solution?*** It is absolutely essential that we continually take those sins our consciences accuse us of to the Cross and plead the cleansing blood of Jesus; because it is only the blood of Christ that cleanses our consciences so that we may no longer feel guilty (Heb 9:14; 10:2). By the way, **the greatest sorrow you can lay on the Father, is to believe that He does not love you**—carefully reflect on that statement. That is why it is so important that we keep the "gospel of grace" before us *every day*—because we sin every day, and our consciences condemn us every day (some more than others), we need the gospel *every day* (actually, many times a day!). The conscience once cleansed no longer retains a charge of guiltiness and of judgment for it. When our sense of guilt is taken away, we are freed up to love God with all our heart and soul and mind. Our love for God will be spontaneous in an outpouring of gratitude to Him and fervent desire to obey Him. The apostle Paul writes, *"The only thing that counts is faith expressing itself through love"* (Gal 5:6). As we by faith feed on the gospel (faith is affirming the truth), that faith will express itself in love—that is, in loving obedience to God. That is the very nature of faith. Jesus said, "He who has been forgiven little loves little" (Lk 7:47); the inverse is also true—"He who has been forgiven much loves much." When we genuinely affirm the reality of all God has done for us, it will dramatically affect the way in which we live. (111–125)

> *Therefore, we can say that the extent to which we realize and acknowledge our own sinfulness, and the extent to which we realize that we have been forgiven and cleansed from those sins, that will determine the measure of our love to God.*

In the pursuit of holiness we must exercise both "discipline" and "dependence"—*Discipline* refers to certain activities designed to train a person in a particular skill. Paul exhorted Timothy to "discipline himself" for the purpose of godliness (1 Tim 4:7); notice that Paul said *"discipline* *yourself"*—thus part of the responsibility for growing in holiness lies on the shoulders of the believer. Notice that Paul does not just tell Timothy to "turn it all over to the Lord and everything will be fine." Furthermore, logic alone tells us that God does not ask us to do something we are not capable of doing. So let us first understand that God is not asking us to long jump the Grand Canyon! or pole vault the Eiffel Tower (spiritually speaking). Therefore, if you are thinking that God is asking you to do something that "you cannot do"—you have misunderstood something—so, study the matter before you throw in the towel. The truth of the matter is God gives us the *responsibility* to "respond" according to our "abilities"—hence the word, response/ability—nothing more, nothing less (Mt 25:15). By the way, to whom He gives much, He requires much (Lk 12:48). Remember these two principles: 1) **God enables us** to do the things He asks us to do; and 2) **God will not do for us** the things He asks us to do for ourselves. There are many passages in Scripture where this concept is taught—"Unless the LORD build the house, its BUILDERS labor in vain" (Ps 127:1). Your responsibility as a believer is to *"do your part;"* when you do, you can depend upon God to *"do His part!"* The builders cannot put away their tools and go fishing and expect God to build the house—by the way, "praying your head off" is not going to get you off the hook! When God gives you "orders" to do something—you do it! Any plea of ignorance or inability will not cut it. Nehemiah, the wall-builder, understood well the principle of *"dependent discipline,"* the idea that we are both responsible and dependent—Nehemiah and his people both "prayed" *and* "posted a guard." Think about that.

Regarding the situation in which you find yourself—you must both "pray" *(that is dependence on God)* and "obey" *(doing your part is the discipline).* It should be noted that there is not a single instance in New Testament teaching on "holiness" where we are taught to "depend on the Holy Spirit" without a corresponding exercise of "discipline on our part." The exercise of "discipline" is often an "agonizing struggle"—because not everything God asks us to do is "easy"—and for that reason many believers get discouraged and give up. Here is where the believer must "put in the effort" to overcome the temptation to give up—the chastening of the Lord will ultimately move the believer toward action, but it is not wise to always take the "detour" to holiness—because it is a lot more painful and frustrating. Let's review: *Our part is to work, but we must do so relying upon God to enable us to do what He asks—God's work does not make our effort unnecessary, rather it makes it effective.* At this point it might be helpful to reflect upon the words of the great Puritan writer **John Owen**—

> *Our duty and God's grace are nowhere opposed in the matter of sanctification—we cannot perform our duty without the grace of God; nor does God give His grace for any other purpose than that we may perform our duty.*

If we are to make any progress in the "pursuit of holiness," we must assume our responsibility to discipline or train ourselves. But we are to do all this in *"total dependence on the Holy Spirit"* to work in us and strengthen us in Christ. Paul said, "I can do all things through Christ who strengthens me" (Phil 4:13). Some ask: "Why doesn't the Holy Spirit always strengthen us?" There may be several reasons why He doesn't—He may be letting us see the sinfulness of our own hearts . . . He may want us to see how weak we are in ourselves and how dependent we really are on Him . . . He may be curbing a tendency toward spiritual pride and causing us to grow in humility. Whatever the reason, which we may never know, our responsibility is to utterly depend on Him. More wisdom from **John Owen**—

> *Even though we have been given a new heart and the principle of spiritual life, that new life needs to be continually nourished and sustained by the Holy Spirit—it does not operate on its own.*

Jesus said, "Apart from Me you can do nothing" (Jn 15:5)—In theory we believe that, but in practice we tend to live as if we *can* do some things—each of us has areas of our lives where we feel fairly confident, and we don't sense the need of the Holy Spirit's aid. But that is contrary to what Scripture teaches—we cannot do anything "spiritually good" apart from the working of God's Spirit within us. If we are going to make any progress in becoming "more Christlike," we will have to learn to rely on the Holy Spirit rather than on our own virtues and abilities. How do we grow in a conscious sense of dependence on Christ? Through the discipline of *"prayer"*—prayer is the tangible expression of our dependence on God. Think about that. Obviously, if our prayer life is meager, in effect we are saying that we can handle most of our spiritual life. One of the chief characteristics of our *flesh* is having an attitude of *"independence toward God."* Undoubtedly, one of the reasons God allows us to fall to temptation so often, is to teach us experientially that we really are "dependent on Him" to enable us to grow in holiness. So if we want to become holy we must pursue, not a spirit of independence, but a *"spirit of dependence"*—and the best means God has given us for doing this is the discipline of "prayer." (127–143)

If we hope to make any progress in the pursuit of holiness, "commitment" is absolutely essential. Paul's call to commitment in Romans 12:1 is this: "I urge you, brothers, in view of God's mercy, to offer your bodies as living sacrifices, holy and pleasing to God—this is your reasonable service of worship." We cannot control what our eyes look at, what our mouths speak, or what our hands and feet do, if our whole being, including our mind and heart, is *not committed to God*. In short, it is a commitment to a life of obedience—*we must make it our firm intention not to sin willfully*. Therefore, we must keep reminding ourselves of the "gospel of grace" every day, because it is only by grace whereby God's Spirit will give us the victory. Furthermore, it is only through making the right choice to obey God's Word that we will break the habits of sin and develop habits of holiness. This is where we desperately need the power of the Holy Spirit to enable us to make right choices. So cry out to God every day for "His help" (Mt 26:41), and then cry out again each time you are confronted with the choice to sin or to obey.

Saying NO to sin involves a struggle between what we "know" to be right, and what we "desire" to do. Paul describes the struggle thus: "The flesh sets its desire against the Spirit, and the Spirit against the flesh; they are in opposition to one another, so that you may not do the things you feel like doing" (Gal 5:17). Since mortification is a difficult work, we need the help of other brothers (or sisters) in Christ to engage in the struggle with us, and who are also willing to be mutually open with us about their own struggles. This act of "humility" results in an outpouring of "God's grace" upon our lives. In the battle of putting sin to death, we need the "mutual encouragement and prayer support" of others—that is why *"spiritual synergism"* is so often taught in the New Testament. For example, we are to admonish one another (Col 3:16); encourage one another (Heb 3:13); confess our sins to one another (Jam 5:16); bear one another's burdens (Gal 6:2); and pray for one another (Jam 5:16). We each need at least "one brother" to *walk* and *encourage* and *admonish* and *pray* with us through the spiritual struggles of life. And yet all the while we must keep going back to the "gospel of grace"—because it continually gives us the courage to get up and keep going even after we have failed for the umpteenth time. It is only "grace" that will allow us to be as honest about our sin as David was about his. It will only come from the gratitude and joy of knowing that however miserably I have failed, God's grace is *greater* than my sin. The only cure for spiritual pollution is to preach the "gospel of grace" to yourself—preach it to yourself *every day!* because it is only the gospel that will keep you living by grace! (145–200)

An old Pogo cartoon years ago expressed it well, "We have met the enemy and it is us!"—Paul called the *"indwelling sin"* in us a law, or a principle, that is at work within us constantly seeking to draw us away from God and into sin (Rom 7:21-25). James referred to this *"principle of sin"* when he said, "Each one is tempted when he is carried away and enticed by his own lust" (Jam 1:14). The evil desire within us constantly searches for occasions to express itself—the "flesh" wants to be its own boss and satisfy itself; it has no desire whatsoever to submit to the lordship of Christ—none! There is the sober warning of Paul: "If you think you stand, take heed lest you fall!" (1 Cor 10:12). And then the words of **John Owen:** "When indwelling sin is least felt, it is in fact most powerful!" The truth of the matter is this: "There is no sin which I am not capable of committing!" As Jerry Bridges said, "Our only safeguard is a sense of deep humility as we realize how powerful indwelling sin still is." And again ***John Owen:*** "When we realize a constant enemy of the soul abides within us, what diligence and watchfulness we should have!" Some years ago Jerry Bridges began to pray this prayer—*"Lord, keep me on a short leash; don't let me get away with the little sins."* A prayer I often pray is this: "Lord, give me neither riches that I deny You, nor poverty that I would steal" (Prv 30:8–9)—this means being continually mindful that I can have "too much" or "too little" of anything; that I need to trust God to give me only whatever is necessary—and to accept it joyfully. (201–231)

CHAPTER 11

A summary of the book...

"HOLINESS BY GRACE"
by Bryan Chapell

Grace is trusting "Christ's work," rather than our own achievements, as the basis of our righteousness; so grace is God's willingness to look at us from the perspective that sees His holy Son in our place. What robs many believers of joy is a misunderstanding of how God continues to view us after we have received the grace of the *new birth*. After initially trusting Christ to make them right with God, many Christians embark on an *"endless pursuit of trying to satisfy God with good works"* that will keep Him loving them—as such, they live with the understanding that though they are saved by God's grace, they are kept in His care and His good graces by their own goodness; this makes the Christian life a perpetual race on a *performance treadmill* to keep winning God's affection and approval. *"Legalism"* makes the believer think that God accepts him on the basis of what he does. Resting on God's grace, however, does not relieve us of our *"holy obligations"*—rather it enables us to fulfill them (Eph 4:7–13).

Having the assurance in our heart that "God really does love us," allows us the freedom of not having to *"strive to please Him"* in order to earn His affection—instead our obedience becomes a "gratitude response" to God's love and grace. So, it is not as though "our works" don't matter—clearly they do—but the *"heart attitude"* that governs our works is the important issue. The realization that our good works will not move God to be more favorably disposed to us runs counter to our "natural reasoning." *True grace overwhelms us with a sense of God's love for us*—thus our heart resonates with the things God desires; as such, His purposes become our purposes. Our soul delights to obey and serve Him because of our love for Him (1 Jn 4:19), and our thanksgiving for "His mercy" makes us long to honor Him. Thus, true grace produces joy and promotes godliness. So, the "focus of the believer" who is growing in holiness, must not be upon the "excellence of his own actions or thoughts"—that is performance-based Christianity—but upon "his complete reliance on *God's mercy* that he does not deserve." If the "heart" is not tender toward God in gratitude for His mercy, the believer will strive to earn God's favor thru good works—once the magnitude of *"God's mercy"* is fully realized, gratitude to God will overflow in the soul; but not until then. Read carefully the words of **Martin Luther** on this subject—

> *I have been preaching and cultivating the message of grace now for almost twenty years, and I still feel the old clinging dirt of wanting to deal so with God that I may contribute something, so that He will have to give me His grace in exchange for my holiness. And still I cannot get it into my head that I should surrender myself completely to sheer grace; yet I know that this is what I should and must do.*

Long-term Christian workers oftentimes find these truths particularly distasteful. It is easy to feel that God, to some degree, owes us *"His favor"* for faithful service—after all, didn't we make significant sacrifices for Him and His work? By the way, if the reason we obey God is to earn His affections with our goodness, we need to be reminded that "God will be no man's debtor" (Job 41:11; Rom 11:35). Our attempts to barter (in some sense) for God's kindness with our goodness and great efforts will not move Him. Remember that one line in the hymn, *"Rock of Ages"*—"Nothing in my hand I bring, simply to Thy cross I cling." We must keep our hands empty of any claim that God must bless us on the basis of our faithfulness or goodness. According to Scripture even our best works are *"filthy rags"* (Is 64:6). Capturing the essence and implications of our limitations, **John Calvin** wrote—

> *To man we may assign only this—that he pollutes and contaminates by his impurity those very things that are good. For nothing proceeds from a man, however perfect he be, that is not defiled in some way.*

Divine blessing flows from "God's mercy" rather than from our merit. Our works do not obligate God to care for us in the way that *we* think is best. We cannot put God on a leash through our goodness. God blesses according to the wisdom of His eternal mercy rather than in proportion to our works of earned merit. Should we *"plead for mercy"* like the man with leprosy (Lk 17:11–19), we must realize that Jesus shows pity to those who have nothing to claim but "desperation." He is moved by a desperate cry for help. So, God is not moved by the deeds that we trophy, but by the desperation that we acknowledge as our own. A corollary of this—*"God gives grace to the humble"* (Jam 4:6). Those who cry out in desperation have more hope of "moving God's heart" than any who would trophy their own righteousness before Him. *Therefore, to experience God's grace, I must readily and repeatedly confess my own hopeless condition.* The assumption that God only loves the righteous will tempt me to "hide the darkness of my heart from Him"—unafraid of God's rejection, I am free to confront the wicked face of my soul, my anger, my lust, my doubt; such honesty moves God to pity us in our desperation. When we understand that our works in themselves earn us *"no merit"* with God, then the only reason to do those works is "love for Him"—thus, we learn to serve God not for personal gain but for His glory. When we grasp how great is God's love for us, our hearts will long to please Him. "He who is forgiven much . . . loves much" (Lk 7:47). (7–37)

Because I am a "new creature" in Christ Jesus, the Spirit of God indwells me and I have the means of grace available to me by which the Spirit teaches, trains, and "rewires" me, so that I can mature in knowledge and righteousness. The Spirit changes our hearts in a way that our own efforts do not. When the Spirit supernaturally reorients our hearts to love and obedience, we have the inclination and power to follow Him. Thus, spiritual change is more than a matter of the practice of "spiritual disciplines," or even of resolving to act on the reality of who we are in Christ. We progress in sanctification as we humbly and prayerfully depend upon the Holy Spirit to mature our wills and transform our affections, so that we stay on the course that He has designed. While Christians sometimes still yield to temptation, they now hate their own susceptibility to the wrong. Once this godly hatred of sin did not exist because the mind, untouched by the indwelling Spirit, loved the world and was hostile to God (Rom 8:5–7; Jam 4:4–5; 1 Jn 2:15). The repulsion we feel for the sin in our lives is our internal witness of the "new nature" that God's Spirit has supernaturally created in us. The new affections of a Spirit-changed heart combined with nurturing instruction of the means of grace mature us in faith, but the processes vary greatly among individuals. Some grow quickly, while the progress of others seems undetectable over many years. We grow according to God's plan and purposes, but there is not a linear math to prescribe our advances. Progress in sanctification requires work from us, but we are made willing and able to work because of our sure relationship with the Lord who gave Himself for us, and now indwells us with that life-changing power.

Some of us, because of our sin or lack of progress, have determined that we are either spiritually stupid or hated by God. Therefore, God tells us our "true status and ability" in His Word. Let's begin with this—because of our union with Christ, we are not hated. Though weakness, wrongdoing, and failings do cling to us, they do not establish who we are. We are the beloved of God. Though sin still exists in our lives, we have the status of the One who gave His life for us and to us—God's own Son. And because of the indwelling presence of God's Spirit, we have the ability to change and progress in our Christian walk. (39–65)

If we fail to understand how we "rely on God's grace alone" to make us right with Him, our Christian walk becomes one of personal achievements and works-orientation. Jesus wants to liberate us from the unappeasable demands of "personal merit." Thus, He must turn us away from the error of somehow believing that the perfection of our performance will gain His favor. Our works will never earn God's affection, just as they will never merit His pardon—though the majority of believers concur with that, still the seeds of such thinking lie deep in their hearts. Reflect upon these thoughts, and ask God to extract this works-orientation from your heart.

The assurance of my pardon provides the "peace of heart" that is the Spirit's ultimate weapon against temptation. After all, when I am perfectly satisfied, then what can tempt me? When I am perfectly loved, then what else do I desire? When I am eternally secure, then what can threaten me? A "legalistic" mode of thinking, however, gives "indwelling sin" an advantage, because nothing destroys the desire to "pursue holiness" as much as a sense of guilt. On the other hand, nothing so motivates us to deal with sin in our lives as does the knowledge that our sins are truly forgiven, and that the dominion of sin is broken through the cross of Christ (Rom 7:24–25). The man who comes to obey God will "love Him" first—the love of God is the beginning of religion. Love of the Savior draws us from the lure of temptation. With much wisdom *Charles Spurgeon* said—(69–110)

> *When I thought God as hard, I found it easy to sin; but when I found God so kind, so good, so overflowing with compassion, I smote upon my breast that I could ever have rebelled against One who loved me so, and sought my good.*

When religious opponents argued with "John Bunyan" in prison, they urged him not to assure his Christian friends of God's unswerving love. "If you keep assuring the people of God's love," the opponents argued, "they will do whatever *they* want." Replied Bunyan, "If I assure God's people of His love, then they will do whatever *He* wants."

The Holy Spirit takes hearts that are hard and softens them toward God (Ezek 11:19–20; 36:25–27). The Spirit changes our priorities, our affections, our cravings—and give us a love for God that is greater than a love for the things of the world. Love for God provides the zeal we need to employ the weapons He provides. This does not mean that the battle will be without effort or without pain. It is, after all, spiritual *warfare*. But with the faith that God has given us, we can stand faithful so long as we truly desire to do so. That desire is also a gift from God, as His Spirit for which we pray stirs within us the love for God that is more compelling than the love for sin. Engaging in spiritual warfare *because* of a compelling love for God is *how* we secure victory over sin.

People drowning in destructive habits are not rescued by simply urging them to act more like Christians—reading the Bible more, praying more, and becoming accountable to fellow believers. They are all good and necessary steps, but in themselves these disciplines will not rescue us from sin that infiltrates the heart. Just as secular psychology may change some people's habits by behavioral techniques, the diligent pursuit of "Christian disciplines" can cause changes in us that have healthy aspects, but do not reflect true spiritual change. So, how do we change the "core level" of our being? The Bible teaches that *"these disciplines"* are powerful weapons for holiness in spiritual warfare, but the power and willingness to use these means must come from a *"constraining love for God"* that replaces our affections for the world. That "change of affections" and "reconstruction of the heart," is the supernatural work of the Spirit for which we must pray. We facilitate this work of the Spirit when we fully comprehend *why* we love Jesus. *Full and consistent apprehension of "why we love God" is the most effective piece of armor in the Christian arsenal*, because the Devil always begins his attack with an alienation of our affections. Note this—spiritual change is more a consequence of *"what our hearts love"* than *"what our hands do."* The "spiritual disciplines" are important, but not as important as *"developing a heart for God."* God's Spirit enables us to "grasp the fullness of God's love that surpasses knowledge" (Eph 3:18–19), and our love is ignited by the flame of Christ's love. Our "love for God" then stirs up within us a large and loving heart for His glory and purposes, and we act as the heart inspires and enables. The heart is the "command center" for every battle (Prv 4:23). (111–156)

God's "discipline" is always loving in its intent. God's process of making us what He wants us to be includes "discipline"—it teaches us that hardship is neither punitive nor pointless (Heb 12:4–11). Saying that discipline is not punitive does not mean that it is without pain. Nine times in Hebrews 12 the term for discipline refers to the correction or training of children. One commentator says that the meaning of discipline is *"to put someone in a state of good order so that he can function as intended."* The goal of God's discipline is to correct, or to set right, or to improve—not to make someone suffer as an act of vengeance or retribution. Incidentally, God cannot, in justice, punish us for sin—that would mean that Christ didn't pay the full payment of our sin, because He would be requiring us to pay a part of it as well; therefore God does not chastise us as a means of satisfaction for sin. Though the means of God's actions may be quite painful, His motive is never to "punish" His children in the sense that He makes them pay some penalty for their sin. Again, the penalty for our sin was fully and completely paid for by Christ on the cross (Heb 7:27; 9:24–28; 10:10, 1 Pet 3:18). Divine discipline is intended to benefit the wayward rather than to exact retribution for wrong. *"God disciplines us for our good that we may share in His holiness"* (Heb 12:10). The writer of Hebrews also tells us why the Jewish Christians needed this reassurance—apparently they were being tempted to let down in their fight against evil, so he gently chides them saying, "In your struggle against sin, you have not yet resisted to the point of shedding your blood" (Heb 12:4). He encourages them to remember that hardship is not a sign of God's abandonment but of His activity in their lives (Heb 12:5–6; Rev 3:19). God ultimately uses affliction and trial to conform our nature to Christ's; that discipline is ultimately for our well-being. Carefully note what the second verse of that centuries-old hymn *"How Firm a Foundation"* teaches—

> *When through fiery trials thy pathway shall lie,*
> *My grace, all sufficient, shall be thy supply:*
> *The flame shall not hurt thee; I only design*
> *Thy dross to consume and thy gold to refine.*

When we face the pressures of declining finances . . . when illnesses ravage our families . . . when dear friends become our critics . . . when trusted workers undermine our leadership . . . when governments act unfairly . . . when people to whom we have given ourselves turn on us . . . and when those we count on remove their support—*there is still cause for joy*. Whether we suffer under the weight of circumstances or under the weightiness of bearing the consequences of the sins of others—these disciplines teach us more of what Christ endured for us. As a result, we know Him to a degree and depth not available through any other means of study or contemplation. When we understand that God has not called us to freedom from all difficulty, His grace begins to flow through us in the most profound ways. Knowing that He communicates Himself through suffering, we find ourselves willing—for the sake of others—to pursue opportunities that are less attractive than others, and endure people whose insensitivities and ingratitude cause us to suffer. (159–182)

God sometimes gives us so much to do that we tend to "lose heart"—The apostle Paul must have known the likelihood of our discouragement, so he precedes all the duties and assignments he outlines in Romans 12 with this exhortation—"I urge you, brothers, in view of *God's mercy* to serve Him" (v.1); thus he encourages us with "God's loving mercy" above all other motivations. The Puritan writer **Samuel Bolton** wrote in 1645, "If the law is merely our command we cannot *delight* to do the will of God. We can perform duties but cannot *delight* in them, even though we may think them needful as something necessary for glory and for heaven." Thus, the inevitable consequence of obedience without *delight* is the erosion of holiness. We cannot continue to do our duty to God if we have no love for the task or the Taskgiver. Paul did *not* say, "I urge you by the guilt you will assume if you are negligent" or "I urge you by the love you will lose if you fail." Paul knew that if we serve God out of "guilt" or "servile duty," then our labors will not be joyful, or strong, or long. God does not want us to serve Him that way—"Serve Me," He says, "by keeping in view not my anger nor your shame, but *My mercy!*" Recall Him whose weight hung on nails . . . so cruel that each breath was torture . . . and remember that it was "our sins" that He bore . . . and then consider His words to us, "Oh, My child, now I will spare you what I go through" (1 Pet 2:24–25; 1 Jn 2:1–2). *"How great is the love the Father has lavished upon us, that we should be called children of God!"* (1 Jn 3:1). Such mercy eclipses all other motivations for our service for Him. His mercy should so fill our vision that gratitude fills our hearts with the longing to do His will. If "thankfulness" does not move us to serve God, then we do not truly understand who our God is and what He has done in our behalf. Without gratitude for Christ's sacrificial love, our duty will become nothing more than drudgery and our God nothing more than a dissatisfied boss. This is why Paul tells us at the outset to service *"in view of God's mercy"* (Rom 12:1).

Many Christians punish themselves to get rid of their "guilt." They believe their *"guilty feelings"* are the penance God requires of them in order to renew His love for them. As a consequence they do not want to be denied their guilt. They will offer God the gifts of their own depression and self-hatred to satisfy His wrath. This thinking comes from the conviction that, if we will make ourselves feel bad enough and carry a burden of remorse long enough, *we will to some degree merit God's grace and forgiveness*. But "who" is the one who really wants us pressed down and paralyzed by a burden of guilt? Satan! Nothing pleases him more than for Christians to beat themselves down into paralyzing depression or unproductive despair. *God* makes us right with God—not guilt feelings—and He does not want us bowed down in despair. God is the *"lifter of our heads!"* (Ps 3:3). We cannot offer loving service to a God who loves us only when we are good—if God's love is conditional, then His love is not any better than "our love," and we would not like Him very much—let alone love Him! Ultimately, we would discover that we love this unappeasable God less and less, as we try to please Him more and more. In time we would become hard, cynical, judgmental, bitter, and despairing, because our God would be nothing more than a *"heavenly ogre"* intent on extracting His pound of flesh from whomever crosses Him.

> **Guilt** should drive us to the cross . . . but **grace** must lead us from it. **Guilt** makes us seek Christ . . . but **gratitude** should make us serve Him.

Lasting service comes when we serve God because "He accepts us," not to get His acceptance—the former kind of service rejoices in His mercy;

the latter seeks to merit His approval. ***J. I. Packer*** said *"the true driving force in authentic Christian living is a heart of gratitude."* The "conditional nature" of many human relationships causes us to think of God's love as that which is subject to the vagaries and degrees of our obedience. The consequences of sin reinforces this misconception. It is wrong to think, however, that because there is a divine discipline or temporal consequence resulting from personal sin, God's love is altered. (183–205)

To properly evaluate the place of "good works" in the Christian life, we must understand that *grace* maintains our value as God's children, apart from our own merit; but we must also understand that God uses our *obedience* to promote our good and His glory. God's honoring of our righteousness does not change the degree of His love for us, or imply that we can earn His affection. Still, His recognition and reward of righteousness does indicate that He values efforts that conform us more to His image—"God rewards those who earnestly seek Him" (Heb 11:6). The righteousness in us that *God* motivates and enables by His grace, He also graciously blesses. Without that understanding, the believer could easily turn his Christian faith into a *"bartering system"* for personal gain—therefore we do not make *"temporal rewards"* the chief motive of our obedience. While we have the privilege of participating in eternal causes, the reason that the righteous and their works endure forever is that God sanctifies our feeble and faulty efforts by instilling His own righteousness in them. *God's grace is not easily reconciled with human logic*—this side of heaven, we will never logically resolve the tension between human responsibility and divine provision in sanctification—but as we learn to acknowledge that God must provide what we need to please Him, the result will be our full dependence upon *His grace*.

Scripture asks the question, "Must we obey God in order to grow in godliness and please Him?" The answer is a definite "Yes!" Scripture also asks, "Where do we get the desire, ability, and faith to obey?" The answer is, we get each of these things from "God!" Then, is God responsible if I do not obey? The answer is "No!" There is no room for boasting before God, because of Him, and through Him, and to Him are all things (Rom 11:36); yet neither can any say that God is to blame because we disobey (Rom 9:19–23; Jam 1:13–14; 1 Jn 1:5). Scripture does not resolve the tensions involved in these questions. *God makes us "spiritually alive," and enables us to obey His Word.* Through regeneration, God sets us free from the dominion of sin, and sets our will free to honor Him. Still, we cannot exercise this freedom rightly without the aid of the *"Holy Spirit."* This makes us responsible for our sin, but dependent on God for our righteousness. This is why the apostle Paul's meditations on God's mercy ultimately lead Him to exclaim—"Oh, the depth of the riches of the wisdom and knowledge of God! How unsearchable His judgments, and His paths beyond tracing out!" (Rom 11:33). The parable of the landowner in Matthew 20 is perplexing to us, because it does not seem *fair* that "the last be first and the first last!" Jesus responds to Peter, "Friend, do not be offended that I am generous." The message of *unfair but generous grace* is for us as well. Our God lavishes us with His grace. Read the following verses of Psalm 103:10–14—

> *God does not treat us as our sins deserve*
> *or repay us according to our iniquities.*
> *For as high as the heavens are above the earth,*
> *so great is His love for those who fear Him;*
> *as far as the east is from the west,*
> *so far has he removed our transgressions from us.*
> *As a father has compassion on his children,*
> *so the Lord has compassion on those who fear Him;*
> *for He knows how we are formed,*
> *He remembers that we are but dust.* (207–243)

CHAPTER 12

A summary of the book . . .

"ENJOYING THE PRESENCE OF GOD"

by Martyn Lloyd-Jones (1899–1981)

The **"fool"** says in his heart **"there is no God"** (Ps 14:1)—As you know, this is a very common attitude in the west. The fool listens too much to "his heart"—he is governed by *"his desires,"* what he likes and what he wants. Instead of listening to that "sense" that is within him—a sense of God—which is innate in every human being; he stifles that and tries to argue it down. When you study anthropology and investtigate the most primitive people groups in the world, you will find that they all have a *"sense of God"*—this they express in various forms of worship. So, those who say, "there is no God," go against the voice of their conscience. We all have a conscience within us—when we do something wrong, our conscience tells us so and it condemns us. It makes us feel miserable. The vast majority of people seek to resolve their wrongdoing through a *"religious belief system"*—the atheist resolves his wrongdoing by simply striving to live up to what he believes is *"his own ethical standards"*—which, unbeknownst to him, is a product of the "law of God" written on his heart; incidentally, that is why there is a *"common morality"* among all people groups (we all have the essence of "God's law" written on our hearts); most people "lower the standards" so that they can meet those standards; as such they are governed by their desires.

The "fool" arrives at a momentous conclusion that "there is no God" on insufficient evidence; he doesn't think things through; instead he jumps to conclusions and is governed by his prejudices and passions. Let me illustrate it—the fool says, *"I don't believe there is a God, because no God would allow wars, disease, spastic children, earthquakes, pain and suffering."* We have all heard the arguments. It is with that kind of reasoning, and that alone, that the fool concludes "there is no God." It is amazing how intelligent people can reason and argue so *"unreasonably."* They never stop to think there might be a *"bigger purpose"* behind all the calamities of life. The psalmist said, "It is good for me that I have been afflicted, because before I was afflicted I went astray" (Ps 119:67, 71). When confronted with such thinking, people generally respond that they had never "reasoned from that perspective"—additionally, if people do not understand themselves or other people, why then do they demand that they *"fully understand the ways of God"*? And rashly conclude that *"God does not exist"* because the things that happen in life are incompatible with how *I think* God should act. (7–23)

Is "communion with God" the supreme thing in the whole of your life? Men and women must realize that they are a needy people (they are lost), and the only people who know what it is to enjoy the blessings of salvation are those who have discovered that fact. The tragedy is that so many people never discover that they are needy—hence, they have never seen the need for Christ. *Only the Christian realizes he has "sin within him"—and that his very nature is twisted and perverted.* He sees there is something wrong and foul in his own heart and the power of sin within him. He realizes that in addition to that, the whole world is set against him, that the flesh is militating against him, and that the devil is behind it all. He no longer says, "Let any temptation come and I can stand up to it." He discovers that one of the most dangerous things in the world is to *think he is strong;* because suddenly he will go down—he went out of the house determined never to fall again, but he fell before he knew where he was. He begins to realize how *"helpless"* he is, and how utterly defenseless. The Christian understands the great *"moral struggle;"* and knows what it is to fight with all his might and yet go down with his enemies attacking him. So, the ultimate secret of every godly Christian, is that he has come at last to realize that the "most priceless thing in life" is his *SOUL*—that thing within us that goes on for all eternity. It is that thing that God has put within us, which God breathed into us—"man became a living soul" (Gen 2:7). It is that thing that stamps men and women as being made in the "image of God." Our *SOUL* is the most precious thing we have. Therefore, Paul says, "I have committed my soul to God and Christ for safe-keeping, and I know whatever may happen to me, God will keep that which I have committed unto Him until that great Day of Judgment. It is eternally safe" (2 Tim 1:12). (24–52)

Jesus said, "Do not waste your time worrying about what you are going to eat, drink or wear . . . rather, seek first the kingdom of God and His righteousness, and all these things shall be provided for you" (Mt 6:25–33). "What shall it profit a man if he gains the whole world, and loses his own soul?" "What shall a man give in exchange for his soul?" (Mk 8:36). The most priceless possession we have is our *SOUL!* Where can I put it that I may know it is "safe" for all eternity? We are going to live on and on and on and on—there is no end to our existence. The ultimate question is this, "Have you become concerned about the future of your soul?" The Lord Jesus, using another analogy, compares us to sheep and Himself to the Good Shepherd. He says, "They shall never perish, neither shall any man pluck them out of My hand" (Jn 10:28). Paul writes, "I am persuaded that neither death, nor life, nor anything in all the universe, can separate us from the love of God which is in Christ Jesus (Rom 8:38–39). Blessed is the man who trusts in Thee. Reflect on the words of a hymn written by **Fanny Crosby**—(52–57)

> *All the way, my Savior leads me, What have I to ask beside?*
> *Can I doubt His tender mercy, Who through life has been my guide?*
> *Heavenly peace, divinest comfort, Here by faith in Him to dwell,*
> *For I know whate're befall me, Jesus doeth all things well.*

The essence of true religion is to "know God"—It is not simply knowing things about God, but truly knowing God. Conversely, true religion is not just a matter of morality. David's secret was that "his strength was in God (not himself), in whose heart are the highways of God!" (Ps 84:5). Blessed therefore is the man who has *"made roads in his heart."* The heart of the unbeliever is like a *"pathless uncharted wilderness;"* there are no paths or highways mapped out; everything is tangled and mixed up—that is a description of what we all are by nature. So, people who are not Christians really have no view or philosophy of life; there is no order or system in their lives. They have no clear ideas; there is no plan in it and no purpose . . . life is entirely aimless . . . they just exist . . . they are like a great uncharted territory. They do not sit down and ask the big questions: "What is man?" "What is life all about?" "What am I meant to do with my life?" "What are these strange intimations that I feel from time to time that I am meant for something bigger and greater?" The thoughts may come, but they dismiss them. They just become victims of what may happen to them. If a bit of good fortune comes they are happy . . . if it is bad they become miserable and disconsolate. If you read the biographies of unbelievers, you will find that this undoubtedly is the case; other than some temporary view, *the vast majority just wander aimlessly.* There is no goal. There is no road. When they find themselves in a crisis or an emergency, there is nowhere they can go for help and sustenance—there is no path. "Blessed is the man whose strength is in Thee, in whose heart are the *highways of God!"* (Ps 84:5). That is the great message of the Christian faith. (58–63)

Christianity is truth, and truth in the mind is "intellectual." The very first thing that happens to people who become Christians is that they begin to *"think straighter"*—the highway of the mind is laid open and they begin to see life as they have never seen it before. It gives them a new understanding and a whole view of life. All of the New Testament epistles are, in a sense, just a *"map of life"*—in it they see themselves as under God and in relationship to Him. The believer can confidently say, "I understand life; I understand myself; and I am not one bit surprised that the world is as it is." *For the unbeliever, the whole world is upside* *down and in a state of chaos—not so for the believer.* The gospel shows us that life is a pilgrimage, and that we are travelers and sojourners in this world—we simply follow the "light" on the road of holiness we travel. Though there are times of testing and trials and tribulations and a valley of tears, *we are still not victims of our circumstances—we are more than conquerors* (Rom 8:37), because "God is with us, and He comforts us" (Ps 23:4). The fact is, our troubles make us think all the more about God and Christ. This is the secret of the Christian life—the more things go against us the more they drive us to Christ, and the more we are with Christ the happier we are. So our valleys of tears turn into springs of rejoicing, and we realize this life is just a temporary journey. Do you know where you are going? Face it honestly, and if you have to admit it scares you, go and admit it to God. *Plead with Him and ask Him to send His Holy Spirit to bulldoze a* **"highway"** *in your soul that will bring you to Himself.* (64–73)

The psalmist reviews the long history of the children of Israel in Psalm 78—they were the people of God, yet they were found grumbling, rebelling, complaining, defeated by their enemies, and sometimes even utterly disgraceful. David said they were "guilty of limiting the Holy One of Israel" (v.41)—they failed to believe God's promises and listen to His voice (Ps 81:11); as such they were living in a state of misery and weakness and sometimes utter dejection; so *"God gave them up to their own heart's lusts; as such they walked in their own counsels"* (Ps 81:11). As Christians, we are God's people and we are meant to show forth His praises, His excellencies, His virtues. Are we guilty in some shape or form of "limiting the Holy One of Israel"? God is sovereign, almighty and omnipotent. There is a tremendous responsibility that comes upon the Church as a whole—we have something to offer to a world that is in utter chaos, despair and hopelessness. Are we "limiting God"? Are we uncertain about our "forgiveness"? Christians who merely go on hoping, wondering whether they are forgiven . . . they are living as the children of Israel were living. We are not meant to live like that. *We are meant to "know" with absolute certainty that God loves us, that we are God's children and joint heirs with Christ, and that our sins are forgiven*—we have been given the Holy Spirit ("Comforter") so that we might truly understand and know these things. (74–82)

Having "assurance" of these things leads to "rejoicing!" God's people are meant to be a rejoicing people (Phil 4:4). Even in tribulation. Christians are not meant to be miserable and unhappy—that is limiting the Holy One of Israel. We should be delighting in God and His commandments; not grumbling and complaining. A corollary of rejoicing in the Lord, is that it leads to enjoying the "peace of God" (Phil 4:6–7). Do we know something of the peace of God that passes all understanding? We can have a peace that nothing can disturb—it is our duty to enjoy it; we are sinning (not trusting) if we do not. Conversely, we should be "resting in Him and in His all-sufficiency." Paul said he had learned in whatever state he was in to be "content" (Phil 4:11); that he can "do all things through Christ who strengthens him" (Phil 4:13). Do you know Christ to be *"all-sufficient"* in times of trouble? Here are five of the most common causes for *limiting God*—

1. Sin and obedience—you will never know the blessings of the Christian life if you are deliberately sinning; to deliberately continue in sin will only bring the chastening hand of God.

2. Self-confidence and self-reliance—the Children of Israel often felt they did not need the power of God; they could gather an army and muster their own forces; as such they challenged their enemies in their own strength, and were defeated. Many churches today believe they can do the work of ministry in their own strength and still be successful; they fail to realize that it is the Spirit who "produces fruit" (not man). This point needs to be expanded upon—when we "do ministry" it is *natural* to routinely do the things we have always done, and simply expect God to bless. To do things in the "power of the Spirit" means *"consciously relying and depending upon Him;"* most ministry is simply "too routine"—mechanical methodology—thus, it is not done in the power of the Holy Spirit; therefore it is neither effectual or fruitful.

3. <u>Ignorance and blindness</u>—ignorance of what is taught in Scripture; ignorance of history. That was the trouble with the children of Israel; they forgot God's works and wonders, and were ignorant of the history of their own past (Ps 78:11).

4. <u>Unbelief</u>—not taking the Bible seriously or interpreting it correctly. They would say things like, "that is only meant for special people, not ordinary people;" a kind of fatalism.

5. <u>Fear</u>—fear of the cost of these things; fear of the consequences; fear of persecution; fear of mockery. (82–91)

A psalm is a song, a kind of poem; therefore it has a message which is complete in and of itself. So, it is always essential to take a psalm as a whole. Psalm 63 was the favorite hymn of John Chrysostom, the "golden-mouthed" orator and preacher of the 4th century. It is generally agreed that David wrote this psalm at the time of the insurrection of his son Absalom—he had to flee for his life. He says, *"My soul thirsts for Thee, O God; my flesh longs for Thee in a dry and weary land, where there is no water"* (63:1). This is true of many individuals in the Church today—they are undergoing grievous problems, with everything apparently against them. A time of trouble or difficult is a *"time of testing"*—what it does is test where we really are spiritually, and how much faith we really have. A time of affluence and prosperity never tests our profession. But the moment things go wrong, you will know exactly the value of what you claim to believe. So the real value of what you claim as your profession of the Christian faith, is to know how you react and how you behave in a time of trouble. *Everyone of us will eventually be in a "wilderness"*—so here is the test: what are we like when we find ourselves in the wilderness? This is the supreme test of our whole profession of the Christian faith, so let's consider the following *three tests* as to how we measure up to being true Christians.

1. <u>Adversity always drives true Christians to God</u>. When something goes wrong many people cry, "Why has God done this to me?" And they turn away from God. But the true believer does the exact

opposite—his immediate reaction is to "draw near to God"—"To whom shall we go but Thee?" There is a kind of instinctive reaction to turn to God.

2. <u>True Christians feel that they have a right to turn to God</u>—because they know Him. David fled to his God, "Thou art my God" (Ps 63:1); there is a consciousness of this personal relationship; he knew that God was his God and that he was God's child. There was no query or doubt about that in David's mind. David goes on to say, "My soul thirsts for Thee—as the deer pants for water, so my soul pants for You, O God" (Ps 42:1).

3. <u>The greatest desire for true Christians is to feel the presence of God.</u> What David wanted was to experience God in that wilderness. David longs for an assurance that God is still with him, and that He will never leave him or forsake him. He cries out for it. This is the thing that the true child of God wants above everything else—*"Tell me Thou art mine, O Savior; grant me clear assurance."* This is always a mark of the children of God; the desire for an intimate knowledge of God is the most important thing in their lives. When we are in the wilderness, our biggest concern as Christians is not with the circumstances—though that is a legitimate concern—it is the assuring presence of God. Says the hymn writer, **Bill Williams**, *"The one who loves always wants to know that he or she is loved in return."* David realizes, "I have known it in the sanctuary, but I know that it is equally possible here" (63:2). The longing of the Christian in all circumstances is just to know that God is with him and is looking upon him—"*My soul thirsts for Thee, my soul longs for Thee*" (63:1). (92–100)

David says, "Thy lovingkindness is better than life" (Ps 63:3). Here is a profound statement. To the true believer, God's lovingkindness is the most precious thing in life. The children of God want this presence of God, this felt realization of God's lovingkindness above everything else. That is why the apostle Paul could say, *"To me to live is Christ"* (Phil 1:21). That is life! "That I may know Him; and the power of His resurrection, and the fellowship of His sufferings" (Phil 3:10). The true child of God constantly realizes that this is a "passing world," a transient life. But the world wants you to concentrate upon it—that is the whole fallacy of man in sin—and everywhere you look, be it the newspaper, books, journals, entertainment, television, you name it, it is screaming that you pay attention to "living life to the full in this world!" But Christians know that life in this world can never really completely satisfy or fulfill them. The child of God is someone who can honestly say, *"I don't know what it is, but I have never found complete satisfaction in this world as such, never!"* This is partly, of course, because it is a world of trials and troubles, but even aside from problems, life in this world has never truly brought satisfaction or fulfillment; it is mainly vain and empty, even at its best and highest—all is but pomp and show. *It is a world where "moth and rust corrupt and where thieves break-in and steal"* (Mt 5:19); that is the world at its best! So the true child of God, like David, has come to see that mere living, mere existence, merely going on, getting out of this hole or this trouble, is not the first thing. No, they have seen it as it is, no longer deluded by its glamour and pretence. (100–103)

Thy "lovingkindness" is better than life! Why? Because there is nothing comparable to it! If you know anything of what it means to "be in love," you know that you desire to be in the presence of the object of your love more than the whole world. *"Love-sick" people are those who are unhappy because they are separated from the one they love.* They still have their money, their houses, and their friends, but they are love-sick and unhappy because the loved one is not there. You can offer them the whole world, but it is useless, for they only want their loved one. This is of more value to them than the whole of life. When you have seen something of God's glory, you will also say, "There is nothing of any significant value when contrasted with this—nothing." Once someone has had any knowledge of God, there is nothing else that one can compare it. Furthermore, David says, he has found a "satisfaction in this intimate knowledge of God"—the world cannot give this kind of satisfaction, but God does give it. He is able to satisfy the soul even in the midst of affliction and suffering—He gives light to the soul of His children even in the darkness. Not only does He satisfy their minds, He also satisfies their hearts. "God's peace passes all understanding" (Phil 4:6). (103–108)

We are living in a difficult and "trying world," and sooner or later, we all find ourselves in some kind of a wilderness, where nothing matters but Christ. When we are bereft of all the things we normally have and enjoy—health, strength, wealth, friends, entertainment—nothing matters except our knowledge of God's lovingkindness. We should never lose sight of the fact that God cares so much for us He died for us, that He is ever-present with us, that He wants us to turn to Him for help, that He wants us to trust Him with our situation, and that He wants us to enjoy His presence in the midst of humbling, difficult circumstances. People are not merely interested in something *theoretical*—but they are interested in *reality!* Our faith is not based on wishful thinking, hopeful desires, or pipe dreams—it is based on the reality of God's character and what He has promised us. In short, it is absolute. The believer must always remember that the dynamic of the flesh is *"feelings"*—if we give more consideration to our feelings than to objective truth, we will struggle tremendously in our *"faith"* (the dynamic of the Spirit)—believing the truth must always trump feelings. Don't worry about your feelings—it is a question of believing. God never commands us to *"feel"* anything, but he does command us to "think and believe and do" certain things—and that is where we must place our focus. Conversely, *the Bible never teaches a cold, intellectual believism,* but an experience which involves the whole person—when we place objective truth in the forefront, and *"affirm its reality,"* that truth will settle in our souls and open a floodgate of joy and peace. Feelings are critically important, but they are not the foundation upon which we make decisions and build our lives—you make decisions based upon objective truth.

Seek God with "great fervor" and God will bless you tremendously— David writes, "My soul follows hard after Thee" (Ps 63:8). ***Isaac Watts*** stated it well in his great hymn: *"Love so amazing, so divine, demands my soul, my life, my all"*—this is that ultimate reality upon which we must build our lives. Remind yourself of what God has done for you in the past, and remind yourself of God's love for you—"Count your blessings, name them one by one; and it will surprise you what the Lord hath done." *It makes no sense to try and "work up your heart," or "work up your* *feelings"—it cannot be done, but you can reflect upon what God has done for you, and as you do you will find that your heart will begin to melt.* But you have to make the intellectual effort, exercise your will, and affirm the truth . . . and God will suddenly come and visit you . . . this is the great art of recollection. Start with what you have, and then go through this process and it will lead you upwards and onwards. "Be anxious for nothing, but in everything with prayer and supplication *with thanksgiving*, let your requests be made known to God" (Phil 4:6). How little do we thank God? How quick we are to grumble and complain? Most of us are always ready to remind Him of things that have gone wrong. So, begin to *"praise Him"* for what you have . . . praise Him for everything (health, strength, faculties, wealth) . . . and, as **William Carey** said, "confidently expect great things from God." **John Newton** wrote this little poem: (109–126)

> *Thou art coming to a King,*
> *Large petitions with thee bring.*
> *For His grace and power are such,*
> *None can never ask too much.*

David was a man of "like passions" as ourselves—he had many troubles; he brought many of them upon himself (as we do); but many came in spite of him . . . he lived a very tempestuous kind of life, yet through it all, with all his sins and faults and failures, you find this man going steadily forward . . . a man who was *"well pleasing in God's sight."* Obviously, such a man has a great deal to teach us. David gives us the secret to life—"I have set the Lord always before me" (Ps 16:8)—*David determined to live life in the conscious presence of God, and as long as he did that "he would not be moved."* Paul said something similar—"Set your affections on things above, not on things of the earth" (Col 3:2). We must get the right perspective; be constantly looking at those things; "setting" implies a determination, an act of the will, meditation and consideration (Heb 12:2). We too must determine and decide, and exercise our will power. We must not allow ourselves to drift and allow life to manipulate us and carry us along. Life seems to be organized for us, and the most difficult thing in the world is just to isolate ourselves and to insist upon controlling our lives, living them as we believe they should be lived. We cannot become so encumbered with the things of this world, that we forget about our immortal souls—we must determine and *"resolve to keep the Lord always before us!"* That is the first thing! (127–131)

There are "two sides" to this Christian life in which we find ourselves— There is the *"divine"* initiative without which nothing happens at all. But, as the result of that divine initiative, we are meant to initiate things *"ourselves."* We must "set our affections" on things above (Col 3:2). We must compel ourselves and discipline ourselves to do this; it involves a very definite activity on our part—it is not just going to *"happen all by itself"* because we are believers. Many believers take the view that they just need to go on as they are and pray that God will do something to us. *No!!* We must "always consciously set the Lord before us!" We must deliberately insist upon setting our minds upon Him. We cannot surrender to the "I don't feel very spiritual today" mood. Passive spirituality will not cut it! You must act! By the way, those individuals who have experienced the most gracious visitations from God have been those who have *"sought Him most diligently."* Remember, "God is a rewarder of them that *diligently seek Him*" (Heb 11:6). Consciously seek the presence of God . . . insist upon it . . . study His Word, and recognize that God is speaking to you! Listen to Him and you will come into His presence. Pour out your heart to Him . . . talking and listening to God are the ways in which you set Him before you. (132–139)

In Psalm 27, David teaches us how to face the whole problem and battle of life and living. The psalmist does not pretend that he is better than he is—he opens his heart and exposes himself exactly as he is. He tells us about his fears and his forebodings and his weaknesses, so we feel that he speaks to our condition. *In our daily lives each of us is involved in struggle—it is a common reality for every believer.* We can expect difficulties and trials simply because we are followers of Christ. Look at His life—though He was the Son of God, He was tried! He was tempted! He was tested! He had to suffer! His life was one of battle and conflict . . .

and if it was true for Him, how much more is it likely to be true for us as His followers? Jesus said, *"In this world you will have tribulations"*—we are not promised an easy life; yet we can be *"more than conquerors."* It is the politicians and philosophers who are always promising us that our troubles will be abolished—they are the dangerous optimists, the idealists, who are always going to make a perfect world. And it is absolute *"nonsense."* The Bible tells us that while men and women are in rebellion against God and are sinners, the world will be full of problems and difficulties. Psalm 27 can be divided up into "three sections"—

1. **The psalmist expresses his "confidence and assurance" in vv. 1–6**—When facing conflicts in life, we must start with a grand strategy of life that *begins in heaven with God;* then having done that, we come down to earth and face the problems of life. Never start with your problems! Never! Never start with earth. Never start with men. Always start in heaven with *GOD!* So, start with your relationship with God. *The whole problem in the world today is that people start with themselves, with the world, with life, and with their problems—and that inevitably leads to failure.* Therefore, we start with the psalmist's confidence—"The Lord is my light and my salvation; whom shall I fear?" He says, in effect, "I am not afraid, nor is there any need to be afraid; even though my enemies conspire together against me, it does not matter; let war rise against me; nothing can defeat me!" This is overwhelming assurance. What is the source of his confidence? Well, he tells us quite plainly that it is nothing in himself—*"I would have fainted, unless I had believed I would see the goodness of God."* He does not say as the poet **W. E. Henley** once said: "I am the master of my fate, I am the captain of my soul"—which is sheer nonsense. So the first great characteristic of us as Christians, is that we are no longer *self-confident;* we know the truth about ourselves—our source of confidence is *"the Lord."*

2. **The psalmist then comes to his "petition and prayer" in the midst of his struggle in vv. 7–12**—After expressing our confidence in the Lord, the psalmist then cries out to the Lord, "Hear, O Lord, when

I cry unto Thee; Thy face will I seek." *The tribulations in life result in darkness*—we do not understand, we do not see what we can do about them—but, *"The Lord is my light!"* We do not believe in something like evolution and hold that the world is getting better and better, because it is painfully evident that is not the case—it is getting worse and worse. We observe the futility and everything else, and we realize it is all due to man's rebellion against God. Therefore, we do not expect any different. We have "light" on the situation . . . we are no longer in the kingdom of darkness . . . we belong to a different realm, though we are still in this world.

3. **The psalmist arrives at his "conclusion" in vv. 13–14**—"The Lord is the strength of my life." This again is the theme that runs right through the Bible. David is fully aware of the power of darkness and his own weakness—but he has a power behind him that is illimitable; therefore *"of whom shall I be afraid?" David knew of God's concern for him, and the fact that God wants us to come to Him when we are in trouble.* God comes to us even when we are overwhelmed by troubles and we are beginning to turn to human expediency and we do not know what to do. When we are utterly bewildered and frustrated, suddenly something says within us, "Why not turn to God?" This is the great word of the whole Bible: "Come to me all who are weary and heavy-laden, and I will give you rest" (Mt 11:28). "Your adversary, the devil, is as a roaring lion, seeking to devour you" (1 Pet 5:8)—therefore "cast all your care upon Christ, because He cares for you" (1 Pet 5:7). He knows all about you. He is supremely interested in all you are going through. Nothing can happen to you apart from Him. He understands all about the travail and the agony and all the weakness of the flesh. He knows it all because He came in the likeness of sinful flesh, and so with His great care and concern, He says, *"Seek My face."* He encourages us to come to Him. He is not only there and ready and willing to help us, He even has to prompt us to come to Him in prayer! God not only listens to our prayers, He inspires them! As one old hymn puts it—

Can a woman's tender care, cease towards the child she bare?
Yes, she may forgetful be, yet will I remember Thee.

There is a point beyond which human love cannot go, even when it wants to. There are agonies of the soul where a father and a mother cannot help. But God still can! Even in death, God is still with us. With such a God, it matters not what rises against us (Rom 8:31). (140–152)

David said, "I would have despaired if I had not believed in the Lord" (Ps 27:13)—that is always the beginning. You cannot have anything without *belief.* "He that comes to God must believe that He is, and that He is a rewarder of them that diligently seek Him" (Heb 11:6). God says, *"I have nothing to offer you if you do not believe in Me."* Accept the revelation, humble yourself, become a little child, and believe the truth. *Belief is the starting point—God must become the "supreme reality" in your life.* He must be the one object of your desire and of your ambition. The Apostle Paul said that his supreme desire was to "know God and the power of His resurrection, and the fellowship of His sufferings" (Phil 3:10)—"this one thing I do, forgetting what is behind, I press toward the mark" (Phil 3:13-14); it is the realization that nothing really matters ultimately in life except my relationship to God—"that I may dwell in the presence of the Lord all the days of my life" (Ps 23:6); that I am ever in communion and fellowship with God. "What I want above everything else in this world is always to be in that *'intimate relationship with God'* so that whatever may happen, I am with Him and He is with me." The whole secret of life is not obeying a set of moral duties—*it is an intimate, passionate relationship with Jesus Christ!* (153–158)

CHAPTER 13

A summary of the book . . .

"ALL THINGS FOR GOOD"
by Thomas Watson (1620–1686)

This book was written by Thomas Watson in 1663, one year after he and 2000 other ministers were ejected from the Church of England. He wrote this book to buoy desponding hearts, by reflecting on the wonderful cordial, Romans 8:28—***"God causes all things to work together for good to them that love God."*** To know that "nothing" hurts the godly, is a matter of comfort . . . that their crosses shall be turned into blessings . . . that showers of affliction water the withering root of their grace and make it flourish more—this should fill the believer's heart with joy until it runs over.

Though the Christian does not have a "perfect knowledge" of the mysteries of the gospel, yet he has a *"certain knowledge."* The Spirit of God imprints heavenly truths in the heart—a Christian may know infallibly that there is evil in sin, and beauty in holiness; he may know that he is in a state of grace (1 Jn 3:14); he may know that he will one day go to heaven (2 Cor 5:1). The Lord does not leave His children *uncertain* with regard to matters of salvation. Let us then not rest in skepticism or doubts, but labor to come to a certainty in the things of our salvation—be well grounded and confirmed in it. If we are doubting Christians, we will be wavering Christians. Believers become dejected because their *"inward comforts"* are darkened, or their *"outward comforts"* are disturbed. Men first question the truth before they fall from it.

All things work together for "good!" The expression *"work together"* refers to medicine. Several poisonous ingredients put together make a medicine that works together for the good of the patient. So, all God's providences, being divinely tempered, work together for the best in His children's lives—therefore, every thing conspires for our good. "All the paths of the Lord are mercy and truth to God's children" (Ps 25:10). The best things and the worst things (from our perspective) work for our good, and it is *"God's power"* that works the good—the verb "works together" is a *causative verb* in Greek. So God's power works for "good" in supporting us in trouble—"underneath are the everlasting arms" (Deut 33:27). Consider the lives of Daniel, Jonah and David. How is a weak Christian not only able to endure affliction, but to rejoice in it? He is upheld by the arms of the Almighty—"My strength is made perfect in weakness" (2 Cor 12:9). ***The power of God subdues our corruptions*** (Mic 7:19)—Is your sin strong? God is stronger! Is your heart hard? God makes the heart soft (Job 23:16). The power of God conquers our enemies—"Thou shall break them with a rod of iron" (Ps 2:9). There may be rage in the enemy . . . malice in the devil . . . but there is power in God! "It is nothing for Thee, Lord, to help" (2 Chr 14:11). The wisdom of God works for good—His wisdom is our Instructor . . . He is the supreme Counselor (Is 9:6). When we are in seeming absolute darkness, God says "I will guide Thee with My eye" (Ps 32:8). The goodness of God works for good to the godly—God's goodness is the means whereby He makes us good—"The goodness of God leads to repentance" (Rom 2:4). The goodness of God is a spiritual sunbeam that melts the heart into tears. God gives *"common blessings"* to everyone . . . but He only gives *"crowning blessings"* to His children—and He crowns them with "lovingkindness" (Ps 103:4). (8–15)

Are we under the guilt of sin?—**"The Lord is merciful and gracious"** (Ex 24:6). God is more willing to pardon than to punish—*mercy is His nature*. The bee naturally gives honey—it stings only when it is provoked.

God does not give mercy because we deserve it, but because *"He delights in it!"* In working for our good, God says, "I will heal their backslidings" (Hos 14:4)—God gives us His Spirit to sanctify, cleanse, purify, and refine us. Are you in great trouble?—*"I will be with you in trouble"* (Ps 91:15). He will stand by you with strength in time of trouble (Ps 37:39). Do we fear outward wants? "They that seek the Lord shall not lack any good thing" (Ps 34:10). If it is good for us, we shall receive it; if it is not good for us, then the withholding of it is good. David: "I have never seen the righteous forsaken" (Ps 37:25).

The mercies of God humble us—David wondered why God would "confer kingship upon him" (2 Sam 7:18). "Lord, what am I, that it should be better with me than others? that I should have the mercies others want? when they are better than I?" *The mercies of God have a "melting influence" upon the soul;* His mercies make us love Him (King Saul; 1 Sam 24:16). The mercies of God make the heart fruitful—when you lay out more cost upon a field, it bears a better crop; conversely, a gracious soul honors the Lord with his substance. *The mercies of God make the heart thankful*—"What shall I give to the Lord for all his benefits towards me?" (Ps 116:12-13). Every mercy enlarges the soul in gratitude. The mercies of God work compassion to others—a Christian is a temporal savior; he feeds the hungry, clothes the naked, and visits the widow and orphan in their distress. Charity drops from him freely. The Word preached works for good—it is a soul-transforming Word (1 Pet 1:23). Prayer works for good—prayer is the key that unlocks the treasury of God's mercy. Prayer keeps the heart open to God, and shut to sin; prayer is the sovereign medicine of the soul (1 Sam 1:18). The Lord's Supper works for good—it quickens the affections of the godly; it strengthens their graces; it mortifies their corruptions; it revives their hopes, and increases their joy.

The "Angels" work for the good of Saints—"They are ministering spirits sent to minister to the heirs of salvation" (Heb 1:14). The whole hierarchy of angels is employed for the good of the saints—the highest angels take care of the lowest saints. Angels do service to the saints in this life—an angel comforted Mary (Lk 1:28); stopped the mouths of lions (Dan 6:22).

Christians have an invisible guard of angels about them—"He shall give His angels charge over you, to keep you in all your ways" (Ps 91:11). As God comforts by His Spirit, so by His angels. As Christ was refreshed by an angel in His agony (Lk 22:43), so are believers in their agony—when the saints breathe their last, their souls are carried up to heaven by a convoy of angels (Lk 16:22).

"Christ's intercession" works for good—Jesus said, "I do not pray for these alone, but for all who shall believe in Me" (Jn 17:20). When a Christian is weak, and can hardly pray for himself, Jesus Christ is praying for him. Jesus prays that believers be kept from sin (Jn 17:15); that they progress in holiness (Jn 17:17); that they be glorified (Jn 17:24). *What a comfort this is—when Satan is tempting—Christ is praying!*

The prayers of "Saints" work for good to the godly—The prayers of saints prevail much; for recovery from sickness (Jam 5:15); for victory over enemies (Is 37:4); for deliverance from hard times (Acts 12:5-7); for forgiveness of sins (Job 42:8). One of the amazing things about the body of Christ is the *"efficacious"* nature of intercessory prayer.

It is not that the "worst things" in life are good in and of themselves, but the overruling hand of God disposes and sanctifies them so that they have a *morally good effect* upon our lives. So things that seem to move contrary to the godly, yet by the wonderful providence of God work for their good. *In all the afflictions that befall us, God has a special hand in them* (Ruth 1:21; Jer 24:5; Ps 119:71). Afflictions to the godly are medicinal. No vessel can be made of gold without fire. Said Joseph, "You meant it for evil, but God meant it for good" (Gen 50:20). As the hard frosts in winter bring on the flowers in the spring, so the evils of affliction produce much good to those that love God. We are prone to question the truth of this, as Mary did to the angel, "How can this be?" **Luther** *said he could never rightly understand some of the Psalms, till he was in affliction*—God makes us know affliction that we may better know ourselves; we see that corruption in our hearts in the time of affliction, which we would not otherwise believe was there. *In the fire of affliction the impurities of the heart, impatience and unbelief raise to the surface.* Afflictions work for good, in that they serve to conform us to Christ. Afflictions also serve to destroy sin—there is much corruption in the best heart; affliction does by degrees work it out, as the fire works out the dross from the gold. (16–31)

The "evil of temptation" is overruled for good to the godly. Satan walks about to tempt the saints; he labors to storm the castle of the heart; he throws in thoughts of blasphemy; he tempts to deny God; he tempts to inflame the passions. Satan will not tempt contrary to the "natural disposition and temperament" of the individual—*the wind of temptation blows as the natural tide of the heart runs.* Satan also knows the best time to tempt—just as a soldier, who after a battle leaves off his armor, not at all thinking of an enemy, Satan watches his time. Satan also makes use of close relationships—he handed over a temptation to Job by his wife (Job 2:9). Satan also uses godly men to tempt us—he used Peter to tempt Christ. *Satan can propose the object . . . instill evil thoughts into the mind . . . and excite and irritate the corruption within.*

These temptations are overruled for good to the children of God. A tree that is shaken by the wind is more settled and rooted; so, the blowing of a temptation settles the Christian more in grace. Temptations are overruled for good in the following ways: Temptation sends the soul to prayer—the more furiously Satan tempts, the more fervently the saint prays. Consider Paul and his thorn in the flesh (2 Cor 12:8). The more a child of God is tempted, the more he fights against the temptation. *Temptation abates the swelling of pride—better is that temptation which humbles me, than that duty which makes me proud.* Temptation is used by God to try us—temptation is a trial of our sincerity. Temptation makes us fit to comfort others in the same distress (Paul and 2 Cor 1:3–4; 2:11). Temptation stirs up paternal compassion in God to them who are tempted. Temptation makes the believer long more for heaven—when believers are ascended to heaven, they will no longer be molested by the old serpent. Temptation engages the strength of Christ on our behalf—if a poor soul was to fight alone with the Goliath of hell, he would be sure to be vanquished—*"through Him we are more than conquerors"* (Rom 8:37). Sometimes temptation foils the believer—Peter was tempted to self-confidence; he presumed upon his own strength, so Christ let him fall; but this wrought good though it cost him many a tear (Mt 26:75). From that point on he would not say he loved Christ more than the other apostles (Jn 21:15)—his fall broke the neck of his pride. Luther said, *"There are three things that make a Christian—prayer, meditation, and temptation."*

Sometimes God "withdraws" from us; however, we desert Him before He deserts us. We desert God when we leave off close communion with Him. So, when God withdraws, there is darkness and sorrow in the soul. Desertion is an agony of conscience—"the arrows of the Almighty are within me, the poison whereof drinks up my spirit" (Job 6:4). In times of desertion the people of God are apt to think that God has cast them off. *There may be the "seed of grace" where there is not the "flower of joy"*—vessels at sea being tossed to and fro in a storm may be laden with jewels and spices. David, in a state of dejection, prays, "Take not Thy Holy Spirit from me" (Ps 51:11). It should be noted that *desertions are but for a time;* God ultimately responds in mercy (Is 54:8; 57:16). The tender mother sets down her child in anger, but she will take it up again into her arms and kiss it. Desertion cures the soul of sloth. Desertion cures inordinate affection to the world—we may use it as an "inn" where we take a meal, but it must not be our home. Desertion makes the saints prize God's countenance more than ever—"Thy lovingkindness is better than life" (Ps 63:3). *God has no better way to make us value His love, than by withdrawing it awhile.* If the sun shown once a year, how would it be prized? Desertion embitters sin to us—can there be a greater misery than to have God's displeasure? What makes hell but the hiding of God's face? And what makes God hide His face but sin? (Ps 66:18). Desertion sets the soul a weeping for the loss of God—when the sun goes down, the dew falls; when God is gone, tears drop from the eyes. Though it be sad to want God's presence, yet it is good to lament His absence. *Desertion sets the soul a seeking after God*—when Christ was departed, the spouse pursues after Him; the deserted soul knocks at heaven's gate by prayer. Desertion puts the Christian upon inquiry—He inquires the cause of God's departure. Desertion gives us a sight of what Jesus Christ suffered for us—if the sipping of the cup be so bitter, how bitter was that which

Christ drank upon the cross? (Mt 27:46). *None can so appreciate Christ's suffering as those who have been humbled by desertion, and have been held over the flames of hell for a time.* Desertion prepares the saints for future comfort—it is God's way to first cast down, then to comfort (2 Cor 7:6). The Lord brings us into the deep of desertion, that He may not bring us into the deep of damnation. (32–44)

"Sinful behavior" against a believer works for his good—Though sin by its own nature is damnable, God in His infinite wisdom overrules it, and causes good to arise from it. God overrules the sins of others for "good" in the life of the believer. Said **Augustine,** *"God would never permit evil, if He could not bring good out of it."* The most heinous evil ever perpetrated by man (the cross)—purchased our salvation!

Why all things work together for "good"?—The grand reason why God causes all things to work together for good in the believer's life, is the love God has for His people—"They shall be My people, and I will be their God" (Jer 32:38). By virtue of this compact, all things must work for our good. Ultimately, all of God's dealings with us, though some are sharp and painful, yet they are safe and bring healing. "As a father chastens his son, so the Lord chastens His children" (Deut 8:5; Heb 12:6)—God chastens not to destroy but to reform. God will not ruin His children, for He is a tender-hearted Father—"As a father pities his children, so the Lord pities those who fear Him" (Ps 103:13). God is the tender-hearted "Father of mercies" (2 Cor 1:3). There is a marriage relation between God and His people—"Thy Maker is thy Husband" (Is 54:5). Jesus calls us "friends"—Augustine described a friend as *"half one's self."* (44–55)

Things do not work together for good of themselves—"God causes" them to work together for good. God is the great Disposer of all events and issues—*"His kingdom ruleth over all"* (Ps 103:19). The things in the world are not governed by second causes, by the counsels of men, by the stars and the planets, but by *"divine providence."* God sets everything a working. That which is by some called "chance" is nothing else but the result of divine providence. Providence mingles the ingredients, and makes up the whole compound. The most dark, cloudy providences of

God have some sunshine in them. *What a blessed condition is a true believer in—when he dies, he goes to God; and while he lives, everything shall do him good.* What hurt does the fire to the gold? It only purifies it! Though affliction has a bitter root, it bears a sweet fruit—"it yields the peaceful fruit of righteousness" (Heb 12:11).

By the "wisdom of God," the worst things imaginable turn to the good of the saints—God can by divine chemistry extract *gold* out of *dross*—"Oh the depth of the wisdom of God!" (Rom 11:33). God enriches by impoverishing; He causes the augmentation of grace by the diminution of an estate. God works strangely. *He brings order out of confusion, harmony out of discord.* He frequently makes use of unjust men to do that which is just—either the wicked shall not do the hurt that they intend, or they shall do the good which they do not intend (Gen 50:20). God often helps when there is least hope, and saves His people in that way which they think will destroy. Incredible as it may seem, He made use of the high-priest's malice and Judas' treason to redeem the world! *"God's ways are not our ways!"* (Is 55:8). God's ways are "past finding out" (Rom 11:33). How stupendous and infinite is that wisdom that makes the most adverse dispensations work for the good of His children! (55–61)

Learn how little cause we have to be "discontented" at outward trials and emergencies. There are no sins God's people are more subject to than *"unbelief"* and *"impatience"*—they are ready either to faint through unbelief, or fret through impatience. Discontent is an "ungrateful sin," because we have far more mercies than afflictions; furthermore, shall we be discontented at that which works for our good? The Lord may bruise us by afflictions, but it is to enrich us. Since afflictions work for us a weight of glory, shall we be discontented? God works out sin, and works in grace—is not that good? "We are chastened by the Lord that we should not be condemned with the world" (1 Cor 11:32). The apostle Paul says, "In everything give thanks" (1 Th 5:18). Why so? Because God makes everything work for our good. Many thank God when He gives; Job thanked God when He took away (Job 1:21). *Being thankful in affliction is a work peculiar only to a saint; only a true saint can be thankful in* *adversity.* Therefore, let us endeavor to make the name of God glorious and renowned—*if God seeks our good, let us seek His glory!* If He makes all things tend to our edification, let us make all things tend to His exaltation. When we have done our best, we must vanish away in our own thoughts, and transfer all the glory to God. The apostle Paul said, "I labored more abundantly than all of them" (1 Cor 15:10)—does that not sound prideful? Keep reading—the apostle pulls off the crown from his own head, and sets it upon the head of "grace"—"Yet not I, but the grace of God which was with me." **Constantine** (Roman Emperor in 337 AD) used to write the *"name of Christ"* over the door—so should we over all our duties and efforts. (61–65)

Expressing "love to God" is an expansion of the soul, by which we breathe after God as the "sovereign good." We love God because of His grace to cleanse us and forgive us, and ultimately to crown us. *He is a sea of goodness without bottom.* God has an innate propensity to dispense mercy and grace to those who will but believe in Him. When we esteem God above all else, everything else vanishes when He appears—like stars vanishing when the sun appears. All creatures vanish in our thoughts when the "Sun" of righteousness shines in His full splendor. We love God not for what He bestows; we love Him for His intrinsic excellencies. You don't hire a mother to love her child—likewise, a soul deeply in love with God does not need to be hired by rewards. Additionally, many waters cannot quench love—neither the sweet waters of pleasure, nor the bitter waters of persecution. Love to God abides firm to the end. (66–73)

Our love to God will be best seen by the "fruits of it"—He who loves God, his thoughts are ever upon the object (Ps 139:18; Heb 12:2); conversely, God is scarcely ever in the thoughts of the unbeliever (Ps 10:4). *He who loves God converses with God* (Word and Prayer)—lovers cannot be long away from each other. Where there is love to God there is grieving for our sins (Mt 26:75). He who loves God will stand up in His cause, and be an advocate for Him—love for God casts out fear; he who loves his friend will stand up for him. He who loves God aches when God is dishonored (2 Pet 2:7). He who loves God purges out sin—the love of God and the love of sin cannot dwell together; our affections cannot be carried in two contrarieties at the same time; *a man cannot love health and poison also.* He who loves God is dead to the world (Gal 6:14); he who is in love with God is not much in love with anything else—love to God swallows up all other love (Acts 4:35). What is there in the earth that we should so set our hearts upon it? *The world has no real intrinsic worth; it is but paint and deception.* He who loves God fears displeasing Him (Gen 39:9). He who loves God is more afraid of the loss of spiritual blessings, than temporal ones. He who loves God loves what God loves (Ps 119:72, 103)—He loves God's law; conversely, the wicked pretend to love Christ as Savior, but hate Him as King and Lord—they would have Christ put a crown upon their heads, but not a yoke upon their necks. *A saint in this life is like gold in the ore; much dross of infirmity cleaves to him, yet we love him for the grace that is in him.* He who loves God thinks good thoughts about God (1 Cor 13:5)—how good is God, that He will not let me alone in my sins, but smites my body to save my soul. It is *Satan* that makes us have good thoughts of ourselves, and hard thoughts of God. He who loves God obeys God (Jn 14:15, 21); does that child love his father, who refuses to obey him? If we love God we will "forgive one another" (Eph 4:32)—this is hard, because we are apt to forget kindnesses and remember injuries; but if we love God we will pass by offences. Love made Christ suffer for us; if we love God, we should be willing to suffer for Him—Love endures all things" (1 Cor 13:7). Stephen was stoned, Luke hanged, and Peter crucified . . . for Christ's sake! He who loves God will proclaim His excellencies, that He will appear glorious in the eyes of others, and induce them to fall in love with Him. Love is like fire—where it burns in the heart, it will break forth in his speech. He who loves God will long for Christ's appearing (2 Tim 4:8)—love desires union; when our union with Christ is perfect in glory, then our joy will be full. *He who loves God will stoop to serve Christ and His members regardless of the cost*—if we love God, we shall not think any work too mean for us, by which we may be helpful to Christ's members—it will visit the sick, relieve the poor, and wash the saints' wounds. (74–87)

"Loving God" is not easy as most imagine—Men are by nature *"haters of God"* (Rom 1:30); they would neither be under His rules, nor within His reach. It is only the almighty and invincible power of the Spirit of God that can infuse love into the soul. *Following are a number of "MOTIVES" for loving God:* It is not duty, but *love to duty,* that God looks at—duties not mingled with love are as burdensome to God as they are to us. *It is by love that we grow in Christ's likeness* (1 Jn 4:16)—love is a grace which most delights in God. We cannot spend our love on a better object; there is nothing in God that can cause a loathing. Love facilitates religion—it oils the wheels of the affections; it takes off the tediousness of duty (cross reference Jacob's love for Rachel); *he that loves God is never weary of serving Him.* God desires our love—what is there in our love that God should seek it? God deserves our love—what a miracle that God should love us, when there was nothing lovely in us. What love, that Christ should die for sinners! **Charles Wesley:** "Amazing love, how can it be, that Thou my God shouldst die for me?" God set all the angels of heaven wondering at His love. Will we love the world more than He? Love to God is the best self-love; it is self-love to get the soul saved; by loving God—to love God is the truest self-love; he that does not love God does not truly love himself (seek his own highest good). *We love God because He first loved us*—knowing we are loved by God, can only result in a heart burning in love for Him.

It is better to "love God" than to love the world—worldly things cannot remove troubles in the soul (1 Sam 28:15); loving God gives you peace when nothing else can; if we love God, He will love us in return (Jn 14:23); *when you love the world, you love that which is worth infinitely less than your soul;* worldly things die and leave you—riches take wings, relations drop away, there is nothing abiding in worldly things. But if you love God, "He is your portion forever" (Ps 73:26). It is better to love God than sin—sin is a debtor—it binds you over to death. Sin is a disease—will you hug a disease? Sin is pollution—it is compared to poison. *Sin is an enemy—it has four stings: shame, guilt, horror, and death.* Will a man seek that which seeks his death? God our Maker is our Husband (Is 54:5)—His spouse is to Him the apple of His eye; He rejoices over her; shall a wife leave her husband? Love to God will never let sin thrive in the heart—love to God withers sin—though sin does not die perfectly, yet it dies daily. Love to God is an excellent means for growth of grace (2 Pet 3:18); love is like watering the root which makes the tree grow. Love to God accrues great benefits to us—"Eye hath not seen, nor ear heard, the things God hath prepared for them that love Him" (1 Cor 2:9); God has promised a "crown consisting in life" to them that love Him (Jam 1:12). *Love to God is the armor of proof against heresy*—men give themselves up to strong delusions when they "receive not the love of the truth" (2 Th 2:10–11); the more we love God the more we despise the heterodox opinions that would draw us away from God. *If we love God, everything in the world shall conspire for our good*—every wind shall blow to a heavenly port. He who loves God will cleave to Him and keep himself from apostasy (Ruth 1:16–17)—*a lack of love for God in the heart, will cause us to* **"fall away"** *in time of temptation.* (88–97)

What shall we do to love God? The answer in a word is to *STUDY GOD!* Did we study Him more, we should love Him more. The angels know God better than we do; therefore they are more deeply enamored with Him. The more we believe, the more we love—faith is the root, and love is the flower that grows upon it. *"Faith worketh love"* (Gal 5:6). Make it your earnest request to God, that He will give you a heart to love Him. Surely this prayer pleases the Lord, and He will pour out His Spirit upon you. If you have love to God, labor to preserve it; don't let it die or be quenched. "Thou hast left your first love" (Rev 2:4). Satan labors to blow out this flame, and through neglect of duty we lose it. *Of all the graces, love is most apt to decay;* therefore we have need to be more careful to preserve it. It is sad to see pastors and professors declining in their love for God. There are *four signs* by which Christians may know that their love is in a state of decaying:

1. <u>When we lose our taste</u>—When we lose our taste, we find no sweetness in a promise; it is a sign of spiritual consumption. Time was, when we found comfort in drawing nigh to God; His Word was like honey, delicious to the palate of the soul, but now it is otherwise—they taste no more sweetness. Have you lost your taste?

2. <u>When we lose our appetite</u>—Time was when we hungered and thirsted after righteousness (Mt 5:6). We minded things of heavenly aspect, but now the case is altered; our hearts no longer burn within us; our love is decaying.

3. <u>When we grow in love with the world</u>—When our thoughts and affections are encompassing the world, that is a sign we are going downhill spiritually. When rust cleaves to metal, it not only takes away the brightness of the metal, but it consumes it.

4. <u>When we make little of God's worship</u>—When duties of religion are performed in a dead and formal manner; conversely, when the strings of a violin are slack, the violin will never make good music; additionally, when men grow slack in duty, they pray as if they prayed not—why? they have left their first love. A soldier may as well be without his weapons, an artist without his brush, a musician without his instrument, as a Christian can be without love. Love is to the soul what natural heat is to the body—there is no living without it. Love influences the graces; it excites the affections; it makes us grieve for sin; it makes us cheerful in God; it is like oil to the wheels; it quickens us in God's service.

How may we keep our love from going out? Watch your heart EVERY DAY! Take notice of the first declinings in grace, and use all means for quickening. Be much in prayer, meditation, and holy conference. *When the fire is going out you throw on "fuel" to get it going again.* Make use of God's promises to keep the fire of your love burning. They who have a few sparks of love should blow up those divine sparks into a flame. *You who love God little, labor to love Him more.* A godly man is contented with very little of this world. The disciples love to Christ at first was weak—they fled from Christ; but after Christ's death it grew more vigorous, and they boldly preached Him. A corollary of "loving God" is "obeying Him"—*we must labor to obey Him (that is faith), if we want our love for Him to grow.* If our love to God does not increase, it will soon decrease. If you do not fan the flame of the fire, it will quickly go out. Christians should above all things endeavor to cherish and excite their love to God; as such, they must *labor in the "spiritual disciplines"*—spend time in the Word, Prayer, Meditation, Worship, Service, Fellowship, and affirming eternal realities (truth). (98–103)

All things work together for good to those who are "called" according to His purpose—When God wonderfully overpowers the heart, and draws the will to embrace Christ, this is the "effectual call" of the sinner to Christ. Before we are called, we are in bondage to Satan; in a state of darkness; without strength to grapple with temptation or inward corruption; in a state of pollution; in a state of damnation—born under a curse. The means of our effectual call is the ministry of the Word through the power of the Holy Spirit—*the Holy Spirit "draws" us to Himself* (Jn 6:44); the Word is the instrumental cause of our conversion (Rom 10:17; 1 Pet 1:23); and the Spirit is the efficient who "opens the heart" to believe (Acts 10:44; 16:14). He comes in a still small voice to some, but to those who are more stubborn sinners, He has to plough up the fallow ground of their hearts by humiliation—whatever the case, the Lord secretly and gradually instills grace into their hearts. *Though God's method in calling sinners varies, the effect is the same—they become "children of God"* (Jn 1:12). It should be noted that God so calls as He allures—He does not force us, but draws us. The freedom of the will is not taken away, but the stubbornness of it is conquered (Ps 110:3)—the soul readily obeys God's call. The call of God calls men out of their sins; as such, they are separated from sin, and consecrated to God's service—therefore the call of God is a *"holy calling"* (1 Th 4:7). Paul responded to God's call as "being obedient to the heavenly vision" (Acts 26:19). Though many have the light brought to them, only a few have their eyes anointed to see—there are many formalists, but few genuine believers. The "Cyprian Diamond" says Pliny, "sparkles like the true diamond, but it is not the right kind—it will break with a hammer;" so will the hypocrite's faith break under the hammer of persecution. There are many pebble stones, but only a few precious stones. God's call is founded upon His decree, and His decree is immutable—"the gifts and the calling of God are irrevocable" (Rom 11:29). By the way, a man can no more convert himself than a dead man can raise himself. As God makes heaven fit for us, so He makes us fit for heaven. The "end" of our effectual calling is that we should live to the "praise of His glory" (Eph 1:12). (104–113)

Scripture exhorts us to "be diligent to make our calling sure" (2 Pet 1:10)—Do not satisfy yourself with an empty profession, but labor to evidence to your soul that you are indeed called of God. He who is genuinely called acknowledges that "he does not have a righteousness of his own" (Phil 3:9); as *Augustine* says, "self-renunciation is the first step to saving faith." Also, he who is effectively called has a "visible change" wrought in his life—he is altered from what he was before . . . his body is the same . . . but his mind is not the same; and he has another spirit. What a metamorphosis grace makes! "For such were some of you; but you are now sanctified and justified" (1 Cor 6:11). Grace changes the heart. There is a three-fold change wrought by an effectual calling—

1. There is a change in the ***understanding***—before there was ignorance and darkness; now there is light that shines

2. There is a change in the ***will***—the will, which before opposed Christ, now embraces Him (Acts 9:6; Heb 2:10). Before, the will kept Christ out; now it keeps sin out.

3. There is a change in the ***conduct***—he who is called of God, walks directly contrary to what he did before he was saved. He walked before in envy and malice, now he walks in love; before he walked in pride, now he walks in humility.

Unbelievers are the same as they were years ago—they have seen many changes in their times, but they have had no change in their heart. (113–117)

He who is called of God esteems this call as the "highest blessing"—A king whom God has called by His grace, esteems it more that he is called to be a "saint," than that he is called to be a king. He values his high-calling more than his high-birth. *Theodosius* thought it a greater honor to be a Christian than to be an emperor. A carnal person can no more value spiritual blessings than a baby can value a diamond necklace—he prefers his worldly grandeur, his ease, plenty, and titles of honor, before conversion. He had rather be called a "duke" than a "saint." He who is effectually called, though he lives in the world, he is no longer of the world—though his body be from the earth, his affections are from heaven. (117–118)

What is it to "walk worthy" of our heavenly calling? It is to walk *regularly*—to walk according to the rules and axioms of the Word (Gal 1:6). It is to walk *singularly*—when others walked with the devil, Noah walked with God (Gen 7:1). It is better to go to heaven with a few, than to hell with a crowd. We must walk in an opposite course to the men of the world. It is to walk *cheerfully*—we are to "rejoice in the Lord always" (Phil 4:4); too much drooping of spirit disparages our high calling, and makes others suspect a godly life to be melancholy. Cheerfulness is a perfume to draw others to godliness. When the prodigal was converted, "they began to be merry" (Lk 15:24). It is to walk *influentially*—to do good to others, and to be rich in acts of mercy (Heb 13:16). Good works honor religion; though they are not the cause of salvation, they are "evidences" of it. God has magnified rich grace toward you as His child—you are called to be co-partners with angels, and co-heirs with Christ—this should revive you in the worst of times. Though the sea roars and the stars are shaken out of their places—you need not fear, for you have been called by the Creator of the universe to share in His glory.

God's purpose is the "cause" of salvation—The reason for our effectual calling is "according to His purpose" (Eph 1:11). What is the reason that one man is called, and not another? It is from the eternal purpose of God. Let us then ascribe the whole work of grace to the pleasure of God's will. God did not choose us because we were worthy—by choosing us He makes us worthy. God "saved us, and called us, not according to our works, but according to His own purpose and grace" (2 Tim 1:9). There is no such thing as merit. *Our best works have in them both defection and infection, and so are but "glittering sins"*—therefore, if we are called and justified, it is God's purpose that brings it to pass. God did not choose us "for" faith, but "to" faith. "He hath chosen us that we should be holy"

(Eph 1:4). What could God foresee in us, but pollution and rebellion. If any man be saved, it is according to God's purpose. *Our graces are imperfect, our comforts ebb and flow, but God's foundation standeth sure.* They who are built upon this rock of God's eternal purpose, need not fear falling away; neither the power of man, nor the violence of temptation, shall ever be able to overturn them.

CHAPTER 14

A summary of the book...

"WHEN YOUR WORLD FALLS APART"
by David Jeremiah

David Jeremiah wrote this book to chronicle "his experience" with near terminal cancer. He begins the book with a poem that was very meaningful to him on his journey—*"A Bend in the Road"*—It reads:

> *Sometimes we come to a life's crossroads*
> *   and we view what we think is the end;*
> *But God has a much wider vision*
> *   and He knows that it's only a bend—*
> *The road will go on and get smoother*
> *   and after we've stopped for a rest,*
> *The path that lies hidden beyond us*
> *   is often the path that is best.*
> *So rest and relax and grow stronger,*
> *   let go and let God share your load,*
> *And have faith in a brighter tomorrow—*
> *   you've just come to a bend in the road.*

He writes: "Somewhere along your own path, you've likely encountered a bend in the road too." Suddenly you have faced circumstances you never expected or wished to encounter, and you read encouraging words from fellow strugglers. Fellow-struggler, **Gordon MacDonald** writes, "None of us enjoy suffering, but pain does have a way of accomplishing the *'greatest good'* in our lives by drawing us closer to God. God uses *'disruptive moments'* to help us keep things in perspective." The apostle Paul writes, *"A thorn in the flesh was given to me, a messenger of Satan to buffet me"* (2 Cor 12:7ff). God told Paul He would not remove the thorn, but would do something else—in the midst of the ordeal, He would give Paul all the *grace* he needed to continue his work—*"My grace is sufficient for you—because My strength is made perfect in weakness."* When we are weak, then we are strong—the weaker we are, the stronger His grace is revealed (2 Cor 12:9–10). It is when we are weak that we really learn to *"rely on Christ,"* and that is when we experience *"His power"* in us and accomplish what He desires.

How quickly we are prone to "strike out against God" when we come to a bend in the road. Our short-sightedness causes us to become discouraged by the event, lose heart, and want to give up. But no matter how disruptive the event may be, we need to remember that everything that happens to us is for the eternal purposes of God—He is training us through the process, with the ultimate goal in mind of "conforming us to the image of Christ." British journalist **Malcolm Muggeridge** wisely explained this to William F. Buckley—*"the only thing that has taught me anything is suffering;* not success, not happiness, not anything like that... the joy of coming in contact with what life really signifies is suffering and affliction." The only road that leads to the destination God desires for us has a number of *sharp bends*—all shortcuts only lead us into the wilderness. **Charles Spurgeon** said,

> *I bear willing witness that I owed more to the fire, and the hammer, and the file, than to anything else in my Lord's workshop. I sometimes question whether I have ever learned anything except through the rod. When my schoolroom is darkened, I see most.*

Your "crisis" is important to God—Whatever your struggle or setback, it is intended by God to empower and purify you. Never forget that. Five principles we as believers need to remember—

1. <u>Disruptive moments are simply Divine appointments</u>—Every trial we face, difficult as it may be, comes from the hand of God, who loves us and wants us to grow. Seeing disruptive moments as *divine appointments* will keep you from giving in to *discouragement.* The moment we accept the fact that our ordeal has been permitted, even intended by God, our perspective will change. You will find yourself saying, "God, You have allowed this in my life. I don't understand it, but I know that it could not have happened to me unless it was filtered through Your loving hands."

2. <u>Progress without pain is usually not possible</u>—We live in a skin-deep world—all the things the world values are cosmetic. Character and substance are shaped in the crucible of adversity. Pain makes us sensitive to God—without pain we simply end up spinning our spiritual wheels, and we go nowhere. Writes David Jeremiah: "Show me someone who lives a carefree life with no problems or trials or *dark nights of the soul*, and I will show you a shallow person." Author **Gordon MacDonald** said: "The spiritual masters have taught us that the one who would get in touch with *'his soul'* must do so with diligence and determination . . . because one must overcome feelings, fatigue, distractions, errant appetites, pain, suffering."

3. <u>The promise of God is the provision of grace</u>—God told the apostle Paul, "My grace is sufficient for you; My strength is made perfect in weakness"—therefore, it is when you are weak, and not relying on your own strength, that you are strong. God must do some pruning in order for us to thrive and bear fruit, but our Gardener is loving and devoted to our well-being. Someone has profoundly said, *"The Father is never closer to the vine than when He is pruning it."* David Jeremiah writes: "Never in all my life have I sensed the closeness and provision of God as I did when I came to the bend in the road;

and never before have I been *more fruitful* than I have been since I came through the bend in the road."

4. Disruptive moments produce dynamic growth—You can *struggle* against the disruptive moment, shake your fist at the heavens, and find yourself exhausted, defeated and in despair . . . or you can *accept* the moment and let it train and strengthen you in your inner man. God allows no pain without purpose. His power will rest upon you only when you have abandoned the idea that you are big enough to go it alone. Every plant must weather a storm every now and then. Listen to the words of **Charles Spurgeon**—

   > *Those who navigate little streams and shallow creeks, know but little of the God of tempests; but those who "do business in great waters," these see His wonders in the deep. Among the huge Atlantic waves of bereavement, poverty, temptation, and reproach, we learn the power of Jehovah, because we feel the littleness of man.*

5. What we receive from disruptive moments depends upon how we respond—"Why this, Lord?" you might ask. "Why now? Why not later? Why not someone else?" We all ask the *WHY* questions. They are a natural part of being human. But we can ask better questions—we can ask *WHAT* questions: "What Lord?" What would You have me do? What are You trying to teach me?" Reflect upon the words of **Psalm 71**—(1–27)

   > *In You, O LORD, I put my trust . . .*
   > *Incline Your ear to me, and save me.*
   > *Do not cast me off in the time of old age;*
   > *Do not forsake me when my strength fails.*
   > *O my God, make haste to help me . . .*
   > *You, who have shown me great and severe troubles,*
   > *Bring me up again from the depths of the earth.*
   > *And I shall speak of Your righteousness all the day long.*

Psalm 71 is an incredible jewel in the Scriptures—Most scholars believe it was written by David when he was going through some heart-wrenching times as a result of his sons. ***Absalom*** had turned on his father and attempted to seize the throne. ***Adonijah*** tried to usurp the throne as well, but David had already promised it to ***Solomon***. The cost to David was horrendously heavy; his aging heart was burdened with a deep grief few of us will ever experience. *God's children have no immunity whatsoever to pain or suffering.* Trials can come through friends, or enemies or aging and bad health, but they can also come from God Himself. Peter wrote, "Beloved, do not think it strange concerning the *fiery trials* you are going through, as though some strange thing is happening to you" (1 Pet 4:12). Some things cannot be learned through lectures or the written word; they must come at the cost of bruised hands and bloody knees—there are an infinite number of different kinds of trials.

God sends trouble into our lives to "strengthen us" and to make us better children in His family. Little by little, over a period of many years, we are stripped of all the things in life that gave us security. It is a season of slowly developing anxiety. David was under attack from his own children . . . in the midst of his insecurity, he found that God was his refuge, his rock, and his fortress. In those times when we feel the hostile forces of the universe pursuing us, we long for a *"strong refuge"*—the kind of security that can only be found in God Himself. *A powerful leader is invariably self-reliant and independent*—it simply comes with the territory. He charts his own course and depends on his own resources. But sooner or later, he reaches his limit, and he finds he is not self-reliant after all. When their power hits its limit, they will seek a power higher than themselves and begin to experience a feeling of dependency. In that moment of transformation, we come to suddenly realize, *"I don't control my world after all! I have no more ideas and nowhere to run or hide! Lord, only You can rescue me! Make haste to help me, O God!"*

Someone has said that Psalm 71 is filled with great praise and great complaining all at once. David's pilgrimage embodies both *"human defeat"* and *"godly victory"*—and that is not an insignificant footnote, for we tend to lack a theology of adversity in the church these days. When David saw the worst life had to dish out for him, he could still remember the perfection and faithfulness of God: "In You, O Lord, I put my trust . . . deliver me in Your righteousness . . . incline Your ear to me." Whenever we face trials, we need to remember who God is—sometimes we get so focused on our *"trials"* we forget to focus on *"Him."* Five times in Psalm 71 David mentions the "righteousness of God" (vv. 2, 15, 16, 19, 24). David understood that there was one thing he must do when trials were swirling around his head—*he must never forget that God is righteous and good, and He is a God who can be trusted.* Things may be bad, but God is never any less in control, nor does He lower His love for us. Ultimately, we fall on our knees and say, *"My Lord and my God, my hope is in You!"*

David reminded himself that God had proved "faithful to him" throughout his life. There in the midst of his suffering, he cried out, *"But still I will continue to hope in You and praise You"* (71:14). This is the mark of the truly godly person. Praising God generally does not happen until we step just far enough outside our own entrenched emotional defenses to take a good look at where God really is. David began to question, "God, now that I am old, are You finished with me?" Never assume God is through with you. Gray hair means nothing. In God's way of doing things, the best is always yet to come. Have you gradually bought into a worldview based on Murphy's Law—*"Whatever can go wrong will go wrong?"* Psalm 71 takes you down a road that leads precisely in the opposite direction. Your cynicism is replaced by faith. You see a godly future in which God bends the world's distorted hopes into His beautiful plan. David has confidence in the future because he has confidence in the One holding it. He writes, "You shall increase my greatness, and encourage me on every side" (71:21).

Trials are for our "benefit," as unwelcome as they are at the time. They make us better men and women. When you have walked through the fire, people begin to listen to you. When you have the wisdom borne of suffering, you begin to have the tools to accomplish something in the world. As God's children, *"We must learn to live with the insecurities and the ambiguities of life,* knowing that we are secure in Christ; for He is our God." The psalmist in Psalm 119 said, "Before I was afflicted I went astray, but now I keep Your word . . . it is good for me that I was afflicted, that I may learn Your statutes" (119:67, 71). Testing makes you walk the straight path, while the untested go astray. **Charles Spurgeon** suffered with prolonged bouts of depression and anxiety, and his psychological and physical ailments were so crippling that he frequently was confined to bed for weeks. But Spurgeon came to see these problems as part of God's work in his life. *His sufferings enabled him to comfort and encourage the many hurting people who were touched by his ministry.* And he found a pattern to his life—His periods of depression invariably preceded seasons of God's special blessings on his ministry. He knew he did not suffer without reason. Here are his own words: "This depression comes over me whenever the Lord is preparing a larger blessing for my ministry; the cloud is black before it breaks." This psychologically frail man, published more than 3,500 sermons, authored some 135 books, and is still regarded today as the "Prince of Preachers" in the modern era. *God is up to something when He sends difficulty our way.* (29–52)

For every pilgrim in this journey of life, the road will "bend" in a different direction. When we meet the bend in the road we must look to God for the *"grace"* to meet that defining moment. The old Swedish hymn *"Day by Day,"* written by **Carolina Sandell Berg** (1832–1903), was one of my father's favorite hymns—he was a devout believer who was born in Sweden in 1898. Berg was never strong as a child, so she spent much time in her father's study and grew especially close to him. When she was twenty-six years old, she accompanied her father, who was a parish pastor, on a short voyage to Goteborg. As they stood on deck, the boat lurched and Pastor Sandell fell overboard—the crew was unable to save him, and he drowned as his daughter looked on. This tragedy inspired many hymns, including this one. This hymn expresses the heart of God's child in the midst of trial and difficulty—

> *Day by day and with each passing moment,*
> *Strength I find to meet my trials here,*
> *Trusting in my father's wise bestowment,*
> *I've no cause for worry or for fear.*

> *He whose heart is kind beyond all measure*
> *Gives unto each day what He deems best—*
> *Lovingly, its part of pain and pleasure,*
> *Mingling toil with peace and rest.*

Even to those of us who follow Christ, the topics of pain and suffering and ultimate meaning are complex and confusing. How can we cope with them? The Bible tells us that life is like a vapor that appears for a little while and then vanishes—it is like grass that grows for a season only to be cut down and scattered by the winds. ***John Bunyan*** paints a masterpiece from that image in his classic book *Pilgrim's Progress*. Life is a journey, and we must all walk the path. So many of the psalms are written for pilgrims on the path—one of the most helpful is that of Psalm 21. In this psalm we can hear the psalmist crying out, "Lord, I need guidance for my journey . . . I've lost my way . . . will You show me where to go?"

> *I will lift up my eyes to the hills—*
>   *from whence comes my help?*
> *My help comes from the LORD,*
>   *who made heaven and earth.*
> *He will not allow your foot to be moved,*
>   *He who keeps you will not slumber . . .*
> *The LORD shall preserve you from all evil,*
>   *He shall preserve your soul . . . forevermore.*

In spite of all the "perils" we encounter, we can trust the Lord. We are never too small for His caring. God's Word reminds us that *"we are pilgrims and strangers in a foreign land"* whose roads are filled with hazards. The road is long, weary, and dangerous. It winds through veils of tears, but the long winding road finally comes to the *City of God*, the place of joy and feasting. That is the biblical view of life in this world. There are numerous passages that describe the *"mountains"* as a place of blessing (Mt. Moriah, Mt. Sinai, Mt. Zion, Mt. Olivet, Mt. Carmel, Mt. of Transfiguration, Mt. Calvary), but we know all too well that mountains can also be a place of danger. Godly pilgrims have always found a sense of majesty in the *"high country"*—the mountains of life—but they have also found a sense of danger and a fear of the unknown. The psalmist says to himself, "I will lift up my eyes to the hills"—then he breaks off and asks the question, *"From whence comes my help?"* He tells himself, "I've looked to the mountains, and I find no help . . . I've looked within, and I find no guidance . . . finally I looked up, and realized the source of my help—*"My help comes from God!"* God is not merely the *Creator* of all things, He is the *Sustainer* of all things as well (Col 1:16–17). If God numbers the hairs on your head, don't you think He's up to date on the larger issues of your life? He will not allow your foot to be moved. Such thoughts should renew our strength to carry on. (53–76)

In every life, at some point, a person finds himself in that "dark tunnel" where no light is visible. In agony you cry out in frustration—*"Lord, I can't take any more!" "I must hear from You today!"* If you find yourself in David's shoes, you fully understand his heartfelt emotions as stated in **Psalm 13**—

> *How long, O LORD? Will You forget me forever?*
> *How long will You hide Your face from me?*
> *How long shall I take counsel in my soul,*
> *Having sorrow in my heart daily? . . .*
> *I have trusted in Your mercy;*
> *My heart shall rejoice in Your salvation . . .*
> *Because You have dealt bountifully with me.*

David was a man after God's own heart, yet he was *a man of anguish and suffering*. One moment he was the toast of the nation, the next he was a young man hiding out in caves. David was a fugitive for eight or nine years! At one point David's band of faithful followers lost their wives and families (as did David) in a raid, and "they turned their anger toward David!" 1 Samuel 30 tells of David's deep distress. David was desperate, and out of this pain he cried out to the Lord—*"How long, O Lord? Will You forget me forever? I have trusted in Your mercy!"* You can see and feel the impatience and desperation David experienced in this psalm (Ps 13). There are some favors that the Almighty does not grant either the first, the second, or the third time you ask Him, because *He wishes you to pray for a long time* and often He wills the delay to keep you in a *state of humility*, and to make you realize the value of His grace.

On those occasions when you struggle with "God's timing," it is good to know these feelings did not originate with you—David expressed such feelings numerous times. On this occasion he was overwhelmed with a sense of the *"permanence of trouble."* "Will you forget me forever?" You too will come to the point that God has forgotten you—it is a common experience. We all pass through such *"dark stages."* We can take a certain amount with our faith intact—but the longer we go without God's peace and perspective in the midst of bad times, the more *our faith begins to weaken.* It was not until Job realized he was in for a *"long term battle,"* that he began to come apart at the seams. Everyone has a point somewhere in the geography of their souls marking *"the limits of their faith"*—it is the point at which faith begins to unravel, and you begin to give up on God. What you really believe is that God has given up on you. The truth of the matter is—God never ceases to care about you. I love the poignant words of Isaiah 49—"Can a woman forget her nursing child? They may forget, says the Lord, *"but I will never forget you! I have inscribed you on the palms of My hands!"* (Is 49:15-16). Remember the words of Jesus on the cross—*"My God, My God, why have You forsaken Me?"* Next time you begin to think about God's forsaking you, remember, Jesus can identify with your pain (Heb 4:15). And then remember His promise, *"I will never leave you nor forsake you"* (Heb 13:5). But that does not mean we will never *"feel forsaken"*—because our emotions will bring us to that point. You can feel free to express your honest feelings to God—He understands. David was frustrated for two reasons:

1. He was frustrated because of his own *"emotions"*—Like David, when we no longer sense that God is blessing us, we tend to ruminate on our failures and get into an emotional funk. And when our emotions take over, it gets us into such an emotional bind that no matter how hard we try, we know we cannot do the things we know we should do. It happened to David. He was frustrated by his emotions.

2. <u>He was frustrated because of his *"enemy"*</u>—David cried out, "How long will my enemy be exalted over me?" David was the *"king in waiting"*—the waiting period ended up being fifteen years! The blood-thirsty monarch "Saul" had once sent 30,000 men after David! Whose side was God on? God seemed to give Saul everything and David nothing. Can you hear David cry out, "Lord, what do You want from me?" By the way, you need to know that if the enemy ever pursues you, he will be relentless, and you will wonder, *"Lord, how am I ever going to get victory over this problem?*—I'm doing everything I know how to do, but it is just too much for me!" It is comforting to know that David had the kind of *"dark days"* we do. The psalm does not stop there: David may have thought he didn't have a prayer, but in fact, he was just where God wanted him!

Our supplications when "God delays"—True prayer is a spontaneous outpouring of honesty and need from the soul's foundation. *In calm time, we say a prayer—in desperate times, we truly pray.* When you come to the end of your own limited resources—that is when you really pray. David seemed to have come to the last page of his life; hence, he poured out his heart to the Lord—Psalm 13. David is certain that Saul will come out the winner; perhaps he feared being humiliated or subjected to mockery. David was desperate and cries out—*"O Lord, help me!" "Please hear my cry!"* He worked honestly through his darkest, most hopeless feelings—then he turned his eyes away from his troubles and fixed his gaze on God. He is suddenly conscious of an exalted and holy God and addresses Him as *Jehovah Elohim*—*Jehovah* reflects God's promises; *Elohim* reflects God's power. David's heart suddenly returned to the conviction that the God who promises is the God who is powerful—at this point *his faith rebounds* and reasserts itself. A similar promise is found in Psalm 138:7–8—"Though I walk in the midst of trouble . . . You will save me . . . *and accomplish what concerns me."* We must come to the point where we hear ourselves saying, "Lord God, my life is devastated; I am overwhelmed by my problems; I can't go on . . . in the midst of all this *help me, O God,* my redeemer."

In the midst of his crying out to the Lord, David breaks into "joyful song" (Ps 13:5–6). David's song is a song of triumph. How did he reach that point? He began to see God. Our troubles can cause us to avoid the places where we are most likely to *"see God."* You need all the church you can get in such a time. Our faith is not a luxury intended for periods of smooth sailing—when trouble comes along, that is when it is wonderful to be a part of a faithful, Bible-believing body of people who will rally around you, and pray for you, and support you, and encourage you, and counsel you. David said, *"I have trusted in Your lovingkindness; I shall rejoice in Your salvation."* David knew what the prophet Jeremiah knew—"The steadfast love of the Lord never ceases, His mercies never come to an end; they are new every morning; great is Your faithfulness" (Lam 3:22). At this point, God counseled David's hurting soul—our Lord never changes. Was David delivered from his plight? No, but his spirit was lifted—and he was once again certain of God's promises. David remembered all the Lord had done in his life, and how faithful He was—*"God has dealt bountifully with me!"* When we become trapped in the claustrophobia of present trials, we desperately need perspective. "I waited patiently for the Lord . . . He heard my cry . . . He brought me up out of a horrible pit, and set my feet upon a rock . . . God has put a new song in my mouth" (Ps 40:1–3). Our problem is that we become preoccupied with our *circumstances;* whereas God is preoccupied with our *character.* He will allow the *"tough times"* for the higher good of our character, until He is finished with the great work that is invisible to our earthly eyes. God is never late, nor does He lose control. (77–102)

We need to "worship" in times of trouble. Life comes crashing down—it happens to every one of us, you are never prepared, and you have no clue where to turn. How wonderful is the moment when you discover you can run into the arms of a Father who loves you and weeps with you. David wrote, "Though I walk in the midst of trouble, You will revive me" (Ps 138:7). Psalm 138 speaks to us about worship in times of trouble. David begins his worship by *"giving thanks to God"*—that takes a certain degree of wisdom and maturity to reach that level. When difficulties come, we must struggle to remember our reasons for gratitude to God—that will not happen if we are preoccupied with self-pity and loss. Focusing on our *"misery"* traps us in our own private dungeon—*"gratitude"* is the key to unlocking that prison. God sends storms to force us to look to Him—the thunder gets our attention, and when we are humbled in fear, we are far more likely to approach Him with our whole heart. David praised the Lord for His mercy and lovingkindness—the Hebrew term *hesed* encompasses both of those ideas. ***Barclay Ron Allen*** penned the wonderful words of the hymn *"I Found a Friend"*—

> *I found a Friend when life seemed not worth living;*
> *I found a Friend so tender and forgiving.*
> *I can't conceive how such a thing could be,*
> *That Jesus cares for even me.*

God is a "very present help" in time of trouble (Ps 46:1). We may think He delays because we have our own timetable in mind, but God hears us the instant we cry out. Whatever He chooses to do about our circumstances, He will *"strengthen"* us for the battle (Ps 138:3)—God fills us with *renewed faith* and resolve (Ps 138:4). The Lord divides people into two groups—the lofty and the lowly. "The *proud* God knows from afar" (Ps 138:6); "the *humble* come to Him with desperate hearts and receive His grace, forgiveness and comfort" (Ps 138:6; Jam 4:6).

Though David was a "man after God's own heart," his life was one long procession of problems. He spent years fleeing the wrath of a king . . . his nation was at war with everyone in sight . . . he had marital trouble . . . his sons openly rebelled against him. David made terrible, fateful mistakes—yet he always remained one of God's favorite children! David sang, *"He restores my soul!* He leads me in the paths of righteousness for His name's sake. Yea, though I walk through the valley of the shadow of death, I will fear no evil—*because Thou art with me!"* (Ps 23:3–4). Reflect upon the following words of God to the prophet Isaiah (Is 43:2–3)—

> *When you pass through the waters, I will be with you;*
> *And through the rivers, they shall not overflow you.*
> *When you walk through the fire, you shall not be burned,*
> *Nor shall the flame scorch you, for I am the LORD your God.*

Every believer knows that when we walk through the valley of tears, "God walks beside us." God is closest in the crises, surrounding us with His presence—this He has promised. When we navigate troubled waters, God is not only the *Master of the waves*—He is also *Master of the ship*. He never abandons us. He will see the voyage through to its final destination (Phil 1:6). *But we are stubborn creatures who struggle to learn*. We learn the least when the sun is shining and the winds are light. Peace and prosperity have never provided effective classrooms. Crisis and catastrophe, on the other hand, offer master's degrees—that accreditation makes you a *"Master of Disaster."* It is the school of hard knocks. Through it all, He is working all things together for our good (Rom 8:28). It is essential that we cling to His promise of continuous perfection—be confident of this! (Phil 1:6). No matter what, you must never forget that when you are deep in the midst of trouble, God is still busy at work in you (Phil 2:13), though He may be doing so out of your sight. Just place a *"God at Work"* sign into that scar where your troubles have taken their toll—He is involved in very expensive renovation. He is perfecting you. You may be paying the bill up front, but you are going to like the beautiful new design and furnishings of your life. When we begin to look at our difficulties from the perspective of the psalms, our depression fades; our hope increases; our love for God is intensified. David's final appeal was that God *"keep up the good work in me!"* (Ps 138:8). "Lord, continue the work you have begun in me!" (103–123)

Nobody expects to sail through life without a "little rain" and a few choppy waves; the fact is, we cannot have "crops" without rain. We never know what lies in the road ahead, and we never know when our world will fall apart. It may come in the active middle years, or perhaps in those mature years. David faced a variety of bitter times of disappointment—his family was ripped by tragedy, bloodshed, and bitterness... his son ***Absalom*** had set his heart on taking the place of power by whatever means necessary—"*he stole the hearts of the men of Israel*" (2 Sam 15:6). David fled into the Judean desert with a number of his followers... while he was there he inscribed the immortal words of *Psalm 63*. David begins by *"calling out for God to come and comfort him."* The king feels a gaping hole in his heart that only God can fill. His own family has deserted him. His subjects had rejected him. His sole consolation was now his Creator. *He is lonely, sad and empty.* David had already sung the words, "My soul thirsts for God, for the living God" (Ps 42:2). And "My flesh longs for You in a dry and thirsty land where there is no water" (Ps 63:1). When David speaks of *"longing,"* he has in mind that he has collapsed in every way. His strength had been drained away. He was desperate to be revived. The *"dry and thirsty land of the desert"* that surrounded David physically is the picture of his soul without God. Only God can bring refreshment and a rejuvenated life. "Lord, show me the path of life; for in Your presence is fullness of joy" (Ps 16:11).

David's heart always makes for a fascinating picture—he was by no means a perfect man; his failures are as legendary as his accomplishments; he was a great leader who happened to be a member of that struggling, stumbling band of creatures known as the human race. David ached for communion with God. The great Christian mathematician **Blaise Pascal** once said—*"the heart has its reasons which the reason does not know."* God's rules fly in the face of logic. Reflect upon this thought—*When we begin to praise God in defiance of misfortune, we align ourselves with the deepest truths of the universe,* the place where God dispenses deep wisdom and spiritual maturity. We unleash His victorious power in the world of pain and suffering.

In the midst of the "lonely desert road," what are you to do? Praise God with every part of your body, mind, and spirit. Learn to *"praise God"* regardless of your personal circumstances, and you will see miracles occur. When treading through life's desert, it helps to remember God's help in ages past. Reflect upon the words of *Isaac Watts'* hymn: *"O God, our help in ages past, our hope for years to come; our shelter from the stormy blast, and our eternal home!"* We also gain a wise perspective by realizing that nothing that is happening to us is a surprise to Him. Furthermore declares the Lord, "I am God, is there anything too difficult for Me?" (Jer 32:27).

David praised God to "dispel the darkness." Helplessness is the real secret and the impelling power of prayer . . . it is only when we are *"helpless"* that we open our hearts to Jesus and let Him help us in our distress. Needless to say, God calmed the troubled waters of David's soul; He dealt with his enemies and gave him victory. Just as David made his *"desert journey"*—like the one you and I must travel—close by our side will be a faithful, powerful God, filled with lovingkindness and plans for us, plans that lead to spiritual victory and personal fulfillment. (124–148)

Some crises are much like an "explosion" that knocks us off our feet, and leaves us stunned and confused. After the explosion, we have no idea what is coming next; we feel we will never again have hearts filled with joy—only fear. Perhaps your life has been shattered by a bomb. The road goes on. There will be many more peaks and valleys along the way. The *"deep valleys"* are places of spiritual dryness and conflict with God—things David faced and chronicled for us in Psalm 30. After David had at long last become king, his first royal initiative was to *establish the ark of the covenant in the city of Jerusalem*, where it would enshrine the idea of worshiping and trusting God. While enroute to the city, the cart carrying *the ark began to wobble*, and a man named Uzzah reached out and touched the ark to steady it. It was a forbidden thing for human hands to do, and *God struck Uzzah dead* on the spot. David became both angry and afraid. David decided to stop transporting the ark to Jerusalem, and had it placed in the home of a man named Obed-Edom the Gittite for three months. Word trickled back to Jerusalem that everything Obed-Edom touched seemed to turn to gold. King David carefully reviewed exactly what the Scriptures had to say about *"moving the ark"*—he then decided to transport it to Jerusalem. As they proceeded to move the ark, they stopped "every six paces" and offered a great sacrifice of oxen and sheep (as prescribed by OT law)—and David worshipped the Lord with great joy and intensity (2 Sam 6:14). Many scholars believe David channeled his heartfelt gratitude into the song we know as **Psalm 30.**

David prayed in his "sickness," and the Lord healed him. He extols the people of God to sing praises to the Lord, "for *His anger* is but for a moment; *His favor* is for life . . . weeping may endure for a night, but joy comes in the morning" (Ps 30:2–5). "Hear, O Lord, and have mercy on me; be my helper!" The time comes when you find yourself at the bottom line of hope or despair—and you cry out saying, "Lord, I need Your mercy! Please help me!" "Lord, You reached down to the darkest depths and pulled me right out of the grave. I was almost gone." When you know you will see the sun rise again, you start waking every morning thanking and praising God. A *"thankful perspective"* is essential for a joyful, positive life. God has a purpose for you . . . He loves you . . . and keeps you alive to bring praise to His name. That should make you see things through different eyes, and cause you to begin each day on your knees. *David reflects upon the purpose for his healing*—"Lord, let me lift up my life today in service for Your purposes!"

David takes us once again to the highest reaches and the lowest depths. He writes, "In my prosperity I shall never be moved . . . but You hid Your face and I was troubled." In effect, David was saying, "I thought back on my life to the time when I had everything I had ever dreamed. And I said to myself, *'I'm set for life—set in stone—I have got it made!'* I am bigger than anything life can throw at me" (Ps 30:6–7). David continues, *"But painful experience has taught me differently—I now realize the great danger of prosperity—how quickly it can all come tumbling down!"* Pride goes before a fall (1 Cor 10:12). A simple phone call with a single sentence from your doctor will instantly cause all your earthly security to go up in flames. Worldly life is fragile. Eternal life is a gift from God. Nebuchadnezzar was the king of all he could see in the great empire of the Babylonians—he thought it was all the result of *"his hands"*—God showed him otherwise, and ripped the kingdom from him in but a moment (Dan 4:31). He spent the next seven years eating grass out in the field like a beast! He learned his lesson the *"hard way"*—afterwards he praised, extolled, and honored the King of Heaven. The message?—*"Eat enough grass and your worldview will change!"* Nebuchadnezzar finally realized that when you are flying high, filled with your own prosperity, *"God is more than able to burst your little bubble."*

Prosperity to poverty can be a "painful negative," but it is God's primary means to bring us to Himself. And when it does, we will identify with the words of David: "You have turned my mourning into dancing" (Ps 30:11). Getting "knocked down" in life is not all negative—consider the *"giraffe."* His mother gives birth by "dropping him from the wound some ten feet!" How is that for an introduction into this world? After laying there for a few moments, the baby giraffe "struggles to its feet." About a minute passes and the mother *"knocks the baby down"*—booting it through the air. The calf goes head over heels through the air landing on its side, puzzled and protesting. The reason for the mother's actions? She wants him to get up—if he doesn't get up, she will do it again. This process is repeated over and over, and the struggle to get on its feet continues. When the baby grows tired of trying, the mother gives the little one another hearty kick. Finally, the calf rises to her feet, wobbly on its little spindly legs. And then the mother kicks it off its feet one more time! The purpose? *She wants the calf to remember how it got up!* You might be thinking, "This can't be true!" It is . . . go look it up!

God nurtures us in much the same "rough way" sometimes. And if we are ignorant as to His methods and purposes, the actions can seem cold and even cruel. When we finally struggle to our feet, it seems as if we get knocked down again. But our heavenly Father knows that love must be tough—and it must take the long view. God knows the world will fall apart, and we must be sturdy travelers to stay on our feet. *We must not forget how we got to where we are.* One of the reasons for some of the challenges in our lives is that God is toughening us up, preparing us for warfare against forces intent on destroying us. Oftentimes we look at God's training and just feel like He's kicking and abusing us. God created the principle of *"rigorous discipline"*—understand it is for the purpose of training us and remaking us into the image of His Son. (149–170)

Praying under pressure—David was a man of faith, but like many believers, he was also a man who struggled with *discouragement* and *depression.* David coped with an abundance of turbulent emotions during his fugitive years. Most scholars believe David wrote at least eight different psalms during his season of flight from King Saul. *When he came to a cave where he could lay low, he poured out his heart to God.* The *"Cave of Adullam"* became David's *"cave of despair."* Most Bible scholars believe King Saul had levied a heavy tax on the people; as such, many were joining David's band in rebellion over the unfair taxation. Goliath's conqueror was still admired by most citizens of Israel. So David, having entered the cave to be alone, finds himself surrounded by the most distressed citizens of Israel. David confesses to us in Psalm 142:3 that his spirit within is *"overwhelmed."* He has come to a place where he has begun to distrust his own judgment. He is no longer certain where to turn. David's spirit is a picture of disorientation. He is pursued by two armies, one made of soldiers out to kill him, the other of suffering comrades. As punishment for harboring his prey, Saul slaughtered the village of Nob. David realized that he was spiritually responsible for the mass slaying of an entire village, and he is nearly driven insane with guilt. He has entered the darkened depths of the cave to better contemplate the darkness in his soul. David closes his eyes with a sinking heart and whispers, *"O Lord God, what would You have me do?"* The following poem regarding men in just such a condition was written by **Charles Spurgeon**—

> *Fits of depression come over most of us.*
> *Usually cheerful as we may be, we must at intervals be cast down.*
> *The strong are not always vigorous,*
> *The wise not always ready,*
> *The brave not always courageous,*
> *And the joyous not always happy.*
> *There may be here and there "men of iron" . . .*
> *But surely the rust frets even these.*

The pit into which his soul had plunged was a "dark one"—David felt everyone had deserted him (Ps 142:4). Problems tend to isolate us. It seems to be a particularly strong tendency for those of us who are males to *"turn inward"* when problems come. We seek the nearest cave that might offer protection from the world. **Alexander MacLaren:** *"The soul that has to wade through deep waters has always to do it alone*—we have companions in joy, but sorrow we have to face by ourselves . . . unless we have Jesus with us in the darkness, we have no one." **Ella Wheeler Wilcox** is famous for saying the same thing: *"Laugh and the world laughs with you, weep and you weep alone."* Elijah suffered from this orientation—it was him against the world. The Lord had to remind him that there were a few thousand more soldiers in His army than the prophet thought. Elijah then reflected upon the bigger picture—the one that included God. Here is what we learn from this passage: *Problems encourage isolation, and isolation nurtures misconception.*

David cries out to the Lord, "I am brought very low" (Ps 142:6). That is what the condition of depression is all about. David's depression approached desperation—all of his hope and joy were gone. He had allowed his circumstances to drive him *inward* instead of *upward*. He had come to fall back on his own resources. He no longer sensed the presence of God in his life. All believers enter the *"dark cave of depression"* at times; this is particularly true of godly leaders. They wear the mantle of greatness with unease, and—quite naturally—great expectations can lead to "great depression." In the grip of his low spirits, David cries out to the Lord, "Deliver me from my persecutors, for they are stronger than me" (Ps 142:6). David locked himself in the dungeon of despair and threw away the key. There can be no doubt that *"discouragement"* defeated David—he had encountered a *"giant"* that could get into his own head. For the people of God, however, there is never a pit too deep to escape.

When David felt that he would like to see his enemies all "die violently," that is exactly what he says. An important point when *"praying under pressure"*—prayer should be a time of honest, no-holds-barred, straight-ahead communication with God. This is when we cut to the root of the problem, and we are not afraid to name names. When that happens, we feel a tremendous sense of unburdening ourselves before the most intimate Friend imaginable. He is listening. He cares. He responds. We can tell Him anything at all. God has said we are to *"cast all our cares upon Him."* Period. ***James W. Pennebaker,*** Ph.D, a professor at the University of Texas, has conducted a study on this subject—

> *Suppressing negative emotions can weaken the immune system and arouse your fight-or-flight system, churning up blood pressure and heart rate . . . articulating trauma helps us deal with the emotion and oftentimes reduces the need for medication; the net effect is that people can move beyond the stressful event.*

It is interesting to me that as science stumbles along in the modern world, it tends to come across truths that we have had for thousands of years in the Word of God. In another study by psychology professor, **Mark. A. Lumley,** Ph.D, at Wayne State University in Detroit—he concludes that it is important for us to honestly express the issues of our lives. That is what the Lord has been trying to tell us all along. Hence, if expressing ourselves in a candid journal or secular environment can be a healthy thing, how much more can *"honest prayerful expression to the Lord"* be healthy? So, tell the Lord exactly what you are feeling, without fear or blame—when you do that, God begins the process of recovery.

Every second David despaired over the lack of God's presence . . . God was right there, as close as ever (Ps 142:3). David could never find a cave where God was not waiting for him! No believer will ever find himself in a place that is not exactly where God expected him to be! David then cries out to the Lord, "Bring my soul out of prison, that I may praise Your name; the righteous shall surround me, for You shall deal bountifully with me" (Ps 142:7). *Prayer will move us from the valleys of despair to the mountaintops of joy*—we can pray our way right through the crises and the losses and the fears. David traveled from prison to praise. (171–193)

Jesus is a "rock" in a weary land . . . a "shelter" in the time of storm— those are the words of a hymn written by ***Ira Sankey.*** When David Jeremiah was stricken with cancer, it moved into his life like a tornado, demolishing his control over his life, his career, and all his plans for the future. He became consumed with his illness; discouragement gave way to depression, yet deep within there was the nagging question of his faith—he could not give up the life commitment he had made to God.

He experienced great spiritual conflict—*How could a believer experience the thoughts and emotions he was feeling? Why had God let him sink into anger, discouragement, depression?* He finally realized that his pain and despair only served to *"draw him closer to God"* than health and happiness ever could. Through the pain, he writes, "I began to know God better . . . I found a genuine *"friend"* in God I had never known before." **Psalm 107** celebrates the friendship and the faithfulness of God—it is a beloved hymn of thanksgiving for God's deliverance. The author paints *"four pictures"* for the reader that portray four great challenges of life:

1. **The Desert**—We might call this one *"Wanderers in the Wilderness"* (Ps 107:4–9). In these verses we read about the experience of being lost in the desert. The psalmist writes, "They wandered in the wilderness in a desolate way; they found no city to dwell in; hungry and thirsty, their soul fainted in them." Many have lost their way in a *"dry wilderness,"* devoid of meaning and purpose. For some the desert is loneliness . . . others routine futility . . . others affluence (not what they thought it would be) . . . the wanderers trudge through the dry sand without hope, seeking the true spiritual home that has always eluded them.

2. **The Prison**—This picture is of a group of prisoners who "sat in darkness and in the shadow of death, bound in affliction and irons" (Ps 107:10–16). People are like prisoners, trapped in the dungeon of their own moral folly. *The wrong choices become patterns of behavior that finally master them*—the drug addict, the alcoholic, the sex addict—people are taken prisoner by their own conduct. Some are trapped by difficult circumstances from which there seems little hope of escape—these prisons might have been constructed by other people's evil, by persecution, or by matters over which they have no control. We do not have to be at fault to become hopeless captives.

3. **The Hospital**—The author writes, "Fools, because of their transgression, and because of their iniquities, they were afflicted; they abhorred all manner of food, and they drew near to the gates of death" (Ps 107:17–22). This is a ward of illness and affliction, and it serves as a

corridor that opens into the darkness of death. Not every illness, of course, is caused by sin . . . but people here have poisoned themselves with their own transgressions. *They are suffering, ready for the release brought only by death.* They lie there in the ward, waiting only for their final moments on this earth. **Dietrich Bonhoeffer** appropriately penned these words—

> *In me there is **darkness**, but with Thee there is light.*
> *I am **lonely**, but Thou leavest me not.*
> *I am **feeble** in heart, but Thou leavest me not.*
> *I am **restless**, but with Thee there is peace.*
> *In me there is **bitterness**, but with Thee there is patience;*
> *Thy ways are past understanding, but Thou knowest the way*
>   *for me.*

4. **The Storm**—This is a picture of men on a ship caught in a furious storm, fearing for their lives. "Those who go down to the sea in ships, who do business on great waters, they see the works of the Lord, and His wonders in the deep . . . *their souls melt because of the trouble.* They reel to and fro, and stagger like drunken men . . . then they cry out to the Lord in their trouble, and He brings them out of their distresses, and calms the storm, and guides them to their desired haven. Oh that men would give thanks to the Lord for His goodness" (Ps 107:23–32). These sailors realize their small stature, their seeming insignificance—out on the open sea. There is no land in sight. There is no one to rescue them in their peril on the sea. David Jeremiah writes, "When I have encountered the storms of my own life, I have taken encouragement from this psalm. Though I feel certain that I am pursuing the will of God for my life, my faith is sternly tested by the wind and the rain." *Great works are done in deep waters.* Jesus tells us to launch out into the deep. This is not only true in the spiritual world, it is also true in the physical world—*play it safe and you will never build a business;* launching a new firm is launching out into the deep. The storms are certain to come, and the winds will howl. *No one ever said it would be easy out in deep waters.* No one ever guaranteed

fair weather and smooth sailing. It is your choice—stay along the shore and you will always be safe from drowning and disaster—but you will also never know the blessings of the deep things of God.

By the way, the storm in this psalm is "from the hand of God" (Ps 107:25)—It is "He" who has commanded it. Conversely, it is God who sends the winds and the rains. We are much more comfortable crediting God with *calming* the storms than with *causing* them. The Bible teaches us that He is Lord of all—and that includes the storms that *"serve His purposes"* along with everything else. Let's be careful, however, before blaming God for every storm. Sometimes we have done just fine on our own bringing on those dark clouds. We make mistakes, and God's place is simply to let us discover how deeply we need Him when we are just about to go under the waves. But in this passage (Ps 107), we are not referring to those *"self-induced tempests."* We are talking about storms brought about expressly by *"divine appointment"*—and those do exist. Listen to the words of the author of **Psalm 66**—

> *You brought us into the net; You laid affliction on our backs. You caused men to ride over our heads—we went through fire and through water; but You brought us out to rich fulfillment* (66:11–12).

Even rebellious, dispassionate "Jonah" knew Who was behind the storms. Here was a God who could trouble the sea. Jonah realized that he could run, but he could not hide. The Lord sent the storm just as He sent Jonah. Jonah was God's messenger to the Ninevites . . . but the storm was God's message to Jonah. Are you experiencing a *"storm"* in your life? Is it intended to cut off your flight from God, as in the case of Jonah? Perhaps it is to draw you closer to God. *If you are weathering a storm, you can be certain the winds are no random weather front—they blow for a clear purpose.* As you are caught up in a tempest, ask God to help you be caught up in His purposes. The psalmist writes, "Their soul melts because of trouble; they reel to and fro, and stagger like drunken men, and are at their wits' end" (Ps 107:26–27). The expression *"at your wits' end"* comes from this psalm. When we find ourselves in one of God's storms we come to the end of all our own ideas and strategies, and the tempest masters the vessel. The wind and the waters are now navigating the ship; the passengers can do little but watch and pray. Writes **_Augustine:_** *"Usually prayer is a question of groaning rather than speaking, tears rather than words—God does not ask for words from men."* The psalmist states, "Then they cry out to the Lord in their trouble, and He brings them out of their distresses. The greater the storm, the shorter and simpler we pray—starting with the most classic of all prayers, *"Help!"* Our only hope is to reach beyond ourselves to *Someone* stronger than we are, and stronger than the shackles that bind us.

God's part in the storm is a sensitive topic for many believers; they fear that if they stopped to consider that God may be the Author of the storm, *they might become "angry" with God.* God knows that *"lesser pain"* is a necessary part of avoiding *"far deeper pain"* later—it hurts to pull out a thorn, but the pain of leaving it in causes the deeper pain of infection. The fact is, God knows that He has to pull out a few thorns every now and then, and that we will cry out in pain and even anger at Him. Furthermore, God loves us enough to bring us to our knees in fresh dependence on Him—*"storm-tossed passionate prayers"* are the most effective prayers we pray. God is especially near to us when we are hurting. When God *"calms the storm"* (Ps 107:29–30), He then gives comfort and relief. It has been wisely said, *"We are far more secure in the storm with Jesus in our boat, than we ever are on the shore without Him!"* If you have chosen to pursue the adventure of following Jesus, you have already discovered that the journey does not occur in a luxury limousine. God will lead you to and through some rough places. In all likelihood, there will come a time when you will say, *"I didn't sign up for this!"* Just cling to the knowledge that you could be in no safer place than a storm of God's making.

"Grace through the storm" is a function of believing that the Creator of the storm is also the Deliverer from it. Downpour or desert . . . dungeon or disease—the specific facts of the crisis ultimately do not matter—for God is in control. Wherever we are, whatever we may be up against, when we cry out to God in our trouble, *He will hear us . . . He* *will calm the waters.* The time may come when He will even let us know the reasons He unleashed them. The purpose of the storms in our lives is to *"guide us to our desired haven"* (Ps 107:30). Crises never leave us the same as they found us. Those of us who love and trust God through the worst of times, find that our hearts have been changed by the time the stillness replaces the storminess. And our goals will have moved closer to His own. Ask Jonah. As incredible as this may sound, God changes our *"want-to"* in the midst of His storms.

When God calms the storm, what is there for us to do but to "praise our God?" If you have been hopelessly lost in a barren wilderness, or shackled mercilessly in a prison, and suddenly you find yourself in a beautiful oasis. What do you do? "Oh that men would thank and praise God for His goodness"—that is the response for each of the four scenarios depicted in this psalm (Ps 107:8–9, 15–16, 21–22, 31–32).

God is our refuge and strength, a "very present help" in trouble (Ps 46:1). The psalms area dotted and drenched with more tear stains than any other part of the Bible. Every conceivable emotion from ecstasy to anger to despair can be found in these pages. If there is one great message in the psalms, it is that *our pain is real, but God's presence is just as real.* The psalms bear witness to the fact that we are not the first to walk down the difficult roads of disappointment and pain and bitterness. Here we find hope in the time of storm, even when the thunder and lightning cause us to run for shelter. There can be no more powerful *"healing balm"* than the wisdom we find in the psalms. Writes Jeremiah:

> *Whenever I have suffered, the psalms have provided my medicine toward healing. When I have most needed these verses, no commentaries or scholarly notes have been necessary. The simple and heartfelt words I have found in the psalms have always been enough. It is in the psalms that I have learned to swim to deeper depths.*

Here is the history behind the writing of Psalm 46—The year was 701 BC. The king of Assyria—**Sennacherib**—was a man who struck terror in the hearts of those in the Mediterranean world. He was obsessed with expanding his kingdom, which had rapidly risen to dominance. He led his army on a ruthless march throughout the Mediterranean world—*the Assyrians consumed and conquered everything in their path.* The Assyrian Empire was a cruel and mighty one, capturing and enslaving numerous kingdoms. Finally, Sennacherib came across a little kingdom called **"Judah"**—the center of which was the city of Jerusalem. In that day Judah was ruled by a godly man named **Hezekiah**—he was absolutely intolerant of idols and statues and pagan shrines that were inconsistent with the God of Israel; he destroyed them and pointed his people back to temple worship and godly sacrifice. *"He did what was right in the sight of the Lord"* (2 Kg 18:35-37). The Assyrian monarch had already conquered the northern kingdom of Israel—he marched them off into captivity to spend the rest of their lives as slaves. Confrontation and destruction was just as certain for Judah. When the Assyrian king taunted the people of Judah, the prophet **"Isaiah"** gave a word of encouragement to Hezekiah. In essence he said, *"Relax, God says that everything is under control; simply ignore the challenges of Sennacherib"* (2 Kg 19). After repeated taunts and a *"letter"* from the King of Assyria, Hezekiah spread the menacing letter out before the Lord—and prayed for God to save them, "that all the kingdoms of the earth may know that Jehovah alone is God" (2 Kg 19:19). The result was *an angel of the Lord came by night and executed 185,000 Assyrians* (2 Kg 19:35). All the people of Judah quickly realized that "this moment" would forever be celebrated in the history of their nation—the psalm penned to commemorate this day was Psalm 46—probably written by Hezekiah or Isaiah. Psalm 46 towers over us today as *a biblical monument to the awesome and limitless power of God.* It shows us that with God "all things are possible." **Psalm 46** divides neatly into three sections—

1. **When trouble comes, "retreat to your refuge"** (vv. 1-3)—Our God is an awesome refuge—this idea is sprinkled throughout the OT (Deut 33:27; Ps 18:2; 91:2). At the first sign of trouble, we naturally rely on our own resources—when that fails, we may call upon a friend or godly counselor to help, but "God" is our refuge—*"a very present help in trouble."* **Martin Luther** based the most important hymn of the Reformation on Psalm 46—*"A Mighty Fortress is our God."*

> *A mighty fortress is our God, a bulwark never failing;*
> *Our helper He amid the flood of mortal ills prevailing.*

This hymn became a great source of strength and inspiration for God's people during the Reformation, especially to those who were martyred for their convictions. If you travel to Germany and visit the place where Luther is buried, you will find the first line of this psalm engraved on his tomb. Our God is a *"very present help in trouble"*—when trouble rolls in, He moves in closer and puts His arms around us and holds us close to His chest. *Therefore we will not fear*, though the earth be moved, and the mountains be carried into the midst of the sea—*God is present*. Read this psalm!

2. **When trouble comes, "rediscover your strength"** (vv. 4–7)—Difficult times force us into the waiting arms of God. When we realize that He is in control, we are overjoyed and immensely comforted. When we come to the sobering realization that our resources are fully spent, that is when we learn that God is more than a refuge—*He is also our strength*. In ancient times, most people feared being cut off from supplies of food or water should powerful invaders come to conquer them—if the enemy waited long enough, he could stop you from getting the things you needed outside the city walls. The city of Jerusalem was a "walled city," and Hezekiah had taken steps to make sure they were well-prepared for an onslaught from Assyria's king, Sennacherib. In the Kidron Valley, just outside the city was a *deep spring called Gihon*—it provided the water supply for Jerusalem, so it was of enormous strategic importance. Hezekiah redirected the spring through a conduit that was 1,777 feet long, hewn of solid rock. He had the spring waters brought into the city beneath the walls of Jerusalem into a reservoir in the middle of the city. Then he covered up all traces of the spring in such a way that Sennacherib would have no idea where the water supply was. If the angel of the Lord had not destroyed the Assyrian army that night, the people of Judah would still have had fresh water for a lengthy period of time. There is reference to this spring in this psalm in verse 4—

*There is a river whose streams shall make glad the city of God,
The holy place of the tabernacle of the Most High.*

The Holy Spirit is the eternal spring that never runs dry for us as believers—He is a secret fountain of life-giving water (Jn 4:13ff; 7:37ff). The message here is this: Why should we look *"outside"* for help when trouble comes? Almighty God lives *"inside"* of us to satisfy our thirst. God is in our midst, and He shall not be moved; God shall help us, just at the break of dawn" (46:5-7); interestingly enough, that is precisely the time the angle of the Lord destroyed the Assyrians. The armies of Judah may have been outnumbered, but there was one Warrior—God—who tilted the scales toward a rout of the Assyrians.

3. **When trouble comes, "redirect your thoughts"** (vv. 8–11)—In times of trouble, God's advice to us is not abstract, but pragmatic. He offers us a sound battle plan. The Lord reminds us that *our mind* is a powerful element in our armory. Our *"thought patterns"* are crucial in the midst of our difficulties. Any soldier will tell you that the moment the enemy can be demoralized, he is beaten. A sanctified mind can stand against any worldly foe. God's Word over and over again instructs us to *"remember the works of the Lord"*—"Behold the works of the Lord; He has wrought desolations in the earth; He makes wars to cease; He breaks the bow and cuts the spear in two" (Ps 46:8-9). The people of God could always look back, even from bondage, and say, *"Remember how the angel of the Lord slew the Assyrians?"* The psalmist writes, *"Be still and know that I am God—the God of Jacob is our refuge"* (Ps 46:10-11). Frequently we are too busy squabbling and playing games and doing everything but listening—God says, *"Be still and know that I am God."* We are enjoined to be silent that we may become aware of His presence and purposes. *"The Lord of hosts is with us"*—think about that! And remember, just *"one angel"* was dispatched from heaven to defend the city of Jerusalem and he destroyed 185,000 Assyrians. The people of Judah needed only one angel—as His children we have the Lord Himself with

us! He is the One who created and empowers the angels! Our God is *Emmanuel—"God with us!"*—He is a very present help in time of trouble.

David knew about the "night seasons" of life—Psalm 16 is the evidence of that. Scholars suggest it may have been written during a brief interlude of peace, immediately after David refused to take Saul's life while sleeping in a cave. Though David's men enjoined him to kill Saul, "David refused to stretch out his hand against *God's anointed*" (1 Sam 26:9); instead, he took Saul's spear and water bottle as proof that he had spared his life when he easily could have killed him. Later Saul acknowledged that he was the one who had sinned . . . he was the fool . . . and he was ashamed of himself. So David now finds himself in a temporary oasis of tranquility. He is no longer running for his life, and he is able to enjoy peace of mind. He takes the time to reflect upon all the good things he has received from the Lord—***Psalm 16*** is the record of his spiritual inventory. This psalm exhorts us to—

1. **Remember Who God "Is"** (vv. 1–4)—David begins at the beginning—he acknowledges who God really is: "Preserve me, O God; in You I put my trust . . . my goodness is nothing apart from You." David looks within himself and gravely observes that he finds *"no goodness apart from God."* Can you say the same thing? That is among the most profound revelation that can ever come to us. There is no good thing within us or about us or connected to us that does not come from God—"every good and perfect gift is from above" (Jam 1:17). One argues, *"I make my own bread"—Oh, is that right?* Where did the grain come from? It grew because God caused the sun to shine and the rains to shower down upon the earth where the grain was planted. Furthermore, David had been surrounded by a group of dedicated friends during his wilderness wanderings—*God had never failed to provide a friend for him;* as such, he never had to be alone. Do you go it alone when times are tough? God never intends you to do so. Loving people and loving God are closely related (Jn 13:35; 1 Jn 3:14; 4:7–8). David reflects upon his relationships with

the people of God—godly friends that God had placed in his life. Who are the godly friends God has placed in your life? Have you ever thanked Him for them? David then goes on to say that the sorrows of the pagan and the ungodly are multiplied—note the contrast.

2. **Reflect on What God is "Doing"** (vv. 5-9)—David now takes a look at God and at what He is doing in his life at the present time. *God never sleeps.* He is always at work, fine-tuning the minute details of our lives. "You, O Lord, are the portion my inheritance and my cup" (v. 5)—the Lord is the One who makes us complete and provides for us whatever we need. This is the answer to the Lord's Prayer when it says, *"Give us this day our daily bread"* (Mt 6:11). Realize what a blessed privilege it is to be provided with the essentials of life. David goes on to say, "You maintain my lot"—*God took care of his circumstances.* David had lost nearly everything, yet he is able to praise God for providing for him in his time of need. Therefore, *the Lord is his contentment*—*"The lines have fallen to me in pleasant places."* Look back on your life and see how God has provided for you over the years—raised in a godly home, had godly friends, godly education—have the lines not also fallen for you in pleasant places? In no way do we deserve the *"blessings"* we have been given. How is it that we come so often to feel just the opposite? Thinking that we have the worst fortune? Nothing ever goes our way? Everyone else has it better? *Check the record.* Self-pity throws everything out of perspective. Stop and think about what it is that we *do* deserve. Contentment is not something that happens automatically—it is something that develops intentionally—all babies are born discontented. We learn contentment through conditioning our minds to *"dwell on our blessings"* (Phil 4:11). David then reflects upon the fact *"the Lord is his counsel"* (Ps 16:7). Scripture tells us that when we lack wisdom, we should simply go to God and ask for it (Jam 1:5). God is always at work in our hearts—even when we are deep in sleep—it is as if He does *His holy maintenance work on our minds and hearts as we rest.* So during the night, a quiet miracle takes place, and you

wake up feeling entirely different about things in the morning. After considering God's blessings, David acknowledges, *"the Lord is his confidence"* (Ps 16:9).

3. **Rejoice in What God is "Going to Do"** (vv. 10–11)—David first rejoices in the fact that one day he will actually be *resurrected:* "For You, O Lord, will not leave my soul in Sheol, nor will You allow Your Holy One (the Lord Jesus) to see corruption" (v. 10). David, obviously, would never refer to himself as "Your Holy One," therefore the Holy Spirit must have given him a glimpse into the future; but we cannot be certain that David grasped the full meaning of the events to which he was pointing. The apostle Peter confirmed that David was referring to *"Christ's resurrection,"* by quoting this passage in his Pentecost Sermon (Acts 2:24–28). David's view into the world of eternity is startling, because it actually surpasses even that of the prophets. David responded to the death of his child, *"One day I shall go to him"* (2 Sam 12:22–23). Thus he knew there is a place called *"heaven"* and *God cares for His helpless little ones.* David then brings a beautiful ending to this psalm by declaring, *"You will show me the path of life; in Your presence is fullness of joy; at Your right hand are pleasures forevermore"* (v. 11). The *"path of life"* leads through all the troubles and cares of the world and right into the holy presence of God. In effect David says, "I'll walk down that path one day, and be in a land where joy is made full, and pleasure can be found at God's right hand." Paul essentially said the same thing: *"To live is Christ."* **Oswald Chambers** makes the following statement—

> *No one experiences **complete sanctification** without going through the burial of the old life. If there has never been this crucial moment of change through death, sanctification will never be more than an elusive dream. There must be the **burial of the old life** and a **resurrection into the life of Jesus Christ**. Nothing can defeat a life like this.*

Can you look beyond the terrible frustrations of poor health, family trauma, or a crisis in business, and believe that God is preparing a sumptuous feast for you? And praise the Lord Jesus because you know He is your rock and your salvation? David was able to do that. Countless believers throughout history have found that *the dark seasons of life have not been defined by the absence of God*, but somehow, by the miraculous, closer presence of God. They have stared at the emptiness of death and realized that it held the fullness of a feast. The bending path can seem like a lonely one, and we must all walk it. *I hope God's Word will be your "beacon" in those dark times.* Never forget the Bible offers us a "storehouse of guidance" in the field of adversity. We continue to fight daily battles with the forces of sin, which want so badly to infiltrate our lives and spread so insidiously. We travel this road for the days that God has ordained for us, taking in the difficult curves as well as some wonderful scenery along the way. The journey is rewarding, and the destination is the only one worth the traveling. The 'ole Irish poet traditionally blessed the traveler with these words—

> *May the road rise up to meet you, with all its snares and hazards, in the grace and wisdom and wonderful sufficiency of God.*

CHAPTER 15

A summary of the book...

"SHATTERED DREAMS"
by Larry Crabb

It is the dream of every believer to be TRULY HAPPY and feel excited about life. The Health-and-Wealth Gospel has devolved into a gospel of *"wish-fulfillment."* Paul writes, "If our hope in Christ is only for this life, we are more to be pitied than anyone in the world" (1 Cor 15:19). As Christians, we need to believe God when He promises to work everything for our good that happens to us—both in our lives and in our souls. We all cling to the *false hope* that happiness we were created to enjoy is available here and now . . . that hope can become a narcissistic, obsessive quest for the spiritual fulfillment we assume we are entitled to. We deny the truth that our deepest desire of fully felt union with God largely remains unsatisfied. The shattering of our deepest dream of *"fulfillment in the present"* becomes the unexpected pathway to genuine happiness. (viii-xi)

God truly wants to bless us (Jer 32:40–41). As His beloved children, there is never a moment in all our lives when God is not longing to bless us. At every moment, in every circumstance, God is doing us good. He never stops. It gives Him great pleasure. God is not waiting to bless us after our troubles end. *He is blessing us right now,* in and through those troubles. He is giving us what He knows is good . . . though we do not always agree. We cannot stop wanting to be happy—our souls long for whatever we think will provide the greatest possible pleasure. Our problem is that we are not yet fully aware that an *"intimate relationship with God"* is that greatest pleasure. In our foolishness we look for that experience in all the wrong places. We dig *"broken cisterns"* to satisfy our thirst and walk right by the fresh spring of water that is God.

An encounter with God is what we really want—we just don't know it. We dream *"lower dreams"* and think there are none higher. We dream of good marriages, talented kids, health and money to enjoy life, rewarding work—and for some reason, we think they are the best things. That is what God means when He calls us "foolish." The greatest blessing is not the blessing of a "good life," it is the blessing of *an encounter with God*. We don't see things that way; we almost always mistake lesser pleasures for this greater pleasure and live our lives chasing after them, so God goes to work to help us see more clearly. *One way He works is to allow our "lower dreams" to shatter*—He lets us hurt and does not make it better. The Holy Spirit uses the pain of shattered dreams to help us discover our desire for God. He leads us into the depths of our being, into the center of our soul where we feel our strongest passions. It is there that we discover our desire for God. Shattered dreams are not accidents of fate; they are ordained opportunities for the Spirit to awaken us to our highest dream—an encounter with God. Through the pain of shattered lower dreams, we wake up to the realization that we want an encounter with God more than we want the blessings of life. Our shattered dreams (suffering) are an opportunity to be embraced, a chance to discover our desire for the highest blessing God wants to give us, an encounter with Himself. (1–7)

God told Paul, "My grace is sufficient for you, for My power is made perfect in WEAKNESS" (2 Cor 12:9). We want God to give us power/ victory over our weaknesses and troubles . . . but God normally gives us the power/grace to *endure them*. Paul was taken up to the third heaven and God revealed some incredible things to him—things that made him vulnerable to pride. As such, God gave Paul a significant weakness (great suffering) to keep him humble. Man is prone to becoming *proud* when things are only positive; so God gives us weakness (suffering) to *humble* us—[think about that]—difficult humbling trials serve to make us more like Christ. Paul's thorn in the flesh was a constant humbling presence of some painful suffering. God sends hardship into our lives to keep us humble—totally dependent on God (not ourselves or our circumstances). *Humility is far more important than our comfort.* It is not in victory that we are made more like Christ, but in difficulty, trial, and suffering. Reflect upon the words of **John Newton's** hymn, *"I asked the Lord"*—it speaks powerfully to our suffering and its purpose:

> *I asked the Lord that I might grow*
> *In faith and love and every grace,*
> *Might more of His salvation know*
> *And seek more earnestly His face.*
>
> *Twas He who taught me thus to pray*
> *And Thee I trust has answered prayer,*
> *But it has been in such a way*
> *As almost drove me to despair.*
>
> *I hoped that in some favored hour*
> *At once He'd answer my request,*
> *And by His love's constraining power*
> *Subdue my sins and give me rest.*
>
> *Instead of this He made me feel*
> *The hidden evils of my heart,*
> *And let the angry powers of Hell*
> *Assault my soul in every part.*
>
> *Yea more with His own hand He seemed*
> *Intent to aggravate my woe,*
> *Crossed all the fair designs I schemed,*
> *Cast out my feelings, laid me low.*

> *Lord, why is this, I trembling cried,*
> *Wilt Thou pursue Thy worm to death?*
> *"Tis in this way," the Lord replied,*
> *"I answer prayer for grace and faith."*
>
> *"These inward trials I do employ*
> *From self and pride to set thee free;*
> *And break thy schemes of earthly joy*
> *That thou mayest seek thy all in Me."*

The man's life was "pleasant"—he attributed it to his faith. So he said, "This will soon pass. God is faithful. Life will again be pleasant." His worship remained shallow . . . God allowed more unpleasant things to happen in this man's life—*"I will be patient,"* thought the man. His worship became a way to convince God to restore his pleasant life. God was not pleased. The man's life became more miserable. Finally, the man got angry. *God still did not move.* The man became increasingly convinced God was becoming increasingly indifferent and uncaring; thus the man could only think of better yesterdays, not of better tomorrows. *He finally lost hope.* God had withdrawn His blessing. The man fell into depression, and his worship stopped. God was not pleased . . . so He released the forces of hell into the man's life. Temptations once manageable, now became irresistible. The man finally "begged" for help—"You owe me help! I don't deserve all this that has happened to me! This pain is not my fault! It's Yours!" God was not pleased, so He even let new struggles come into the man's life. The man finally concluded, "I have no choice but to conclude that *God is not good."* The battle waxed hot. But a flicker of hope remained. "I'm trying to maintain faith in you, God—doesn't that impress you? if not, what does?" God was not pleased. So He allowed the man's trials to continue unabated. He provided the man no comfort. God had a greater dream for the man than a return to a *pleasant life*—He wanted the man to find *true joy.* The fog around the man's soul thickened . . . and all that was left was the mystery of a bad life and a good God.

He remembered Jacob—so he began to fight! For the first time he cried out to God to *"Bless me!"* "Bless me! Not because I am good and deserve your blessing, but because You are good. You owe me nothing. I appeal only to who You are." He still saw his pain . . . but now he also saw God. It was a cry for whatever God wanted to do. The man felt something different—it was the beginning of humility. *The man had forgotten himself and discovered his desire for God.* Fresh water bubbled up from a spring in the desert of his soul. It was a dream of actually knowing God and representing Him in an unpleasant world. He had never before felt grateful for his troubles. *His suffering became to him a doorway into God's heart.* Suffering actually made him feel closer to God. The man thought, "My soul is thirsty—a pleasant life is not water for my soul; whatever comes from God—this is the only true water, and this water is enough." *The man worshipped God, and God was pleased.* So God kept the water bubbling up out of the spring in the man's soul. When the man failed to drink every morning from the spring, or return every evening to drink again, his thirst became intolerable. Some things in his life got better, some stayed the same, some got worse. But the man was dreaming new dreams, greater dreams than merely a pleasant life—and he found the courage to pursue them. He was now a man with hope, and that brought him joy . . . and God was pleased. (8–12).

Larry Crabb: "Sometimes God seems like the 'least responsive friend' I have." My real problem with God becomes apparent when long-held and deeply cherished dreams are shattered and He does nothing. And these are good dreams, not dreams of money and fame. We long for a job we really like . . . to serve God in a fruitful way . . . but nothing happens. Depending on an unresponsive God in the middle of crumbling dreams can be tough on one's faith. *Live long enough and dreams important to you will "shatter."* Some will remain shattered. God will not glue together the pieces of every Humpty Dumpty in your life. The divorce will go through . . . cancer will claim a loved one . . . Alzheimer's will not be arrested . . . broken friendships will not be restored despite your best efforts to reconcile . . . your marriage will not be satisfying no

FAITH VS. FEELINGS

The dynamic of the flesh is FEELINGS; the dynamic of the Spirit is FAITH. As human beings, when we don't "feel good" our inner self becomes dark, anxious, discouraged, depressed, dissatisfied, angry, and full of pain; in short, we feel miserable and set out to do whatever we can to make ourselves *"feel better."* One of the reasons we don't like temptation is that it is a very uncomfortable feeling. We would love to just be able to push the right button and experience instant deliverance and feel better; but that is not the economy under which we live. Since feelings are a by-product of our thoughts, the key is to walk by the Spirit and think right thoughts (Phil 4:6–9). When *"anxiety"* rules in our hearts, peace and joy exit, and discontentment and frustration enter. Our initial response to temptation as believers is to "pray" that God would simply take it away—after all, we don't want to sin; so why should we be subjected to the "hound of hell" beating on us until we finally cave in to it? There is a reasonableness to that argument, but it completely misses out on *"God's purpose"* for temptation—God uses temptation to test us, to prove us, to purify us, to purge the sinful dross that remains within us, to humble us, to strengthen us in our faith, to mature us in Christ, to conform us to the image of Christ, to sanctify us, and to keep us mindful of how weak we are in and of ourselves, and how much we need His mercy and grace. So to expect God to operate in a way that runs contrary to His purposes, is foolish—it is simply not going to happen. Thus anxiety will reign in our hearts until we determine to "fight the fight of faith."

When we truly trust God—believe Him, walk by faith, walk by the Spirit—instead of being overwhelmed by our anxious feelings, we will experience His peace and His joy (Phil 4:6–9). Therefore our problem is a *"faith"* problem, not a *"feeling"* problem. Obviously, when we are *feeling good,* nothing feels better . . . but the reality is, good feelings quickly grow wings and fly away, especially when we are confronted with trials and temptations. The biggest problem we have with this thing called "feelings" is that we so desperately want to "feel good," that we actually think it is God's supreme desire for us. The flesh would have us believe that *God genuinely desires that we feel good about ourselves, and that we are really happy and content*—that may sound good, but that is not what Scripture teaches, and it is not God's supreme desire for us. Sadly, this wishful thinking, Santa Claus kind of theology, is very popular here in the West; people buy into it—hook, line and sinker—because that is

> what they really *want* to hear (2 Tim 4:3). I have heard many professing Christians say, "I could not believe in a God who did not want me to feel good about myself and be happy in life." Yet that is not what Scripture teaches. The Bible teaches that God, above everything, wants us to enjoy *Him* and live a life of faith and obedience—those two positions are radically different from each other. Though God does care about our feelings, they are not His *primary* concern; they are of *secondary* importance. By the way, those who enter into an intimate, joyful relationship with Christ, and live a life of faith and obedience, experience far more peace and joy and contentment and happiness than anyone else in the world—why? because such things are the *by-products* of right living.

matter how many counselors you consult . . . your singleness will not be tolerable . . . your ministry will not be gratifying. You will feel low for a long time . . . the dark tunnel will lengthen with no end in sight. You will be miserable . . . *AND GOD WON'T DO A THING*—that's the problem with Him. (13–21)

When dreams shatter, we hurt and the pain won't go away. But it can be numbed for a time by working hard, seeing lots of movies, dining out a lot, sometimes a regime of rigorous self-discipline, sometimes a season of private pleasures. Whatever the means, the goal is the same—*Handle Pain!* Find some way to keep going in spite of the hurt. Don't think about it. Stay strong. Do whatever it takes—spiritual retreat, leaning on family, talking to a counselor, reading books, whatever—handle the pain! The question is, *"What do we do with how we are feeling toward God?* What we want is good. Why won't God let us have it? He promised us an abundant life—we are not seeing the abundance. In the midst of the pain of crumbling dreams, God so often seems to pull away. *When we cry the loudest, He sometimes turns a deaf ear.* When we pray earnestly for relief, He sometimes adds new pressures to our pile. And nothing improves inside us. We pray for love, joy, peace—and feel anger, despair, and fear. It is hard to escape the fact that God is not coming to help us—He is unresponsive to our pain.

Crabb's thoughts here remind me of an "Old Papa Polar Bear" who once took his son fishing. The story goes like this—after the old bear and his little cub were out on the ice for a couple of hours, and hadn't caught anything, the little fella finally looked up at his dad and asked him a question, "Papa, am I one hundred percent polar bear?" Old papa bear looked down at his son and said, "Sure you are, son . . . my father was a polar bear; my mother was a polar bear; and all of our descendents were polar bears." The little guy still had a "puzzled look on his face," and said, "You sure, Papa?" At that point old papa bear looked down at his son and said, "Yes, Son, I'm absolutely positive! Why do you ask?" "Well," the little cub said to his father, "I'm freezing!" Sometimes each of us as believers might begin to wonder whether we have the *"spiritual DNA"* we're supposed to have—it happens to all of us when we go through seasons of darkness, especially when God is silent and unresponsive . . . but it is during these times that God is doing a very significant and painful work in our lives . . . our faith is being tested, and some of the dross is being purged from our hearts. *Keep seeking Him during those dark times—the sun will shine in the morning.* God never stops the work He is doing in us. Never! He fully understands our anxieties, and won't suffer us beyond that which we are able to endure (Heb 12:11; 13:5; Jam 1:2–4; 1 Pet 4:12, 18; 5:10; Phil 1:6; 1 Th 4:3; 5:24).

Trusting God is dangerous business. In his college days, ***Ted Turner*** trusted God. When a loved one contracted cancer and, in spite of his prayers, died a painful death . . . he turned from God. He could no longer depend on God. He was right. *God cannot be trusted to always minimize our suffering in this life.* When dreams shatter, we lose hope. When the capacity for soul-pleasure is lost, we become irresistibly attracted to *"lesser pleasures"*—power, popularity, sex, prowess in business or sports, eating, drinking. That is my problem with God—to people whose souls have been inundated with pain, God seems so unresponsive. We pray and nothing happens. The problem sincere Christians have with God often comes down to a wrong understanding of what this life is meant to provide. We assume we are here for one fundamental reason: *to enjoy life and have a good time*—if not good circumstances, then at least good feelings. We long to experience a compelling pleasure that eliminates all pain. We give up immediate pleasure in order to later experience a deeper kind of pleasure—but we expect to feel that pleasure soon, certainly before we die. We insist on the internal good time of peace, of self-respect, of feeling at least pretty good if not fully alive. Sometimes all that separates believers from unbelievers is our understanding of how to produce those good feelings—*the pursuit of "soul pleasure" remains primary;* it continues to be the aim behind our choices. As long as our purpose is to have a "good time," to have "soul pleasure exceed soul pain," *God becomes merely a means to an end, an object to be used . . . never a lover to be enjoyed.* When God fails us—we feel betrayed, let down, thoroughly disillusioned. He neither reverses the tragedy nor fills us with peace and joy. He typically remains aloof . . . our souls remain unsatisfied . . . and eventually, we may even learn to hate Him. Going to church doesn't help, and Bible study becomes boring. We lose hope. Nothing gives us a good time . . . things remain hard and we continue to feel bad.

How are we to "find hope" when God's kindness hurts, when bad things happen that God could have prevented? We must discover a hope that thrives when dreams shatter, when sickness advances, and poverty worsens, and loneliness deepens. It is harder to discover our desire for God when things go well. Shattered dreams are the truest blessings; they help us discover our true hope. But it can take a long, dark time to discover it. Does Christianity genuinely offer anything in this life other than a good ethic to follow? Is there anything we can hope for in this life? Shattered dreams destroy false expectations, such as the *"victorious Christian life"* with no real struggle or failure. They help us discover true hope. Pain always has a purpose. It will not go away, without doing its work. It will stir an appetite for *a higher purpose—the better hope of knowing God well enough now to love Him above everything else, and trusting Him no matter what happens.* Suffering has an important function in this life—as nothing else can, it moves us away from demanding what's *good* . . . toward desiring what's *better* . . . until heaven provides what's *best.* (22-33)

When we think of "hope," most often we think of things "getting better." In the Old Testament the idea of salvation almost always means deliverance from tough circumstances. That is the kind of hope we want. But then the writer of Hebrews goes on to talk about others who were "not delivered"—their gratification was delayed until heaven (Heb 11). Apparently God is pleased with people who suffer terribly, but who keep on trusting. What the Bible wants us to *hope for in this life* is very different from what most of us think. Some of our fondest dreams will shatter, and we will be tempted to lose hope. God will seem callous, or worse—weak; unresponsive to our pain. As we struggle with dashed hopes, we will fail, just as Peter did. You will then feel discouraged with yourself to the point of *"self-hatred."* And God will seem to withdraw from you and do nothing. When this comes to pass, *"do not lose hope"*—a plan is unfolding that you cannot clearly see. What God is saying to us is this: "In the deepest part of your soul, you long more than anything else to be a part of My plan, to further My kingdom, to know Me and please Me and enjoy Me. I will satisfy that longing. You have the power to represent Me well no matter what happens in your life. That is the 'hope' I give you in this world. Don't lose it." (34–43)

God could have done something, but He did nothing. Why is God so inconsistent, so maddeningly unpredictable? A faithful missionary for sixty years recently died an agonizing death from lung cancer. He had never smoked a day in his life. His final days were spent screaming, "Where is God? I can't find Him! All I can feel is darkness!" The Lord did nothing to preserve the dreams **Naomi** once thought were essential to her happiness (Book of Ruth)—if Naomi could speak to us now, she would probably report, "Everything worked out for the best. It was extremely difficult . . . but don't let pain cause you to miss the power of shattered dreams to change your life for good, forever." From Naomi we learn—

1. <u>Our fondest dreams for this life must be *"fully abandoned"* if we are to know God well.</u> Shattered dreams are necessary for spiritual growth.

2. Shattered dreams sometimes produce *"excruciating pain,"* and we emerge from the experience as "changed people" (though not always for the better). The pain is not evidence of weak faith; it is evidence that we are *"normal."* Something wonderful survives everything terrible, and it surfaces most clearly when we hurt.

3. Some cherished dream will *"crumble"* in your life—that's inevitable; no one makes it unscathed to the end. Whether we believe God caused the trial (as Naomi did), or that God merely allowed the trial, one thing is clear—God could have prevented the trial, and that fact creates within us a tension with God, which results in a battle with Him.

4. Only an experience of *"deep pain"* develops our capacity for recognizing and enjoying true life.

5. Most people never discover *"true life."* Not many Christians drink deeply from the well of living water. As a result, our worship, our community, and our witness are weak.

6. The past is *"irreparable,"* but no matter what happens in life, a wonderful new dream is always available, that if pursued will generate an unfamiliar, radically new internal experience. That experience, strange at first, will eventually be recognized as *joy*. (44–51)

We like to remain "naively happy." Other people get cancer, suffer through divorce, lose their jobs, and experience a friend's betrayal. With adolescent maturity we declare that *"God is good"* when we ace a test or when a biopsy comes back negative—and when blessings come, we should of course enjoy them. In His mercy, God takes away the good to create an appetite for the better. It comes down to this: God's best is available only to those who are willing to sacrifice the merely good. If we are *satisfied* with good health, responsible children, enjoyable marriages, close friendships, interesting jobs, successful ministries, we will *never hunger* for God's best. Furthermore, we will never really truly worship. Only a few people believe an *"intimate relationship with God"* is the greatest blessing—and those who believe that appear to have developed that conviction only through *suffering*. Happiness must be stripped away, before joy can surface. Most Christians can envision nothing higher than *"circumstance-dependent happiness"*—marriage, children, nice house, health, financial security (what every culture calls "the good life"). When this kind of happiness is not experienced, life can be very depressing (actually, downright miserable). Naomi called God "Shaddai," the Almighty One, the invincible mountain, the force that cannot be resisted; God does what He wants—we can do nothing but endure His choices. And we conclude that most tragedies are a discipline for our wrong choices or for some other reason, but *whatever the reason, tragedies are God's doing. He could prevent them, but He doesn't*. Happiness is taken away, and is replaced by despair. *God is working when we see nothing but darkness*. We are being taken to an experience of joy along the path of suffering—there is no other way to get there; God is creating within us an appetite for a *"better dream."* We cannot rush the process—the water of life will find its way down the mountain to fill the lake from which we can drink. (52–59)

Gautama Siddhartha one day announced he was "Buddha" (the awakened one), when he gained the insight that the way to end suffering is to end desire. Buddhists seek to *"feel less"* when confronted with pain ... to find some way to deaden the desires that bring pain. Jesus taught the opposite—His way is to *awaken a passion within the soul* that transcends all other passions. So instead of deadening the pain, He emphasized deepening the desire. Gautama Siddhartha made it his life's mission to understand suffering and discover its solution. His awakening consisted of the *"four noble truths"*—

1. <u>Life is *suffering*</u>—suffering is the gap between what we desire and what we experience.

2. <u>The cause of all suffering is *desire*</u>—people suffer because they don't experience their desires.

3. <u>The way to end suffering is to end desire</u>—if you want nothing, then nothing can disturb you.

4. <u>Spend your life learning to eliminate desire</u>—Gautama's "eight-fold path" shows you how.

Jesus directs us to a different path. He tells us to not let our hearts be troubled; He teaches that—

1. <u>Life includes suffering, but life is good</u>—in this world everyone will suffer tribulation.

2. <u>The cause of all suffering is *separation from God*</u>—we are deceived into looking elsewhere for joy.

3. <u>The way to handle suffering is to *discover your desire for God*</u>—then everything, both good and bad, becomes redemptive; everything moves us toward the God we desire.

4. <u>The new life provided through Jesus must be accepted as a gift of love</u>—we spend the rest of our days discovering our desire to know God better, and we come to realize it is a desire whose satisfaction no shattered dream can thwart.

Remember what "brokenness" is—it is the awareness that you long to be someone you are not and cannot be without divine help. Never pretend to God or to yourself that you *feel* what you don't or that you *are* what you are not. Be completely honest with yourself and God. No one discovers the fullness of their desire for God without entering the fullness of *"lesser desires."* We must feel the soul-piercing pain of disappointment and despair before we can enter the depths of our souls. Beneath our troubled emotion is a desire for God that in rich measure can be satisfied now. Every Christian, no matter the depth of his pain, can discover that desire. It takes time, agonizing time, characterized more by despair than hope, but discovery can be made. *Don't let your hearts be troubled—in the middle of shattered dreams, discover a desire that Christ pledges Himself to satisfy.* The desire will surface like bubbling water from a spring that can no longer be held back. When that desire is discovered, we wake up to a new world of passion, a quiet world of genuine rest—spiritual disciplines become our favorite things to do. People who insist on happiness never find joy; they only allow themselves to feel those desires that are met. The effect is to feel happy for a season, but it is a selfish happiness. They live for the ongoing satisfaction of desires other than the desire to know God. They become *"self-absorbed."* God stripped Naomi of happiness to prepare her for joy. *Desperate people* discover that desire—happy contented people never do. (60–72)

Everything helps me to God—He causes "all things" to work together for good in the believer's life. St. John of the Cross found "light" in his darkness, knowing God was at work in ways he could not see. Impatient Westerners want *"quick sanctification"*—bring your soul to a counselor/pastor and get it fixed right away. Wisdom knows the deep workings of the hungry, hurting, sin-inclined soul and patiently follows as the Spirit moves quietly in those depths, gently nudging people toward God. There is no Concorde that flies us from immaturity to maturity in a few hours—there is only a narrow, bumpy road where a few people walk together as they journey to God. Naomi was on that path . . . she was not doing well . . . life was very cruel and difficult . . . she couldn't shake the feelings of depression . . . and she was mad at God . . . she believed she was a victim of His ruthless sovereignty. It was at a point like this that **Ted Turner** dismissed God, and learned to live like a functional atheist—*"There is no God I can depend on; He offers me no real help."* Churches are filled with worshipers who have reached that conclusion.

Believers need to know that "God's Spirit" is working quietly in their souls, redeeming everything that has happened to direct them to Himself. We need to interpret all of life's hardships not as problems to fix, or struggles to relieve, or pains to deaden, but as important elements in a much larger story. Believers need to accept wherever they are on the journey, whether happy or miserable, as the place where God will meet them, where He loves them, where He will continue to work in them. *The last thing suffering saints need is to hear sermons that leave them feeling scolded and pressured and falsely hopeful, because biblical principles are presented as formulas for making life work.* God never stops His work of making His children aware of a dream that remains alive beneath the rubble of every shattered dream, a new dream that when realized will release a new song of joy in our hearts. (73–80)

The function of pain is to carry us into the inner recesses of our being that wants God. We need to let *"soul-pain"* do its work by experiencing it fully. If we deny how badly we hurt, we remain unaware of our desire for God and aware only of *"lesser desires."* We need God. He is all we need. But until we realize that fact, we experience lesser desires as "needs" and devote our energy to arranging for their satisfaction. That is the essence of *"addiction"*—addictions are not the product of psychological disorder; they are not the expression of internal damage caused by difficult backgrounds; they are rather the fruit of the flesh, that natural tendency in all of us to fill our empty souls with some pleasure other than God. Obedience to God is a fruit of the Spirit's revealing the sweetness of Christ to our spirits so that we actually enjoy obedience more than sin.

When the deepest desire we feel within our hearts is for something "other than God," a spirit of entitlement develops. We see ourselves as needing something we don't have and we believe we should have. Whatever brings satisfaction relieves pain for the moment, then creates deeper emptiness, that in turn clamors for even greater relief—the will then becomes a slave to whatever *god* makes us feel better. Only *"true worship"* expresses our deepest freedom, but we do not properly worship until we discover our deepest desire for God. The decision to live for whatever brings instant pleasure turns us into addicts (alcohol, porn, being obsessed with growing great kids, closing the next big deal, accomplishing the next big task, etc). When second-place desires become first-place priorities, we don't discover our core longing for God. *The flaw is in the premise—God wants us happy.* Our generation wants what it wants *now*. Unsatisfied desire has become to us like a bad toothache that demands quick relief at any cost.

When El Shaddai allows terrible pain to come into our lives, He is removing "some satisfaction" that keeps us happy and content whether or not we know God well. He is taking away *"good food"* to make us hungry for *"better fare."* When the pain of shattered dreams helps us discover our desire for God, God seems to disappear. His absence becomes obvious, and we discover how badly we long to know Him. It is this frustration of our desire for God that deepens it. We cry out, "How long, O Lord, before you deliver me from all my distress?" The psalmists were realistic—they didn't see God as a divine vending machine that could be manipulated. Naomi endured ten years of pain and suffering . . . ten years with no visible evidence of God's involvement. But it is in the midst of pain that she ultimately discovered her desire for God. It was then that she faced the truth that there was no other answer. To whom else could she go? *Only God has the life our souls so desperately need.* In the midst of our pain, we come to really believe that. So we abandon ourselves to Him . . . and wait. There is no formula for making it happen.

No longer do we live for blessings; no longer do we pray, "God, here is what I need; give it to me!" We learn to say, "God, whoever You are, whatever You do, that is all I want. I demand nothing. I will wait for You." If you are seeking God in the middle of shattered dreams, but are having trouble finding Him, be encouraged that it bothers you. The more you are bothered by not finding Him, the more aware you are becoming how badly you want Him. Abandon yourself to Him. Let the cross bring you confidence that He is with you and will reveal Himself to you. When you realize that your desire for God is the most passionate yearning of your heart, you are in the spiritual condition to recognize God's hand when He makes it visible. To paraphrase Naomi's words: *"The Lord has not discarded me. He has always been there, but now I can see His kind heart at work. My pain is still real, but now something matters more."* She did not give herself over to lesser pleasures. She refused to settle for inferior joy. She did not become an addict. When God moved, her heart leaped. But, as is so often the case, when God began to visibly move in Naomi's life, He did not create a smooth path. There was more Naomi needed to learn before she could worship. Through the agony of shattered dreams, her soul was ripped open so she could discover her desire for God. Now she needed to discover God's desire for her. (81–89)

All of us are trapped by "addiction" to a desire for something less than God. For many *women*, that something is *"relational control"*—"I will not be hurt again, and I will see to it that what I fear never happens." For *men*, it is more often an addiction to *"nonrelational control"*—"I will experience deep and consuming satisfaction without ever having to relate meaningfully with anyone." Men keep things shallow and safe; their commitment is twofold—to never risk revealing inadequacy by drawing close to people, and without breaking that commitment, to feel powerful and alive. Power in business and illicit sex are favorite strategies for reaching that goal. *The only cure for addiction is the "gospel"*—we will not find the power to resist the pull toward *"lesser desires"* until we discover a more powerful desire that we long to fulfill, a desire the Spirit creates within our hearts when the Father forgives us. We must discover our *desire for God*—as we discover that desire, we come to see that we cannot pursue God and a lesser source of pleasure at the same time. The desire for God and the desire for anything else are competitive—only one can serve as the *"guiding rule"* of life.

When we attempt to serve "two masters," we end up bowing before the one who is more apparently responsive to our needs and hating the other. An hour of porn reaps more immediate dividends than an hour of prayer. We will not win the battle against addiction without discovering *our desire for God*. Therefore, if you want to know God, welcome shattered dreams. Nothing reveals our desire for Him so effectively. But we must also discover *God's desire for us*—God is constantly at work in our lives . . . all with the purpose of breaking us, so that we might become formed to the image of Christ. Only a fulfilled desire for God provides the power to consistently resist the lure of lesser pleasures, and to stay anchored in Christ when life's storms rage.

How do we experience the reality of God? That is not easily answered. It was really much easier when we were satisfied with "lesser things." Until we realize how badly we need God, how empty we are without Him, we can enjoy a kind of happy indifference to whether we discover Him. For many people, when things go reasonably well, they feel pretty good. When their path hits a bump, they pray and things get better. They expect God to do something, and He does. Why does God seem to provide for the *"pleasantly committed"* and withdraw Himself from the *"seriously committed"*? In **Exodus**, every time the Israelites complained, God blessed them; He straightened things out. But, in **Numbers**, when they were farther along on their trek to Canaan, God changed tactics, and usually refused to bless them.

Who wants to become "mature"? Answered prayer seems to be more frequently reported among younger Christians. God, it appears, accommodates our immaturity not to keep us there, but to give us a confidence in His Presence that will sustain the search for a deeper, more relational expression of His Presence. The farther we travel on our spiritual journey, the less responsive God becomes to our requests for a pleasant life. Things go wrong and God does nothing. He becomes the elusive God. *Live long enough and important dreams will shatter—things will go wrong that God will not fix.* He could fix them, but He chooses not to. Then, when the pain of unmet desires puts us in touch with how desperately we long to discover the gentle *Presence of God* in our lives, we become more aware of His absence. From the depth of our being we then cry out, "God, where are You? Don't You care? Let me find You!"

It is one thing to discover our desire for God; it is quite another to discover "His desire for us;" to know with absolute certainty when life is at its worst that His Presence is real, that He is with us, and that He really cares. We discover God's desire for us, first, by looking at Scripture. God exists—He exists both in heaven and on earth. Most important, He exists in us. Therefore, our search for God is an "inward" search. *Silence and solitude are essential to discovering His Presence.* We must block out the noise of life and become aware of our interior world if we are to find God. Beneath every heartache, moral failure, shattered dream, a divine Presence is waiting to be discovered. Only when we discover a desire for Him that is stronger than our desire for relief from pain will we pay the price necessary to find Him. If we are to encounter the divine Presence, we must enter the interior sanctuary of our heart, and like Jesus in the temple, become indignant over what we find. There is no way to God but through the rubble of our lives. The process is what spiritual people call BROKENNESS and REPENTANCE.

We must let our souls live in a "private monastery," in an attitude of contemplation that helps us see that all of life is sacred, where we remain alert to the Spirit's revelation of ourselves and God. When life gets tough and God does nothing, the Spirit is telling us that this world is not our home—He is exposing the rubble that must be cleared away. If we fail to be quiet enough to hear all that the Spirit is saying, we will be in danger of discovering *our desire for God* and never discovering *His desire for us*. When we first met Naomi, she was living the pleasant life of the immature, the good life of the untested. Then her world fell apart. Huge dreams were shattered. She was heartbroken with life and bitter toward God. God was moving, but she couldn't see it. Then, her daughter-in-law (the widow Ruth) met Boaz, a rich relative who could make new dreams come true. Naomi's hope returned. Her desire for God to move in her life was reawakened. When we discover our passion for God, He reveals His passion for us. First, we are reduced to exhilarating humility, to an interior darkness, a silencing darkness, that lets us see God in the richest way He can be seen in this life. (90–98)

More than ever before, people are self-consciously "hungry for God," for spiritual renewal, for deep satisfaction of the soul. The search to discover God requires that we *"abandon ourselves,"* that we give up control of what matters most, and that we place our confidence in Someone we cannot manage. As we respond to our desire for God by looking for Him, we make a fundamental assumption: it is this—*God can be experienced!* In our shallow, sensual way of looking at life, we tend to measure God's Presence by the kind of emotion we feel. But the Spirit's invitation to experience God appeals to something far deeper than easily produced emotions—it appeals to a capacity of soul that carries us toward a higher dimension than mere emotions can reach. *True abandonment*, giving ourselves to God in utter dependence on His willingness to give Himself to us, pleads only mercy. It allows no room for control. Only suffering has the power to bring us to this point. Followers of Christ live under His mercy always. We serve at His pleasure as well, not ours. There is nothing we can do to make Him show up. We merely invite Him to do so. God chooses whether or not to respond. We are entirely dependent on what He wants to do.

When in the midst of terrible pain we cry out to God, we abandon ourselves more to Him . . . then a confidence emerges, a sense of His Presence, that only the awakened spiritual capacities of the soul can identify. Writes Iain Matthew: "This confidence is a kind of companionship and inner strength that walks with the soul and gives it strength." *To the degree that pain teaches us that our deepest desire is for God, we will abandon ourselves to Him.* We will do whatever it takes to create an awareness of space in our souls that only He can fill. And in His mercy, we will find a confidence developing that He is there, that He has indeed entered our space. The soul's capacity to abandon itself to God and to enjoy confidence in Him is a capacity that the Spirit's companionship inspires. It develops most fully when our capacity for *"lesser pleasures"* is frustrated. As the process slowly unfolds, we become aware of God's desire for us. (99–106)

God never promised us a rose garden until heaven, but sometimes life here and now is just too hard. Things that matter so deeply to us, sometimes don't seem to matter at all to God. Sometimes it is difficult to get past the thought that *real love would not let us suffer like we do.* It is hard to think of an absent nurse as caring. There are basically "three options" to mounting an assault on an unresponsive God:

1. <u>Dismiss Him, turn from bad thoughts about Him to no thoughts at all</u>. Handle life as best you can with your own resources.

2. <u>Confess anger at God with how He handles things as blasphemous irreverence and heinous rebellion</u>. Remind yourself that God is the Almighty Sovereign Lord of the universe, then kneel before Him. That is the hardest option. It requires that I smother my soul, that I kick the life out of myself in order to get along with God.

3. <u>Scream and holler until the terror of life so weighs you down that you discover solid ground beneath your feet.</u> The solid ground . . . is Him. God is not mad at us. He is not indifferent. He is not helpless. His character is love. Right now He is "cutting the wedding cake," eagerly awaiting the Father's signal to clear a way for His return. If we believed this, we would rest. Jesus is restraining Himself from ending our pain, for reasons we cannot fully understand. Rather than sorting through His reasons for not responding as we would like, we are encouraged to focus on the passion that makes it difficult for Him not to swoop down in power and solve all our problems. A close look at what Naomi told Ruth might help us see that our unresponsive God is really a restrained lover. Don't let your heart be troubled; rest with confidence in His love. (107–114)

God's restraining has a purpose. From our perspective, he could do something . . . but He does nothing to deliver us from our pain. Why? To deepen our desire for His Presence, to strengthen our passion to pursue Him, to help us see how preoccupied we are with filling our God-shaped souls with something less than God. Only when we want *HIM* as we want nothing else will there develop in our hearts a space large enough for Him to fill. When our discovery creates a secret space that nothing else can fill, and when we know that to be true . . . *He will enter.* Through the pain of shattered dreams, God is awakening us to the possibility of the pleasure of His Presence—that is the nature of our journey; it is what the Spirit is doing.

The *SECULAR JOURNEY* ends in this life—this world is home to secularists; they are not pilgrims passing through. The primary purpose of those on the *SPIRITUAL JOURNEY* is neither to enjoy this life, nor the people they meet, nor themselves—it is rather to enjoy God. At best, the *secular man* feels good about this life; at its worst, he views this life as disappointing. The *spiritual man* on his journey to God experiences an appetite that is never fully satisfied; eventually he discovers his desire for God is stronger than all other desires. *Making his life more comfortable is a secondary concern.* Satan's masterpiece is not the prostitute or the skid-row bum—it is the *"self-sufficient believer"* who has made his life comfortable. (115–124)

We want people, including ourselves, to *FEEL GOOD*. We further assume that if there is a God, His job is to do what we cannot do to make life work as we want. But, suppose we believe God is "not" committed to making our lives work well enough for us to feel good . . . that God is "not" cooperating with us to make life work so we can feel now all that He has created us to feel. There are two problems with that view: One, better circumstances can never produce the joy we were designed to experience; only an intimate relationship with Perfect Love can provide that joy. Two, in this life, we can never feel what God intended us to feel, at least not in full measure. To be completely happy, we must experience *"perfect intimacy"* with Perfect Love—that will not occur until we get to heaven. Therefore—we cannot count on God to arrange what happens in our lives in ways that will make us feel good; but we can count on God to patiently remove all the obstacles to our enjoyment of Him.

God is committed to "our joy," and we can depend on Him to give us enough of a *"taste of that joy"* in spite of how much pain continues to plague our hearts. God's intense desire is to intimately relate with us. For His desire to be realized, He must remove the obstacle within us that, more than any other, stands in the way of intimacy with Him. That obstacle is this—we devote our central energies to *feeling better* and to justifying whatever does the job. The belief that there is no higher good than feeling better now—this is the single biggest obstacle to our enjoying God's Present. The Bible calls it the *FLESH*.

When life is hard and we feel bad, we turn to God to change things— if not our circumstances then at least our emotions. When He proves unresponsive, we naturally turn and seek out some method to *ease the pain*. To realize what we most "deeply want"—*to feel good*—is not a viable option in this life. God simply won't permit sinful human beings to go through life "feeling good" through false gods and false beliefs. Why would he bless sinful human beings with such a quality of life? Good feelings would then become the basis for our joy. In this world, the dream of feeling as good as we want to feel will shatter. Shattered dreams create the opportunity for God to work more deeply than ever before, to further weaken our grasp on our empty selves. It is through *"pain"* we are made aware of our real needs. When dreams shatter, we resolve more than anything to *"feel better"*—that resolve is the *FLESH*. (125–141)

The FLESH—it is the way we think; it is the energy that pushes us to do what we do; it is the energy that drives us to evaluate everything that happens in our lives according to how it makes us feel. We are victims of a fickle world, an unresponsive God, a variety of insensitive people. Our chief aim is to *feel better*—that is the way of the flesh: something bad happens . . . we hurt . . . we feel unhappy . . . we long to feel good . . . we ask God for help . . . God is unresponsive . . . we are resolved to feel better . . . so we do whatever we can to make that a reality (eating, entertainment, sex, sports, shopping, travel, television, etc.).

The way of the SPIRIT is this: we long to feel good, but we trust God; His pleasure matters more than our own, so we abandon ourselves to His pleasure; we live to please Him; and at some point we discover joy. We shift from walking in the *flesh* to walking in the **Spirit**, when the pain of life destroys our confidence in *"our ability"* to make life work—that is the experience of *BROKENNESS*. (142–149)

Lesson #1 on Brokenness—The good news of the gospel is "not" that God will provide a way to make lives *easier* . . . but that He will make our lives *better*. We have a hard time understanding the nature of our journey through this life—we still think that things should go well and that we should feel good. The closest friends of Jesus had the same problem—they assumed He would free their nation from Roman oppression. It made no sense to them to think that Jesus was not committed to feeding them well, keeping them healthy, and restoring their status as a special people. We also expect things to go well, at least not too badly. We are looking for a way to feel good now. When dreams shatter and God does nothing, we move in one of two directions—either we *rebel* in some form, or we try to *become spiritual* enough to experience peace and joy. Either we enjoy the pleasures of sin or we strive to arrange for the pleasures of His Presence—the first is doable, but stupid; the second is impossible. *We continue to think life should work well and we should feel good.* The nature of our spiritual journey, we assume, is that God's glory will be revealed in our prosperity (financial, relational, physical or emotional). It seems so natural to think the Presence of Jesus has no greater purpose than to *improve the quality of our journey through life* . . . with quality defined as a pleasurable, satisfying, self-affirming existence. If dreams never shattered, we would continue to believe that lie and value only what God can do for us now. In addition, we would not be willing to pay the devastating price required to experience His Presence now. Without suffering and trials, only spoiled brats would enter heaven.

Lesson #2 on Brokenness—When God seems most absent from us, He is doing His most important work in us. We should encourage pastors to publicly admit when they don't *"feel"* God's Presence; furthermore, they should also share the deep letdown that strangles their souls during those *"dark nights."* It is a normal experience. It is part of a good journey. Seasons of personal suffering are opportunities for God to do His deepest work. When the dark night comes, we tend to numb our desires, seek relief where available, get mad at God, eat too much, feel afraid of God, or busy ourselves. When dreams shatter and God disappears we need to realize that He vanishes from our sight to do what He could not do if we could see Him. In the spiritual journey, I know of nothing so difficult to believe—but it is true. Think of those three hours of darkness on the cross—Jesus screamed in agony, *"God, where are You?"* And God said—Nothing! It was during that exact time God was in the Son reconciling the world to Himself!

Lesson #3 on Brokenness—It is not always good to be blessed with the good things of life. Bad times provide an opportunity to *"know God"*—blessings alone can never provide that. Healthy, normal people feel wonderful *when good things happen.* They should. But *when things go badly,* do we get mad at God? Do we question Him? Do we voice our displeasure? Suffering is required if we are to discover a desire for God strong enough to help us decline the world's invitation to an immediately good time. Remember the flesh's argument: *God made us to feel happy.* When we don't "feel happy," nothing matters more than finding some way to feel happy or feel good. When things go well, we may think "happiness" is our birthright. Only *trials* have the power to break that argument. Only *pain* exposes our commitment to happiness for what it is, an arrogance that displaces God from His rightful place. So God teaches us three important lessons about *faith* through brokenness—

1. <u>The journey to God will always, at some point, take us through darkness where life makes no sense</u>. Life is not easy; it is hard—sometimes very hard.

2. <u>The felt absence of God is a gift to gratefully receive</u>. During those seasons of darkness He is doing His deepest work in us.

3. <u>Feeling good is not the goal</u>. When we feel bad, we have the opportunity to do battle against the enemy within that keeps us from entering the Presence of God with no greater passion than to glorify Him. *Faith* is about looking beyond our circumstances to a person. (150–156)

True obedience to Christ springs from a "deep passion" for Christ. No one can choose to feel genuine affection when they feel mad or indifferent. So, where does passion come from? In our day of *"feel good Christianity,"* we have come up with a wrong view of our spiritual journey. We think of suffering as something abnormal, as evidence that we *"lack faith."* We work so hard to escape suffering that we fail to realize what good things might be happening in us as we suffer. *The pain created by trouble carries us into the depths of our being, where everything revolves around us;* it is a place we actually believe God has failed us, that He has given us a raw deal. Our deepest desire is for a kind of life only mercy makes possible, a life only grace provides—a life that is *from* God, *with* God, *for* God. "Lord, only You, on Your terms, can satisfy my soul. Like Jabez, I ask that you bless me. I ask that you satisfy the highest dream my heart can envision—an encounter with You." The dream to experience God rises from deep within the soul quickened (broken) by suffering. (157-163)

When God said, "I will never stop doing you good," He meant it. He delights in doing His people good (Jer 32:40–41). I believe that is true. But still we cry, *"Lord, help my unbelief!"* There is no higher dream than experiencing God as He moves through every circumstance of life.

Martin Luther struggled with seeing Christ as his best friend. He once wrote, "I expect more from Kate my wife than from my sweet and blessed Savior; yet I know for certain that neither she nor any other person on earth will or can suffer that for me which He has suffered. Why should I be afraid of Him? *This foolish weakness of mine grieves me very much.*" Then he added, "Oh! His grace and goodness toward us is so immeasurably great, that without great assaults and trials it cannot be understood." That has been my experience as well. How does that coincide with what you have experienced?

We naturally think we would appreciate God's immeasurable goodness if we could measure it by fewer trials and more blessings. Good friends make our lives easier, not harder—so we think. But God insists that in our suffering He is doing us *good*, a greater good than relieving our suffering. *The problem is with our blessing-based, happiness-centered understanding of goodness.* And with our small idea of goodness, we dream small dreams, and small dreams lead to small prayers. Luther's idea of God's goodness was different—it was big, so big that "without great assaults and trials" it could not be understood. Here is how Larry Crabb puts it—(164–172)

> *We will not encounter Christ as our best friend, as the source of all true goodness, as the One who provides the sweetest pleasure to our souls, until we abandon ourselves to Him. And full abandonment, real trust, rarely happens until we meet God in the midst of shattered dreams, until in our brokenness we see in Him the only sufficient answer to our soul's deepest cry.*

Christianity is not primarily about escaping hell and going to heaven—it is about "knowing Jesus." If Luther is right—that only in suffering do we learn to fully delight in God's goodness—then it becomes immediately clear why our enjoyment of God is so shallow. *We don't like to suffer.* We actually arrange our lives to minimize suffering. And we believe Christianity offers a God who will cooperate with that plan. *J. I. Packer* looked over the modern church and observed: "There is something narcissistic and, to tell the truth, nutty in being more concerned about *godliness* than about *God*." We struggle to believe that God is our greatest pleasure! How can this be?

Listen to the testimony of "Augustine," arguably the church's greatest theologian after Paul. As a young man, Augustine struggled with sexual lust. Despite his best efforts, he could not control it. The commandment to confine sexual activity within marriage was not a light burden to him. It was a maddening demand that only made his problem worse and stirred his sinful passions. He felt completely powerless to change. *He knew what was right, but he could not do it—that reality tortured him most.* He was crushed by his inability to do what God required. God's holiness and his sinfulness were the chief sources of his torment. Augustine identified the exact center of his battle as his inability to enjoy God more than sex. Freedom came for Augustine—when he *"encountered God!"* It was an encounter with God that provided more pleasure than sex—*"Lord, You are sweeter than all pleasure!"* Only a thrilling, soul-pleasuring encounter with God that generates more pleasure than sin will free us from our addiction to sin. God longs to give us an encounter with Himself. It simply requires that we enter the pain of living in a world where good dreams shatter. (173–179)

Perhaps you are aware of how badly you long to "experience God." You want to enjoy Him and know His power. You want to change and find the strength to resist sinful urges. You are reading your Bible, praying, attending church, and even serving—all good activities that can contribute to spiritual formation. You want to *"encounter God and experience His joy."* To do so, begin by asking yourself two questions:

1. How do I think about GOD? Scripture tells us that God is *"absolutely holy."* Our culture now thinks of God as being more "paternal" than "holy"—that means we are more apt to view God as being "strict

but understanding," as opposed to being "justifiably enraged." Few Christians view God today as an irate judge who violently hates our sin—He is now more flexible, more tolerant, still insistent that we measure up to at least some of His standards, but gracious and understanding when we don't. It's what **Dietrich Bonhoeffer** calls *"cheap grace."* So, we reduce the holy God of passionate wrath to a fatherly God with strict standards—and we do it in the name of grace. Many dismiss God's standards by attacking them as holdovers from legalism. God has now become the *"helpful God"* of useful principles—as such, we spend our religious energy seeking to know the principles a helpful God provides for handling our lives; principles that will make our lives better. The result is that we never encounter God.

2. <u>How do I think about MYSELF?</u> Most Christians believe their happiness, and having a sense of well-being, matters more than anything else. We believe *"self-interest"* is a virtue—God tells us it is the essence of evil, that *God* is the point, not us. Our evil demand—that our sense of well-being be honored above God's glory—deserves punishment. It arouses God's wrath. We want our own way—in His justice, God is going to let us have it—hell is the enjoyment of our own way forever! Most Christians see themselves as *"minor offenders"* who perhaps deserve a scolding, but not a whipping! In our Christian culture, we have weakened our understanding of personal sin, and focused too much on our longings and needs. We want to *"feel good"* about ourselves; we long for enjoyable relationships. *"WE"* become the point and we see nothing really wrong with it. Because we focus more on "our longings" than "our evil," we see ourselves not as hopelessly arrogant, worthy of eternal misery, but as scoldably selfish, deserving of a *slap on the wrist*. We admit that our minor offenses warrant a *reprimand,* but we really believe that if someone knew what we have been through and the pain we feel, the scolding would actually give way to a *sympathetic hug*. Yes, we struggle and make some mistakes, but given our hurt and how poorly the people in our lives have responded to our longings, our struggles are quite understandable. If God really loves us, then He ought to "helps us."

When understandable strugglers meet a "helpful God" of useful principles, they use Him to make their lives more comfortable. But they never experience a "deep change" in their inner soul, and as such never encounter God as their greatest pleasure. Their experience of God remains shallow—*they simply remain spiritual narcissists, self-centered people who live only to "feel better."* By the way, that is the "norm" in western Christianity.

When arrogant people who know they deserve "eternal misery," tremble before a holy God of passionate wrath, they "discover grace." They encounter the depths of God's kindness and love, and they fall on their knees and worship Christ as Lord and Savior. They know they don't deserve a hug, no matter how badly they are hurting . . . but they get an eternal one anyway! That is the grace that takes their breath away. With abandon they seek God . . . and they are startled when they discover that their interior worlds are changing. *They discover that they actually want to obey God.* They become spiritual people and dream the dream of knowing Christ even better. As such, they welcome shattered dreams as friends. They learn slowly. More dreams must shatter before they experience their deepest joy in Christ. The Holy Spirit uses the pain of shattered dreams to help us discover our desire for God. The journey to joy takes us through shattered dreams. (180–189)

SOME CONCLUDING THOUGHTS—The enormous challenge of trusting a seemingly unresponsive God, requires a change in how we naturally look at life. More than ever before in history, believers assume we are here for one fundamental reason—to have a good time; if not good circumstances, then at least good feelings. *Furthermore, we "invent biblical strategies" for seeing to it that our dreams come true. When our life's purpose is to "have a good time, to have soul-pleasure exceed soul-pain," God becomes merely a means to an end, an object to be used, never a lover to be enjoyed.* It is hard to discover our desire for God when things "go well"—we may think we have, but more often all we have found is our desire to use God, not to enjoy Him. Shattered dreams destroy false expectations, such as the "victorious Christian life" with no real struggle or failure. They help us discover true hope.

We like to remain naively happy—when we signed on to the Christian life, that is what we thought the deal was. We do what we are told, and God stacks presents under the tree. With adolescent maturity we declare that "God is good" when we ace a test or the biopsy comes back negative. When blessings come, we should of course enjoy them. Apparently, only a *few believers* in any generation believe that the weight of *"knowing God"* is a blessing far greater than any other. And those who believe it appear to have developed that conviction only through *suffering*. Happiness must be stripped away (forcibly), before joy can surface.

We don't like to suffer. We see no value in suffering. We arrange our lives to *"minimize suffering."* And we believe Christianity offers a God who will cooperate with that plan. The cure for every form of slavery to something other than God is *"worship"*—worship that creates deep pleasure in the One who receives it and the one who gives it. Only a thrilling, soul-pleasuring encounter with God that generates more pleasure than sin will free us from our addiction to sin.

CHAPTER 16

A summary of the book . . .

"TRUE FACED"
by Bill Thrall, Bruce McNicol, and John Lynch

This book draws a clear distinction between two very different underlying motives—my determination to *"please God"* or to *"trust God."* One results in a striving that never feels it has done enough to please Him; the other results in a trust that experiences His full pleasure. As believers, our motives will either keep us in unresolved sin and immaturity, or free us into God's astonishing dream for our life.

God wants you to discover "your destiny" and walk into the reasons He placed you on this earth. He has a ticket of destiny with your name written on it—no matter how old, how broken, how tired, how frightened, or how many times you have failed. The dreams many believers have simply become "cruel mirages"—shimmering pools of a once naïve hope. Here is the reality—God's dreams for you and me are ultimately not really about *"us,"* they are about *"others"*—for their benefit—loving them, guiding them, serving them, influencing them. There are no other types of God dreams. Nothing less or else will compel, attract, or seem worthy of this *"God heart within you."* It is all about *His glorious kingdom,* and others being freed, healed, and convinced of who they really are.

Think about it—God's dreams for us reflects "His heart." One of God's dreams is that we would influence others far more out of *"who we are"* than out of *"what we do."* So, above all else, your destiny requires that you be a *maturing person*—maturing into the "likeness of Christ." *True Faced* was written for those who pant for a life worth living; for those longing to see their God with eyes no longer filtered with fear, self-disgust, desperate proving. In a very real sense, we are all *performers*—because of sin we have lost confidence that we will always please our audience, so we have put on *masks*. As an unintended result, no one, not even the people we love, ever get to see *our true face*. Do you remember how mask-wearing got started? In the garden of Eden—*"I was naked, so I hid myself."* Nakedness cried out to be covered—Adam and Eve fashioned leaves to hide what was true about them. When we lose all hope that we can be changed or "fixed," we cover up. Mask wearers fall into 3 groups:

1. We live in the land of "doing just fine"—The truth is, we are not; we are weary of hurting, and we feel betrayed . . . even by God.

2. We look for "new techniques" that promise to help change us—We've admitted life isn't fine. Those in this group grow increasingly more disillusioned and skeptical. We have convinced ourselves that there are answers, but we are befuddled that we can't find them. What's wrong with me? Nothing I try works. Maybe my performance disqualifies me. We start to lose all hope that we can change. We feel stuck in our deep insecurity and shame.

3. We are the "together folk"—We don't need help. We've got it all together. We are the standard by which the industry is judged. We intimidate others . . . we know it's because they are jealous. If they had our self-determination and discipline they wouldn't have to be intimidated. We deny that we even wear a mask . . . but the truth about us is this: those who know us best wish they could tell us that . . . the truth is, we are emperors wearing no clothes.

Most of us have deep, painful feelings . . . distorted, dysfunctional thoughts . . . and befuddling behaviors that we feel an almost involuntary need to *mask*. Whenever we are unable or unwilling to deal with the guilt or hurt of sin done by us or to us, then pain and confusion floods our lives. When sin remains unresolved, it causes a nagging sense in the heart that won't go away. We start trusting techniques, conscience-numbing medication, pop psychology, spiritual fads, and other nicely packaged teachings. Next thing we know, we are looking for a top-of-the-line mask . . . all the while, our heart whispers, "You're a fake! an impostor! a loser!"

It is very expensive to wear a mask. For one thing, no one—not even those we love—ever gets to see our face; even though there are moments when some hint of the real me bleeds through. Mask-wearing thwarts our maturing. Sadly, our masks deceive us into believing that we can hide our true selves. Not so, and most of us realize that. In time, others can usually see what we are trying to hide. Many of us are hurting. We harbor painful junk that is eating us alive. God allows our masks to crack and chip because He loves us so much. The book *True Faced* was written to help the believer begin, by God's grace, to reveal their true face. We are all on this same journey of learning these truths. (13–36)

"Two roads diverged in a wood—I took the one less traveled, and that has made all the difference." Those are the words of Robert Frost. The day will come when we will arrive at a pivotal place on our journey with God, and we will be forced to choose—and our choice will make all the difference. Either we choose the path that says *"Pleasing God,"* or the one that reads *"Trusting God."* There is no third path, by the way, and we must choose one. Only one. Pleasing God and Trusting God represent the *primary and ultimate* **motives** *of our hearts*.

1. <u>On the path of determining to **"Please God**,*"* and striving to be all God wants us to be</u>, this one is referred to as the *"Room of Good Intentions."* An enormous banner on the back wall reads: *"Working on My Sin to Achieve an Intimate Relationship with God."* Sounds a lot like, "Be holy as your heavenly Father is holy." Gradually, almost imperceptibly, the road of Pleasing God has turned into "What Must I Do to Keep God Pleased with Me?" In this room you will

get tired of pretending and keeping up appearances. Ultimately, you will decide to retrace your steps and head out for the "Trusting God" trail.

2. <u>The path marked **"Trusting God"** has a room with a sign above it that reads,</u> *"Living Out of Who God Says I Am."* Where is the part where I get to prove my sincerity? Where are my guidelines? When do I get to give God my best? I stoop down and read what it says on the doorknob—*"Humility."* This particular room is referred to as the *"Room of Grace."* On the back wall is a huge banner that reads—*"Standing with God . . . with My Sin in Front of Me . . . Working on It Together."* I can't help but notice that in this room everyone seems *vitally alive*. The people are obviously imperfect, full of compromise and struggle, but they are *authentic* enough to talk about it and ask for help. Many people in this room have a level of integrity and freedom I never saw in the Room of Good Intentions.

Our "motives" direct what we value and how we act. For example, if we are motivated by money, we will value lucrative careers and people who can help us make money. That value will then shape how we act. It will influence us to pursue certain education, experience, jobs. We get the word *"motion"* from *"motive"*—our motives ultimately determine our actions; God designed us this way. Our motive as followers of Christ will either keep us *enslaved* in unresolved sin and immaturity, or it will *free us* into God's astonishing life for us. The key to our maturity and freedom lies in the *"dominant motive"* that governs our relationship with God. It all starts with motive.

Hebrews 11 declares, "Without *faith* it is impossible to *please* God." Did you recognize the two paths in this verse? Trusting and Pleasing God? If our primary motive is *"Pleasing God,"* we never please Him enough and we never learn trust. That is because life on this road is all about *"my effort"* and *"my striving"* and *"my ability"* to make something happen. On the other hand, if our primary motive is *"Trusting God,"* we find out that He is incredibly pleased with us. So, pleasing God is actually a by-product of trusting God.

Here is the deadly trap—If my life motive is determining to *"Please God,"* then my values will be "Striving to Be All God Wants Me to Be" . . . and my action will be "Working on My sin to Achieve an Intimate Relationship with God." When we live in the *"Room of Good Intentions,"* our theology sets us up to fail and to live in hiddenness. Furthermore, it disregards the godliness and righteousness that God has already placed in us [at infinite cost], and will sabotage our journey. We can never resolve our sin by working on it, nor can our striving to sin less keep us from future sins. A theology of "more right" and "less wrong" will ultimately cause us to lose hope; *sin-management theology will break your heart.* Many believers have spent their entire lives serving God, yet they are lonely, broken, defeated, and full of despair. They have embraced a theology of *"rebuilding their old barns"* and have placed all their efforts in *"trying to be good."* Cain was "trying to be good" on his terms—when his offering didn't please God, he felt dishonored. Early in his reign, King Saul struggled with trusting God, just like the Galatians whom Paul corrected. Saul ended up trying to keep God pleased with him. He thought his sacrifice would please God enough to give him success against Israel's enemies. But God told him, "To obey is better than sacrifice" (1 Sam 13:5–15; Heb 3:18–19; 4:2)—He knew Saul's obedience would be the evidence of his trust.

Pleasing God is an incredibly good longing, but it cannot be our primary motivation, or it will imprison our hearts. Pleasing God is not a *means* to our personal godliness; it is the *fruit* of our godliness, the fruit of trust. We will never please God through our efforts to become godly. Rather, we will only please God—and become godly—when we trust God (Heb 11:6). When our motive is to *"Trust God,"* our value will be "Living Out Who God Says I Am." Have we already been changed? Yes! We have received a new heart . . . we are a new creation . . . with a brand new identity . . . we have been changed, and now we get to mature into who we already are (2 Cor 5:17). God paid an infinite price to buy us back, to redeem us, and make us new creatures in Christ (Eph 1:3–14). So He gets deeply disappointed (it grieves Him) when *we choose not to believe* what He says is now true about us. He values our high-priced identity, and He wants us to do the same. How can we show that we really value our identity? By *"believing"* what He says is true about us.

Let's review what we've learned—"If my motive is *Trusting God,* then my value will be "Living Out Who God Says I Am," and my action will be "Standing with God, with My Sin in Front of Us, Working on It Together." *God has given us the DNA of godliness*—we are righteous saints, and nothing we do will make us more righteous than we already are. Furthermore, nothing we do will alter this reality. God knows our DNA. He knows that we are "Christ in me" (Col 1:27). And now He is asking us to join Him in what He knows is true. Remember, it is not what you and I do—it is what God is doing, and He is creating something totally new, a free life! (Gal 6:15).

Here is the "Great Disconnect"—Many people talk as if they have taken the *"Trusting God"* path, but in reality they live in the "Room of Good Intentions." So many people say the right thing, but then live the wrong life! This chasm exists everywhere in the body of Christ. Jesus warned us about this very thing when He said, "Be wary of false preachers who smile a lot, dripping with practiced sincerity . . . don't be impressed with charisma . . . look for character." Who preachers *are* is the main thing, not what they *say*. The reality is this—

> By taking the path marked **"Pleasing God,"** *many Christians never fully understand or live out what it means to be* **"in Christ Jesus."**

We discover in the "Room of Grace" that the almost unthinkable has happened—God tells us:

- He has taken away all elements of *fear* in condemnation, judgment, and rejection.
- He *loves* us and will always love us.
- He *loves* us right now, no matter what we have done.
- He *loves* us just like He loves His only Son.
- There is *nothing* we can do to make His love go away.

- He doesn't keep a log of past *offenses*, of how little we pray, how often we have let Him down.
- We actually have the *righteousness of Christ*, therefore we should stop beating ourselves up.
- We can stop being so *formal*, stiff, and afraid around Him.
- There is *nothing* we can do to make Him love us less or love us more.
- We are going to *heaven* no matter what—that is a done deal.
- It is ok to *be who we are* at the moment, with all our junk.
- He will *never punish us* when we mess up.
- He will *never hurt us* even if we should hurt Him.
- Life is not about *self-effort*, but about allowing Him to live His life through us.
- This is the way of life in the *Room of Grace*—it is the way home to healing, joy, peace, fulfillment, contentment, and release into God's dreams for us.

If we don't enter the "Room of Grace," we will constantly strive in the "Room of Good Intentions." In the Room of Grace we grow up and mature into something that is already true about us—godly. God is not interested in changing you. He already has. The new DNA is set. God wants you to believe that He has already *changed* you, so that He can get on with the process of *maturing* you into who you already are. **Trust** *opens the way for this process*—if you do not trust God, you cannot mature, because your *"focus"* is messed up. You are still trying to change enough to be godly. If you are living in the Room of Grace, you are not making desperate attempts to improve yourself. You know you cannot change yourself; you can only mature because of who you already are in Christ—a spiritually new creation born of the Spirit, a saint maturing into the image of Christ.

On the road of "Pleasing God," effort got me into the Room of Good Intentions. On the road of *"Trusting God,"* effort is never a means of pleasing God or getting God's grace or changing us. Effort born out of striving to please God never ceases to tire us or renew us. When we reverse *"trusting and pleasing,"* it is like switching "trust & obey" to "obey

& trust." Placing obedience before trust locks us into a mindset of obeying to *please God,* to earn His favor and His pleasure. (37–58)

Let's explore the "Room of Grace" and see how grace works, how grace resolves our sin issue. The following five truths give us lasting answers for this question.

1. **Grace is attracted through "humility"**—Humility requires trust—it is her core feature. We define humility as *"trusting God and others with me."* Remember, "God resists the proud, but gives grace to the humble" (Jam 4:8). In Scripture we learn that *grace can never be earned,* but it can be spurned through untrust, the absence of humility. We never deserve grace—it is always unmerited—but we can invite grace into our lives . . . we can attract it. How? *By trusting God.* God gives His grace to those who trust Him—to the humble. Trust, humility, and grace guide us into an astonishing life. Prideful striving brings God's resistance.

2. **Grace changes our "life focus"**—When we became Christians, something happened that actually changed who we are . . . yet, in this life we will always have *"sin issues,"* and we will always have the *"identity God gave us"*—and "trusting who God says I am." These two realities are constant—the key question is, "Which one of these two constants defines my life focus?" If we opt for the *"sin issues,"* we will never experience "trusting who God says I am." Do you see why the path of "Trusting God" is so important? We will never know our identity in Christ—and we will never live out of our identity—unless we start on the path of Trusting God. *To resolve our "sin issues" we must begin trusting who God says we are.* If our life focus is on "sin issues," if we strive to eradicate our sin issues so we can somehow create a "new me" or a "changed me," we will always keep "me" bound to "my sin" and we will remain immature. *Trusting Who God Says I am lays the foundation for maturity.* Many of us say we believe that salvation brings a *"new birth,"* a *"new identity,"* but the way we view ourselves betrays our words—we don't believe its reality in us for a second. Instead we think we must *"keep striving"*

to become someone who will be better. And all along we deny the mind-boggling truth that we have already become that someone. The *"Great Disconnect"* is the gap between who we say we are, and who we actually believe we are. This is the reason this book teaches that how we *view ourselves* is the most revealing commentary of our theology. It tells me . . .

- About my relationship with God
- About my relationship with others
- Whether my trust is in myself or in God
- If I am maturing into Christ's likeness

3. **Grace lets "God handle sin"**—Many Christians know God loves them and wants to be with them, but they also believe their sin has put an impossible mass between God and them. As such, *"they believe they will have to settle for rare moments of intimacy with Him."* They know themselves too well, and there is no way they are ever going to be able to keep from sinning. *They believe God loves them, but they also believe He's pretty disappointed with them.* That is as good as it gets on this earth . . . or so they have come to believe. Why do millions of Christians, now possessing the righteousness of God, feel distant from God, imagining that a pile of sin separates them? It is as if their salvation never took place. Ironically, striving to achieve this relationship with the Father will keep us in unresolved sin and immaturity. It produces just the opposite of what we are looking for!

People in the "Room of Good Intentions" hold this view. There, piles of sin separate each person from God, who is on the other side of the pile. Supposedly, *"moral striving"* will save the day, so everyone in the room keeps trying to chip away at that mound of sin, all the while realizing they are creating a bigger pile. When they finally achieve some level of success, they think they have accomplished something big—thus, this process breeds pride, not humility . . . sin, not maturity. The truth is, *"sin will not be managed."* Our efforts will not make us godly.

Grace teaches us to "trust that God can handle our sin—and only God." Our thoughts begin to run like this—I can't handle my sin. I can't change myself. Thank you, God, for already making me godly. *Lord, thank you there is "no pile of sin and junk between us."* If there were, I wouldn't stand a chance of intimacy with you. I know I can't survive away from You. Father, as we look at my sin together, I am learning to trust Your assessment of what will truly satisfy me. I trust You, Lord, for the next step. This *"heart-set"* changes our entire approach to sin—for only in the "Room of Grace" do we take sin seriously. In the Room of Grace, Jesus Christ is honored, depended upon, and submitted to for the resolution of our sin issues.

Now when we mess up, we can say: "Lord, I hate that I am prone to sin. This sin doesn't surprise me in the least. I expect that sinful desires will trip me up at times. Experience tells me that I cannot stop sinning. That is how powerful I believe sin is. Lord, I need You." Do you really think God would make it so hard to live a life that pleases Him? What if we didn't have to work so hard? What if our sin doesn't affect how close we are to God? What if God meant it when He said, *"I will never leave you nor forsake you"* (Heb 13:5). What if we truly believed we were without condemnation? (Rom 8:1). What if grace was that strong? Welcome to the "Room of Grace"—amazingly, the more we depend upon Jesus and His full ability to heal the effects of our sin, the less we sin.

4. **Grace melts "masks"**—Striving leaves us dysfunctional and immature because it creates hiddenness. Masks abound in the Room of Good Intentions. Grace creates *authenticity,* and reveals our true face. In an environment of grace sin issues and striving gradually start sliding off of us. Grace brings us adoption into God's family, a new identity, a new life, new power, and God's full protection—with absolutely no strings attached. *Grace is more than a theological position—it is an actual environment, a realm, a present-tense reality.* The triune God lives in the realm of grace. Trusting God means trusting that such a realm exists. God does not ask us to get our act together or to stop sinning so much before we can enjoy this realm. God wants only

one thing from us—He wants us to become more *dependent* upon Him. He wants us to walk on the path of Trusting God.

5. **Grace changes how we "treat each other" and "our sin issues"**—When we live in the Room of Grace, we begin to relate to others differently. We begin to experience true intimacy. We no longer feel we must compete with each other. We stand in front of each other "true faced." We see one another as saints who sin, rather than as sinners who are saved. If we truly believe in our hearts that we are saints, then we are able to stand with each other in the reality of our sin. When we trust God, we live by this value—*the godly are those who trust God with themselves.*

Resolving sin is only the starting point of life in the Room of Grace. God's ultimate goal is maturing us into who He says we are, and then releasing us into the dreams He designed for us before the world began (Rom 8:28; 1 Pet 1:3–5). Note the sequence of truths—

- We cannot profoundly influence others without *maturing*.
- We cannot mature without finding resolution to our *sin issues*.
- We cannot find resolution to our sin issues without *trusting who God says we are*.

God's ultimate dream for us is that we bring significant beauty into the lives of others—that is what the Room of Grace ultimately prepares us for. The fragile, the goofed-up, the compromised, the failed, the inadequate, the squirrelly, those full of pain and despair, even the arrogant and the controling—all mature into health when they enter the Room of Grace. Those who are *genuinely humble,* even with their warts and boils, become a healing balm to others. The Room of Grace is tricky business for those who have believed that *"self-made excellence"* makes the man. Either we learn to rest in the sufficiency of Christ in us, or we will soon return to the Room of Good Intentions. When you think you don't belong in the Room of Grace, because you are unfit or because you have failed, others in the room will say to you, "That's all you got? You're welcome here!"

Do you see how the "Room of Grace" helps people trust who God says they are, and then deal with sin in a new way that enables them to mature? Grace allows them to strip away the veneer and trust God with their sin, their healing, and their growth. They are vulnerable people who rely on God's strength in the midst of their often-compromised existence. *The power is in the "grace"*—and you can attract grace through a *humble heart.* God loves to give excessive amounts of grace to humble people. Trust God and others with you. Initially, we come to Christ *"me-centered,"* and we struggle to progress beyond that condition. The wonderful dreams God has for us often remain unclear because *"unresolved sin"* issues block our view. God thinks about *"our influence on others"* all the time—He designed us to influence others. *Every so often we catch a glimpse of the destiny God has planned for us, and new longings stir within.* We fill up with fresh motivation to learn how grace works and to follow God's voice into a land of adventure and fulfillment. Then we struggle to remember the entry point to that great land. It is the door that teaches us how to live out of who God says we are by turning the doorknob of *Humility,* and stepping into the *Room of Grace*—remember, humility is the doorway of grace; it results in the infusion of more grace in us, which in turn transforms our lives! (59–81)

THE SUPREME GIFT OF GRACE is "LOVE"—When you enter the Room of Grace, Jesus has some gifts for us . . . gifts of grace . . . and the greatest of all gifts is *"love"*—it acts as a balm that can begin to heal our unresolved sin. The gift of love is not about learning to love more or better. In God's world *receiving love* comes before *giving love.* We learn how to love only when we first learn how to receive the love of God and others—*"we love because He first loved us"* (1 Jn 4:19; Lk 7:47). We so much want to "do" something, rather than let something "be done to us." We have not learned to *"receive love,"* because we have been urged to *"give love."* Knowing we are loved and experiencing that love are two different things. Experiencing God's love means the following:

1. **I understand that I have needs**—We see our needs as weaknesses; sin influences us to define our innate needs as weaknesses. Our weakness

also stem from our unwillingness to accept our *limitations*. If we see needs as weaknesses, we will hide our needs, or we will pretend that we have no needs *(call it independence)*. Or we may believe no one should ever have to meet our needs *(call it strength)*. Or we believe that as we grow more *"spiritual,"* we outgrow them *(call it maturity)*. Needs do not come from sin, and they are not sin—Adam and Eve needed the love of God long before they sinned. *The problem is sin has distorted our understanding of needs.*

2. **I realize that having my needs met is experiencing love**—Every day we need to be loved, and every day God wants to meet our needs for: attention (Jn 13:5–20)—acceptance (Rom 5:5, 8)—security (Zeph 3:17)—trust (Lam 3:32–33; Jer 31:3)—guidance (Heb 12:6)—truth (Ps 33:4; 119:160; Heb 6:18)—protection (Ex 34:14–15; Hos 11:1–12)—significance (1 Tim 1:12)—affirmation (Jer 31:3). These needs never go away. *Sadly, if we cannot identify our needs, we cannot know love*—conversely, if we deny we have needs, we will not experience love. If we don't know love, we will be stuck with open wounds that will not heal. Thus when our needs go unmet, we are not happy people.

3. **I freely admit that I desire to be loved**—Deep within each of us resides the desire to be loved. Oh, but the pain and risk of love! Therefore we creatively fashion masks to make others think, at least in our case, that love is optional. Many of us have spent years perfecting *self-protection routines*. Some of us had good reasons for *erecting walls and barriers*. These walls, however, have never truly protected us—*they have simply kept us isolated and alone*. These walls won't come down until we *admit* we have needs . . . we can only experience love when our needs are met . . . and we really, really want to be loved.

4. **I choose to let you love me—on your terms, not mine**—People who are unable to *trust* will never experience love. Ever. Despite years of abuse and the *lonely life*, we can learn to trust ourselves to God and others. Grace, when it is conceived in trust, begets astonishing resolution, healing, maturity, and powerful influence. Many people who deeply want to be loved are not loved, because they won't turn

the doorknob of *"Humility"*—"trusting God and others with me." They stand out in the cold, outside the Room of Grace, in pain (and blame), because people don't love them. The truth is, the people God wants to use to love you deeply and to meet your needs stand right on the other side of that door—turn the knob. Learning to let others love us on their terms is part of what it means to *"submit to one another out of reverence for Christ"* (Eph 5:21; as a result of 5:18–20). If, despite our need for acceptance and people's attempts to include us, we continually reject them because we want them to meet our needs on our terms, we will remain unloved and in the darkness of our unresolved sin. We cannot experience another's acceptance, love, or guidance unless we let that person give us these things. Neither should we wait for people to *love us perfectly* or *trust perfectly*—remember, this is the Room of Grace, and *"Grace is the face love wears, when it meets imperfection."*

Learning to love or trust perfectly is not the point—it is learning to receive love. We can't wait for perfect people before we trust people. We live in an imperfect world—it is simply not going to happen. In the Room of Grace we learn that God won't let us down, even when others do. When they turn away, we remember He won't. He is our safety net—He has our back. *Trusting God frees us to move into these relationships.* Trusting God frees our hearts to experience His safe, constant, intimate sufficiency. Trusting God, who can't let us down, allows us to move toward others in love despite the risk . . . and that propels us into a different dimension of living.

5. **I am fulfilled when I have experienced love**—Trusting God is the path that leads us into the Room of Grace where we gradually receive the supreme gift of grace—love. If we have spent our lives building walls of self-protection, it will take time and trust for us to unwrap this gift. But when we receive love—when we are loved—we feel fulfilled. *Love completely satisfies* our longings, ambitions, and potential. God, the ultimate fulfiller, invites us to trust Him. Those who hang out very long in the Room of Grace always experience too

much love to return to a life without such a gift. *Received love turns frightened pretenders into confident dreamers*, and even turns violent lions into humble and tender receivers of love.

6. **I am now able to love others out of my own fulfillment**—Having our needs met by receiving the love of God and others is not just about "feeling better;" it is about fulfillment/being satisfied. *When the requirements of our soul—our needs—are met, it satisfies us.* This fulfillment produces inward peace, contentment, and healing for our wounds. As our wounds heal, we can turn away from them with a fresh passion, confidence, and love for others. To serve others out of a contented, fulfilled soul is like rubbing eucalyptus oil onto the sore muscles of a friend. The person experiences healing. If it is unerringly true that each of us enjoys only the love we will allow in, and if it is equally true that God went to unending lengths to bring us love in a way that we would allow in, then it becomes stunningly obvious that the carriers of God's love ought to be wildly driven to learn to give His love in a way that can be easily put on. *To give love that can be trusted changes everything—this is where life gets worth living.* When others experience God's love past their double-bolted defenses, they wonder out loud what took them so long. And they almost involuntarily begin to offer to all around them a love as rich and freeing as what they are taking in . . . and the world around them dramatically changes, through one refreshing act of love at a time. (83–98)

THE SWEETEST GIFT OF GRACE is "REPENTANCE"—When men don't know how to deal with their sin, they will try to hide it; it has been that way since Adam and Eve in the Garden. Repentance is a gift of God's grace because it doesn't have a chance without *"grace."* Grace alone resolves sin. Grace alone heals. And grace alone gives power over sin. Yet many of us act as if repentance is a matter of the *"will"*—it is not. We cannot make a decision to stop sinning. We cannot "will" ourselves into change. *Repentance isn't doing something about our sin; repentance means admitting that we can't do anything about our sin.* All of our striving and willpower have only momentary, external value when it comes to fighting an opponent as crafty, persistent, powerful, and experienced as sin—to confirm that simply look at the legalistic Judaizers. *God did not design us to conquer sin on our own.* To think we can is an incalculable undervaluing of *"sin's power,"* and a huge over-valuing of our own *"will power!"*

Some of us fool ourselves into believing we can "manage our sin"—sin cannot be managed. Our goal is not to solve all of our sin issues. Our motive is to *"trust God"* so we can live out who God says we are—so that *"together"* we can work on our sins issues. When we try to manage our sin through willpower, the process looks something like this: Sin—confess—do better for a while—then sin again and again and again. Despair, anger, shame, distance from God, guilt, self-loathing, and sin again. Disillusionment, doubt, self-pity, resentment at God—"Why doesn't He hear my prayers?" "Why doesn't He do something?" More disappointment . . . more anger.

Confession does not resolve our sin either. Agreeing that we have done something wrong is not the same as *"trusting God"* with what we have done. Confession is not the same as truly needing God to free us of the sin we have committed. Sin is resolved when we are cleansed of it, and only dependence upon the *"Cross of Jesus"* cleanses us from sin (1 Jn 1:7). There is power there. When grace introduces us to repentance, the two of us become best friends. When anything else introduces us to repentance, it feels like the warden has come to lock us up. When *"grace"* gets involved, the truths of repentance reveal a fabulous world of "life-freeing beauty." Repentance is about *"trusting"* not *"willing."* Yes, there is a choice involved, but if our motive is a determined straining to please God, all our striving will be a pile of filthy rags (Is 64:6). In repentance we depend on God to turn water into wine. Trust in our act of repentance releases the gift of God's grace to transform our hope into reality.

Trusting God with ourselves allows us to "receive love"—His love, and the love of others. Because we are loved, we can face what we have done to others and ourselves without having to retreat to a cave of hiddenness. Love acts as a safety net that can keep us from destruction as we admit the truth about ourselves. We know that nothing we do can change how God sees us. When we feel safe, we let go of our self-defense and call out to Him saying, "God, I no longer have anything to prove. I have nothing to hold on to. I want only what You want for me." Every act of repentance depends on an act of redemption. To *redeem* means *"to release from debt or blame."* Willpower, no matter how sincere, cannot buy you this freedom. By the way, there is no difference between the power to *save*, and the power to *resolve sin*. Healing requires that we face God with what is true about us and to trust God to cleanse us. We must stop walking down the road of self-effort, and start walking down the road of **"*Trusting God.*"** When we repent through trust, it is exclusively and entirely a *"gift of God's grace."* That is where the power is. This kind of repentance actually provides a real power over sin. The work of Jesus is not just the *forgiving* of every sin, but the *healing* that is needed as a result of every sin (Tit 3:4–6).

In the event that we attempt repentance in the "Room of Good Intentions," it will be out of a motive to make God happy with us, to become more godly. But trying to repent without grace is like trying to swim without water. In a *"grace-filled community,"* this community expects and anticipates imperfection—we honor others in the community as saints, but we also face the reality of each other's sin. We applaud vulnerability and view godliness as something much more than the presence of good behavior and the absence of bad behavior. The individuals in this community trust God to mature them from the inside out, by the power of His Spirit. It is a community of saints . . . who sin. Such a community will make a *mask-shattering difference,* because these folks will treat you for who you are—a saint—and will stand by you with outstretched arms, and *accept you* . . . as such, you will learn to receive their love. In such an environment repentance becomes a way of life. And when that happens, grace heals, matures, reconciles, and unleashes the love of God through people. When failing strivers stumble into a community of grace, safety, and vulnerable repentance, it radically disrupts their game plan. Suddenly, they are face to face with a real, tangible option of sweet freedom. And as the community treats them as they have never been treated before, their confidence grows that grace can support the full weight of their sin.

Give up trying to look good and sound like a saint. The principles of God's grace play off of each other—grace begets repentance, and repentance nurtures forgiveness. Trust attracts grace, and grace helps saints to trust—even goofed-up, compromised, failed, and confused saints. Especially them. The truth always sets us free—free to love God and others, free to trust even more truth, free to heal, free to follow our callings and dreams. The question is, do we really believe the God we trust is strong enough and powerful enough to heal us? That is the bottom line. As we exercise our trust, we receive His grace—just like we did the first time we met Him. So, trusting God for His grace in repentance prompts us to ask:

- God, are you strong enough to heal my patterns of self-destruction?
- God, do you always have my best interests at heart?
- God, are you able to take care of me if I live without the mask?
- God, are you able to vindicate me if I do not vindicate myself?
- God, are you able to deal with my sin if I make the decision to turn away from my willpower and trust in your power?
- God, are you able to protect me when in disclosure I am vulnerable to others when they know what is true about me?

In the Room of Grace no one is above anyone else. No one brags about his/her accomplishments. No one keeps score. No one is shunned. No one can lose membership for blowing it. This room is not a utopian ideal—it is simply a home where people live together. When you are ready to trust God's provision for resolving your sin, you will pray something like this—"God, here we go. Here is a sin I trust you to do something about. I am convinced I cannot deal with this sin. I trust what you did at the Cross is powerful enough, not only to bring me to heaven one day, but powerful enough that it can break this very sin's power that is now plaguing my life." (99–116)

THE MOST MYSTERIOUS GIFT OF GRACE is "FORGIVENESS"—Forgiveness breaks down walls, frees hearts, restores families, and draws out the best in us. It can turn hatred into tenderness. It is more powerful than any weapon, government, or wealth. Nothing else can bring such profound healing. Like repentance, forgiveness is a matter of the heart—when we forgive, it makes us ready to love again. *Forgiveness releases us from bitterness and resentment—when we forgive, our heart heals;* such is the miracle of God's grace in our heart. Forgiveness forms the foundation of our relationship with God. Have you ever noticed that Jesus waits for our repentance before He forgives us? Think about that. God's forgiveness isn't realized until we repent. By receiving it in humble trust that God can actually free our heart and heal our relationships, then the miraculous can happen. Forgiveness brings alienated enemies together. *Here are the seven keys of forgiveness—*

- Admit something happened.
- Forgive the consequences of the act done against you.
- Tell God what happened to you.
- Forgive the offender for your benefit.
- Forgive the offender when they repent, for their sake.
- Distinguish between forgiving and trusting your offender.
- Seek reconciliation, not just conflict resolution. (117–130)

MATURING INTO GOD'S DREAMS FOR YOU—Life in the Room of Grace teaches us to wait for God's exaltation rather than to pursue position or power. The timing is perfect. For one thing, our dreams are being clarified as our sin is being resolved, our wounds are being healed, and we are in the process of maturing. You never stop returning to the Room of Grace, for your heart and protection reside there. *Now you get to draw others into the Room of Grace*—that is what this dream is ultimately about—your place in God's Kingdom. It is a kingdom where God uses healing and maturing people to bring His grace to hopeless and hurting people. You get to use your gifts, passion, and healed heart to show the glory of Jesus, who has loved you beyond telling from the beginning of time.

God's goal for us is never just healing, safety, rest, or even receiving love, as astounding and stunning as those gifts are, *His goal is that we be released into these dreams we've not been able to shake all of our lives.* Ever since we were children we have had dreams and hopes of destiny. Some of these dreams are our own, but others came from the very hand of God—and *God's dreams never go off the radar screen*; not even time, failure, or heartbreak can make us forget them entirely. Still, most of us have tried to stuff them into the attic. We have been rudely awakened out of too many of them, too many times, and each time we lost a little more of the dream. Yet even if we have forgotten the fiber of those dreams, God has not. *God has a ticket of destiny with your name written on it—no matter how old, how broken, how tired, or how frightened you are.* No matter how many times you may have failed. God longs for the day when He gets to hand you that ticket.

People in the Room of Good Intentions never get released into the dreams God has for them. We may become competent and skilled, and even achieve impressive stuff . . . but without *humility* we will miss *"God's destiny"* for our lives. Remember, there is no humility without choosing to walk a road called **"Trusting God."** Those of us in the Room of Grace have come to believe who God says we are—we aren't trying to change into another person. God has made us exactly who He wants us to be, and we have come to believe it. Any change that takes place in us comes from maturing into the person we already are—much like a caterpillar matures into a butterfly.

In the Room of Grace we must learn to trust . . . to wait . . . to rest in God's promises, to grow in health and authentic relationships, so we will mature toward the day of God's releasing us into our destiny. We wait to receive God's authority, His exaltation of the humble.

We patiently wait for God to give us the desires of our hearts. We are no longer in a hurry. We know He cares about our destiny more than we do. We depend upon God and His power and resources. We are free to trust Him for repentance. We are free to trust Him so we can forgive others and be forgiven. Most of all, the mature have a childlike joy and freedom. We are playfully alive. *But such maturity does not happen overnight.* God uses many others for our benefit in this process—teachers, counselors, friends, pastors, spouses, siblings, children, mentors, disciplers. *Spiritual disciplines* are practiced in the Room of Grace as part of the process of maturing and releasing the saint to minister the gospel of the kingdom. These disciplines are no longer seen as a means of entry to the Room of Grace—*they are disciplines designed to help us be active and effective in the spiritual realm of our own heart,* now spiritually alive by grace in relationship to God and His kingdom. Maturity in the Room of Grace occurs in three general phases—

1. <u>Healing the Needy Christian</u>—Everyone who enters the Room of Grace is *"me-centered."* In this room we become acquainted with the power of love, grace and truth. We identify various wounds we carry, and we embrace the significance of our new identity. We also discover the process of unresolved sin issues as well as the cycle and power of sin. We become immersed in the person and work of Jesus, the Holy Spirit, and the Father. In this room, teachers and mentors help us learn the priority of disclosing who we really are—thus setting us free to be who we really are.

2. <u>Maturing the Healing Christian</u>—In time we become more *"others-centered."* In the previous stage, the emphasis was on introduction and new awareness of truth. In this stage we focus on applying, developing, and processing the truths we learned in phase one. For example, we learn to apply love, grace, and truth to our life situation and circumstances, and so our wounds begin to heal. We begin living out our new identity and apply truth

to the dynamics of sin. We are in the process of developing a vitally wonderful relationship with Jesus, the Holy Spirit, and the Father. In this phase, we are looking around our world and beyond to see how God wants us to love others. This stage more fully introduces the reality of *"suffering."* God uses suffering to mature the humble as they come under His influence and obey His truth, out of a heart of love. As they grow in trust during this suffering, God will enlarge their sphere of influence, because the humble can be trusted with truth. At this stage we are looking for and encouraging vulnerability, made evident by our new level of *authenticity.* We no longer hide. We don't arrive at this stage by taking an eight-week crash course—maturity is a process that takes time. Don't rush the pace.

3. <u>Releasing the Maturing Christian</u>—In this stage our life becomes more **"Christ centered."** We naturally respond to life out of our "new identity"—a Christlike identity—that we live through grace and truth. In this stage we are looking around our world and beyond to see how God wants us to love others through His particular plans and destiny for us. We gauge maturity by how we live with others who are maturing. Mature Christians delight in God's exaltation of others. We do not fear others' strengths; we understand them, submit to them, and benefit from them. The mature are always learning, studying, and inviting others to speak into our lives and meet our needs.

God's grace is perfected in our imperfection—The Room of Grace is not a place where we do not sin; rather, it is a place where we are protected by those who love us . . . by people we have learned to trust with the deepest part of our pain, ugliness, fear, and failure. When we grow in grace we come to realize ever more clearly that *"we are really loved by God"* . . . and our identity in Christ becomes our lifeline. Though we are daily made aware of how prone we are to engage, at any moment, in unhealthy behavior, and continue to struggle with sin, yet we believe God that *"we are really who He said we are."* When that is the case, we can be honest about all of who we are . . . and can trust others to help us heal. The truth is, *we are by faith who God says we are, even on our worst day* . . . yet, in humility, we never deny that we are capable of great wrong.

The life in the Room of Grace is not conjecture or wishful thinking; neither is it a utopian state where no one lives. Many people all over this world live there. The play has been written; the good works have already been created for us to walk in (Eph 2:10). We are believing who God says we are, and we are actually choosing to trust it in spite of what we act out every day. We are astonished by the reality that a life beyond appearances can truly be ours. In grace, God has made it possible for us to live *"True Faced."* (131–146)

CHAPTER 17

A summary of the book . . .

"THE NEW NATURE"
by Renald Showers

The "New Nature" and the "Old Nature" are opposite dispositions toward God—One's "nature" is that inherent disposition that affects the conduct and character of that person. Since the Fall, all human beings inherit an inborn sinful disposition with an impure heart and evil lusts and desires—as such, all human beings are naturally inclined and disposed to live contrary to God and His commandments. The old and new natures are frequently referred to as *"dispositions."* The **Old Nature** is a contrary disposition against God; the Bible refers to this as enmity with God (Gal 5:17; Eph 2:15-16). Since enmity against God is sin, the Bible calls the old nature "sin"—many theologians call it "the sin nature." The *New Nature* is a favorable disposition toward God; it consists of the "law of God" written in the human heart (the Holy Spirit places it inside the believer at the moment of regeneration/new birth). When man rebelled against God in Eden, he became what the Bible refers to as an *"old man"* (unregenerate man)—his total being became enslaved by a disposition of enmity against God. In this state of "total depravity" fallen man received the position of "slave to the old nature," so the old nature gained the position of *"master"* over him. This condition of slavery obligated unregenerate man to obey the dictates of the old nature.

Before we continue, let me share a special word with you the reader—
The material that *Renald Showers* discusses in his book provides the believer with an understanding of what it means to be a Christian, and yet still have a "sinful nature" dwelling within him. Admittedly, this material is somewhat deep and requires careful consideration and reflection. In all likelihood you will need to read parts of this summary more than once—don't opt out of wrestling through this chapter just because the content becomes too heavy for you. Not one of us has a full understanding of this topic. Prayerfully work your way through it, knowing that the more understanding God gives you on this subject, the greater will be your peace and sanctification. Reflect carefully on the following—

When a person trusts Jesus Christ as his Savior, several major changes happen to him—

- He ceases to be an *"old man"* (unregenerate man).
- He is no longer a *"slave"* to the old sin nature (the old nature is no longer his "master").
- He becomes a *"new man"* (regenerate man).
- He receives a *"new nature"* (a favorable disposition toward God; His Laws are written on his heart).
- He receives the *"Holy Spirit"* as his permanent indweller.

Although the Old Nature loses its position of "master" over the born-again person at the moment of conversion (regeneration), it does not leave the believer during his lifetime. It continues to dwell in him until the believer is present with the Lord. The Old Nature actively tries to exercise controlling power over the Christian, in spite of the fact that it no longer has the right to rule him. The believer continually has the potential for *"internal spiritual struggle,"* because he has two opposing natures dwelling in him. The ***Old Nature***, because it is a disposition of enmity against God, tries to control the believer in opposition to God's rule. The ***New Nature***, because it is a favorable disposition toward God (the law of God in the heart), prompts the believer to concur with the rule of God, and *will* to obey Him. The New Nature, however, does not give the believer the *"power"* necessary to overcome the power of the old nature. The Christian, therefore, needs more than the new nature if he is to do God's will.

Whenever the believer relies upon the Old Covenant Law or himself for the power necessary to overcome the power of the old nature, he is defeated. The Old Nature takes him captive against his will and prevents him from doing the will of God. This does not mean, however, that the believer is doomed to be continuously defeated. At the moment of regeneration the *"Holy Spirit"* permanently indwells the believer—*He is the source of power necessary to defeat the power of the old nature in the believer.* Because the Holy Spirit permanently indwells the believer, His power is constantly available to him; however, that power will not operate in the Christian's life unless he personally appropriates it by faith. Moment by moment he must trust the Holy Spirit rather than himself to empower him for victory over the power of the Old Nature.

Prior to the Fall of man Adam possessed a "disposition" which was favorably oriented toward God. He joyfully fellowshiped with God and willingly accepted and obeyed His commands. Man's original disposition has been called a *"holy disposition."* Satan tempted Adam to disobey God and choose to be "his own sovereign—his own master;" since the temptation apparently was too great to pass up, he disobeyed God and fell. Adam's sin of rebellion essentially consisted of two things: rejection of the sovereignty of God, and an assertion of his own sovereignty; in effect, *he declared his independence*—he desired to be his own master (his own sovereign lord) . . . he wanted to run his own life . . . *he refused to subject his will to the will of God.* Therefore, instead of God being the chief end of man, man became the chief end of man. When Adam sinned he lost his favorable disposition toward God, and became thoroughly confirmed in a disposition of enmity *against* God.

The resultant tragic condition of Adam was that he became "polluted" in every area of his being; sin took possession of his heart and made it exceedingly corrupt (Jer 17:9). Like a cancer sin permeates the whole person—body and soul. The effect of Adam's sin was that he became locked into a master-slave relationship with his sinful disposition; thus he became helplessly enslaved to a continuing state of sin. Theologians refer to this state as *"total depravity"*—the contagion of sin spread through his entire being, leaving no part of his nature untouched. Romans 8:7 says, "The mind set on the flesh [or man himself] is hostile toward God; it does not subject itself to the law of God; it is not even able to do so" (Gal 5:17). Sin is not a matter of occasional deviation from the right way, but a consistent expression of the natural tendency of one's being. Sin has been inscribed so indelibly upon human hearts that it is the governing disposition of their lives (Jer 17:1, 9; Rom 3:10–12). It is because human beings are already sinners by *nature* that they think wrong thoughts and perform wrong actions. What unregenerate man needs is someone to redeem him from this slavery, and give him a *"new disposition"* or *"new nature"* which is favorably oriented toward God. The good news is—God in His grace has provided such redemption and a new nature for man.

All "unregenerate (unsaved) men" inherently possess a degree of moral and natural truth; as such, he is "not without excuse" when he sins (Rom 1:20)—"he suppresses the truth in unrighteousness" (Rom 1:18); correspondingly John writes, "men love darkness rather than light" (Jn 3:19). Paul tells us in Romans 1:19–21 that God has clearly manifested Himself to everyone through all He has made, so men know Him through this natural revelation, yet they still reject Him. *The truth of the matter is men rebel against the knowledge of God that they have (however much that is).* Furthermore, Scripture tells us that "all men have the knowledge or the works of God's Law written in their hearts" (Rom 2:15), and their *"conscience"* bears witness to this fact. So that there is no confusion regarding what God does in the hearts of His born again children through the New Covenant, it is important to note that Paul, here, does <u>not</u> say that the *"law itself"* is written in the hearts of all men; instead he says, it is the *"work of the law"* that is written in their hearts—there is a radical difference between the law and the work of the law; the work of the law is not the same as the law God writes on the hearts of His people in the New Covenant, as we will see in the next paragraph. Suffice it to say at this point, the work of God in the heart of the *believer* is far more comprehensive than the work of God in the heart of the *unbeliever*. Through this "work of the law" in the hearts of all men (regenerate and unregenerate alike), *their "conscience" serves as a monitor,* confirming the instinctive knowledge of divine moral truth. Thus it should be understood that the unregenerate (unsaved) do have an *"inherent moral consciousness."*

God's "Old Covenant Law" failed to produce obedience in people's lives because it was *external*, and was opposed by an *internal* sin disposition. The *"New Covenant,"* however, would be written on the hearts of God's people (Jer 31:31–34; Ezek 36:26), thus internalizing His Law. The "heart" is the seat of man's disposition, the fountain of his actions, the center that determines his moral conduct, whether it be sinful or holy (Mt 12:34–35). So the inner law written on the heart of the believer governs his life, not by external regulations like the Mosaic Law, but by the continual control of the heart and conscience by the Holy Spirit. Therefore the *law of God* written upon the heart is the *"new disposition"* that God places in His people—it is a disposition that desires to do God's will, and be conformed in both thoughts and affections to the holy nature of God. Therefore the new disposition in a certain sense is the *"divine nature"* planted in a man (2 Pet 1:4), that is, he receives a disposition which is an expression of the holy nature of God. The ultimate goal of regeneration is that the individual *"be transformed into the image of Christ"* (Rom 8:29; 2 Cor 3:18). In addition to this new disposition, He also places the Holy Spirit in him so that he will have the "power" to obey Him and walk in God's ways (Ezek 36:26–27). Throughout his book Renald Showers essentially explains Paul's teachings of the Christian faith as presented in Romans 6–8, so open your Bible to the book of Romans and carefully follow along with me.

In Rom 6:12–13, Paul pictures "sin" as a governing disposition that demands obedience. As Paul attempts to explain the relationship of human beings to sin and God, the instrument that he uses most frequently is the analogy of the *"master-slave relationship."* Paul goes on to assert that people are slaves either to sin, impurity, and lawlessness . . .

or to righteousness, obedience, and God (Rom 6:6, 16–22); the unregenerate (unsaved) man exists in a "master-slave relationship" with his sin disposition—Paul says, before you were saved "you were slaves of sin" (Rom 6:17, 20). This means that *unsaved* man is obligated to render complete obedience to the dictates of the sin disposition. Paul indicates that when an unregenerate man becomes a Christian he is then identified with the death, burial and resurrection of Christ (Rom 6: 1–13). Paul teaches that there is some sense in which the unregenerate man actually *"dies with Christ"* when he becomes a Christian (Rom 6:6); thus freeing him in some sense from his sin disposition (Rom 6:7). When Paul applies his teaching, he exhorts Christians to "reckon themselves as dead to sin" (Rom 6:11). If this is really true, however, then why is it that Christians "struggle with sin"?

In Rom 7:14–25, Paul describes the "great spiritual struggle with sin" that he experienced. According to Paul (Rom 7:14–25 and Gal 5:16–24), the "sin disposition" is still very much alive and active in the Christian. In Galatians, Paul says "he was crucified with Christ" (Gal 2:20), but note carefully what he did not say—he did not say "his sin disposition was crucified." So what Paul is teaching us here is this—there is some sense in which the *"unregenerate person"* actually dies when he becomes a Christian; that means the unsaved person dies with Christ in the sense that he ceases to be an "unregenerate man." Before regeneration he was an unregenerate or "old man"—at the moment of the new birth he ceases to be an *"old man,"* and he now becomes a *"new man"* (Rom 6:6; Eph 4:22–24; Col 3:9–10). Although the Christian remains the same person metaphysically, the Scriptures do regard him as a "different person" in some sense—according to Scripture, the Christian is a "new creature" (2 Cor 5:17), a "new creation" (Gal 6:15); a "newborn babe" (1 Pet 2:2). The difference is a *"spiritual difference"*—therefore, when we were crucified with Christ, we were crucified with Him in some "spiritual sense."

In Rom 6:10, Paul was talking about a "once-for-all death" that was completed on the cross by Christ (2000 years ago) for the Christian. Paul exhorts Christians to consider themselves to be *"dead to sin"* (Rom

6:11); he does not exhort them to consider themselves to be *"dying to sin."* The language implies that they are to reckon themselves as being in a "fixed state of death" (not in a continuing process of dying). So the *"co-crucifixion with Christ"* is a once-for-all, completed act in the past for the Christian (that is the essence of the aorist tense in Greek); it is not in an ongoing process of happening.

In Rom 6:2, Paul declares that the Christian has died with reference to "sin"—as noted earlier, in this context the term "sin" refers to the *"sin disposition."* Paul is saying that the Christian has died with reference to the personal relationship which he had with his sin disposition while in the unregenerate (unsaved) state. Therefore, through his death with Christ, the Christian loses completely and once-for-all the "master-slave relationship" which he had with his sin disposition while in the unregenerate state—*this means he is no longer a "slave of sin," and no longer is sin "his master."* Paul declares that one purpose for the old man's crucifixion with Christ is "that our body of sin might be done away with" (Rom 6:6); that we would no longer use our bodies as instruments of sin. Though the body of the unregenerate man is not the *source* of sin, it serves as the *instrument* of the sin disposition—in this sense the human body is the "body of sin" (Rom 6:12–13; 7:23; 8:11).

In Rom 6:14, Paul states that another purpose for the unregenerate man's death with Christ is that *"we might walk in newness of life."* Romans 6:5 explains why this walk in newness of life is possible—the person who is united with Christ in His death is also united with Him in His resurrection. Paul here is teaching that there is some sense in which a person actually experiences "resurrection with Christ" when he becomes a Christian—he becomes a "regenerate person;" a "new man" with a "new disposition;" and is "indwelled by the Holy Spirit." This is a *"spiritual resurrection"* in which he now has newness of life.

In Rom 6:7, Paul states the result of death with Christ—the person who has died is *"freed from sin;"* in other words the person is "freed from his sin disposition" (his sinful nature), in the sense that his sin disposition is no longer his "master." Though the sin disposition is still within him, it no longer holds its legal position of master over him. In Paul's day a master held a legal position of authority over a slave; this gave the master the right to control every aspect of the slave's total being; the slave was obligated to render complete obedience to the dictates of his master. This legal "master-slave relationship" was terminated only by the death of the slave. By analogy, Paul is teaching that the sin disposition holds the legal position of "master" over the unregenerate (unsaved) man, and the unregenerate man holds the position of "slave" under his sin disposition. *The unregenerate man is obligated to render complete obedience to the dictates of his sin disposition.* This "master-slave relationship" is terminated by the unregenerate man's death with Christ. Thus, death with Christ results in legal freedom from a legal "master-slave relationship"—*as such, the regenerate man is no longer a "slave to his sin disposition"* (Rom 6:6). Paul tells his readers, in the past they had been slaves of their sin dispositions, but now they have been freed and have become *"slaves of righteousness"*—they now have a new master (Rom 6:17–22). By the way, if you are struggling with what Paul is teaching

---

FEELING CONFUSED?

I liken Showers' teaching on this subject to that of learning to play a new piece of "sheet music" on the piano . . . if you have ever played the piano, or any other instrument, you know the first time through a piece of music can be a grueling experience—you stumble through the music in such a way that the "rhythm" is completely lost; it is only after playing through the music three or four times that you begin to sense the flow of the melody. If this is your "first time" through the subject that Renald Showers is teaching, you may be feeling overwhelmed—that is "normal"—don't give up on this "vital topic" so easily; God's Spirit will awaken you to its truths as you wrestle through it a few times. This material focuses on the essence of the "believer's identity" in Christ—it is absolutely essential that one grasp it if he is to progress in holiness and sanctification. Remember, the Holy Spirit has been given to you to "enlighten" your understanding—that is His work when it comes to the apprehension of spiritual truth (Jn 14:26; 15:26; 16:13; Acts 16:14; 1 Cor 2:12–14; 1 Jn 2:20, 27).

here in Romans 6–8, be sure you are following along with your Bible "open," and that you are carefully reading the text—don't move on to the author's next teaching without grasping what is presently being taught. Essentially, Renald Showers is giving us a "running commentary" on Romans 6–8, therefore it is critically important that you follow along in the text—if you don't, you may find this subject matter somewhat confusing. If you are confused, start over.

Rom 6:11–13 teaches that the Christian has certain responsibilities in light of his freedom from the sin disposition and resurrection with Christ. First, the Christian is no longer obligated to serve his sin disposition. The sin disposition, however, will do everything in its power to continue to dominate its former slave (you), even though it has no legal right to do so any longer. According to Scripture, the regenerate man will succumb to the demands of his sin disposition, if he does not take into account the fact that he is "truly dead to it," so Paul *commands* the Christian to "reckon himself dead to his sin disposition" (Rom 6:11). This command is in the present tense, so just as the "sin disposition" keeps on trying to take control, so the believer needs to *"keep on considering himself as being dead to it"*—that he is no longer obligated to obey it; thus he needs to refuse to render service to it. The practical application is this—as a believer, *daily* you need to reckon yourself as indeed being *"dead to your sin disposition,"* you no longer *have* to sin . . . sin is no longer your master . . . if you do sin, you do so simply because you *choose* to do so. Secondly, the Christian is to reckon himself *"alive to God"* in Christ Jesus (Rom 6:11). The Christian has been resurrected spiritually with Christ—thus the regenerate man has a "new disposition," along with the indwelling presence of the "Holy Spirit" (Rom 6:4–5). Now that he is a *"new man,"* the believer is *spiritually alive* with reference to God; as such, he has tremendous potential to live a new kind of life. It should be noted, this command is also in the present tense, therefore the believer needs to *"keep on considering himself to be alive to God in Christ Jesus."* Every time the sin disposition tries to encourage the Christian to commit sin, he should remember the fact that he now has a unique living personal relationship with God.

"THERE ARE TWO SPIRITUAL REALITIES"

Ultimately, there are just TWO SPIRITUAL REALITIES—God and Satan—Good and Evil. Following are some of the various ways Scripture contrasts these two realities:

KINGDOM OF GOD	KINGDOM OF SATAN
Children of God	Children of Satan
Disciples of Christ	Disciples of the Devil
Slaves of Christ	Slaves of the Devil
Regenerate	Unregenerate
Believers	Unbelievers
Born Again	Not Born Again
Eternally Alive	Eternally Dead
Spiritually Alive	Spiritually Dead
Spiritual Perspective of Life	Fleshly Perspective of Life
Godly View of Life	Selfish View of Life
Slaves of Righteousness	Slaves of Unrighteousness
Free from Sin	Enslaved to Sin
Dead to Sin	Alive to Sin
Alive to God	Dead to God
Lovers of Light	Lovers of Darkness
Children of Light	Children of Darkness
Walk in the Light	Walk in Darkness
Live According to the Spirit	Live According to the Flesh
Mind set on the Spirit	Mind set on the Flesh
Submissive toward God	Hostile toward God
In the Spirit	In the Flesh
Anti-Satan	Anti-Christ
Redeemed Sinners	Unredeemed Sinners
Holy and Pure	Unholy and Impure

Godly and Righteous	Ungodly and Wicked
Have spiritual sight	Are spiritually blind
Angelic support	Demonic support
Love the Church	Love the World
Heavenly minded	Worldly minded
Indwelled by the Spirit	Controlled by Satan
Produce spiritual fruit	No spiritual fruit
Serve God and Righteousness	Serve Satan, Self and Sin
Haters of the Flesh	Lovers of the Flesh
People of Faith	People of Unbelief

Every human being is "ALIVE" to one of these realities, and is "DEAD" to the other reality; that is, every one of us is "rooted," has his "being," has his "life source" in one of these realities. Every one of us is either a citizen of the Kingdom of God, or a citizen of the Kingdom of Satan. The problem for us as believers, however, is that "both of these realities" reside within us; hence, we live in a state of "constant conflict!" (Rom 7:14–25; 8:5–9,13, 18; Gal 5:17). Therefore we are enjoined to "fight the fight of faith" (1 Tim 1:18; 4:7; 6:12). The Christian life is a life of "continual warfare between the flesh and the Spirit," and a life where we "practically work out" what "God has worked into us" (Gal 2:20; 5:16–17; Eph 4:11–16, 22–24; Phil 1:6; 2:12–13; 3:13–14; Col 1:13; 3:1–5; 1 Pet 1:3–7; 4:12–13; 2 Pet 1:3–10).

When Paul says that we have "died with Christ" (Rom 6:3, 6, 8), he is describing the process whereby we as believers become children of God—because we were children of the Evil One before we were saved, it was necessary to have our "sin problem" resolved. This was accomplished by the Holy Spirit when He mysteriously took us back in time some 2,000 yrs and "placed us in Christ;" i.e., we were "spiritually baptized into Christ"—the resultant effect was we actually experienced the death of Christ for our sins; thus, we now (like Christ) are "dead to sin." Furthermore, just as we "died with Christ," we were also "raised with Christ" to newness of life (Rom 6:4–5). Through this work of the Holy Spirit, we have become "brand new creatures in Christ" (2 Cor 5:17). This incredible work of God's Spirit miraculously and totally changed us; as such, we are no longer children of Satan, but children of God!

(continued)

You say, "But my own heart wants to dispute the fact of the new birth, because I feel so very much alive to sin and temptation." Due to the fact that "our behavior" (which is often sinful) does not fully reflect "our new identity" (being children of God), we are naturally inclined to dispute the fact (with Satan's prompting) that we are really born again. Here is where it is critically important for us to understand the "three steps of salvation"—once we are saved, we enter into a stage where "we are in the process of being transformed into the image of Christ" by the Holy Spirit (2 Cor 3:18). Though we indeed are "fully God's children" (Jn 1:12), we start out as "babes in Christ" (1 Pet 2:2; 1 Cor 3:2), and are exhorted to "grow-up and mature in our faith" (Eph 4:15; 2 Pet 3:18); the more we grow, the more we reflect His image. This is the "sanctification aspect" of salvation—at the moment of conversion we experience "justification" (we are made righteous); after conversion we experience "sanctification" (we grow in holiness); when we get to heaven we then experience the final stage of salvation called "glorification" (at that point, we are fully transformed into the image of Christ). The second stage of sanctification is the "participatory stage," where we get involved in the process; growing in Christ is not just a matter of "what we do," however, it is also a matter of "what God does in us." The truth is, God's work in us is in this stage is far more transformational than our work, even though we often feel like "we're doing all the work!" Paul puts it this way, "Work out your salvation with fear and trembling, but work with the realization that you're not working alone, God is also at work in you both to will and to do His good pleasure" (Phil 2:12–13).

The reality is, you have been "crucified with Christ" and have "died to sin." Therefore the tyranny or mastery of sin over you has been broken—though you were once a helpless captive of sin, you have now been set free from sin. Sin's dominion or absolute dominance over you has been shattered—that is a fact! You are now a new creation in Christ! That is the reality for every Christian! No matter how much you struggle and stumble in sin, you are a child of God. So what do you do with this TRUTH? You reckon or consider it as indeed being "true;" that is, you believe what God says about you—that is FAITH! The first step in living a "holy life" is that of believing who you now really are! As a believer, your primary appetite is no longer sin and self, it is now God and righteousness. As Paul puts it, "You have been given a new mindset . . . a brand new way of thinking!" (Rom 8:5–9; 12:2; Eph 4:22–24; Col 3:9–10).

> **The "big hurdle" for us as believers in affirming the reality of Rom 6:11,** is the fact that we are, in some sense, <u>alive to the principle of sin</u> that dwells within us; i.e., to our sin nature, our flesh, our sin disposition. Though sin is no longer our master (we are dead to its mastery), we are still under its persistent, antagonistic presence. Therefore, when interpreting this passage, it is important to remember that the emphasis of this verse is on our IDENTITY, not on our BEHAVIOR. As believers we are "dead to sin as the ruler of our lives," and "alive to Christ as the ruler of our lives." Another way of putting it is this—we are "dead to being against Christ" and "alive to being for Christ." The "constitution" or "mindset" under which we as believers now live and process life is GOD, not SATAN. Hence, being "<u>dead to sin</u>" and "<u>alive to God</u>" describes our essence—these two spiritual realities are two sides of the same coin; one states it in positive terms, the other in negative terms. As Paul says, we need to move and grow in the direction of who we are in Christ—thus becoming more and more like Him. As Christians, we have a brand new Master! a brand new life! a brand new identity! The key to the Christian life is "growing in the grace and knowledge of our Lord and Savior Jesus Christ" (2 Pet 3:18); without growing in faith, joy and assurance decline, and sin and guilt increase. By the way, there is "no automatic spiritual cruise-control" in the Christian life—faith and obedience are essential!

Another responsibility the Christian has is that he is "not to let sin reign in his mortal body that he should obey its lusts" (Rom 6:12). When the person was unregenerate (unsaved), his sin disposition reigned like a king over his physical body, making it a "body of sin." Because the person's death with Christ ended his master-slave relationship with his sin disposition, *the believer is to "keep on refusing to allow his sin disposition to use his body as an instrument"* (note the present tense verb "keep on"). He is to say "no" every time the sin disposition stirs up "his inward desires" and tries to dominate his body (Jam 1:14). Instead, the believer is to "present himself to God as one who is alive from the dead" (Rom 6:13). The *command* here is this—the Christian is to present his total being to God to be *"God's slave"*—he is to make God is new Lord and Master.

Rom 6:14 focuses on the believer's "release from the Law"—The Christian who has died with Christ will never have the "sin disposition" as master again, because he is "no longer under the law," but "under grace." Those who are *"under the law"* are subjected to ***law*** as a governing principle; those *"under grace"* are subjected to ***grace*** as a governing principle. As a governing principle for daily living, grace is able to do what external law cannot do—only grace can release a person from the mastery of his sin disposition (that is an incredibly important truth to grasp). Paul goes on to develop this truth further in Romans 7. Paul is declaring here that Christians are not under any "external law" as a means of sanctification—*no external law can set a person free from the mastery of his sin disposition*. Paul uses the illustration of *"marriage"* to make his point—he says a woman is bound by law to her husband as long as "he" lives; however, that bondage is abolished by death. If the woman's husband dies, she is released from the law that bound her to her husband and is free to be married to another man. The first husband represents the "sin disposition" in this story—just as the wife is bound to her husband, so the unregenerate person is bound to his sin disposition as master. Furthermore, just as a woman is released from the law which bound her to her husband when death takes place, so the believer has been released from the Old Covenant Law. Paul here teaches that the believer has been released from the "entire old covenant law" as a rule of life or as a means of sanctification.

The purpose of the believer being married to the resurrected Christ is "to bear fruit for God" (Rom 7:4). While married to the "sin disposition," the unregenerate person bore the fruit of death; by contrast, being married to the resurrected Christ, the believer is to bear the fruit of God. Romans 7:1–6 teaches the following: in order to experience any victory over one's sin disposition, and achieve any practical sanctification, a person must be totally freed from the old covenant law. Romans 7:14–25 describes the effect of the "old covenant law" upon the believer who attempts to use it as the means of practical sanctification—instead of *enabling* the person to live righteously, it actually *hinders* him from living righteously. The old covenant law has the effect of *"arousing the sin* *disposition"* to assert its authority over the person; and the more the law asserts itself, the more the sin disposition exercises its power to cause the person to violate the law. Thus, Paul teaches an ironic fact—the old covenant law, which is holy and opposed to sin, actually serves as an instigator of more sin through its effect upon the sin disposition. The result of being released from the Old Covenant Law is that *"we serve God and bear fruit in newness of the Spirit, not in old covenant law*—as such, the believer has a new, internal disposition and a dynamic source of divine power. The regenerate person is not to try to bear fruit for God by using the old covenant law as his rule of life or means of sanctification. Paul tried it, and it was a disaster (Rom 7:14–25).

Rom 7:14–25 describes the struggle Paul experienced as a Christian; it was a struggle that ended in defeat. The antecedent of Romans 7 is Romans 6:14—there Paul declares that never again will the Christian have the "sin disposition" as his master, because the Christian is not under law but under grace. Paul relates what happened to him when he tried to use the law as the means of practical sanctification. *In spite of the fact that he had a new "holy disposition" in him, the law still did not enable him to live righteously.* If the Christian is to be free from the dominance of his sin disposition, he must never use the law as his means of practical sanctification. Paul in this section describes the experience of the regenerate (saved) person who struggles against the power or influence of his sin disposition through his own *self-effort*—Paul uses the word **"I"** twenty-four times in these twelve verses, and the last **"I"** he makes *very emphatic* by the way he positioned it and by adding the word "myself." The self-effort is the result of using the old covenant law as the means of sanctification. *The problem with the law is that it does not provide us with the "power" to do what is right and abstain from what is wrong.* As previously noted, the old covenant law actually arouses the sinful disposition. Paul joyfully concurs with the law of God—he says "in my mind I serve the law of God" (Rom 7:16, 22, 25). These expressions indicate that during his struggle Paul had the old covenant law ever before him in his thinking as a rule of life to be followed—the problem was he was attempting to keep the law for the purpose of sanctification.

All believers try to sanctify themselves by keeping the law—and we all fail miserably in that attempt.

Paul concludes, "We know that the Law is spiritual; but I am of flesh, sold into bondage to sin" (7:14). The context indicates that he learned this contrast by painful experience. The struggle and defeat which Paul describes in the remainder of the passage provides the evidence that "he is of flesh," and as such cannot be sanctified by the law. So Paul is saying here, *"in spite of the fact that he is a regenerate man, he still is made of flesh;"* and as *"flesh"* man is weak (Mt 26:41; Rom 6:19). Thus Paul is emphasizing the fact that, even though he is a regenerate man with a new disposition, two things are true of him: 1) he is still only a man, and 2) apart from divine empowerment he is powerless to do the will of God. The expression, *"sold into bondage to sin,"* implies bondage to the sin disposition. So what he is saying here is that there is some sense in which he as a Christian is still in bondage to the sin disposition. Earlier it was seen that the sin disposition loses its position of "master" over a person when he becomes regenerate. In that sense the regenerate person has been *"freed from bondage to sin"* (Rom 6:7). But the sin disposition continues in the regenerate person throughout his earthly life; as such the regenerate person is susceptible to the power of his sin disposition whenever he relies upon his own *"self effort"* rather than the power of the *"Holy Spirit"* for enablement to live a godly life. The regenerate person, then, as a result of being made of flesh, is still in bondage in the sense that the sin disposition remains present in him, and in the sense that he is susceptible to that disposition's power. It is in these senses that Paul, as a regenerate man, could say that he is of flesh, having been sold into bondage to sin.

On the one hand, Paul knew that the law was good, but on the other hand he ended up doing the evil which he hated, and not doing the good which he wished to do (Rom 7:15, 19). This great contrast between *"desire and performance"* caused real consternation in Paul's mind. He could not understand why he could not live right since the law was good, and since he agreed with it and desired to keep it, and the fact that he had a "new disposition." Since the new disposition consists of the law of God written in the heart, it seemed natural to Paul to expect that the new disposition would cause him to be favorably oriented toward the old covenant law. Paul states, "For the *wishing* is present in me, but the *doing* of the good is not. For the good that I wish I do not do; but I practice the very evil that I hate" (Rom 7:18–19).

If the regenerate person had only the "new disposition" inside him, he probably wouldn't have any problem doing the will of God. But, as seen earlier, he also has the *"sin disposition"* inside him. The believer is still subject to its presence and influence. Paul talks about "sin which indwells me" (7:17); "sin which dwells in me" (7:20); "evil is present in me" (7:21); and "the law of sin which is in my members" (7:23). By the way, if the sin disposition were not in the Christian, then the struggle between the Holy Spirit and the flesh of the Christian would not take place (Gal 5:17). Paul indicates that God gave him his "thorn in the flesh" to prevent him from exalting himself (2 Cor 12:7); if Paul had not had the sin disposition within him even as an apostle, there could have been no danger of his exalting himself.

Paul makes it clear that not only is the "sin disposition" inside him as a regenerate person, but that it is also an *"extremely active force."* It exercises great power to make him go contrary to what his inner self wills. In Romans 7:17 (also v. 20) Paul pictures the sin disposition as an unwanted guest that not only lives in another person's house, but also takes control of that house against the owner's wishes. In essence, Paul is saying, "Now that I am regenerate, I hate the fact that the *sin disposition* is still in me; it continually tries to usurp control of me against my will." In Romans 7:23 Paul portrays the sinful disposition as an armed soldier that wages war against the law of his mind and makes him a prisoner of itself. Since law is intended to function as a "controlling factor," it would appear that by "the law of my mind" Paul is referring to his mind as a controlling factor. "The law of sin" is a reference to the sin disposition as a controlling factor. *The "sin disposition" works to cause the believer to go contrary to what his inner self wills in accord with the holy nature and will of God.* It strives to take the regenerate person and illegally exercise controlling power over him.

The outcome of Paul's struggle can be stated in one word—defeat. Paul says that he ended up doing the evil which he hated, and he failed to do the good which he willed to do (Rom 7:15–16, 19–20). He was in the exasperating situation of being held a prisoner contrary to his will (7:23). In all his efforts to do right and to abstain from evil he was blocked by a power which he could not overcome (7:22–23). In great frustration he gave vocal expression to the wretchedness which he felt (7:24). *In spite of his being a regenerate man with the new disposition, all his efforts ended in utter, degrading defeat.* Paul recognized the reason for his defeat when he says, "For the wishing is present in me, but the doing of the good is not" (7:18). The "old covenant law," which he was relying upon as his means of sanctification, did not give him the power to overcome his sin disposition and do good. Instead, it actually aroused his sin disposition to a greater exercise of its power over him (7:7–13). Since the law did not provide Paul with the power of performance, he was forced to resort to *"self-effort"* in his struggle with his sin disposition. But that did not work either, because his regenerated humanity by itself lacked the power of performance. The "new disposition" within his inner self did positive things for him, but it did not give him the *power* to overcome the power of the sin disposition and do good. Whenever Paul resorted to self-effort to do good, the sinful disposition rendered him helpless. The reason for his defeat was a *"lack of power."* Paul's defeat gives insight concerning three matters—

1. The *old covenant law* is powerless as a means of sanctification even for the believer.

2. Although the *new disposition* does positive things for the believer, it has no power.

3. If the Christian is to do what God says is right, he must not only *"will"* to do it, he must also have the *"power"* to do it. Living the righteous life is more than a matter of the "will"—to have will without "power" leaves the believer frustrated and unable to accomplish his purposes.

SANCTIFICATION

Sanctification is a state of being "made holy" or "set apart unto God." All of God's children are "holy" unto God (Lev 20:26; Col 3:12; Heb 3:1; 10:10; 1 Pet 2:5). The Bible identifies all believers as _"saints"_ (Rom 1:7; 1 Cor 1:2; Phil 1:1); they have all been "set apart unto God" for His purposes. The Greek word _"hagios"_ can be translated holy, sanctification, holiness, or saint (Jn 6:69; 14:26; 2 Cor 7:1; 1 Th 3:13; 1 Pet 1:15–16). Though every believer has been permanently "set apart unto God," yet they are all in the process of _"growing in holiness"_ while they live in this world. God's goal for all believers is that they ultimately become conformed to the _"image of Christ"_ (Rom 8:29; 2 Cor 3:18; Gal 4:19; Phil 1:6). Paul reminds us that none of us achieves a state of perfection this side of heaven (Phil 3:12–14; 1 Jn 3:2). Though all believers are new creatures in Christ (2 Cor 5:17), they are all at various stages of growth—some are "babes in Christ" (1 Cor 3:1)—nevertheless, they are all holy.

Due to the fact that no believer reaches a state of perfection in this life, Jesus prayed to the Father that He would "sanctify them in the truth through the ministry of His Word" (Jn 17:15–20). God's will for us is _"our sanctification"_ (1 Th 4:3); we are to be "vessels for honor, sanctified, useful to the Master, prepared for every good work" (2 Tim 2:21). All of God's children are to earnestly pursue a life of practical holiness (Rom 12:1; 2 Cor 7:1; 1 Pet 1:15–16; Heb 12:14); and central to that is making the Word of God an integral part of our daily lives. Over and over again, sanctification is said to be the work of the _Holy Spirit_ in Scripture (Rom 15:16; 1 Cor 6:11; Eph 4:30; 1 Th 4:7–8; 2 Th 2:13; 1 Pet 1:2); but this work is not accomplished in the believer without his faithful cooperation and participation in the process—i.e., the believer's work of faith (Gal 2:20; Phil 2:12–13). The believer has a responsibility to humbly submit to the Holy Spirit's direction in life (walk according to the Spirit), and when he does the Spirit then makes his walk efficacious (1 Cor 3:6; Gal 5:16)—carefully note the need for "dependence on the Holy Spirit" and an "intimate connection with the Spirit."

In Rom 7:14–25, Paul taught us that it is impossible to achieve sanctification by obeying the law. Where we err as believers is that we like a _"mechanical"_ kind of solution to all of our problems—so that "we can fix them." We want God to tell us what to do, give us the ability do it, and once we do it, experience the reward of a job well done. Thus we are prone to look at life as a series of right and wrong actions. The approach we use is similar to the one Paul

(continued)

used; his efforts at "living by the law" not only made him miserable (because he failed so often), it also did not result in making him more like Christ. The chief problem with this kind of thinking is that it makes _"our actions"_ the ultimate game changer; thus the emphasis is on what _we do_, rather than on what _God does_. When we live by the law "our behavior" becomes the central focus of our lives, and our behavior cannot make us holy—only the _Holy Spirit_ bestows holiness. The believer can no more make himself holy than he can save himself; thus he must focus on the "Holy Spirit" rather than his own efforts. Paul put it this way: "Are you so foolish? having begun by the Spirit, are you now going to perfect yourself by the flesh?" (Gal 3:3). Human effort cannot make us holy. It is only by _God's grace_ and _God's Spirit_ that we are transformed into the image of Christ. The good news is, God has provided us with the grace we need—a new disposition and the indwelling Holy Spirit—as such, we must _rely upon the Spirit_ if we are to become more and more like Christ. This _humble perspective_ (admitting we don't have the capacity to make ourselves like Christ) results in God activating His grace within us, and effectuating our transformation when we walk humbly before Him (Mic 6:8; Rom 12:2; Eph 4:23). "It is not by might nor by power, but by My Spirit and My Word" (Zech 4:6; Eph 6:17).

The _object_ of our faith cannot be "our behavior"—it must be "Christ and His Word." When we focus in any way on "our own efforts," God has a way of making it very evident to us that our own personal performance is not sufficient to accomplish our sanctification (Is 64:6). This _"humble condition"_ keeps us ever on our knees before the Father . . . ever in His Word . . . ever at His mercy . . . ever depending on Him . . . and ever striving to walk with Him (that's faith)—when we do these things, God keeps His transforming grace flowing in and through our lives (Mt 18:4; 23: 12; Jam 4:6, 10; 1 Pet 5:6; Ps 69:32; Is 66:2). As Peter said, "Humble yourself under the mighty hand of God that He may exalt you at the proper time" (1 Pet 1:6). Therefore we conclude: 1) we cannot transform our lives into the image of Christ by our own efforts; 2) we cannot live a holy life without a significant dose of humility; and 3) we cannot live a holy life without cultivating an intimate relationship with Christ—then and only then is it possible to experience God's transforming grace in our lives. Remember, the Christian life is not about obeying a set of rules or believing certain doctrines (as important as those things are), it is primarily about _cultivating an intimate relationship with Christ_. What is the _main thing_ you are focusing on? Rules, doctrine or Christ? (Read Heb 12:2 and Col 3:2). Chapters **18 & 22** expand upon this teaching in considerably more detail.

In Rom 7:24 Paul calls himself a "wretched man"—this term expresses a wretchedness which comes through the exhaustion of hard labor. Paul had struggled so long and strenuously through self-effort against his sin disposition that he had exhausted all his strength. With no reserve left to draw upon, he collapses in the clutches of his sin disposition. *Finally, Paul recognizes that he himself does not possess the power necessary to overcome the controlling power of his sin disposition and do good.* It dawns upon him that if he is ever to get victory over sin someone else must provide that victory for him. Thus, in desperation, he cries for help: *"Who will set me free from the body of this death?"* "Who will rescue me from the controlling power of my sin disposition?" Immediately after uttering his plea for help, Paul interjects a strong, sudden expression of gratitude: *"Thanks be to God through Jesus Christ our Lord!"* (7:25)—the Lord Jesus Christ does for us what neither the law nor our own power can effect. Paul learned that the Christian is not condemned to live in constant defeat (Rom 8:1). In Romans 8 Paul presents what God has done through Christ for victory—whenever he appropriates what God has provided, he can experience victory. Paul's struggle as recorded in 7:14–25 has led to several conclusions:

- The *regenerate person* cannot defeat the power of his sinful disposition thru self-effort.
- The *new disposition* causes the believer to agree with the will of God in the inner man.
- The *sin disposition* is still present and active in the believer, and wages war against him.
- The *new disposition* is limited in what it can do; it does not provide the power needed to obey.
- The *regenerate person* is not condemned to live in a permanent state of defeat.

The Holy Spirit is related to the new disposition—He is the agent by whom Jesus Christ implanted the new disposition (2 Cor 3:3); and He works together with the new disposition to enable the Christian to do God's will. The **New Disposition** prompts the believer to "will" to do what is right, and the ***Holy Spirit*** supplies the "power" necessary to put that will into effect. According to Ezekiel 36:26–27, the Holy Spirit is in the regenerate person for the purpose of *"empowering"* him to do what God wants. As a result of this special endowment of divine power men are able to do that which they are otherwise quite unable to do. In Paul's writings, the Spirit of God takes hold of a man, controls him, and gives to him a power that is not his own.

Immediately after talking about the "defeat of the Christian" and God's provision of victory through Jesus Christ, Paul enlarges upon the provision by writing Romans 8:1–4. In verse 1 he makes the following announcement: "There is therefore now 'no condemnation' [to a life of servitude to his sin disposition] for those who are in Christ Jesus!" Notice the *CONTEXT—penal servitude to one's sin disposition!* Paul is teaching that there is no reason why those who are in Christ Jesus should go on doing penal servitude as though they had never been pardoned and never been liberated from the prison-house of sin. Again note the *CONTEXT*—Romans 6–8 deals with the subject of *"sanctification,"* not *"justification."* Also note the next verse (8:2)—it presents the reason why believers are under "no condemnation"—this verse deals with *"freedom from the controlling power of the sin disposition,"* not with freedom from guilt. And also notice that verse 1 is joined to what immediately precedes it with the word *"therefore"*—thus, Romans 8:1 is a conclusion drawn from what Paul has just said in Romans 7. Since Paul has just dealt with the problem of the believer being overpowered by the sin disposition and God's provision of deliverance from the power of that disposition (7:24–25), his conclusion in Romans 8:1 must be referring to no condemnation with regard to the power of the *sin disposition*, not to no condemnation with regard to *guilt*. Thus Paul is saying this: "Since God has provided the believer with deliverance from the power of his sin disposition, he is not condemned to a life of servitude to that disposition." Paul's use of the word "now" in his announcement of no condemnation indicates that "the believer is free from this condemnation *NOW,* during this present lifetime."

Paul begins Rom 8:2 with the word "For"—this indicates that he is giving the *"reason"* for the believer not being condemned to a life of servitude to the sin disposition: "The law of the Spirit of life in Christ Jesus has set you *FREE* from the law of sin and death." In other words, God has provided a means of deliverance—*"the law of the Spirit of life."* Paul refers to two distinct laws in verse 2—the law of the Spirit of life and the law of sin and death. *LAW,* no matter what kind it may be, is established for the purpose of governing or controlling. In light of this, *the law of the Spirit of life* is the controlling power of the Holy Spirit, which controlling power produces newness of life (Rom 6:4; 7:6). As noted earlier (7:23), *"the law of sin"* is the controlling power of the sin disposition, which controlling power works death. The *reason* that the believer is not condemned to a life of servitude to his sin disposition is that the controlling power of the Holy Spirit has set him free from the controlling power of the sin disposition.

The freedom from the sin disposition to which Paul refers in Rom 8:2, is different from the freedom from that same disposition to which he refers in Romans 6:7—carefully note the *CONTEXT.* Paul uses two distinct words for freedom in these passages. The word in 6:7 is a "legal term." The word in 8:2 is not a legal term. Furthermore, the freedoms of these two passages are obtained through two different means—the freedom of 6:7 is obtained through death with Christ; the freedom of 8:2 is obtained through the controlling power of the Holy Spirit. Plus, the freedom of 6:7 involves freedom from a position; and the freedom of 8:2 involves freedom from a controlling power.

As seen earlier, in Rom 6:1–14, Paul teaches that through "death with Christ" the person's position of slave and his sin disposition's position of master are terminated once-for-all. Never again will the sin disposition hold the position of master over that person. Although the sin disposition has lost its position of master over the believer, it still remains with him and tries to exercise control over him; hence the issue of *spiritual warfare.* Unless someone more powerful than the sin disposition intervenes on behalf of the believer and sets him free from the controlling power of his former master, the believer is doomed to *a life of servitude* to a disposition which has no right to exercise power over him. In Romans 8:2, Paul is saying that someone more powerful than the sin disposition has intervened on behalf of the believer and has set him free from the controlling power of his former master—that someone is the *Holy Spirit*.

Although the Holy Spirit set the believer free at the time of regeneration, the believer does not always *experience* that freedom. When the believer uses *self-effort* against the power of his sin disposition as the means of sanctification, he experiences the domination of sin. Only when he appropriates the controlling power of the *Holy Spirit,* as a result of relying upon *God's grace* as the means of sanctification, does he experience the freedom that is his. Union with Christ in His resurrection (power) is what frees the believer from the controlling power of his sin disposition—this is what makes it possible for the believer to "walk in newness of life" (Rom 6:4) and "bear fruit for God" (Rom 7:4). The believer has been set free to do what his spiritual inner self wills to do—the will of God.

The grace of God through the power of the Holy Spirit is able to do what the old covenant law through the self-effort of the believer is not able to do—free the believer from the controlling power of his sin disposition. The old covenant law pronounced a sentence of judgment upon sin, but it could not execute judgment upon it in the sense of nullifying its power within a human being—in actuality, the old covenant law "aroused the sin disposition" to a more vigorous exercise of its power. The reason why the old covenant law could not nullify the power of the sin disposition is that it was "weak through the flesh" (Rom 8:3). The law could not produce holy living because of the weakness of man's flesh—the problem was not with the law, but with fallen human nature.

Rom 8:4 says that the purpose for which God condemned sin in the flesh is "that the requirement of the Law might be fulfilled in us;" that the holy life required by the old covenant law might be fulfilled in us. The "passive voice" of the verb indicates that the believer does not produce this holy life in himself; the *Holy Spirit* produces it in him and for him through His power. Thus, the Holy Spirit produces what the old covenant law demanded but could not produce. Verse 4 says the holy life required by the old covenant law will be fulfilled in those "who do not walk according to the *flesh*, but according to the *Spirit*." The power of the flesh is no match for the power of the sin disposition. Those who walk according to the power of the Holy Spirit will have the holy life required by the law fulfilled in them. The power of the Spirit will overcome the power of the sin disposition and enable the believer to do God's will.

The appropriation of the power of the Spirit is not a once-for-all act which delivers the believer from the controlling power of his sin disposition forever. *Just as walking is a step-by-step procedure, so the appropriation of the controlling power of the Holy Spirit is a* **moment-by-moment procedure.** The key is "depending on the power of the Holy Spirit." In Ephesians Paul prays for Christians that God would "strengthen them with power through His Spirit in the inner man" (3:16)—the fact that Paul prays for this to happen indicates that the potential for strengthening is there. The actual strengthening depends upon the appropriation of the power of the Spirit by the believer. The Spirit comes to reside in each believer at regeneration, but must be relied upon continually to furnish power for Christian living. Since the "new disposition" in the inner man prompts the believer to will God's will, he needs to be strengthened with power through the Spirit in his inner man in order to do God's will. Paul says the intended purpose of being strengthened with power through the Spirit is "that Christ may dwell in your hearts" (Eph 3:17).

Paul obviously is not praying that Christ may dwell in their hearts as Savior; He is already doing that (see Rom 8:9). He is speaking of a further and richer dwelling or filling (Eph 5:18). Thus the dwelling of Christ in the believer that Paul is referring to is a *"progressive thing"*—and the means by which this dwelling of Christ takes place is *"through faith."* As the believer trusts the Holy Spirit rather than his own humanity to make him more like Christ, the Spirit empowers him to experience the progressive fulfillment of that goal. According to Ephesians 3:19, Paul wants Christians to "be filled up to all the fullness of God's [moral character];" *i.e., becoming fully Christlike—this is the essence of progressive* *sanctification*. The believer is *sanctified step-by-step throughout his lifetime* as the Holy Spirit gives him one victory after another over the controlling power of his sin disposition. Many skirmishes can be won during the course of one's life as he appropriates the power of the Holy Spirit, but the whole war is not completed in victory until the believer has gone to be with Christ.

The "old man" is not the sin disposition . . . it is the unregenerate man. The old man is a slave to his sin disposition, and is characterized by the sinful way of life. Through death with Christ the person stops being an old man—the old man dies in the sense that the believer ceases to be an unregenerate man. Since the old man is not the sin disposition, the new man is not the new disposition. *The **"new man"** is the regenerate man*—that man that is free from the position of slave to the sin disposition. Through resurrection with Christ (Rom 6:4–5) the person becomes a new man; the believer is resurrected in the sense that he becomes a regenerate man. *As a new man he possesses the new disposition, but the new disposition is "not" the new man*—the new man and the new disposition are not the same. The new man is the regenerate man, but the new disposition is the law of God written in the heart of the regenerate man—though the new disposition is in the new man, it is not the new man.

Paul teaches that the regenerate person is being "transformed" into the moral image of God—"we are all being transformed into the moral image of God from glory to glory" (2 Cor 3:18)—since Jesus Christ is "the image of the invisible God" (Col 1:15), and "the exact representation of His nature" (Heb 1:3), to be transformed into the moral image of God is to become like Jesus Christ. Paul teaches this when he says, "For whom He foreknew, He also predestined to become conformed to the image of His Son" (Rom 8:29). Since man's disposition toward God has significant influence upon the moral image of God in man, the new disposition which is favorable toward God must play a key role in the reversal of the corruption of the image of God and Christ in the believer.

The transformation of the regenerate man into the image of God and Christ is not an instantaneous, once-for-all event—*it is a gradual,* *step-by-step process throughout the life of the believer.* Paul says, "We all *are being transformed* into the same image from glory to glory" (2 Cor 3:18). The regenerate person passes from one stage of glory to another in a progressive movement forward. The process is emphasized again in Colossians: "The new man is being renewed to a true knowledge according to the image of the One who created him" (Col 3:10). The present tense of this statement indicates that the renewal is a *process.* The process of transformation will not be completed until the believer sees Christ (1 Jn 3:2). Christians start as babes and *grow* into the fullness of the stature of the Lord Jesus Christ (Eph 4:13). They are Christians all the while, but they grow—*a believer should never stop growing*. During this life it is impossible to reach the perfection to which the believer shall attain when he sees his blessed Lord as He is (1 Jn 3:2). Paul himself tells us that he had not attained to this state of perfection (Phil 3:12). *Although perfection is impossible during this life, steady progress toward that final goal is to be made.* The believer is to become more and more like Christ in his daily living. The process of being transformed or renewed into the moral image of God has been called *"sanctification."* The essence of sanctification is now to be found in the *gradual transformation of man's character into the moral image of God.*

Through "grace" God's holy precepts are administered internally in the form of a holy disposition which consists of the law of God written in the heart. The regenerate are the only ones who possess this *"holy disposition"* or a *"holy internal administration."* Because the administration through grace is inward in nature, the Christian is not under the law of God—Paul declares, "If you are led by the Spirit, you are not under the Law" (Gal 5:18). To be led by the Spirit must involve more than guidance or simply pointing out of the right way, for the old covenant law gave such guidance, but Paul sets the Spirit in contrast with the law. *Being led by the Spirit includes the "controlling power of the Holy Spirit."* The reason those who are controlled by the Holy Spirit are not under the law, is the fact that the Spirit produces so much righteous fruit in the lives of those whom He controls, no external law is necessary to be directed against their actions—"The fruit of the Spirit is love, joy, peace, patience, kindness, goodness, faithfulness, gentleness, self-control—against such things there is no law" (Gal 5:22–23)—therefore it is possible for the Christian to be free from the old covenant law without being lawless.

Being under the "grace of God" involves the possession of the new disposition and the Holy Spirit in the believer's life. As the new disposition causes the Christian to *"will"* to do the will of God, and as the Holy Spirit *"empowers"* him to do that will, the Christian denies the lawless way of life and lives the righteous way of life. This is the essence of what grace teaches the Christian. *The Holy Spirit is the powerful ally of the new nature inside the believer.* At the time of regeneration the Holy Spirit set the believer free from the controlling power of his sin disposition. If the believer "relies upon the grace of God" to give him victory, the Holy Spirit will "enable the new nature" to govern the whole person.

CHAPTER 18

A summary of the doctrine . . .

"WALKING BY THE SPIRIT"
by Donald W. Ekstrand

In Gal 5:16 Paul says, "Walk by the Spirit, and you will not carry out the desire of the flesh." To walk *in* or *by* the Spirit is to allow Him to direct the way in which you live your life; it is to make decisions in the light of His holiness; it is to remain in communion with Him; it is to be occupied with the person of Christ, because the Spirit's ministry is to engage us *"intimately"* with the Lord Jesus. Carefully note—walking by the Spirit is <u>not</u> a mystical, translike state in which the believer enters and mysteriously lives; nor is it some kind of far out, ethereal experience as some have postulated—any such thinking along those lines is completely "cultic" in its orientation. To walk by the Spirit is to live under the direction of the Holy Spirit and to walk by faith in God's Word. Consider for a moment what Jesus taught His disciples the night before He went to the cross—He told them He was going to return to heaven, but would send *His Spirit* to live within them to guide and instruct them in much the same way He had. Jesus referred to the Holy Spirit as the *Paraclete*—this Greek word means the Holy Spirit is "called alongside" to *Help, Comfort, Encourage,* and *Counsel;* since His function is to *Guide* and *Instruct* in the truth, He is referred to as the *Spirit of truth* (Jn 14:16–18, 26; 15:26; 16:13–15). Scripture tells us it is only by the indwelling presence of the Holy Spirit that we are able to grasp and understand spiritual truth (Acts 16:14; 1 Cor 2:12-14). So to walk in the Spirit is to live in the light of truth, and walk by faith in God's Word.

When we walk in the Spirit, the flesh or "self-life" is rejected and treated as dead. We cannot be occupied with both Christ and sin at the same time; so being led by the Spirit means being lifted above the flesh and being occupied with Jesus. It should be noted, the verse that immediately follows this injunction (Gal 5:17ff) shows that the "flesh" is still present in the believer's life; thus the idea of the eradication of the sinful nature is refuted. ***Awareness, Reliance*** and ***Dependence*** are key words when it comes to giving definition to walking in the Spirit—walking in the Spirit involves *a conscious awareness of His presence,* and *a conscious reliance and dependence upon Him to guide and direct our lives.* The knowledge of His abiding presence, and this reliance and dependence is clearly taught in Scripture. Since the parameters of walking in the Spirit are revealed to us in God's Word, we embrace these truths by *"faith,"* and we *"act upon them"* with an attitude of submission to God's will (Jam 1:22).

Therefore to be occupied with the things of the Spirit, is to be occupied with "living a life of faith." The walk of faith is one in which we submit to the truths of Scripture—it amounts to studying, believing, trusting, obeying, and affirming those truths. I want to strongly emphasize the concept of *"affirming truth,"* because, in a nutshell, that is the essence of faith; *you affirm the truths of scripture over and over again, until they find complete peace and rest in your soul*—this involves wrestling with the truth, meditating upon it, and confirming it with other passages of Scripture. When you fully affirm a particular truth it will settle confidently and peacefully in your soul. So when you really believe a truth, you are able to confidently "lean upon it with all your weight" (Prv 3:5-6). The most incredible truth any believer can affirm is the fact that *"God really loves them."* Sadly, most Christians question God's love for them, because deep down they know they really aren't *"lovely"*—but that is not the issue! The truth is, no human being is lovely! God does not love us because we are lovely—He loves us because *He is love!* Knowing that truth is incredibly liberating! *Nothing* we do can make God love us more, or make God love us less. That is the wonderful reality of the God we worship. Affirm the truth of that reality every day of your life! Only when you truly believe that God really loves you, will it transform your life!!!

Paul said, "Be filled with the Holy Spirit" (Eph 5:18), and "Let the Word of Christ dwell in you" (Col 3:16); essentially, the *Spirit* and the *Word* are direct equivalents in these two verses. Paul said, "the life I now live, *I live by faith"* (Gal 2:20); "we live and walk by *faith,* not by *sight"* (2 Cor 5:7). We live and walk by the *Spirit,* not by *feeling.* We must *believe* what God says in His Word. Just as we began the Christian life "by the Spirit," so also are we to live the Christian life (Gal 3:3; Col 2:6)—"since we live by the Spirit, let us walk by the Spirit" (Gal 5:24). We were "justified by faith" (Gal 3:24); we "live by faith" (Gal 3:11); and we received "the promise of the Spirit by faith" (Gal 3:14). "Faith is the victory that overcomes the world !" (I Jn 5:4). We walk in the Spirit (live by faith in the Word) when we obey Christ from the heart (Gal 5:8–10). We are to live life by being occupied with the things of Christ in every respect—"to live is Christ," says Paul (Phil 1:21).

We are transformed by the "renewing of our minds"—by faith (Rom 12:2; Eph 4:23). We walk in the Spirit when we *love Christ* with all our heart, soul, mind and strength, and give allegiance and preeminence to Him in all things (Col 3:18). Said Paul, "Keep seeking those things which are above, where Christ is; set your minds on things above, not on the things of this world" (Col 3:1–2) . . . we are transformed and renewed through a true knowledge of Christ (by faith) (Col 3:10) . . . we are to "do everything in the name of the Lord Jesus Christ" (Col 3:17) . . . and "take every thought captive to the obedience of Christ" (2 Cor 10:5). God has not called us to impurity, but to sanctification and holiness (1 Th 4:7). We are to "pray without ceasing" and "give thanks in all things" (1 Th 5:17–18). The goal of our instruction, writes Paul, "is love from a pure heart and a good conscience and a *sincere faith"* (1 Tim 1:5). We are to "fight the good fight of faith" (1 Tim 6:12). Only a life of faith *"pleases God"* (Heb 11:6). We are to be "doers of the word and not merely hearers" (Jam 1:22). This is pure and undefiled religion—"caring for those in need" (Jam 1:27). "Let us not love with word or with tongue, but in deed and truth" (1 Jn 3:18). "Faith without works is useless" (Jam 2:20). "Long for the pure milk of the word, that by it you may grow in respect to your salvation" (1 Pet 2:2). "Sanctify Christ as Master in your hearts" (1 Pet 3:15). "Grow in the grace and knowledge of our Lord Jesus Christ" (2 Pet 3:18). "Fix your eyes on *Jesus,* the author and perfecter of faith" (Heb 12:2). We walk in the Spirit through a life of Bible study, prayer, conscious submission to His will, worship, fellowship, obedience, serving, and witnessing. To walk *effectively* in the Spirit is to do these things *habitually*.

The Spirit and the flesh are in constant conflict. God could have removed the *"fleshly nature"* (the sin disposition) from believers at the time of their conversion, but He did not choose to do so. Why? He wanted to keep us continually mindful of our own sinfulness and weakness . . . He wanted to keep us continually dependent on Christ as our High Priest and Advocate . . . and He wanted us to continually praise the One who saved such undeserving ones. Instead of removing the old nature, God gave us His own Holy Spirit to dwell in us. God's Spirit and our flesh are perpetually at war, and will continue to be at war until we are taken home to heaven. The believer's part in the conflict it to *"yield to the Spirit."*

"Walking in the Spirit" is the essence of our stewardship in God's divine economy, and is the criteria by which God will evaluate each of us as believers. Paul made "walking in the Spirit" the central element of the believer's responsibility. The Old Covenant saints were expected to glorify God by living in conformity to the **Mosaic Law;** today, God's children are required to glorify God by walking in the **Spirit.** Paul teaches us that the Holy Spirit lives within every born-again believer, but not every believer lives in submission to the Spirit; possessing the Holy Spirit is not sufficient—believers must allow the Spirit to possess them (Cf. Ananias & Sapphira in Acts 5:3). The word "walk" is a New Testament metaphor for "live," as illustrated by Paul—"We are His workmanship, created in Christ Jesus for good works . . . that we should *walk* in them" (Eph 2:10). To walk in the Spirit means to live in complete submission to the control of the indwelling Spirit of God (Rom 6:12–13). "Walking in the Spirit" is the opposite of "walking in the flesh"—Paul contrasted the results of these "two walks" in his letter to the Galatians (5:19–23). Walking in the Spirit accomplishes the following:

1. It prevents walking in the flesh, which is our *"default mode"* (Rom 6:12–13; Gal 5:16).

2. It proclaims God's glory because we submit to His stewardship in this economy (1 Cor 6:19–20).

3. It preserves the grace principle, which we forfeit if we default to the flesh (Gal 5:4; Jam 4:3–10).

4. It prevents death, the natural result of anything accomplished in the flesh (Rom 6:23; 7:5,24; 8:2–7). The fruit of the flesh is death; nothing of the flesh has any eternal value; it is simply rubbish.

As a believer submits to the Spirit's control, he moves forward in his spiritual life. Step by step the Spirit moves him from where he is toward where God wants him to be. Though the *Spirit* is the source of all holy living, it is the *believer* who is commanded to walk (Gal 5:16). This *apparent paradox* of the divine and the human is seen throughout all aspects of salvation (Jn 6:35–40; Phil 2:12–13). Both in the justifying work of Christ and the sanctifying work of the Holy Spirit, *"man's will is active"* and commitment is called for. The Christian is not to sit on the sidelines, as it were, and simply watch the Holy Spirit do battle for him (Rom 6:11–13; Gal 6:9–10). The believer who is led by the Holy Spirit must be willing to go where the Spirit guides him and do what the Spirit leads him to do. The life we live when we walk by the Spirit is the *"Christlike life;"* it is the life whereby the believer's thoughts are saturated with the truth and love of Christ, and with a heartfelt desire to be like Him in every way. It is to live in *"continual consciousness"* (that is faith) of His presence and His will, "letting the word of Christ richly dwell in him" (that is faith) (Col 3:16). When the believer fails to walk by the Spirit, he *"walks by the flesh"*—there are no other options. The flesh is that part of a believer

WALKING BY THE SPIRIT
(Supplemental Notes)

The Greek word "walk" is *peripateo;* it is a compound word that is made up of two words—the preposition *peri* means "about, concerning, around;" and the main verb *pateo* means "to tread, to walk along"—thus *peripateo* means *"to stroll or walk about."* This Greek term is used ninety-five times in the New Testament as a metaphor for *"live,"* as illustrated by Paul in Ephesians: "We are His workmanship, created in Christ Jesus for good works, which God prepared beforehand that we should *walk* in them" (Eph 2:10). As stated earlier, to "walk in the Spirit" is to live in complete submission to the control of God's indwelling presence—"we are not to let sin reign in our mortal body that we should obey its lusts, and we are not to present our members as instruments of unrighteousness to sin; instead, we are to present ourselves to God as being alive from the dead, and our members as instruments of righteousness to God" (Rom 6:12–13).

The figurative meaning of "walking" refers to conduct—

- Believers are to <u>conduct their way of life</u> in the paths indicated by God (2 Kg 20:3).

- The sons of righteousness <u>walk in the light</u>, rather than <u>walk in darkness</u> (1 Jn 1:7).

- The heathen way of life is to <u>walk according to the flesh</u> (Rom 8:4; Eph 2:2; 1 Cor 3:3).

- <u>Believers are to . . .</u>

    <u>walk in Christ</u> (Col 2:6—that is our "position" in Christ)

    <u>walk according to the Spirit</u> (Rom 8:4—according to His leading)

    <u>walk in the Spirit</u> (Gal 5:16—that is the realm in which we are to walk)

    <u>walk in love</u> (Rom 14:15; Eph 5:2; 2 Jn 1:6—that is the essence of a godly walk)

    <u>walk as children of light</u> (Eph 5:8—that is the sphere in which we are to walk)

    <u>walk in good works</u> (Eph 2:10—our lives are to produce fruit)

    <u>walk in newness of life</u> (Rom 6:4—we are to live in this new reality)

> walk in a way that pleases God (1 Th 4:1—by obeying God we please Him)
>
> walk by faith, not by sight (2 Cor 5:7—we must trust God and walk accordingly)
>
> walk in the light and walk in the truth (1 Jn 1:7; 2 Jn 1:4; 3 Jn 1:3) (the whole way in which one lives proves fellowship with God—1 Jn 1:6ff; 2:6)
>
> walk in a manner worthy of their calling (Eph 4:1; 1 Th 2:12; Col 1:10) (conduct your life in a way that corresponds with your high and holy calling)
>
> **Applying this figuratively**—Imagine yourself *"walking with a friend down a path"* where you find yourself continually dialoging and sharing with that person. Notice, you are not just silently walking beside this person with very little communication taking place . . . where a disquieting silence is only interrupted by him telling you to do something. Also notice you are *"walking together in the same direction"*—you don't wander away from your friend off the path, and start walking with someone else; you walk together with your friend. The reality that underlies all of this is that you are *"enjoying the intimacy of the other person's company"*—furthermore, this is your very best friend and he loves you unconditionally. This is a description of "how" you are to live as a believer. This is the essence of walking *with* God . . . walking *in* the Spirit . . . walking *by* the Spirit . . . or walking *according to* the Spirit—don't let the prepositions create a difference in your mind as to what this *walk* means (all of these translations or expressions are equally valid). "Draw near to God—*walk with Him*—and He will draw near to you!" (Jam 4:8; Jn 15:13–15).

that functions apart from and against the Holy Spirit; it actually stands against the work of the Spirit in the believer's heart (Gal 5:17); in short, the flesh is the believer's propensity to *"walk in sin,"* and live according to the dictates of his selfish fallen nature.

The most effective way for a Christian to strongly oppose the flesh is to "starve it" to death—"to make no provision for it with regard to its lusts" (Rom 13:14). The surest way to *fall into sin* is to allow oneself to be in situations where inevitable temptation exists—"don't go near her house!" (Prv 5:8; 7:25); therefore, the safest way to *avoid sin* is to avoid situations that are likely to pose temptations. A believer who is not actively involved in resisting evil and seeking to do good, obviously is *not* being "led by the Spirit"—the faithful believer is not an observer, but a *"good soldier of Christ"* who is engaged in the "active service" of his Lord (2 Tim 2:3–4) . . . "he runs in such a way that he might win . . . he buffets his body and makes it his slave" (1 Cor 9:24–27). The Christian life involves both the *believer's* yieldedness and commitment, and the *Spirit's* guidance and power (Gal 2:20; Phil 2:12–13). Though this mystery consists of a paradoxical balance that cannot be fully understood or explained, it can be fully experienced.

How do believers "Walk by the Spirit"? Walking in the Spirit is both simple and profound. Being born again is so simple a child can experience it; yet it is so profound theologians cannot plumb its depths. Bill Bright, the late founder of *Campus Crusade for Christ*, pointed out that there are three things necessary for walking in the Spirit—Desire, Confession, and Yielding."

1. **Desire**—Walking in the Spirit begins with "desire." Jesus said, "Blessed are those who hunger and thirst for righteousness, for they shall be filled" (Mt 5:6). Although He was speaking about a different type of filling, the principle is the same. To live in the "new nature" rather than the "old nature" (our default mode), *we must pursue life in the Spirit.* This is the reason for Paul's imperatives: "walk in the Spirit;" "be filled with the Spirit;" "put off the old man;" "put on the new man" (Gal 5:16; Eph 5:18; 4:22, 24). If we simply respond to life as it comes, without a determination to walk in the Spirit, inevitably, we will lapse into the ungodly carnal behavior of the old sin nature—*walking in the flesh is both natural and easy; it is our "default mode."* Don't be fooled by the popular *"automatic cruise-control"* kind of Christianity that is being so widely preached today—where you just sit back, enjoy the ride, and let God do it all!—this theological teaching is not only rubbish, it is dangerous! (Phil 2:12; 3:14; 1 Tim 3:15b; 2 Tim 2:15; 3:1–5; 4:1–3).

2. **Confession**—Walking in the Spirit requires "confession of sins." Sin interrupts fellowship with God; hence, believers must confess their sins to maintain their intimacy with God. Confessing sins means "to agree with God from the heart about our sins;" literally, "to say the same thing about our sins that God says about them." The application is this: "If we confess our sins, He is faithful and just to forgive us of our sins, and cleanse us from all unrighteousness" (1 Jn 1:9). Incidentally, *"sin" is that which is "not of faith"* (Rom 14:23)—therefore any time we are "living for ourselves," it is sin, because we are called to live for Christ; hence, sin is not just doing something that is "overtly evil," as many believers think—it is living without giving primacy to the will of God in any matter; it is to disregard God's input. God requires that we acknowledge the nature of what we have done and how offensive it is to Him; much the same as parents require of their children (parents want their children to "agree with them" that poor behavior is "wrong"—that is confession). The indwelling Holy Spirit "convicts us of sin"—if we "fully agree" with Him, the Father then "cleanses" us of all unrighteousness. The key to confession is *"removing self"* from the throne, and *"placing Christ"* on the throne.

3. **Yielding**—Walking in the Spirit requires "yielding control of one's life to the Holy Spirit." The Spirit does not take control of our lives without us yielding that control to Him. Once we have genuinely confessed (agreed with God from the heart about our sin), the resultant effect is that we are then prepared to *"surrender control"* of our lives to the Holy Spirit. If we have regard for iniquity in our hearts (i.e., living life our way), "the Lord will not hear us" and take over (Ps 66:18). You cannot serve "God and mammon" (money/self). When the Spirit takes control, He directs what we do and what we experience . . . He teaches us what is needed for life . . . He provides experiences He wants us to have . . . and He leads us down the road to maturity. This control remains until believers re-exercise their own control and live according to their own desires, thereby rescinding the authority delegated to the Spirit. *"Cruise control"* on an automobile

illustrates this principle well. Once a driver activates it, he removes his foot (his will) from the gas pedal. The cruise control governs the vehicle's speed until the driver steps on the brake or accelerator to override it. To restore the Spirit's control, a believer must "remove his foot" from the gas pedal of life (confess) and "submit (yield) to the Holy Spirit."

Achieving "spiritual maturity" requires a consistent walk under the control of the Holy Spirit. Living according to the flesh (carnality) results in spiritual immaturity (1 Cor 3:1–3; and Heb 5:11–14). Spirituality requires regular maintenance—Bill Bright called this process *"spiritual breathing."* Our bodies require us to *exhale impurities* (CO_2) from the lungs, and *inhale oxygen* that is carried throughout our cells to maintain physical life. Similarly, spiritual life requires us to confess *(exhale)* that which produces death, and yield to the Spirit *(inhale)* who produces life. Spiritual breathing is required every time we permit an impurity to enter our spiritual lives—which is "often!"

A corollary of walking in the Spirit is being "Filled with the Spirit"— this is an extremely significant ministry of the Holy Spirit. It involves the Spirit's empowering people to do things they are incapable of doing by themselves—living the "God-life." The Apostle Paul exhorts us "not be drunk with wine . . . but be filled with the Spirit" (Eph 5:18). People filled with wine are prompted to do foolish things that they otherwise *would not do;* on the other hand, believers filled with the Holy Spirit are empowered to do significant things that they otherwise *could not do.* The resultant effect of "walking in the Spirit" is living a life that produces the "fruit of the Spirit" (Gal 5:22–23). Therefore, in every area of stewardship, it is imperative to acknowledge that it is the Holy Spirit who makes the effort efficacious. Though we are told to diligently study the Word—should we interpret it correctly, it is because of the teaching or illuminating ministry of the Holy Spirit. Likewise, when we struggle to be faithful in the discipline of prayer—should our prayers prove effectual, it is because of the Holy Spirit's intercession for us. In the same way, when we "walk in the Spirit," it is God Himself who lives His life in and through us (Gal 2:20).

Another aspect of the believer's Spirit-filled walk is that of "Praising God"—C. S. Lewis writes in his book *"Reflections on the Psalms"* that he actually found the Scriptural command to *"praise God"* a stumbling block for him (Lewis, *Reflections*, pp. 90–98). The suggestion that *God Himself demanded it* seemed troublesome to him. He noted how much we despise the crowds around the filthy rich and the celebrity, who gratify that demand. The Psalms were especially troublesome in this way—"Praise the Lord!" "O praise the Lord with me!" Worse still was the statement put into God's own mouth—"Whoever offers Me thanks and praise, he honors Me" (Ps 50:23). It was hideously like saying, "What I most want is to be told that I am wonderful and great." In Psalm 54 the poet begins with "save me," and then adds an inducement, "I will give sacrifices to and praise Thy Name" (Ps 54:6). Again and again the speaker asks to be saved from death on the grounds that if God lets His supplicants die, *"He will not get anymore praise"* from them, because the spirits in Sheol cannot praise (Ps 30:10; 88:10; 119:175). The mere quantity of praise seemed to count—*"seven times a day do I praise Thee"* (Ps 119:164). It was extremely distressing. It made me think what I least wanted to think . . . gratitude to God, reverence to Him, obedience to Him, I thought I could understand, but not this *perpetual eulogy*.

C. S. Lewis goes on to say that he found it best to approach the idea that God "demands" praise from the perspective of *admiration*. He writes, *"God is that Object to admire"*—which is simply to be awake and to have entered the real world. The incomplete lives of those who are tone deaf, those who have never been in love, never known true friendship, never cared for a good book, never enjoyed the feel of the morning air on their cheeks, are faint images of it. By the way God does not only *"demand"* praise as the supremely beautiful and all-satisfying Object, He *"commands"* it as Lawgiver. The Jews were told to "sacrifice"—as Christians we are under obligation to "go to church." Says Lewis: *"I did not see that it is in the process of being worshipped that God communicates His presence to men."* Though it is not the only way, for many people the "fair beauty of the Lord" is revealed chiefly or only while they worship Him together—in the central act of our worship it is God who gives and we who receive. The miserable idea that God should in any sense need or crave our worship, is akin to asking our dog to "bark approval" of our written books. Of such an absurd Deity one cannot even conceive.

"The most obvious fact about praise—whether of God or anything—strangely escaped me," writes Lewis. "I thought of it in terms of compliment, approval, or the giving of honor. *I had never noticed that all enjoyment spontaneously overflows into praise.*" The world rings with praise—readers praising their favorite poet, lovers their mistresses, walkers praising the countryside, sportsmen their favorite games and fellow competitors—praise of weather, wines, dishes, actors, cars, horses, universities, mountains, flowers, gardens, political leaders, scholars. *I had not noticed how the humblest minds praised most, while the malcontents praised least.* The good critics found something to praise in many imperfect works. The healthy could praise a very modest meal. Praise almost seems to be inner health made audible. Says Lewis, "I had not noticed either, that just as men spontaneously praise whatever they value, so they spontaneously urge us to join them in praising it!"—"Isn't she lovely?" "Wasn't it glorious?" "Don't you think that is magnificent?" "Isn't that great?"

The psalmist in telling everyone to "praise God" is simply doing what all men do when they speak of what they *care about*. I think we delight to praise what we enjoy because the praise not merely expresses but completes the enjoyment—it is its appointed consummation. It is not out of compliment that lovers keep on telling one another how beautiful they are—the delight is incomplete until it is expressed. It is frustrating to have discovered some mountain valley of unexpected grandeur and then to have to keep silent because the people with you care for it no more than for a tin can in the ditch . . . or to hear a good joke and find no one to share it with. *To praise something means the object is fully appreciated and our delight has attained its perfect development.* The worthier the object, the more intense this delight would be. It is along these lines that I find it easiest to understand the Christian doctrine of *"Heaven,"* where angels now, and men hereafter, are *perpetually employed in praising God.*

To see what the doctrine really means, we must suppose ourselves to be in perfect love with God—so drunk with love that bliss flows out from us incessantly again in effortless and perfect expression. Remember, *"man's chief end is to glorify God and enjoy Him forever!"* To fully enjoy God is to glorify Him—therefore, in commanding us to glorify Him, God is inviting us to really *enjoy Him!* As for the element of bargaining in the Psalms—*"Do this and I will praise You"*—that silly dash of paganism certainly existed. Remember, the flame does not ascend from the altar pure. Furthermore, you and I are not in a position to criticize even the crudest psalmists on this score. C. S. Lewis says, "I have often on my knees been shocked to find what sort of thoughts I have . . . what infantile placations I was really offering . . . obviously, there is a pagan, savage heart in me somewhere" (Lewis, *Reflections*, pp. 97–98; also cf. Ps 50:21).

Another corollary of walking in the Spirit is that of living according to the "will of God," and the only way to know the mind or the will of God is to know the Scriptures (2 Tim 2:15; Jam 1:22; 1 Pet 1:23; 2:2)—they alone give us an understanding of His ways, His will and His purposes. Through the agency of *God's Word* the Holy Spirit guides the believer into all truth, thus the Spirit plays an instrumental role in helping us know and understand God's will for our lives (1 Cor 2:12; Jn 16:13; 1 Jn 2:27). Scripture teaches us a number of things that should characterize our lives as Christians—here is just a short list of things that are *"the stated will of God"* for us:

- "It is God's will that we believe in His Son"—Jn 6:40; Jn 1:13; Eph 1:5
- "Understand what His will is"—Eph 5:17; Col 1:9; 2 Tim 2:15; 3:16–17
- "Be willing to do His will"—Jn 7:17
- "Take up our cross (die to our own will) and follow Christ"—Mt 16:24
- "Lose our life (die to our own will) for the sake of Christ"—Mt 16:25; Lk 14:26–27; Jn 12:24–25
- "Die daily to our own will"—Rom 6:5; 8:36; 1 Cor 15:31; 2 Cor 4:11; Eph 4:22–24
- "Obey His will"—Jn 14:15, 21; Heb 13:21; 1 Pet 1:2; 1 Jn 5:3
- "Walk by faith"—Rom 12:2; 2 Cor 5:7; Gal 2:20; 3:11; Eph 4:23; Col 3:2; 2 Tim 6:12; Jam 1:22; Heb 12:2

- "Sanctify and purify ourselves"—Phil 2:12; 3:14; 1 Th 4:3; 1 Tim 4:7; 6:12; Heb 12:1–2; 1 Pet 2:2; 1 Jn 3:3
- "Live for Christ"—Rom 11:36; 14:8; 1 Cor 8:6; Gal 2:20; Phil 1:21; Col 3:23; 1 Pet 4:2
- "Serve Christ and serve one another"—Rom 6:18, 22; 1 Cor 12:7; Eph 4:11–12, 16; Eph 6:5–6; Jam 1:27
- "Walk according to His Spirit"—Rom 8:4; Gal 5:16; Eph 5:18; Col 3:16
- "Be thankful in all things"—Eph 5:20; Phil 4:6; Col 3:17; 1 Th 5:18
- "Seek His Kingdom and His righteousness above all else"—Mt 6:33
- "Love one another"—Jn 13:34; Gal 6:2; Phil 2:4–5; 1 Tim 1:5; 1 Jn 3:16, 18; 4:7
- "Do not forsake assembling with other believers"—Heb 10:25
- "Be transformed by the renewing of your mind, that you might prove what His will is"—Rom 12:2; 2 Tim 2:15; 3:16–17; 1 Pet 2:2; 2 Pet 3:18

When the Lord Jesus taught His disciples "how to pray," He told them the bottom line in praying was that all of their requests were to be subservient to the *"will of God"*—there was to be the subjugation of their will to the will of the Father. Jesus Himself modeled this when He poured out His heart to His Father in the Garden of Gethsemane the night before He went to the cross—"Father, if it is possible, let this cup pass from Me; nevertheless not My will, but *Thy will* be done" (Mt 26:39). In Matthew 6:9–13, Jesus gives His disciples a *"model"* by which to pattern their prayers. In the verses that immediately precede this passage He told them how "not" to pray—First, they were not to pray in order to be *seen by others* that they might impress them (Mt 6:5); instead, they were to pray in private, in secret (Mt 6:6) . . . Second, their prayers were not to consist of *vain repetitions* (Mt 6:7); God only wants to hear the sincere expressions of the believer's heart, not just a bunch of words, no matter how pious or lovely they may sound. Furthermore, since God already knows what we need, even before we ask Him, then it is reasonable to ask the question, *"Why should we pray at all?"* The reason is twofold: *in prayer we acknowledge our need and dependence on God*, and *through prayer we align our will with His will*. Hence prayer is essentially the basis of communicating what is in our heart to God. It should also be noted that God does things in answer to prayer that He would not otherwise do—writes James: "you have not, because you ask not" (Jam 4:2). James also tells us, "the effective prayer of a righteous man accomplishes much" (Jam 5:16). With that said, let us look at the various components of the *"prayer model"* Jesus gave to His disciples—they include:

1. **The recognition of God's preeminence** (v. 9)—All our prayers should be addressed to God the Father in acknowledgement of His sovereignty over all creation. The main verb of verse 9 is an imperative, thus the petitioner is literally saying, *"May Your name be hallowed"*—that is, "May Your name be revered, for You alone are holy." So when we pray we begin by first ascribing praise and honor to God who is so worthy of it—this is the *attitude* with which we are to pray. By acknowledging His preeminence, we are reminding ourselves just who it is we are praying to—the *Creator* of all things . . . and who we are as supplicants—His *creatures;* not the autonomous beings our flesh wants us to think we are; the fact is, we are mere mortals, only a breath away from the grave; furthermore, we don't even have a say in when we draw our last breath—that happens according to God's plan (Ps 139:16; Lk 12:20). Reflect upon that when you are inclined to think God simply exists to *serve you*—how diabolical can the mind of man be to actually think that that might be the case?

2. **The advancement of God's kingdom** (v. 10)—After we worship God for who He is, we should pray for the advancement of His cause, putting His interests (His kingdom) first; after all, everything that exists is His. Prayer is not a matter of getting *"our will"* done in heaven, but of getting *"God's will"* done on earth. Perhaps that is the reason so many Christians are disappointed in their prayer life—they never seem to get what they want from God no matter how much they beg Him. Prayer is not about getting "our will" done—it's about getting "God's will" done (Mt 6:10; 26:39; Jam 4:3)—and therein lies the problem. By definition, being dedicated to God's will is being opposed to Satan's will, and anything that is contrary to God's will. Therefore, to pray ***"Thy will be done"*** is to rebel against the worldly idea that sin is normal and inevitable and should therefore be acquiesced to or

at least tolerated. It is to rebel against the world system of ungodliness, the dishonoring and rejecting of Christ, and the disobedience of believers. To accept *"what is,"* is to abandon a Christian view of God and His plan for redemptive history. You should also notice there are *no singular pronouns* in this prayer—thus, it is important to remember that we are part of God's worldwide family of believers. Our primary concern must be that God's answer will ultimately be a blessing to all of His people in some way. So in this petition we acknowledge that God knows what is best and that we surrender our will to His—hence, many have rightly defined prayer as *"the aligning of our will with God's will."*

3. **The request for daily sustenance** (v. 11)—Once we have placed God's concerns first, we are then ready to bring our own individual *needs* before Him. Obviously, God is concerned about our needs and knows them even before we mention them (Mt 6:8, 32). This petition acknowledges our absolute *dependence on God* for daily needs—both spiritual and physical. The expression *"daily bread"* is a reminder of God's supply of *"manna"* to the children of Israel when they wandered in the wilderness—as His children now, we also have need of His daily supply in our lives.

4. **The request for forgiveness and our forgiveness of others** (v. 12)—This petition refers to the parental forgiveness that is necessary if the *experience of joyful fellowship* with our Father is to be maintained. If we as believers are *not willing to forgive* those who wrong us, how can we expect to enjoy the sweet fellowship and forgiveness of the Father? Why should God forgive us if we are unwilling to forgive others? An unforgiving spirit is an unloving sinful spirit—God's call upon our lives is that we reflect His character, and not be *hypocrites*. How can we even ask for mercy if we are not willing to be merciful? How can we express hate and expect to receive love? Scripture is very clear on this: we cannot expect to be the recipients of God's loving mercy, if we are not willing to extend mercy to others (Ps 66:18; Mt 5:21–24; 18:33; Eph 4:32; Jam 2:13).

5. **The request for protection from temptation and evil** (v. 13)—The request, "not to be led into temptation," at first may appear to contradict what James teaches—"God does not tempt anyone" (Jam 1:13). However, God does *allow* His people to be tested and tried and tempted by Satan. In this petition we are asking God to "guide us so that we will not get out of His will and get involved in a situation of temptation" (1 Jn 5:18), or get involved in a situation of tempting God so that He must miraculously rescue us (Mt 4:5-7). This petition is similar to the one Jesus gave to Peter, James and John in the Garden of Gethsemane, the night before He went to the cross—He said to them, *"Pray that you may not enter into temptation"* (Mt 26:41). Therefore, this petition expresses a healthy distrust of one's own ability to resist temptations or to stand up under trial, and acknowledges *complete dependence* on the Lord for preservation. The heart's cry of all who desperately desire to be "kept from the power of sin and Satan" in their life, is that God would *"deliver them from evil."*

In light of the foregoing, it becomes readily apparent that as believers here in the West, we have developed a strange way of looking at the Christian life—at the forefront of our concerns is that our lives be comfortable, happy and trouble-free. When our circumstances prove difficult and challenging, we ask God to *"change them"* . . . when we become sick and don't feel good, we ask God to *"heal us"* . . . when the road we travel becomes too bumpy for us, we ask God to *"make it smooth"*—in short, nearly all of our requests are self-serving with the goal of *"making life more enjoyable, and making us feel better."* By the way, it is "natural" for us to pray this way, because that is our self-centered nature—it naturally argues: "Who in their right mind enjoys being miserable and unhappy?" The problem here is **the believer's focus**—our primary focus is on *ourselves*—not *God*. Western Christianity has developed a **theology of life** that essentially is *self-centered*—not *God-centered*. The God of the Bible becomes our *"Loving Caretaker"*—He is there to take care of us . . . to manage our lives for us . . . to protect us . . . to provide for us . . . and, principally, to keep us happy, fat and satisfied. What a great God! The benevolent lover of our souls! No!!! That is the God of our *desires* . . . not the God of the Bible!!! (Jn 6:66-69).

"LEAD US NOT INTO TEMPTATION"

The truth is, temptation is a relentless, perplexing, frustrating reality in every believer's life—it is the "norm;" none of us get an exemption from it (Rom 7:18–19, 24; 1 Cor 10:13; Jam 3:2; 1 Pet 1:6–7; 4:1, 12–13; 5:8–10; 1 Jn 1:10). This "goliath" frequently overwhelms us and wracks havoc upon our souls; and try though as we may, it often leaves us discouraged and defeated. Jesus tells us to pray to the Father that "*He lead us not into temptation*" (Mt 6:13). The thought that God would actually "lead us into temptation" is actually quite troubling to most believers—why on earth would Jesus ask us to pray that God not lead us into temptation? This injunction has disturbed many Christians down through the ages, and caused them to wonder what Jesus really meant by these words? To answer this question, we need to first "define" what the Greek term peirasmos (translated "temptation") means.

The MEANING of *peirasmos*—This word is translated a number ways in English: temptation, test, trials, afflictions, tempting, testing and trying to name a few (Mt 4:1ff; 1 Cor 10:13; Jam 1:13–14; 1 Pet 4:12; Jam 1:2, 12). The "context" determines how one translates the term. This word could be rendered a "sore trial" in the passage before us—*peirasmos* comes the word *peira*, which means to "*pierce through, as with a spear;*" many Greek scholars use it in this way. The word not only implies violent assaults from Satan, but also sorely afflictive circumstances, none of which we have, as yet, the grace or fortitude to sufficiently endure. Trials and afflictions "test" our virtue; hence, it is possible that this is the meaning here (see Lk 22:42). Most scholars, however, translate this word "temptation," because the context strongly points in that direction—since Jesus is referring here to the evil one or evil, and we are always tempted to do evil, this phrase is translated: "Lead us not into temptation." It should be noted that "*temptation accompanies every trial*"— they are two sides of the same coin; with every trial there will be temptation. The psalmist David offered up a prayer similar to the one we find in the Lord's Prayer: "O LORD, do not incline my heart to any evil thing, to practice deeds of wickedness with men who do iniquity" (Ps 141:4). Since God obviously does not tempt man to do evil (Jam 1:13), this injunction then must be used in the sense of "*permitting*"—"Lord, do not suffer or permit us to be tempted in such a way that we sin"—"Do not lead us into a trial that will present such a temptation to us that we will not be able to resist it." It is a heartfelt appeal to God to protect us from sin. The good news is that God is able to *"save us from the tempter's power"* if we will but call upon Him for help.

The SOURCES of temptation—It should be noted here that we are not being taught to "pray against temptation;" it is often needed and useful; rather, we are to pray that it not have the power over us, or that it destroy us. There are a number of sources of temptation—there are the <u>temptations of God</u>, who may be said to tempt, not by infusing anything that is sinful, or by soliciting to sin, but by enjoining things hard and disagreeable to our nature, as in the case of Abraham . . . or by afflicting us either in body or estate, as was the case with Job . . . or by permitting and letting loose the reins to Satan, and a man's own corruptions . . . or by withdrawing His presence and withholding the communications of His grace, that we may be humbled; that our faith and patience may be tried; that we may see our weaknesses and need of Christ; and that we may be stirred to prayer and watchfulness. In addition to the temptations of God, there are also three other sources of temptation: the <u>temptations of Satan</u>, which lie in soliciting to evil, suggesting hard and blasphemous thoughts of God, and filling our minds with doubts and fears . . . the <u>temptations of the world</u>, which arise from poverty and riches, from the men of the world, from the lusts of it, and from both its frowns and its flatteries . . . and the <u>temptations of man's own heart</u>. In the petition before us, the children of God are encouraged to pray that they be kept from every occasion and object of sinning; from those sins they are most inclined to; and that God would not leave them to Satan and their own corrupt hearts . . . but that in the issue besetting them they might experience "God's way of escape" and be victorious (1 Cor 10:13; Jude 1:24).

The PROCESS of temptation—When tempted, writes James, "Let no one say that God is doing the tempting, for God cannot be tempted by evil, nor does He tempt anyone; rather, each one is tempted when he is carried away and enticed by *his own lust*" (Jam 1:13–14). As sinful humanity, we are always ready to *"shift the blame"*—if we cannot blame God for temptation, then we are inclined to blame others or our circumstances, but none of these are the cause of sin. Some believers actually go so far as to say that sin is a sickness not of their own making; but sin is not a sickness—it is a moral failure for which every individual will one day have to give an account. Sin comes from within us—it comes from dwelling on temptations rather than driving temptations from our minds. Genesis 3 describes the four-step process of temptation:

(continued)

- **First, temptation begins with a simple evil thought**—and this is the stage you must shut it down!
- **Second, there is the consideration of the thought**—at this stage the devil gets you on his turf!
- **Third, there is delight in entertaining the thought**—at this stage you start selling yourself on it!
- **Fourth, there is the consent of the will**—at this stage lust is conceived and sin results (Jam 1:15); a man may be tempted without entering into the temptation (Mt 4:1ff); entering into it implies giving way to it and embracing it.

The PURPOSE of temptation—Though God does not bring temptation, He does allow it, according to His supreme wisdom and unsearchable providence (Deut 8:3; Job 1:1–12; Mt 4:1ff; 2 Cor 12; Eph 6:11; Jam 4:7; 1 Pet 5:8). Why? Scripture gives us at least four reasons: **_First, to show us how frail, sinful, and helpless we are, so that we will run daily to Christ for grace_**; without a strong sense of our sinfulness we would not pursue Christ (Ps 32:3–5; Rom 7:18, 24–25; Gal 3:24). The writer to the Hebrews tells us that "we have a high priest who can genuinely sympathize with our weaknesses, because He was tempted in every way that we are, yet did not sin;" as such we can "come boldly to the throne of grace to receive mercy and grace to help in time of need" (Heb 4:15–16). But why the necessity to pray? We need to be conscious of the fact that in and of ourselves we do not possess the ability to resist temptation—(none of us do!)—therefore we need to fully rely upon God to overcome it. The Apostle Peter denied the Lord Jesus after he failed to avail himself of the opportunity to *pray* in the Garden of Gethsemane; apparently he was tired and did not realize how critically important it was to pray. Jesus told His disciples, "Watch and pray that you not enter into temptation; the spirit indeed is willing, but the flesh is weak" (Mt 26:41). If we desire to <u>not</u> perpetually be caught in the grip of sin, then we need to continually claim the promises of God in prayer that we not succumb to temptation—the message is clear, if we do not watch and pray we will succumb. Christians grossly underestimate the necessity of prayer in overcoming temptation. **_Second, to wean us from the corrupt, death-producing pleasures of this world_**; sin has bitter consequences; thank God we reap what we sow, or we would never desire to get out of the mud (Ps 32:3–5; 73:25; Prv 5:3–4; Ecc 7:26; Gal 5:19–21; 6:7; Phil 3:8; I Jn 2:15–17). **_Third, to make us more like Jesus_**; evoking within us a hunger and thirst for righteousness. It is never God's desire for us to be "led into sin," but He does allow us to be put into tempting situations for the purpose of strengthening our faith and character (Job 23:10; Ps 66:10; Mt 5:6; Rom 5:3–5; Heb 12:4–11; Jam 1: 2–4; 1 Pet 1:6–7; 5:12–13). And **Fourth, to make us long for heaven and be rid of sin altogether;** to be glorified (Rom 8:18, 23; 2 Pet 3:12–13; 1 Jn 3:2–3; Rev 22:17).

The RESPONSE to temptation—Jesus tells us in this prayer that a "_healthy distrust of self_" should characterize every child of God . . . that we should continually be conscious of our own weaknesses and the schemes of the one who seeks to destroy us. We are not to have any false assurance about our ability to do as well as Jesus did when He was "_put to the test_" by Satan in the wilderness—(read that statement again!)—instead, we are to recognize our inclination to be headstrong like Peter, thinking he was confident to handle any challenge that might come his way (Lk 22:31–34, 54–62). Though we as God's children never have to give in to temptation—for God provides a way of escape (1 Cor 10:13; 1 Pet 5:10; 2 Pet 2:9; Jude 1:24)—we must be extremely aware of our own personal lack of strength and vulnerability. Jesus therefore emphasized the need for "_humble dependence on God_." He called us to recognize our human frailty and to acknowledge that, "on our own," we are no match for our triple foes: the world, the devil, and the flesh. Therefore we are called to "_trust the Lord_" (not ourselves) for the strength to resist temptation before it becomes sin. Remember, it is not the temptation itself that leads us to sin, but the lack of resistance and trust in the Lord for deliverance. It is crucial that the believer understand the fact that he is not able to resist temptation without God's grace. As Christians, we are in a constant fight with the desires born of our sinful natures, to either please ourselves or God (Gal 5:17). Therefore we must "put on the full armor of God to _stand_ against Satan and the forces of evil . . . and _pray_ in the Spirit at all times" (Eph 6:10–18; 1 Th 5:17). In prayer we humbly take all of our failings, weaknesses, evil tendencies and struggles to God . . . and express our gratitude to Him for His unending love and faithfulness to us . . . and acknowledge our total dependence on Him to walk in the light and be obedient to His will (Jn 15:5, 7, 16; 16:23; Rom 7:24–25; 8:31–37; 2 Cor 12:9; Eph 3:20; Phil 1:6; 2 Tim 2:13; Heb 7:25; 13:20–21; Jude 1:24). In closing, here's a good exercise for you—place yourself in the Garden of Gethsemane the night before Jesus went to the cross . . . after hearing Jesus warn you to "_watch and pray_," how would you pray? what would you say? Construct a prayer that incorporates the various elements that would make your prayer most efficacious.

With that in mind, let's return to the subject at hand—"the will of God." Let's begin by carefully defining those absolute realities that underlie the governance of the universe—*"God's interests"* are first and foremost—not "our interests," as we want to think. *"God's kingdom"* is to be the focus, not "our kingdom;" *"God's will"* is preeminent, not "our will." The problem with western Christianity is that we dedicate the vast majority of our spiritual energies to our own *"self-interests"*—to our own personal happiness and our overall well-being; if you don't believe that, monitor all of your thoughts throughout the course of a day. Our primary problem as believers, is that it is very difficult for us to get our eyes off of ourselves—*we are obsessed with ourselves*—that's the functional reality of indwelling sin (Rom 7:14–21). The writer of Hebrews exhorts us to, "Fix our eyes on *Christ*, the author and perfecter of our faith" (Heb 12:2). That injunction identifies the solution—instead of focusing on **ourselves**, we are to focus on **Christ**. The Great Commandment tells us that we are to "Love the Lord our God with all our heart, soul, and mind;" and that a second is like it—we are to "Love our neighbor as ourselves" (Mt 22:37–39). For some reason, the western church in the last half of the twentieth century began embracing and teaching something called *"self-esteem theology."* Essentially it says, "we must first learn to love ourselves if we are ever going to learn to love others." The problem, according to this way of thinking, is that *"we don't love ourselves enough"*—if we would just learn to love ourselves more, we would start loving others more! Therefore, all we need to do is learn to *"love ourselves more!"* That's the solution! No!!! That is not the solution!!! That is the problem!!!

Scripture is very clear on this—our problem is <u>not</u> that we don't love ourselves enough; everyone loves himself more than anything in the world—and that is the problem! Listen to what Paul has to say to husbands: "Love your wives as your own bodies" (Eph 5:28)—the given here is, *"men love their own bodies."* We all love ourselves—I didn't say *like*, I said *love*—obviously, many of us don't particularly like ourselves. But all of us *care about ourselves* more than anything else in the entire world—*SELF* is our first love—and therein is the problem. What Paul says is this: *"We are to love our wives <u>like</u> we love ourselves."* Conversely, we are to *"love our neighbor **as** we love ourselves."* (Mt 22:39). Paul goes on to say in Philippians, "we are not merely to look out for our own personal interests (which we essentially do non-stop!), but we are to look out for the interests of *others*" (Phil 2:4). Loving God and loving others is where we need to direct our spiritual energies—obviously, this is difficult work for us as believers, because it is not something that is easy or comes natural; it requires the operating presence of the very Spirit of God in our lives (Lk 18:27). Our problem as human beings has never been a *"lack of self-love"* (we have never had any problem with looking out after "number one!")—it has always been about *"loving God and loving others!"* (i.e., putting others "first"). Incidentally, this is not some radical new understanding of the Christian faith; theologians have been screaming for years at the "self-centeredness" of Western Christianity. I am simply one more voice among thousands who is calling for a return to *"biblical Christianity!"*

Scripture tells us that our life is to be all about *"GOD"—NOT US*— we are to have a *"God-focus,"* not a *"self-focus."* For some reason, that statement seems to rub a lot of Christians the wrong way. They rebel against it, because it is too intrusive . . . and some even argue that it is not reasonable. The Bible, however, emphatically teaches that God made us *FOR HIMSELF*—He didn't make us to just sit around enjoying His playground and all of the fun stuff He put in it. He made us *"for Himself"* (Rom 11:36; 1 Cor 8:6; Col 1:16; Heb 2:10; Rev 1:6)—we were not made *"for us!"* Remember, He is the Creator, and we are the creature—since when does the *creature* (that which is made) define the parameters of its existence? And how is it that he is even able to do so? From whence does his intelligence come? From himself? Is he not the product of the One who made him? And yet, he argues for autonomy? How do such inane thoughts even enter the minds of men? Where does such nonsensical thinking come from? Since when does the *creature* dictate to the *One who made him* what shall be? What are the grounds for such a position? Assuming you are a proponent of that position, how would you litigate your case? Do you really think your case has merit? To see its farcical nature, imagine the following—you become the creator of something, and then "that created thing" actually has you incarcerated, through some judicial system of sorts, for being morally perverse. I concur, it seems ludicrous to even imagine such a scenario, but that seems to be "moral character" of the defiant soul of man. He just refuses to accept the fact that he is *"the creature."* I agree this is an absurd argument—but apparently there are many within Christendom who need to hear this message. Let's return again to the subject at hand: God made us *FOR HIMSELF*, which means *HE IS TO BE OUR REASON FOR LIVING*—not ourselves (Mt 16:24–25; Gal 2:20; Eph 1:4–5; Phil 1:21; 2:13; Heb 13:21). As long we have a *"self-centered independent focus in life,"* we will increasingly find life to be an empty, lonely, unpleasant, unfulfilling experience. Why? Because we were not created for *"self-centered living"*—God created us for Himself and for others, as the Great Commandment clearly states: "You are to love God and love others!" (Mt 22:36–39). Until that becomes *your heartfelt conviction,* you will simply live a life of delusion and spin your wheels spiritually. My advice—stop trying to make a case for your own autonomy; that is a deadend street! By the way, that is the same road Satan traveled! (read the last chapter of this book!).

Some go on to argue that God must be a *"selfish ogre,"* if He just made us for Himself! After all, if He were really a loving God, He would have given us *"freedom"* to make our own choices, rather than making us bow down and serve Him! Isn't it amazing how warped our sinful minds are? Contrary to the imperceptive nature of the sinful soul, many believers need to be reminded that God graciously gave us *"complete freedom"* to do whatever we want in life—we are even free to impugn the very character of God with benign nonsense! For those of you who are still convinced that God is a selfish ogre, remind me, if you will, how is God being selfish? I find it ironic that some of you would actually argue from "the most selfish of all vantage points"—who is the *hellion* here who wants "his freedom"? Who is the self-centered egotistical maniac demanding his rights? Here we are—*the served*—accusing the Great Servant of all—*Christ Himself*—of being selfish? (Mt 20:28; Jn 13:14; 2 Cor 8:9; Phil 2:7). How can one logically make such an argument? Think with me for one more moment—Jesus came to this world and emptied Himself of all

His prerogatives—including the very glory of heaven itself!—was made in the likeness of lowly man . . . took on the form of a bond-servant . . . was mocked and ridiculed and spat upon by ingrates . . . and then went to the cross and subjected Himself to the cruelest death imaginable—for them! (Phil 2:6–8). I'm not quite seeing how you can call that act "selfish"? Help me here if there is something I am missing in all this. So how is it that we have the audacity to call God "selfish!"? It is utterly amazing how twisted and perverse the minds and hearts of men are—but such is their mental condition (Jer 17:9; Rom 1:25; 7:18).

In a study I did years ago, I was introduced to America's preeminent psychiatrist—Dr. Karl Menninger; he was a member of the famous Menninger family of psychiatrists who founded the *Menninger Foundation* and the *Menninger Clinic* in Topeka, Kansas. Dr. Menninger graduated cum laude from Harvard Medical School in 1917. By 1925, he had attracted enough investors to build the *Menninger Sanitarium.* After World War II, Karl Menninger was instrumental in founding the *Winter Veterans Administration Hospital* in Topeka—it became the largest psychiatric training center in the world. In 1981, Menninger was awarded the Presidential Medal of Freedom by Jimmy Carter. Menninger wrote a number of influential books including *The Human Mind, The Crime of Punishment,* and *The Myth of Mental Illness.* I state the foregoing for a purpose—Dr. Menninger believed the vast majority of the so-called *"mentally ill"* were only "slightly different" from the so-called *"mentally healthy,"* and that their problems were not at all what many so-called *"professionals"* were making them out to be—in most cases, Menninger actually felt professional psychiatric diagnosis was a *medical fraud.* Obviously, that's a pretty strong indictment against many of those in the psychiatric community. To continue—Menninger had gained nationwide acclaim for his ability to *help patients* who were struggling with mental illness—i.e., depressed mood, loss of interest, feelings of guilt or low self-worth, disturbed sleep or appetite, low energy, and poor concentration—as a result he was being inundated with requests by people seeking his help. He took on thousands of patients, but only with the understanding that they would "promise to follow his advice"—if they would not make such a promise, he would not see them. Menninger believed the vast majority of individuals who were struggling with psychological problems, were so *self-absorbed and obsessed with themselves that it had made them sick!* When he would meet with a patient, this is what he would instruct them to do—"Go down south of the tracks . . . find someone who really needs help . . . then help meet that person's need." Invariably, Menninger found, the person's psychological problems would vanish overnight! Menninger believed it was critically important that people get their focus onto something or someone other than *themselves*—in short, *"Get your eyes off yourself!"* Isn't it amazing how even a secular psychologist can stumble upon a universal truth? Self-centered living is destructive! It will ruin your life! So stop focusing on yourself, and start focusing on Christ and others—God commands you to *"Love Him and love others!"* (1 Jn 3:16–18; Gal 5:6; 6:2, 7–10). Obviously, I am not an authority on "mental illness," but I do believe in listening to the admonitions of Scripture—walk according to the expressed will of God, and become that person God wants you to be. By the way, you *will* reap what you sow (2 Cor 9:6–11).

CHAPTER 19

A summary of the book . . .

"TRUE SPIRITUALITY"
by Francis A. Schaeffer (1912–1984)

The question is this: What is the Christian life (true spirituality) really all about, and "how" is it lived out? Obviously, one must first be a Christian in order to live the Christian life. The reason for this is that all men are separated from God because of their *true moral guilt* . . . and only the finished, substitutionary work of Christ upon the cross is enough to remove it; hence, it is Christ *plus nothing* on our part. The only *instrument* for accepting the work of Christ is *faith*—not faith in faith, but simply believing the specific promises of God. Furthermore while the new birth is necessary as the beginning, that is only the beginning. The important thing after being born spiritually is *to live*—this is the area of *SANCTIFICATION*. True spirituality is not a matter of refraining from certain behaviors *or* actually performing certain behaviors in a mechanical sort-of-way, yet neither is it a rejection of such a list and living a looser life.

Likewise, the Christian life (true spirituality) is not to be seen as "outward" at all, but as "inward." The climax of the Ten Commandments is the Tenth Commandment—*"Thou shat not covet"*—this commandment is an entirely inward thing. Actually, we break this commandment before we break any of the others. Paul states very clearly in Romans that this was the commandment which gave him a *"sense of being sinful"*—"I would not have come to know sin except through the Law; for I would not have known about coveting if the Law had not said, *'You shall not covet.'* But sin, taking opportunity through the commandment, produced in me coveting of every kind" (Rom 7:7–8). What Paul is saying here is this: "I did not know I was a sinner; I thought I would come out all right, because I was keeping these outward things and was doing well in comparison with other people." He had been measuring himself against the externalized form of the commandments which the Jews had in their tradition. But when he opened the Ten Commandments and read that the last commandment was not to covet, he saw he was a *"sinner."*

The great commandment in the Bible is to "Love God with all your heart, soul, mind and strength" (Deut 6:5; Mt 22:37). We must see that "loving God" means "not coveting against God" . . . and that "loving our neighbor" means "not coveting against him." When we do not love the Lord as we should, we are actually *"coveting against Him."* The word *"covet"* in the Greek is *epithumeo*—which means *"to fix the desire upon; to long for; to lust after."* Therefore, when we do not fix our desire upon God, we are longing for something or someone else; so when we do not love God as we should, we are coveting against Him. Jesus said, "You cannot covet both God and mammon—you will hate one and love the other" (Mt 6:24). *"Thou shalt not covet"* is the internal commandment which shows the man who thinks himself as being "moral," as really needing a Savior. The average "moral man" who has lived comparing himself to other men can feel like Paul, that he is actually doing all right. But suddenly, when he is confronted with the *"inward command"* not to covet, he is brought to his knees.

Says Schaeffer: This is a very "central concept" if we are to have any understanding or any real practice of the true Christian life or true spirituality. We can take man-made lists and we can seem to keep them, but when we come face to face with the *"Law of Love,"* we can no longer feel proud, and the reality of our sinful self becomes quite clear. In this life we can never say, "I have arrived! it is finished! look at me! I am holy!" When we talk of the Christian life or true spirituality . . . when we are talking about freedom from the bonds of sin . . . we must wrestle with the *"inward problems"* of not coveting (fixing our desires) against God and men, of loving God and men, and not merely some set of externals. This immediately raises the question of whether or not "all desire" is sin—the Bible clearly teaches that it is not. Schaeffer says, *"desire becomes sin when it fails to include love of God or men—we are to love God enough to be contented, and love men enough not to envy."*

If we do not love God enough to be contented, our natural and proper desires will bring us into revolt against God—and revolt is the whole central problem of sin. When I lack proper contentment, either I have forgotten that God is God, or I have ceased to be submissive to Him. By the way, *a quiet disposition and a thankful heart at any given moment is the real test of the extent to which we love God at that moment*. God's own standard for Christians is that "we not let immorality or any impurity, or greed, or filthiness, or silly talk be named among us, as is proper among saints; but rather giving thanks" (Eph 5:3-4). *"Giving thanks"* stands in contrast to the dark list of items. Paul goes on to say we are to *"always give thanks to God for all things"* (Eph 5:20). We are not to worry or be anxious for anything—rather we are to pray with *thanksgiving* about everything (Phil 4:6). To the Colossians he writes, "Let the peace of God rule in your hearts and *be thankful* . . . and whatever you do, do all in the name of the Lord Jesus, *giving thanks* to God" (Col 3:15, 17). Elsewhere he states, *"In everything give thanks,* for this is the will of God for you in Christ Jesus" (1 Th 5:18). I think we can see all this in its proper perspective if we go back to what Paul wrote in the first chapter of Romans: "For even though they knew God, they did not honor Him as God, *or give thanks;* rather their foolish hearts became darkened" (Rom 1:21). Again, the central point is that they were *"not thankful"*—the beginning of man's rebellion against God was, and is, the lack of a thankful heart. Do you genuinely *"desire and long for God"*? or something else?

The truth of the matter is, if we are not content and grateful, we are not loving God as we should; rather we are *"coveting against God."* It is this *inward* area that is the first place we lose true spirituality; the *outward* is always just a result of it. Inward coveting—lack of love toward God and man—soon tends to spill over into the external world; it cannot be kept in the internal world completely. The apostle Paul tells us that *our longing in love* should be to seek the other man's good—not just our own—"though all things are lawful for us, all things are not profitable for edification; therefore let no one seek his own good, but that of his neighbor" (1 Cor 10:23–24; Phil 2:4). "Love is long suffering . . . and does not seek its own" (1 Cor 13:4–5). Schaeffer writes, "If we can only get hold of this—that the *internal* is the basic, and the *external* is always merely the result—it will be a tremendous starting place."

Paul writes, "I have been crucified with Christ, it is no longer I who lives, but Christ lives in me; and the life which I now live in the flesh I live by faith in the Son of God" (Gal 2:20). Note the *negative* and the *positive*—we have been **crucified** (death) that we might walk in **newness of life.** Paul shares the same force in his letter to the Romans (6:4). Paul also says: "Our old self was crucified with Christ, that our body of sin might be done away with, that we should no longer be slaves to sin" (Rom 6:6). Therefore as Christians, we *died* with Christ . . . but we also *rose* with Christ—hence, there is to be an external positive manifestation of the inward positive reality. We are not just dead to certain things . . . we are to love God . . . we are to be alive to Him . . . we are to be in communion with Him (in this present moment of history). Since we have been justified (made righteous) by Christ, we should desire a *"deeper life of true spirituality,"* one that springs forth from within—"the love of God has been poured out in our hearts through the Holy Spirit" (Rom 5:5); the fruit of the Spirit should be produced in us—love, joy, peace, longsuffering, gentleness, goodness, faith, meekness, and self-control (Gal 5:22–23). (1–17)

At this point let's return to the "negative considerations"—"We were *buried* with Christ through baptism into death" (Rom 6:4); "our old self was *crucified* with Him" (Rom 6:6). Paul says, "I have been crucified with Christ" (Gal 2:20); "God forbid that I should boast in anything except the cross of our Lord Jesus Christ, through which the world has been crucified to me, and I to the world" (Gal 6:14). In these statements we find that as Christians *"we died with Christ"* (that is the reality) when we accepted Him as our Savior. But there is more—in practice *"we are to die daily!"* (Lk 9:23; 1 Cor 15:31)—and that cuts into the hard stuff of normal life. We already saw that God's Word is definite when it tells us to be contented and thankful in "all things"—and that includes the hard things. In essence, that means we are to say *"no"* to the dominance of things and self. We are to be willing to say *"no" to ourselves*, in order that the command to love God and men may have real meaning. We are not to seek our own, but to seek another man's good (Phil 2:4). Obviously, anyone who is thinking along honestly at this point, must say that this seems like an *extremely hard position* that Scripture is presenting to us. After all, we are surrounded by a world that says "no" to nothing! In the society in which we live, everything must give in to affluence and selfish personal peace. Furthermore, this environment of *"not saying no"* fits exactly into our individual natural disposition—ever since the fall of man, we do not want to deny ourselves. This was the very crux of the fall—when Satan told Eve she would *"be like God"* if she ate of the fruit, that is what she *"wanted"* (Gen 3:4ff); she wanted to run her own life; she did not want to say "no" to eating the fruit, even though God had told her to say "no." If we stand in the normal perspective of fallen man, it is very hard indeed to say "no" to ourselves. But if we shift our perspective, the whole thing changes.

Consider Jesus' words: "If anyone wishes to come after Me, let him deny himself, and take up his cross daily, and follow Me" (Lk 9:23). This is the same thing we read in Corinthians—not seeking our "own things" even if we have rights to them. This perspective is the antithesis of the world's perspective—the perspectives of the Kingdom of God and that of the fallen world and of our own fallen nature are diametrically opposed to each other. When we step out of that very black perspective and into the perspective of the Kingdom of God, then these "negatives" which are laid upon us take on an entirely different aspect. The *"death of Christ"* is the central message of the Christian faith—not the life or the miracles of Christ. The first promise of the coming of the Messiah (Gen 3:15), tells us that He would be bruised—how else is "sinful man" to be clothed except with skins requiring the shedding of blood? (Gen 3:21). In the celebration of Passover, the Passover Lamb died—this looked forward to the coming of Jesus (Ex 12; Is 53:7; Jn 1:29; 19:14). The center of the Christian message is the redemptive death of Jesus Christ. The apostle Paul writes, "All have sinned and fall short of the glory of God, being justified as a gift by His grace through the redemption which is in Christ Jesus" (Rom 3:23–24).

Conversely, as believers, we are to take up our cross "daily" and follow Christ (Lk 9:23). "For whoever wishes to *save his life* shall lose it, but whoever *loses his life* for My sake, he is the one who will save it" (Lk 9:24). Here Jesus takes the *order* that was so necessary for our redemption, and applies it to the Christian life—Jesus was *slain* and then *raised*. That is precisely the order of true spirituality—there is no other. By the way, *Jesus is talking here about "our death" by choice in the present life.* Jesus carries this concept of *being slain* down into a very practical situation—saying "no" to self in an alien world. Just as Christ's death preceded His resurrection in the order of redemption, so our death to things and self is the first step in the order of true and growing spirituality. Just as Christ's death was *central* to our redemption, *so also is our continuing death by choice central to our spiritual growth in Christ.* We must not think that we can rush into true spirituality without being slain. Carefully and prayerfully reflect upon the foregoing—these truths are absolutely essential for growing and maturing in Christ.

The very First Commandment set forth a call to say a "strong negative" towards wanting to be in the place of God. This is the key to the whole thing—wanting to be at the center of the universe. By choice *"we are to die to running our own lives and doing our own thing."* The Last Commandment, "Thou shalt not covet," shows us that these negatives are not related just to outward behavior, but to *inward attitudes*. In reality, here is our death. We are to say "no"—by choice—to self at that point in living when we are confronted with things that are wrong, and that we might very well find enjoyable. Thus, here in the midst of life, where there is battle and strife, there is to be a *"strong negative"*—by choice, and by the grace of God. It is not, for example, a matter of waiting until we no longer have strong sexual desires, but rather than in the midst of the movement of life, surrounded by a world that grabs everything in rebellion first against God and then against its fellow man, we are to understand what Jesus means when He talks about denying ourselves and renouncing ourselves in regard to that which is not rightfully ours.

There will be some pain here—there are splinters in the Christian's cross. Keep in mind the order of things for Jesus on the way to the cross: "The Son of man must *suffer many things,* and be rejected by the elders and chief priests and scribes, and be killed, and be raised up on the third day" (Lk 9:22)—*suffering must precede any possibility of knowing anything about the risen life*. Christ called His followers to take up the cross *daily*—there is this daily moment-by-moment aspect that so many of us seem to ignore. Note carefully Jesus' words: "Whoever does not carry his own cross and come after Me cannot be My disciple" (Lk 14:27). Jesus is not saying that a man cannot be saved without this, but that you are not a disciple of Christ—in the sense of following Him—if this is not your way of life; rejected and slain daily! This is not an abstract principle we are talking about—it is intensely practical (Lk 14:26); He sets it among the realities of daily life. This is where we must die—calculate the cost! (Lk 14:28–30). Believers must ever keep before them the fact that part of being a growing Christian is the element of *"bearing one's cross daily."*

Paul writes, "We have been buried with Christ through baptism into death, in order that as Christ was *raised* from the dead through the glory of the Father, so *we to* might walk in newness of life" (Rom 6:4). Schaeffer says, "we are in peril if we ignore the element of *dying*—the way to freedom is *through* death, not around it!" *The order is absolute—dying, then being raised*. Paul goes on to say: "Knowing this, that our old self was crucified with Christ (we must know this before we can get on to the second half of this verse), that our body of sin might be made powerless *(done away with)*, that we should no longer be slaves of sin" (Rom 6:6). As Schaeffer puts it, "One does not get on the other side of a door without going through it; likewise, we do not get to the joyous second part of this verse without passing through the first part." If we want to know anything of true spirituality in the Christian life, *"we must take up our cross daily."* After *death* to self, there continues to be a *resurrection* (Gal 2:20).

Paul says, in the present life we are in practice to "live by faith," as though we are now dead (Rom 6:6)—"Consider yourselves to be *dead to sin*, but *alive to God* in Christ Jesus" (Rom 6:11). We are called in faith to reckon ourselves *dead* (in practice) at this present moment of history—so by faith we are to live now as though we have *already died*. Conversely, we are to live by faith now, at this moment of history, as though we had *already been raised*—thus, we are to "walk in newness of life" (Rom 6:4). That is the message of the Christian life. How do we do this? *By faith*—"Consider yourselves to be dead to sin, but alive unto God in Christ Jesus" (Rom 6:11). The word translated "consider" is *logizomai*—it signifies "to take account of" (2 Cor 10:7)—as believers we are exhorted to think and consider certain things as being true—that is faith—we are trusting what God says as indeed being true. As believers we are called to "live by faith" (Rom 1:17; 4:3). When we believe God, we please God—"without believing Him, we cannot please Him!" (Heb 11:6). The basic consideration of the Christian life in a nutshell is this—we are to "count or reckon ourselves as indeed being *dead* to sin, and *alive* to God" (Rom 6:11)—these two truths are not only "facts," they are to be practiced and lived out—that is the essence of faith! As believers we are to turn our faces toward God—away from ourselves and sin—and keep our eyes fixed upon Him (Heb 12:2). Writes Schaeffer, "This is the place in which, by faith, at the present moment of history, we are to be."

A NEW CREATION IN CHRIST
(Supplemental Notes)

The death and resurrection of Jesus Christ are not only historical facts and significant doctrines, but they are the personal experiences of every believer through *"union with Christ."* As believers, we have each been *"baptized into Christ"*—spiritually speaking, that means *"we died with Christ"* and *"we were raised with Christ,"* that we might walk in newness of life (Rom 6:3–4). The essence of the mysterious union we have with Christ is this—God's Spirit spiritually placed us *"in Christ"* 2000 years ago at the cross, so that when He died, *we died with Him* . . . and when He was raised, *we were raised with Him* (Rom 6:5; Gal 2:20; Col 2:20; 3:1). That is the *spirituality reality* of every believer; they are all *"in Christ;"* that is their "position" if you will (Rom 6:3–4, 11; 1 Cor 1:30; Gal 3:27; Eph 2:6; 2:10; Col 3:3). Christ *"died to sin"* in the sense that He bore sin's penalty (Rom 6:23); as a result sin has no more claim or demand upon us . . . because we died with Him. As Christians we are no longer *"alive to sin"* and *"dead to God"*—we are now brand *new creations* in Christ (2 Cor 5:17); therefore we are *"dead to sin"* and *"alive to God."* We were *"crucified with Christ"* that our old self might be done away with, that we should no longer be slaves to sin—that means we are freed from sin (Rom 6:6–7); we now have the capacity to walk in newness of life (Rom 6:4); we didn't have that capacity as unbelievers. Because we died with Christ, we have been set free from the law of sin and death (Rom 8:2).

It is important for the believer to understand that "his flesh"—his old nature—is not dead. The old corrupt nature is still alive and active in regenerate believers; so much so that we are exhorted over and over again not to obey its lusts (Rom 6:12–13; 13:14; Eph 4:22–24). God has given us the *Holy Spirit* for the precise purpose of subduing and controlling the flesh (Rom 6:4; 8:11, 13). Therefore, as believers, we have *died to sin* in the sense that in Christ we have borne its penalty—thus *our old life ended (died),* and *a new life has begun* (2 Cor 5:17). The apostle Paul exhorts believers to *"reckon"* these things as being true—you have been united with Christ in His death and resurrection (Rom 6:11). "Reckoning" is not pretending that your old nature has died when you know perfectly well that it has not. We are rather to realize that *"our old former self died with Christ,"* thus paying the penalty of its sins and putting an end to its career—we are now *"new creations in Christ!"* Therefore, reckon these things

(continued)

> as true—you are indeed <u>*dead to sin*</u> and <u>*alive to God*</u> in Christ Jesus! This is the reality of *"what is"* for the believer.
>
> **Grasping this truth is paramount to experiencing the transformation, liberation and sanctification of your soul.** You must know *who you are* as a believer in Christ; this is your *new identity* as a believer! Study this concept over and over again . . . let your mind play upon these truths . . . prayerfully meditate upon them until you grasp them firmly, and your soul is really at peace with them. Remember, all of the foregoing is true because God's Spirit placed you *"in Christ!"* Without a firm understanding of the truths presented above, you will often struggle with a "lack of assurance" regarding the fact that you are really saved . . . you will frequently question the fact that God really loves you . . . you will try to please God by trying to live up to His standards, and always feel that you fall short—which you do! That is the essence of performance-based living . . . and more often than not you will feel discouraged and defeated as a Christian. Unless you really know who you are *"in Christ,"* the Christian life can be an exhausting, debilitating experience. Therefore, believe what God says about you, and walk with Him through life . . . and in doing so, you will experience His power, His peace, His presence, and His joy. Any other kind of living will simply leave you joyless, frustrated and disheartened.

When [through faith] we are dead to ourselves and this world, and we are face to face with God, then we are ready *by faith* to live in this present world, as though we have already been *raised* from the dead. Once we "consider ourselves dead to sin and alive to God" (Rom 6:11), Paul then says, "we are not to let sin reign in our mortal bodies by obeying its lusts" (Rom 6:12); rather, "we are to present our bodies as instruments of righteousness to God" (Rom 6:13)—that is faith. *Obviously the Christian life is not just a mystical life of "sheer passivity."* Though there are passive aspects to the Christian life, God will not bring forth fruit in your life without the *activity of faith*—we are called to cooperate with God by believing and obeying Him (Jn 15:5, 8; Phil 2:12–13). Perhaps the concept of "passivity" should be explained here—in the New Testament language of Greek, when the verb is *passive,* that means "we are *recipients* of the action;" when the verb is *active,* that means "we are the ones *initiating* the action." Though much of what we experience in the Christian life is the "direct action of God upon our lives"—thus we are *recipients* of His action—there are aspects of the Christian life where we are called to *"initiate action,"* and therein is the essence of submitting to and obeying God. So . . . just as we yielded the members of our bodies as instruments of *unrighteousness* as unbelievers (by obeying the lusts of the flesh), we are now called to yield the members of our bodies as instruments of *righteousness* (by obeying God). This calling is a *choice*—we are called to live in such a way that God is glorified, and that means believing, trusting, and obeying Him. Though **Justification** is a once for all thing—it happens at a single moment in time—**Sanctification** is a moment-by-moment thing, where we die to ourselves and the world moment-by-moment, and live to God moment-by-moment; living as though we have been raised from the dead. (18–45)

Believers naturally ask the question, "How" is it practically possible to live this way? What do I begin to do? Do I begin to whip myself in order to get it accomplished? Do I begin to seek some sort of ecstatic experience? No. Neither of those. The answer is an intensely practical one. The apostle Paul writes, "While we are in this tent, we groan and are burdened, because we do not wish to be unclothed, but to be clothed with our heavenly dwelling, in order that what is mortal may be swallowed up by life. Now it is God who has made us for this very purpose and has given us the Spirit as a pledge, guaranteeing what is to come" (2 Cor 5:4-5). Paul draws two factors together here: 1) *we will be with Christ when we die*, and 2) *we are indwelt by the Holy Spirit*. To die is to be with the Lord—it is not just an idea, but a certain reality. At the same time, Christ lives in us at the present time (Jn 14:16–17; Gal 2:20; Col 1:27). Here is the essence of true **Christian mysticism**—it is not based merely on an experience without content, but on the reality of historic biblical truth. Whereas **Eastern mysticism** is grounded in the loss of the individual's personality, it is not so with Christian mysticism. Christian mysticism is *"communion with Christ"*—it is Christ bringing forth fruit through us, with no loss of personality.

So "bearing fruit" is not simply done in our own strength—the glorified Christ does it through us through the agency of the Holy Spirit. As Paul writes, "the love of God has been poured out within our hearts through the Holy Spirit who was given to us" (Rom 5:5). It is this reality upon which we are to act. The Holy Spirit is not just an *"idea,"* but the *"living presence of God"* within us. Paul expresses it this way—"if by the Holy Spirit you are putting to death the deeds of the body, you will live" (Rom 8:13). There is not enough strength in ourselves to bear fruit; it is the indwelling presence of the Holy Spirit that empowers us to do so. But we have a part—we are to abide in Christ and obey Him, and when we do God produces the fruit! (Jn 15:4-5; 1 Cor 3:6). The Holy Spirit is the *"Prime Mover"* in our lives (Phil 2:12-13). As we look in the book of Acts, we find in the early Church not just a group of strong men laboring together, but the power of the Holy Spirit working in and through them, bearing fruit to the praise and glory of the risen Christ—so it must be for us also. Obviously, this is not merely a *passive* role on the believer's part—for example: when Mary was told she was going to give birth to a child, she could have rejected the idea and said, "No, I don't want it" . . . or she could have said, "I will have a child in the same way other women have children (through Joseph) . . . or, she could have responded as she did: "Be it unto me according to your word" (Lk 1:38)—there was *"active passivity"* on Mary's part. She took her own body, by choice, and put it into the hands of God to do the thing that He said He would do—and Jesus was born.

If we are to bring forth fruit in the Christian life, or rather, if Christ is to bring forth this fruit through us by the agency of the Holy Spirit, there must be a *constant act of faith,* of thinking: "Upon the basis of Your promises I am looking for You to fulfill them, Lord Jesus—bring forth Your fruit through me into this poor world to Your praise" (note carefully that it is the presence of God in your life that is making your actions efficacious and fruitful—you are called to obey believing, and God brings forth the fruit). That is what Schaeffer means by *"active passivity."* Thus true spirituality is not achieved in your own energy. The *"how"* of the Christian life (true spirituality) is stated in Romans 6:11—"Consider yourself to be *dead to sin,* but *alive to God* in Christ Jesus" (that is the faith perspective; the foundational consideration for your entire life). This is the *"how"*—there is no other. The Christian life is not just a matter of right actions (irrespective of faith), it is a matter of humble submission to will of God with a *proper heart perspective* (faith), knowing that His Spirit is doing a special work in and through your life in that particular moment—it is the power of the risen Christ, through the agency of the Holy Spirit . . . *by faith.* You must have *confident assurance in the moment* that "God is at work in you to will and do His good pleasure" (Phil 2:13; Heb 11:1)—by the way, the faith you exercise one moment doesn't get credited to the actions you take the next moment; you must *consciously exercise faith* at all times. Again reflect upon the words of Paul to the Galatians—"It is no longer I who live, but Christ lives in me; and the life which I now live in the flesh, *I live by faith* in the Son of God" (Gal 2:20). So, fruit-bearing Christians "live by faith," that the "power of God might live in them" in the person of the Holy Spirit—when we live by faith, God is involved in the work. It is then that the believer can say with Paul, *"I live, yet not I, but Christ lives in me."* (45–59)

One of the problems of our western world is that it is essentially "naturalistic"—that is, it believes everything works by "natural processes;" as such, it excludes *"supernatural causation"* as an explanation of reality. Naturalists believe scientific laws are adequate to account for all phenomena. If the believer is not careful, even though he claims he is a *"supernaturalist,"* naturalism can easily make inroads into his thinking without his recognizing it, primarily because it is the prevalent philosophical position here in the west. As soon as this happens, Christians begin to lose the reality of supernaturalism in their Christian lives. *While we say we believe one thing, we allow the spirit of the naturalism of our age to creep into our thinking, unrecognized.* Christian spirituality is related to the scriptural view of the universe—this means the universe is not the naturalistic universe the western world says it is. So instead of living in an *"impersonal universe,"* we live in a universe where the *"personal God of creation"* is its central figure. Since the Bible clearly teaches that we live in a supernatural universe, the central tenet of Christianity is the existence of a *"personal God."* Due to the fact that the default mode for the believer is *"his flesh,"* this makes him high susceptible to the danger of thinking in a naturalistic fashion.

The true Bible-believing Christian is one who lives in practice in this "supernatural world." That doesn't mean, however, that a person is "unsaved" if he fails to live in practice in this supernatural world—happily this is not so, or none of us would go to heaven, because none of us live this way consistently. According to the biblical view, there are two parts to reality: the *natural world* that we see normally, and the *supernatural world* which we do not see (that is the reason we call it supernatural). So the biblical Judaistic-Christian view of the universe is that reality has two halves—one part is *seen,* and the other is *unseen* (Rom 8:24; Heb 11:1). Schaeffer states that it is perfectly possible for a Christian to be so infiltrated by twentieth-century thinking, that he lives most of his life as though the supernatural were not there—he says "all of us do this to some extent." *But being a "biblical Christian" means living in the supernatural now.* Unhappily, the Christian all too often tends to vacillate between these two realities—at one moment he lives in the realm of *faith,* and at another moment he lives in the realm of *unfaith.* If I am trying to live the Christian life in the realm of unfaith, I am only *"playing at it,"* rather than *"living it."* Since the real battle is not against flesh and blood, but is in the *"heavenlies,"* we cannot participate in that battle in the flesh (Eph 6:12). Furthermore, the Lord's work done in human energy is not the Lord's work any longer—it is something, but it is not the Lord's work.

Is the supernatural world remote? The answer, very decidedly, is "No." The supernatural world is not only not far off, but is very close indeed. Perhaps the classic passage on this subject is that found in 2 Kings—here Elisha is surrounded by an enemy, and the young man who is with him is terrified. So Elisha says to him: "Do not fear, for those who are with us are more than those who are with them." At that moment, Elisha prayed saying, *"Lord open his eyes that he may see."* And the Lord opened the servant's eyes, and he saw—"and behold the mountain was full of horses and chariots of fire all around Elisha" (2 Kg 6:16–17). The only difference was that the young man's eyes had to be opened to see what Elisha already saw—the supernatural was not something far off, it was right there. God gives his faithful children *"eyes of faith"* to see and understand the unseen world (Jn 16:13; Acts 16:14; 1 Jn 2:27). Little by little, many Christians in this generation find this reality slipping away—the reality tends to get covered by the barnacles of naturalistic thought. ***Doctrine is important, but it is not an end in itself—there is to be an experiential reality, moment by moment.*** This is "how" to live a life of freedom from the bonds of sin—not perfection, for that is not promised to us in this life. This is the Christian life—true spirituality. In the light of the Scripture, the *"how"* is the power of the crucified and risen Christ . . . through the agency of the indwelling *Holy Spirit* . . . *by faith*. (60–70)

The apostle Peter writes, "You are a chosen race . . . a people for God's own possession, that you may proclaim the excellencies of Him who has called you out of darkness into His marvelous light" (1 Pet 2:9). As Christians, we are a people set apart for a *purpose*—and that is to show forth the praises of God. The supreme purpose of man is that he love God with all his heart, all his soul, and all his mind (Mt 22:37). Furthermore, it was always God's intention that His children be the evidence and demonstration of Christ's victory on the cross. Every Christian is to be a *demonstration* at his own point of history and to his own generation—not only of God's character, which is a moral demonstration, but of God's very existence. Though the Christian is called to *believe right doctrine*, Scripture also places an importance on *what he does* as well as *how he does it*—in Christian service, the *how* is as important as the *what*.

The Christian is to live a "conscious life of faith" moment-by-moment throughout his present life. Writes John, "This is the victory that overcomes the world—*our faith*" (1 Jn 5:4). On the basis of the finished work of Christ, a conscious moment-by-moment life of faith is *"the victory."* But be absolutely clear about this: the basis is not "your faith"—it is what our faith is in: the *"finished work of Christ."* Faith is simply the instrument to receive what Christ purchased for us on the cross—it is the channel through which we receive what God has done for us. *The Christian life—sanctification—is a moment-by-moment experience that operates on the basis of "faith" in God's promises*—if we try to live the Christian life in our own strength *(without faith)*, we will have sorrow . . . on the other hand, if we serve the Lord in the power of the Holy Spirit *(with faith)*, we will have His joy and a song in our heart. That is the difference. The *"how"* of the Christian life is the power of the crucified and risen Lord . . . through the agency of the indwelling Holy Spirit . . . by faith (moment by moment) (Gal 2:20). Remember, we serve and worship a "personal God," with whom we have a "personal relationship;" we don't just focus on a bunch of ideas and principles. "May this [personal] God of hope fill you with all joy and peace in believing . . . by the power of the Holy Spirit" (Rom 15:13). This is our calling, through the agency of the Holy Spirit. (71–80)

Is it possible for a Christian to bring forth the same kind of "fruit" he bore as a non-Christian? Absolutely. Why? Because he is yielding himself to that old master of his, the devil. If we are not living a life of faith toward Christ, we are being unfaithful toward Him—this is *spiritual adultery*—such living produces the fruit of the flesh (Gal 5:19–21), as opposed to the fruit of the Spirit (Gal 5:22–23). Living according to the flesh both grieves the Holy Spirit (Eph 4:30), and quenches the Holy Spirit (1 Th 5:19). As Schaeffer says: There are *"oceans of grace"* awaiting the believer—if they do not flow through the Christian's life, it is only because the instrumentality of *"faith"* is not being used. Thus, the real sin of the Christian is not to possess his possessions, by faith. Paul tells us, "that which is not of faith is sin" (Rom 14:23); so anything that is not brought forth from faith is "sin." When I am not allowing this fruit, which has been purchased at such a great price, to flow forth through me, *I am unfaithful,* in the deep sense of not believing God—remember, *not living by faith is not believing God.*

One of the reasons we don't bear the kind of spiritual fruit in life that we should is "ignorance." If that is the case, in all likelihood, we were never taught the meaning of the work of Christ for our present lives—as a result, we may have thought the Christian life was to be lived in our own strength; as such, we were never instructed that *"there is a reality of faith to consciously be acted upon"* after becoming a believer. *So what is needed is the knowledge of the meaning of the work of Christ in our present life, for our present life, and then for us to act upon it in faith.* We may agree with doctrinal positions mentally, without making them ours; in the final analysis, it is never doctrine *alone* that is important—it is always doctrine *appropriated* that counts. Just as in **Justification** we must see, acknowledge, and act upon the fact that *we cannot save ourselves . . .* so in **Sanctification** we must see, acknowledge, and act upon the fact that *we cannot live the Christian life in our own strength,* or in our own goodness. In justification the instrument by which we receive the free gift of God is *faith . . .* in sanctification the instrument by which we receive the free gift of God is *faith*—it is exactly the same thing. There are two differences, however, between the practice of justification and sanctification—justification deals with *our guilt,* and sanctification deals with the problem of the *power of sin in our lives . . .* justification is a *once for all* occurrence, and the Christian life is a *moment by moment* occurrence. Carefully reflect upon the dynamics of these two critically important doctrines.

Life is only a succession of moments—we live "one moment" at a time. No one lives his whole life in a single moment in time—we all live it one moment after another in time. So we must believe God's promises at this one moment in which we now are. In believing God's promises, we apply them for and in this one moment. Schaeffer says, *"If you grasp this, everything changes!"* As we believe God for this moment, the Holy Spirit is not quenched; and through His agency, the risen and glorified Christ (the vine) brings forth His fruit through us *at this moment* (Jn 15:5). By the way, this morning's faith will never do for this afternoon. In every moment of time, our calling is to *believe God . . .* raise the empty hands of faith (we bring nothing to the table!) . . . and let fruit flow out through us. Furthermore, Christian faith is never faith in faith, it is never without content, it is never a jump in the dark, *it is always believing what God has said.* And Christian faith rests upon Christ's finished work on the cross.

We were created for "moment-by-moment communication" with God Himself! Think about that. This moment-by-moment quality brings us back to the purpose for which God has created us. This being the case, it is obvious that there is *"no mechanical solution to true spirituality"* or the true Christian life. Anything that has the mark of the mechanical upon it is a mistake. It is not possible to say, read so many chapters of the Bible every day, and you will have this much sanctification . . . or pray so many hours . . . or do anything else! True spirituality can never have a mechanical solution. *The real solution is being in "moment-by-moment personal communion" with God Himself,* and letting Christ's truth flow through you through the agency of the Holy Spirit. The most basic teaching of the Bible is that God exists, that God is personal, and that we have been made in His image—thus, our relationship to God is to be personal, not mechanical. We are not machines; we are created in the image of God—therefore we are personal, rational, moral beings, who were *created for a purpose*—to be in a *personal relationship with God,* in loving communion with Him—by choice—the creature with His Creator. The only difference between our relationship with God now, and that which it would have been if man had not sinned, is that now it is under the *covenant of grace,* and not under the *covenant of works;* therefore it rests upon the basis of Christ's finished mediatorial work on the cross. That is the only difference. The *will,* the *mind,* and the *emotions* are all involved—the complete man—in this moment-by-moment, one moment at a time, believing God's promises about the significance of the work of Christ in our present lives. We are to believe God every moment, one moment at a time—this is the Christian life—true spirituality. (80–89)

Now we consider the question of "freedom in the present life" from the results of the bonds of sin. First, it is important that we keep things in the right order—don't get them reversed—*sin causes bondage and the results of sin.* Sin *causes* the bondage . . . not the other way around. The dilemma of the human race is *"moral"*—the basic problem of the human race is *"sin and guilt."* We have sinned *against* a holy God (sin is not just a matter of violating an impersonal law—it is *against* God), so we are guilty before a holy God against whom we have sinned. Regarding the question of freedom from our conscience—*there are two attitudes which the Word of God and a study of Church history warn us against:*

1. <u>Perfectionism</u>—This is the teaching that a Christian can be "perfect" in this life; this teaching is the result of something known as a "second blessing" that follows conversion—once received the individual never sins again. The early John Wesley taught this; not the later Wesley, for he began to see that this could not be consistently held. Obviously, perfectionism does not align with the teaching of Scripture. Schaeffer reflects: "The more the Holy Spirit puts His finger on my life and goes down deep into my life, the more I understand that there are *deep wells* to my nature—in a sense we are like the *"iceberg,"* one-tenth above the surface and nine-tenths below it; as such, it is a very, very simple thing to fool ourselves." (Jer 17:9; Jam 3:2; 1 Jn 3:10). Schaeffer continues, "As the Holy Spirit has wrestled with me down through the years, more and more I am aware of *the depths of my own sinful nature,* and the depths of the results of that awful fall in the Garden of Eden." Man is actually separated from himself *(more on this later).*

2. <u>We sin daily in thought, word, and deed</u>—That is the emphasis of the Westminster Catechism. Though this is not wrong, it can be *distorted by our sinful hearts* into something which is exceedingly wrong. As we teach our children that we all sin daily in thought, word, and deed, we must be very careful to warn them of the danger of thinking that *they can look lightly or abstractly at sin* in their lives. Furthermore, if we count on Christ's victory at the cross for our entrance into heaven, dare we deny Him the glory of what the victories would produce in the battles of the present life? And the battles before men and angels and the supernatural world? What an awful thought!

The Bible makes a clear distinction between "temptation" and "sin." Christ was tempted in every point like as we are, yet He never sinned (Heb 4:15); therefore, there is a difference between temptation and sin. Scripture goes on to tell us that the victory that overcomes the world is *"our faith"* (1 Jn 5:4). It is not *we* who overcome the world in our own strength—we do not have a power plant inside ourselves that can overcome the world. The overcoming is the work of the Lord Jesus Christ, as we have already seen. There can be a victory, a practical victory, if we raise the *"empty hands of faith"* moment by moment and accept the gift. God has promised a way of escape that we might not succumb to temptation (1 Cor 10:13).

Schaeffer: "As a born-again child of God, I have been practicing the reality of true spirituality, as Christ has purchased it for us . . . and yet there are times when *sin re-enters.* For some reason my moment-by-moment belief in God falters; *a fondness for some specific sin* has caused me at that point not to draw in faith upon the fact of a restored relationship with the Trinity. The reality of the practice of true spirituality suddenly slips from me . . . *my quietness and my peace are gone.* It is not that I am lost again, because justification is once for all. But as far as man can see, or even I myself, at this point there is no exhibition of the victory of Christ upon the cross . . . because God still holds me fast I do not have the separation of *lostness,* but I do have the separation from my Father in the *parent-child relationship* . . . and I remember what I had."

At this point the question arises: Is there a way back? Or is it like a piece of fine china that has been dropped on a tile floor and smashed beyond repair? Thank God, the gospel includes this. *The Bible is always realistic*—it is not romantic, but deals with realism—with what we are. There is a way back, and the basis of the way back is *"the blood of Christ"*— the finished work of the Lamb of God on the cross. And the first step of the way back is not new either—no man becomes a Christian until he *acknowledges he is a sinner;* likewise, the first step in the restoration of the Christian after he has sinned is to *admit to God that what he has done is sin* (1 Jn 1:4–9). He must not blame it on someone else (like Adam) . . . he must not call it less than sin (like Saul) . . . and he must be sorry for it (like David). Hence, "if we confess our sins, He is faithful and just to forgive us our sins, and to cleanse us from all unrighteousness" (1 Jn 1:9). This is the gentle dealing of God with His children after they have fallen. This is the purpose of God's chastisement of the Christian—it is to cause us to acknowledge that the specific sin is indeed *"sin."*

If we have sin in our lives, and we continue in it, and God does not chastened us, then we can conclude that we are not children of God, because God chastens (disciplines) those He loves (Heb 12:6-8). It should be noted that *"discipline is not joyful, but sorrowful;* yet those who have been trained by it, afterwards it yields the peaceful fruit of righteousness" (Heb 12:11). Thus, God disciplines (chastens) us for a *"purpose"*—that we might have peace in the midst of these things. That is God's loving care for us. God the Father's chastening is to cause us to acknowledge that a specific sin is sin; His hand can grow increasingly heavy until we come to acknowledge that it is sin and stop trying to get out from under it by blaming it on others or excusing it in some way (Ps 32:3-5). Do you want restored fellowship with God? You can have it as His child, but you will not receive it until you are willing to call specific sin *"sin."* It is a matter of telling God that you want *"His will"* in this matter that you acknowledge it to be sin—"not my will, Lord, but Thine be done" (Mt 26:39; Jn 6:38).

In practice we may not comprehend all that is involved in the sin, and especially if a person is psychologically disturbed; he may not always be able to sort out what really is sin, and what is just confusion on his part. Here is the concept of the *"iceberg"* again—nine-tenths below the surface, and only one-tenth above it, so that we cannot always sort out all that we are in the midst of our sin. Much of the sin may be *below the surface,* much may even be in the *subconscious* boiling up, just showing itself in spots. But whatever evil may be *above the surface*—the portion that we do comprehend as sin—that portion we must take with honesty before the One who knows our whole being, and say to Him, *"Father, I have sinned."* There must be real sorrow for the sin that we know, that is above the surface. Just as the first step in justification is the acknowledgement that *we are a sinner,* so the first step in living the Christian life as God intended is the acknowledgement that *we cannot live the Christian life in our own strength or in our own goodness.* Again, we must bring the specific sin under the blood of Jesus Christ *"by faith"* (1 Jn 1:9). (93-103)

Martin Luther, in his commentary on Galatians, shows a great understanding of the fact that our salvation includes salvation from the *"bondage of our conscience."* It is natural and right that as we become Christians our consciences become *ever more tender*—this is a work of the Holy Spirit. But we should not be downcast by our conscience year after year over sins which are past. When your conscience, by the Holy Spirit, makes you aware of a specific sin, you should at once call that sin "sin" and *bring it consciously under the blood of Christ*—when you do this it is then *"covered,"* so by continuing to *"worry about it,"* you not only dishonor the finished work of Christ, but you impair your relationship with God, either by thinking that you must "suffer sufficiently" to merit his forgiveness, or by "doubting" that God is that loving and merciful—hence, your fellowship with Him is short-circuited. Writes Schaeffer: "To worry about it is to do despite to the infinite value of the death of the Son of God." As you consciously say, *"Thank you"* to God for a completed work, your conscience should come into rest. By applying the blood of Christ to your sin, your fellowship experience with God is restored.

Writes Schaeffer: "For myself, through the twenty years or so since I began to struggle with this in my own life, I picture *my conscience* as a 'big black dog' with enormous paws which leaps upon me, threatening to cover me with mud and devour me. But as this conscience of mine jumps upon me, after a specific sin has been dealt with on the basis of Christ's finished work, then I turn to my conscience and say, in effect, *'Down! Be still!'* I am to believe God and be quiet, in my practice and experience. My fellowship with God has been supernaturally restored. I am cleansed, ready again to resume the spiritual life, ready again to be used by the Spirit for warfare in the external world. I cannot be ready until I am cleansed, but when I am, then I am ready. And I come back for cleansing as many times as I need, on this basis." For us as Christians, the point of reality is this: "My little children, these things I write to you that you not sin *(so naturally the call is not to sin)*, but if any man does sin, we *(the apostle John includes himself in this category)* have an advocate with the Father, Jesus Christ the righteous" (1 Jn 2:1).

Schaeffer continues: "This is the point of reality for me personally. If I lay hold upon the blood of Christ in faith, reality rests here—not in trying to live as though the Bible teaches perfectionism. That is no basis for reality; that is only a basis for despair. But there is reality here—the reality of sins forgiven; the reality of a certainty that when a specific sin is brought under the blood of Christ—it is forgiven. *This is the reality of restored relationship.* Reality is to be experienced, and experienced on the basis of a restored relationship with God through the finished work of the Lord Jesus Christ on the cross."

One more thing needs to be said on this subject—"If we judged ourselves rightly, we would not be judged. But when we are judged by God, we are chastened by Him that we should not be condemned with the world" (1 Cor 11:31-32). *This teaches us that we do not need to wait to be chastened before our fellowship with God can be restored.* God's chastening (discipline) is not a *punishment*—our punishment was altogether dealt with on the cross. Instead, God's chastening is *corrective in nature;* its purpose is to bring us back to fellowship with Himself. The chastening of a child of God does not have a penal aspect—that was finished on the cross. There is no "double jeopardy" when the holy God is the Judge. Our guilt is gone—once and forever! Therefore if we judge ourselves, we are not chastened. Since God is not going to have us *condemned* with the world, he will *chasten* us. But if we judge ourselves, and call the sin *sin,* and bring it under the blood of Christ, then He will not have to chasten us. As such, it is overwhelmingly better not to sin! But is it not wonderful that when we do sin, we can hurry to the place of restoration?

So God means us to have, as one of His gifts in this life, freedom from a false tyranny of conscience. Most, if not all, Christians find that the first step in the *"substantial healing"* that they can have in the present life is the substantial healing of the *"separation from themselves"* that is a result of the fall and of sin. Man is first of all separated from God . . . then from himself . . . and finally from his fellow man and from nature. The blood of Christ will give an absolute and perfect restoration of all these things when Jesus comes. But in the present life there is to be a substantial healing, including the results of the separation between a man and himself. This is the first step towards *"freedom in the present life"* from the results of the bonds of sin.

Thoughts precede actions—the external is a product of the internal. All behavior begins in the mind. Paul tells us to *"present our bodies a living and holy sacrifice*, acceptable to God, which is our spiritual service of worship"* (Rom 12:1). Notice verse one cannot be separated from verse two—"Do not be conformed to this world, but be *transformed by the renewing of your mind,* that you may prove what the will of God is, that which is good and acceptable and perfect" (Rom 12:2). So in contrast to being conformed to this world, we are to be transformed by the renewing of our mind, and that is internal. Paul exhorts us to not walk as other Gentiles walk, "in the futility of their mind" (Eph 4:17); rather, we are to be "renewed in the spirit of our mind" (4:23). You will notice this is not simply a "feeling"—it is a matter of "thoughts" with content (4:24). Paul goes on to say, "Walk not as unwise men, but as wise, making the most of your time, because the days are evil; so do not be foolish, but understand what the will of the Lord is" (Eph 5:15-17). Thus our *"thought-life"* is critical in the area of true spirituality. *"As a man thinks, so is he"* (Prv 23:7). Jesus also emphasized this: "the mouth speaks out of that which fills the heart" (Mt 12:34); "out of the heart come evil thoughts and all manner of evil" (Mt 15:19)—if the internal condition of the heart is not right, one cannot bring forth proper results. John writes, "Whoever hates his brother is a murderer"(1 Jn 3:15)—hate in the heart (mind) does not just lead to murder; morally it *is* murder. In the story of Joseph, his brothers "hated him"—their internal hate was the root of the whole problem; his brothers "envied him" (Gen 37:4ff).

So this is where true spirituality in the Christian life rests—in the realm of our "thought-life." As believers we must understand the reality of communion with God and loving God—it must take place in the *"inward self"* (Mt 22:37). Therefore the real battle of man is in the world of ideas, rather than in that which is outward. Ideas are the stock of the *"thought-world,"* and from the ideas burst forth all things external—painting, music, buildings, love and hate. Where a man will spend eternity depends on his reading or hearing the truth content of the gospel, and his believing it. Thus, the battle for man is centrally in the world of "thought"—the spiritual battle, the loss or victory, is always in the thought-world. (104–122)

Consider the following with regard to your "thought-life"—While we are awake, our minds are almost *continually reflecting upon something.* Sometimes it's mere trivia . . . at other times it's focused on work or some activity we are doing . . . yet at other times it's entertaining issues and circumstances that challenge or provoke us in some way. It is in this last category where we are most confronted with *potentially sinful thoughts*—how we respond to these thoughts determines whether or not we are sinning. Being as our "default mode" is our fleshly nature (our sin disposition), it is only logical that we frequently entertain thoughts about *subject matters that potentially lead to sin*—these may include being critical or angry with others, thinking negatively about others, entertaining juicy gossip, envying and being jealous of others, dwelling on immoral and lustful thoughts, dwelling on relationship issues that perturb us, thinking vengeful thoughts, thinking derogatory thoughts about others, being angry because of negative circumstances, being angry due to world injustice, political anger, sports-world anger, traffic anger, impatience with life, frustration with circumstances, and even being angry with God because we lost our job, we have been stricken with cancer, we have been hospitalized, our kids don't like us anymore, our teenage daughter has come home pregnant, our car broke down, our spouse is angry with us, or our business partner is suing us for everything we own. Obviously, the foregoing is a pretty short list of things—but it is sufficiently long enough to *make us mindful of how often we entertain "sinful thoughts."* The truth of the matter is—whether we admit it or not—each of us sins over and over and over again in our "thought life" throughout the course of a day . . . because of the *"sin disposition"* that dwells in us! What compounds the problem of our thought-life, are the *strong feelings and desires* that frequently accompany our thoughts—hence, the difficulty of refraining from dwelling on potentially sinful matters.

THE "THOUGHT LIFE" OF THE BELIEVER

Temptation generally starts as a subtle voice in the back of "our mind"—if it is allowed to germinate, it results in sin (Jam 1:14–15). At the earliest moment of recognition we must apply sudden death to it, or it will plant its deadly seed within us. **Dr. Caroline Leaf,** one of the world's leading authorities on the "cognitive neuroscientific aspects of the brain," has studied the brain and the "science of thought" for more than 30 years. She is a devout Christian with a PhD in "Communication Pathology" from the *University of Pretoria* in South Africa. Dr. Leaf says the average person thinks over 30,000 thoughts a day (our minds never rest while we are awake). Think about that number with the understanding that many of our thoughts have a fleshly orientation and are evil in nature—since evil thoughts have an "ally" in our flesh, they can be extremely stubborn and difficult to overcome once they are firmly implanted. Dr. Leaf goes on to say that 87–95% of all the illnesses we experience are a direct result of our "toxic thoughts"—our thoughts quickly influence our emotions, which in turn cause a physical reaction in our body; <u>positive emotions</u> cause our body to release helpful chemicals; <u>negative emotions</u> cause the release of harmful chemicals. By not controlling our thoughts, we create the conditions for illness—research shows that "fear alone" triggers more than 1400 known physical and chemical responses, and activates more than 30 different hormones in the body. Science believes that thoughts are basically <u>neurological responses to stimuli</u> that are shaped by past experiences—therefore it is important for us to exercise extreme care with regard to what stimuli we allow to enter into our thought processes. Toxic waste generated by "toxic thoughts" causes the following illnesses: diabetes, cancer, asthma, skin problems, and allergies just to name a few. Everything we see, hear, or read has the potential to shape our thinking, and what we think about affects us physically and emotionally. Dr. Leaf's message to both Christian and secular audiences is that <u>they detox their brains by consciously controlling their thought lives</u>—this means engaging interactively with every single thought we have, and analyzing it before we decide to accept it or reject it. Her message parallels that of the apostle Paul: <u>*"Bring every thought captive to the obedience of Christ"*</u> (2 Cor 10:5). Our mind will either be our best friend or our worst enemy—it all depends on how we choose to use it (Leaf, *Who Switched Off My Brain?*).

Richard Rohr, a popular writer, Franciscan Friar, and Catholic Priest, citing psychological studies, says 90–96% of our thoughts are repetitive and generally negative, and that many Christians mistakenly believe that their "thought life" actually has a life of its own; that their thoughts are so strong that they dictate what goes on inside their heads, rather than they themselves. *The truth is we are the masters of our thoughts, and the controllers of our self talk*. Surprisingly, many Christians believe that Satan somehow controls their thoughts and that they are just too weak to resist him, but that is not what scripture teaches—"Greater is He who is in you than he who is in the world" (1 Jn 4:4). Because our thoughts have much to do with the *"formation of our character,"* we must be extremely concerned about what goes on in our thought life. Those who would not fall prey to Satan's devices must guard the avenues of the soul—they must avoid reading, seeing or listening to anything that causes impure thoughts; furthermore, the mind must not be left to wander at random upon every subject the adversary of our soul suggests (Phil 4:8; 1 Pet 1:13–15). This requires earnest prayer and unceasing watchfulness, aided by a diligent study of the Word, and the power of the Holy Spirit (Ps 119:9, 11; Prv 4:23; Mt 26:41; Jn 14:26; 16:13; Rom 8:6; 12:2; 2 Cor 10:5; Phil 4:6; 2 Tim 3:16–17). Guarding the gates of our minds against the invasion of sinful thoughts is a *continual responsibility* for the believer (Rohr, *Hope Against Darkness*).

Ralph Waldo Emerson said, "A man is what he thinks about all day long." Your thought life determines the life you live, who you are, and what you become (Prv 4:23; 23:7). *Either you master and rule your thoughts, or they will master and rule you*—our thoughts influence our feelings, choices and behaviors; therefore, we must monitor our thought life so that it is spiritually healthy. **Dr. Don Colbert** is the medical director of *Divine Health Wellness Center* in Orlando, Florida, and the author of more than 40 books, including the New York Times Best Seller, *"The Seven Pillars of Health."* Over the years, he has worked with thousands of people who have discovered that once they made a *sincere effort* to tackle their dysfunctional thought patterns, they experienced a significant reduction in depression, anxiety, anger, grief, shame, jealousy, and all other toxic emotions. Dr. Colbert maintains that replacing Satan's lies with God's truth is not really that difficult—*"it just takes intentional and consistent effort."* He goes on to say that replacing toxic negative thoughts with spiritually healthy thoughts requires an ongoing intentional study of the Word (Colbert, *Deadly Emotions*). Remember the words

(continued)

of Jesus: "If you abide in My word . . . you shall know the truth, and the truth shall make you free" (Jn 8:31–32).

Dr. James P. Porowski is the Director of *Family Life Resource*, a counseling center in Raleigh, North Carolina, and Professor of Child and Family Development at *Southeastern Baptist Theological Seminary*. He says that unsuccessful attempts at changing one's thought patterns results from an <u>unwillingness to change them</u>, because they simply enjoy their misery, woundedness, lustfulness or pride more than they desire godliness. He goes on to say that the Holy Spirit empowers the change process when we are truly repentant and want His control (Gal 5:17; Jam 4:8). Mind control is the responsibility of all growing Christians. Toxic negative thoughts are the enemies of a victorious life—if you give attention to toxic thoughts, they will intensify significantly and sin will result (Porowski, *With All My Mind*).

Controlling our "thoughts" is neither easy, nor is it a spontaneous action—it is a battle! And if you are not into fighting this battle you are going to be defeated (Eph 6:11–18; 1 Tim 4:7; 6:12). The devil's attack is focused primarily on the thoughts of our minds. Together with the flesh, Satan interjects *"toxic thoughts"* into our minds—these thoughts need to be quickly removed with holy aggression and replaced with "spiritually healthy thoughts" (Rom 12:2; Col 3:1–2; Phil 4:8). God's plan for you is to have an abundant and victorious life (Jn 10:10), and that means experiencing victory over sin, Satan, and the flesh. Why are people anxious, depressed, loveless, angry, worldly and immoral? The origin of all such problems lies in the thought life. Nearly every *"mental illness"* and psychological disorder is the result of a toxic thought life—depression, low self-esteem, anxiety disorders, schizophrenia, paranoia, psychotic illness, personality disorders, psychosexual disorders, sleep disorders, reactive disorders, excessive grief. Remember, if you allow impure destructive thoughts to germinate in your mind—sin will conceive; be it in the heart or outward expression (Jam 1:14–15).

So what practical steps can a believer take to develop a spiritually healthy thought life? There are four things a believer can do, and each one of them is absolutely essential: *1)* <u>You must have a daily quiet time with the Lord</u>—this is the number one priority; it is the Word of God in conjunction with the Spirit that lifts us out of ruts, gives us hope, and renews our minds (Rom 10:17; Gal 5:16; Col 3:16; 2 Tim 3:16–17; Jam 4:8; 1 Pet 2:2). The spiritual impact of not having communion with God, can be likened to your body going without physical nourishment—without spiritual manna you will suffer spiritual paralysis. *2) You must safeguard those areas of your life you can control*—your reading, conversations, radio, television, movies, internet, music; if you compromise on this level and you will fall (Prv 4:23; 5:8; 7:25; Rom 13:14). *3) You must dwell upon the truths of God's Word*—set your mind on the things of the Spirit and those things which are above; things that are good, right, pure (Ps 1:1–3; 19:14; 119:11; Rom 8:6; 12:2; 2 Cor 10:5; Phil 4:8; Col 3:1–2). God wants us to be healthy and mature in our thinking (1 Cor 14:20; Phil 4:8–9). And *4) You must pray that you not enter into temptation*—by praying we humbly admit that we are ever in need of God's mercy and grace; none of us have the capacity to stand in our own strength (Mt 6:13; 26:41; 2 Cor 12:9–10; Eph 6:18). Remember the encouraging words of the Lord to the prophet Isaiah: "God will keep him in perfect peace whose mind is stayed on Thee" (Is 26:3; Rom 8:5–6; Phil 4:6–9).

To change our thoughts is to "change our life"—the process of sanctification starts with the "renewal of our thoughts" (Rom 12:2; Eph 4:23). Obviously, we will never achieve sinless perfection in this life, but we are to "press on toward that goal" (Phil 3:12–14; 1 Pet 1:15; 2 Pet 3:18). The reality of the Christian life is that it includes a lot of joy, suffering, and sin (Jn 15:11; Rom 14:17; Gal 5:22; Rom 8:17; Phil 1:29; 3:10; 2 Tim 2:3; 1 Pet 4:1, 13; 5:10; Mt 6:12; Phil 3:12; Jam 3:2; 1 Jn 1:10)—*we are all a work in progress* (2 Cor 3:18). To the degree that we press on toward the goal, and fight the good fight of faith, and cultivate an intimate relationship with Christ . . . to that degree we will experience the joy of the Lord and the fruit of the Spirit in our lives. The more we sin and the less we strive with God, the more chastening we will experience, the darker our world will be, and the greater our pain will be (Ps 32:3–4, 9; Prv 18:14; Rom 5:3–5; Heb 12:4–11; 1 Pet 4:12). The Christian life is a *"lifelong journey"* in which the believer is exhorted to press on to maturity and cooperate with the Holy Spirit in order that he might become conformed to the "image of Christ" (Rom 8:28–29; 12:2; 2 Cor 3:18; Phil 2:12–13; 3:13–14; I Jn 3:1–3); and central to this transforming work is the believer's *"thought life."* May your prayer be that of the psalmist David: "Let the words of my mouth and the meditation of my heart be acceptable in Thy sight, O LORD, my rock and my redeemer" (Ps 19:14; 26:2). Remember, without cultivating an intimate relationship with Christ (Phil 3:10; Jam 4:8), setting your mind on the things of the Spirit (Rom 8:6; Col 3:1–2), fighting the fight of faith (1 Tim 6:12), and growing in grace (2 Pet 3:18), your progress in sanctification will be minimal (Jn 15:4–5; 1 Cor 3:12–15; Gal 6:7–8). This is your calling (1 Th 4:3a).

The apostle Paul tells us not to worry or be anxious about anything, but to dwell only on those things that are true *and* honorable *and* right *and* pure *and* lovely *and* worthy of praise (Phil 4:6–9). That's a tall order, but that is the imperative God gives us as Christians. Humbling, is it not? By the way, God would not tell us to do something that is not possible. The Bible teaches that we *can* control what we think, so we cannot offer as a defense that "we simply cannot help it when our minds are filled with unwelcome thoughts." The fact of the matter is we *can* help it. The secret lies in *"thinking godly thoughts"* rather than *"fleshly thoughts"*—the most enlightened psychologists and psychiatrists of the day have come to agree with the Apostle Paul on this matter—thus they stress the dangers of negative thinking. The essence of Paul's teaching here in Philippians is that God does not garrison (v. 7) the thought-life of a man who does not *want* it to be kept pure. Obviously, the believer who desires true spirituality must be diligent in guarding his mind. The "key" to being successful in the war of the mind is *becoming proficient at wielding the sword of the Spirit—the Word of God—against all sinful thoughts and forces of darkness* (Eph 6:10–17).

Next, let's consider the Christian life in relation to "psychological problems." This is the problem of man's separation from himself, and his relationship to himself in the world of thought. Just as God is a person—he thinks, acts, and feels—so, we are persons who think, act, and feel. Therefore as humans we are *personal, rational,* and *moral* beings. God created us in His image. As a result of the fall, however, we are separated from God and trying to exist outside the realm in which God made us to exist—as such, we are trying to be what we are not. As Schaeffer puts it, "our rationality damns us . . . by not bowing to God, with a loud shout of rationality, we simply end up jumping in the dark, and are torn within ourselves." It is not enough for man to rationally begin with himself and work outward—his very existence demands purpose . . . being the sinful man that he is, he is not able to bring resolution to such demands; he is not only confounded by his limitations, and naturally "separated from himself," but knows nothing of a tranquil heart that is at peace.

In the area of "morality" we find exactly the same thing. Man cannot escape the fact of the notions of a true right and wrong in himself—not just a sociological or hedonistic morality, but true morality, true right and true wrong. Yet beginning with himself he can neither bring forth *"absolute standards"* nor keep the *"poor relative ones"* he has set up. Thus in the area of morality, as in the area of rationality, trying to be what he is not, he is crushed and damned by what he is. *Man is thus divided against and from himself in every part of his nature*—he is divided from himself because of his rebellion—in rationality, in morality, in his thinking, in his acting, in his feeling . . . by rebellion he is *divided from God* by true moral guilt, and he is damned by what he is—wanting to be God, which obviously he is not, because he is not infinite. At some level of consciousness man cannot forget the fact that he is *"finite man"*—surely at some point there will be a cry within him, that there must be a real answer in this life to the "separation from himself." And the answer is an emphatic, "Yes, thank God, there is!"

How is it that the psychologists who act as if God is there *(but merely pragmatically),* like Carl Gustaf Jung, are able to help their patients to some degree? Schaeffer writes, "I think it is because that which really helps is always in the direction of *the reality of what is.*" At least a man like Jung has the word *"God"*—behind which there may be at least a sense of some *universal purpose* accepted blindly and irrationally, as Viktor Frankl does. And this is the proper direction. To these men these things are a piece of theater; but without their really knowing it, it *is* in the direction of what is. The fact is—*He really is there,* a personal God, who is holy in a moral sense. Not bowing to Him, however, they do not acknowledge Him for who He really is—yet pragmatically they find they must *act* as if He is there.

To say there is "no real guilt" is futile, for man as he is knows that there is "real moral guilt." But when I know the real guilt is really met by Christ, so that I do not need to fear to look at the basic questions deep inside myself, then I can see that the *feeling of guilt* that is left is really just *"psychological guilt,"* and only that. This does not mean to say that psychological guilt is still not cruel—but now I can be open with it and see it for what it is. *This also does not mean that we will be perfect in this life psychologically any more than we are physically.* But thanks be to God, now I can move forward, not expecting to be perfect. We will wait for the second coming of Jesus Christ and the resurrection of the body, to be perfect morally, physically, and psychologically—but there *now* can be a *substantial overcoming* of this psychological division in the present life on the basis of Christ's finish work. It will not be perfect, but it can be real and substantial. Let's be very clear about this—all men since the fall have had some psychological problems. It is utter nonsense to say that a Christian never has a psychological problem. *All men have psychological problems.* They differ in degree and they differ in kind, but since the fall all men have more or less a problem psychologically—that is the essence of "fallen man." None of us are even close to perfection.

A very practical thing for ourselves and for those whom we would help is that it is not always possible to sort out *true guilt* from *psychological guilt*—at this point the *"iceberg concept"* is helpful once again. Man is more than is on the surface. All too often the evangelical Christian acts as though there is nothing to man except that which is above the surface on the water. Since the fall *man is divided from himself,* and so since the fall *there is that which I am which is below the surface*—in psychological terms, there is the unconscious, subconscious aspect of our humanity. It should not be a surprise to any of us that there is something which we are which is deeper than that which is on the surface—hence, as we said earlier, it is not even possible to say at this given moment that we are perfect, free from all known sin. This is true even at our best moments (1 Cor 4:3–4). We all have our problems . . . we all have our storms . . . and some of us can have exceedingly deep storms. In the midst of these storms that break over us, it is wonderful to know that we ourselves do not need, in every case, to sort out true guilt from psychological guilt. God knows the line between our true guilt and our guilt feelings (Heb 4:12). Our part is to function in that which is *above the surface,* and to ask God to help us be honest. Our part is to cry to God for the part of the iceberg that is above the surface and confess whatever we know is true guilt there, bringing it under the infinite, finished work of Jesus Christ . . . *and God graciously applies this to the whole,* and gradually the Holy Spirit helps us see deeper into ourselves. Once we have applied the blood of Christ to all our known sin, we can be confident that the *guilty feelings* that remain are not true guilt, but a part of *the awful miseries of fallen man.* The comprehension, moment by moment, of these things is a vital step in *freedom from the results of the bonds of sin,* and in the substantial healing of the separation of man from himself. (123–133)

"REPENTANCE OF THE BELIEVER"

It is generally supposed by many Christians that repentance is only the gateway of faith; that it is necessary only at the <u>beginning of the Christian life</u> (Mt 3:2; Mk 1:15; Lk 24:47; Acts 2:38; 17:30; 2 Cor 7:10; 2 Pet 3:9). But there is a very distinct repentance that is <u>necessary for "believers" as well</u>—if they are to grow in grace. God tells the churches of Ephesus and Laodicea in Revelation 2–3 to <u>"repent."</u> The **Ephesians** were reminded of the height from which they had fallen; as such, they were told to repent and return to their first love (Rev 2:5; Mt 22:37). The **Laodiceans** had become spiritually lukewarm and spiritually indifferent; God reminded them that He rebukes and chastens those whom He loves; thus they needed to be zealous and repent (Rev 3:19; Heb 12:6). The promise to those who repent is that "Jesus will dine with them" (Rev 3:20); the picture is one of intimacy and enjoying one another's company. The apostle **Peter,** after his threefold denial of the Lord Jesus, was said to have "wept bitterly" (Mt 26:75); experiencing the emotional component of repentance. **David** frequently expressed his repentant grief over his sin (2 Sam 12:7-13; Ps 32:3-4; 40:12; 119:176). Godly sorrow will lead to the open acknowledgment, confession, and repudiation of sin—read David's two penitential psalms (Ps 32:5 and 51:3-4). **Job,** likewise, repented or turned from his sin (Job 42:1-6). When **Martin Luther** nailed his 95 theses to the door of the Wittenberg Church on October 31, 1517, his very first thesis was on "repentance." It read—<u>"When our Lord and Master Jesus Christ said, "Repent," He willed the entire life of believers to be one of repentance."</u>

The Greek word translated "repent" is "metanoeo"—it is a compound word made up of two words: The first word <u>"meta"</u> indicates a change or transformation, and appears in many English words,

(continued)

such as "metamorphosis," which means a change in condition. The second word is from the root word *"nous,"* which we translate "mind." So *metanoeo* literally means to *"change your mind"*—by extension it means to turn about, to express regret or adopt another view. Whenever the Bible says you should repent or turn away from unrighteousness, its main emphasis is on your will, changing your mind or purpose—thus turning to God from unrighteousness is a function of the mind. The fact that God *demands* repentance shows that it involves the mind—it is something we must *choose* to do. A Christian's mind plays a vital role in his relationship with God as he learns what God expects of him and chooses to please Him (Rom 12:2; 2 Tim 2:15; 3:16–17; 1 Pet 2:2). So biblical repentance has an *intellectual* component (change in thinking) . . . an *emotional* component (remorse and godly sorrow) . . . and a *volitional* component (an inward turning from sin to God), which is evidenced by fruit (Mt 3:8; Lk 13:5–9; Acts 26:20).

In what sense do we "repent as believers"? John Wesley asked the question: "Are we *fully purified* from a carnal mind . . . and *wholly transformed* into the image of Him that created us? Far from it!" he says. "We still retain a depth of sin . . . there still remains a whole body of sin in our hearts, weakened indeed, but clearly not destroyed . . . and it is the consciousness of this indwelling sin which constrains us to groan for a full deliverance . . . and cry out in our souls"—

> *I sin in every breath I draw,*
> *Nor do Thy will, nor keep Thy Law*
> *On earth, as angels do above:*
>
> *But still the fountain open stands,*
> *Washes my feet, my heart, my hands,*
> *Till I am perfected in love.*

Writes Wesley: "It is not seldom long before he who imagined all sin was gone, that he sees an overwhelming evidence of it in his life." Let's recount the ways—*we think more highly of ourselves than others* (sin of pride) . . . *we feel self-will in the heart*; a will that is contrary to the will of God . . . *we feel the desire of the flesh*, the *desire of the eye*, and *the pride of life* . . . without continually watching and praying, we feel the assaults of inordinate affection and become lovers of pleasure more than lovers of God . . . we find within ourselves *attitudes that are contrary to the love of our neighbors*—jealousy, envy, evil surmisings, criticisms, malice, hatred, anger, and outright bitterness . . . we find <u>*resentment and revenge*</u> in our hearts when we are injured or affronted, especially against those whom we had labored to help or oblige in some way . . . we see how <u>*covetous*</u> we are when we discover how tight a grip we have on our money, and how much we desire more of it . . . we see how *"carnal"* we are, and how prone we are to *"<u>wander</u>"* and depart from the God we love . . . and how sin cleaves to <u>*our words*</u>—many are mixed with sin, but some are altogether sinful (backbiting, tale-bearing, gossip, and outright lies); as Wesley says, "much sin cleaves to even the best conversation of believers." And then there is the matter of our *"<u>sins of omission</u>"*—writes Paul, "To the one who knows the right thing to do, and does not do it, to him it is sin" (Jam 4:17). Are there not a thousand instances where we might have done good—be it to our enemies, to strangers, to friends, to our brothers, and did not do it? How many opportunities to share the faith have we neglected? So aware was that holy man, **Archbishop Usher**, of his sinfulness, that he cried out with almost his dying breath—*"<u>Lord, forgive me my sins of omission!</u>"* Yet even besides these outward omissions, do we not also find within ourselves <u>*inward defects without number*</u>? It is good for us to remember the confessions of Job, Isaiah, Peter, and Paul—

- **Job**—"I abhor myself, and repent in dust and ashes" (Job 42:6).
- **Isaiah**—"Woe is me, for I am ruined! Because I am a man of unclean lips" (Is 6:5).
- **Peter**—"Depart from me, for I am a sinful man, O Lord" (Lk 5:8).
- **Paul**—"I know that nothing good dwells in me, that is, in my flesh" (Rom 7:18).

Writes Wesley: "By all the grace which is given at justification we cannot extirpate [our sinful dispositions]. . . . therefore, if there be no <u>*instantaneous deliverance after justification*</u> [of all sinful behavior in this life] . . . if there be none but a <u>*gradual work of God,*</u> then we must be content, as much as we can be, to remain [in this condition] till death." Because of the presence of sin in our lives as believers, <u>*we are to live lives of repentance*</u>—unless we do so, we will not grow . . . and unless we understand our disease, we will live despairing lives. We must believe the glad tidings of the great salvation of the gospel of Christ that God has prepared for us—we must believe the He is able to save to the uttermost all that come to God through Him . . . that He is able to save us from all the sin

(continued)

that still remains in our hearts . . . that He is able to save us from all the sin that cleaves to all our words and actions . . . that He is able to save us from sins of omission, and supply all that is lacking within us. It is true, this is impossible with man; but with God all things are possible (Mt 19:26).

Therefore, as believers, we must continue to believe in Him that loved us and gave Himself for us—and when we go from faith to faith, and have faith to be cleansed from indwelling sin, and faith to be saved from all our uncleanness, then we may say with full assurance, <u>*"Every moment, Lord, I have the merit of Your death!"*</u> For by faith in the life, death, and resurrection of Jesus Christ, and His continual intercession for us, we are being renewed moment by moment, and being fully cleansed. Furthermore, there is neither condemnation for us now, nor punishment awaiting us in the future as was the case before. The Lord is continually at work within us, cleansing both our hearts and our lives. By <u>repentance</u> we feel the sin remaining in our hearts, and cleaving to our words and actions; and by <u>faith</u> we receive the power of God in Christ, purifying our hearts, and cleansing our hands. By <u>repentance</u> we have an abiding conviction that there is no help in us; by <u>faith</u> we receive not only mercy, but grace to help at every point of need.

> *Repentance says, "Without Him I can do nothing."*
> *Faith says, "I can do all things through Christ who strengthens me."*

Therefore, through Christ we can love God with all our heart, mind, soul, and strength, and walk in holiness and righteousness before Him. Will we do so perfectly? Of course not. We inhabit sinful flesh. Richard Owen Roberts in his book, *"Repentance: The First Word of the Gospel,"* gives us some practical advice—<u>*"practice immediate repentance!"*</u> Since intimacy is broken by sin, "seek to walk with God in such a way that there is no accumulation of sin or even any time lag in dealing with sin." And in spite of your efforts, know this—the operative grace of God is continually producing in you that which is pleasing in His sight. As difficult as that is to believe, that is the miracle of "grace!" Without which "none of us" would see the Lord. Read Jn 6:39; 17:12; 18:9; Rom 8:28–33; 2 Cor 4:17; Eph 1:5; Phil 1:6; 2:13; 1 Th 5:23–24; Heb 13:21.

(Much of the foregoing material was extracted from a sermon John Wesley preached at Londonderry—April 24, 1767)

Though there is the possibility of "substantial healing," that does not mean "perfect healing." The Bible makes the possibility of miracles very clear, but both Scripture and experience show that while sometimes God does heal, sometimes He does not. Furthermore, this is not always a matter of faith, or of the lack of faith—God is personal, and He has His own purposes. It is exactly the same with psychological healing—a person may be healed psychologically but that does not mean he will become psychologically perfect the rest of his life. Lazarus was raised from the dead, but no doubt suffered physical infirmity at various times the rest of his life—he may even have had psychological depression; we must remember that eventually he died again. *The results of the fall will continue until the second coming of Christ.* We deny the doctrine of the fall, and we build a new romanticism, if we fail to accept the reality of our limitations, including our psychological struggles. Thus we lose "substantially" in beating ourselves to bits, trying to be what we cannot be. This is not only true in the psychological area, but is also true in all the *relationships of life*—some married couples believe they must have the *"ideal love affair"* of the century just because they are who they are. Such couples refuse to have less than what they have set as a romantic ideal, forgetting that the fall is the fall. Another may want *"sexual experience"* beyond what one can have in the midst of the results of the fall—thus you see marriages destroyed simply because they have set such proud standards and refuse to have the good marriage they can have.

The basic psychological problem is "trying to be what we are not." The basic problem for us as believers is *"not being willing to be the creatures we are before the Creator."* We need to *"be real."* Since the fall, we all have points of weakness—with some of us it tends to be physical, with others it tends to be psychological. Fear can be small, or it can be the horror of great despair—many modern men who have come to a philosophy of despair have gone through the horror of a great darkness. Many psychologists, for example Carl Gustav Jung, will meet this fear simply by telling the patient to *"act as if God were there!"* Alcoholics Anonymous attendees refer to it as *"their higher power!"* The wonderful truth for the Christian is the fact that *"God really is there!"* And He really loves and cares for us! So whenever we find these points of tension and conflict within us, we are not at a dead end, because the blood of Jesus Christ can cleanse us from all true guilt, not just once—but as many times as we need it! There is *always* the possibility of a *truly new start* within a totally rational framework—because of the redemptive work of Christ on the cross.

In this modern age we have become very much aware of psychology and "psychological problems" as never before. Though modern psychology often provides valuable insights, this is not enough because it is an *insufficient base*. If men act and live according to the teaching of the Word of God, however, they have in practice a *sufficient psychological base*. There is no real answer to man's psychological need and crushing load apart from the Creator-creature framework, the comprehension of the fall, and the redemptive work of Christ on the cross. God is good to His people. Therefore, to the extent that a man lives in the light of the command of Scripture, he has a solid psychological foundation. If, as believers, we refuse our place as the *creature* before the Creator and do not commit ourselves to Him for His use, this is *"sin"*—and anything else is also *"misery."* To live moment by moment through faith on the basis of the blood of Christ, in the power of the Holy Spirit, is the only really integrated way to live. Furthermore, this is the only way to be at rest with yourself—to do otherwise is to throw away your own place of peace and rest. As Christians, we are not just acting *"as if,"* like the secular psychologists recommend, we are actually following the invitation of the infinite-personal Creator—*"Cast all your care upon Me, because I care for you!"* (1 Pet 5:7). God says, *"Come to Me and I will give you rest"* (Mt 11:28)—this is not only an invitation to the non-Christian, but to the Christian as well. God invites us to roll our cares upon Him, and not someone else.

As believers we stand in a "living relationship" with a living God who loves us, to the extent that Jesus died on the cross for us. *Fear diminishes* when we see we are not giving ourselves to impersonal situations, or a world of men devoid of eternal wisdom—but we are offering ourselves to God who loves us, and He is not a monster, but our heavenly Father. Furthermore, He will not use us as a weapon without showing tremendous care for the weapon itself. To the extent that we bow our will in practice to God in this present life, we will experience communion with God, and not be divided against ourselves. This is the meaning of *true spirituality* in our relationship to ourselves. (134–147)

Regarding substantial healing in "personal relationships," the key is the fact that God is a *personal* God; the emphasis on His *"personality."* Throughout Scripture God deals with us on the basis of who He is, and what He has made us—as such, He always deals with us on a basis of *personal relationship*. It is always a person-to-person relationship—His dealing with us is *never mechanical*. Of course there is the distinction that He is the Creator and we are creatures—therefore in all our thoughts and acts toward God we must keep the creature-Creator relationship in mind. This, however, does not alter the "person-to-person nature" of our relationship. The command for man is to *"love God* with all his heart, soul, and mind" (Mt 22:37)—as such, God is satisfied with nothing less than our loving Him. *We were created to be in "personal fellowship with God and to love Him."* Prayer is to be seen as a person-to-person communication with God, not merely some kind of devotional exercise. Conversely, our thinking must not be just *things about God*, but a *relationship with God*—loving, embracing, praising and worshipping Him.

Man, having put "himself" rather than God at the center of the universe, constantly tends to turn *inward* instead of outward. He has made himself the last integration point of the universe. This is the essence of his rebellion against God. When we turn *"inward,"* there is no one to communicate with—this is the tragedy of man. This not only leads to *psychological problems,* but it also *destroys our relationships with others*. We must recognize that no human relationships are going to be supremely sufficient—*the only ultimate sufficient relationship can be with God Himself.* When our relationship with God is that preeminent relationship in life, *our human relationships* can be valid without being the ultimate sufficient thing. As sinners, acknowledging that we are "not perfect" in this life, we do not need to cast away every human relationship, including the relationship of marriage, or the relationships of fellow-Christians inside the church, just because they prove not to be perfect. On the basis of the finished work of Christ, it is possible, once we have seen this, to begin to understand that our relationships can be *substantially healed* in the present life. By the way, since we are finite, do not expect to find *final sufficiency* in any human relationship, including marriage—final sufficiency can only be found in our relationship with God. In this matter of "human relationships," always keep in mind that all men are God's image-bearers. (148–180)

CHAPTER 20

A summary of the book...

"SLAVE"

by John MacArthur

To be a Christian is to be a "wholehearted follower of Jesus Christ." Jesus said the following: "My sheep hear My voice and *they follow Me*" (Jn 10:27) ... "If you continue in My word, then you are truly disciples of Mine" (Jn 8:31) ... "If you wish to come after Me, you must deny yourself, and take up your cross daily and *follow Me*" (Lk 9:23; Jn 12:26). Time and again throughout the pages of Scripture, believers are referred to as *slaves of God* and *slaves of Christ*. We are told to obey Christ without question, and follow Him without complaint—Jesus Christ is *our Master* and *our Owner;* we are His possessions; He is the King, and we are *His subjects*.

The Greek word for slave is *"doulos"*—it appears 124 times in the original text. The *problem* is that it has been translated *"servant"* (rather than "slave") in nearly every instance in the various English translations of the Bible. While it is true that the duties of slave and servant may overlap to some degree, there is a key distinction between the two—servants are *hired;* slaves are *owned*. Servants have an element of freedom in choosing whom they work for and what they do; slaves, on the other hand, have no freedom, autonomy, or rights. In the Greco-Roman world, slaves were considered *property*—they were regarded as *things* rather than *persons*.

So, why have modern English translations consistently mistranslated *"doulos"*? There are at least three answers to this question. **First,** given the *stigmas attached to "slavery" in Western society,* translators have understandably wanted to avoid any association between biblical teaching and the slave trade of the British Empire and the American Colonial era. For the modern reader today, the word *"slave"* does not conjure up images of Greco-Roman society, but rather depicts an unjust system of oppression that was finally ended by parliamentary rule in England and by civil war in the United States. In order to avoid both potential confusion and negative imagery, modern translators replaced slave language with servant language. **Second,** from a historical perspective, in late-medieval times it was common to translate *doulos* from the Latin word *servus*, which is more naturally translated "servant." **Third,** the term "slave" in 16th century England generally depicted someone in *physical chains or in prison*—since this is quite different from the Greco-Roman idea of slavery, the translators of early English versions (like the King James and Geneva Bible) opted for a word they felt better represented Greco-Roman slavery in their culture—that word was servant. But whatever the rationale behind the change, something significant is lost in translation when *doulos* is rendered *"servant"* rather than *"slave."* The gospel is not simply an invitation to become Christ's associate; it is a mandate to become His slave.

Early Christian leaders, like ***Ignatius*** (he died around AD 110) and his co-workers, saw themselves as *"fellow slaves of Christ."* ***Polycarp*** (AD 69–155) instructed the Philippians, "Bind up your loose robes and serve as God's slaves in reverential fear and truth." ***Augustine*** (AD 354–430) asked his congregation this question, "Does the Lord not deserve to have you as his trustworthy slave?" ***Chrysostom*** (AD 347–407) comforted those who were in physical bondage with these words, "You are the slave of Christ; He is your Master." ***Charles Spurgeon*** (1834–1892) states, "Where our Authorized King James Version softly puts it *servant*, it really is *bond-slave*. The early saints delighted to count themselves Christ's absolute property, bought by Him, owned by Him, and wholly at His disposal. The ***Apostle Paul*** even went so far as to rejoice that he had "the marks of his Master's brand on him." The Scottish pastor **Alexander Maclaren**, a contemporary of Spurgeon, echoed these same truths: "The true position, then, for a man is to be God's slave . . . absolute submission, unconditional obedience, on the slave's part; and on the part of the Master complete ownership, the right of life and death." There are numerous other individuals who expressed the same message throughout the history of the Christian Church.

Our slavery to Christ has radical implications for how we think and live. We have been *bought with a price* . . . we *belong to Christ* . . . we are part of a people for *His own possession*. True Christianity is not about adding Jesus to *my life*—instead it is about devoting myself completely *to Him;* submitting wholly to His will and seeking to please Him (by believing and obeying Him) above all else. It demands dying to self and following the Master, no matter the cost. Hence, to be a Christian is to be *"Christ's slave."* (1–24)

Slavery was a pervasive social structure in the first-century Roman Empire. About one-fifth of the empire's population were slaves. Initially, the Roman slave population came through military conquests, but by the first century the majority of slaves inherited their place in society by being born into slavery. Most slaves, then, had never known freedom. For many slaves, life was *difficult*—especially for those who worked in the mines or on farms. Slaves who lived in the cities, working alongside their masters as part of the household, life was often considerably *easier*. Depending on their training and on their masters' needs, slaves functioned as teachers, cooks, shopkeepers, and even doctors—slaves were involved in a wide variety of occupations. *Household slaves* received greater honor than other slaves because they worked more closely with their masters—they would do such things as take care of their master's children, manage his house, or even administrate his business interests. A wicked slave was a great liability and could cause serious damage to the owner's welfare; but a loyal hardworking slave was a wonderful asset to his master. Conversely, the faithful slave could look forward to possibly even receiving his freedom one day—a reward that owners often used to motivate their slaves toward full compliance. Slaves did not have to worry about where their next meal would come from or whether or not they would have a place to stay—their sole concern was to carry out the interests of their owner.

To be careful not to present an overly romantic impression of first-century slavery, being a slave was to be someone else's possession, totally subjugated to one's master in everything. The Greek philosopher *Aristotle* defined a slave as a human being who was considered an article of property, someone who belonged completely to another person. *Ancient Rome* viewed slaves the same way—"The slave had, in principle, no rights, no legal status whatsoever; he was a chattel owned by his master." One's experience as a slave, then, ultimately depended on the demands and goodness of the master—one's life could be miserable, or exponentially better. Slavery in the Roman world was as diverse as the number of masters who owned slaves. Each slave owner defined the nature of his slaves' lives. For their part, slaves had only one primary objective—*to please the master in everything* through their loyal obedience to him.

Jesus and the apostles spoke about slavery, using it as an illustration to describe the Christian life. But to fully understand this New Testament metaphor, we also need to briefly consider slavery as it existed in Old Testament Israel. The Hebrew word for slave *"ebed"* appears in the Old Testament 799 times as a noun and another 290 times as a verb—so this was a common word during Old Testament times. The most fundamental meaning of *ebed* is also that of a *"slave."* Slavery was part of Israel's history from her earliest days as a nation. *Joseph* was sold into bondage by his brothers . . . the descendants of Jacob (renamed *Israel*) were eventually enslaved by the Egyptians. The exodus of the children of Israel from Egypt did not give them complete autonomy; rather, it issued them into a different kind of bondage—they now became *"the Lord's possession"* (Ex 19:5). Later God told Moses, "The Israelites are My slaves whom I brought out of the land of Egypt" (Lev 25:55). The Hebrew people had been delivered from one master in order to serve another. God would be their sovereign King, and they would be His loyal subjects. Sadly, throughout Israel's history, the Jews frequently forgot that God was their Master—God responded by allowing the surrounding nations to conquer and oppress them. If His people were unwilling to be His slaves, they would once again become the slaves of their enemies. The book of Judges details Israel's repeated failures in this regard. In spite of the nation's unfaithfulness, God remained faithful—He was always quick to deliver His people, when they cried out to Him in heartfelt repentance. The nation's idolatrous path eventually led to its complete removal from the promised land when they were exiled in Babylon . . . yet once again the Lord would deliver them (Ez 9:9). Many of Israel's heroes, including **Abraham, Moses, Joshua, David, Elijah, Nehemiah** and the *prophets*, are specifically referred to as *"His slaves"* (Jdg 2:8; 1 Kg 18:36; 2 Kg 18:12; Neh 1:5–6; Ps 89:3; 105:42; Is 48:20; Ezek 38:17; Dan 9:11). Like all slaves in the ancient world, their lives were characterized by the ideas of total dependence, the forfeiture of autonomy, and the sense of belonging wholly to another.

The believer's relationship to Christ is one of complete submission and subjugation to the Master. When the apostle **Paul** referred to himself as a *"slave of Christ"* (Rom 1:1; Gal 1:10; Phil 1:1; Tit 1:1), his readers knew exactly what he meant. Paul's life revolved around the Master—nothing else, including his own personal agenda, mattered. The blood brother of the Lord Jesus, *James,* writes: "If the Lord wills, we will live and do this or that" (Jam 4:13, 15). Such language draws heavily on the slave/master relationship; slaves could not go and do whatever they wished; they were bound to follow the will of the master. **Peter, Jude,** and *John* all likewise designated themselves as slaves bound to do the work of the Lord (2 Pet 1:1; Jude 1:1; Rev 1:1). The apostles eagerly embraced the title for themselves (Acts 4:29; 16:17; Col 1:7; 4:12; 2 Tim 2:24). Incidentally, the word *doulos*, or *slave*, is even used throughout the book of Revelation to describe *the believer's eternal relationship to the Lord* (Rev 7:3; 10:7; 19:2). All believers at the very end of Revelation are called slaves collectively (Rev 22:3–4). (25–38)

The truth of God's Word is always "countercultural," and the notion of becoming a *"slave"* is certainly no exception. Western society, in particular, places a high premium on personal liberty and freedom of choice. So, to present the good news in terms of a *"slave/master relationship"* runs contrary to everything our culture holds sacred. When one examines the teachings of Jesus, however, we find that many of His illustrations and parables were taken from the *"slave world"* of His day. Christ repeatedly used slave imagery as the best analogy to clarify profound spiritual realities. From His teaching we learn that slaves are not greater than their master . . . they are not privy to their master's plans . . . they are accountable to the master for how they use his resources, even in his absence . . . they are also liable for how they treat their fellow slaves . . . they are expected to obey and honor their master without complaint, though the faithful slave will be honored for his diligent service (Mt 10:24; 18:23, 26–33; 24:45–50; 25:14–30; Lk 6:40; 12:37–47; 17:7–10; 19:13–22; Jn 13:16; 15:15–20). Discipleship, like slavery, entails a life of total self-denial, a humble disposition toward others, a wholehearted devotion to the Master alone, a willing to obey His commands, an eagerness to serve Him even in His absence, and a motivation that comes from knowing He is well pleased (Mt 24:44–46; 25:21; Mk 10:44; Lk 6:46; 12:37; 14:26–33; 16:13; Jn 14:15, 21). Though they were once the *slaves of sin*, Christ's followers receive spiritual freedom and rest for their souls through their saving relationship with Him (Jn 8:34, 36; Mt 11:28–30). A slave's life was one of complete surrender, submission, and service to the master—and the people of Jesus' day would have immediately recognized the parallel. Christ's invitation to follow Him was an invitation to that same kind of life. Consider the following *five parallels* between biblical Christianity and first-century slavery:

1. Exclusive Ownership—Roman law considered slaves to be property under the absolute control of an owner. Though we were born *"slaves of sin,"* we were purchased by Christ through His death on the cross (Rom 5:18–19; Eph 2:1–3; 1 Pet 1:18–19). We were bought with a price, therefore, we are no longer under the authority of sin . . . instead we are now *"slaves of righteousness"* (Rom 6:17–18), and Christ is our new Master. We are a "people for His own possession" (Tit 2:14) . . . we

belong to Christ Jesus (Gal 5:24) . . . we worship Him as our "Master in heaven" (Col 4:1). Just as first-century slaves would receive new names from their earthly masters, so will we each be given a new name from Christ. Believers in the eternal state will serve the Lord as His slaves forever (Rev 3:12; 22:4).

2. <u>Complete Submission</u>—Being a slave meant being always available to obey that person in every way. The slave's sole duty was to carry out the master's wishes. The New Testament repeatedly calls believers to faithfully obey the Master (Col 3:22–24; 1 Cor 6:19–20; Phil 1:22). Submission to the lordship of Christ—a heart attitude that works itself out in obedience to Him—is the defining mark of those who are genuinely converted (1 Jn 2:3; 3:22; 1 Pet 1:2; Rom 12:1; 1 Cor 6:20). The New Testament describes false teachers as "slaves of corruption" (2 Pet 2:19) . . . slaves of their own appetites (Rom 16:18). The true man of God, by contrast, is *"the Lord's slave"* making himself "useful to the Master, prepared for every good work" (2 Tim 2:24, 21).

3. <u>Singular Devotion</u>—Slaves had only one primary concern: to carry out the will of their master. Like slaves in the first century, we are to be fully devoted to our Master alone—*"you cannot serve God and mammon"* (Mt 6:24). Exclusive devotion makes it impossible to serve God and other masters at the same time. Believers are to *"please God"* in all things (Col 1:10; 1 Th 4:1; Rom 14:18); we are called to seek His glory in everything we do (1 Cor 10:31; Col 3:17).

4. <u>Total Dependence</u>—As part of the master's household, slaves were completely dependent on their owners for the basic necessities of life, including clothing, food, and shelter. Because their needs were met, they could focus entirely on serving the master. The parallels to the Christian life are striking—we can focus on the things God has called us to do, trusting Him to meet our needs. Jesus said, "Seek first My Kingdom and My righteousness, and I will provide for all your needs" (Mt 6:25–33; also 1 Tim 6:8). Paul writes, "My God shall supply all your needs according to His riches in glory in Christ Jesus" (Phil 4:19; also 2 Cor 9:8; 12:9).

5. Personal Accountability—In everything they did, first-century slaves were fully accountable to their owners. If the master was pleased, the slave would benefit accordingly; if the master was not pleased, the slave could expect appropriate discipline. Rewards and punishments provided powerful stimulation for slaves to work hard and do well. Believers likewise are to be impelled by the realization that one day they will stand before Christ and *"give an account"* (Rom 14:12; 2 Cor 5:10). Each of us, like the diligent slave pictured in Matthew 25, longs to hear the Lord say, *"Well done, good and faithful slave—enter into the joy of your Master!"* (Mt 25:21, 23). In the context of the early church, a significant number of believers also would have been Roman slaves. Paul encouraged believers to "obey your earthly masters . . . and to remember that they were ultimately serving the Lord, who will reward them" (Col 3:22–24; Eph 6:5–8). Christian masters also needed to remember that they had a "heavenly Master," and that they needed to deal justly and fairly with their slaves (Col 4:1; Eph 6:9). Knowing we have a *Master in heaven* should be a powerful motivational force for us as well. (39–54)

Scripture teaches that Jesus Christ is the "head of the church" (Eph 5:23; Col 1:18; also Eph 4:15; Col 2:19); to say that Christ is the head of the church is to say that He is the Lord and Master over the church. The overwhelming testimony of Scripture is that Jesus Christ is *"Lord of all"* (Rom 10:12; Phil 2:9–11), and the "Head over all things" (Eph 1:22). When we call Jesus "Lord," we are acknowledging Him as our sole Master. The Greek word for *"Lord"* is *kyrios,* and it occurs nearly 750 times in the New Testament. Its fundamental meaning is *"master"* or *"owner,"* making it the relational counterpart to the word *"slave" (doulos). Kyrios* and *doulos* are two sides of the same relationship. To be a *doulos* was to have a master; and vice versa, a *kyrios* by definition was the owner of slaves. In New Testament times, the *kyrios* had full authority over the life of his slaves (Mt 8:9; 13:27–28; 18:31–34; 21:34–36; 24:45–51; 25:23, 26–30; Mk 13:34–35; Lk 12:37; 14:16–24; 17:7–10). The complete supremacy of the master over the slave was so culturally ingrained that Jesus could even use it as a truism in His teachings. The Greek word for *"head"* was *kephale*—it was synonymous with the word *despotes*, from which we derive the English word *despot*. When the term is applied to God or to Jesus, it emphasizes absoluteness of ownership, or authority, and of power. To confess Jesus as *"Lord"* (Rom 10:9), is to simultaneously acknowledge one's own obligation to obey Him with total submission. In that context, Christ's words in Luke take on the full weight of their meaning: "If anyone wishes to come after Me, he must deny himself, and take up his cross daily and *follow Me"* (Lk 9:23). To follow the Master is to *come to the end of oneself and submit completely to His will.* Anyone who would be His disciple must also be His slave (Mt 10:37-39). Paul calls himself *"the slave of Christ"* (Rom 1:1; Phil 1:1; Tit 1:1)—he was no different than any other slave; he was completely at his Master's disposal. Therefore, Paul could exclaim, *"It is no longer I who live, but Christ lives in me"* (Gal 2:20). Elsewhere, he exhorted his readers with these words, "Do you not know . . . that you are not your own? You have been bought with a price: therefore glorify God in your body" (1 Cor 6:19-20). Over and over again, Paul writes that Jesus is his Master, and he is but a slave. (55-82)

The New Testament writers repeatedly spoke of themselves and fellow believers as "slaves of Christ." The apostles understood that Jesus Christ was "Lord" over every other lord—that He is *"Lord of all"* (Acts 10:36), possessing the full weight of divine authority (Col 2:9-10; Lk 22:69) . . . that He upholds all things by the word of His power" (Heb 1:3; Col 1:15-19) . . . that all things have been put "in subjection under His feet" (Eph 1:22) . . . and that His throne "is forever and ever" (Heb 1:8). According to Scripture, "slaves of Christ are to be "always abounding in the work of the Lord" (1 Cor 15:58) . . . "trying to learn what is pleasing to the Lord" (Eph 5:10) . . . ever seeking to "understand what the will of the Lord is" (Eph 5:17) . . . and rightly regarding themselves as "a people for His own possession, zealous for good deeds" (Tit 2:14). The only right response to Christ's lordship is wholehearted submission, loving obedience, and passionate worship. *Loving obedience* is the defining evidence of salvation. Genuine conversion is always marked by the fruit of repentance and the fruit of the Spirit (Lk 3:8; Gal 5:22-23). Though many call themselves "Christians," the true condition of anyone's heart is ultimately seen in *"how he lives."* As the saying goes, actions speak louder than words. The profession of faith that never evidences itself in righteous behavior is a *"dead faith"* (Jam 2:17), being no better than that of demons (Jam 2:19). This is not to say that true believers never stumble. They do—but the pattern of their lives is one of *continual repentance and increasing godliness* as they grow in sanctification and Christlikeness.

Because the "Lord" is our Master, we can trust Him to take care of us in every situation and stage of life. Even in the most difficult of circumstances, He will provide all that we *need* in order to be faithful to Him (Mt 6:31-33; Phil 4:19; 2 Cor 9:8). As such, we should be "free of anxiety" (Phil 4:6), because of the assurance we have that "God causes all things to work together for good to those who love Him, and are called according to His purpose" (Rom 8:28). We are right to trust Him completely, for He is sovereign not only over our lives, but also over everything that exists (Mt 28:18; Rom 14:7-9; Eph 1:20-23; Col 2:10; Jam 4:13-15). God Himself said, *"I will never leave you or forsake you"*—therefore, we can boldly say, "The Lord is my helper; I will not fear. What can man do to me?" (Heb 13:5-6). As David declared, "The Lord is my Shepherd, I shall not want . . . I will fear no evil, for You are with me" (Ps 23:1-4). The blessings of being "His slave" go beyond mere *provision;* to be the slave of Christ is also a *position* of great privilege, for we are in the company of none other than the King of the universe. It was considered a great honor to be "a slave of one of the Caesars"—it is infinitely more so to be the *"slave of Christ!"* the King of kings! To be His *doulos* is an incomparable honor; therefore let us *"boast of Him!"* (1 Cor 1:31; 2 Cor 10:17; Phil 3:8) whose name is above every name! (Phil 2:9). And then to think that *"His name"* will be written on our foreheads for all eternity! (Phil 2:9-11; Rev 22:4). Along with the saints of every age, we will never cease to marvel at the fact that, in spite of our own faults and frailties, the Lord chose us to be His own! (Eph 1:3-4; 1 Pet 2:9; Tit 2:14; also Ps 95:1-3, 6-7). (83–98)

In order to fully grasp what it means to be made a "slave of Christ," we need to understand our previous *"slavery to sin"*—a universal reality. *John Newton,* the author of the hymn *"Amazing Grace,"* had not only been the captain of a slave ship, he had also been subjected to slavery himself as a young man—he writes, "I was destitute of food and clothing, and became depressed to the lowest degree of human wretchedness." Ultimately, Newton, in conjunction with his friend **William Wilberforce**, helped the abolitionist cause in Britain reach its goal—just ten months before Newton died in 1807, the British Parliament passed the *Slave Trade Act*. Newton's past experiences helped him understand what it truly meant to be a *slave of sin*—to be hopelessly oppressed and exploited by a wicked master. Throughout his letters and hymns, Newton repeated contrasted bondage to sin with the redemption he received through Jesus Christ. He portrayed himself in his lost condition as *"the willing slave of every evil"* and *"Satan's blind slave"* who, if Christ had not rescued him, would have *"been a captive still."* In the following words penned by Newton, we are given an accurate description of the essence of unbelievers:

> *By nature how depraved — how prone to every ill,*
> *Their lives to Satan how enslaved — how obstinate their will.*
> *Satan reigns — and keeps his goods in peace.*
> *The soul is pleased to wear his chains — nor wishes a release.*
> *Jesus being stronger far than he — in His appointed hour,*
> *Appears to set His people free — from the usurper's power.*
> *He sees us willing slaves — to sin and Satan's power;*
> *But with an outstretched arm He saves — in His appointed hour.*

Newton also understood the ethical implications of his "liberty in Christ." Though he had been rescued from the evil oppression of sin, he now had a *new Master*, the Lord Jesus Christ. But unlike sin—the most wicked and cruel of all oppressors—Christ is the *perfect Master*, being righteous, just, gracious, and good. Therefore, **Newton** could exclaim:

> *Farewell world, thy gold is dross — Now I see the bleeding cross.*
> *Jesus died to set me free — from the law and sin and thee.*
> *He has dearly bought my soul — Lord accept and claim the whole.*
> *To Thy will I all resign — now no more my own but Thine.*

Having been rescued from the slavish bonds of sin, Newton was eager to obey Christ with all of his heart. He compared the Christian's deliverance from sin to Israel's deliverance from Egypt. Like Pharoah, sin is the harshest of taskmasters. But Christians, like the Israelites, can rejoice in being rescued by God's grace.

> *Beneath the tyrant Satan's yoke — our souls were long oppressed;*
> *'Till grace our galling fetters broke — and gave the weary rest.*
> *Jesus, in that important hour — His mighty arm made known;*
> *He ransomed us by price and power — and claimed us for His own.*
> *Now, freed from bondage, sin, and death — we walk in wisdom's ways;*
> *And wish to spend our every breath — in wonder, love, and praise.*
> *Ere long, we hope with Him to dwell — in yonder world above;*
> *And now we only live to tell — the riches of His love.* (99–114)

Sin is a cruel tyrant—it is the most devastating and degenerating power to ever afflict the human race, such that "all creation groans and suffers the pains of childbirth together until now" (Rom 8:22). It corrupts the entire person—infecting the soul . . . polluting the mind . . . defiling the conscience . . . contaminating the affections . . . and poisoning the will (Jer 44:15–17; Jn 3:19–21; Rom 1:21; 2 Cor 7:1; Tit 1:15). Sin is a life-destroying disease that grows in every unredeemed heart like an incurable gangrene. But unbelievers are not just *infected* by sin, they are *enslaved* by it. Jesus said, "Truly, truly I say to you, everyone who commits sin is the *slave of sin*" (Jn 8:34). Peter described false teachers as *"slaves of corruption; for by what a man is overcome, by this he is enslaved"* (2 Pet 2:19). Paul reminded the Romans that, before their salvation, they were *"slaves of sin"* (Rom 6:17). Every human being, until the moment of redemption, is under the domain of darkness and the *dominion of sin*—completely incapable of freeing himself from it. The very notion of such absolute enslavement is commonly known as *"total depravity."* Motivated by pride, the depraved mind thinks itself much better than it really is, but God's Word cuts through that deception by declaring sinful humanity as being incurably sick, and *incapable of any spiritual good* (Jer 13:23; 17:9; Rom 3:10–12; 8:7–8; 2 Cor 4:4; Eph 2:1; Col 2:13). The Bible teaches that unbelievers whole-heartedly love their sin (Jn 3:19–20; 2 Tim 3:2)—they not only are utterly *incapable* of freeing themselves from its corruption, they are obstinately *unwilling* to do so (Mt 19:26; Jn 1:13; Rom 9:16). Left to his own natural reason and volition, the unredeemed sinner will always choose slavery to sin over obedience to God. Until the Lord intervenes, the sinner is neither able nor willing to abandon his sin and serve God in righteousness. Both his will and his reason are utterly corrupt.

It is from "slavery to sin" that God saves us, rescuing us from the *domain of darkness* and transferring us into the kingdom of His Son (Col 1:13). Our redemption in Christ results in both *freedom from sin* and *forgiveness of sin*. Not only are we liberated from bondage to our former master, we are also exempt from sins's deadly consequences—namely, the eternal wrath of God. Paul writes, "The law of the Spirit of life in Christ Jesus has set us free from the law of sin and death" (Rom 8:2). Because we are now in Him, all our sins—past, present and future—have been forgiven for His name's sake (1 Jn 2:12). Hence, we should no longer fear our former master, nor fear the wrath of God. Christ defeated sin at the cross. Note the contrast between slavery and freedom—when we were *slaves to sin*, we were "free in regard to righteousness" (Rom 6:20); but now that we have been redeemed we are *slaves of righteousness* and "free with regard to sin" (Rom 6:18, 22). One of the classic paradoxes of the Christian faith is this—"one slavery" is terminated in order to allow "another slavery" to begin. **Sin** is the cruelest of masters . . . and **Christ** is the most loving and merciful Master. **Charles Wesley** wrote more than six thousand hymns, many of which we still sing today. The fourth verse of one of his best known hymns, *"And Can It Be,"* summarizes the glorious reality of God's redemption from sin, along with the believer's subsequent duty to follow and obey his new Master:

> *Long my imprisoned spirit lay,*
>   *Fast bound in sin and nature's night;*
> *Thine eye diffused a quickening ray,*
>   *I woke, the dungeon flamed with light;*
> *My chains fell off, my heart was free,*
>   *I rose, went forth, and followed Thee.*

The hymn concludes with the resounding truth of the glorious hope that all believers in Christ share—

> *No condemnation now I dread,*
>   *Jesus, and all in Him, is mine;*
> *Alive in Him, my living Head,*
>   *and clothed in righteousness divine,*
> *Bold I approach the eternal throne,*
>   *and claim the crown, through Christ my own.*

Having been bought with a price—the blood of Christ—believers are now "Christ's possession." As the redeemed, we are now not only *His slaves* but also *His friends* (Jn 15:14–15), citizens in *His kingdom*, and adopted children in *His family*. The very idea of **adoption** is filled with ideas of compassion, kindness, grace, and love (Jn 1:12; Rom 8:15–17; Gal 3:26, 29; Eph 1:5; Phil 2:15; Heb 12:5–11; 1 Jn 3:1–3). In ancient Rome, the act of adoption immediately granted the former slave his freedom, permanently placing him into the family of his master. So also, as the adopted children of God, we have been set free from slavery to our old master (sin and Satan)—he no longer has control over us. Once adopted into God's family, we become a child of God forever (Jn 6:39–40; 10:27–29; Rom 8:35–39; Phil 1:6; 1 Th 5:24; 1 Pet 1:5); hence, we are simultaneously *sons* and *slaves* forever—forever we will be in His glorious servitude (Rev 22:3). (145–176)

Jesus compared the "kingdom of heaven" to that of a man who went on a long journey; in doing so, he entrusted the management of his estate to his slaves—he gave responsibilities to each of them according to their individual abilities (Mt 25:14–30). When he returned, he inspected their work—those who were faithful in their duties he *rewarded,* and those who were not he *disciplined.* Jesus likened this parable to Himself and His slaves (believers)—Jesus would be leaving them for awhile, but would one day return and *"settle accounts with them"* (Mt 25:19; Mk 13:33–37; Jn 14:2–3; 1 Cor 3:8). The central message of this parable is that of *"being faithful"* with what God has entrusted to us, and to look forward to hearing our Master one day say, *"Well done!"* (Mt 25:21) and then be welcomed into His heaven—that is the greatest reward we could ever receive! This parable specifically refers to our Lord's judgment at His second coming (Rev 11:18). As Christ's slaves we are ultimately *accountable* to Him (1 Cor 3:12–15; 4:3–4; 2 Cor 5:9–10; Eph 6:5–9; 2 Tim 4:7–8). Our obedience and sacrificial service in this life will not go unnoticed or unrewarded by our sovereign Lord (Mt 5:12; 10:42). Even if our faithfulness to Him is costly and painful, we can rejoice in knowing that "this momentary, light affliction is producing for us an eternal weight of glory far beyond all comparison" (2 Cor 4:17). The apostle John, in his final description of the *"eternal state,"* expands on the glories that await us as believers—

> *The throne of God and of the Lamb will be in [the New Jerusalem], and His bond-servants [douloi/slaves] shall serve Him; they shall see His face, and His name shall be on their foreheads. And there shall no longer be any night; and they shall not have need of the light of a lamp nor the light of the sun, because the Lord God shall illumine them; and they shall reign [with Him] forever and ever* (Rev 22:3–5).

Our study of slavery has reminded us that we were once the "wretched slaves" of the cruelest master imaginable—sin, and in the midst of our helplessness and hopelessness, God intervened and redeemed us through the blood of His Son (Eph 2:13; Phil 2:7–8). As Christians, we have become *"slaves of Christ"*—we no longer live for ourselves and sin, we now live for Christ and righteousness (Mt 6:33; Gal 2:20; Phil 1:21). Every person is a slave—either to sin or to God. Slavery to Christ not only means freedom from sin, guilt, misery, and condemnation . . . it also means freedom to obey and please God, and to live the way our Creator intended us to live—enjoying intimate fellowship with Him.

Though as Christians we do fall into sin from time to time, we are never again the *"slaves of sin"* as we were before—sin no longer has dominion over our souls. Having been redeemed by Christ and empowered by the Holy Spirit, the believer has everything he needs to gain victory over temptation and sin. So God not only calls us to be *dutiful slaves*, He also enables us to serve Him with loving, joyful, faithful obedience (Jn 14:15; 1 Cor 15:10; Eph 2:10; Phil 2:12–13; 1 Th 5:24). ***Augustine*** when writing of the salvation of the Lord said, "You awake us to delight in praising You, for You have made us for Yourself, and our hearts are restless until they find their rest in You." (177–212). In closing, reflect upon the words to Stuart Townend's hymn, *"How Deep the Father's Love for Us"*—

> *How deep the Father's love for us,*
> *How vast beyond all measure;*
> *That He would give His only Son*
> *To make a wretch His treasure.*
>
> *How great the pain of searing loss,*
> *The Father turns His face away,*
> *As wounds which mar the Chosen One*
> *Bring many sons to glory.*
>
> *Behold the Man upon a cross,*
> *My guilt upon His shoulders;*
> *Ashamed, I hear my mocking voice*
> *Call out among the scoffers.*
>
> *It was my sin that held Him there*
> *Until it was accomplished;*
> *His dying breath has brought me life,*
> *I know that it is finished.*
>
> *I will not boast in anything,*
> *No gifts, no powr's, no wisdom;*
> *But I will boast in Jesus Christ,*
> *His death and resurrection.*
>
> *Why should I gain from His reward?*
> *I cannot give an answer;*
> *But this I know with all my heart,*
> *His wounds have paid my ransom.*

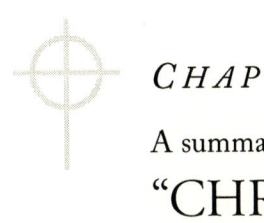

CHAPTER 21

A summary of the book . . .
"CHRISTLIKE"
by Bill Hull

Christians are to be followers of Christ—"little Christs"—in the world, touching the lives of people around us with the love of Christ, one person at a time. Love cannot be resisted. C. S. Lewis wrote, "The church exists for nothing else but to draw men to Christ, and make them *little Christs.*" The result of being a *"disciple"*—a follower of Christ—is that we influence others through our ordinary lives. Jesus said, "I have come that you might have life, and have it to the full" (Jn 10:10)—life as God intended can be *full* only when Christ Himself embodies us. When we *"follow Christ"* we grant Him permission to rule us, and when He rules us the transformation of our culture becomes possible. It does not happen quickly or easily or automatically—it requires *intentionality* and is anything but passive.

The problem in the church is that far too many Christians "don't act" like they "believe." The Greek term translated *"gospel"* is the word *euaggelion*, which means "good news." There is a lot of misinformation in the church today regarding the gospel—some believe it is just a *"forgiveness-only gospel"* that simply focuses on becoming a Christian, and ignores the life that is to be lived . . . others believe it is a *"social gospel"* that emphasizes the need of helping others . . . others see it as a *"relevant* *gospel"* that seeks God in a more personal way with the intent of being relevant to the watching world, yet it rejects the idea that absolute truth can be known on the human level . . . another gospel is the *"prosperity gospel"* that believes the physical blessings of health and wealth are as sure as the saving of the soul—to these, material blessing becomes one of the ways you know God is blessing you . . . but the *"consumer gospel"* is by far the most popular of the gospels that is being preached in the United States today—this gospel caters to one's self-interest; it combines the appeal of forgiveness with the abdication of any obligation to discipleship. Since we live in a world of consumption and assertiveness, we endorse churches that are impatient and impetuous—everything must be faster and bigger; the gospel of speed and fame is a natural by-product of our culture, which is driven by a mania to succeed. As such, this gospel is preoccupied with the youth program, the type of music, the time and length of services, and the personalities of the clergy.

The consumer gospel does not welcome "discipleship" (the intentional commitment to follow Jesus and live for others). That is why Dallas Willard states, "The reason why the Christian faith has failed to transform the masses and to make a more just and peaceful world, is because *it has failed to transform the human character."* Discipleship is not an essential part of the church today. Most American Christians embrace a hybrid kind of gospel that melds the *forgiveness-only* with the *consumer gospel*—this creates Christians who live by *"formulas"* and interpret the Christian message as primarily a narrative about *"their own needs."* The world is in orbit around the individual's need for personal peace and affluence. Those in this camp find themselves trapped in little enclaves of the evangelical subculture that believes the only things that count are "saving souls" and "church work." (1–40)

Jesus said things like, "I must preach the Good News of the Kingdom of God . . . that is why I was sent" (Lk 4:43). The Kingdom of God is a locality where God rules, where His will is done. That locality can be anywhere, including the human heart, the home, the workplace, the marketplace, any place. Jesus said His kingdom was not of this world.

He instructed His disciples to *"seek it first"* and everything else that is important will fall into place (Mt 6:33). The full force of the *Kingdom of God gospel* is that followers of Jesus are transformed in their spirits . . . they are reborn people set on their way by a new life . . . they are driven by the Spirit of God to make the world right. Those same people become Jesus to the world around them—feeding the hungry, helping children, assisting the poor, caring for the needy, and doing it in the name and power of the living Christ. The gospel of the kingdom is not only about saving souls; it is about the saved changing and caring for their world—this is the gospel that Jesus, Paul, Peter and the early church believed and taught.

The early church grew to about "ten thousand" by the end of the first century. It continued to grow exponentially until it peaked with regard to population at around 34 million in 350 AD—or 56 percent of the Roman world. The church did not sponsor organized evangelistic meetings to speak of—instead Christians impacted the world through their *deeds*. One of the reasons for the rise of the faith was the church's protection of human life—the early church was against *infanticide and abortion*, which were routinely practiced in the Greco-Roman world; Christians took care of *orphans and widows* in a culture that discarded them (Jam 1:27); and most dramatic of all, they stayed in the cities and *nursed the sick,* even during plagues when everyone else abandoned them—early Christians risked their lives to nurse the sick because it was a value lived out in the faith community. *This was Christian character at work.* By the way, the church did not have dedicated buildings during this period—as one wise sage put it, "The church was at its best when it had the least."

The church in the West has responded in a number of good ways to the needs of the world . . . by building hospitals, providing on-the-ground health care and emergency services such as the Red Cross, drilling wells to bring clean water where there is none, erecting schools where there are none, teaching people to read and to right, establishing written languages where there are none, fighting against corruption in government, fighting for freedom of religion and speech, etc.—these Christian global missions have been conducted primarily through Western philanthropy. But the "kingdom effect" has nearly been lost in the West during the past fifty years, in large part, because western Christians have *"privatized"* their spirituality—the problem is, personal spirituality was never meant to be *private;* it was always meant to be *public,* that it might affect the world around us. *The local church was simply meant to be an "outpost" in the larger world of the kingdom—it is just a part of the kingdom.* The church has grown significantly in the United States over the last three hundred years, but it is now on the wane because it has seriously compromised its values. Dallas Willard writes: "Widespread transformation of character through *wisely disciplined discipleship to Christ* can [renew the church and] transform our world. It can disarm the structural evils that have always dominated humankind and now threaten to destroy the world." (41–56)

When we first become Christians, most of us have a fairly naïve vision of our religious future. We generally assume that with a few more Bible studies and a little training, that *temptation* will get easier to handle . . . that our *prayer life* will soon become as natural as eating or sleeping . . . that our desire for *material things* will quickly be brought into submission . . . and that our *spiritual growth* will soon let us float above the fray! Life takes these naïve impressions and shatters them on the hard rocks of reality. Being formed into the image of Christ is a *lifelong journey.* Furthermore, it is really naïve to think that becoming more spiritual will eliminate the *sinful desires of the flesh.* The Scriptures tells us that we must be constantly on guard against the flesh, because it is crouching at the door ready to pounce without warning (Gen 4:7). The flesh never improves; it is actually in a state of continual degeneration, where it is getting worse and worse! (Eph 4:22)—your flesh was not nearly as corrupt when you were ten years old as it is today; that is just the reality of the *flesh* (your sin nature); get used to it, because your fallen nature is going to be with you until that day when you enter into God's presence. *But that does not mean it has to be in control!* The battle is a spiritual one—as such, Scripture exhorts us to train our bodies to become our *servants*—not our *rulers* (1 Cor 9:24–27).

The new life in Christ does mature with "intentional discipleship," but it is a competitive struggle, and the opponent will *score points*. With that said, there are many Christians for whom spiritual maturity is a far-off fantasy, because they believed that after a time of basic training, the Christian experience would become *"more natural"* and *"more easily managed."* That is why there is disillusionment and confusion as to why one stops making progress and why more heinous sins continue to have a grip on us. The truth of the matter is, throughout our life our primary enemy is *"self"*—the desire to please self, and to interpret life through our own limited perspective. The goal of *Christlikeness* is to live in such a way that God is pleased, to interpret life from His perspective, and to live for others—incidentally, when we stop exercising spiritually, we regress. Remember this wise old saying, "What do you have to do to get out of shape?"—"Nothing!"

The problem for many of us is that we begin to live on "yesterday's manna," and our biblical knowledge base. When that happens, we begin to go soft on prayer, Bible reading, meditation, worship, fellowship, and service, and start *"spiritually regressing."* Regression is gradual—it is a product of a negative pattern, and negative patterns are most often characterized by *"ease."* Ease comes naturally; you do not need to practice it—you just drift into it. A positive pattern requires *intentional discipline*, and almost always, *the fellowship and input of godly friends*. Structure and accountability empower people, and enable them to practice what makes them successful. (57–74)

Dietrich Bonhoeffer distilled the meaning of a disciple's life thus: "It is nothing else than bondage to Jesus Christ alone . . . Jesus is the only significance . . . He alone matters." The apostle Paul tells us the purpose of the believer's life is that he *"becomes like Christ"* (Rom 8:29). **C. S. Lewis** expressed it this way: *"We are to become little Christs."* We are not to be conformed to "this world"—that is, we are not to let the pressures of the world influence us in its direction (Rom 12:2); this is an ever-present problem for believers, and that is the battle that must be fought. What is it that causes people to conform? **People conform when there is more**

to gain from conforming than from not conforming. Rather than being conformed to this world, we are to be *"conformed to the image of Christ"* (Rom 8:29), and this happens *"by the renewing of our minds"* (Rom 12:2). Paul writes, "We are to have the same attitude that Jesus had" (Phil 2:5)—that attitude was one of *"humility."* Humility characterizes the person who understands that all gifts, talents, possessions, opportunities, and accomplishments are from the hand of God. Humility attracts God's grace—pride distances one from it. Without humility, conformity to Christ is impossible, because it only happens by grace (Jam 4:6). *When we lose our pride, lay aside our desire to control, decide to obey and live for others, humility becomes our habit.* Humility makes its way into our character through the regular practice of prayer, the assimilation of God's Word, and living for others.

According to Philippians, submission, obedience, and sacrifice were hallmarks of Jesus' character (Phil 2:5–8). *"Submission"* is motivated by love—Jesus submitted to the Father's will because of love. The more He submitted to God's will, the more joy it brought Him because He was pleasing the one He loved—this is the model of all human relationships (Eph 5:21). When a person submits and serves from a basis of love, that person is free from self-interest, and joy results. Jesus' humble submission led Him to *"obedience"*—Jesus never thought of obedience as just a sterile act of courage; rather it was His heart responding to His Father in love. The natural result of humility, submission, and obedience is *"sacrifice"*—Jesus' sacrifice on the cross was the greatest act of *selfless giving* in all God's creation. Just as Jesus bore our sins, we are now free to do the same for others. The goal of Christian disciples is that they take on the *character of Christ*. (75–90)

Is character transformation more BEING than DOING? more INTERNAL than EXTERNAL? There are a number of proponents on both sides of this issue—the truth of the matter is, God works both *inside out* and *outside in*. The classic position is that people *"change on the inside"* and that change works itself out in the world. Solomon states a very ordinary manifestation of the relationship between internal and external:

"A glad heart makes a happy face; a broken heart crushes the spirit" (Prv 15:13). Dallas Willard is a proponent of this view. He writes, "Spiritual formation is formation of the inner being of the human [soul] resulting in transformation of the whole person . . . [but] spiritual formation is never merely inward." So God works *inside out* through prayer, Bible reading, and the practice of spiritual exercises. The question remains: Does *action* that is against one's natural desire create a new or different spirit in a person? Consider the following—let's say you have a strong dislike for someone . . . as a disciple of Christ, you know you are to love even your enemies . . . so how will you treat this person? Is it not true that an *"act of loving obedience"* will also work a change in your own heart? And isn't this what Jesus meant when He taught us to "love our enemies"? Compulsory kindness is not only likely to produce a "change" in the heart of the recipient, but also create something positive in the server's inner life as well—both people are changed. When a person acts like God would act, it shapes that person's attitude as well as his heart. When the intention of the action is to serve others as a "little Christ," the reward is a *transformed spirit*. Conversely, if we repeatedly act kind, even when we are not feeling kind, we begin to be kind—the external action will change the internal disposition. God rewards kind acts in His children through the law of reaping—we reap what we sow—*actions* become *habits* that become *character*.

The Bible says transformation begins in the "mind" (Rom 12:2)—loving acts of kindness first begins in the mind and the heart. The transforming work of the Spirit starts with God's Word acting upon our hearts and minds (Jn 14:26; 16:13); the Word of God is necessary to our spiritual formation because it uses the vehicle of language to make God's thoughts our thoughts. "The Word of God is living and active, sharper than any two-edged sword . . . discerning the thoughts and intentions of the heart" (Heb 4:12). God does *transforming spiritual surgery* in our hearts by His Word through the agency of His Spirit. True thoughts find their way into the disciple's mind through the reading of the Word and prayerful reflection. God uses both internal and external stimulus to change us into the image of His Son. Writes Hull: "My memory comes alive when I recall a close friend slipping a five-dollar bill into my hand years ago when my wife and I had nothing for groceries." Spiritual formation begins *within*—a mind thinking God's *thoughts*, fueled by a Holy Spirit-birthed *desire*, creates new *actions*, which become *habits*, and habits are what make our *character*. (91–108)

So what kind of "relationship" is God inviting us to have with Him? Jesus claimed to be *"friends"* with His disciples (Jn 15:15). Obviously friendship with God is different than friendship with humans—He is preeminently holy and separate from all others; as such He is to be revered and feared. Since He is not like us, it makes sense that our relationship with Him would be different than one with our fellow man. As human beings, we feel most comfortable and secure around those friends who *accept us* for who we are—when that's the case, we don't feel as if we have to hide anything or pretend to be different than we are; we *trust* these friends and feel comfortable around them; we like being with them; that is friendship at its best. Writes Hull: "I want to become the kind of friend to Jesus that He [genuinely] enjoys being around, someone who is not always asking for something. And I would like to get to the point where I can be with God and not think *He's trying to fix me*, because such thoughts either make me avoid Him or keep me on guard when I am with Him."

We can't be a friend of God's if we are always disagreeing with Him about the way He does things. That's the lesson we learn from Job. It is worth noting that God allowed Job to complain; He listened to every word of Job's lament—even when Job cursed the day he was born. But look at where Job arrived after spewing out the pain that was deep within him—"I am vile; I repent in ashes; I have said too much; I will say no more" (Job 40:1-5). All the anger, all the pain, all the confusion, all the sense of betrayal—Job spit it all up; there was nothing left inside to get out. His final response was a matter of logic—Job realized who *God* was and who *he* was, and that settled the matter. We need to do the same. *Unless we accept God for who He is, then we will begin to avoid Him altogether.* Bill Hull puts it something like this: "There is one image that helps me relax around God—I imagine that I am having dinner with

THE CALL TO CHRISTLIKENESS

John Stott in his book *"The Radical Disciple,"* asks the question: "What is God's purpose for His people?" The Westminster Shorter Catechism says, "Man's chief end is to glorify God and to enjoy Him forever." There is also the scriptural dictum, "We are to love God and love others." And the idea that *"God wants us to be like Christ."* It is this last one that Stott finds the most satisfactory. The biblical basis for the call to Christlikeness is found is three texts—

- **Romans 8:29**—God has "predestined His people to be conformed to the image of His Son." God's eternal pre-destination occurred in eternity past; thus, this is the historical "past" tense."

- **2 Corinth 3:18**—As Christians, "we are all [in the process of] being transformed into the image of Christ." This is the present ongoing transformation of our lives by the Holy Spirit—the "present" tense.

- **1 John 3:2**—John writes, "Beloved, now we are children of God, and it has not yet appeared what we shall be; for when He (Christ) appears, we shall be like Him." This is the "future" tense. (Stott, pp. 29–31)

Stott goes on to say that one of the reasons our "evangelistic efforts" are so often fraught with failure is that "we don't look like the Christ we proclaim." John Poulton in his book *"A Today Sort of Evangelism"* writes:

> *The most effective preaching comes from those who embody the things they are saying. They are their message . . . they need to look like what they are talking about. It is people who communicate primarily, not words. . . . what communicates [best] is personal authenticity.*

A Hindu professor once commented to one of his Christian students: *"If you Christians lived like Jesus Christ, India would be at your feet tomorrow."* It should be remembered that Mahatma Ghandi, the twentieth century Hindu holy man (guru) of India, was known to have loved the teachings of Jesus more than any other ancient writings; those were the moral teachings he tried most to emulate. Another example is that of Reverend Iskandar Jadeed, a former Arab Muslim, who said: *"If all Christians were Christians [in the biblical sense] there would be no more Islam today."* Those are

(continued)

some pretty profound statements to those of us who profess to be followers of Christ. The big question for us is this—Is it possible for us as Christians to live _Christlike_ lives? Obviously, in our own strength it is not, but God has given us His Holy Spirit to enable us to fulfill His purpose. _God's purpose_ is to make us like Christ, and _God's way_ is to fill us with His Holy Spirit. (Stott, pp. 35–37)

Stott summarized the Christian scene in the world today as "growth without depth"—"There is superficiality of discipleship everywhere," he writes. The leadership of the rapidly growing African church states, "It is growth without a strong biblical foundation." Likewise, the leadership of the fast growing Asian church says, "It lacks godliness and integrity." The New Testament apostles rebuked their readers for their _"immaturity"_ and urged them to _"grow up."_ Writes Paul: "I gave you milk, not solid food, because you were not yet ready for it" (1 Cor 3:1–3). In another passage he says, "We proclaim Christ, admonishing and teaching everyone with all wisdom, so that we may present every believer fully mature _[teleios]_ in Christ; it is to this end that I strenuously labor" (Col 1:28–29).

What is maturity? To be mature is to have a mature relationship with Christ in which we worship, trust, love, and obey Him. **J. I. Packer** in his book _"Knowing God"_ says that we are _"pygmy Christians"_ because we have a _"pygmy God;"_ that is, a distorted Christ. So if we want to develop true Christian maturity, we need above all a fresh and true vision of Jesus Christ. **Jerome,** one of the early Church fathers, wrote that "ignorance of Scripture is ignorance of Christ." Therefore, we can say that knowledge of Scripture is knowledge of Christ. Nothing is more important for mature Christian discipleship than a fresh, clear, true vision of the authentic Jesus. Writes Stott: "The discipleship principle is clear—the poorer our vision of Christ, the poorer our discipleship will be; whereas the richer our vision of Christ, the richer our discipleship will be." Maturity in Christ must be the goal for ourselves as well as our ministry to others. (Stott, pp. 38–48)

God and a number of other close friends . . . all of us feel accepted . . . we are all laughing, telling jokes, and having fun together, and Jesus is enjoying the moment as much as we are . . . the look on His face tells us that He really likes being with us, that He really accepts us, and that He is thrilled that we are becoming more and more like Him . . . all of us feel affirmed—even in our weaknesses."

In order to enjoy such a relationship, you need to abandon your "stiff, legalistic approach" to prayer and Bible reading. Take your relationship with God and run! Run from the *moralists* who tell you that the more time you log with God, the more accepted and spiritual you are . . . run from those who tell you that you are only heard by God when *tears* are found upon the pages of your Bible . . . run from those who champion a *rigid monasticism* that uses self-denial as a means of making you feel better about yourself . . . and run from those who propose that you are *free from any responsibility* or discipline in connection to knowing God. Leave both extremes behind, and find the healthy place modeled so beautifully by Christ Himself. Karl Barth is reported to have said, *"I have read many books, but the Bible reads me."* When we learn to *read the Bible reflectively*—to read it, to obey it, to confess, to apply it to our life—the revolution will begin. The very center of spiritual transformation is *"being with God"*—spiritual transformation is about reconciliation and closing the distance. In eternity, the distance fully disappears. This life has much more promise than what most disciples experience. We have the prospect of being *God's friend* and of developing the friendship by reflecting on His Word and learning to hear His voice. Living close to God is what He created us for—that is what abundant living is all about. (109–122)

When you sit down in the morning for your time in the Word with God, picture yourself as entering into an *"inter-active relationship"* with someone who really loves you and wants to share His heart with you—expect to be spoken to, and when His Word enters your heart you will *"taste it!"* The prophet Jeremiah expressed it this way: "Thy words were found and I ate them, and they became for me the joy and the delight of my heart" (Jer 15:16). Likewise, the apostle John said, "I went to the angel and told him to give me the small scroll, and he said to me, *'take and eat it'*—it will be sweet as honey in your mouth, but it will turn sour in your stomach!" (Rev 10:9). John ate the book—it metabolized in him. It made him feel . . . it made him happy . . . it made him sad . . . it gave him pleasure . . . and at times it even made him sick to his stomach. It has the same effect on us today. The word of God is food—it is to be taken in, tasted, chewed, savored, swallowed, and digested. The psalmist David said, "How blessed is the man who delights in the law of the Lord, and in His law he *meditates* day and night" (Ps 1:2; cf. Ps 63:6). The word *"meditate"* in Hebrew is the same word that is used of the cow *"chewing his cud."* Cows actually have four stomachs—each serving a different purpose—when he is out grazing in the field, he initially swallows the food into his upper stomach that holds more than twenty gallons of partially digested food; later on "he brings the food back up again to chew on"—this is what it means for a cow to chew his cud. As believers we need to *"bring God's Word up again for reconsideration"*—to prayerfully reflect upon . . . to taste it . . . to be encouraged by it . . . to feed our souls on it . . . to be renewed by it . . . to be satisfied by it. This would not be possible, however, if we were negligent in getting into the Word in the first place.

Millions of believers read the Bible every day, but getting the Scriptures into their lives and hearts is another issue entirely. Eugene Peterson put it this way: "The challenge regarding the Christian Scriptures is getting them read as God's revelation . . . what is neglected is reading them formatively in order to live"—that is, reading the Scriptures in a way that changes you, that impacts the way you live. The Bible is a book that requires some intellect and study to grasp, but it is also food for the soul (Heb 5:11–14; 1 Pet 2:2). One of the functions of the Holy Spirit is to guide and teach us what God's Word means (Jn 14: 26; 16:13) . . . but how will He do that if we neglect spending time in it? One of the largest churches in America—*Willow Creek Community Church*, in Barrington, Illinois—commissioned a study of their church along with hundreds of other churches a few years ago: they discovered that not much has changed in 2,000 years. Of the 80,000 people surveyed, 87% said that *understanding the Bible* was their first priority. But the finding was even more specific—those who had reached maturity said that *reading the Scriptures in a reflective manner* was the main reason they had grown.

Sadly, reading Scripture "reflectively" is uncommon among most evangelicals. The emphasis has been on reading and studying for *understanding and knowing* the Bible. As a result, the Scriptures get into our *heads*, but not our *hearts*. That is why there has been a stampede of interest lately in the *spiritual disciplines*. Saint Bonaventure expresses it well: "To know much and taste nothing—of what use is that?" One of the monastics' finer contributions was *"reflective reading"* and *"meditation"* on Scripture—they developed a time-tested method called **lectio divina,** or *divine reading*. It contains the following four movements:

1. Lectio—First, select a short passage, and then with a listening heart, slowly and deliberately *read the text aloud.* When you find a phrase that speaks to your heart, pause in your reading.

2. Meditatio—Second, *meditate or reflect* upon the words. Think about them. What do they mean? What does the passage say? Allow God to settle the truth of His word into your soul. Allow it to probe your attitude, emotions, and aspirations.

3. Oratio—Third, return the passage you have just read to the Father by praising Him for its work in you. Talk to the Father about your reading. *Pray the words,* interact with God, and ask the Holy Spirit to teach you the *special applications* for your life.

4. Contemplatio—The final stage is *resting* in the Lord's presence. This is the act of simply being with God. Review your immediate life, attitudes, and conflicts. Now *live* what you have read.

One of the benefits of thinking about "developing good habits" is to remember the practices of the ancient church. What the Reformation took away from many of our traditions is the unity of the seven major practices of the church—the first was *communion,* the second *tithing,* and the third was *fasting.* These have largely survived the divide between Protestant and Catholic. The next four major practices mainly have been lost. The fourth had to do with the hours of the day that the church would pray—according to Jewish tradition, *they would pray six times a day:* prayer would be at six, nine, noon, three, six, and at retiring. This was also the practice of the early church—though they would only stop and pray for minute or two, they did faithfully pray. It is easy to understand the importance of communicating with God throughout the course of the day. The fifth practice was the *Sabbath*—a time of worship, rest and reflection; were you thinking "relaxation"? The sixth was the *church year* or church calendar, which would condition a person to experience the steps of redemption, incarnation, preparation for the passion of Christ, His death, His resurrection, His ascension, and the sending of the Holy Spirit at Pentecost. The last ancient practice was *pilgrimage,* where once in a lifetime a Christian would go to a special place to pay homage and for reflection. It didn't need to be a Holy Land tour—it could have been their family home, the place they met Christ, or significant friends who have contributed to their spiritual life. There is power in structure and tradition—by appreciating them, these things assist us in knowing God better and in knowing Him more personally.

Jesus posited Himself as the "Good Shepherd." There are a number of qualities He attributed to His relationship with His flock—His sheep recognize His voice . . . He calls his sheep by name and leads them out . . . His sheep don't follow a stranger because they don't know his voice . . . His sheep listen to His voice (Jn 10:3-5, 14, 16). Four times in this passage Jesus claims that His people *know His voice and follow Him.* How can we know if God is speaking to us? Most of us don't have any trouble knowing if God is speaking to us from Scripture . . . but what about at other times? Entire books have been written on the subject of hearing God's voice—one of the best is **Dallas Willard's** *Hearing God.* Most people who are sensitive to what God has to say to them, consider His voice an *"inner voice"*—a prompting, an impression, an inner urge that simply won't go away. Remember, "God is at work in you, both to will and to work for His good pleasure" (Phil 2:13). **F. B. Meyer** said the following about God's speaking to us: "God's *impressions within* and *His word without* are always corroborated by *His providence around,* and we should quietly wait until those three focus into one point. If you do not know what you ought to do, stand still until you do. My mentor in ministry used to say, "When in doubt, don't!" When the time comes for action, circumstances, like glowworms, will sparkle along your path. *You will become sure you are right when God's three witnesses concur."* **C. S. Lewis**

said he found the exercise of *setting aside time just to hear from God* very frustrating, even though he did subject himself to it on a semi-regular basis. Lewis found *"walking tours"* much more conducive to being with God than the *"sitting still and trying to shut everything out"* routine. For me personally, I have also found *walking tours* much more helpful and beneficial when I need to hear from God—I can spend hours every day in study, but when there is *"angst"* in my soul, I need to get out and *"take a walk with God"*—just the two of us—where we can interact together. Others I know find "sitting still" more helpful. Both of these are viable options. (123–144)

Most people innately believe the healthiest form of spirituality is to have a "heart to please God," and from that heart of passion to respond to Him in obedience. The ancients believed *action* followed *essence*, that our actions are consistent with the reality of our hearts. The flip side, however, is the fear that if we depend on feelings, passions, and emotions, we will sin, giving in to the powerful self-interest deep within our hearts . . . and as **Reinhold Niebuhr** states, "Sin is the precise sense of self-centeredness and the struggle for power." Hence, there is great danger in depending too much on passion or desire. The *"heart"* is the innermost center of man—it encompasses the will, the mind, and the spirit, and it can see, feel, know, reflect, and be turned toward or away from God. *Spiritual formation is the development of a "heart for God"*—the spiritual heart directs the transformation of the entire person to reflect Jesus Christ; it denotes a passion and warmth of relationship, in which there is an honest interchange including disappointment, disagreement, forgiveness, and reconciliation.

A regenerate heart desires to be at one with God and please Him (Eph 1:17–18). In 1928, **William Law** published the popular book, *A Serious call to a Devout and Holy Life*; it was a powerful influence on a number of spiritual giants including Samuel Johnson and John Wesley. In it he asks why is it that so many professing Christians *live contrary to the principles that they say they believe*. He responds by saying that believers are in *constant negotiation with God about who is in charge*—but a holy and devout life calls for *surrender*, not *negotiation*. Thus, we must go into *training* in order to gradually grow out of the grip of our own corrupted hearts and strengthen our spiritual hearts (1 Cor 9:24–27). The facts are, we can have a *new heart* (one that God has put in us) and a *deceptive heart* at the same time (Jer 17:9). **Richard Foster** describes our inner person this way: "We are, each and every one of us, a tangled mass of motives: hope & fear . . . faith & doubt . . . simplicity & duplicity . . . honesty & falsity . . . openness & guile . . . and God is the only one who can separate the true from the false, the only one who can purify the motives of the heart."

Can a person's intention genuinely be changed? The answer is an unequivocal "yes," or there is no sense in continuing this discussion. Paul prayed that *"the eyes of our heart be enlightened"* (Eph 1:18); that the heart would see more the way God sees. As we experience the good and the bad of life, we start seeing life more like God sees it. It is surprising how this change takes place. It is what we call the common, or ordinary life. When we sincerely desire to *please God* in all our actions, we allow Him to dig down deep inside us and to get at the deepest why reasons we do what we do (Ps 139:23–24). If we really believe that pleasing God is what will make us happiest, and that we won't miss anything when we abstain from sin—*the spiritual heart must believe this*—then we will win over lust and lying and every other vice, because we will know that we aren't missing a thing when we refuse to engage in sinful behavior. The problem for most believers is that they really don't believe, in the moment, that they will be happiest by refraining from sin—hence, they capitulate.

Heart work is "hard work," because making ourselves available to God requires "discipline." Paul told Timothy, "Discipline yourself for the purpose of godliness" (1 Tim 4:7). By discipline, Paul meant the *will* and *structure* needed for repeated exercise—this is evident by his mention in the next verse about bodily exercise. This discipline comes from two sources—the Holy Spirit and fellow members of the body of Christ who join with us on the journey. *Lone-ranger believers don't make it, because that is not the way God designed the process—and to fight His wisdom, is to* *lose the battle!* So, don't stubbornly persist on redesigning the process! If you submit to the process as we have previously discussed, God will begin to *"change your heart."* There is great mystery in all this—just submit your spirit and start asking God to, *"Change my heart, shape my spirit, do Your work."* King David was reported to be a man after God's own heart . . . though he was a flawed man like all of us (he had a sin disposition just like you and me), he still had a strong heart and passion for God. David sincerely desired to please God, in spite of his human frailties and shortcomings. (145–154)

Is "obedience" to God ever easy? Some believe so. Easy behavior comes as a result of a transformed nature—it is the product of the ancient practices called the *"spiritual disciplines."* Here is the way Bill Hull puts it: "Part of me will never stop wanting the *doughnut*, but given enough time and training, a better part of me will cause me to desire the better thing, the *carrot* (see Gal 5:16–17). The difference would be that I might taste the Lord and His ways and find them more delicious than anything else in life" (Ps 34:8). Hull concludes, "If the Lord can't taste better than a carrot, then I have a problem, because carrots don't have a chance against doughnuts!" **Dallas Willard** advocates that through *spiritual exercise*, we can become the kind of people who are far more inclined to do the things Jesus did—though this is only possible when we develop *"relational closeness"* to God. Relational closeness comes from investing time in submission to the *practices* that nurture the relationship—being with God, spending time in His Word, and hearing His voice. To the degree that you enter into the *spiritual exercises*—to that degree will you experience the power and joy of a transformed life. It is the old law of *"reaping what you sow"* (Lk 6:38; 2 Cor 9:6; Gal 6:7). If you invest little, you will reap little . . . if you plant soybeans, you will reap soybeans—you do the math. Jesus taught us that when we *"love someone,"* we desire to please and do things that benefit the one we love, even when we don't naturally want to do those things (Mt 26:39; Jn 14:15). "God loved us so much that He gave His one and only Son . . . that we might have eternal life" (Jn 3:16).

No one is transformed by "wishing" it could happen—it is a "choice." It takes place only when a disciple engages in a *sustained effort* with the spiritual disciplines. If you think *"soul transformation"* (sanctification) is solely the work of the Holy Spirit—that God does it all—you are confused about the nature of grace. Our salvation (justification) is the work of God alone, but our sanctification requires the believer's participation—in that sense, it is a "co-operative;" both the believer and the Holy Spirit are involved (Phil 2:12-13). Grace is what we call the act of God whereby He captures our hearts, implants new life in us, and gives us the desire to serve Him, and through the Holy Spirit, the power to do it. Grace is not opposed to *effort*—but it is opposed to *earning*. God's grace is a gift and is not for sale or given to the hardest worker. However, grace endows one with the power and resources to give a full effort (Eph 2:8-10). Paul worked hard; he struggled, but it was with God's power that he did so. That is the divine dance we do every day—we join hands with Jesus . . . He leads and we follow. When we choose to take action, employing the tools God has given us, we are demonstrating our desire to please God—these tools are commonly known as *spiritual disciplines;* their usefulness in forming Christ in us is essential. For the record, the **spiritual disciplines** are normally understood to be the following—reading Scripture, studying it, believing it (affirming the truth of it—that's faith), meditating on it, memorizing it, prayer, solitude, worship, evangelism, service, stewardship, fasting, submission, and frugality. These disciplines are the exercises of Christian training that enable us to experience God's presence in our lives and hear His voice. They are to the Christian what *physical training* is to the long-distance runner. The spiritual heart can be trained by employing these God-given disciplines—we start with the desire to be like Christ, and through sustained effort and God's power (grace), we become more Christlike. Here is the formula: *"Paul planted, Apollos watered, but God gave the increase"* (1 Cor 3:6). Paul and Apollos worked hard, but GOD was the one who brought forth the fruit (the increase). You may work diligently in your garden, but you are not the one who causes the plants to grow—God does—yet without you doing your part, there will be no plant growth. You think about that.

Jesus also practiced these disciplines. So evangelical critics who claim that spiritual disciplines are simply the product of medieval monasticism—that they are Catholic in origin—are simply misinformed. What the critics miss is that the disciplines were embedded in Jesus' life—He prayed alone, fasted, spent extended time alone, and lived a life of frugality. Furthermore, His life was a model of service, submission, sacrifice, and evangelism. Thus, we do these things because Jesus Himself did them. The objective for practicing the spiritual disciplines is to have Christ formed in us. If we choose to *practice* them, they then become a *habit*, which affects our *character*, and the result is a *spiritually transformed heart*.

Sadly, many churches in the West have reduced the Christian faith to "intellectual agreement" that is divorced from "action," and that kind of faith, says James, "in useless" (Jam 2:20). Only the continued practice of the spiritual disciplines *in community* eventually transform the heart—one of the joys of life together in Christ is that of helping one another keep our commitments to God; and only humble people will submit themselves to others and allow their character to be developed in community. God created His people to *"live in community"* with other believers (Acts 2:42; Heb 3:13; 10:24-25); in so doing, those who *"jointly practice the spiritual disciplines"* discover their hearts being transformed. The life of transformation takes *time*—training is a *process*, it is the spiritual equivalent of the athlete who is in training to win a *marathon*—as such, it leaves plenty of room for *patience*. Believers on the road to maturity understand that *the spiritual life is a long journey*—thus they take the long view. (155-170)

Dietrich Bonhoeffer understood how much Christians "need each other." He writes, "The Christian needs another Christian who speaks God's Word to him—in particular when he becomes discouraged and uncertain" (Ecc 4:9, 11, 12; Jn 13:34; Rom 14:19; Gal 5:13; Col 3:16; 1 Th 5:11; Heb 10:24; Jam 5:16; 1 Pet 4:10; 1 Jn 4:7), for such is the common plight of us all—none of us is without the need and support of a brother. There may be much to commend itself for *staying away from church people*—obviously they have their foibles like everyone else—but despite the many reasons for staying away from the body . . . we need it . . . though some within it may be difficult to live with . . . we cannot live without it. What we have described here is simply *structure* and *accountability* clothed in love and relationships—that is the way God designed His Church. **By the way, you cannot program "transformation"—it is too organic to be organized!** Let me say it again, *"Soul transformation is impossible for the lone-ranger believer,"* so get into a good Bible-believing church, and connect with other brothers and sisters in Christ who need you as much as you need them (1 Cor 12:12ff). Obviously, the Christian life is a tougher obstacle course than any of us would have designed, but we were not the ones who were assigned to the design team . . . keep in mind, you are not the Creator, you are the creature . . . God has placed us on planet earth to be *"little Christs"* to sinners just like ourselves—and in order to be as effective as possible in that assignment, we need to submit ourselves to the *discipline and training* that God has outlined for us—He asks us to cooperate with Him throughout the process, and in doing so, He has promised to *transform us into the image of His beloved Son* (Rom 8:29). Seems impossible, doesn't it? I fully understand why you might feel that way—we are all made of the same stuff—and if it were only left up to us, obviously it would not happen. The good news with regard to our transformation is this: *"God is also at work in us to will and to do His good pleasure"* (Phil 2:13)—so what is not remotely possible for you and me, is imminently possible for God (Mt 19:26).

The "local church" is the most significant organized influence for spiritual growth, so the activities of the church naturally emerge as important catalytic factors. Therefore the best advice for Christians is that they *"go to church"*—and once they are there, latch on to those who are doing the spiritual practices. This point is absolutely critical for the believer who wants to grow in Christ—*spending time with fellow followers of Christ who are of kindred spirit is vital to spiritual growth*. By the way, over a lifetime, you will need several different kinds of people to walk with you—there are different seasons, different challenges—but they are all to be found among fellow Christ followers.

THE CALL TO SIMPLICITY

John Stott in his book _"The Radical Disciple,"_ writes about an international consultation on _"Simple Lifestyle"_ he attended in England in 1980. It affirmed that _"Life"_ & _"Lifestyle"_ belong together—since the life we have as believers is new, the lifestyle we have should also be new. The _Lausanne Congress on World Evangelism_ in 1974 ultimately concluded: _"Those of us who live in affluent circumstances accept our duty to develop a simple lifestyle in order to contribute more generously to both relief and evangelism."_ The Congress was convened to listen to the voice of God, through Scripture and the cries of the hungry poor—in so doing, they became more mindful of the unevangelized, the oppressed and the suffering in the world, and, regrettably, the Church's complicity in it. As such, they were stirred to fresh resolves which they expressed in a commitment to _"develop a more simple lifestyle."_ The commitment involved:

- **Creation**—In His generosity God has given us everything to enjoy and we receive it from His hands with humble thanksgiving (1 Tim 6:17). His creation is marked by rich abundance and diversity and He intends its resources to be husbanded and shared for the benefit of all. Therefore we denounce environmental destruction, wastefulness and hoarding, and we deplore the misery of the poor who suffer as a result of these evils.

- **Stewardship**—When God made man, He made him in His own image and gave him dominion over the earth (Gen 1:26–28). He made him a steward (not a proprietor) of its resources; as such, he became responsible to God as Creator, to the earth which he was to develop, and to his fellow man with whom he was to share its riches.

- **Poverty and Wealth**—We affirm that involuntary poverty is an offense against the goodness of God. God's call to rulers is that they use their power to defend the poor, not exploit them. We must remember the words of Jesus about wealth: "Beware of coveteousness—a person's life does not consist in the abundance of possessions" (Lk 12:15). We are to "be rich in good works, generous and ready to share" (1 Tim 6:18). Jesus Christ Himself, "though He was rich, He became poor that through His poverty we might become rich" (2 Cor 8:9)—it was costly and sacrificial.

(continued)

- **The New Community**—The early Church loved one another to such an extent that they voluntarily sold and shared their possessions to meet the needs of others—"none of them said that anything he had was his own" (Acts 4:32). Though some private property was retained, they were free from the selfish assertion of proprietary rights (Acts 5:4). As a result, "there was not a needy person among them" (Acts 4:34). Christ calls us to be the world's salt and light, in order to illumine its darkness and hinder its social decay; it is only then that we truly affect the world for Christ.

- **Personal Lifestyle**—Jesus summons us to holiness, humility, simplicity and contentment. We lay down no rules or regulations for ourselves or others, yet we resolve to renounce waste and oppose extravagance in personal living. We also accept the distinction between necessities & luxuries, modesty & vanity, service to God & slavery to fashion.

- **International Development**—One quarter of the world's population enjoys unparalleled prosperity, while another quarter endures grinding poverty. This gross disparity is an intolerable injustice, and we refuse to acquiesce to it.

- **Justice and Politics**—The Christian community, along with the rest of society, is inevitably involved in politics which is "the art of living in community." As servants of Christ we must express His lordship in our moral, political, social, and economic commitments, and our love for our neighbors by taking part in the political process.

- **Evangelism**—The credibility of our message is seriously diminished and compromised whenever we contradict it by our lives. It is impossible with integrity to proclaim *Christ's salvation* if He has evidently not saved us from greed, or *His lordship* if we are not good stewards of our possessions, or *His love* if we close our hearts against the needy.

- **The Lord's Return**—The Old Testament prophets denounced the idolatry and injustice of God's people and warned them of His coming judgment. Those who have ministered to Him by ministering to one of the least of His children will be saved—saving faith is exhibited in serving love (Mt 25:31–46; Lk 10:25–37; Eph 2:10; Phil 2:4; Tit 2:8; 3:8, 14; Jam 1:27; 2:14–18; 1 Jn 3:16–18; 4:7–8). (Stott, pp. 60–82)

The "spiritual exercises" that make up this training are—reading, studying, memorizing, meditating, and praying through the Scriptures; periodically getting alone with God for times of solitude and reflection; loosening your grip on your selfishness through giving, serving, frugality, and fasting; and exercising your spiritual gifts in the service of others—such as mercy, helps, teaching, exhorting, and so on. In the best of churches, the pastor teaches the value of discipleship and spiritual exercise. Then the *group life of the church* is organized around these practices so that people can grow together in Christlikeness. People cannot become Christlike without *accountability*, and they cannot have accountability without *structure*, but that structure can be as simple as, "We will meet every Tuesday morning at eight and discuss chapter 8 of our book on the spiritual disciplines" (or whatever). In order to flourish, people need to be part of a community that has the qualities of trust, grace, humility, submission, and affirmation. These essential elements *create community*—their polar opposites (suspicion, criticism, pride, self-will, and competition) *destroy community*. Let's look at each one of these qualities in more detail—

- **Trust**—This is the most important requirement for spiritual development; finding at least one person in your community that you can trust. Trust is based on *integrity*—you can trust a person who has proven to be reliable and honest. It is only when you find someone you can trust, that you can be vulnerable with that person, and allow yourself to come under that person's influence. Choose the person carefully because his or her character will help shape yours. If you can't find such a person, pray fervently until you do! God will be faithful in giving you such a person.
- **Grace**—In order to grow in Christlikeness, you will also need to be part of a community that offers you grace, particularly when you stumble and fall. To offer grace means treating others better than they deserve to be treated. It means looking past peoples faults, and offering people a place where they feel safe, affirmed, and able to risk—without an environment of grace, people will be reluctant to open up and be transparent.

- **Humility**—A community that will foster spiritual growth is one that will teach you how to humbly receive life as it comes hurling at you. Humility is simply the acknowledgement of who you are *dependent on*. When your answer is Christ, then you will have humility. Peter exhorts us to, "Humble yourselves under God's mighty hand, that He may exalt you at the proper time" (1 Pet 5:6). Without humility, there is no submission . . . without submission, there are no relationships of trust . . . without relationships of trust, you won't make yourself vulnerable . . . without being vulnerable, no one can influence you . . . and without the influence of others, you won't change.
- **Submission**—Submission is a love word. We submit to others because we desire to enter into a relationship that benefits us and those around us. When we practice submission in community, three things happen: 1) our needs get met; 2) we get to practice humility, the character trait that allows us to submit; and 3) we allow others to love us. This makes us growing disciples who then influence others with our Christlikeness. Nothing could be more radical or counter-cultural than Christians who submit to other people's needs. This is a key place where churches and ministries should invest their energy.
- **Affirmation**—We all need affirmation—it confirms our identities. It lets us know that others appreciate our strengths and contributions, and this helps us risk coming out of our shells. Affirmation is powerful—it creates an environment that gives people permission to drop their defenses, and that allows deep change to take place. Affirmation becomes a way of life in an environment of grace. It reminds people that God values them. (171–188)

Jesus taught that what comes out of the heart reveals the "content of the heart" (Lk 6:43–45). By the way, what is in people always comes out . . . what is inside their hearts cannot remain hidden, because that is the essence of who the person is—the simple fact is, we cannot be who we are not (Mt 7:16–18; Jam 3:12)—the heart is reflected in the way people behave. Disciples who are truly alive in Christ are like a *"match"*—they will start a fire. Jesus said believers are *"the light of the world*—they are like a city on a hilltop that cannot be hidden;" as such, they are to "let their light shine for everyone to see" (Mt 5:14–16). True faith begins within us, in the privacy of the heart, but it cannot remain there—it must be displayed. Faith that springs from inside us shines—it talks, it walks, it interacts, it loves, it cares—it is God's active presence in the world. The mark of the Christian society is *love* (Jn 13:35)—it is disciples giving themselves to others, regardless of the cost. The key to changing the world is a vibrant transformation on the inside that focuses on a person at one with Christ.

Dallas Willard states, "Widespread transformation of character through wisely disciplined discipleship to Christ can transform our world; it can disarm the structured evils that have always dominated humankind and now threaten to destroy the world." The process of transformation is not a short-term experience—it lasts our entire lives—and it is not a passive life, but one of sustained effort. It will require tools, structure, and discipline. Most of all, it means living in community with others, because in order for transformation into the image of Christ to have meaning, we must seek to serve and love others . . . and in order to make a difference—we need to be different. (189–195)

CHAPTER 22

A summary of the doctrine of . . .

"SIN AND MAN'S ETERNAL PURPOSE"
by Donald W. Ekstrand

Temptation is part of Satan's crafty plan that appeals to our "NATURAL DESIRES" (flesh) in an attempt to cause division between us and God; hence, it is an invitation to live a *self-serving life* that leads to rebellion against God. Temptation is Satan's invitation to give into his kind of life and give up on God's kind of life. Satan tempted Eve to doubt God's goodness, implying that He was stingy and selfish for not wanting Eve to share His knowledge of good and evil (Gen 3:1–7). Satan made Eve forget all that God had given to her, and instead got her to focus on what was prohibited. We fall into trouble too, when we dwell on the few things we don't have rather than on the countless things with which God has blessed us.

Temptation generally hits hardest in our "AREAS OF WEAKNESS." For all his wisdom, King Solomon had numerous weak spots—he couldn't say "no" to compromise or lustful desires. You may have strong faith, but you also have significant weak spots. All of us do. The three major areas of temptation categorized for us in Satan's temptation of Jesus are: 1) *Physical needs and desires;* 2) *Possessions and power;* and 3) *Pride* (Matt 4:1–11; 1 Jn 2:15–16). Jesus was tempted in every way in which we are tempted, but He did not give in to temptation—He knows firsthand the difficulties of temptation; as such, *He sympathizes with us* and *wants to help us* in our struggles (Heb 4:15-16). The devil often tempts us when we are most vulnerable—when we are under physical or emotional stress—but he also tempts us where we think we are strong, where we are most susceptible to pride. That is why the believer must be on guard at all times against his attacks.

Without exception, sin results when temptation strikes a sympathetic chord in "OUR HEART." Because it operates in the realm of "*feelings*" (wants, desires, lusts), that's what makes it so difficult. The reason all of us sin is that "*we feel like it*"/"*we want to*"—if we didn't feel like it or want to, we wouldn't sin. *The simple truth is this: "our flesh is not a paragon of virtue!"* Obviously, feelings can be extremely difficult to overcome—it is the main reason people "divorce" each other . . . they no longer have "feelings" for each other. Society's number one message is that we should do what we "feel" like doing—it places an inordinate emphasis on *feelings* rather than *oughts*. The dynamic of the flesh is "*feelings*," and the dynamic of the Spirit is "*faith*"—so either you live your life according to how you *feel* (flesh), or you live your life according to the *truth* (faith). By the way, nowhere in the Bible does God ever command us to feel anything, because we cannot directly control our feelings—feelings in large measure are a *byproduct* of our thoughts; hence, the need to control our thoughts.

To pray that God would take away a particular temptation is to ask God to take away our "FEELINGS"—that is not going to happen. Let me illustrate it: If you are physically *attracted* to someone outside your "eligible arena of candidates" . . . and you pray about it . . . do you think God is going to remove the *God-given attraction* He placed within you in the first place? No. That's absurd. We are all *naturally attracted* to some members of the opposite sex—that is not the problem; the problem is our "corrupt flesh" seeks to take advantage of that attraction and express it in a manner that is inconsistent with God's will. Furthermore, for us to pray that God would remove our *feelings,* essentially is to ask God to remove our flesh—our sin disposition. Again, that is not going to happen. Yet, that is precisely the way most believers pray! Why would God remove the very thing that He uses to *"mature us"* in our faith? Our problem is we are not into this *spiritual warfare stuff* and fighting the fight of faith! Trial and temptation is the *"primary method"* God uses to accomplish His sanctifying work in us, to build our faith and spiritual character (Jam 1:2-3, 12-16). Incidentally, the words *trial* and *temptation* are the same word in Greek—*peirasmos*—this word literally means to test, try, prove, or tempt; thus, inherent in every trial is the temptation to do evil.

Some "PASSIONATE FEELINGS" can be very difficult to overcome—anger, lust, jealousy, and hatred can be brutally tough at times—because when they arise in our hearts, we tend to *fan the flame* before we even think about trying to extricate ourselves from them. Feelings can grow in intensity very quickly, and oftentimes we do not begin to fight against them until we have a *raging inferno* inside of us! To feed "inappropriate feelings" in our minds only *"fans the flame"*—so the battle is one that is "lost" in the mind. Feelings always follow *"thoughts"*—what you *think* causes you to *feel* the way you do. Adam and Eve opted for the satisfaction of *"desire"* rather than for *"obedience"* to the commandment of God. It should be noted, there are only these two ways of living—the *feeling-oriented life of desire* that is oriented toward "self" . . . and the *commandment-oriented life of holiness* that is oriented toward "God." The first is motivated by *feeling,* and the second is motivated by *obedient faith* in God. Satan got to Adam and Eve through "desire"—all sin grows out of the desire-oriented life. Again, we all sin because we desire or want to sin! Many Christians say they just can't control their "thoughts"—yes, you can! it may not be easy! but God commands it! (Mt 22:37; Rom 8:6; 12:2; 2 Cor 10:5; Eph 4:23; Phil 4:8; Col 3:2, 16; 1 Pet 1:13; Prv 4:23; 23:7). Without a disciplined mind the flesh will rule . . . an undisciplined mind is the devil's workshop . . . a disciplined mind is not a spiritual option.

The two most common GOALS for most believers are these:

1. That they *not sin*—which is certainly a noble goal to have, but completely unrealistic.

2. That they *enjoy life*—that is, that they have a happy "feel good" life; another unrealistic goal.

Obviously these are qualities of life every believer would *"like"* to have—by the way, they are also the qualities of unbelievers as well. But these qualities cannot be the *"number one desires"* of our lives—because the number one desire for the believer must be to *exalt God* by living a life of faith and righteousness that pleases Him (Mt 6:33; 1 Cor 10:31; Phil 1:21; Heb 11:6)—anything less than that is to embrace an anti-God position of *"self-centered living."* The self-centered individual says, "To heck with God, I'm doing what I feel like doing! I don't want anybody telling me what to do! It's my life and I'll live it the way I feel like living it!" This worldview completely misses out on the "Creature/Creator" relationship—man was created by God, for an intimate relationship with Him (Rom 11:36). To reject intimacy with Christ is like rejecting "the love of your life" for a ten dollar spending spree at some supermarket! or trading an "incredible jewel" worth millions for a little plastic ring out of a bubble gum machine! How warped and perverted can we be? Obviously, there is no way to adequately contrast the comparison—because we are talking about something of eternal value vs. temporal value.

The number one goal for every believer must be that of "cultivating an intimate relationship with Jesus Christ"—which is vastly superior to having a goal of simply refraining from sin (as noble a goal as that may be). By concentrating on the *"sin issue,"* the believer becomes consumed with a *"performance behavioral-oriented life"*—as such, he has a *"self-focus"* rather than a *"God-focus."* Living righteously and not sinning are *byproducts* of "walking intimately with Christ" or "walking in the Spirit." When you make the byproduct the goal of your life—you are placing the cart before the horse, so-to-speak; such a goal will result in certain failure. Therefore, when you make *"not sinning"* the goal, you will sin—often!

THE "SIN PRINCIPLE" WITHIN

The "sin principle" is referred to by theologians and Scripture as the sin nature, the old nature, the flesh, the sin disposition, and human nature—in short, it is weak, low, debased, inclined toward evil, and tends toward ungodliness and vice (Mt 7:11; 15:19; Rom 3:9–10; 5:12, 19; 7:14–17, 21; 8:3, 5, 6; Eph 2:1–3; 2 Tim 2:26). Nothing good dwells within the flesh (Rom 7:18). The propensities of the sin nature ("fruit of the flesh") are immorality, impurity, sensuality, idolatry, sorcery, enmities, strife, jealousy, outbursts of anger, disputes, dissensions, factions, envying, drunkenness, and carousings (Gal 5:19–21). Each of these qualities reside in each of us, and these cravings and fleshly desires incite to sin (Mt 26:41; Mk 14:38; Jam 1:14–15). So the *flesh* of man is inherently corrupt, diabolical, and fully against the rule of God in a person's life (Gal 5:17)—God and the flesh are diametrically opposed to each other, and they "both" have taken up permanent residency in our lives.

Because the "sin principle within" has some degree of freedom to operate in our minds, its influence at times seems to overwhelm us to the extent that our inner man "strongly identifies with its passions and cravings." This exerting influence causes some believers to "feel" as though they are not just a "little corrupt," but "fully corrupt to the core;" as such, they are prone to question whether or not they are really "new creations in Christ"—after all, how could a believer think such sinful thoughts? (a typical questioning strategy of Satan). When "fleshly thoughts" enter our minds, many of us have such a strong tendency to identify with those thoughts, that we actually feel as though "those thoughts" express the essence of who we really are—Satan works at trying to convince us of such. Because the "flesh" is so influential in our minds and hearts, many of us try to "transform our old sinful natures through religious regimen"—but *the flesh* cannot be transformed, no matter how hard we may try to change it! The truth of the matter is our flesh is actually becoming more corrupt every day! (Eph 4:22), so forget trying to change it! The lack of success in trying to transform it causes many of us to conclude that we *(our spirits)* are "not being transformed into the image of Christ." It is extremely important that the believer understands that the *flesh* and the *spirit* are "two distinct entities" co-existing within us; and these entities are in direct opposition to each other—complete opposites. We are called to "identify with the *spirit*"—not the *flesh* (Rom 6:3–11)—so that our lives are Christlike rather than ungodly (Rom 6:4).

(continued)

> **As a believer, what are you to do to combat this problem?** First, you have to come to the point where you accept the fact that "<u>your sin nature</u>" <u>is going to accompany you all the way through life</u>, yet you have to realize that "<u>it is no longer the real you</u>" that is now a child of God. Your sin nature is that "<u>sin principle</u>" in you that continually tries to influence your life for evil. The sin nature is extremely stubborn and persistent, and it will <u>never lay down its arms</u>; it operates like a "<u>heat-seeking missile</u>"—when it sees something in your life it wants to hone in on, it fires one of its missiles, and the battle is on! <u>As a believer, you need to be able to look at yourself from outside yourself, in a sense, and see that **your sin nature** is that part of you that is **"really not you;"**</u> though you accept the fact that it is still present in your life . . . spiritually speaking, your sin nature is no longer the real you (Rom 7:17). So, when it rears its ugly head, you don't have to think "<u>that's the real me</u>," because it is not! We are not playing games with language here. Knowing this fact should cause you be tremendously grateful that it indeed is "<u>no longer you!</u>" It is now just an ugly sinful voice within you that is screaming for attention. On the one hand, the transparent admission that "sin dwells in you" is very humbling; on the other hand, it causes you to give God all the praise (Rom 7:25). By the way, for you as a believer to think that your flesh is not going to "desire to do evil" is ludicrous—it is going to! That's the reality of the sin disposition. Your flesh is like another person (<u>a totally sinful person</u>) who is going to walk beside you throughout your entire life; he is going to talk to you almost non-stop expressing his desires. The good news is, you no longer have to obey your sin nature . . . or strive to transform it . . . or be embarrassed by its corruptness . . . or grieve over how diabolical it is! <u>You are no longer to identify with "the sin nature" within you</u>—***because it is no longer YOU!*** It is just a part of the total package that will accompany you as a participant in the cosmic battle of which you are now a part. If God didn't want it in your life—it wouldn't be there! If He didn't want you to have to deal with it—He would remove it! This concept will be more fully developed throughout the remainder of this chapter.

Study the teaching of Jesus about the Vine and the branches—the essence of abiding in Christ is walking intimately with Him (Jn 15:1–11). Once again, the "preeminent focus or goal" of every believer's life must be that of ***"cultivating an intimate relationship with Christ!"***

So, the Christian life is about having a "Christ focus" rather than a "Self focus"—If your focus has anything to do with *"your performance,"* you're on the wrong track! Get off that train, and get on the right one! The train you are on is the one Satan wants you on, and it will make you as miserable as you can possibly be! You are going in the wrong direction! This perspective is essential for the believer's emotional, psychological and spiritual well-being. Many believers are experiencing *"spiritual paralysis"*—bewilderment, disillusionment, discouragement, and depression—because the life of faith *(being all God wants you to be)* seems out of reach for them. If you are on the "performance track," you're right, it is out of reach! If you are on the performance track, your problem is that you have a *"wrong focus"*—self, behavior, performance, not sinning—"fix your eyes on Christ, the Author and Perfecter of your faith!" (Heb 12:2). *Stop fixating on the problem (sin), and start focusing on the solution (Christ)—cultivate intimacy with Him!* Is it easy to cultivate intimacy with Christ? No. Not at all . . . but it does bring substantial peace and joy to your life in the midst of the journey! Cultivating intimacy with Christ is God's *lifelong call* upon our lives as His children (Phil 3:10; 2 Pet 3:18; Jer 9:23-24; Mic 6:8)—trying to refrain from sin is not the life we are called to. Achieving intimacy with Christ is difficult because we inhabit *"sinful flesh;"* the resultant effect of living with the flesh, is that it *continually* insists on having its way in our lives—therefore the battle oftentimes gets heated! That is the norm! Expect it! Prepare yourself for it! Furthermore, this battle is won by *faith* . . . by believing God! Yes, it is a battle—it is the mother of all battles! (Eph 6:10ff; 1 Tim 6:12; 2 Tim 4:7).

Following are some thoughts on SIN from the viewpoint of an 'ole Master Practioner—Me. I am approaching 70 years old; I have served in the ministry for nearly 40 years; and I have been an ardent student of the Word for every one of those years; all told, I have more than 11 years of college and seminary education under my belt . . . and I have struggled with the issues of temptation and sin just like every other believer. *Those who say they don't struggle with temptation and sin are either lying, fooling themselves, or they are not a believer—this stuff is common to every believer . . . no man on planet earth walks on water.* Personally, I have been as exasperated and frustrated with "my walk" at times as all of you have been—you are not alone—eventually, we are all subjected to spiritually dark seasons in life, and the experience can oftentimes be downright debilitating. Rest assured, even during those times, God is *very active* in your life. The fact is, those spiritually gut-wrenching times cause us to do some serious thinking and questioning—*which is good*—though we never discover all the answers, we do discover significant pieces of the puzzle that confirm in our minds the miraculous work God is doing in our hearts . . . and with that comes a deep abiding peace. God has wired me with a spiritual DNA that "demands answers"—like some of you, I am always asking the "why questions." Those of us with this particular DNA probably experience a frustration level a little higher than the majority. God simply won't let me rest with simple little spiritual clichés that we all seem to learn on our journey with Christ—such answers don't satisfy the excessively obsessed soul. I hate temptation and sin with a passion—can't imagine too many believers out there hating it much more than I do . . . though I may be wrong on that point. If I had my choice—clearly I don't—I'd opt for a far easier road to spiritual maturity than the one I have traveled. But that is not the "divine economy" under which we live—God did not design an "easy way" to make us like Christ . . . He could have—He is God—but He chose not to. He could have designed a system of salvation whereby He would not have had to go to the cross—but He did not. Why? A part of the answer to that question is found in Scripture. Let me share a little of it with you. Lord willing, it will help answer some of the questions of your heart, like it has mine. Let me begin by first presenting to you the following thesis statement—

> *God has placed you on the grand stage of the universe (planet earth) to be a participant in the cosmic battle between good and evil.*

Think carefully with me about what that statement above really means—that statement explains *your primary purpose for existence*—you are to be a *participant* in the cosmic battle between good and evil. Your purpose is not to live on this beautiful planet, seeking out all of its pleasantries, and enjoying them to the max; nor is it to accrue as many toys as you can for yourself, or indulge in all the pleasures this world has to offer—*those are not your God-ordained reasons for existence.* As believers in Christ, you and I play an integral role in the *battle of all battles*—we are all to be *combatants* in a war of cosmic significance against the forces of darkness and evil . . . you may not like the fact that you have been designated to be a part of that war, but if you are a believer, you have been; so stop trying to create a *Disneyland experience* out of your life—put on your armor and become an active participant with the forces of light in defeating the forces of darkness (Eph 6:10–17). Remember what Jesus said, "Either you are *for* Me, or you are *against* Me" (Mt 12:30)—there is no neutral or middle ground (that is a sober reality)—"You cannot serve two masters; you cannot serve God and yourself" (Mt 6:24). Either you choose to live for *"self,"* or you choose to live for *"God."* Admittedly, that is not an easy choice. Your *old sinful nature* and your *new godly nature* are arch rivals, and they are continually fighting against each other to control your life. That is why it is called *"spiritual warfare."*

The big picture involves a "COSMIC BATTLE" between good and evil. Paul exhorts us as Christians to "put on the *full armor of God* that we might be able to stand against the schemes of the devil . . . [and to be mindful of the fact that] our struggle is not against flesh and blood, but against the rulers and powers and spiritual forces of darkness" (Eph 6:10–12; Eph 2:2; Col 1:13). Conversely, Peter tells us that "Jesus bore our sins in His body on the cross, that we might *die to sin* and *live to righteousness*" (1 Pet 2:24). "Shall we continue in sin as believers because God is gracious?" Paul asks. "May it never be! How shall we who died to sin still live in it?" (Rom 6:2). Since we died with Christ, "do not let sin reign in your mortal body that you should obey its lusts and desires . . . but present the members of your body to God as instruments of *righteousness*" (Rom 6:12–13). "Fight the good fight!" (1 Tim 1:18–19; 6:12; 2 Tim 2:3f).

So what is the "biblical context" for the BIG PICTURE? Let's go all the way back to the day God created Adam and Eve and placed them in the *"Garden of Eden."* The word "Eden" in Hebrew literally means "delight"—obviously, the Garden of Eden was a place of perfect delight; nothing was lacking that could contribute to man's legitimate joy, fulfillment or happiness. God placed Adam in charge of the garden, making him His delegated authority; i.e., God's "regent" on earth (Gen 1:26–30). The duties that fell to Adam's lot seem to have been entirely satisfying and enjoyable, while at the same time not too taxing or onerous. There are, however, a number of questions the creation account raises—

Why did God create "MAN" in the first place? What is the purpose of human history? Is there any relationship between the events of eternity past and human history? Why were humans, a lower creature than angels, created "after" God had already created angels? In order to answer all of these questions, all we can do is chronologically reconstruct the complete testimony of Scripture and see where that leads us. The Bible tells us some very interesting things that occurred *"prior"* to creation that help us connect the dots and provide us with some significant insight.

When you ask Christians why they exist, most respond with the typical answer: *"Humanity exists for the glory of God,"* and they quote a number of passages that support that statement (Ps 19:1; Is 43:7; Rom 1:20). The Book of Proverbs tells us that God created everything *"for His own ends"* (Prv 16:4; cf. Rom 11:36; 1 Cor 8:6; Col 1:16); that all creation is an "expression of His will, His wisdom, His power" (Rev 4:11). So, according to the Bible, we see that human beings were created for *"God's glory."* But that raises another question: *"Why did God need glory?"* If He is God, doesn't He have enough glory? Surely God is not so egocentric that He needs us to reassure Him—right? Or did something occur in the history of the universe prior to the Genesis account of creation, that precipitated His creating man? Was that something instrumental in bringing about the creation of humanity? Again, we need to go to Scripture to see if it indeed has anything to say about "events" that may have occurred in eternity past.

SIN AND SALVATION

On the "Temple to Apollo" in Greece, an inscription summed up the wisdom of that day—*"Know Thyself."* Those two words embodied the deeply held conviction that "the chief study of mankind is man;" that our wisdom consists in the accuracy and depth of self-knowledge. On one level Christianity has no quarrel with that analysis, so long as it corresponds with a personal knowledge of God, and our intrinsic need for salvation. What Christianity does deny is that we can know ourselves apart from God—though it is true that we can know much about man, we cannot know man as he is in himself apart from God's revelation. That is why Reinhold Niebuhr says, "Man has always been his own most vexing problem." Nothing explains the *"nature of man"* except the truths of Christianity.

According to the book of Genesis, God placed man in the Garden of Eden to be His vice regents on earth. He gave them maximum freedom, authority, and dominion over all the earth (Gen 1:28). There were no apparent restrictions on how they were to do it, except one—they were not to eat of the tree of the knowledge of good and evil (Gen 2:17). The fruit was a tangible symbol of the fact that the man and woman were God's creatures—they were not God—as such, they were responsible to Him: *"for in the day that you eat of it you shall die"* (Gen 2:16–17). A contradiction of the veracity of God's Word is the issue in Satan's temptation of Eve—*"you shall not die"* (Gen 3:4–5). Here, then, is the first revelation of sin's nature and of what is basically wrong with mankind: 1) Sin is *unfaithfulness*—it is to doubt God's goodness and truthfulness, leading inevitably to an act of outright rejection; 2) Sin is *apostasy*—it is rebellion against that sublime nature and destiny God made for man; and 3) Sin is *pride*—in the woman's case, it was the conviction that she knew what was better for herself and her husband than God; incidentally, this was the original sin of Satan (Is 14:14). So man's sinful nature is characterized by the fact that it is faithless, rebellious, and full of pride; sin is everything within our being that is contrary to the expressed will of God (Rom 3:20; 4:15; 7:7; Jam 4:12, 17). The sinfulness of sin lies in the fact that it is always *"against God,"* whatever the sin may be (Ps 51:4).

The questions arise, "How bad is man? How bad is sin?" Some believe man is only *"slightly flawed,"* that he is just "sick"—observers differ over how sick he is: acutely, gravely, critically, or mortally. The Bible says man is "dead" (Eph 2:1), that he is *"totally flawed."* Furthermore,

(continued)

the tragedy of human existence is overwhelmingly visible to anyone who will honestly view the mounting starvation, suffering, hatred, selfishness, and indifference on our planet. The fall affected every part of man—<u>his spirit died</u>, for his fellowship with God was broken . . . <u>his soul began to die</u>, for he began to lie and cheat and kill . . . <u>his body eventually died</u>, for God had said, "You are dust, and to dust you shall return" (Gen 3:19). So man is now <u>alienated from God</u> . . . and that, says John Stott, "is the most dreadful of all sin's consequences." The threefold result of man's alienation is expanded upon by the apostle Paul in Romans 3:10–12—1) "<u>No one is righteous, not one;</u>" that is the essence of the moral side of every man. 2) "<u>No one understands;</u>" sin has also polluted our intellect and our spiritual understanding. 3) "<u>No one seeks for God;</u>" this is the area of our will—we have no desire to come to God; instead we make gods of our own making, in the hope that they will fill the spiritual vacuum in our lives. As Luther says, "We are wholly given over to sin"—we are enslaved to sin (Rom 6:6, 17, 20); therefore, the only proper thing for us to do is to humbly acknowledge our sin, and call upon the eternal God for mercy.

What does "sin" really look like in the heart of man? According to Scripture, man is totally corrupt, and has placed his own interests above all other interests; hence, man is fully <u>*"self-centered."*</u> His entire life is totally oriented toward himself—<u>man loves himself</u>; as such, God commands him to "love others!" (Mt 22:39). The sum of all the commandments is "love"—thus sin in its nature is egotistical and selfish; self is put in the place of God (Rom 15:3; 1 Cor 13:5; 2 Tim 3:1–2; 2 Th 2:3–4). By the way, <u>*"self love"*</u> is one of the signs of the last days (2 Tim 3:2). Ultimately, men have their own <u>self-interests</u> at stake in everything they do; in some way, their intent is always to satisfy and gratify themselves. Paul writes, "Don't merely look out after your own personal interests, but also look after the interests of others" (Phil 2:4)—why does Paul say this? Because we "naturally" have a self-focus in life, and we need to be reminded to focus on others. Since our number one concern is <u>*"us,"*</u> everything we do in life is to make us feel good and gain the approval of others; it is natural (that's the essence of "flesh") to want others to <u>*"like us,"*</u> so we behave in ways that elicit favorable responses from others. When people don't like us, or respond negatively toward us, we become angry, discouraged, depressed, or hurt—because our own "self interests" have been impinged. Remember, every human being operates this way; even the so-called "lovely people" of this world—they are just more disciplined in their behavior than others—the fact is *by "nature" we are all sinful and self-centered*.

When we became Christians, we obviously experienced a "radical transformation" within us. Scripture tells us that we were *"saved from something"* and we were *"saved to something."* According to the Bible, we have been *"saved from the law of sin and death"* (Rom 8:2); sin is no longer our master, and eternal death is no longer our destiny. The Bible also tells us we have been *"saved unto eternal life"*—we have been "made alive in Christ," and we will live and reign with Him forever (Jn 3:16; 10:10; Rom 6:4, 11, 23; 8:9; Eph 1:5; 1 Jn 5:13). If you are a child of God, you are a *new creation* (Jn 3:3; Rom 6:4; 2 Cor 5:17; Gal 6:15); your sins are *forever forgiven* (Rom 6:23; 8:2–3; Jn 5:24; Eph 4:32); though your sins were as "scarlet," they have been "white" as snow! (Isaiah 1:18). You have been made *righteous* with the righteousness of Christ—the very DNA of Christ Himself has been given to you (1 Cor 1:30; 2 Cor 5: 20–21). You are now *indwelled* by the Holy Spirit, that you might walk in newness of life (intimacy with Christ), just as God intended at the day of creation. As believers we have been *re-created!* (Jn 14:16–17, 26; 16:13; Rom 8:9; 1 Cor 6:19–20). *By the way, though you stumble and mess up over and over and over again, as all of us do, and though you are even faithless at times, God will never abandon you, or give up on you, because You are now* **"His possession!"** (Jn 6:37, 39; 10:11, 14; 1 Cor 6:20; 2 Tim 2:13; Tit 2:14; 1 Pet 1:18–19; 2:9), and He has promised to see the transforming work in your life through to the end! (Ps 138:8; Prv 24:16; Rom 8:28–31; Phil 1:6; 2:12–13; 1 Th 5:24; Heb 13:5; Jam 3:2).

Now, if the foregoing is indeed the case, that He bought you in the slave-market of sin and made you His own, you should be an excited, rejoicing, exuberant follower of Christ . . . and fully engaged in the work of Christ in the world! If you are not fully engaged— why? Are you *ashamed* of the gospel? (Mk 8:38; Rom 1:16; 2 Tim 1:8, 12, 16; 1 Cor 1:18). If it embarrasses you—study the *"cross"*—you have lost your focus! If you are disappointed or discouraged in your faith, or are seemingly too weak to fight the good fight or stand for Christ in your area of influence, you have taken your eyes off of Christ, and are once again preoccupied with *"yourself."* If that is the case, it is only *natural* that the things of this world consume you, and the destiny and concerns of others, essentially, are irrelevant issues to you. The remedy for your problem? Stop focusing on yourself! and get your focus back on Christ! (Heb 12:2; 1 Jn 3:3). By the way, this is a very common problem for believers. The fight of faith must be

(continued)

> *intentionally fought*—we must be intentional about eliminating all the clutter and noise in our lives, find a quiet space, still our hearts before God, and actively pursue intimacy with Him. There is no such thing as *"spiritual cruise-control"* in the Christian life—either you are progressing or you are regressing. Embrace the spiritual disciplines with renewed vigor and regain your focus. Reflect again upon what the Scriptures have to say—James writes, *"Draw near to God and He will draw near to you"* (Jam 4:8); Jeremiah puts it, *"You will find Me when you seek Me with all your heart"* (Jer 29:13). Jesus said, *"Ask and it shall be given to you; seek and you shall find; knock and it shall be opened to you"* (Mt 7:7—the present tense verbs in this verse emphasize the importance of *"continually"* asking, seeking, and knocking; spiritual growth is not something that occurs at just "one moment in time"—it is a process that continues throughout your entire life; hence, it is a lifestyle of daily drawing near to the Lord Jesus). God has made *our* whole-hearted movement toward Him a condition of *His* drawing close to us—though God is ultimately the *"First Cause"* in our becoming like Christ, the process includes our cooperation, participation and obedience (Phil 1:6; 2:12–13; Heb 11:6).

Scripture tells us of the creation and fall of the most "magnificent creature" to ever come from the hand of God—LUCIFER. In Ezekiel 28:11–19, the magnificent nature of this creature is mentioned during a section of Scripture in which Ezekiel excoriates the king of Tyre for his arrogance and compares him to Satan, as he predicts the fall of this king. The passage reads:

> Thus says the Lord God, "You had the seal of perfection, full of wisdom and perfect in beauty. You were in Eden, the garden of God; every precious stone was your covering . . . the workmanship of your settings and sockets was in you. On the day that you were created they were prepared. You were the anointed cherub who covers, and I placed you there. You were on the holy mountain of God; you walked in the midst of the stones of fire" (probably a reference to the 'wall of fire' that surrounded the throne room of God and point to Satan's unfettered access to God's presence as the guardian cherub). "You were blameless in your ways from the day

you were created, until unrighteousness was found in you. By the abundance of your trade you were internally filled with violence, and you sinned; therefore I have cast you as profane from the mountain of God and I have destroyed you, O covering cherub, from the midst of the stones of fire. Your heart was lifted up because of your beauty; you corrupted your wisdom for the sake of your splendor; I cast you to the ground. . . . By the multitude of your iniquities, in the unrighteousness of your trade, you profaned your sanctuaries. Therefore I have brought fire from the midst of you; it has consumed you, and I have turned you to ashes on the earth in the eyes of everyone. All who knew you among the peoples are astonished at you; you have become a horror, and you will be no more."

Lucifer's fall is described in a section of Scripture where Isaiah denounces Babylon, the center of power and false religion during his ministry to Israel. Isaiah 14:12–17 reads—

How you have fallen from heaven, O star of the morning, son of the dawn! You have been cut down to the earth, you who have weakened the nations! But you said in your heart, "I will ascend to heaven; I will raise my throne above the stars of God, and I will sit on the mount of assembly in the recesses of the north. I will ascend above the heights of the clouds; I will make myself like the Most High." Nevertheless, you will be thrust down to Sheol, to the recesses of the pit. Those who see you will gaze at you and ponder, "Is this the man who made the earth tremble, who shook kingdoms, who made the world like a wilderness and overthrew its cities?"

Lucifer in his original rebellion had "REFUSED TO SUBMIT" to the authority of God and had declared himself "independent of God." In the Genesis account of creation, *Adam* (in this new form of the kingdom of heaven) was being *"tested"* to see whether he would submit to the authority of God out of recognition of God's right to rule, or whether he, *like Satan,* would reject God's right to rule and declare himself to be independent of God's law. Just how long Adam and Eve remained in a state of obedience and continued as citizens of the kingdom of heaven on earth, we don't know, but the time came when their obedience was *"tested by Satan"* (Gen 3). Would man properly execute God's delegated authority, or would he succumb to the temptation to be *"like God"* and appropriate the arrogance of Satan in his moral fall? Scripture tells us that man ultimately fell, succumbing to Satan's luring lies . . . and ended up giving dominion over the earth to Satan. Therefore, Satan ultimately succeeded in transferring a third of the angelic realm and all of God's human creation into his domain (Rev 12:4; Jude 1:6). The earth then became a province of Satan's kingdom. The earth's government changed from a ***theocracy*** to a ***satanocracy***. This is the reason Jesus called Satan "the prince of this world" (Jn 12:31; 14:30; 16:11), and Satan had authority to offer all the kingdoms of this world to Jesus (Lk 4:5–6). In addition, some of the angels of Satan are called "the world rulers of this darkness" (Eph 6:12). Paul called Satan "the god of this age" (2 Cor 4:4).

Instead of becoming "completely independent" as a result of his choice, Adam was brought under the dominion of a new king—SATAN. His original King was a loving, benevolent Ruler who offered him life, peace, happiness, and fulfillment in return for willing obedience—his new king was a hard, selfish taskmaster who offered him death, sickness, conflict, grief, and frustration in return for service to him. Adam was transferred from membership in the ***kingdom of God*** to membership in the ***kingdom of Satan*** (Eph 2:1), from the *kingdom of Light* to the *kingdom of Darkness*. Instead of improving himself by rebelling against God, Adam prevented himself from obtaining the fullness of his original potential. Adam's rebellion had confirmed him so strongly in his tragic predicament that he was rendered totally incapable of rescuing himself from it. Nothing short of supernatural, divine intervention would be able to save him (and his future offspring) from the predicament he had brought upon himself and his progeny by his own choice (Is 43:11—Showers, *What on Earth is God Doing?* pp. 16–17).

From the passages in Isaiah & Ezekiel, we have an understanding of the nature of "Satan's fall" at a point in *eternity past,* as well as the judgment that was pronounced upon him at the time of his fall. Obviously, the execution of his sentence is still in the future since he has not yet been cast into the Lake of Fire (Rev 20:10). The delay between the pronouncement of the sentence and the execution of the sentence is the span of time equal to *"human history."* This fact establishes the relationship between an **angelic conflict** and **human history.** A careful reading of the biblical account of Satan's fall certainly allows for there to have been a *"period of unspecified duration"* between the moral fall of Lucifer and the creation of the universe, including earth. After human history has run its course and the decisions of billions of humans have been made, God will have demonstrated His attributes. In addition, a lower creature, man, will have vindicated the integrity of God's essence every time the lower creature responds positively to God's holy requirements. From the beginning of creation to the conclusion of the *Great White Throne Judgment,* human history will serve as permanent evidence of the integrity of God's essence. In their observation of humans, angels will witness proof after proof of Satan's own culpability, and proof after proof of God's perfect justice (Job 1:6; 2:1–3; Lk 15:7, 10; 1 Cor 4:9; 11:10; Eph 3:10; 1 Tim 3:16; 5:21).

HERE'S THE ETERNAL PERSPECTIVE: The great, governing cherub (Lucifer) became the *"malignant enemy of God"* and *war was declared.* God (being God) was neither surprised nor astonished, because He knew before it happened that it would happen, and He had His perfect plan ready to be put into effect. **Although God had the power to destroy Satan with a breath, He chose not to do so.** It was as though an edict had been proclaimed in heaven—*"We shall give this rebellion a thorough trial . . . we shall permit it to run its full course. The universe shall see what a creature, though he be the 'highest creature' ever to spring from God's Word, can do apart from Him. God's entire creation shall watch this experiment, which shall take place during a brief interlude between eternity past and eternity future—a period called "time." In it the spirit of independence will be allowed to expand to the utmost. And the wreck and ruin which shall result will demonstrate to the universe—and forever—that there is no life, no joy, no peace apart from a complete dependence upon the Most High God, Professor of heaven and earth"*

(Barnhouse, p. 51). The course of God's purpose in creation, it seems, is to make a sufficient and *final trial* of every claim of His adversaries; and when this age, with all its developments, shall have passed by, every mouth will be stopped, and the whole world and Satan will know their own failure and sin before God. They will stand *"self-condemned,"* and nothing could accomplish this but the testing—*by actual trial*—of all the self-sufficient claims of Satan and man (Chafer, p. 24).

Satan and a third of all angels "did not keep their proper domain, but left their own abode" (Jude 1:6; Rev 12:4); they rebelled against God in eternity past. Scripture discloses that Satan has an organizational structure for his angelic forces that consists of principalities, powers, and rulers of the darkness of this age" (Eph 1:21; cf. 6:12; Rom 8:38). Satan governs a portion of the angelic realm and that governance will continue until Satan's trial is concluded at the end of human history at the *Great White Throne Judgment* (Rev 20:10–15). ***Human history will have served its God-intended purpose of demonstrating to all creation that God is love, and the only absolute righteousness and sovereign authority. Human history will have established the integrity of God's essence as a fact not ever again subject to challenge.*** Satan's challenge of God's essence in eternity past as documented in Isaiah 14:11–17 and Ezek 28:12–19 will have been answered with irrefutable evidence for all eternity. Once the evidence of human history has been completely presented, the Only Sovereign over all creation will never again be subject to question or doubt.

Angels were already in existence when God created the material universe—they "shouted for joy" as they observed what was being made (Job 38:4–7). They were fascinated *"observers"* when God was laying the foundations of the earth. The fact that there is a strong interest in human history on the part of God's angelic creation is strongly supported throughout Scripture (note the following activities by His heavenly angels—Job 38:4–7; Lk 15:10; Act 1:10; 7:38, 53; Gal 3:19; Lk 2:13; Mt 4:11; 13:37–39; 24:31; 25:31; 28:2–4; 2 Th 1:7–8; Rev 14:9–10). All these passages, and many others not listed, attest to a keen interest in the affairs of human history on the part of the angelic realm. This fact raises an important question: Why? Why are angels interested in the outcome of human history? Why would human history be a focal point of attention and activity from such a superior creature as angels? Why were humans (significantly lower creatures) created *after* angels anyway?

Satan's case, and that of his followers, has already been adjudicated and his ultimate fate pronounced. At the conclusion of human history, Satan will face the execution of his sentence (Rev 20:10; Is 24:21–22), a verdict adjudged before human history began. Why the delay in judgment? Why didn't God simply plunge the devil and his minions into the fires of hell immediately after their just condemnation? The answer to all such questions is intimately bound up with God's creation of another species of morally responsible creatures—MAN. Until the fires of hell receive Satan and his followers, God grants them a degree of *"freedom"*—and during this interlude of time, Satan goes about the earth in search of believers whose defenses are down, seeking to destroy them (1 Pet 5:8). *The creation of MAN is meant as a response to Satan's rebellion, a living refutation of the devil's slanderous lies against the character of God.* When all is said and done, God's righteousness will have been affirmed before all creation, and proved beyond a shadow of a doubt through the merciful salvation of believing mankind. Human beings who choose to *reject* God's gracious gift of Jesus Christ, will share the fate of the devil and his followers in the lake of fire (Rev 20:11–15); and *everyone*, whether rebellious or regenerate, will eventually bow before the God of all creation and acknowledge His majesty and righteousness, and confess that Jesus Christ is LORD to the glory of God the Father (Rom 14:11; Phil 2:9–11). *Everyone* will be present on that day.

So the TRIAL OF EVIL is the ultimate reason for the MAN'S EXISTENCE—Evil is on trial right now—that is what our existence is all about. Let's return again to the biblical account of creation—Adam and Eve were in the most idyllic setting imaginable . . . a place of absolute perfection and beauty. Nothing could have been added to make it a better, more enjoyable place. Consider this—in this beautiful setting God placed the serpent, **Satan!** Obviously, that was *intentional;* he just didn't *happen* to show up; God *purposely* placed him there. And then God gave a *"moral charge"* to Adam, "From any tree of the garden you may eat freely; but *from the tree of the knowledge of good and evil you shall not eat*—in the day that you do eat from it you shall surely die" (Gen 3:16–17). God's plan was now set in motion—He had created a new species—MAN—and placed him in a perfect Garden *with Satan*. The "moral charge" was given, and the inevitable occurred—Adam disobeyed God! Was God surprised? Absolutely not. God knew the end from the beginning. Furthermore, God's purposes were now about to be executed. The story of man's creation and fall, and his subsequent redemption, was the *plan of God* from all creation (Is 46:9–11; 55:11; Jn 1:13; 7:30; Act 2:23; Eph 1:4–6; Rev 22:13)—*"Christ was slain from the foundation of the world"* (Rev 13:8). God planned the end from the beginning. There are no surprises with God—He is in absolute control of all things; nothing happens outside of His divine providence.

The issue most believers struggle with is how God could include "sin" in His divine economy for the universe. After all, how could a *"perfectly holy God,"* who admittedly "cannot look upon sin," incorporate it into His plan? That's a fair question, and one most students of Scripture have asked. Perhaps one of the keys to answering this issue is to understand that *"God did not create sin"*—that is, He is not its author—but that "He did create the potential for sin," by not programming His creatures to choose only that which is good. Furthermore, because God created the potential for sin, and included it in His divine plan, obviously it has a *"purpose"* in His economy. Think about this for a moment: the "worst sin" ever committed—the crucifixion of Christ—purchased our salvation, and brought the *greatest glory possible* to our Savior in heaven (Phil 2:5–11; Heb 2:9; Eph 1:18–23). That in itself is an astounding thought. Therefore to think that God could not possibly bring glory out of "some sin we might commit" is ludicrous—if God was glorified through the horrible sin of crucifixion, how much easier is it for Him to be glorified through our sins? Consider this: every time you and I sin as His children, we turn toward our heavenly Father and tell Him we "fully agree with Him regarding our sin" (that's confession); in doing so we denounce our sinful behavior, and glory in the blood of the cross of His Son. The response in heaven every time we confess? All the angelic host "rejoice!" So every time we sin, we ultimately (through confession) put another "stake" in the corpse of evil! God has multiple purposes for including sin in His plan—sin causes us to turn to Christ (2 Cor 7:9) . . . it causes us to see how utterly sinful we really are (how else would we ever learn that?), thus keeping us humble before God . . . it causes us to trust God more (as we repeatedly sin and confess our sins over and over again, our faith in Christ is built up and strengthened) . . . it helps us see how great and wonderful and loving and forgiving God really is (how would we ever come to know the unfathomable riches of His grace and love were it not for our repeated sinning and His repeated forgiveness). By "continually experiencing the forgiveness of God," we learn that He loves us with an everlasting love—there is absolutely no end to it! (Ps 100:5; 106:1; 118:1–4; 136:1–26; Jer 33:11; Mt 18:22). Though *"sin"* is a big issue in the sight of God (He sent His Son to the cross for it!) . . . the fact is *"God's love and grace"* are far bigger issues to Him! (Rom 5:20; 8:35–39).

Always remember, God is "GOD"—there is no other! (Is 40:13–18, 25–26; 43:1, 7, 10–13, 25; 44:6, 22; 45:5–7, 22–25; 48:10–11; 50:2; 53:5–6; 55:8–11). History is "His story!" The unfolding of "His plan!" All that happens is according to "His will!" Think of it this way—if God never wanted *"sin"* to exist, it would never have come into existence. Never. To think that God somehow "lost control" in the process of bringing about the created order, is ludicrous. If He lost control, then He is not the omniscient, omnipotent God of the Bible. Clearly, "sin" was not an accident. Nothing is so high that it is above God's providence (Jer 32:17, 27); nothing is so bad but that God cannot draw good out of it (Gen 50:30); and nothing is so wisely plotted that God cannot disappoint it (2 Kg 19; Mt 2:13). **Richard Sibbes** in his book *The Soul's conflict* writes: "God's divine providence cannot but bring incredible security to the believer's soul; to know that in all variety of changes and intercourse in good and bad events, HE hath a disposing hand . . . whatever befalls us serves His eternal purpose. . . . The most casual and disordered things are all subject to divine providence. It is important for believers to know that they are *'under a providence'* that is above their own" (Sibbes, *Conflict,* pp. 144–151). Humanity is prone to question God's dealings, as we see in Gideon, Asaph, Habakkuk, and others—"If the Lord be with us, why then has all this happened to us?" (Judg 6:13). After some struggling between the flesh and the spirit, the conclusion will be (however matters go), "Surely God is *good* to Israel, to those who are pure in heart!" (Ps 73:1; Rom 8:28). God's ways often seem to us full of contradictions, because His course is to frequently bring things to pass by *"contrary means."* "God works all things after the counsel of His own will" (Eph 1:11). Thus David yielded himself up to God: "Here I am, let the Lord deal with me as seemeth good unto Him" (2 Sam 15:26). Even the Lord Jesus prayed, "Father, not My will but Thine be done" (Lk 22:42; Acts 21:14). Out of our inferior reasons we may desire that God remove the cup; but when we look to the supreme reason of reasons—the will of God—here we must stoop and kiss the rod, and humble ourselves under His mighty hand. Whatever our condition and lot in life let us echo the words of **Richard Sibbes:** "If Thou wilt have me serve Thee in this condition I am in, I will gladly do so; it is enough to me that Thou wouldst have it so. I desire to yield readily, humbly, and cheerfully to Thy disposing providence" (Sibbes, *Conflict,* pp. 151–159). Rejoice in the fact that God is GOD!

Return with me to the story of CREATION—Scripture begins with Satan in the garden (Gen 3:1), and it ends with Satan being thrown into the Lake of Fire (Rev 20:10). The bookends of "human history" involve *SATAN*. Why? He was the very reason for man's existence. It was his actions in eternity past that precipitated God's plan of creation and redemption. The book of Genesis tells us that man was *"created in the image of God"* (Gen 1:26). When man fell, that image was defiled. God's plan of redemption was the **miracle of re-creation**—*"creating us in the image of Christ"* (Rom 8:29; Gal 4:19; 1 Cor 15:49; 2 Cor 3:18; Eph 1:3–6; Phil 1:6; 3:21). John writes, "Beloved, we are *children of God,* and it has not appeared as yet what we shall be . . . we know that when Christ appears we shall be *like Him* (emphatic!), because we shall see Him just as He is" (1 Jn 3:2). As redeemed sinful humanity, we shall one day be like the perfect, sinless Son of God who took our sin upon Himself in order that we might share not only *His righteousness!* but *His glory!* (Read Jn 17:22; Rom 8:21, 29–30; 9:23; 1 Cor 15:43; 2 Cor 3:18; 4:17; Eph 1:3–6; Col 1:27; 3:4; 2 Tim 2:10; Heb 2:7, 10; 1 Pet 1:7; 5:1, 10). Think about it—sinful creatures sharing God's glory! It is beyond human comprehension! So, what flows from the work of Jesus Christ is not only forgiveness and right standing with God, but *a systematic reversal of everything that was lost because of sin.* As *"new creations"* we now share the very *DNA of GOD!* (2 Cor 5:17).

In closing, the incredible news of God's Salvation is that He has made us "CO-HEIRS with CHRIST." Unbelievable as it may sound, God's Spirit now resides in us as His children (Rom 8:9; 2 Cor 1:22; Eph 1:13–14), and is "transforming us into the image of Christ" (2 Cor 3:18). By the way, this work is assured! Guaranteed! No matter how lousy you may be performing, or how much you may doubt it, God says *"He will complete the work He has started in you!"* (Phil 1:6). If you want to *enjoy* the journey, then cooperate with Him! (Phil 2:12–13; Gal 5:22). The believer's source of incomparable glory is GOD—who has **adopted us as His own children . . . and made us heirs with His Son** (Mt 25:34; Rom 8:17; Eph 1:11; Col 3:24; Heb 6:12; 9:15; 1 Pet 1:4)—as John Wesley would say, "How can this be!" It is mind-boggling! God appointed Jesus Christ to be the *"heir of all things"* (Heb 1:2), and because we are *"fellow-heirs with Him,"* we are destined to receive all that He receives! Every adopted child of God will receive the *"full inheritance"* with Christ, and everything that Christ receives by divine right, we will receive by *divine grace!* That is why it is called ***Amazing Love! Amazing Grace!***

As believers, we will one day enter into the "ETERNAL GLORY" of our Master (Mt 25:21; Jn 17:22), "who for the sake of the joy before Him endured the cross . . . and is now seated at the right hand of the throne of God" (Heb 12:2). As believers we will one day sit on the heavenly throne *"with Christ"* and rule there with Him forever (Rev 3:21; 20:4; Lk 22:30), bearing forever His very image (1 Cor 15: 49; 1 Jn 3:2). Writes the apostle John, *"Everyone who has this hope [think about that certain reality] fixed on Christ purifies himself, just as He is pure"* (1 Jn 3:3). The hope and expectation of sharing in God's glory should motivate every believer to dedicate himself to living purely while here on this earth. One day every believer will "obtain an inheritance that is imperishable and undefiled, and will not fade away"—this inheritance is reserved in heaven for us! (1 Pet 1:4).

Imagine with me what it must have been like for God's heavenly hosts to look down upon God's new creation and watch the events of human history unfold. Can't you just hear them say, "What in heaven's name is going on?" In the fullness of time they see the Sovereign God of the universe enter into *human history* in the person of Jesus Christ! They cry out, "How can this be? This is incredible! How can God empty Himself of His divine glory and take on the form of a bondservant? and be made in the likeness of a lowly human being? (Phil 2:6–7). What is He doing? Can this really be happening?" And then, they are stunned when they watch Christ subject Himself to the abuses of sinful humanity! They are aghast! "What in the world is God doing? This can't be! He is GOD!" And when the climax of human history unfolds, and God lets these despicable sinners crucify Him on a cross! (Phil 2:8), they are overwhelmed! completely speechless! "How can this be!!!" Then they are told that "God loves humanity so much, that He was willing to absolve them of all their guilt by going to the cross and paying the penalty for their sin!" (Jn 3:16). "Who is like our God!? How can He be so loving and gracious to such 'sinful creatures'! This doesn't make any sense!" And then they're completely blown away when they learn that the Sovereign God of the universe is actually making them *"HIS OWN SONS!" & "FELLOW-HEIRS WITH CHRIST!"* Not even the angels of glory are His heirs!!! (Rom 8:15–17; Gal 4:7; Jam 2:5; Rev 21:7). And they never violated God's law or His love!!! And then they finally learn that *this was God's response to the rebellion in heaven of Lucifer* that they had all witnessed before this new era of creation began. *GOD'S PLAN* was to demonstrate the deplorable nature of sin and the glorious majesty of His love and grace! Completely overwhelmed at all they had witnessed . . . with one voice the angelic host of heaven then shouted aloud before all creation—

*"Worthy art Thou, our Lord and our God,
to receive glory and honor and power!"* (Rev 4:11)

*"Great and marvelous are Thy works,
O Lord God, the Almighty!"* (Rev 15:3)

*"Hallelujah! Salvation and glory and
power belong to our God!"* (Rev 19:1)

*"Hallelujah! For the Lord our God,
the Almighty, reigns!"* (Rev 19:6)

God has placed YOU on the grand stage of the universe to be a participant in the cosmic battle between good & evil! Rejoice in that honor! and fight the good fight of faith!

EPILOGUE
(Concluding Remarks)

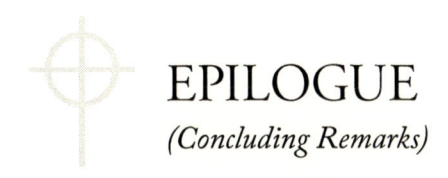

Eugene Peterson has rightly stated, "A quest is not a conclusion." The quest or pursuit of holiness and spirituality is a process—a work in progress—not an instantaneous experience. Furthermore, it is not aimless wandering, but a distinct objective to be pursued. And every step of assent toward God arrives at a place where "joy" is experienced—not only is there more to be enjoyed the more progress that is made, there is an increased ability to enjoy it. "Best of all," writes Peterson, "we don't have to wait until we get to the end of the road before we enjoy what is at the end of the road" (Peterson, p. 192). The noted nineteenth century tractarian and vicar of St. Mary's University Church in Oxford, England, **John Henry Newman,** writes—

> *May it be our blessedness, as years go on, to add one grace to another, and advance upward, step by step, neither neglecting the lower after attaining the higher, nor aiming at the higher before attaining the lower. The first grace is faith, the last is love; first comes zeal, afterwards comes lovingkindness; first comes humiliation, then comes peace; first comes diligence, then comes resignation. May we learn to mature all [of the] graces within us; fearing and trembling, watching and repenting, because Christ is coming.* (Newman, p. 211)

The 17th century theologian "John Owen" has long been recognized by evangelicals as one of the greatest English-speaking theologians in the history of the Church. Owen's thinking touched both the depths of sin and the heights of grace. Many of his readers have come away from reading him on such themes as temptation and indwelling sin, feeling that Owen knew them through and through. The truth is, through a constant and intensive study of both Scripture and the human heart, Owen had come to know himself and God like few before him. His theology is marked by prodigious learning, profound thought and acute analysis of the human heart. It was out of the riches of his studies that he preached and wrote on the loftiest themes of Christian theology. During his lifetime he published over sixty titles of varying lengths, and a dozen more appeared posthumously. In the 19th century, W. H. Goold edited a twenty-four volume edition of all Owen's writings titled *Works*. In his writings *Works XII (p. 52)*, Owens writes—

> *What am I the better if I can dispute that Christ is God, but have no sense of sweetness in my heart from hence that He is a God in covenant with my soul? What will it avail me to evince [by arguments], that He hath made satisfaction for sin, if through my unbelief, the wrath of God abideth on me, and I have no experience of my own being made the righteousness of Him . . . [with] my sins imputed to Him and His righteousness imputed to me? . . . It is the power of truth in the heart alone that will make us cleave unto [God's quickening work of grace within us] in an hour of temptation.* (Ferguson, p. 281).

John Owen, in a challenge to "personal godliness" says the directions for the actual work of mortification are only two—the first is to live wholly and solely in your trust of Christ, and the second is to seek the Holy Spirit who alone mortifies sin. *Regarding trust in the sufficiency of Christ*, he writes: "Avoid the entanglements of lust by filling your soul with the realization of all the provisions available in Christ Jesus. [Without knowing them you will flounder.] Moreover, ponder that you are in no way able, in and by yourself, to contend against your sinful condition.

When you are weary of the struggle and ready to give up, [know this] there is always enough in Jesus Christ to give you relief" (Phil 4:13). Let your soul declare: "The corruption of the flesh is too hard for me to cope with by myself; I have been deceived too many times to believe that I have finally obtained victory over sin . . . yet I know that the everlasting God, the Creator of the ends of the earth . . . giveth power to the faith, and to them that have no might He increaseth strength (Is 40:27–29); and He assures us that His grace is sufficient" (2 Cor 12:9—Owen, pp. 189–190). The author of Hebrews writes: "Since Christ Himself was tempted in that which He suffered, He is able to come to the aid of those who are tempted. . . . We do not have a high priest who cannot sympathize with our weaknesses, but one who has been tempted in all things as we are, yet without sin. Let us therefore draw near with confidence to the throne of grace, that we may receive mercy and may find grace to help in time of need" (Heb 2:18; 4:15–16).

Regarding seeking the Holy Spirit for the mortification of sin, it is the Holy Spirit who convinces the heart of the evil and guilt that needs to be mortified (Jn 16:8). Though we have sufficient light in our souls to behold our sinfulness, we do not have the wherewithal "in ourselves" to mortify the sin. Unless we are convinced of the unique power of the Holy Spirit, we shall go on living in futility about sin. Owen reminds us that the Holy Spirit alone reveals to us the fullness of Christ for our relief, and brings the cross of Christ into our hearts with its sin-killing power (Rom 6:6). The Spirit is the author and finisher of our sanctification—He provides the resources and new influences of grace for holiness and sanctification; He does this when the contrary principle of the flesh is weakened (Eph 3:16–21). The Holy Spirit is the conveyor of faith that prevails with God (Rom 8:26—Owens, pp. 192–193).

In this book we have examined the essence of what it means to be "spiritually transformed" . . . the work of Christ that makes it possible . . . the work of the Holy Spirit throughout the process . . . and the experience of the believer and the need for his participative cooperation. This study was written to provide the believer with an understanding of the ups and downs of the Christian experience, and the path wherein to walk with God in holiness and sanctification. The subjects discussed are—

- The process whereby one truly becomes a genuine child of God
- The process whereby the believer's life becomes conformed to the image of Christ
- The reason the believer struggles in his pursuit of holiness and spirituality
- The believer's predisposition to sinning and living by the law
- The believer's struggle with guilt, discouragement and spiritual depression
- The believer's struggle with performance-based living
- The believer's struggle with walking in the Spirit
- The believer's struggle with trusting God during difficult times
- The reason the believer's feelings often run counter to the will of God
- The believer's struggle to believe that God really loves him
- The reason the believer's peace and joy seem to grow wings so easily and fly away
- The reason the believer's lack of perfection is so discouraging and self-defeating
- The believer's obsession with his sins and his poor performance
- The believer's struggle to overcome temptation
- The believer's struggle to be the person God wants him to be
- The reason God seems to withdraw Himself at times from the believer's life
- The reason the will of God so often seems contrary to our spirits
- The reason it is so difficult for the believer to abandon "his will" for "God's will"
- The reason the believer's "new nature" seems so much weaker than his "old nature"
- The steps whereby the believer can maximize his growth in holiness and sanctification
- The steps whereby the believer can experience the fullness of God's grace in his life
- The steps whereby the believer can experience the joy of intimate fellowship with God

These are significant issues in every believer's life. They are issues we all wrestle with. Obviously, the journey of becoming like Christ is no picnic in the park or day at the beach—it is a challenging, painful pilgrimage through a wilderness of death, war and pestilence. Since when are these pleasant experiences? True, God does provide us with spiritual manna daily, just as He provided the children of Israel with a daily supply of physical manna some 3400 years ago in the Sinai, and there are those wonderful moments of joy, peace and rest . . . yet the enemy of our soul is always just around the corner waiting to wrack havoc upon us, and God's supreme work of *"soul transformation"* is once again front and center in our lives (Is 48:10; Rom 5:3–4; Heb 12:5–11; 1 Pet 5:8–11). It is precisely the painful issue of soul transformation that prompts so many believers—and regrettably, many pastors—to opt for a *"more positive narrative"* about the Christian life: one that only focuses on the positives; one that promises victory at every turn; name it and claim it prosperity; financial success; and happy pain-free living. Yet it is this lack of attention given to "soul transformation issues" that keeps the vast majority of Christians struggling with holiness and living spiritually joyless, defeated, discouraged lives.

In closing, let me earnestly implore you to expose yourself to the teachings of "soul transformation" on a continual ongoing basis. I would encourage you to read through this book once a year—that's just two chapters a month—to keep yourself grounded in the realities of the work of God's Spirit in your soul. My own experience and the testimonies of countless other believers all around the world, is that when "matters of the soul" are not a continual part of the believer's spiritual diet, he will find himself drifting from the joyful fellowship of God in Christ Jesus. It is inevitable. There is no such thing as automatic cruise control spirituality, one day a week (Sunday) spiritual maturity, or a chapter a day keeps the devil away theology. It does not exist. If that is the track you're on, get off that train! You are going in the wrong direction! Stop fooling yourself! Pull up your spiritual boot straps and learn what it means to "walk with God" moment by moment! It cannot be said more passionately—there is no other way! Though the believer's journey does involve pain and suffering (Ps 32:1–5; Rom 5:3–5; 2 Tim 2:3; Heb 12:5–11;

1 Pet 4:1, 12–13, 17–19; 5:10; 2 Cor 4:8–9), there is also simultaneous joy that accompanies it (Jn 15:1–11; 17:13; Phil 4:4; Jam 1:2; 1 Pet 1: 6–9; 1 Jn 1:4) when there is the ongoing pursuit of holiness and sanctification. Did you catch the caveat of that last statement? Without an ongoing quest to experience the life of Christ, your default mode (the flesh) will overwhelm you and you will find it extremely difficult to "quickly and properly adjust your focus" in the hour of temptation (Rom 12:2; Phil 4:6–8)—the result will be a profound awareness of uncontrollable fleshly thinking. The cure for fleshly thinking? Godly thinking (Gal 5:16ff; Phil 4:8; Col 3:2; Heb 12:2). As James puts it: "Draw near to God and He *will* draw near to you" (Jam 4:8). The key to the Christian life? *Make walking with Christ your life's ambition!* Let me close with this benediction from Hebrews—"May the God of peace, who brought up from the dead the great Shepherd of the sheep through the blood of the eternal covenant, Jesus our Lord, equip you in every good thing to do His will, working in you that which is pleasing in His sight, through Jesus Christ, to whom be the glory forever and ever. Amen" (Heb 13:20–21).

BIBLIOGRAPHY

Angelica, M. Mother. *Healing Power of Suffering.* New York, NY: Doubleday, 1977

Barnes, Albert. *Barnes' Notes on the New Testament.* Grand Rapids, MI: Kregel Publications, 1980

Barnhouse, Donald. *The Invisible War.* Grand Rapids, MI: Zondervan, 1965

Boice, James M. *Foundations of the Christian Faith.* Downers Grove, IL: InterVarsity Press, 1986

Bridges, Jerry. *The Discipline of Grace.* Colorado Springs, CO: NavPress, 1994

Brown, Steve. *A Scandalous Freedom.* West Monroe, LA: Howard Publishing, 2004.

Chafer, Lewis S. *Satan, His Motives and Methods.* Grand Rapids, MI: Kregel Publications, 1990

Chapell, Bryan. *Holiness by Grace.* Wheaton, IL: Crossway Books, 2001.

Colbert, Don. *Deadly Emotions: Understand the Mind-Body-Spirit Connection that can Heal or Destroy You.* Nashville, TN: Thomas Nelson Pub., 2006.

Crabb, Larry. *Shattered Dreams.* Colorado Springs, CO: WaterBrook Press, 2010.

Ekstrand, Donald W. *Christianity: The Pursuit of Divine Truth.* Maitland, FL: Xulon Press, 2008

Elwell, Walter A., editor. *Evangelical Dictionary of Theology.* Grand Rapids, MI: Baker Book House, 1992

Ferguson, Sinclair B. *John Owen on the Christian Life.* Carlisle, PA: Banner of Trust Truth, 1987.

Gill, John. *Gill's Exposition of the Entire Bible.* Grand Rapids, MI: William B. Eerdmans Publishing Company, 1993

Hull, Bill. *Christlike.* Colorado Springs, CO: NavPress, 2010.

Jeremiah, David. *When Your World Falls Apart.* Nashville, TN: Thomas Nelson Pub., 2000.

Leaf, Caroline. *Who Switched Off My Brain?* Nashville, TN: Thomas Nelson Pub., 2009.

Lewis, C. S. *A Grief Observed.* New York, NY: Harper Collins Publishers, 1961.

Lewis, C. S. *Reflections on the Psalms.* New York, NY: Harcourt Brace Jovanovich, Inc., 1958.

Lloyd-Jones, Martyn. *Enjoying the Presence of God.* Ann Arbor, MI: Servant Publica., 1991.

Lloyd-Jones, Martyn. *Fellowship with God.* Wheaton, IL: Crossway Books, 1993.

Lloyd-Jones, Martyn. *Let Not Your Heart be Troubled*. Wheaton, IL: Crossway Books, 2009.

Lloyd-Jones, Martyn. *Spiritual Depression*. Grand Rapids, MI: Wm. B. Eerdmans Pub., 1992.

Lull, Timothy. *Martin Luther's Basic Theological Writings*. Minneapolis, MN: Fortress Press, 1989.

MacArthur, John. *Slave*. Nashville, TN: Thomas Nelson, Inc., 2010.

Moulton, J. H. and G. Milligan. *Vocabulary of the Greek Testament*. Grand Rapids, MI: Baker Book House, 1995

Newman, John Henry. *The Preaching of John Henry Newman*, ed., W. E. White. Philadelphia, PA: Fortress Press, 1969.

Owen, John. *Sin & Temptation*, ed. James M. Houston. Portland, OR: Multnomah Press, 1983.

Peterson, Eugene H. *A Long Obedience in the Same Direction*. Downers Grove, IL: Inter-Varsity Press, 1980.

Porowski, James P. *With All My Mind, God's Design for Mental Wellness*. Nashville, TN: Life Way Press, 2002.

Rohr, Richard. *Hope Against Darkness*. Cincinnati, OH: St. Anthony Messenger Press, 2001.

Ryle, John Charles. *Holiness*. Chicago, IL: Moody Publishers, 2010.

Schaeffer, Francis A. *True Spirituality*. Wheaton, IL: Tyndale House Publishers, 1971

Showers, Renald E. *The New Nature*. Bellmawr, NJ: Friends of Israel, 1986.

Showers, Renald E. *What on Earth is God Doing?* New York, NY: Loizeaux Brothers, 1973.

Sibbes, Richard. *The Bruised Reed*. Carlisle, PA: Banner of Truth Trust, 2008.

Sibbes, Richard. *The Soul's Conflict*. Charleston, SC: BiblioLife, 2011.

Sibbes, Richard. *Glorious Freedom*. Carlisle, PA: Banner of Truth Trust, 2000.

Stott, John. *The Radical Disciple*. Downers Grove, IL: InterVarsity Press, 2010.

Thrall, Bill; Bruce McNicol and John Lynch. *True Faced*. Colorado Springs, CO: NavPress, 2004.

Watson, Thomas. *All Things for Good*. Carlisle, PA: Banner of Truth Trust, 2008.

Wesley, John. *Repentance of the Believer*. Londonderry, England: Sermon dated April 24, 1767

Winslow, Octavius. *Soul-Depths and Soul-Heights*. Carlisle, PA: Banner of Truth Trust, 2011.

GLOSSARY

adoption. The believer's "placing as a son," emphasizing the believer's rights and privileges in his new position in Christ.

agape. Greek word for "love" in the New Testament, meaning God's love for humans and the selfless love that should bind them. Contrasted with Greek *eros*, meaning the type of love characterized by longing and desire.

alienation. The estrangement of oneself from God.

allegory. Type of interpretation of scriptures that minimizes the literal meaning of a text in favor of a symbolic or hidden spiritual meaning.

anxiety. Emotion characterized by uneasiness, apprehension, dread, concern, tension, restlessness, and worry.

apologetics. Literally, "defense;" in philosophy, the discipline of rationally justifying one's beliefs.

apostle. "One sent" with a message; a messenger; the first twelve disciples or followers of Christ; any Christian sent forth as a messenger of Christ.

asceticism. Practices of self-restraint such as fasting and celibacy undertaken to attain closeness to the divine.

assurance. This term is most commonly employed to denote the firm persuasion of one's own salvation. It is the product of the Holy Spirit (Rom 8:16; 2 Cor 1:22; Heb 6:11; 10:22; 11:1).

atheism. The belief that there is no God or ultimate reality; the universe is all there is.

atonement. In orthodox Christianity, the biblical doctrine referring to the substitutionary death and sacrifice of Jesus Christ on behalf of mankind, effecting salvation and making possible the reconciliation of the human race to God.

Augustine (A.D. 354–43). Augustine is sometimes called the greatest theologian between Paul and Martin Luther. Augustine stressed the total depravity of man and the grace of God.

carnal. It is mere human nature, the earthly nature of man apart from divine influence, and therefore prone to sin and opposed to God. It is the governance of human nature in the soul of man, rather than the Spirit of God.

catechism. A manual of Christian doctrine, usually in the form of question and answer, for the use of religious instruction.

chastening. The action of the Heavenly Father toward His wayward and disobedient children, that they should not be condemned with the world; the disciplinary process is corrective in nature and its ultimate goal is their restoration.

Christ. Greek word for "Messiah;" in Hebrew it stands for "Anointed One". The Messiah is the Jewish term for an anointed one of God. Christians believe that Jesus was the expected Messiah referred to in the Old Testament.

Christian counseling. Relationship in which one individual, by virtue of both spiritual and psychological insights, seeks to help another individual recognize, understand, and solve his or her own problems in accordance with the Word of God.

church. The word literally means "a called-out group." The term may refer to a local church (1 Thess 1:1) or the universal church; all who have believed from Pentecost until the Rapture. The universal church is also called "Christ's Body" (Eph 1:22–23).

circumcision. Removal of the male foreskin as a sign of the covenant in the Old Testament. It signified membership within the Hebrew community.

clinical depression. State of sadness that is severe enough to have observable physiological symptoms, such as insomnia, anorexia, and fatigue.

conversion. A term denoting the "turning" of a soul from sin to God; it is the human response to regeneration, the infusion of new life into the soul by a divine act of grace. Therefore, conversion has both a divine element and a human element.

covenant. A pact between two parties. In Judaism, the covenant is a major theological concept referring to the eternal bond between God and the people of Israel that calls for the nation's obedience to the divine commandments and instruction (Torah). The first covenant is with *Noah* (covenant of the rainbow); the second with *Abraham* (circumcision); the third with *Moses* on Mount Sinai (Ten Commandments). For Christianity, God made a new covenant (thus, "New Testament") with the *followers of Jesus* the night before He went to the cross, superseding the old covenant (thus, "Old Testament") with Moses at Sinai. (See Old Covenant and New Covenant.)

creation ex nihilo. The Christian view that God created all things "out of nothing" and is thus the ultimate cause and source of meaning for the whole created order.

creed. A formal summary of the Christian faith, held in common by Christians. The most important creeds are those generally known as the Apostles' Creed and the Nicene Creed.

deism. The belief that God created the world and is transcendent but has no continuing involvement with the world.

demon. In Christianity, an evil spirit that works contrary to the divine will.

denial. A defense mechanism used to prevent thoughts, feelings, wishes, or motives from surfacing to consciousness.

denomination. A sectarian branch of Protestant Christianity whose congregations are united by a single administrative body; for example, Baptists, Presbyterians, Methodists, Lutherans, etc.

depravity. A term used to refer to the corruption of sin extending to all people and affecting the entire person—his intellect, emotions, and will—so that nothing in the person can commend him to God.

depression. A morbid sadness, dejection, or melancholy that results from "wrong thinking."

devil. The highest ranking angel *Lucifer*, who fell from prominence and is now the "slanderer" who accuses believers before God.

doctrine. Statements of the basic beliefs of the Christian faith.

Elohim. The most common Hebrew term for "God" in the Old Testament. Though the term is plural it is used to designate the one God of Israel. It is also a synonym for "Yahweh," the self-revealed name of the God of Israel.

emotion. Term that refers to intrapsychic feelings and may range from love or hate to fear or sadness.

epistemology. The division of philosophy that studies how we know truth and what assumptions and presuppositions we make.

eschatology. Beliefs concerning the end times or last things: death, heaven, hell, judgment, resurrection, reincarnation, end of the known world.

essence. Qualities or attributes of a thing which are necessary; its nature.

eternal. That which exists without beginning, end, or change; not simply of endless duration, but the absence of time.

ethics. The study of human values and moral conduct; the study of right and wrong.

evangelical. Protestant Christian tradition of enthusiastic preaching, literal authority of the Bible, salvation by faith in Christ, and conversion (born again) experience.

faith. Attitude of belief in, trust, and commitment to the teachings of Scripture. When believers live by faith, they live in accordance with the will of God as expressed in the Bible; when believers exercise faith, they "affirm" the truths of Scripture in their minds and hearts as indeed being true. Faith can also refer to the beliefs of Christianity, "the faith," which is passed on from teachers to believers.

fall of man. The historic event described in Genesis 3 in which Adam disobeyed God with the result that sin and death entered the human race (Rom 5:12).

false prophets. Those who claim to speak for God but whose predictions fail to come to pass, or who preach the wrong god(s).

fatalism. The belief that events are fixed in advance for all time in such a manner that human beings are powerless to change them.

fellowship. The basic meaning conveyed by the Greek term *koinonia* is that of two or more beings sharing something in common; it is frequently translated sharing, partaking, companionship or partnership. As such, believers are to enjoy their fellowship with God and with one another.

fidelity. Refers to that grace in the servant which shows him to be worthy of his Master's trust. Thus our Lord says, "Who then is that faith and wise steward" (Lk 12:42). Here then is the essence of fidelity: the Master commits a trust, and the trustworthy servant shows fidelity in all things. Fidelity extends to the whole of life.

finite. Having specific boundaries or limits.

flesh. Spiritually speaking, it refers to the sensuous, sinful human nature of man; the earthly nature of man apart from divine influence, and therefore prone to sin and opposed to God; it includes in the soul whatever is weak, low, debased, tending to ungodliness and vice.

foreknowledge. Scripture uses this term for God's prescience or foresight concerning future events; hence, it is an aspect of God's omniscience—nothing is outside of His perfect knowledge; neither the past, the present, nor the future. In His foreknowledge, God is the presupposition of all things, and nothing we do can inform or surprise Him or impose conditions on Him.

forgiveness. The legal act of God in removing the charges against the sinner because atonement for the sins has been made. The believer's ceasing to exercise the feeling of resentment toward an offender, thus pardoning the individual and giving up his claim to requital.

fundamentalism. The doctrine that the Bible is directly inspired by God and therefore inerrant and infallible on all matters to which it speaks.

God. In Greek it is the word *Theos*. The supreme being who is Creator and Ruler of the universe. The study of God is referred to as "Theology."

gospel. In Christianity, the "Good News" that God has raised Jesus from the dead and in so doing has begun the transformation of the world. Also one of the four founding texts telling of Jesus' life—Matthew, Mark, Luke, John.

grace. In Greek it is the word *charis*. Unmerited favor. God's grace is extended to sinful humanity in providing salvation and forgiveness through Jesus Christ that is not deserved, and withholding the judgment that is deserved.

guilt. The state of a moral agent after the intentional or unintentional violation of a law, principle, or value established by an authority under which the moral agent is subject. The law may have been established by one's own authority, the head of a social order, or by God in His effort to lead and protect the highest well-being of humankind. The word *guilt* carries with it the concept of deserved punishment. Clouding the modern understanding of guilt is the common but erroneous use of the words "guilt" and "guilt feeling" as though they were interchangeable. Guilt is an after-the-fact reality, whereas guilt feeling is a painful conglomerate of emotions that usually includes anxiety in anticipation of punishment, shame, humiliation, the need to hide, grief, and a diminished sense of self-worth, dignity, and self-esteem.

hedonism. The ethical view which claims that pleasure is the greatest good.

heresy. A religious belief that contradicts the official teachings of a church. Such a belief is thus regarded as spurious and potentially dangerous for faith.

holiness *or* godliness. The manner of life that is centered on God, with special reference to devotion, piety, and reverence toward Him. It can be defined as the conjunction of an attitude of devotion to God and of the consequent right conduct. The Greek word corresponding to godliness or piety is *eusebeia*—it's original meaning, spiritually, was the appropriate attitude to that which inspires the reverence and awe of God.

Holy Spirit. The third person of the Trinity. God the Father, God the Son, and God the Holy Spirit constitute the eternal Godhead in Christianity. The Spirit inspired biblical writers, makes known the saving work of Jesus Christ, and as God is present in and with the church and all believers.

humanism. The belief that the dignity of man is the highest value in the universe.

humility. Christian humility is that grace which makes one think of himself no more highly than he ought to think. It requires us to feel that in God's sight we have no merit, and in honor to prefer our brethren to ourselves, but does not deman undue self-depreciation or depressing views of one's self, but lowliness of self-estimation and freedom from vanity.

idealism. The philosophy which holds that reality consists of minds and ideas rather than matter.

idolatry. In a general sense idolatry is the paying of divine honors to any created thing; the ascription of divine power to natural agencies, be it inanimate objects, animals, higher powers, hero worship, deceased ancestors, idealism, or the worship of other gods.

immortality. In religious thought, the doctrine that man will live forever.

imputation. Means "to place on one's account" whether as a charge or a credit. The three biblical concepts of imputation are: the sin of Adam is *charged* to all humanity; the sin of all humanity is *charged* to Christ; Christ's righteousness is *credited* to all who believe on Him.

incarnation. Meaning "in the flesh," the incarnation defines the act wherein the eternal God the Son took to Himself an additional nature, humanity, through the virgin birth. By that act Christ did not cease to be God but remains forever fully God and fully man—two natures in one Person.

inerrancy. The term used to describe the Bible as being wholly without error in all that it affirms in the original autographs (writings).

infallible. The term used to describe the Bible as being absolutely correct and perfectly reliable in all that it teaches.

infinite. Without limits or boundaries.

inspiration. When used in Christian thought, inspiration refers to the teaching that the Bible is "God-breathed". It is, therefore, accurate in all it addresses. The authors of the Bible were inspired of God; that is, they wrote under the divine guidance of God.

Jehovah. A name for God in Jewish and Christian tradition. (See Yahweh.)

justification. Comes from a Greek concept meaning "to declare righteous." It is a legal act wherein God pronounces that the believing sinner has been credited with all the virtues of Jesus Christ. Whereas forgiveness is the negative aspect of salvation meaning the subtraction of human sin, justification is the positive aspect meaning the addition of divine righteousness.

Kingdom of God or **Kingdom of Heaven**. God's sovereign reign and rule in the individual and in the world. The main theme of Jesus' teaching. The fullness of the kingdom is in the future tense, although it has also come in the person of Jesus Himself. Christian reign of God where God's will is done and His power is evident, both in the present and future.

law. Usually a designation of the law that God gave to Moses. The law can be divided into: (1) civil law, which legislated the social responsibilities with neighbors; (2) ceremonial law, which legislated Israel's worship life; (3) moral law, found principally in the Ten Commandments, which identified God's timeless standards of right and wrong.

legalism. Spiritually speaking, the essence of legalism is "living by the law." When one lives by the law he puts rules above God, and as such he is "enslaved to the law" rather than to a loving, merciful God.

liberalism. An anti-supernatural approach to Christianity and the Bible that arose because of rationalism. Liberalism denied the miraculous element of the Scriptures, stressing the importance of reason; whatever disagreed with reason and science was rejected.

logic. The study of valid thinking and argument.

love. Conscious choice that occurs when a mature person loves another person because he or she chooses to love that other person and to behave lovingly toward that person. (See agape.)

lust. In the ethical sense lust is used to express sinful desire—sinful either in being directed toward forbidden objects, or in being so violent as to overcome self-control, and to engross the mind with earthly, carnal, and perishable things. Every natural appetite may be perverted by the lustful desires of the flesh to sinful expression.

Luther, Martin (1483–1546). The most prominent leader of the Protestant Reformation, who was excommunicated from the Roman Catholic church because of his persistent efforts to change some of the church's doctrines and customs. Luther nailed his "ninety-five theses" (a list of topics for debate about Roman Catholic doctrine) to the door of the cathedral in Wittenberg, Germany on October 31, 1517, thus beginning the Protestant Reformation.

Lutheranism. The founding principles of the Protestant Reformation. Martin Luther, a German priest/professor began to teach in 1517 the priesthood of all believers (apart from church clerics), justification by faith (apart from the works of the law), and the sole authority of the Bible (apart from church tradition). Also a later Protestant denomination.

martyr. The Greek word means "witness." A general term for persons who endure persecution, usually leading to death, for the sake of their religious witness.

materialism. The belief that all of reality is material, and that no spiritual entities, such as the soul or God, exist.

meditation. A private devotional act, consisting in deliberate reflection upon some spiritual truth or mystery, accompanied by mental prayer and by acts of the affection and of the will. Meditation is a duty which ought to be attended to by all who desire to grow in spirituality.

mercy. Mercy is a form of love determined by the state or condition of its objects; their state is one of suffering and need, and they may be unworthy or ill-deserving—mercy is the ministry of love for their relief.

Messiah. "Anointed One." In Greek it is the word *Christos*, from which we get our word *Christ*. The Messiah was the redeemer figure descended from the royal dynasty of David who would restore the united kingdom of Israel and Judah, bringing in an age of peace and justice. The concept of Messiah has been taken to mean a time of radical new beginnings, a new heaven and earth, after divine judgment. The title was applied to *Jesus* by Himself and by His followers.

miracle. A general term for special events that seem inexplicable by normal (rational) means. Miracle reports are frequent in Jewish and Christian scriptures and early traditions.

monasticism. The religious practice of monks and nuns, usually celibate, who live in an exclusive community according to a life of prayer, work, study, meditation, and service to others.

mortification. To mortify means "to put to death." The believer was moritified by God through the death of Christ (Rom 7:4); and the believer, in response to God's act, is responsible to mortify the deeds of the body (Rom 8:13)—this is the essence of breaking league with sin, and declaring open hostility against it, and strong resistance of it (Gal 5:24; Eph 6:10). The chief agent in carrying on this moritification is the Holy Spirit, with prayer, faith, and dependence upon God as the means.

mysticism. The belief that there are states of mind or reality beyond sensation or reason.

natural law. In ethics, the view that there are innate or natural moral laws known by all men. In physical science, the principles which describe the normal operation of the universe.

naturalism. The belief that the universe is all there is; everything operates by natural law; therefore it precludes any supernatural intervention in the natural order.

New Covenant. An unconditional covenant in which God promised to provide for forgiveness of sin (Jer 31:31–34). The death of Christ is the foundation of forgiveness—unlike the blood of animals being sacrificed as part of the Old Covenant, His blood (because He is God) would truly remove the sins of all who put their faith in Him. And Jesus' sacrifice would never have to be repeated; it would be good for all eternity (Heb 9:23–28). The prophets looked forward to this new covenant that would fulfill the old sacrificial agreement (Jer 31:31–34).

Old Covenant. In contrast to the New Covenant which was a covenant between God and all people, the Old Covenant was a [conditional covenant] between God and the nation of Israel; it was a covenant of law with all its outward institutions and ritualistic services. In Old Testament times, God agreed to forgive people's sins if they brought animals to the Temple for priests to sacrifice. When this sacrificial system was inaugurated, the agreement between God and man was sealed with the blood of animals (Ex 24:8). But animal blood did not in itself remove sin (only God can forgive sin), and animal sacrifices had to be repeated day by day and year after year—God's forgiveness of sin in the Old Testament all looked forward to the future finished work of Christ on the cross. Israel's obedience to the commands of the law was to be rewarded by God's constant care for her, temporal prosperity, victory over enemies, and His presence in their midst (Ex 23:20). The seal of this covenant was "male circumcision" (Gen 17:10–11).

omnipotent. All-powerful. When designating an attribute of God, it means God has the power to do anything He desires; naturally, it would only include those things that would be in agreement with His own essence and character. For example, He would not commit sin, because that would be a violation of His holiness.

omnipresent. Everywhere present. When designating an attribute of God, it refers to the doctrine that everything is immediately in the presence of God, not that God is somehow intrinsically a part of everything, which would be pantheism. God transcends creation, He is not creation itself; but He is present everywhere in creation.

omniscient. All-knowing. When designating an attribute of God, it refers to God's complete and perfect knowledge; that is, He knows everything there is to know—past, present and future.

orthodox. From the Greek for "correct opinion/outlook," as opposed to that which is heretical or spurious. Historically, the term orthodox has come to denote the traditional, classical, or mainstream, such as rabbinic Judaism, Roman Catholic, or Orthodox Christian churches.

Paraclete. A title meaning "one called alongside." It is used only by the apostle John to refer to the Holy Spirit (John 14–16—translated "Comforter" [KJV], "Helper" [NASB], and "Counselor" [NIV]) . . . or to Jesus Christ (1 John 2:1—where it is translated "Advocate" [KJV and NASB], and "one who speaks . . . in our defense" [NIV]).

parable. The New Testament term *paraballo* means "to lay by the side of, to compare." One of the most popular teaching methodologies Jesus used in teaching spiritual truths was the "parable;" that is, He frequently used an idea or object with which His listeners were familiar, as a comparative way of teaching some "spiritual truth." In short, He would place an "unknown" alongside a "known," in order to give clarity to the unknown; hence, it is illustrative, used to make truth intelligible and more vivid. Four of the most common parables in Scripture are: the Sower, the Tares, the Mustard Seed, and the Leaven.

paradox. A statement or tenet that is *seemingly* contrary to or opposed to common sense and yet is true. The various paradoxical anomalies in Scripture are not completely outside the realm of reason, but must be fully examined if one is to appreciate their propositional wisdom. A common paradox in New Testament Scripture is that "we must die in order to live" (Lk 9:23–24; Gal 2:20).

Pentateuch. The Greek word used to describe the Torah. It was a Jewish designation for the first five books of the Hebrew (Old Testament) Scriptures.

philosophy. Literally, "love of wisdom." Careful thought about the fundamental nature of the world, the grounds for human knowledge, and the evaluation of human conduct. Essentially, it is a logical explanation of reality.

pluralism. A situation in which no single worldview or religion is dominant. Religious pluralism believes there is good in all religions, that people need to be open and tolerant of all views.

pragmatism. The philosophy which makes practical consequences the criterion for truth.

prophet. A mediator or spokesman between God and men who received direct revelation from God, revealing God's will to man.

Protestant Church. Term for people who "protested" against the corruption and power of the Roman Catholic Church. A general term for the Christians who broke away from Roman papacy at the Reformation. The Catholic monk, Martin Luther, was a central figure in this movement. Protestants emphasize the sole authority of the Bible, justification by faith, and the priesthood of all believers—that all believers have direct access to God. Denominations include Presbyterians, Baptists, Methodists, Lutherans, Anglicans, Episcopalians, Brethren, Quakers, and numerous other groups.

providence. A term in theology which designates the continual care which God exercises over the universe which He has created. This includes both its preservation and its governance. Divine providence isn't fully reconcilable to man because of the narrow limits of human understanding. Broad obsrvation and right reason preclude the idea of a government of the world by chance or blind force, thus confirming the belief that there is a power in the world that makes for righteousness. Scripture itself attests, "we only know in part" (1 Cor 13:9); for every mind less than the infinite, providence must have its mysteries. Our faith at this point, as at others, must therefore find its chief support and guidance from the word of God.

psalms. Israel's ancient collection of hymns of praise and worship, widely used in temple and synagogue worship. This part of the Hebrew Scriptures is referred to as the "Psalter," and has been particularly cherished by God's people in every age. The Psalter is largely composed of devotional hymns and heartfelt praise and personal testimonies of praise and thanksgiving to the Lord.

psychotic. Loss of contact with reality.

rationalism. A general term for the belief that everything is actually or potentially understandable by human reason.

reconciliation. Through sin man was alienated from God, but through Christ's death peace with God, and salvation itself, was made possible for all who believed in Jesus.

redemption. Comes from several Greek terms that cumulatively mean "to set free by the payment of a price." It emphasizes that through His death, Christ set the believer free from enslavement to sin.

Reformation. The Protestant Christian movements (and the period itself) in the sixteenth century which opposed Roman Catholicism in the interest of reforming Christianity to what was considered its earliest known form (found in the New Testament).

regeneration. The work of the Holy Spirit in giving life to the believing sinner, effecting the new birth.

relativism. The modern position that affirms that everything is relative to the particularities of the given situation, and that no absolutes exist.

religion. Religion consists of a strong belief that there is an *unseen order* in the universe that controls human destiny, and that our supreme good lies in harmoniously adjusting ourselves unto it. The term is often used interchangeably with faith or belief system.

repentance. A term used especially in Protestant Christianity to indicate the subjective state of sorrow, regret, and concern over sin, on the way to salvation. The Greek word *metanoia*, translated *repentance*, literally means "to change one's mind" [for the better]. Therefore, theologically, repentance is a fundamental and thorough change in the hearts of men from sin and toward God.

repression. This is the banishing of unacceptable ideas, feelings, impulses, or motives from conscious awareness or preventing unconscious ideas, feelings, impulses or motives from coming into conscious awareness.

revelation. Means "unveiling" and describes the unveiling or disclosure of truth from God to mankind that man could not otherwise know.

Roman Catholic Church. This Church is headed by the pope, bishop of Rome. Roman Catholics believe in the authority of the papacy; in addition to the Scriptures, they give significant emphasis to tradition, and the authority of the Roman church as the repository of truth; they center the entire Catholic Mass on the Eucharist; and they require that priests be male and celibate.

sacrament. An outward sign established by God to convey an inward or spiritual grace. Although Roman Catholic theology and church practice recognize seven sacraments (Eucharist, baptism, confirmation, marriage, ordination, penance, and unction), Protestant theologians generally argue that only two (Eucharist or Communion and baptism) are found in the New Testament itself.

sanctification. Comes from a Greek verb meaning "to set apart." It is used in two ways: (1) the believer is positioinally sanctified; he stands sanctified before God; (2) the believer grows in progressive sanctification in daily spiritual experience. Hence, sanctification is the gradual process whereby a Christian believer is becoming more like Jesus Christ.

Satan. Hebrew for "adversary," refers to the archangel Lucifer who rebelled against God and was banished from God's presence.

secular. A term that describes culture without any religious influence; it denotes the absence of religion, or the essence of irreligion.

secular humanism. That branch of philosophical humanism that denies specifically the existence of God.

secularism. The ideology of the secular world without reference to religious thinking.

sin. A transgression of the law of God; "missing the mark" of God's standard for all people; i.e., the holiness of God as seen in Jesus Christ. It also refers to the state of rebellion against God that results in self-rule in a person's life rather than God-rule.

skepticism. The belief that one should doubt or suspend judgment on philosophical questions.

soul. The active principle present in living things.

sovereign. With reference to God, it means that God is the supreme ruler and authority, that He ordains whatever comes to pass, and that His divine purpose is always accomplished.

spirituality. The state of deep conscious relationship with Christ, and a life of personal obedience to the word of God. Genuine spirituality is marked by the realization that in spiritual things, we mortals are utterly and completely dependent on the Lord (Ps 127:1; Jn 15:5).

subjectivism. In ethics, the belief that there are no objective, universal principles of conduct. In epistemology, the view that a statement is only true when considered to be true by the individual.

syncretism. The religious practice of selecting religious beliefs, symbols, or practices from different sources and combining them.

telos/teleological. Greek term for the "end," completion, purpose, or goal of any thing or activity.

temptation. The enticement of a person to commit sin by offering some seeming advantage; temptation craves the gratification that is offered. The sources of temptation are Satan, the world, and the flesh. We are exposed to them in every state, in every place, and in every time. James writes, "Every man is tempted, when he is carried away and enticed by his own lust" (Jam 1:14). Paul writes, "No temptation has overtaken you but such as is common to man (1 Cor 10:13).

testament. Latin for "Covenant." The Old and New Testaments are the Old and New Covenants.

theism. The worldview that affirms the existence of a personal, infinite Creator of the world, who is immanent in the world, unlimited in power and in love.

theology. Derived from two Greek words—*theos* and *logia*—meaning "study of God." A general termtt for discussions pertaining to God and religious matters. A person who engages formally in theological studies is called a theologian.

Trinity. The Christian belief that God is a unity composed of three persons: Father, Son, and Holy Spirit. Though God is composed of *three persons*, He is regarded as *one in essence*. Just as a human being is body, soul and spirit—he is one person—so God is three persons, yet He is one. It should be noted that Christianity does not believe in "three gods," as Muhammad assumed when writing the Koran; he apparently thought the essence of Christianity was that God the

Father and His wife Mary cohabitated and bore a child named Jesus. Obviously, this is not what Christianity believes.

universal. That which is true at all times and all places. The general concept or idea of a thing, as opposed to a particular instance or example.

Westminster Confession. A statement of Calvinistic theology formulated at Westminster in London, England, in 1643–1646 by over 150 English and Scottish delegates.

Yahweh. The personal covenant name for God in His relationship with Israel (Ex 6:2–3)—it is based on the sacred Hebrew *tetragram* YHWH, and is generally translated *Lord* or *Jehovah* in English Scripture. By inserting vowels in the tegragram, the word is rendered *Yahweh* or *Jehovah*. The name YHWH is probably derived from the Hebrew verb "to be," suggesting God is the eternally existing One. Considered by some Jews to be too sacred to speak, YHWH is replaced by the Hebrew word *Adonai*.